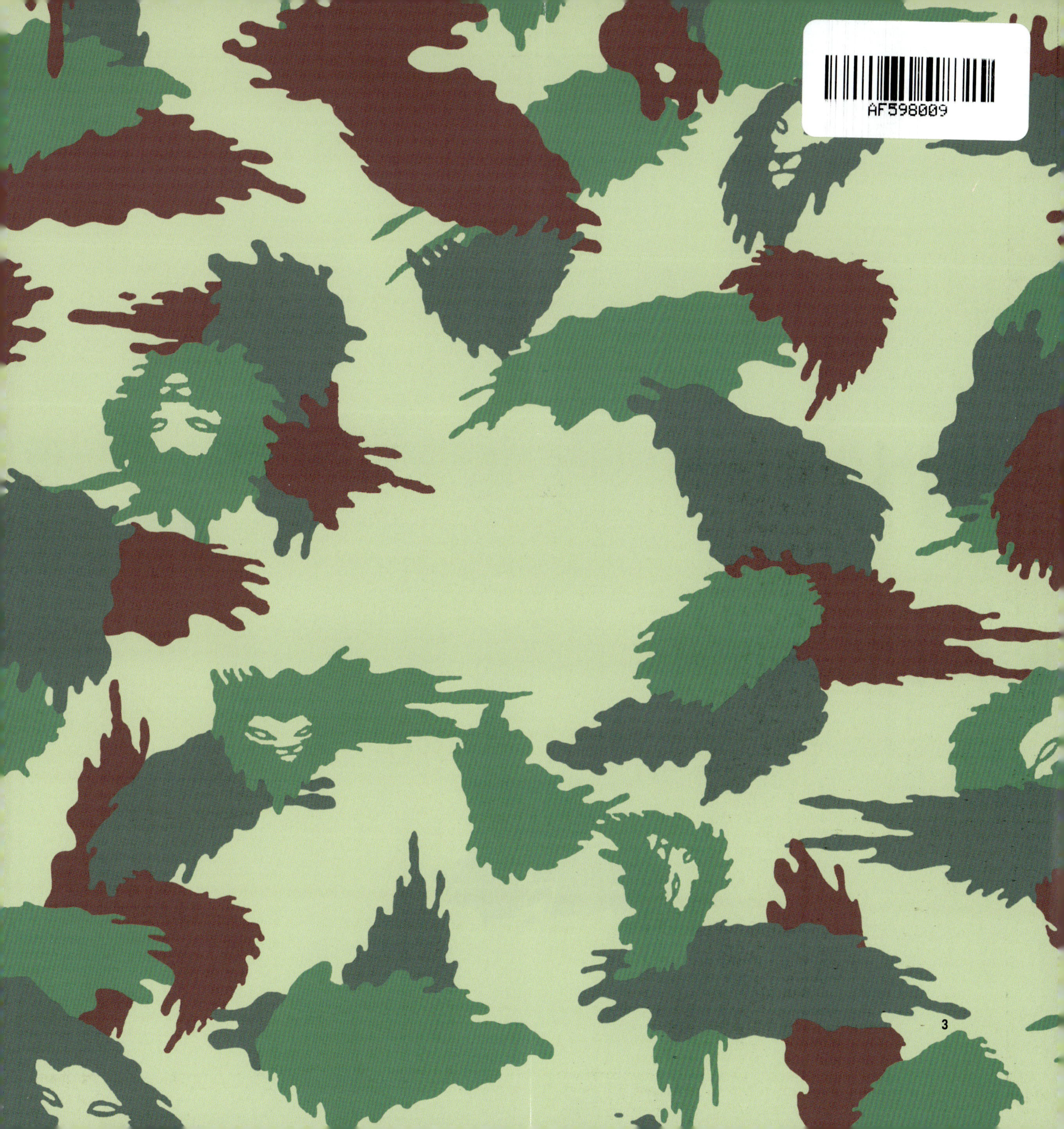

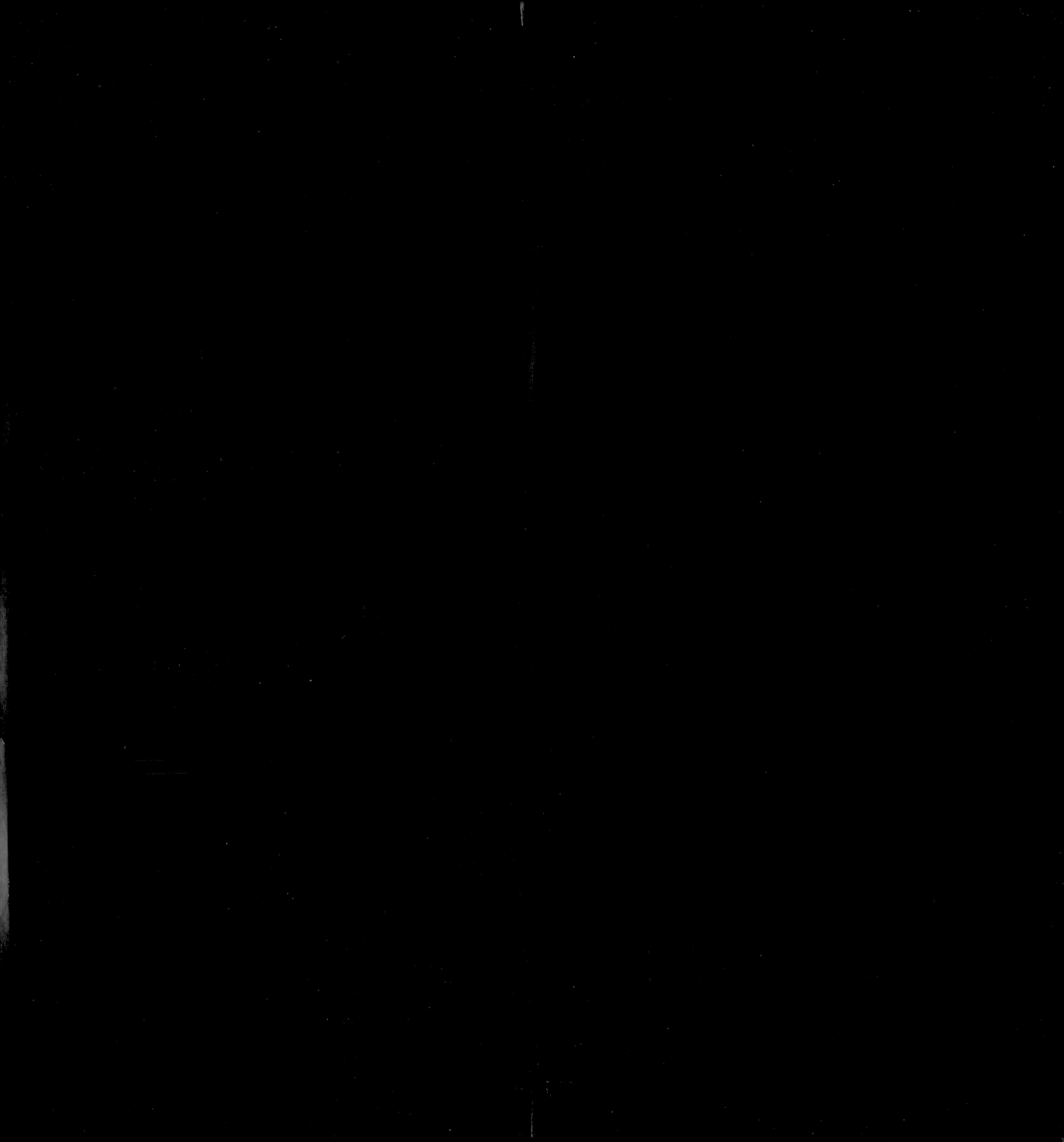

MAU MAU . .

TALKING OUT OF MYARST

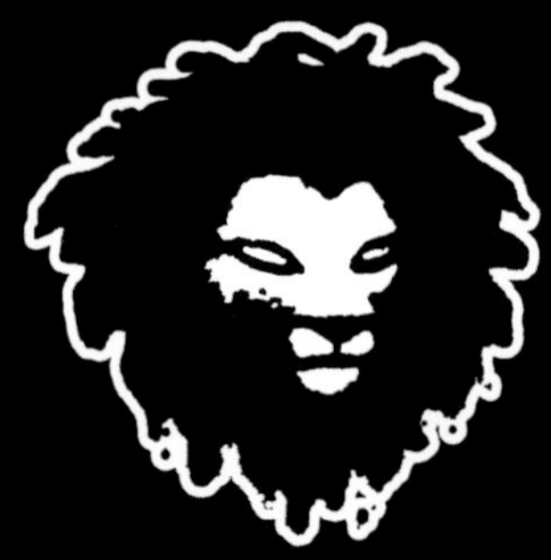

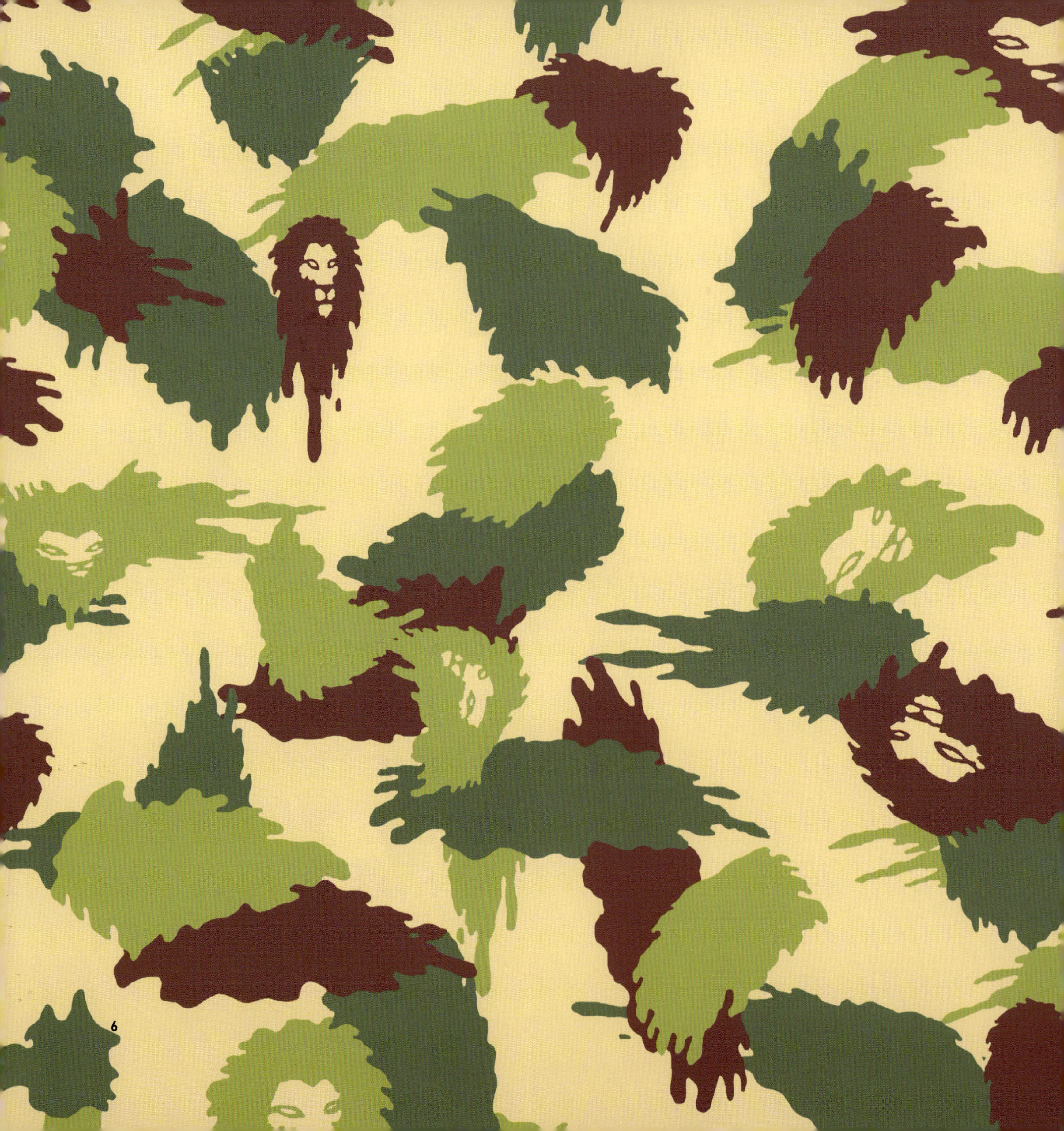

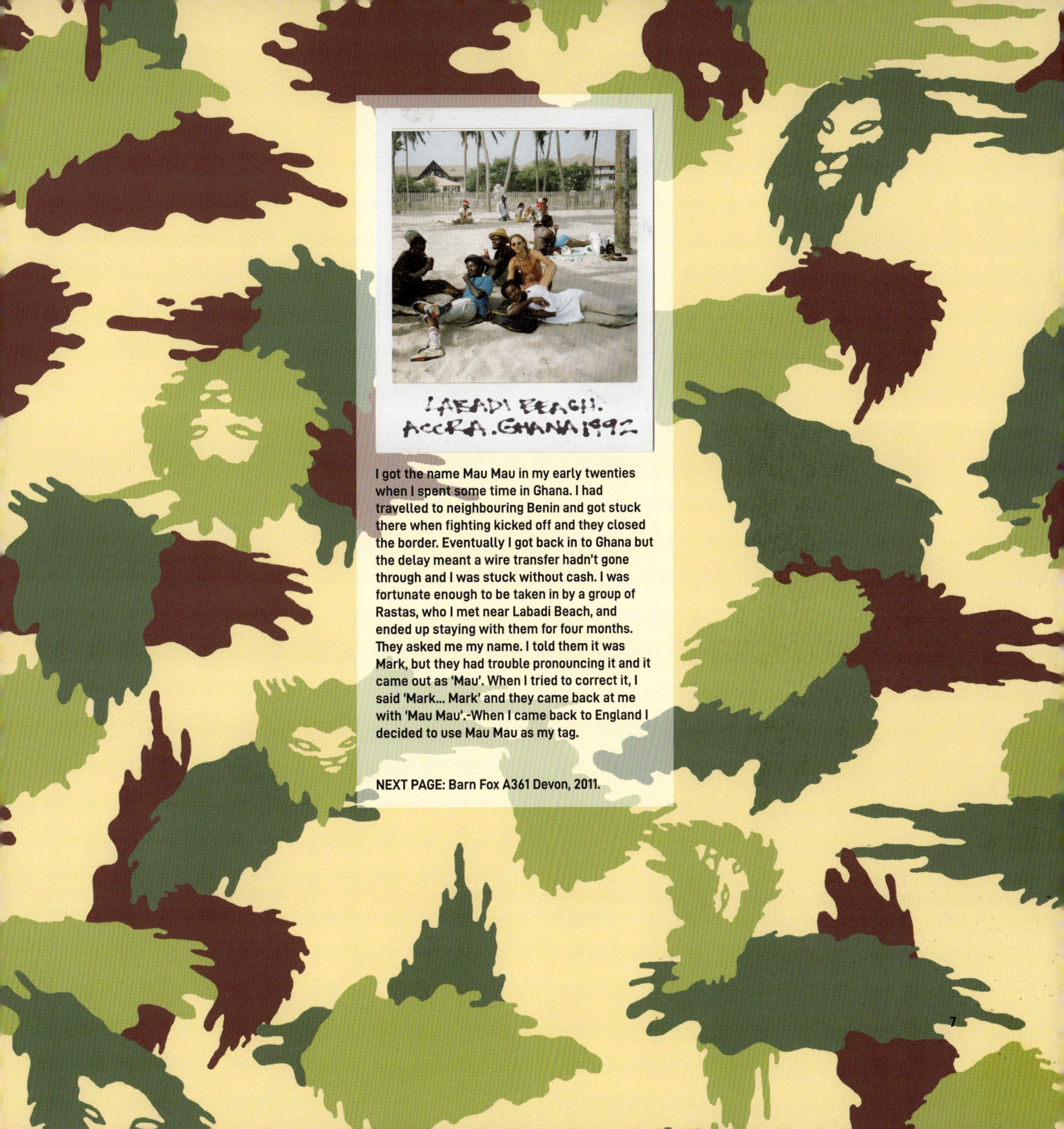

LABADI BEACH.
ACCRA. GHANA 1992

I got the name Mau Mau in my early twenties when I spent some time in Ghana. I had travelled to neighbouring Benin and got stuck there when fighting kicked off and they closed the border. Eventually I got back in to Ghana but the delay meant a wire transfer hadn't gone through and I was stuck without cash. I was fortunate enough to be taken in by a group of Rastas, who I met near Labadi Beach, and ended up staying with them for four months. They asked me my name. I told them it was Mark, but they had trouble pronouncing it and it came out as 'Mau'. When I tried to correct it, I said 'Mark... Mark' and they came back at me with 'Mau Mau'.-When I came back to England I decided to use Mau Mau as my tag.

NEXT PAGE: Barn Fox A361 Devon, 2011.

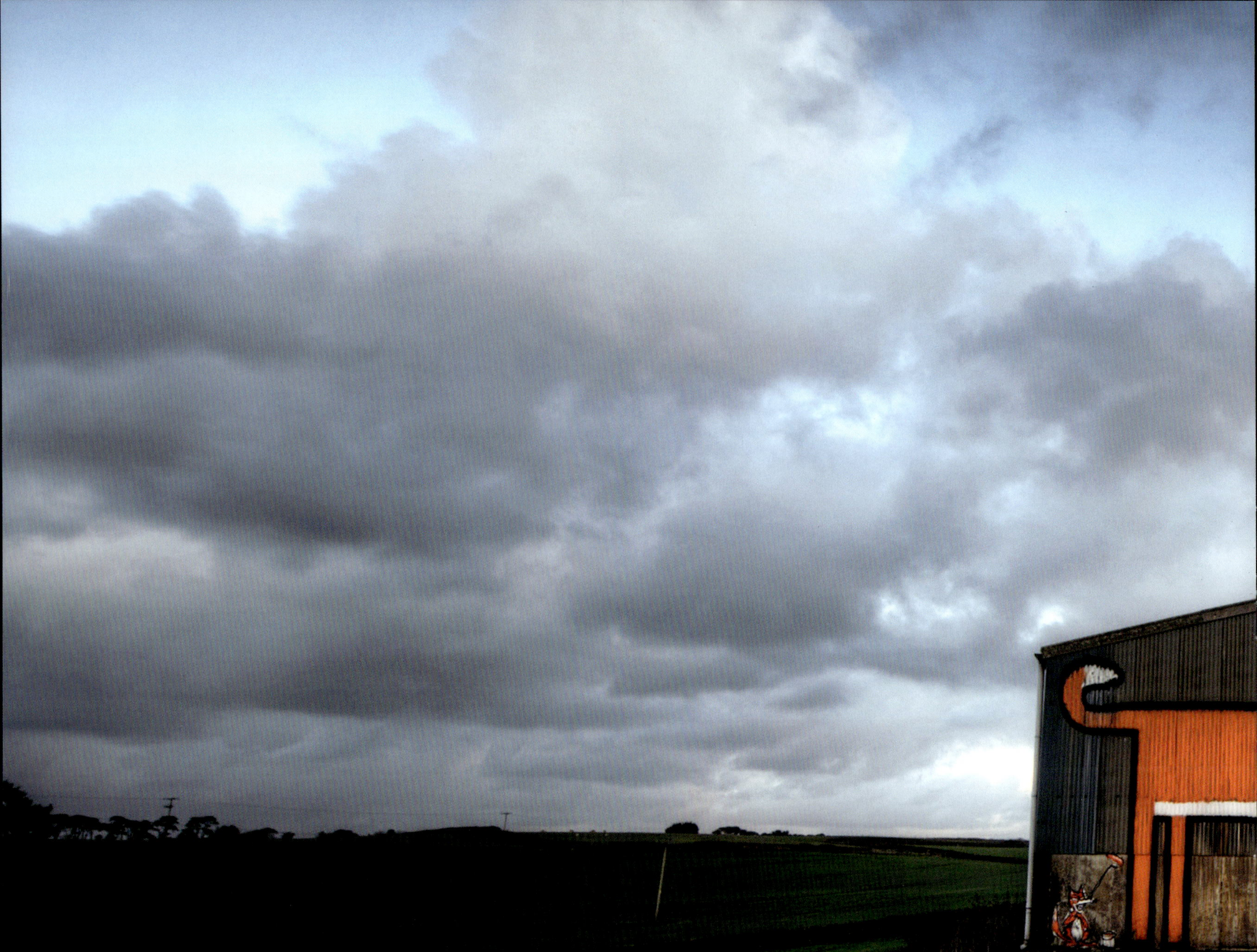

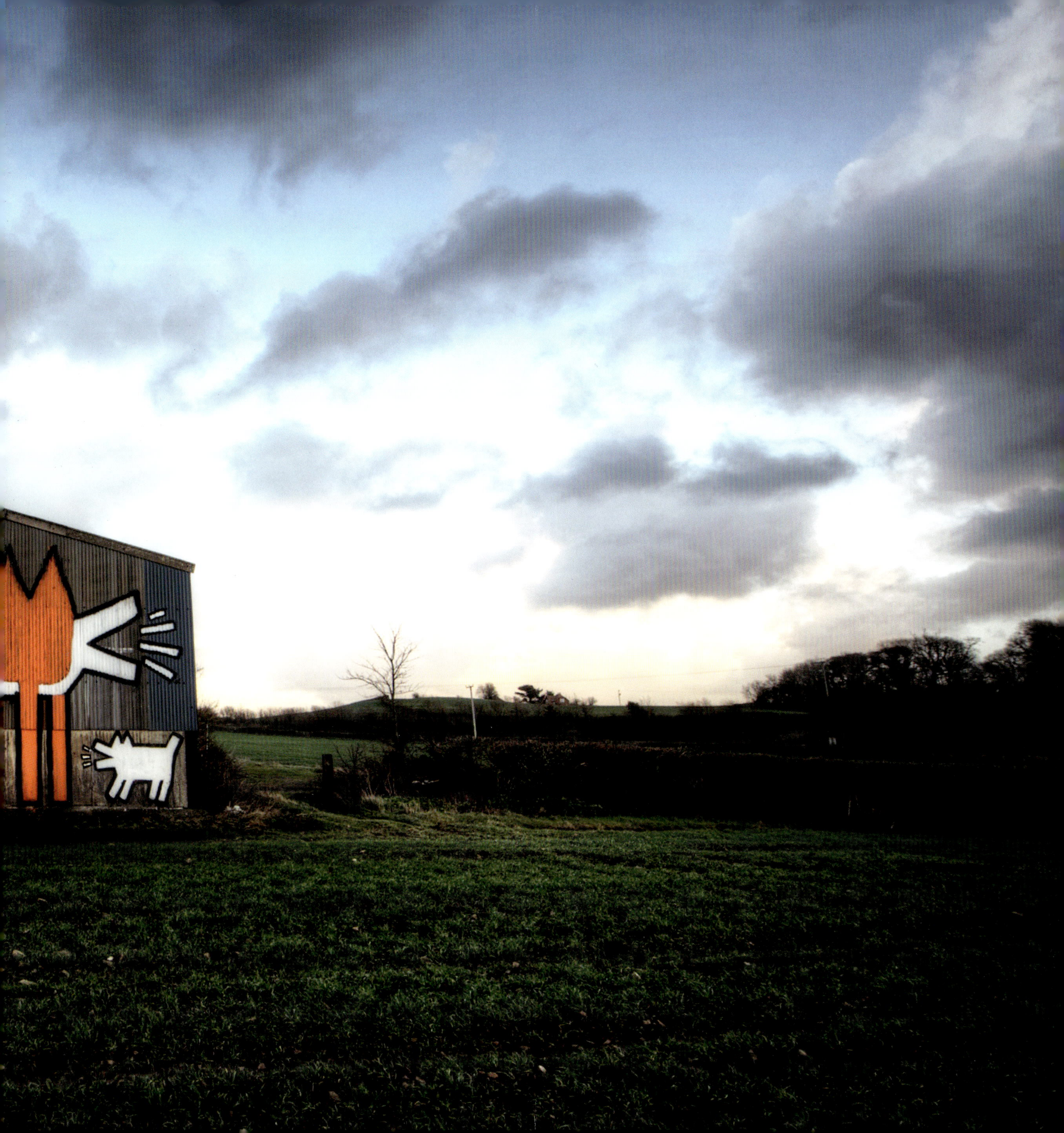

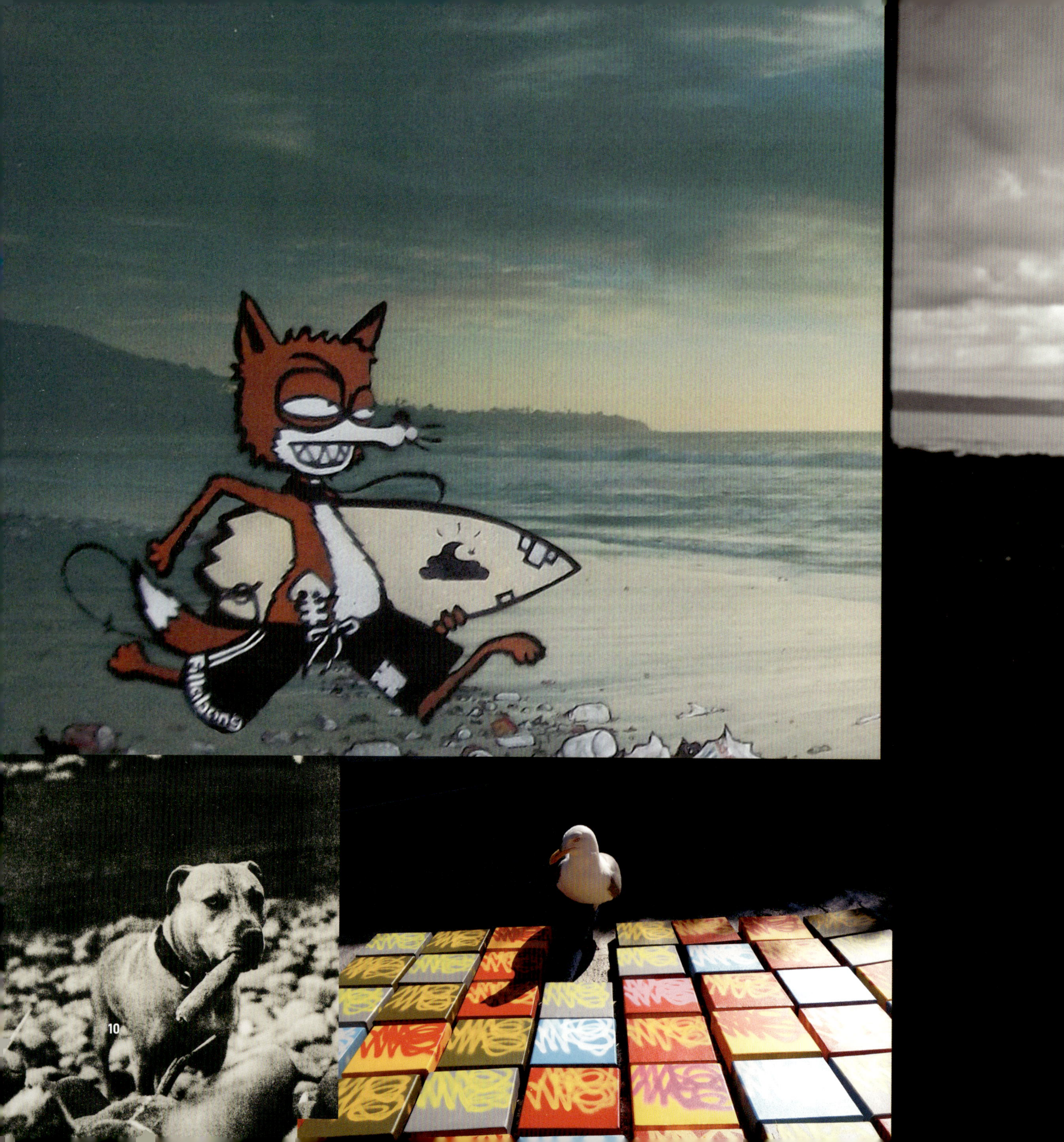
10

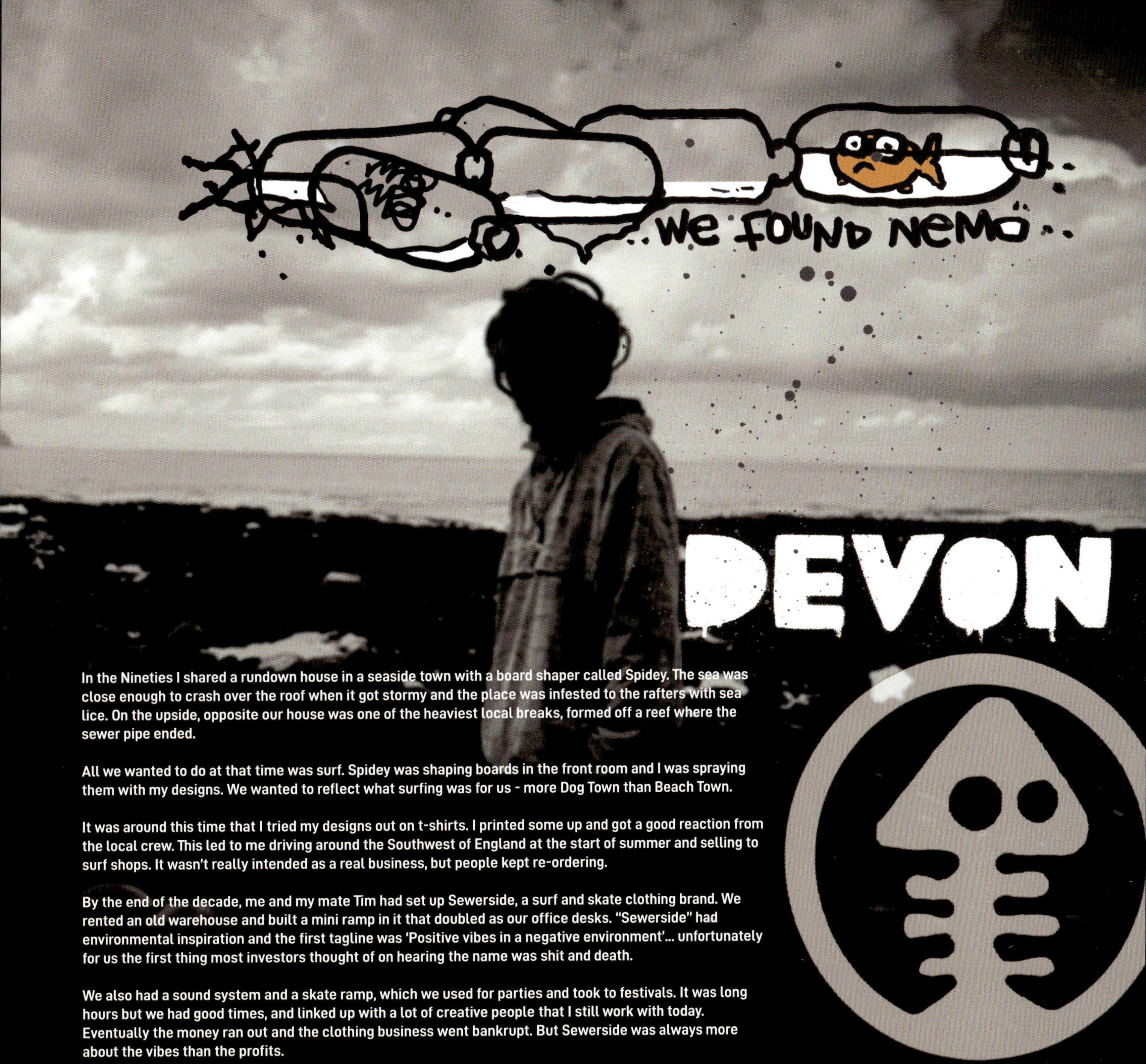

DEVON

In the Nineties I shared a rundown house in a seaside town with a board shaper called Spidey. The sea was close enough to crash over the roof when it got stormy and the place was infested to the rafters with sea lice. On the upside, opposite our house was one of the heaviest local breaks, formed off a reef where the sewer pipe ended.

All we wanted to do at that time was surf. Spidey was shaping boards in the front room and I was spraying them with my designs. We wanted to reflect what surfing was for us - more Dog Town than Beach Town.

It was around this time that I tried my designs out on t-shirts. I printed some up and got a good reaction from the local crew. This led to me driving around the Southwest of England at the start of summer and selling to surf shops. It wasn't really intended as a real business, but people kept re-ordering.

By the end of the decade, me and my mate Tim had set up Sewerside, a surf and skate clothing brand. We rented an old warehouse and built a mini ramp in it that doubled as our office desks. "Sewerside" had environmental inspiration and the first tagline was 'Positive vibes in a negative environment'... unfortunately for us the first thing most investors thought of on hearing the name was shit and death.

We also had a sound system and a skate ramp, which we used for parties and took to festivals. It was long hours but we had good times, and linked up with a lot of creative people that I still work with today. Eventually the money ran out and the clothing business went bankrupt. But Sewerside was always more about the vibes than the profits.

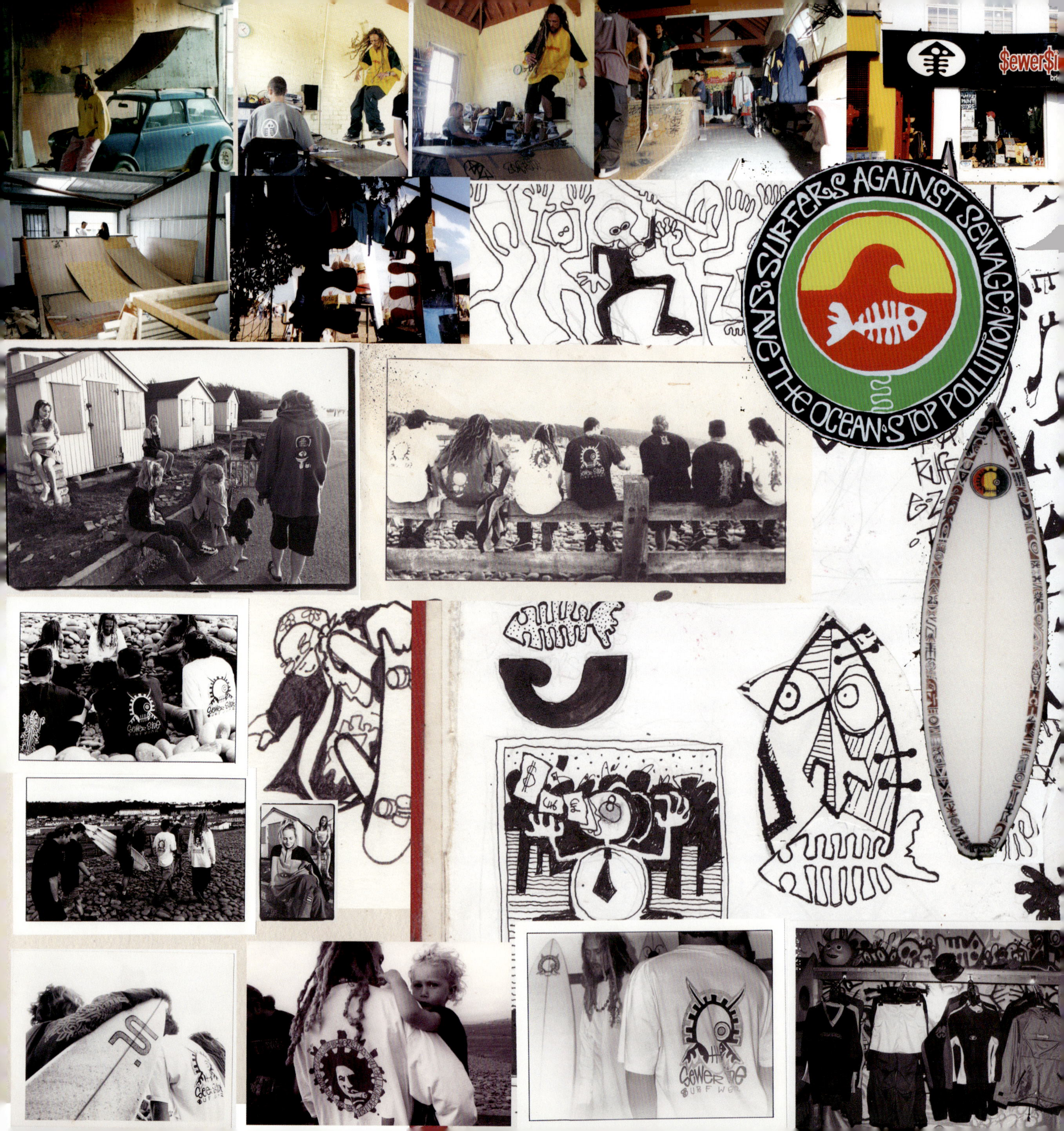
SURFERS AGAINST SEWAGE
SAVE THE OCEAN STOP POLLUTION

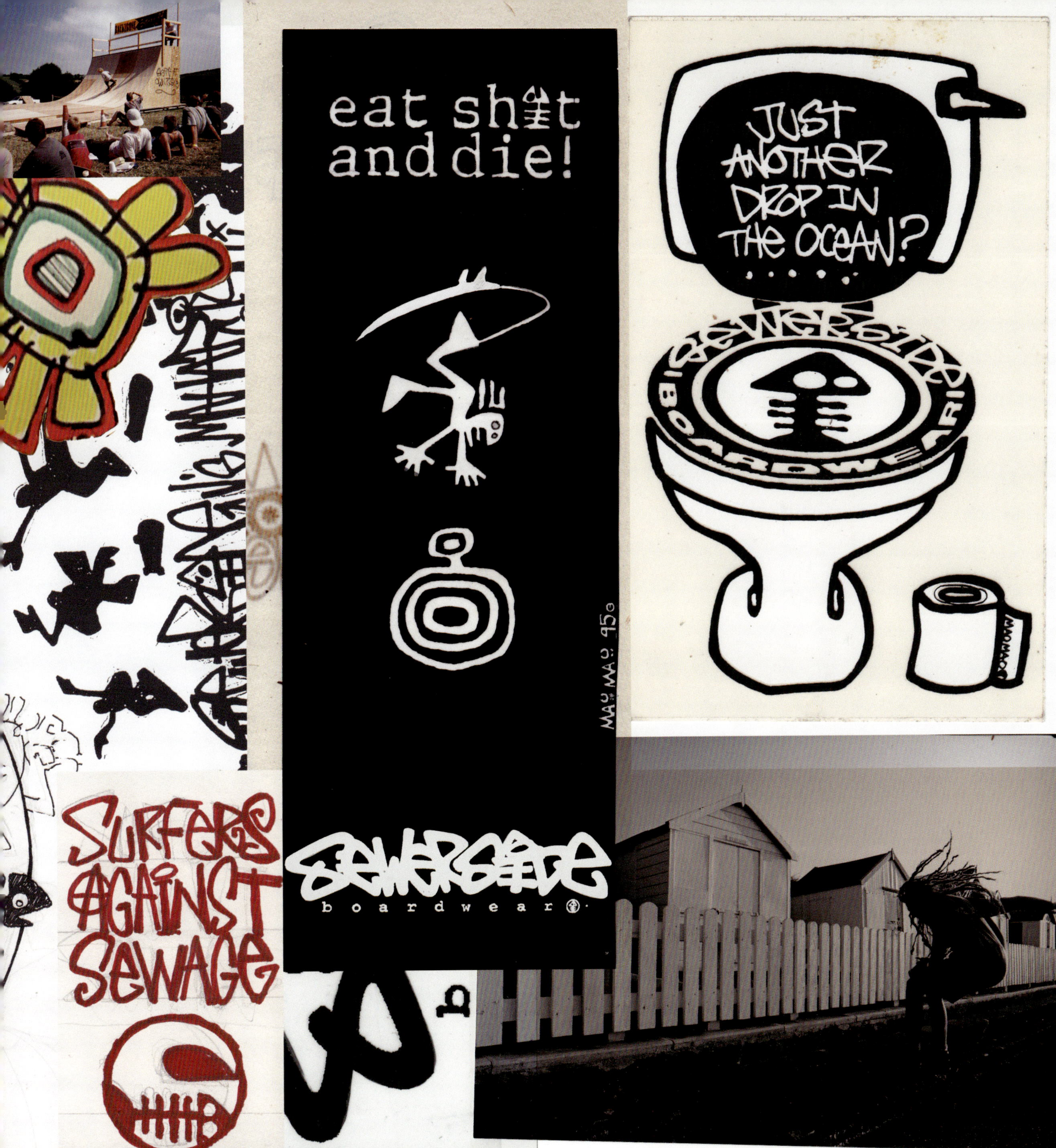
eat shit
and die!
JUST
ANOTHER
DROP IN
THE OCEAN?
SEWERSIDE
BOARDWEAR
SURFERS
AGAINST
SEWAGE
boardwear

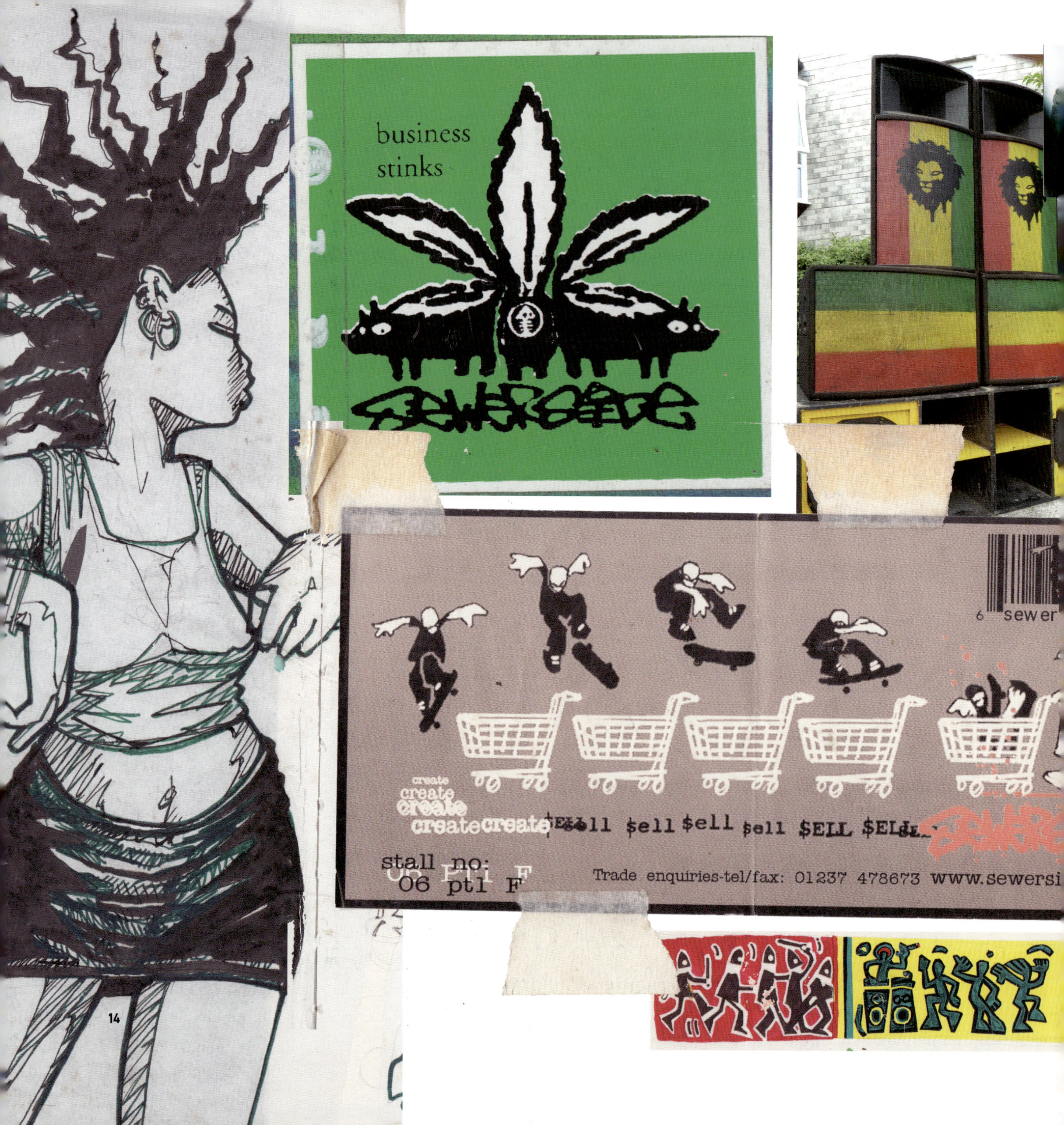
business
stinks
6 sewer
create
create
create
createcreate
$ell $ell $ell $ell $ELL $EL
stall no:
06 ptl F
Trade enquiries-tel/fax: 01237 478673 www.sewersi

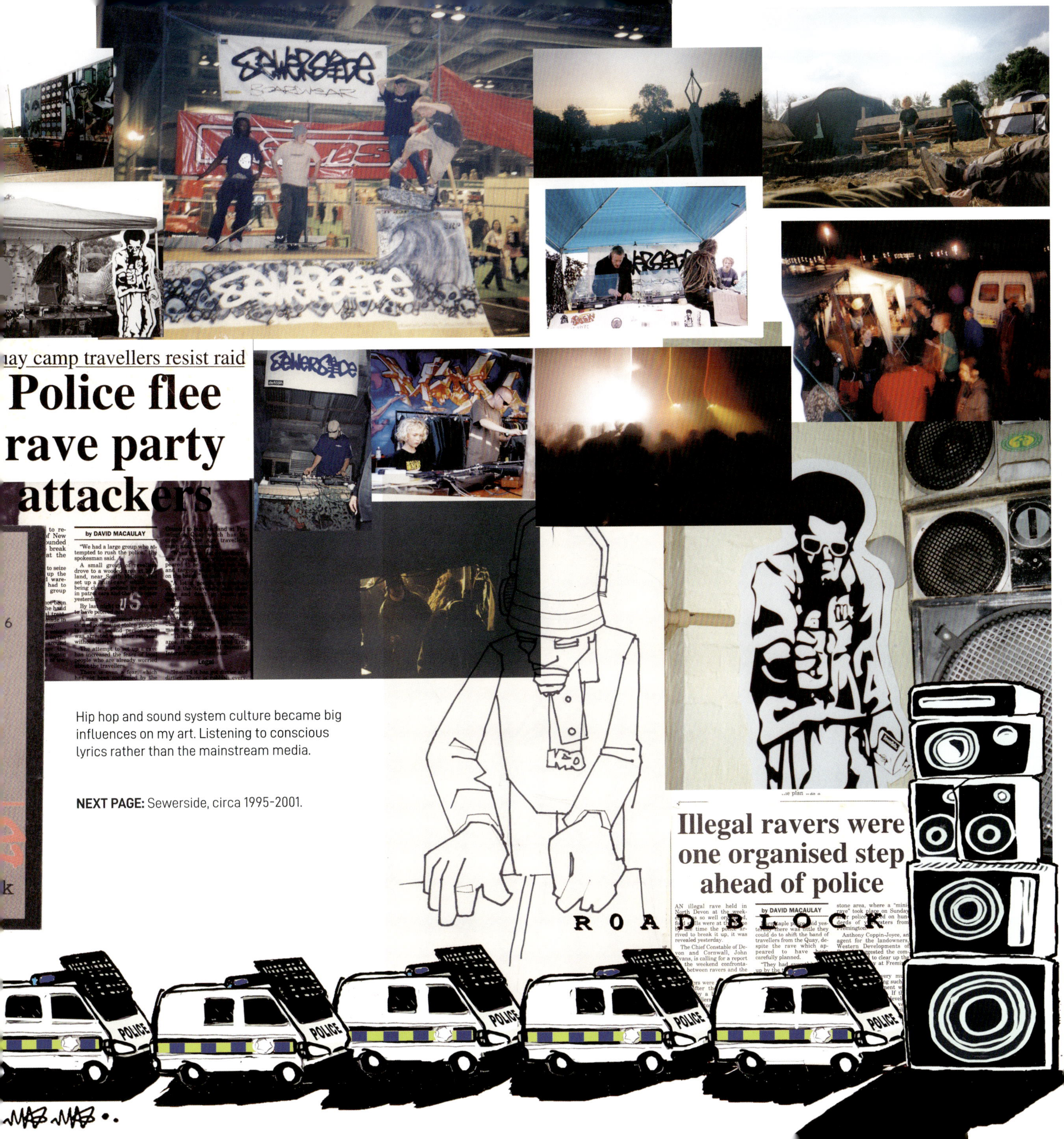

Hip hop and sound system culture became big influences on my art. Listening to conscious lyrics rather than the mainstream media.

NEXT PAGE: Sewerside, circa 1995-2001.

Sewerside circa 1995 – 2001.

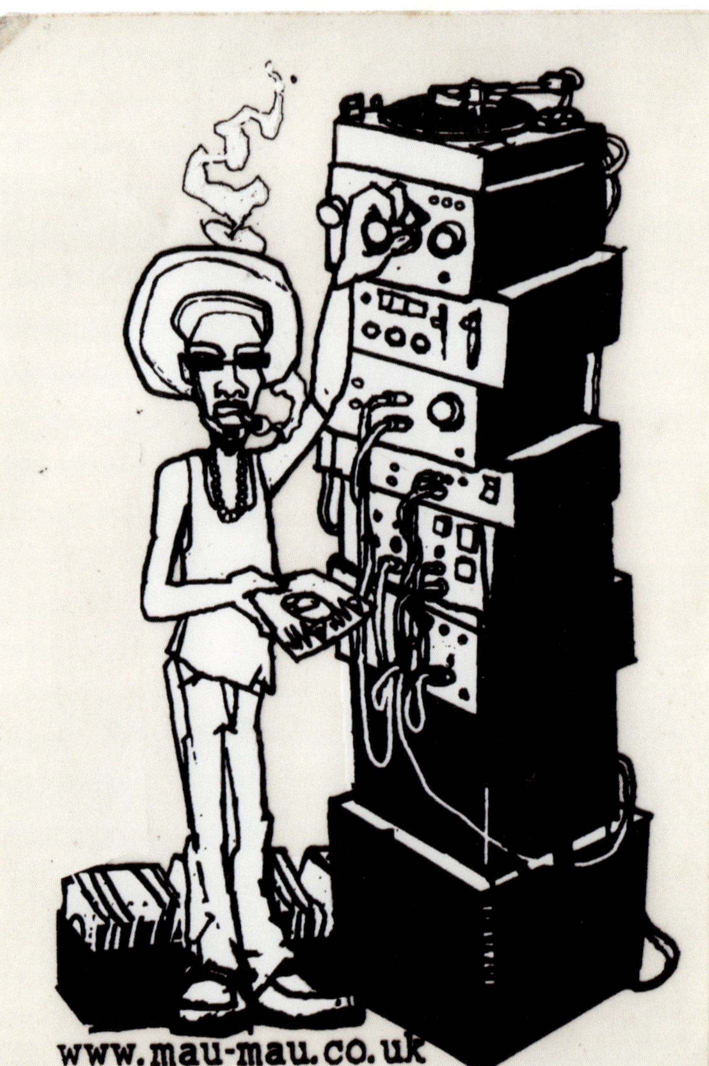

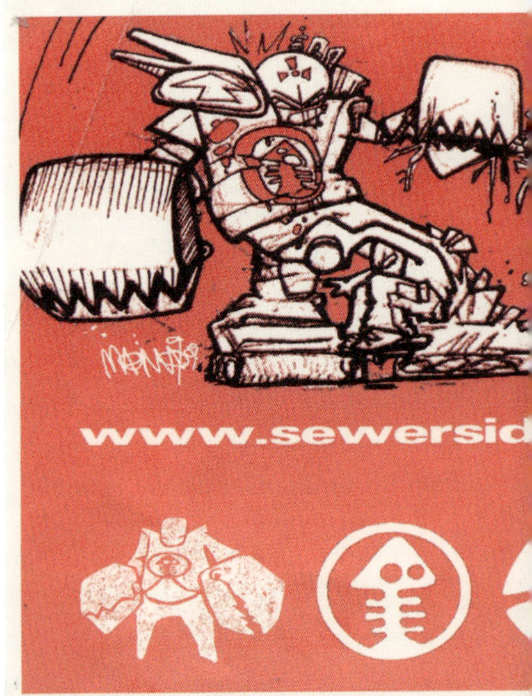

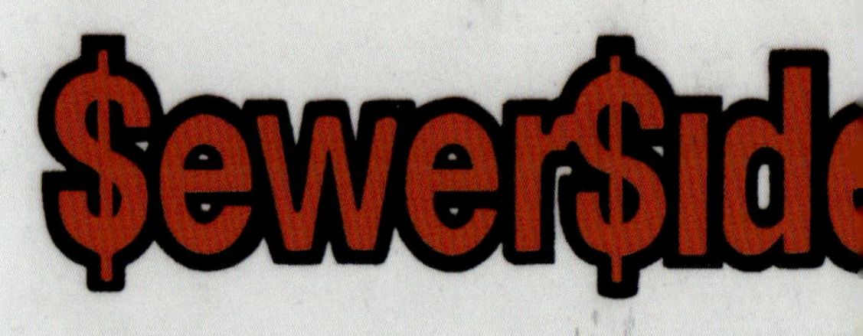

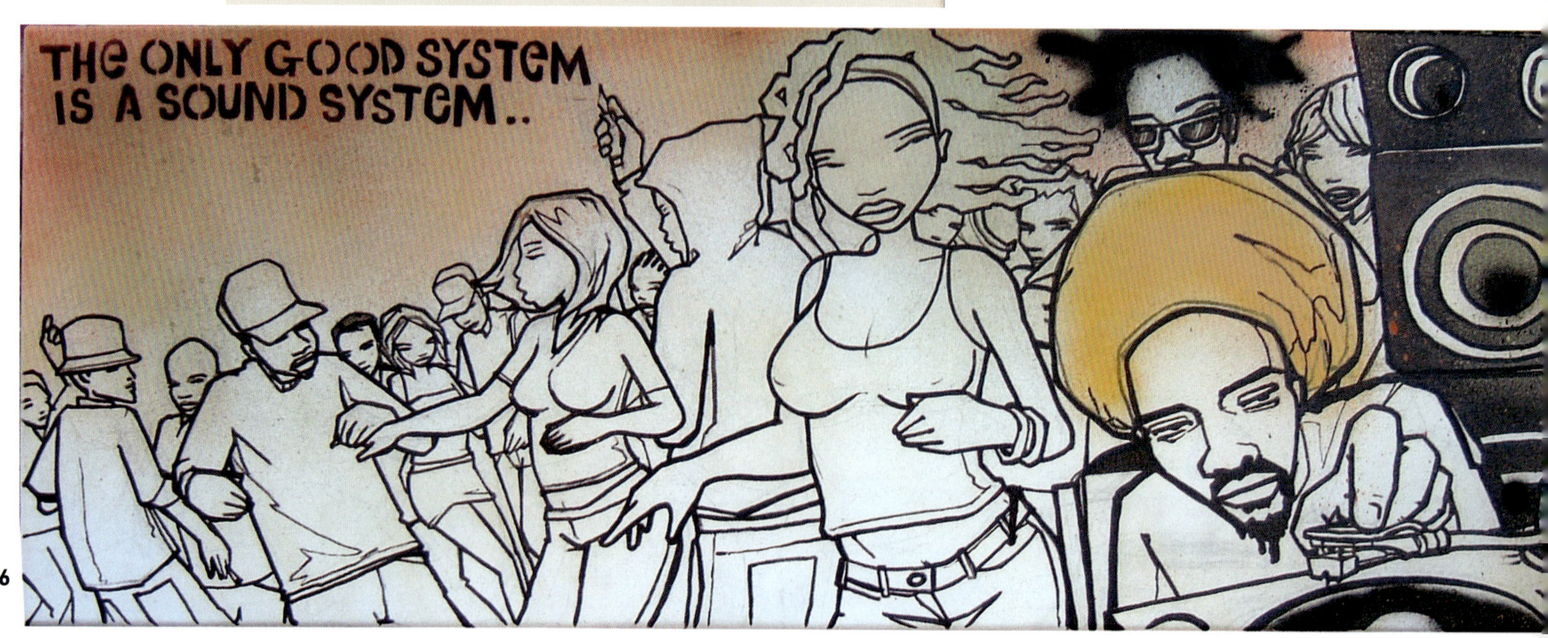

.uk
trade enq : tel/fax :01237 478673.
stand no :
06 PT1 F

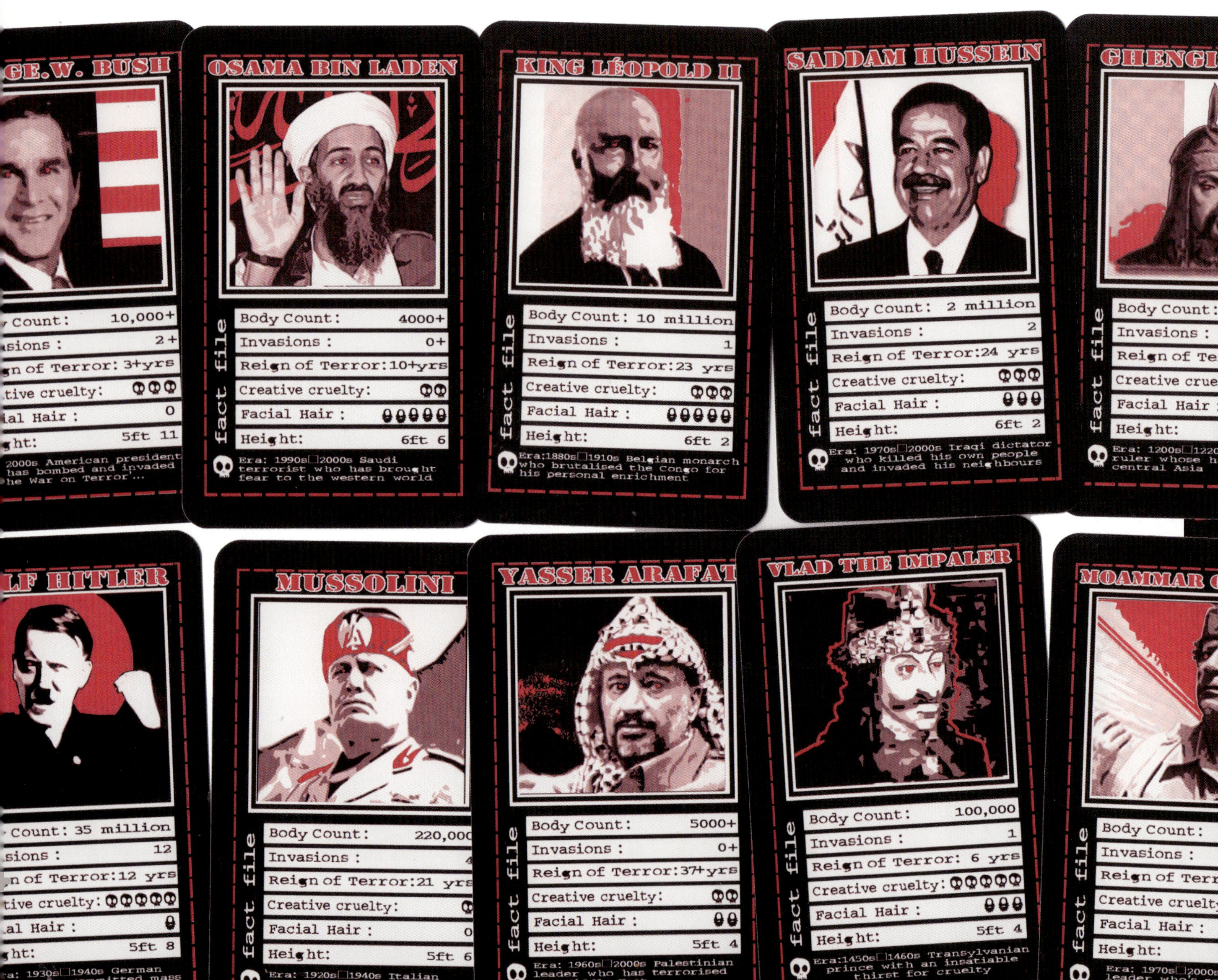

Terror Top Chumps, 2003.

After 9/11 came the War on Terror (following on from the War on Drugs) which defined the early years of the 2000s; George Bush, Tony Blair, the Iraq and Afghanistan wars and the new digital age...

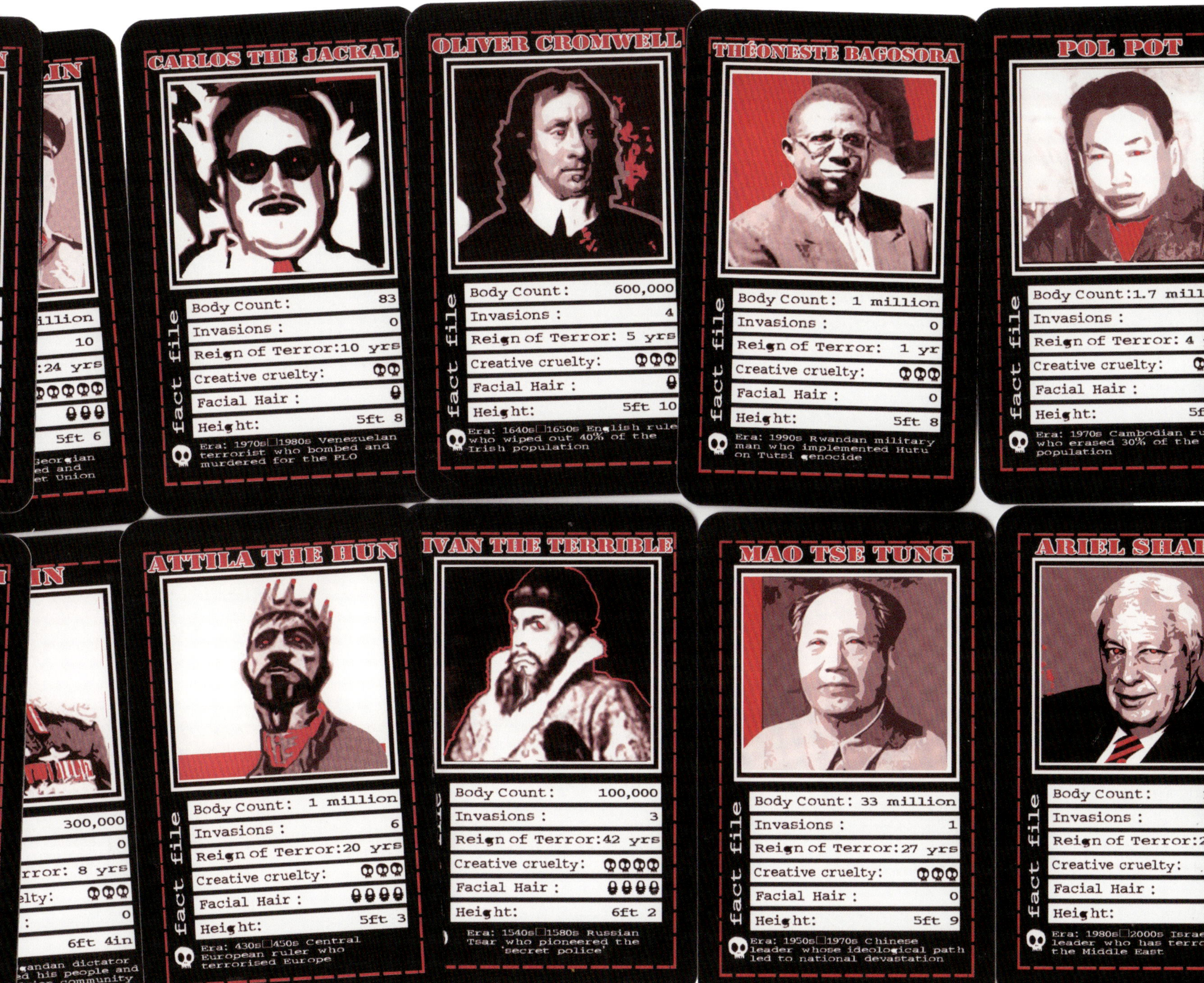

Disclaimer: The information provided is intended solely for the purpose of playing a game. It should not be used as a revision aid or for the basis of a government dossier [Terror Top Chump card game rules].

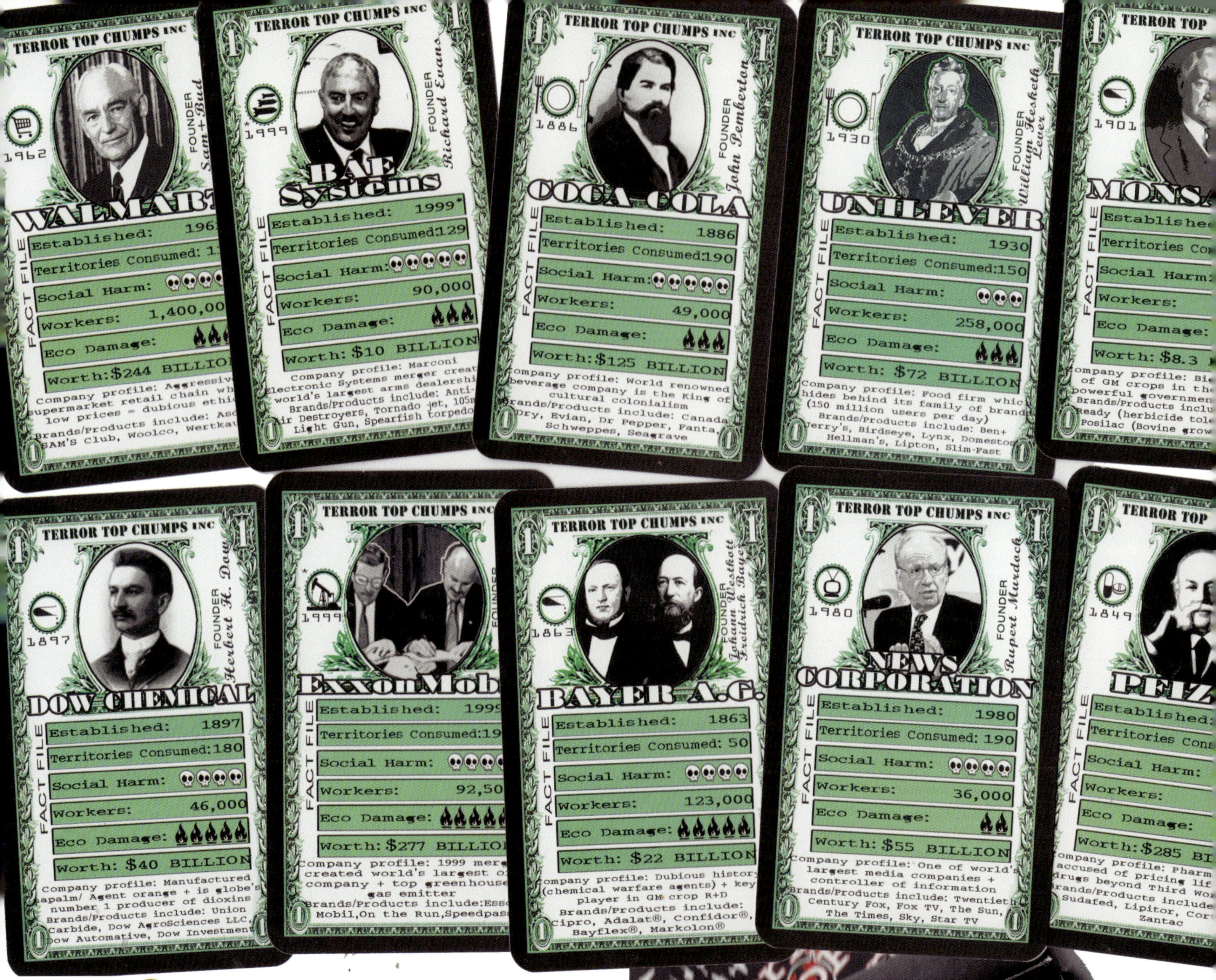

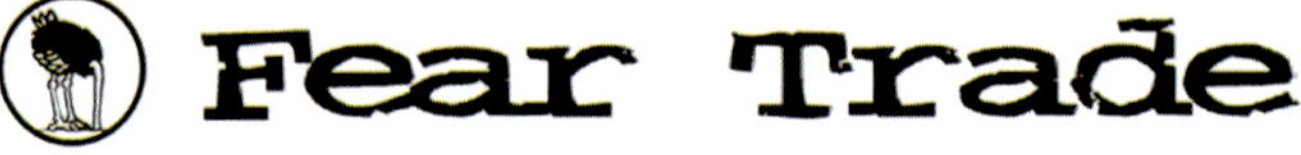

Corporate Top Chumps, 2005.

Disclaimer:
The information provided is intended solely for the purpose of playing a game.
It should not be used as a business aid or the basis of a hostile takeover [Terror Top Chumps Inc card game rules].

PAGE RIGHT: Protection Against Terror (alternative to UK government) leaflet, 2005.

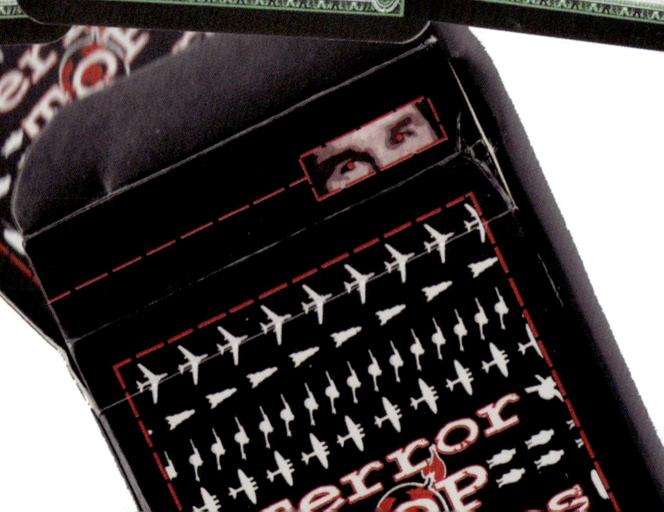

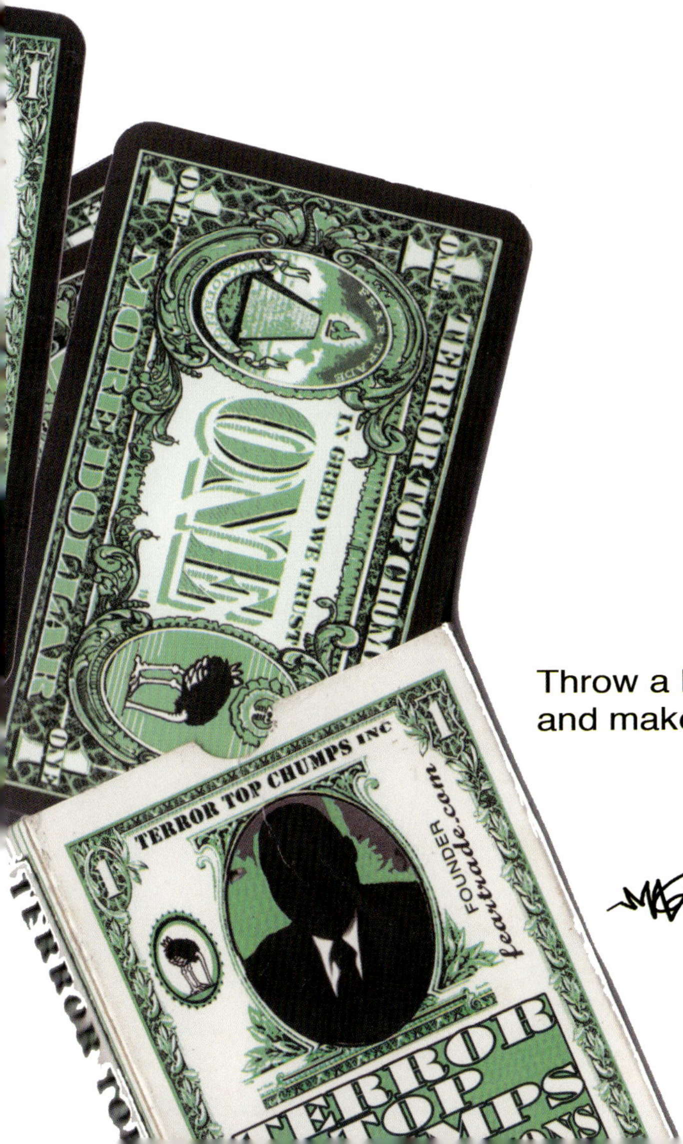

PROTECTION AGAINST TERROR

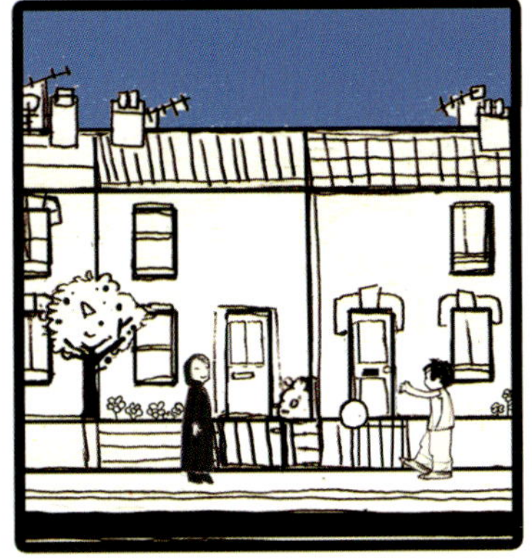

Tune in, turn on, believe..

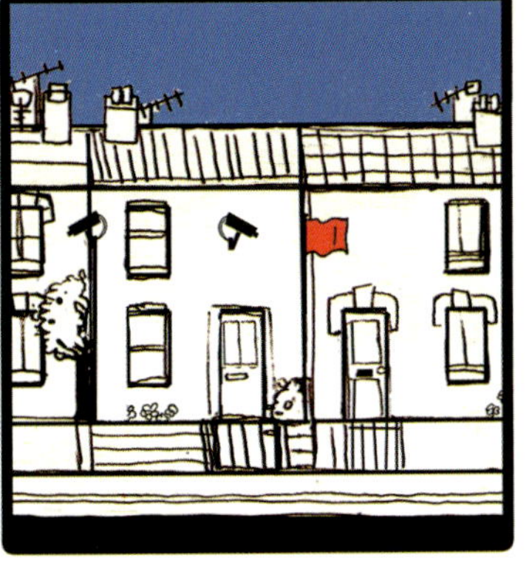

Trust no-one, spy on your neighbours...

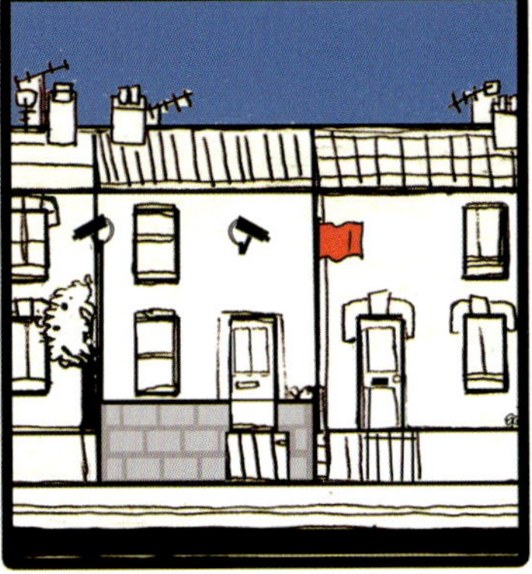

Raise your flag, lock your doors, paranoid

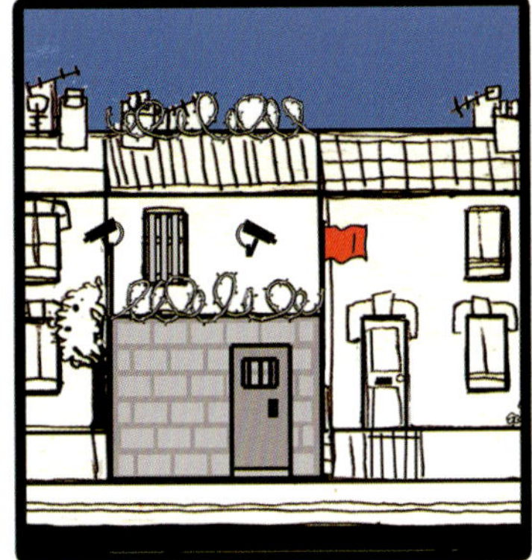

Stay safe, stay inside, do not go out....

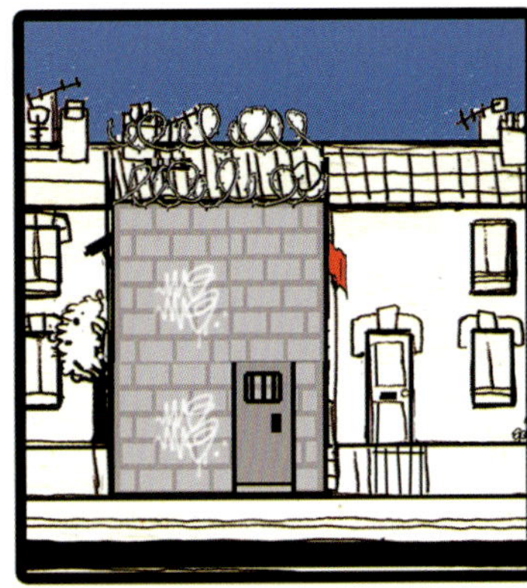

..ever again...

OR...

Throw a block party and make new friends..

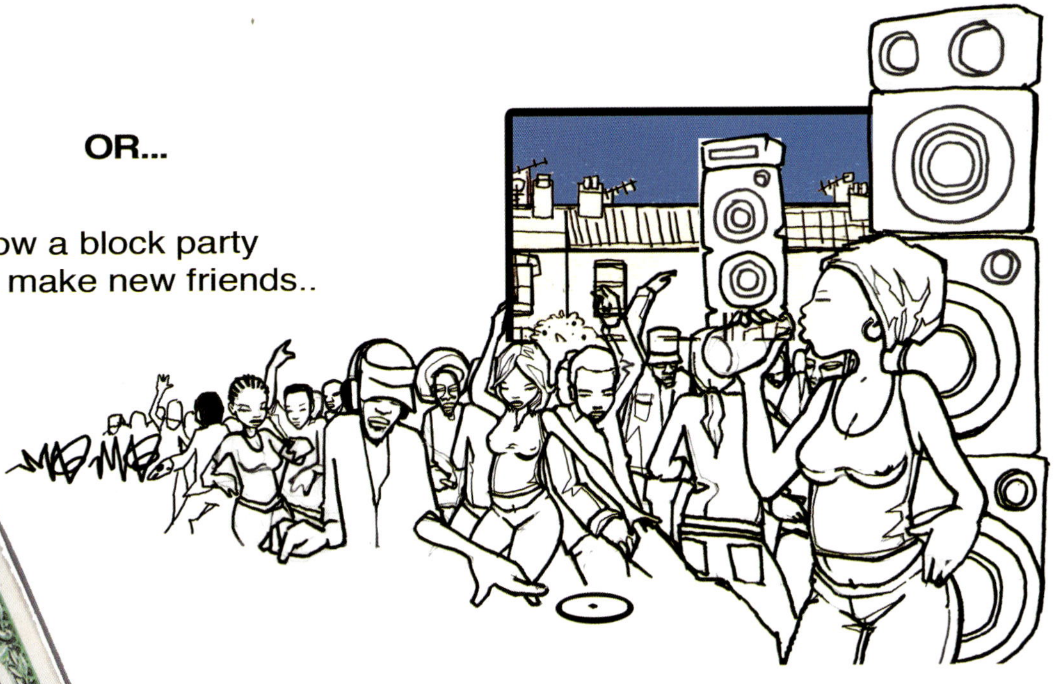

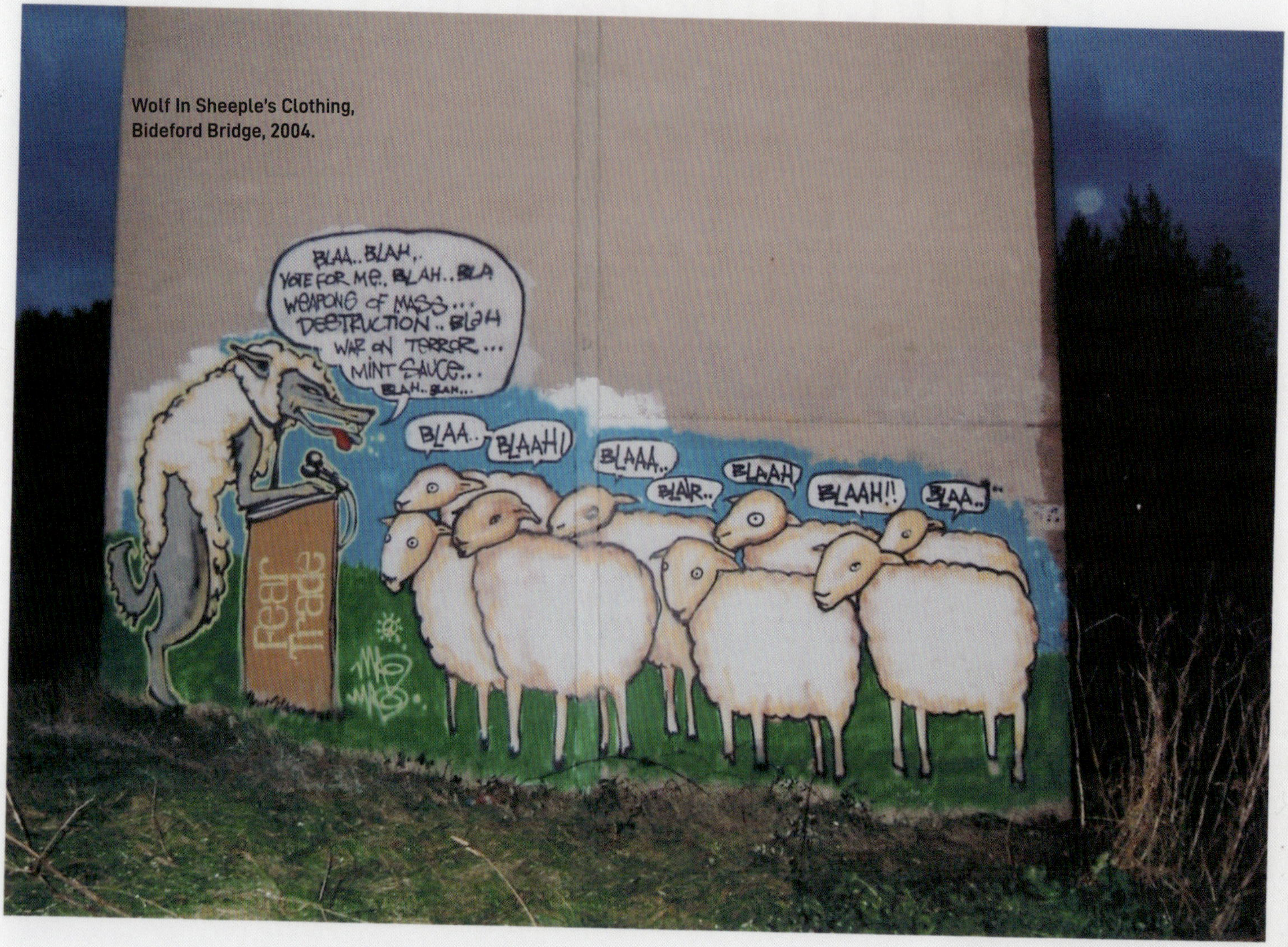

Wolf In Sheeple's Clothing, Bideford Bridge, 2004.

Corporate Undertaker, early stencil, North Devon, 2003.

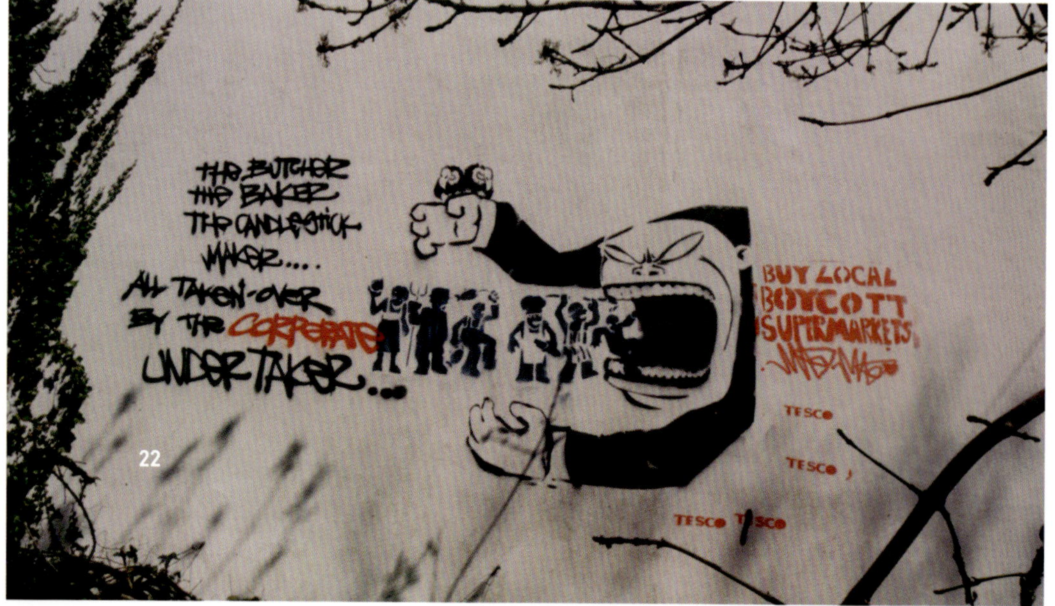

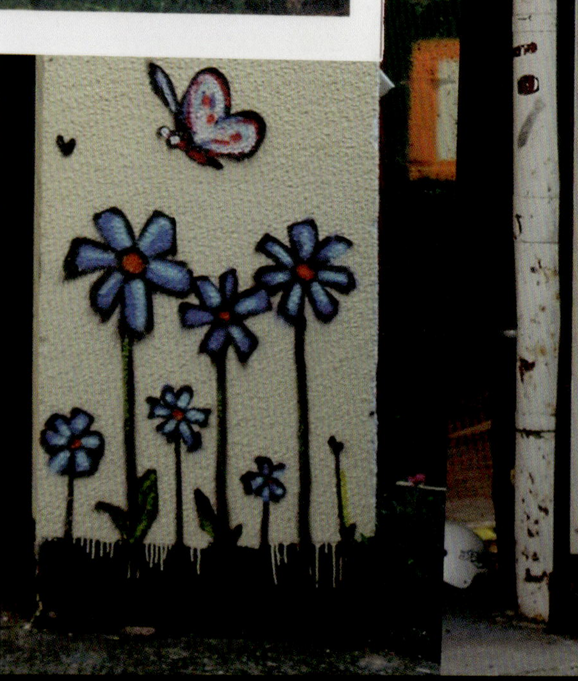

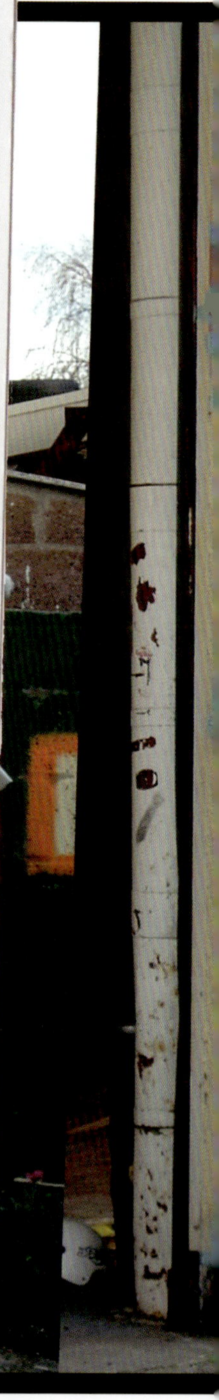

When Sewerside wrapped up, I began to focus more on painting. There wasn't much of a scene in Devon so I used to paint on my own a lot. My inspiration was to paint pieces that had a message.

Wac Ronald, SRP Skate Park, 2003.

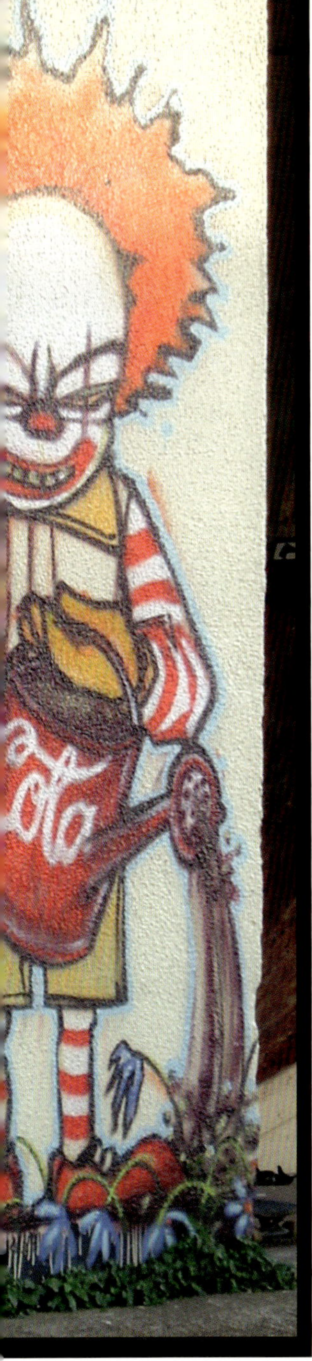

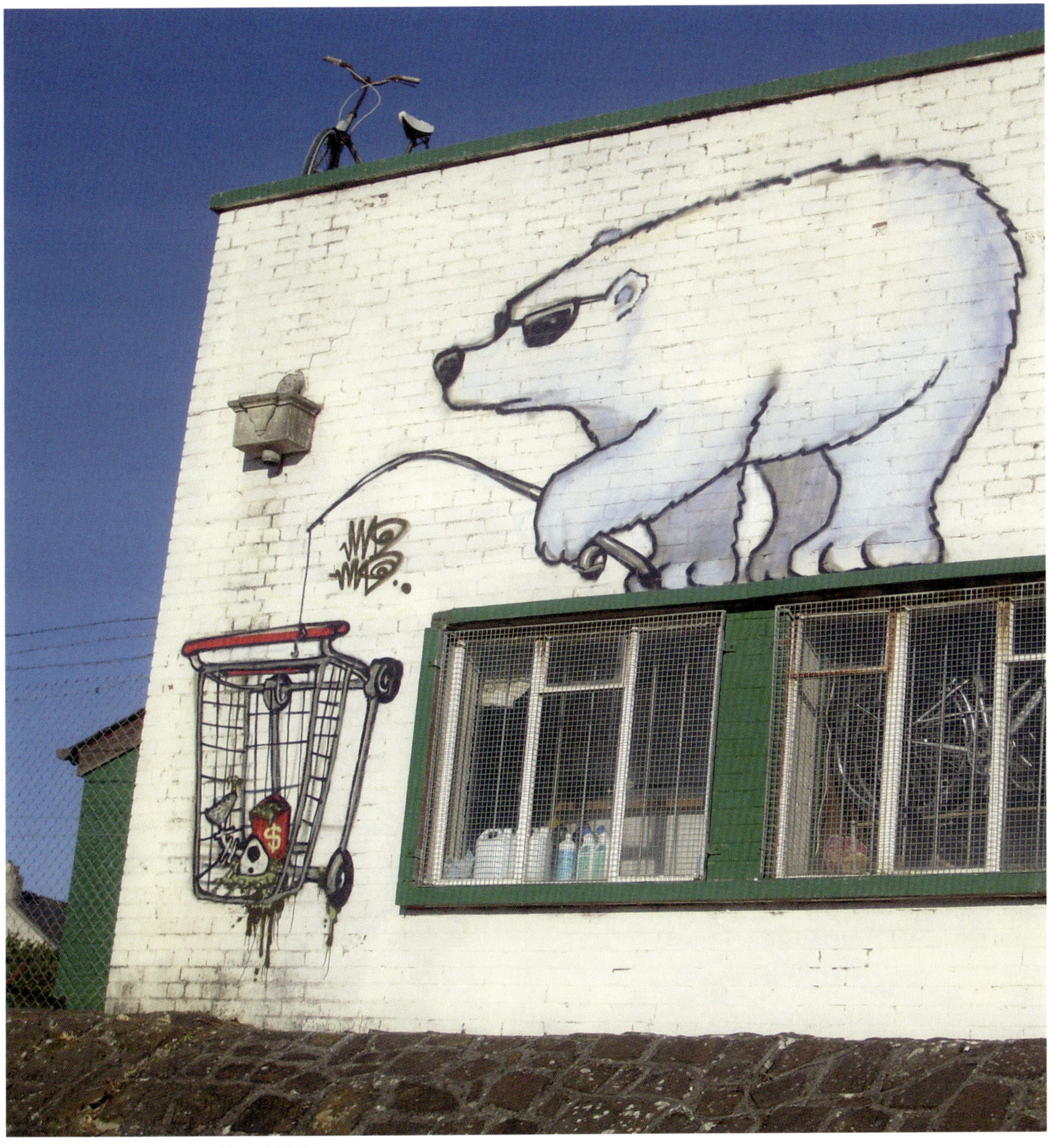

Bear Rubbish, River Torridge, 2004.

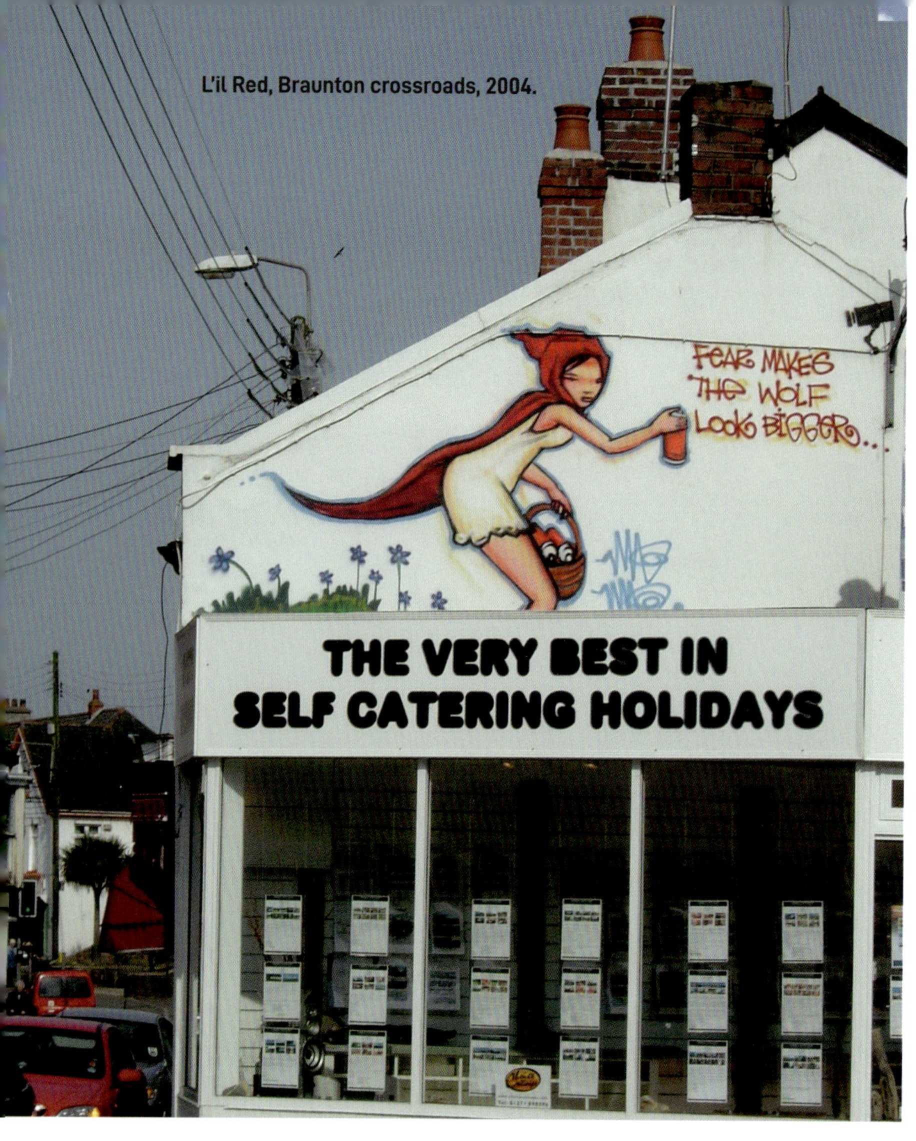

L'il Red, Braunton crossroads, 2004.

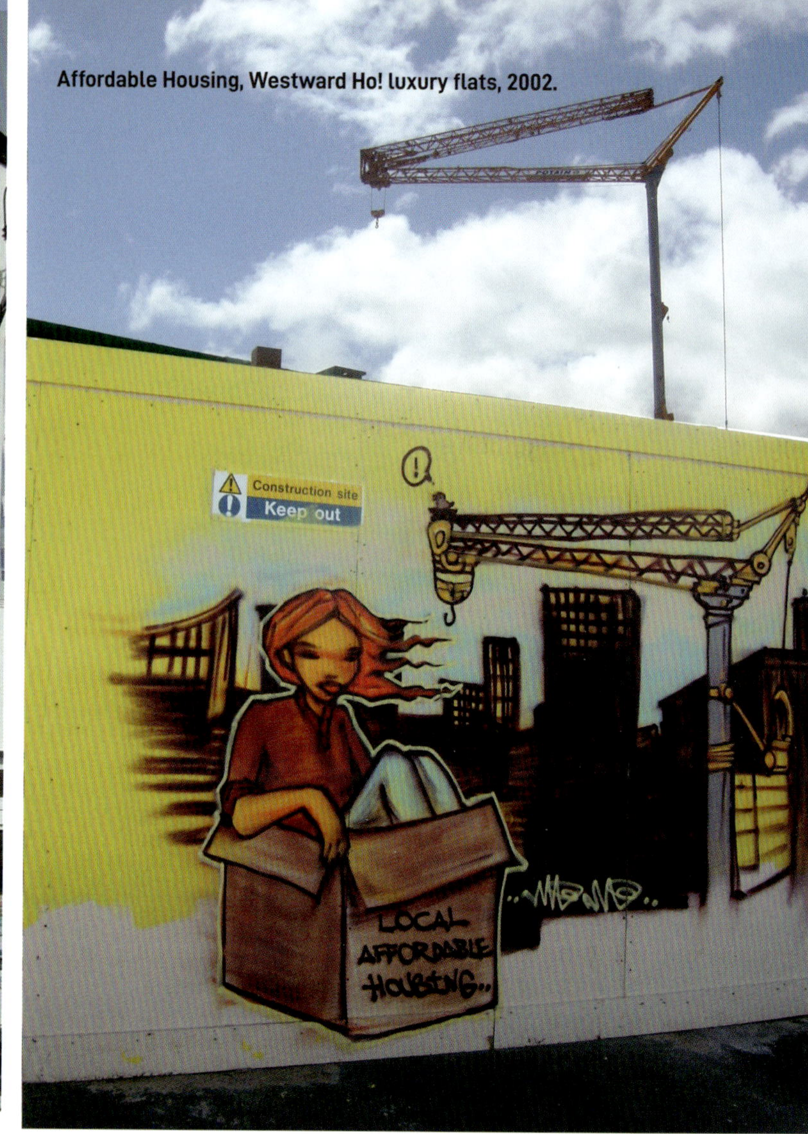

Affordable Housing, Westward Ho! luxury flats, 2002.

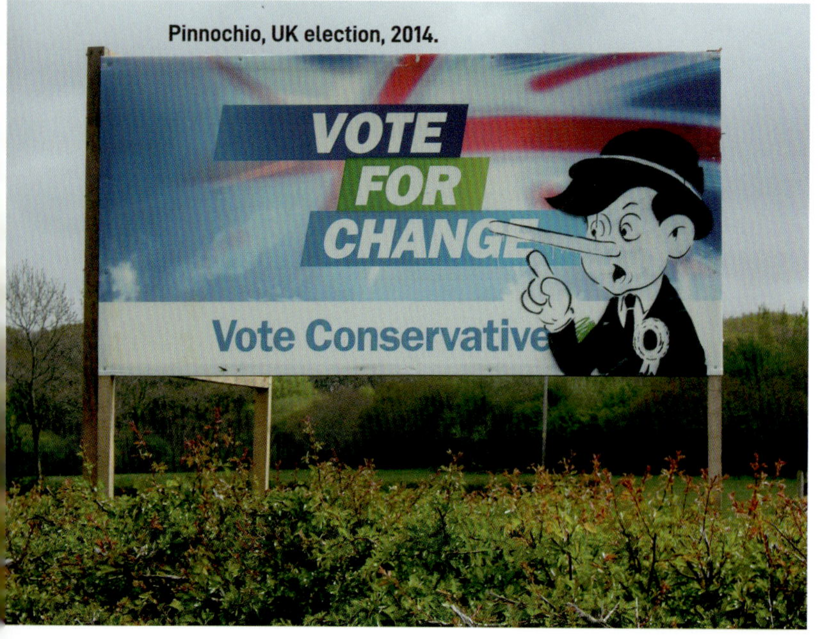

Pinnochio, UK election, 2014.

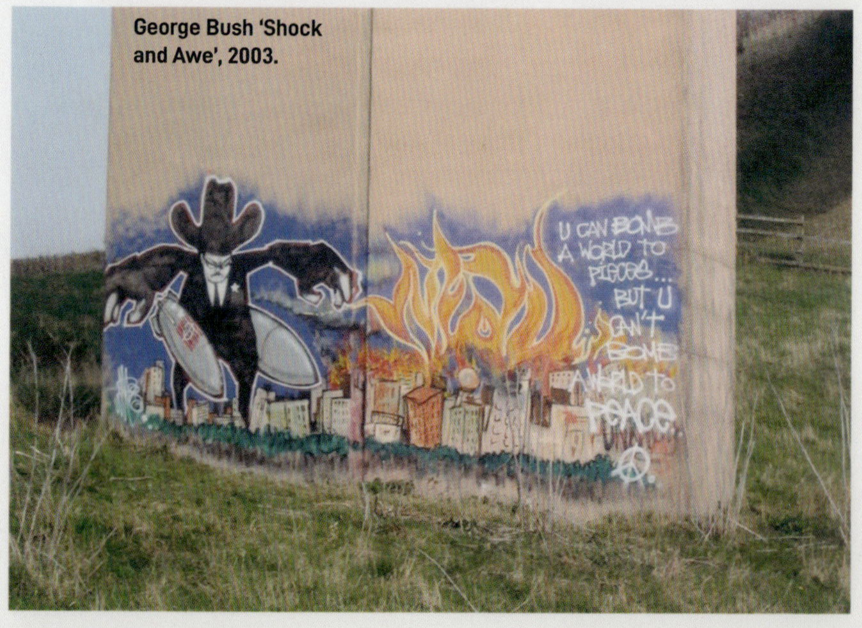

George Bush 'Shock and Awe', 2003.

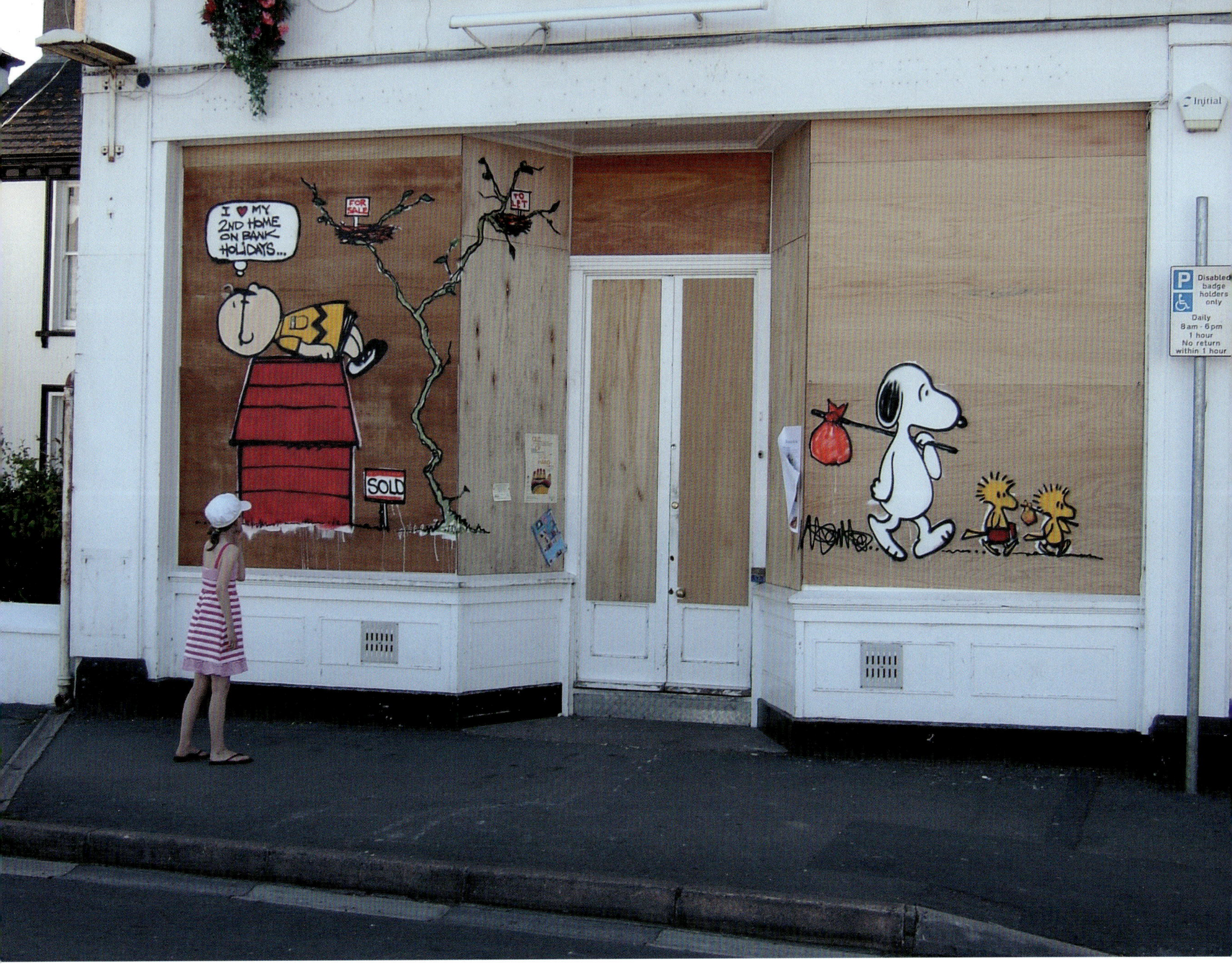

I Love My Second Home On Bank Holidays, 2005.

There was no CCTV to worry about and some spots were so remote that you could paint them in daylight. Being a holiday destination, random spots like a barn or a ship wreck that were deserted during winter became busy in summer.

I painted pieces about what was happening around me – from the lack of local housing to the global War on Terror. It was around then that street art started to become more popular – and I started to get emails asking if my pieces could be bought anywhere. One day a friend put a canvas on eBay and it sold instantly. That was a turning point...

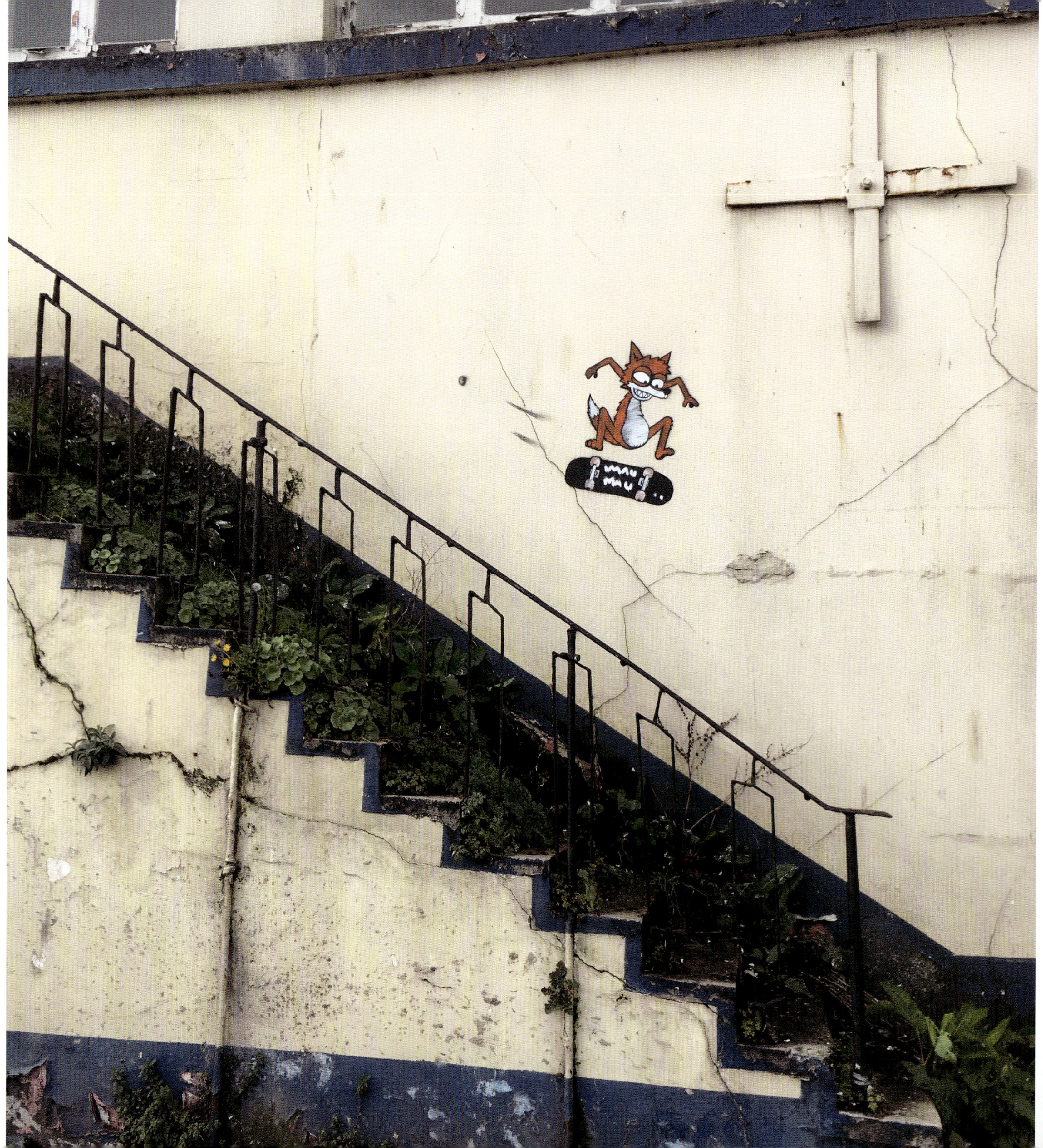
MAU
MAU

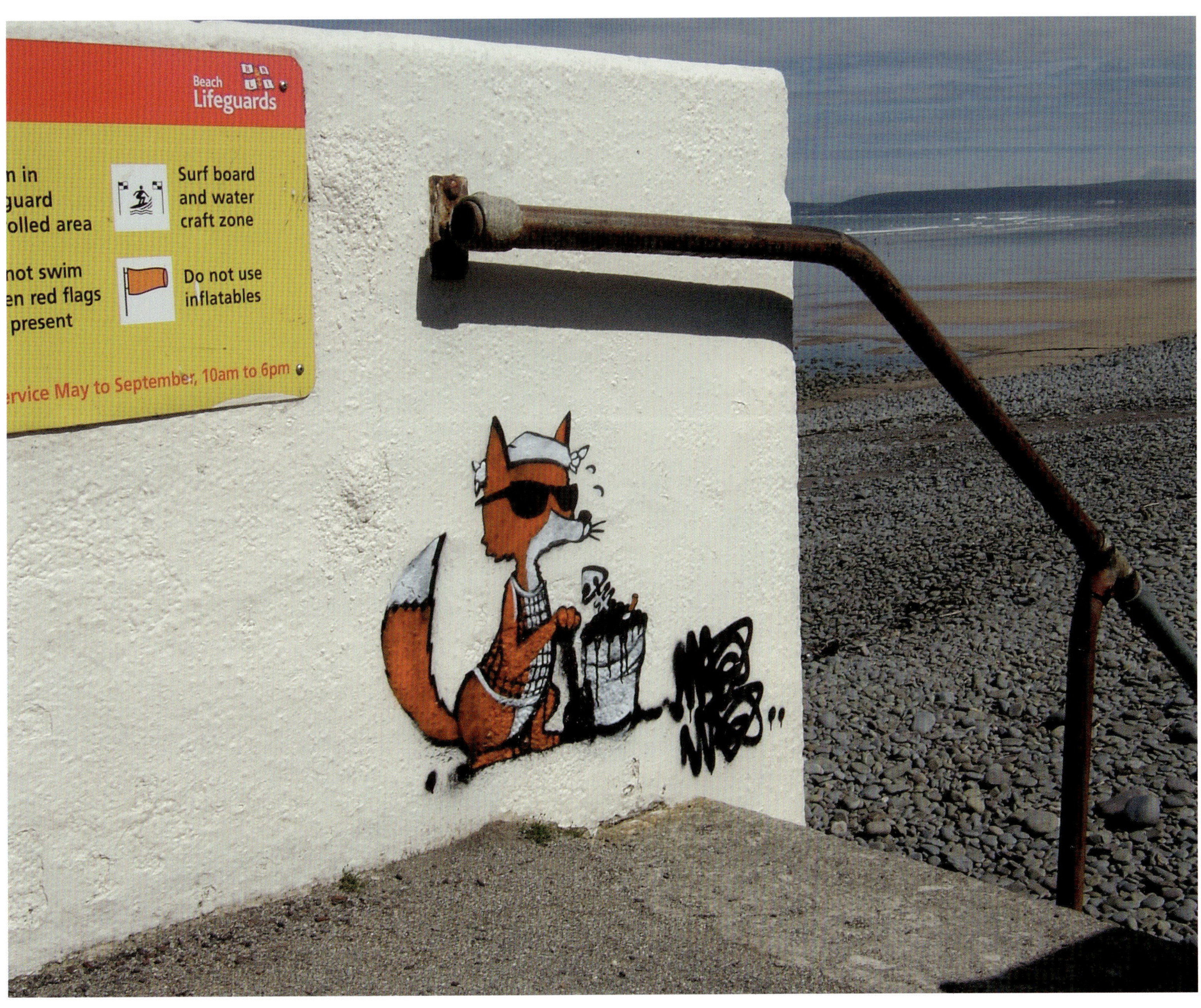

Beach Fox, Westward Ho!, 2013.

Skate Fox, Bideford, 2018.

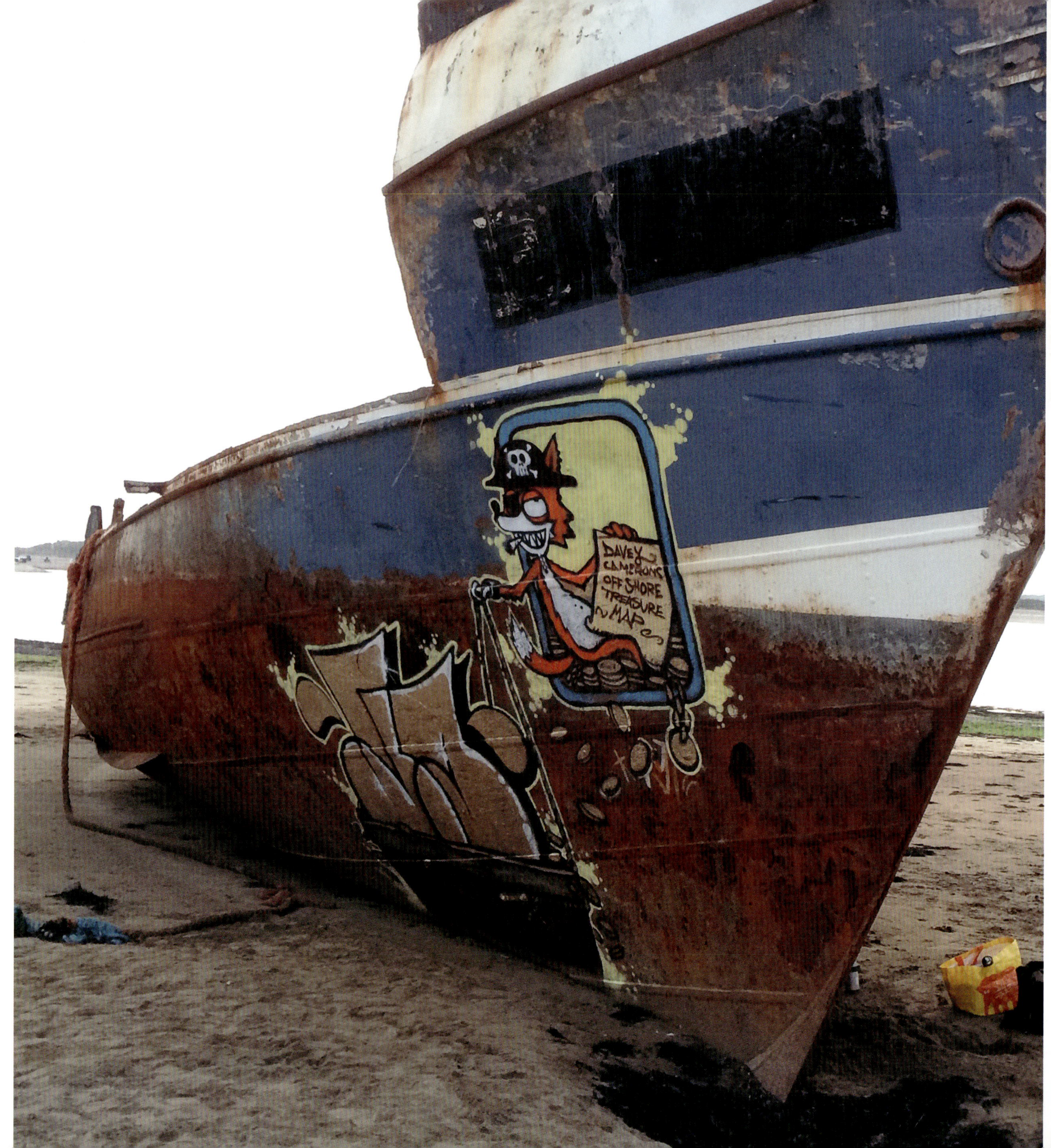
DAVEY CAMERON'S OFF SHORE TREASURE MAP

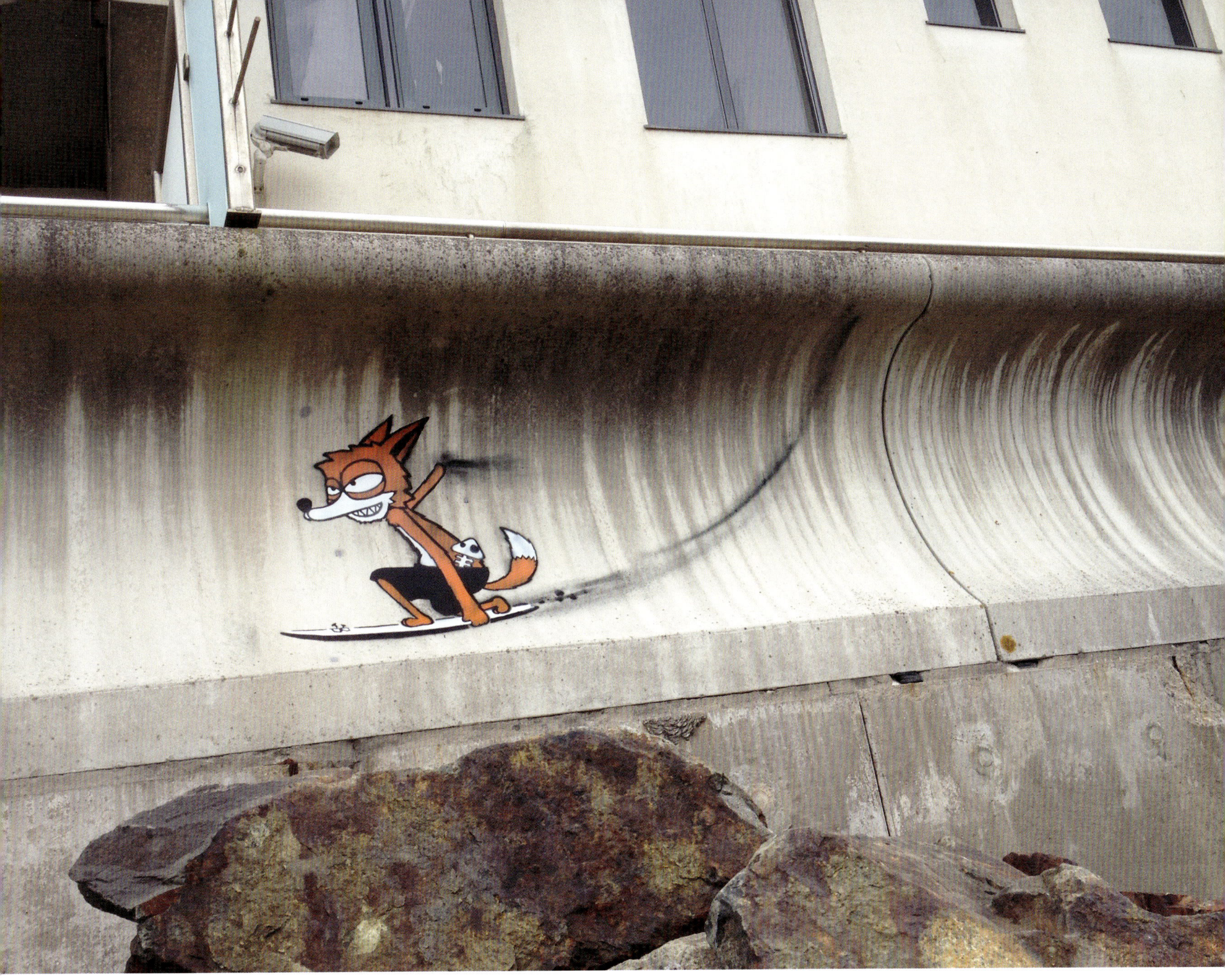

Surfing Fox, Westward Ho! sea front, 2017.

Offshore Treasure Map, Yelland Quay, 2016 (Zhe 155, Mau).

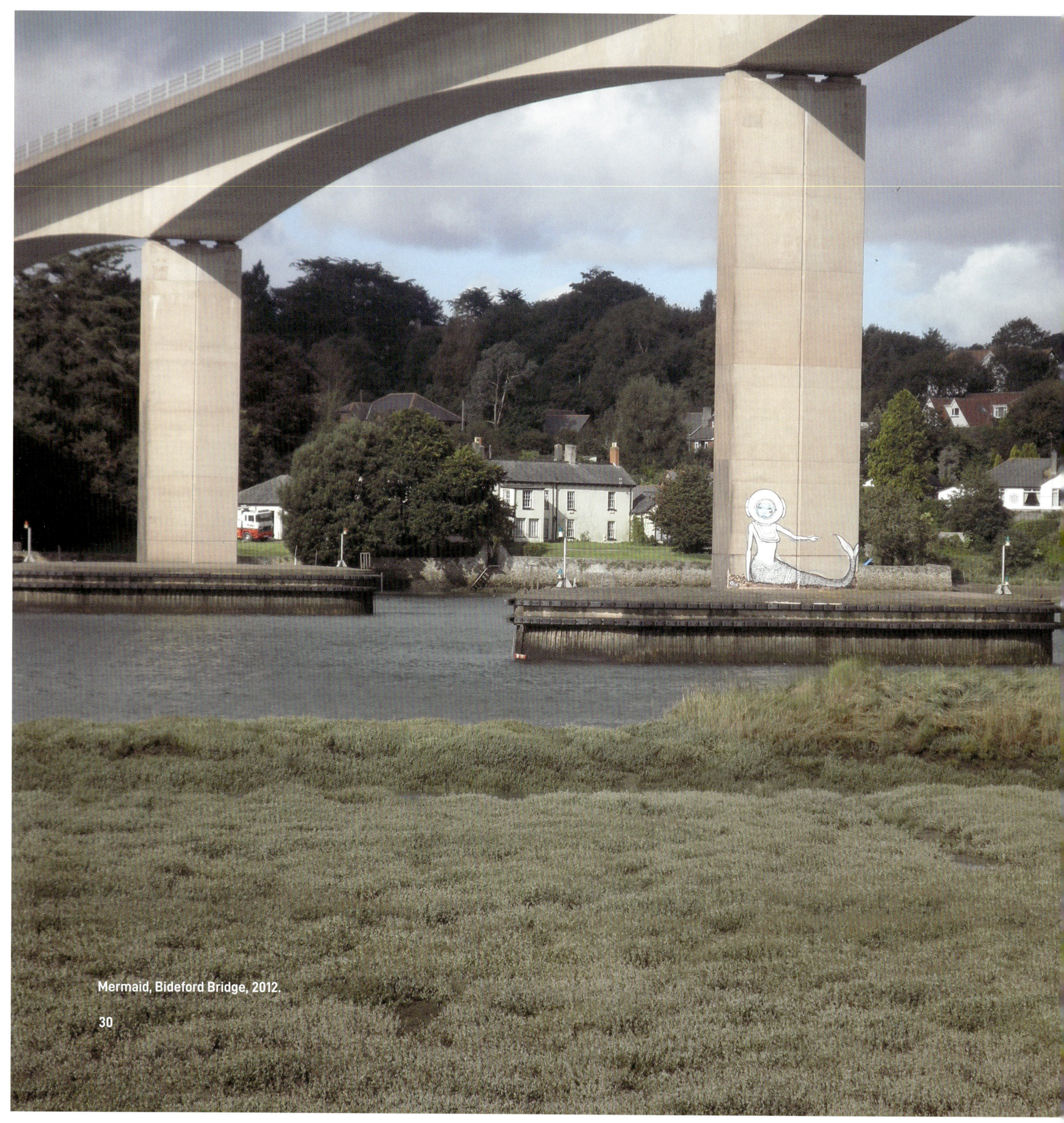

Mermaid, Bideford Bridge, 2012.

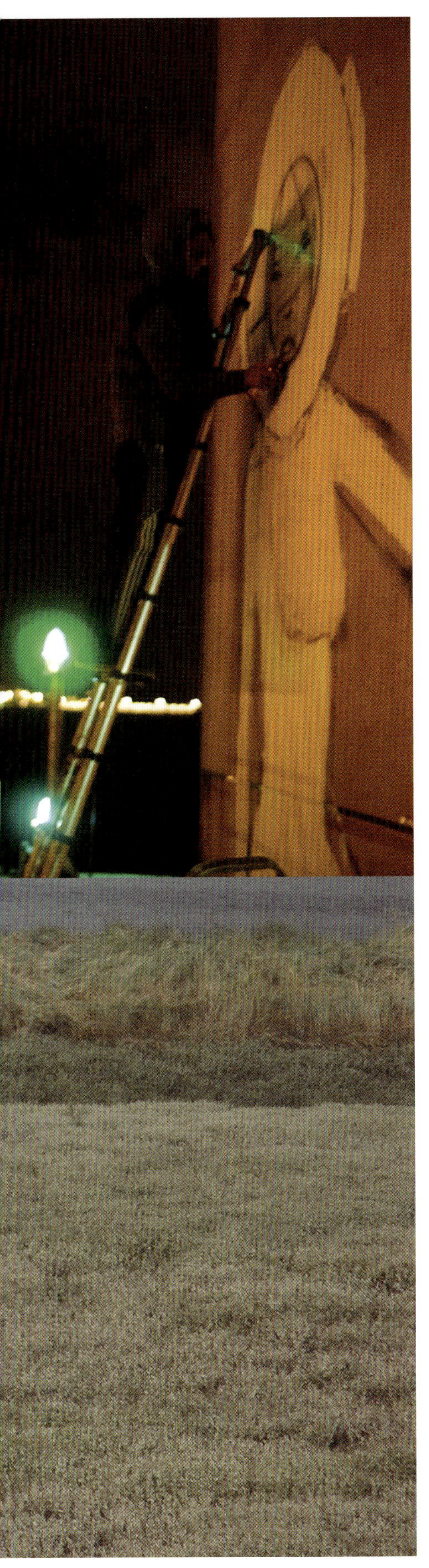

Mermaid Story

Longman was a bit of a local legend and always up for adventure, like when a cargo of wood came off a ship in a storm and got washed up on a local beach, he took it and used it to build a beach shack at a secret spot for the locals. It was his idea to paint the Mermaid on the bridge. He and his mate were heading off in a boat at high tide to go night fishing. He took me and Beejoir out with him (more about him later). It was summer, but it was in the middle of the river and it was windy and freezing cold. We had a couple of hours to do the piece before they came back with the tide. We weren't sure how it would turn out, but we knew it wouldn't get buffed...

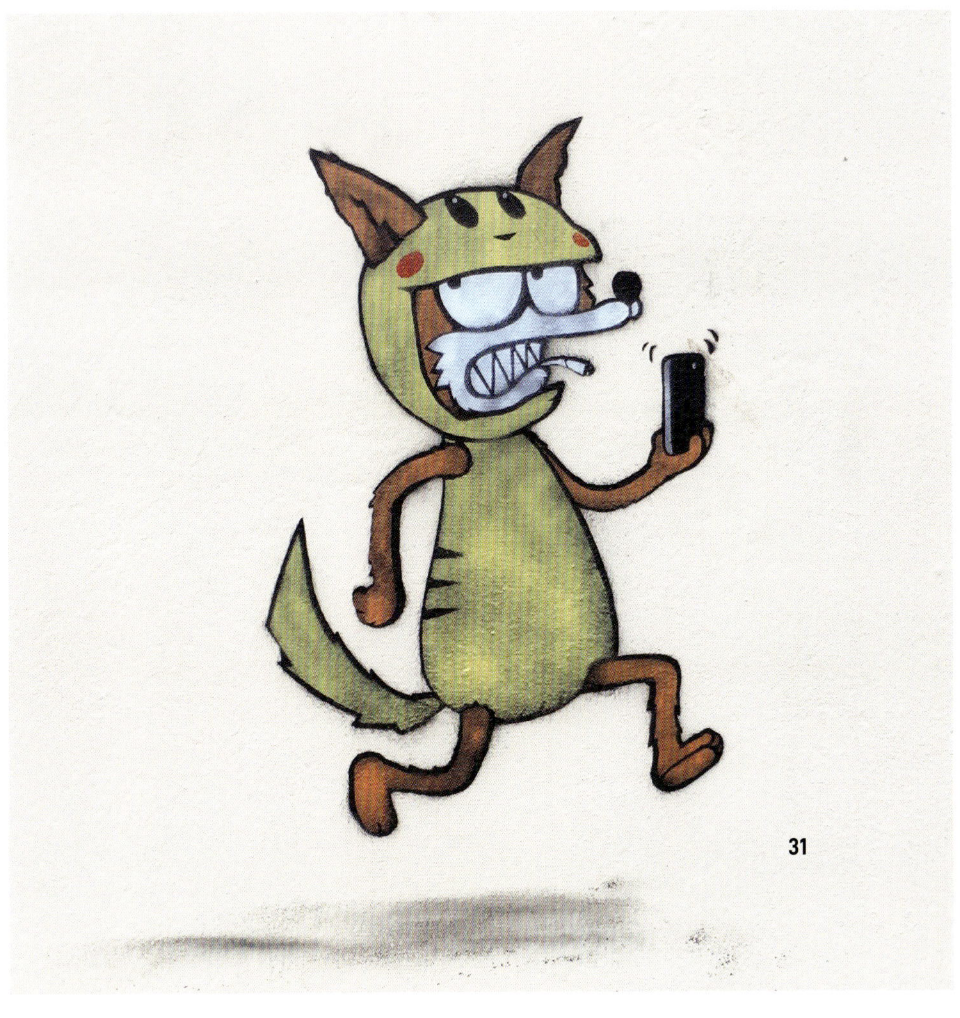

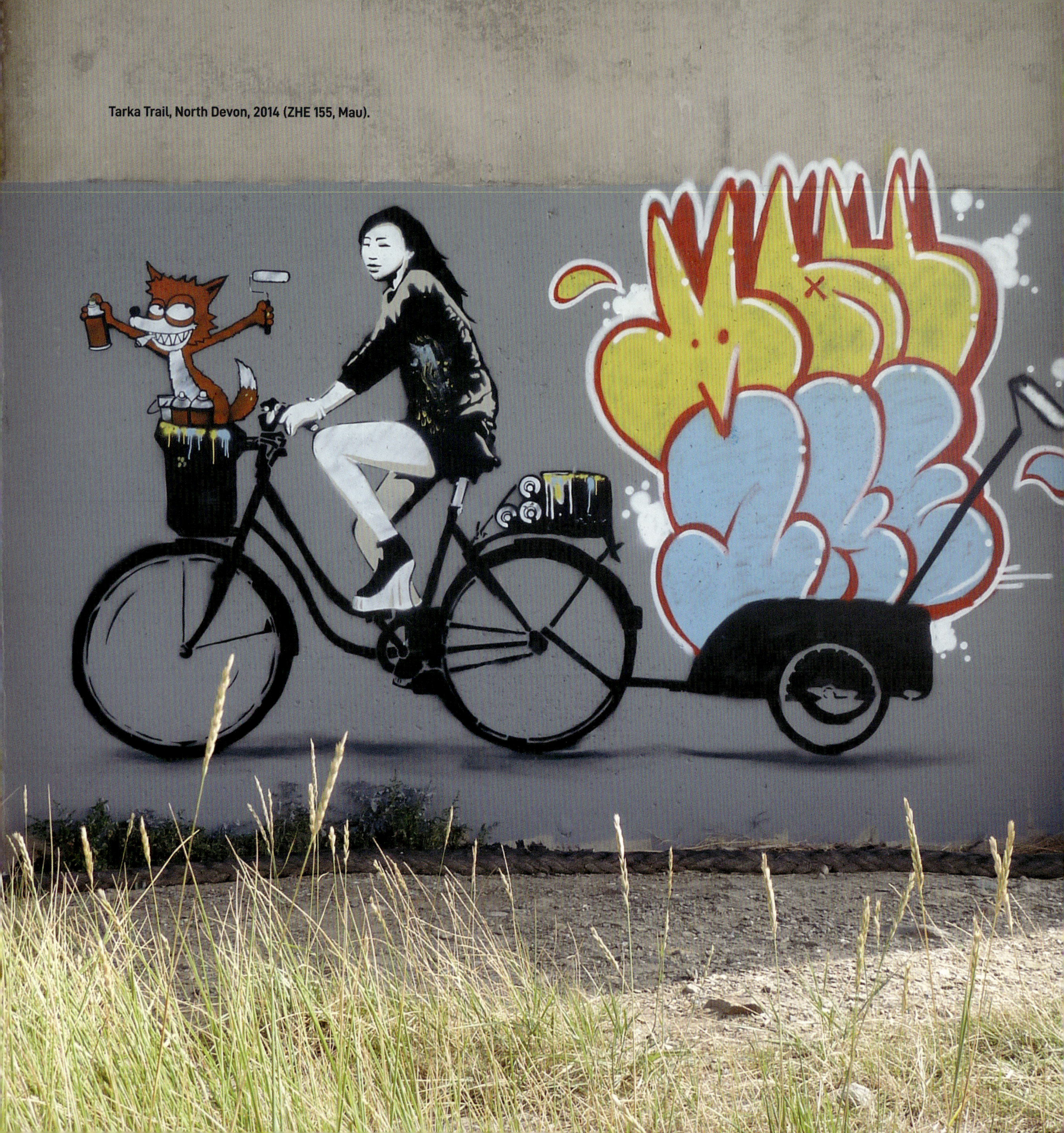

Tarka Trail, North Devon, 2014 (ZHE 155, Mau).

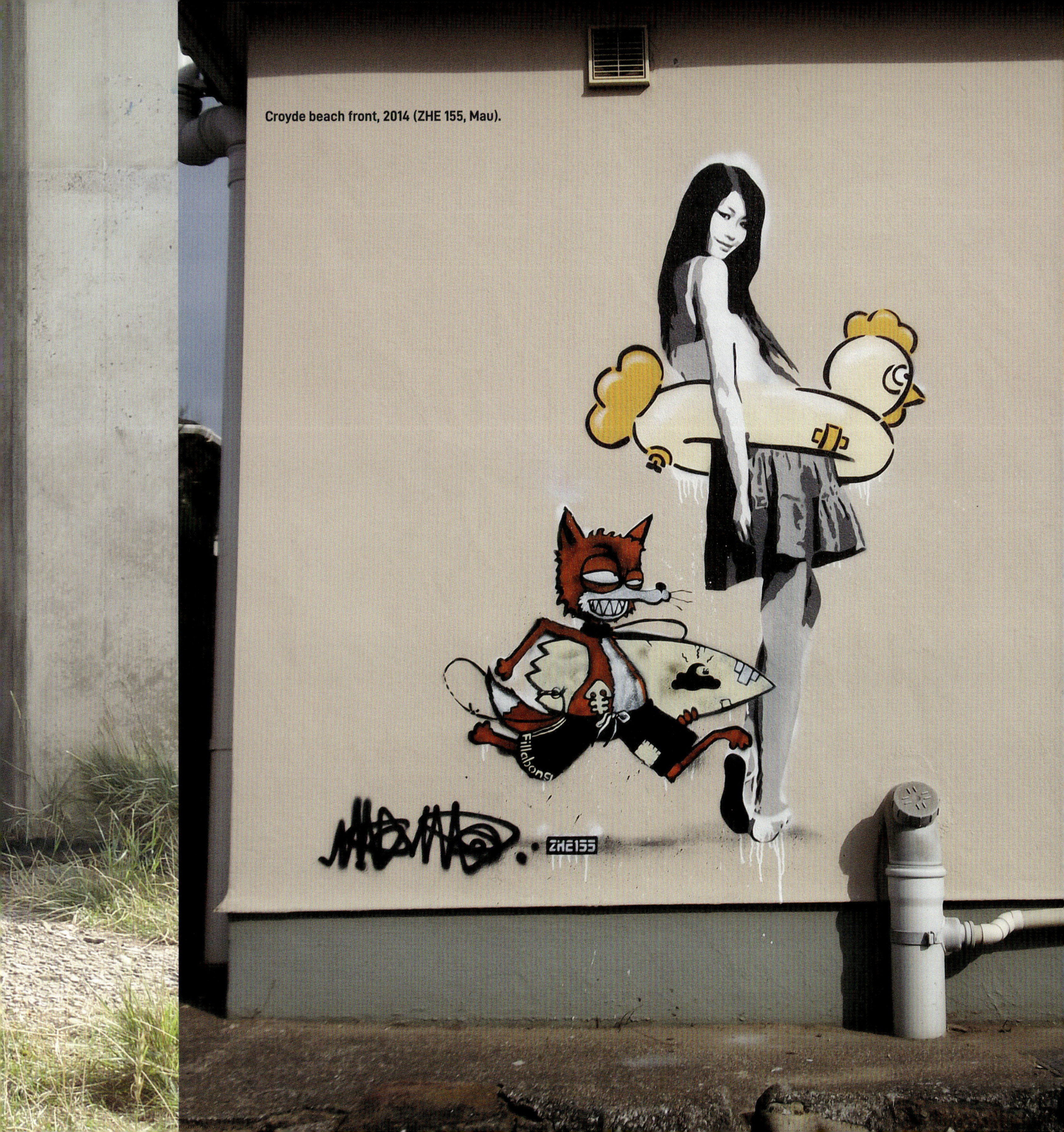

Croyde beach front, 2014 (ZHE 155, Mau).

TV Fox, Barnstaple, 2013.

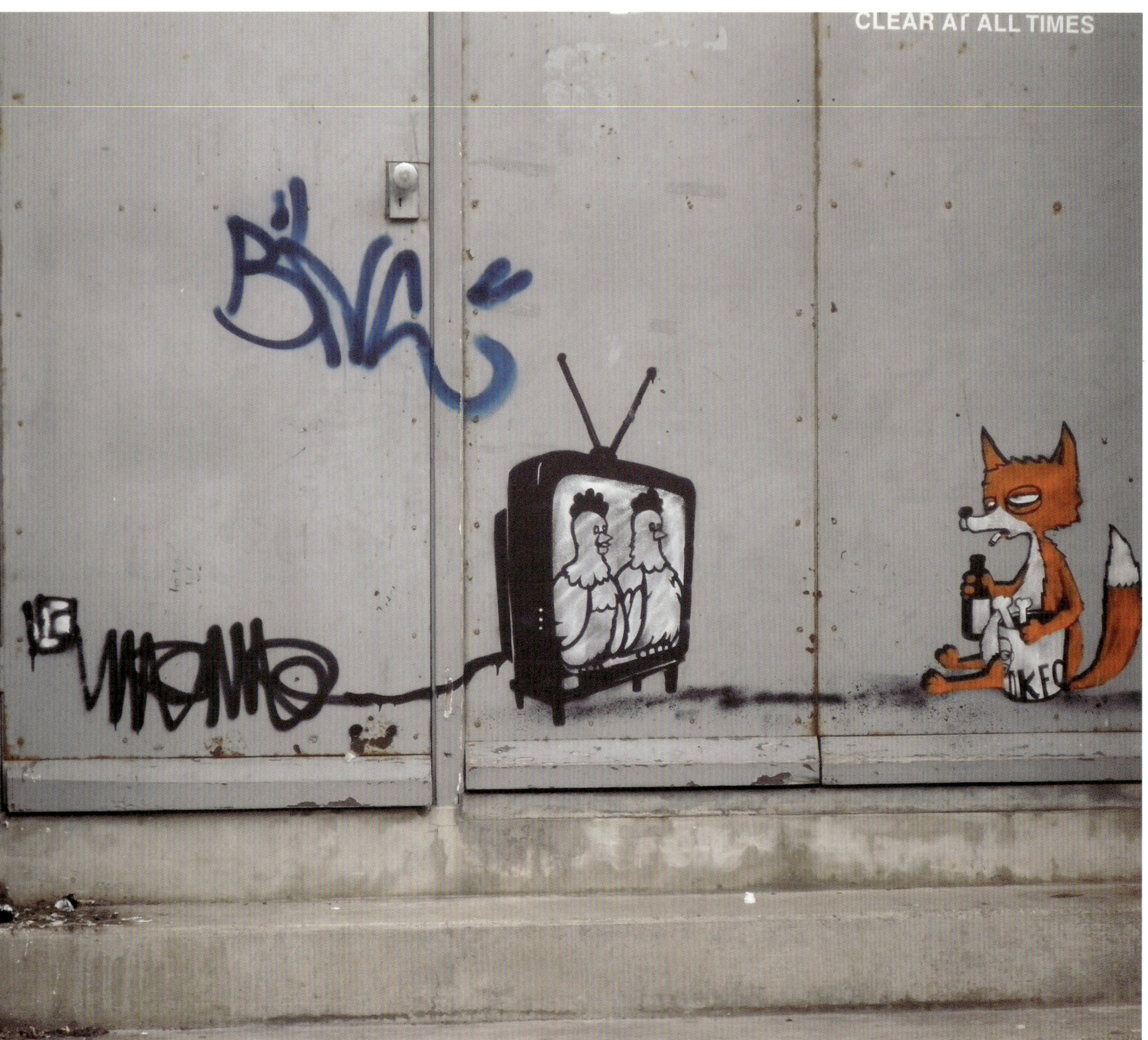

Jubilee Fox, (Shagger's alley) Bideford, 2012.

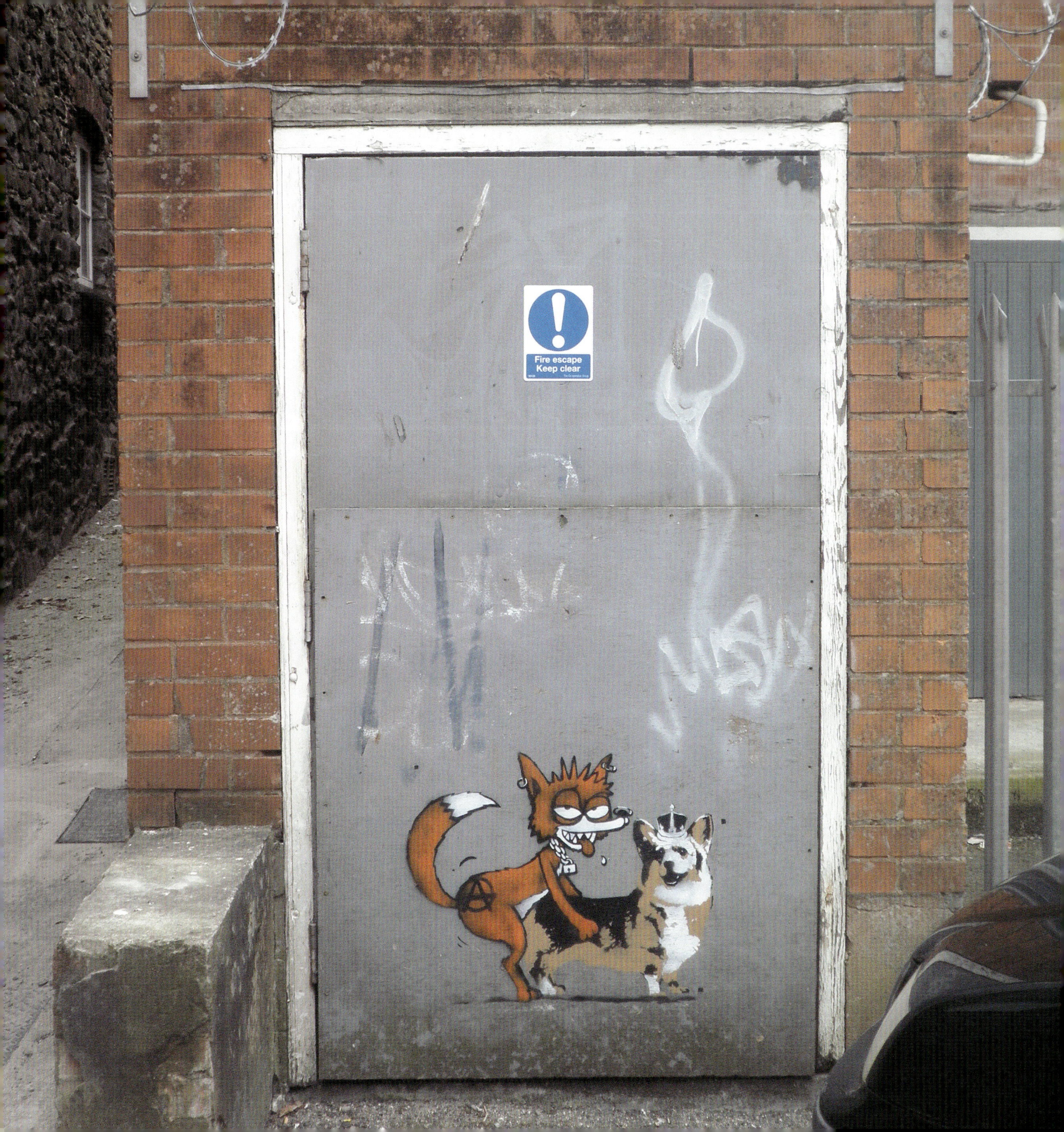
Fire escape
Keep clear

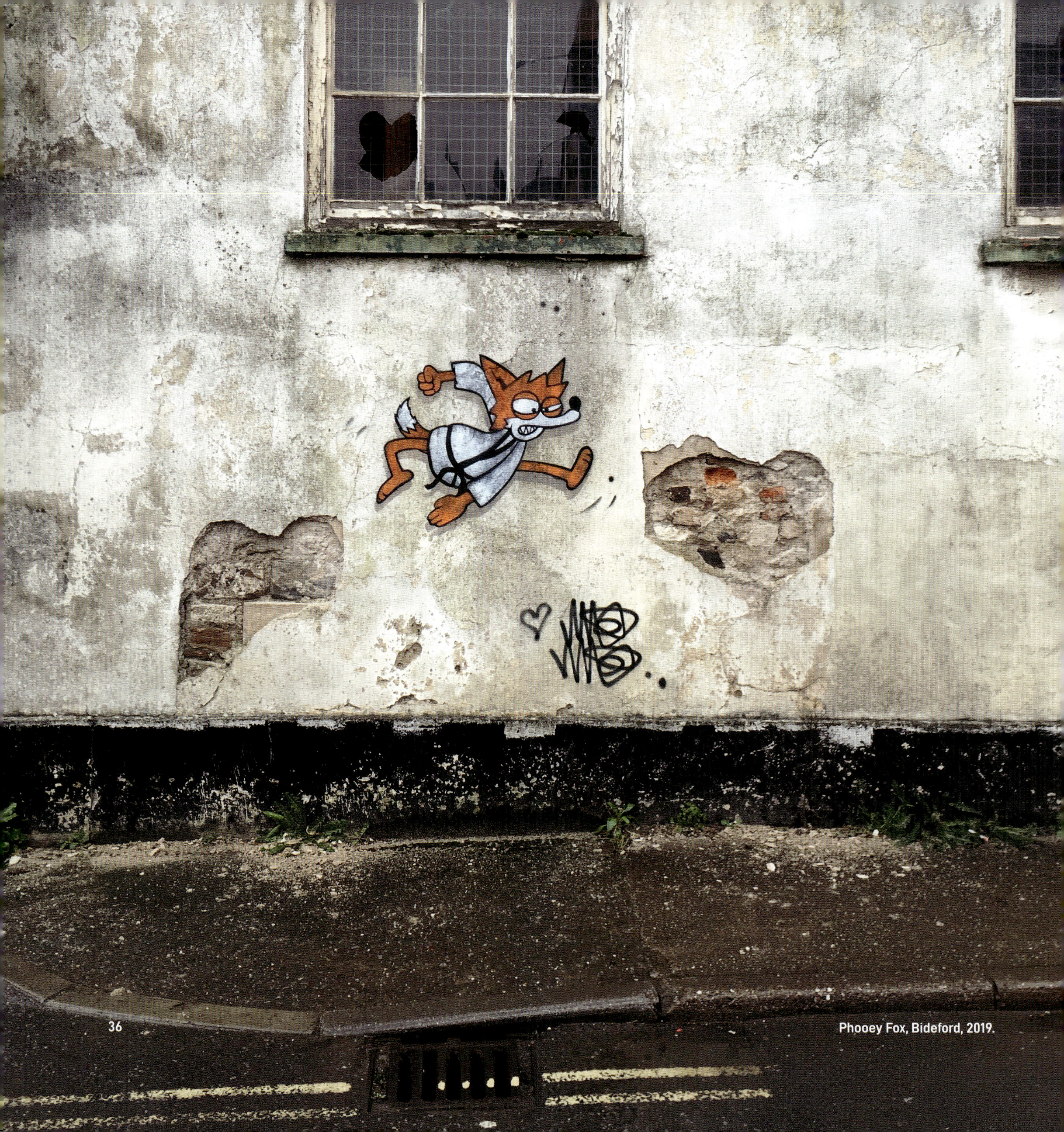

Phooey Fox, Bideford, 2019.

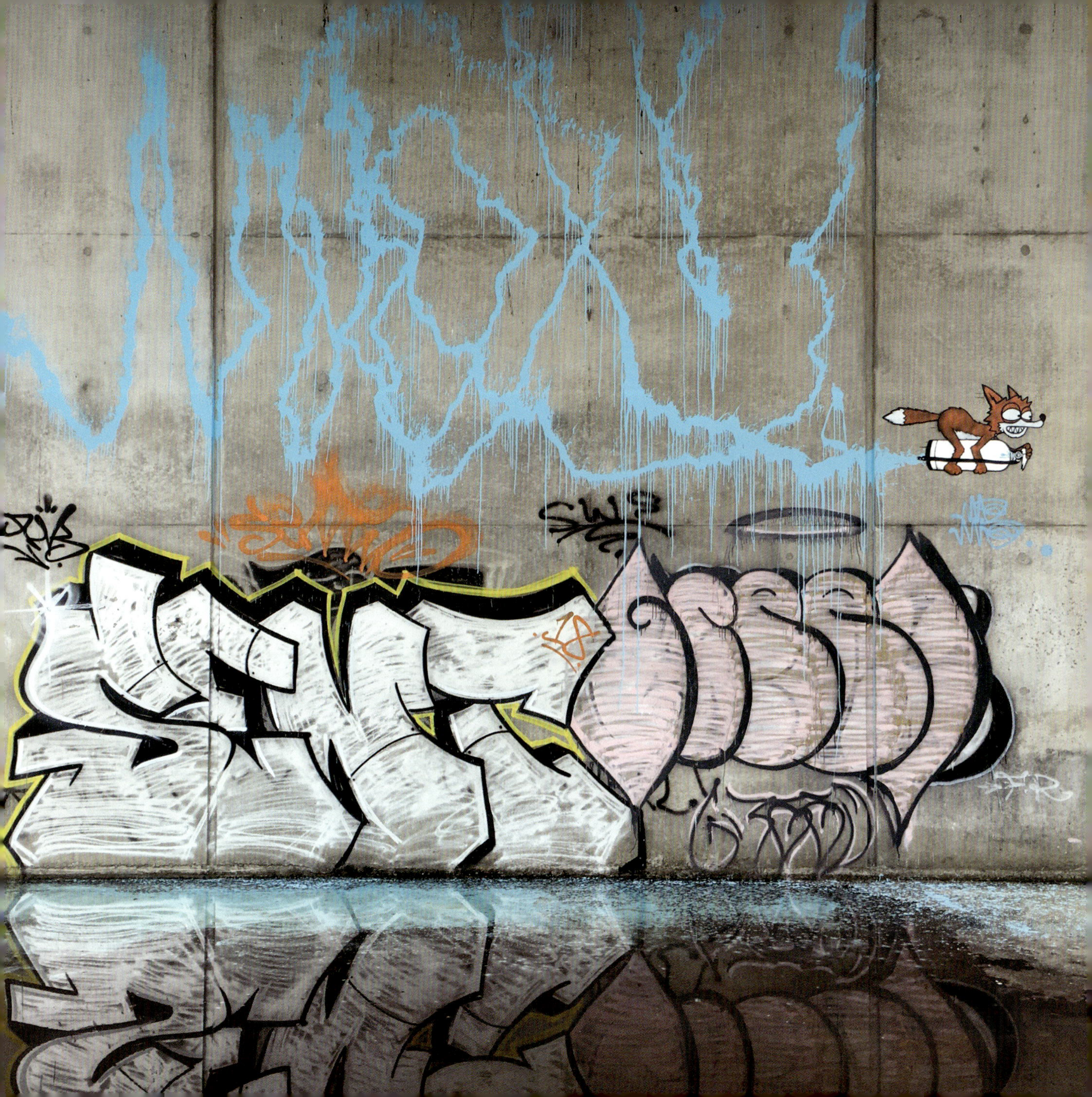

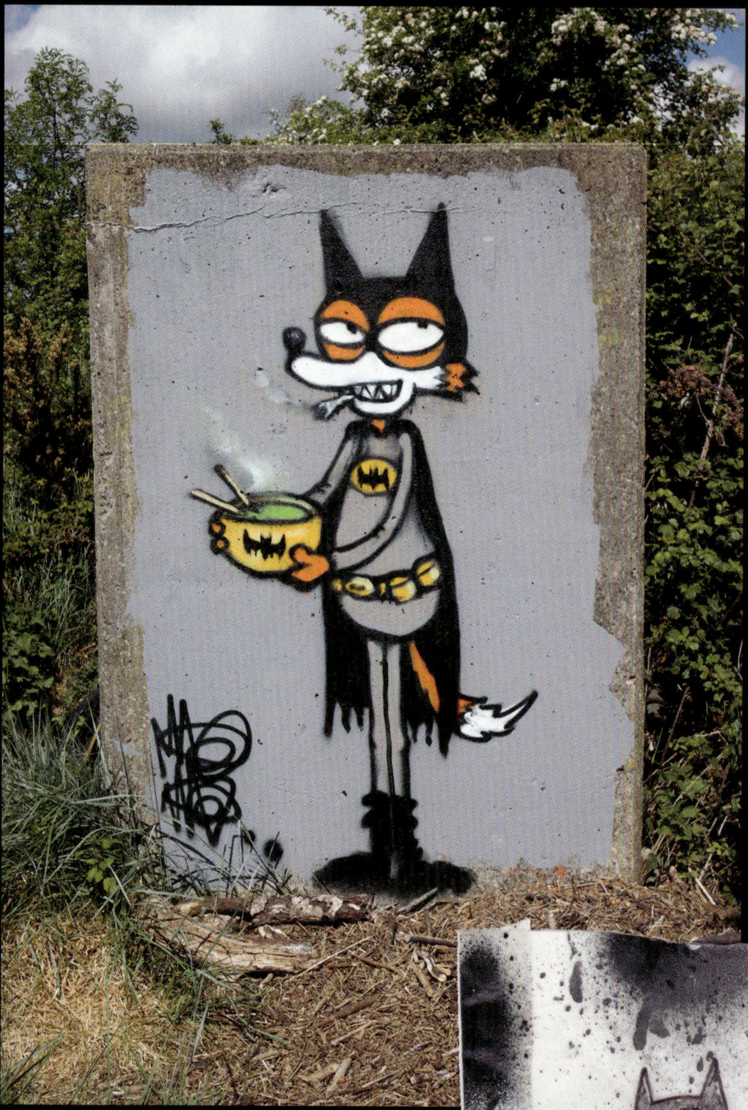

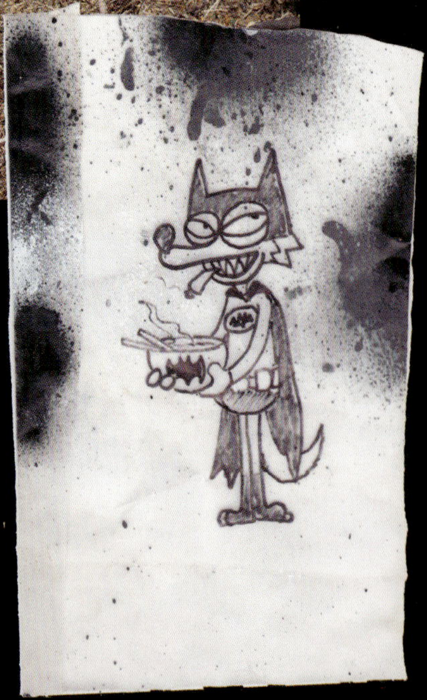

Bird Flu, Swine Flu, Bat Soup?...
Braunton, 2020.

International Earth Day,
Bideford, Lockdown, April 2020.

NEXT PAGE: Where The Woods Was,
Retail Park Site, Bideford, 2013.

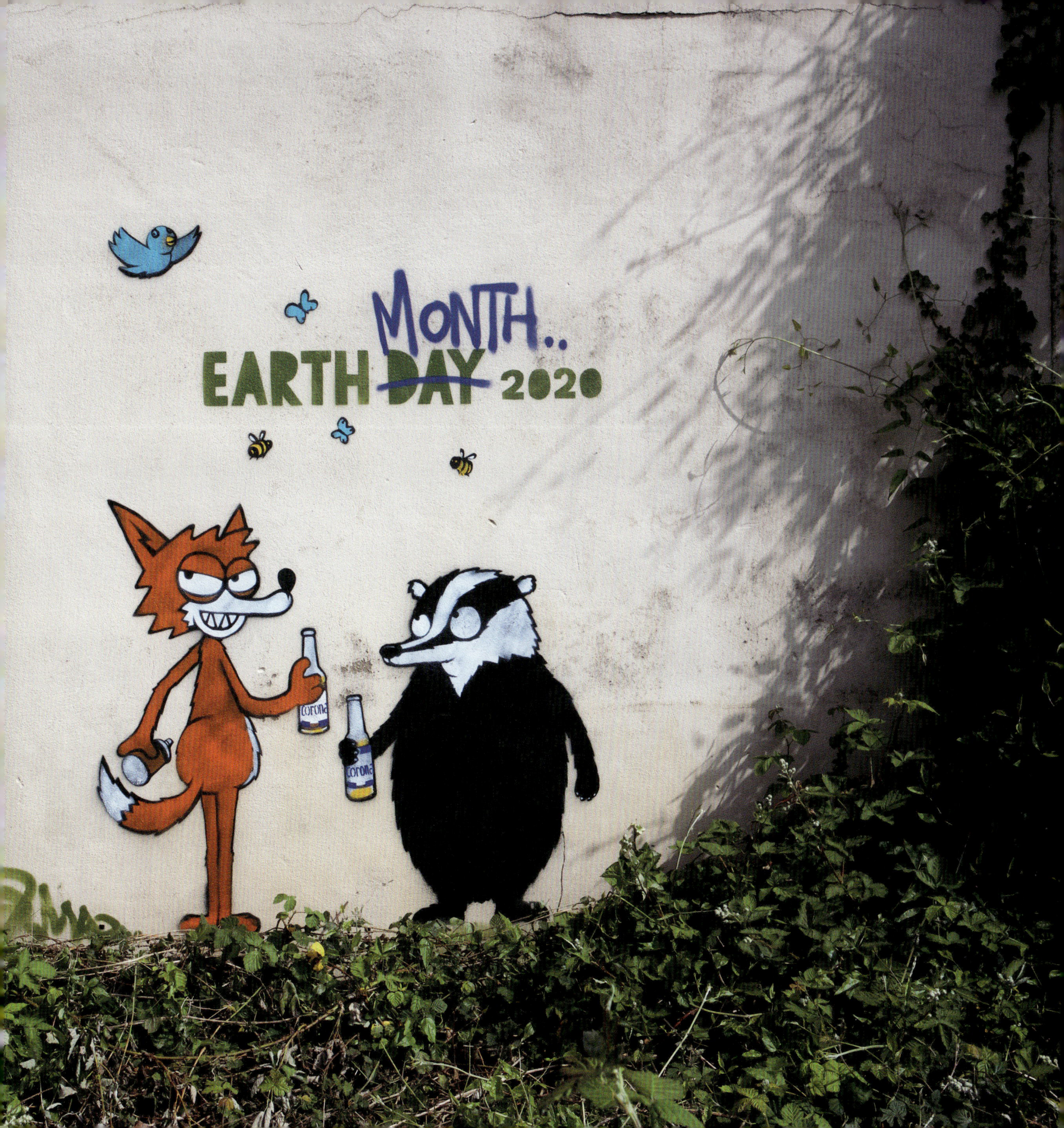
MONTH..
EARTH ~~DAY~~ 2020
Corona
Corona

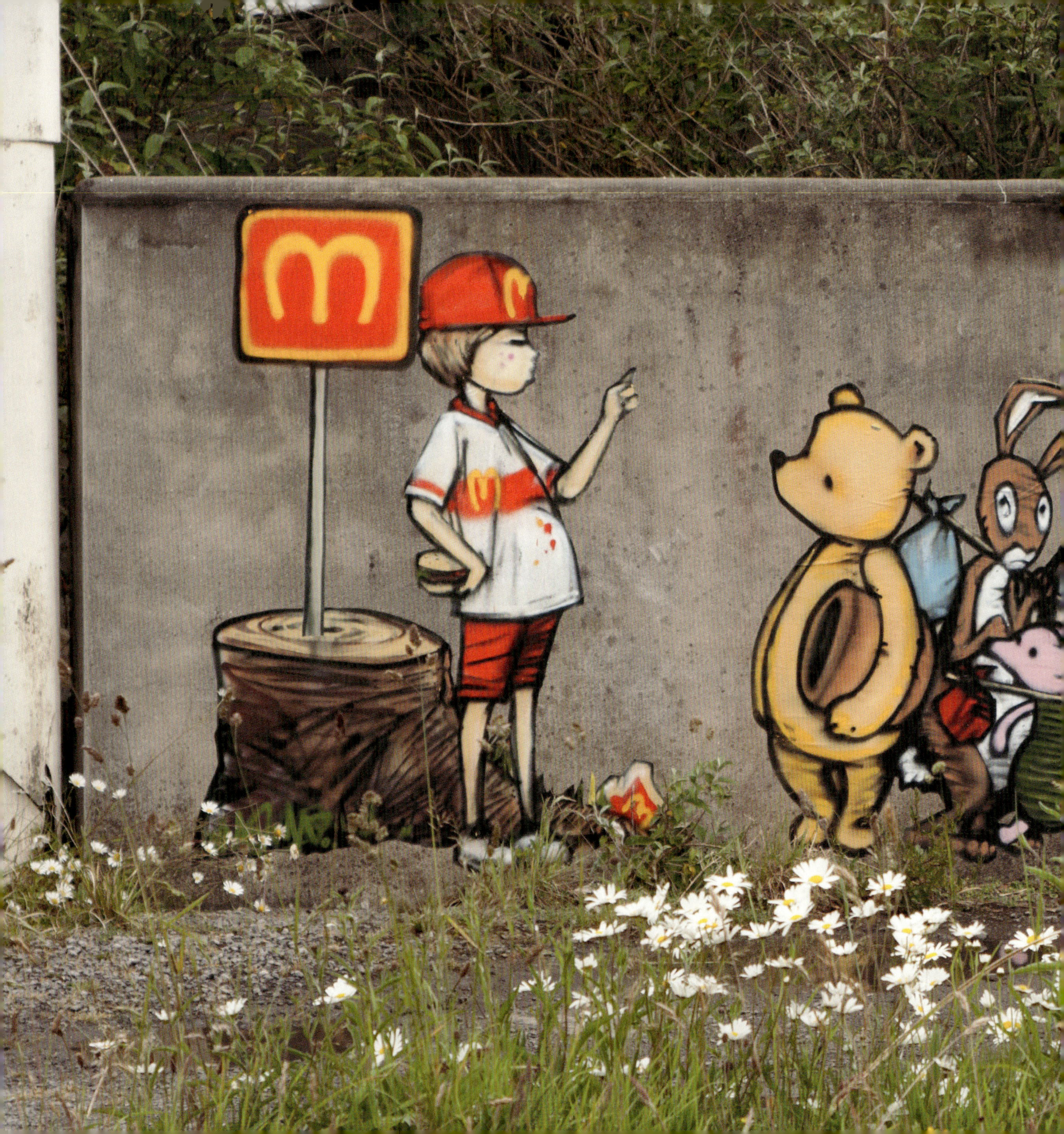

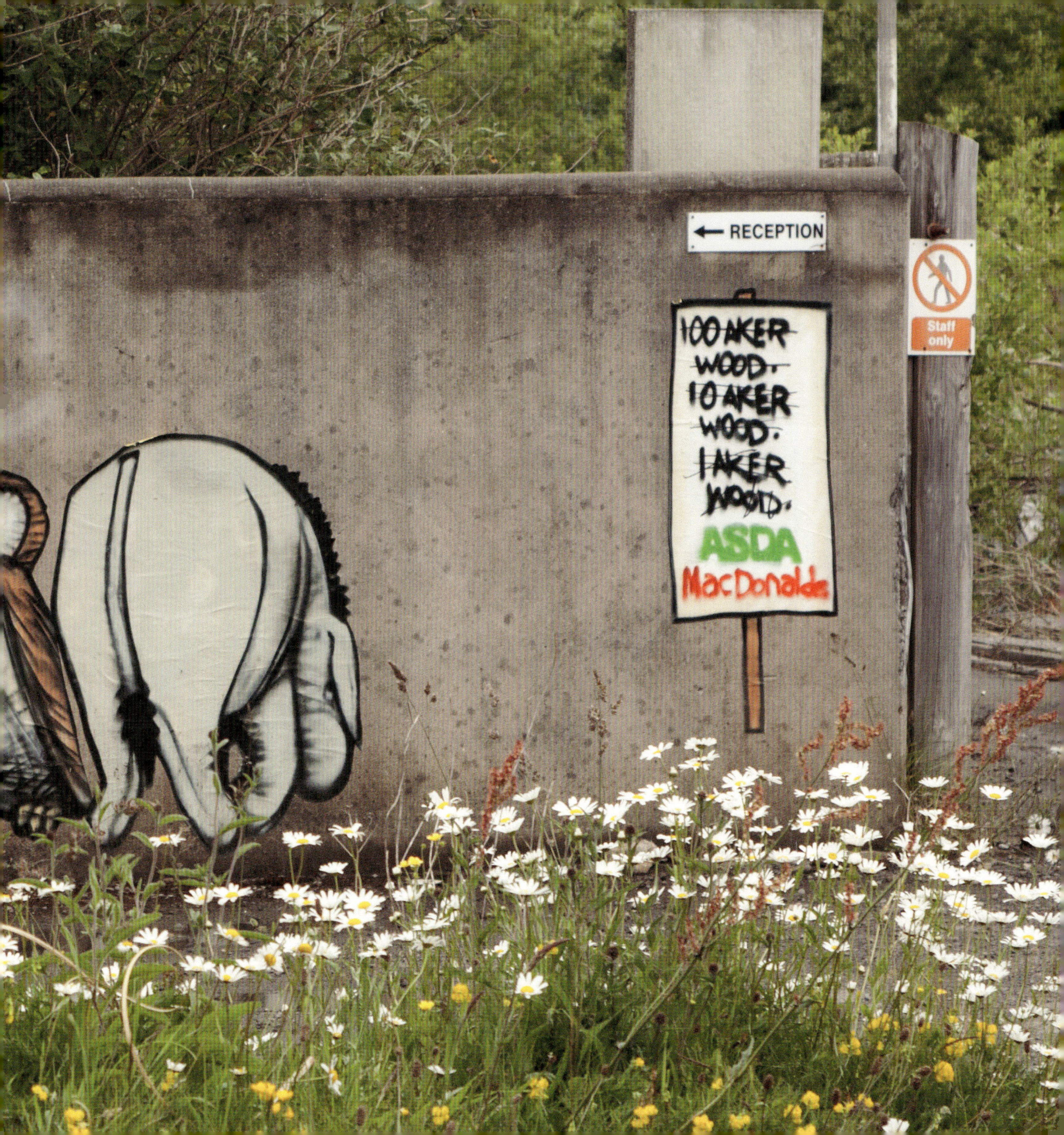
RECEPTION
100 AKER
WOOD.
10 AKER
WOOD.
1 AKER
WOOD.
ASDA
MacDonalds
Staff
only

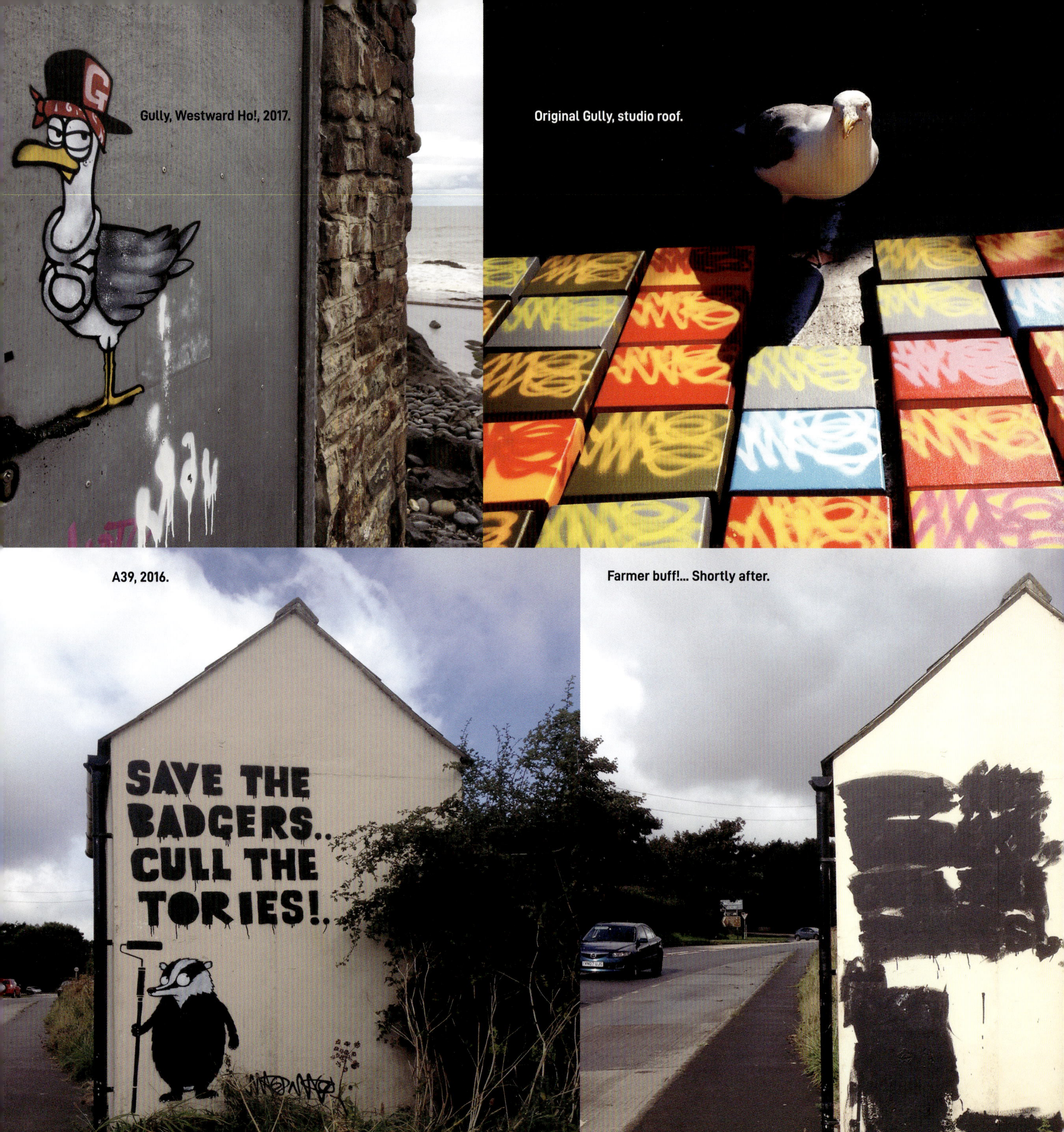

Gully, Westward Ho!, 2017.

Original Gully, studio roof.

A39, 2016.

Farmer buff!... Shortly after.

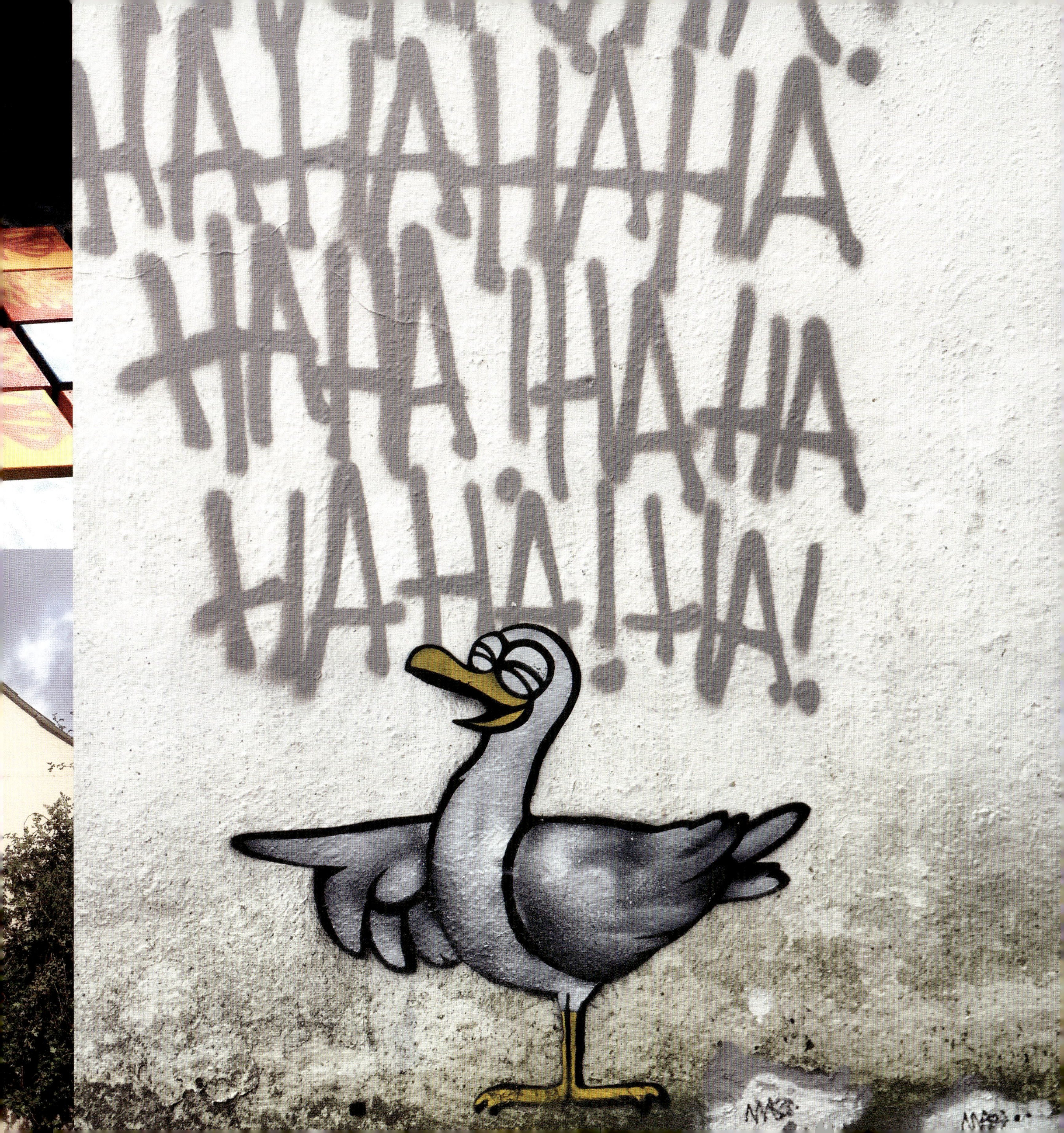
HAHAHAHA
HAHAHA!

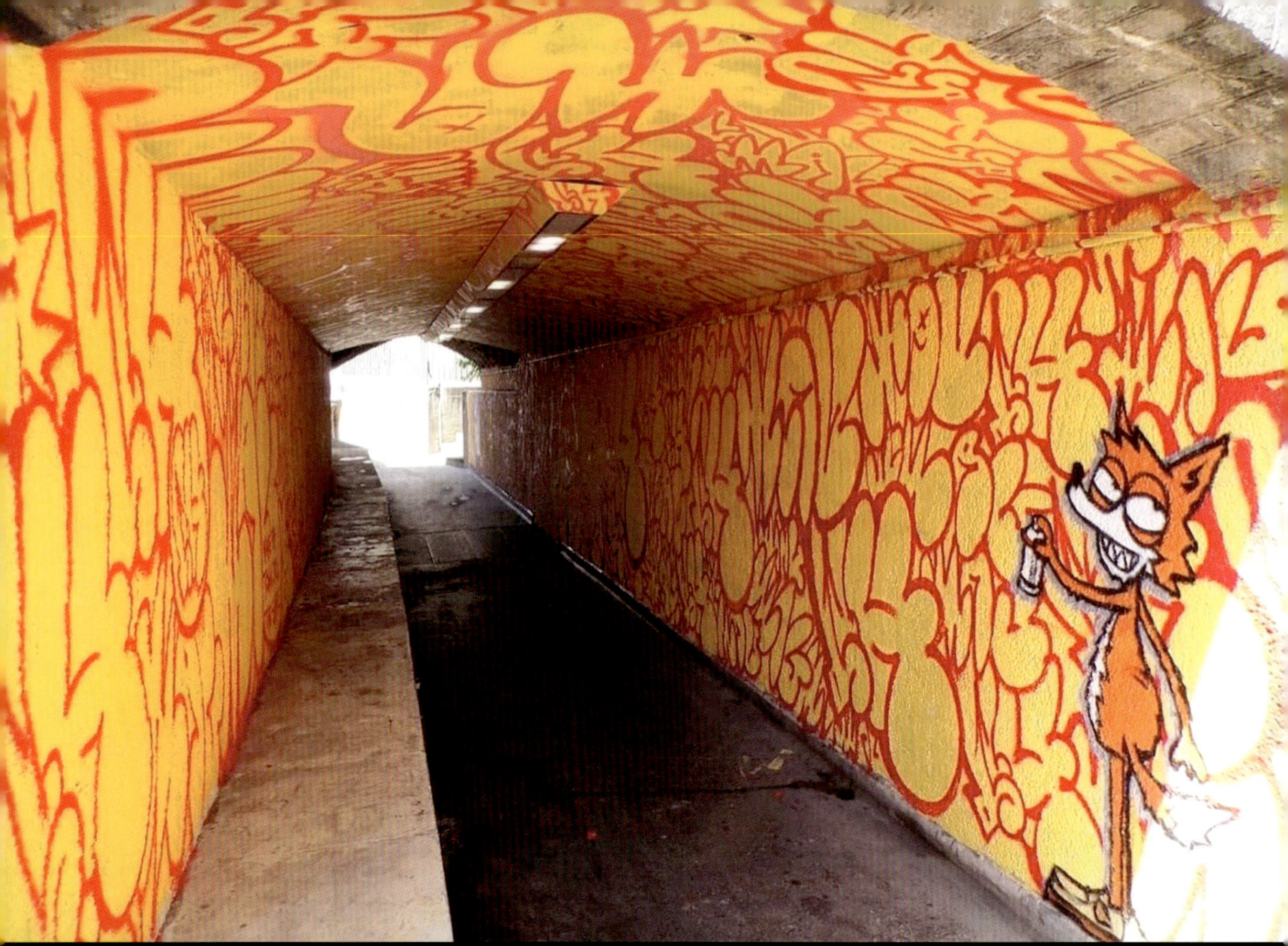

Dub Tunnel, Barnstaple, 2021.

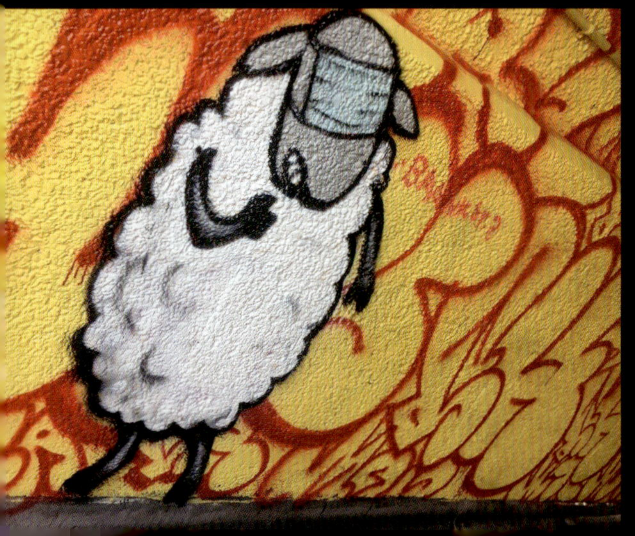

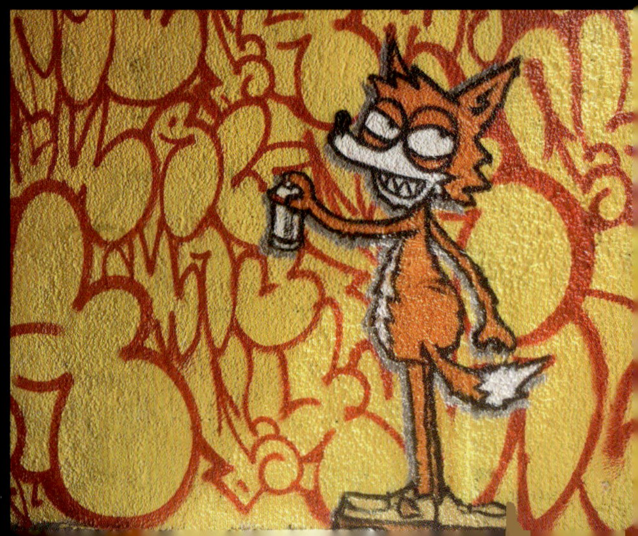

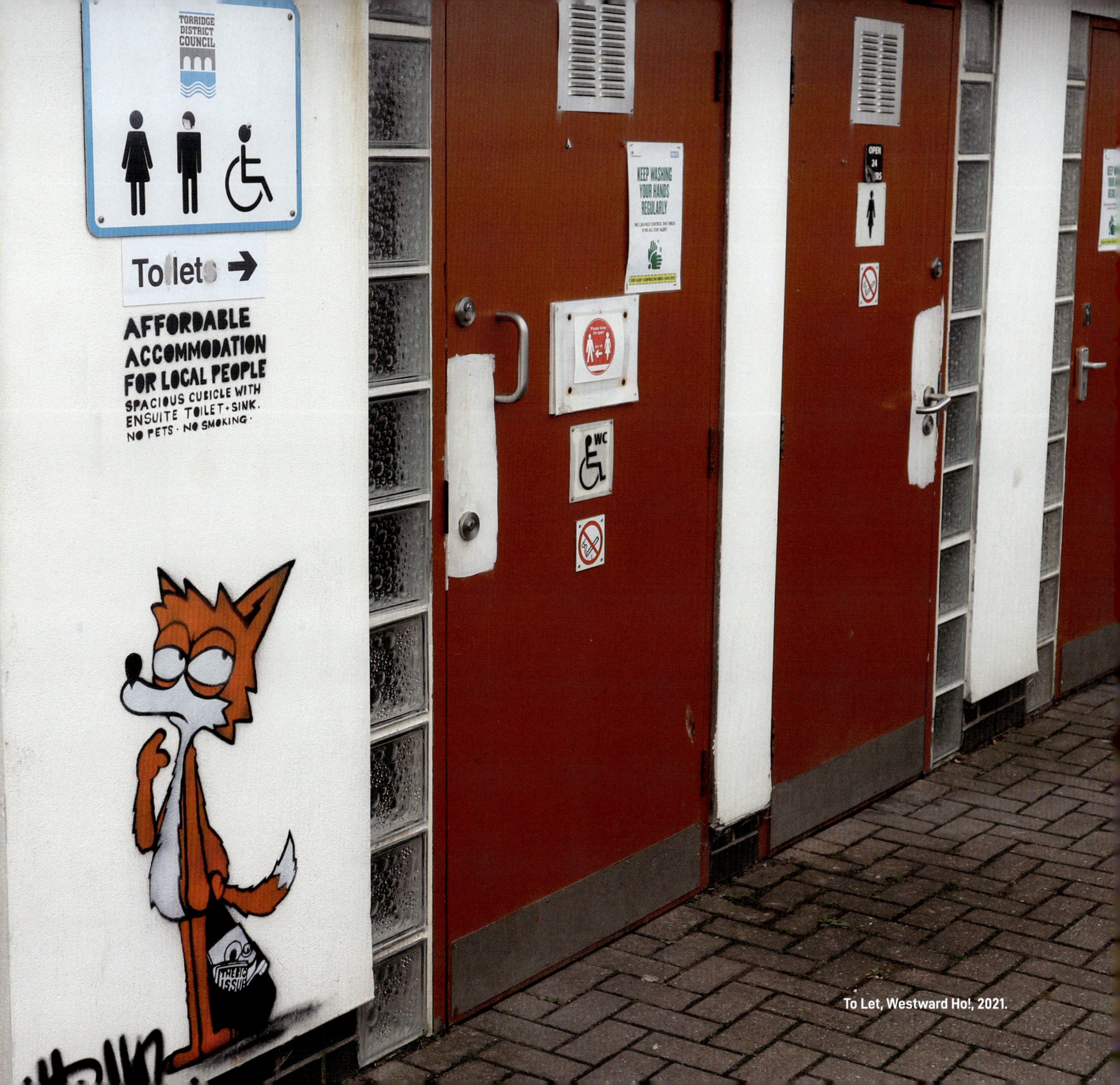

To Let, Westward Ho!, 2021.

My Precious, Barnstaple, 2020.

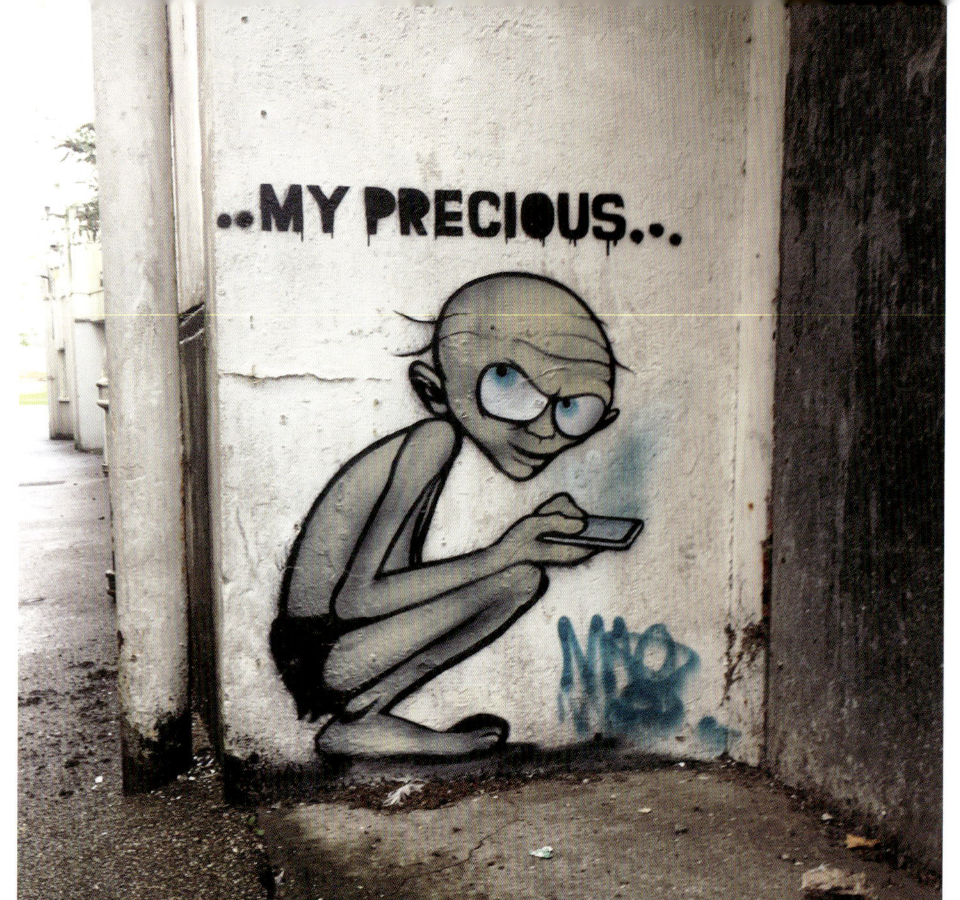

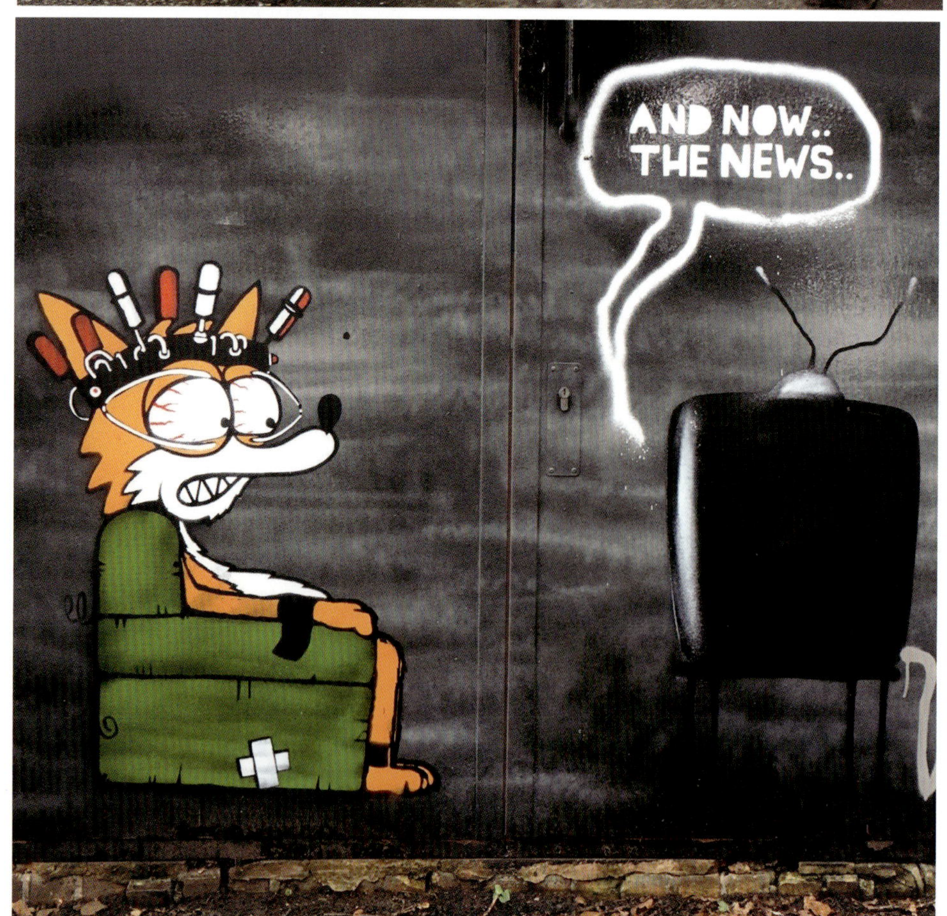

Now the News, 2021.

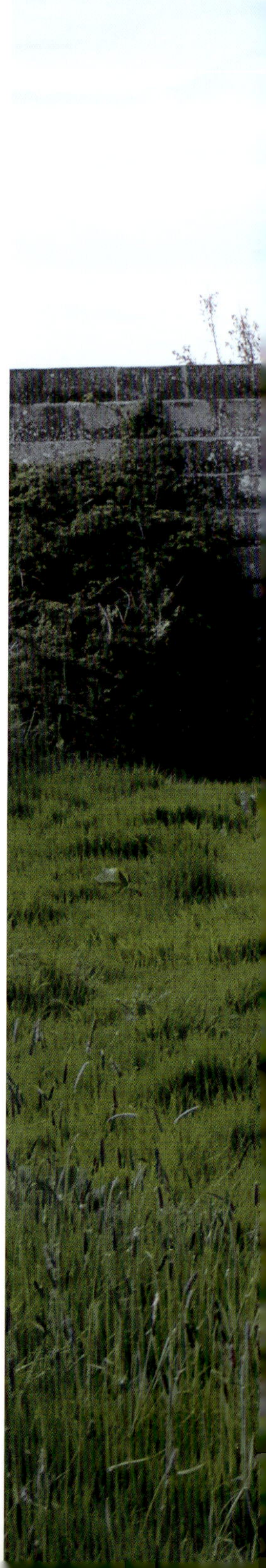

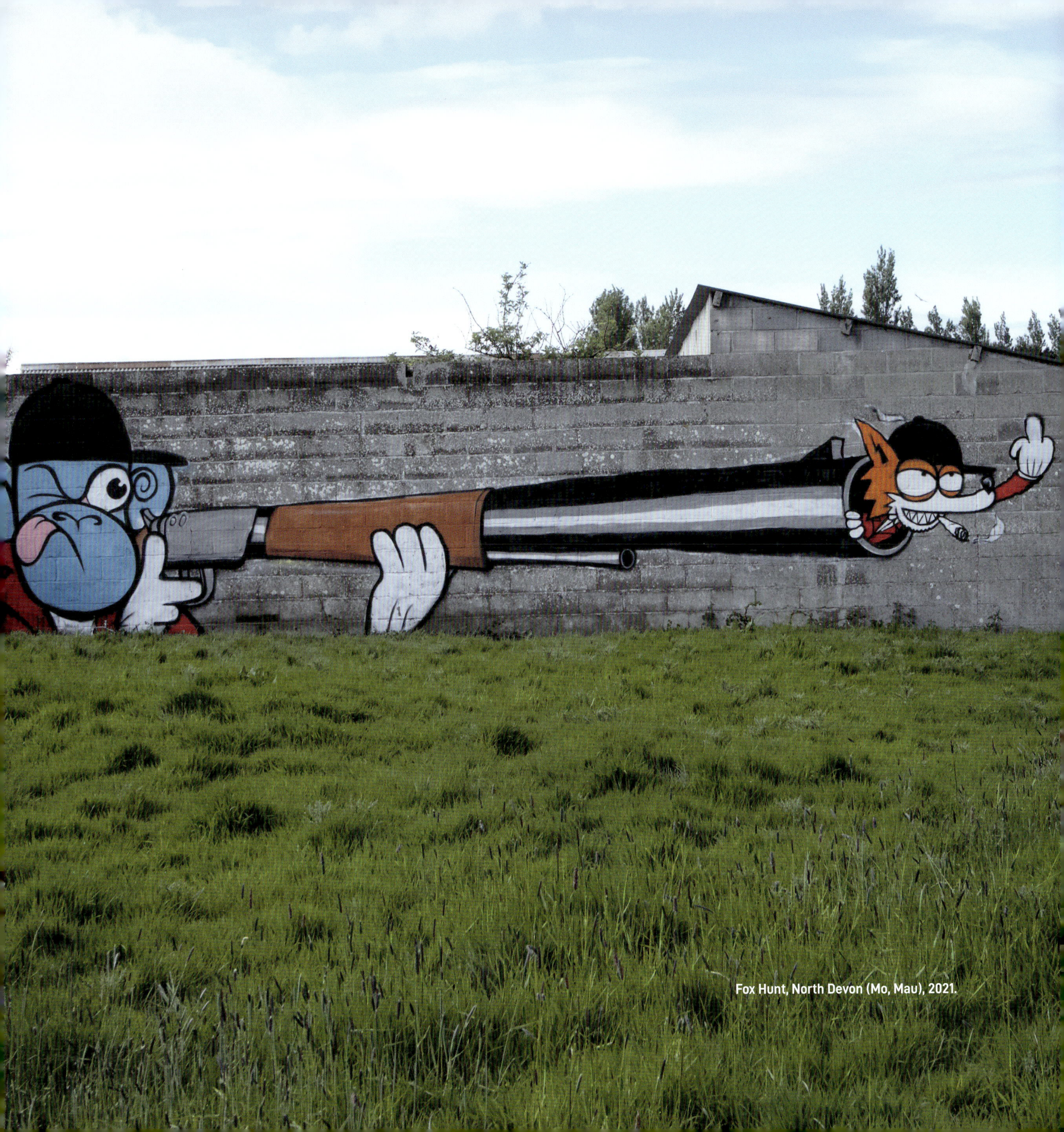

Fox Hunt, North Devon (Mo, Mau), 2021.

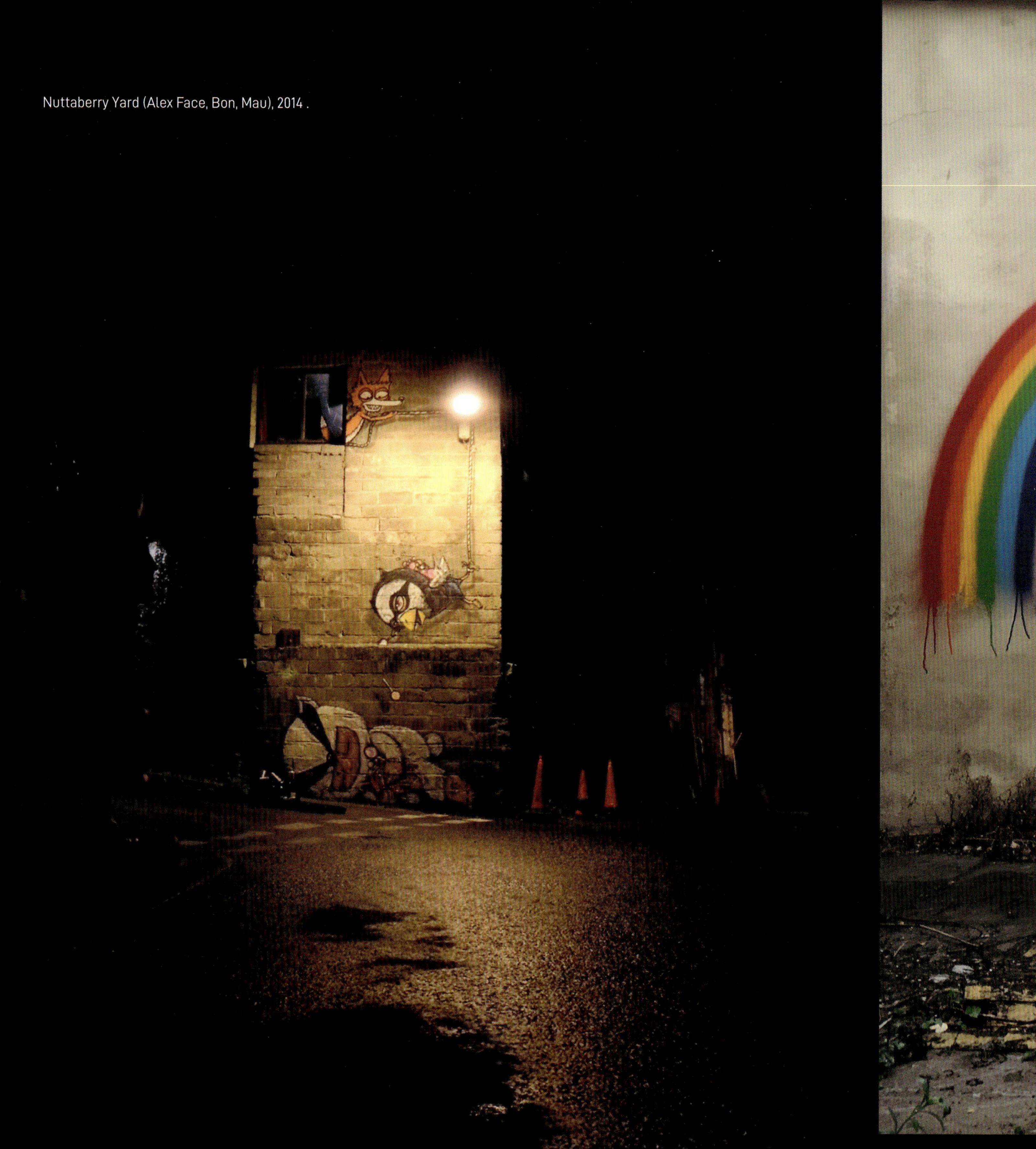

Nuttaberry Yard (Alex Face, Bon, Mau), 2014 .

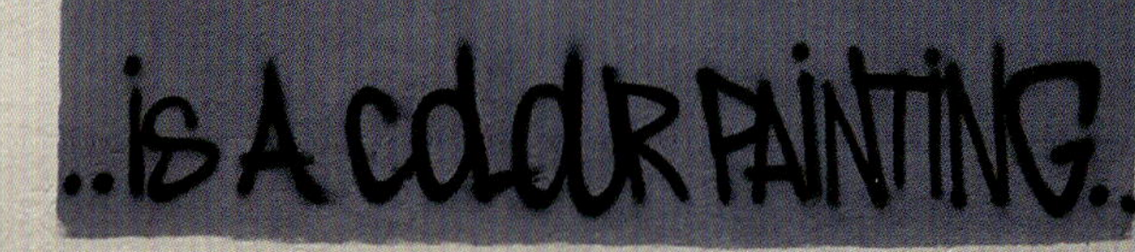

North Devon, 2020.

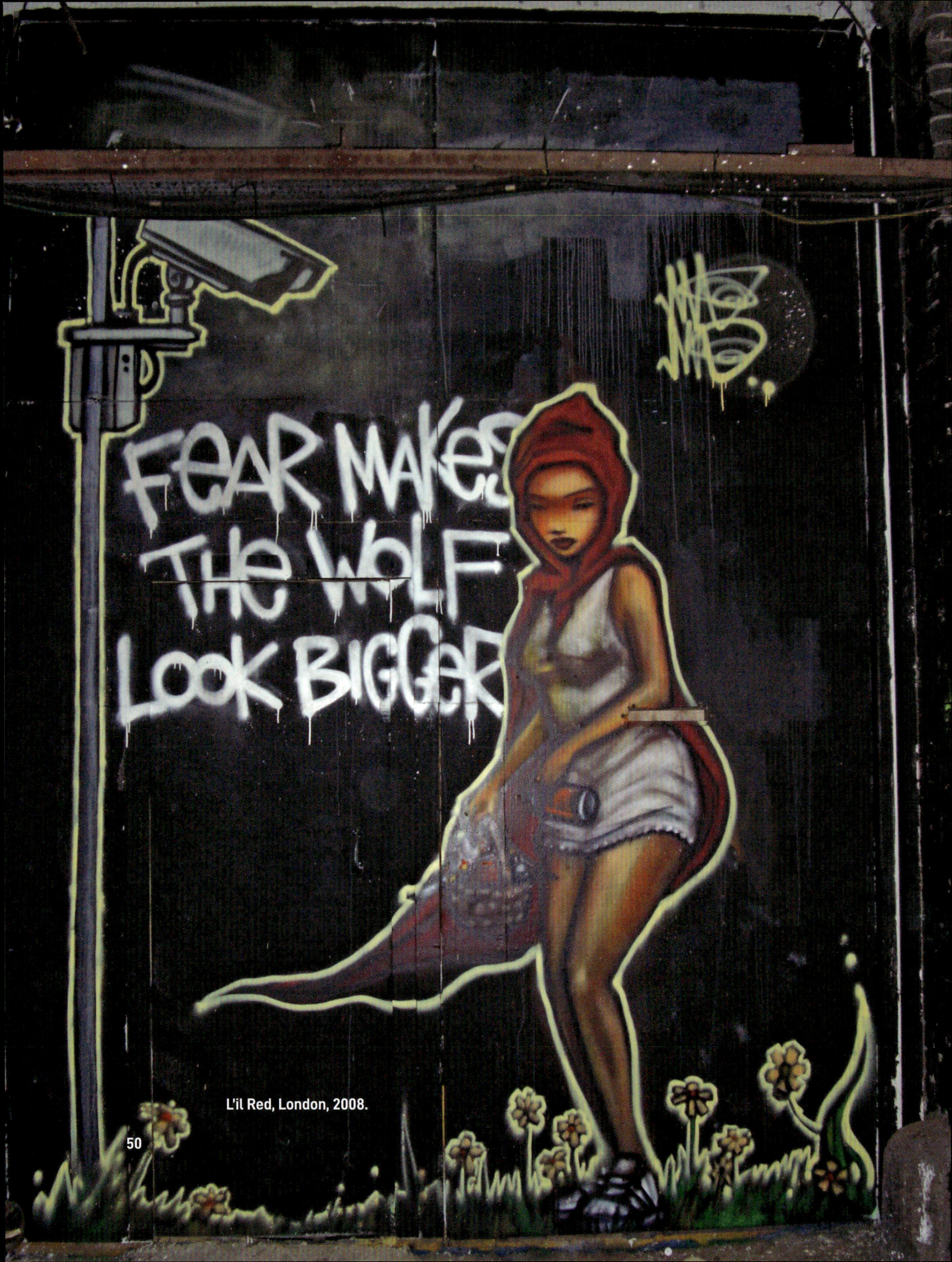

L'il Red, London, 2008.

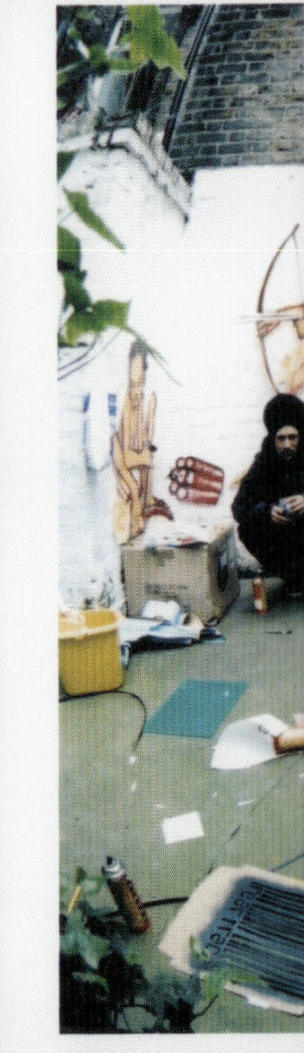

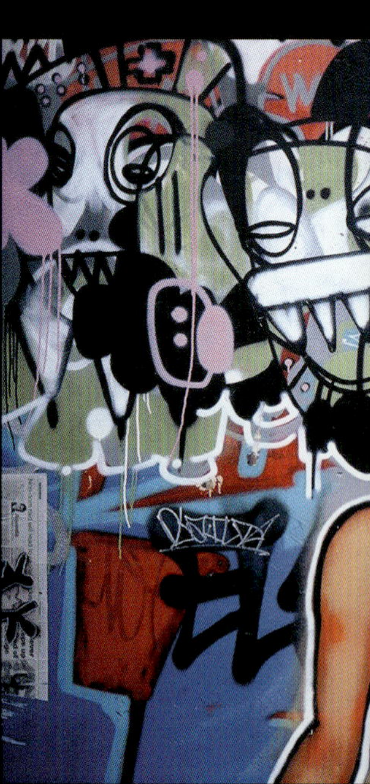

BRISTOL LONDON

Eventually it got to the point where I wanted to go out painting without the pressure of having to do something that carried a message. I enjoyed painting characters more than letters and I started using iconic characters relating to stories that people already knew so I had a narrative to work with – like Little Red Riding Hood, Winnie the Pooh or Snoopy.

It was also around this time that I linked up with Bristol artists Inky, Banksy, Sickboy and the TCF and Burning Candy crews and went out bombing pieces in Bristol. It was helpful to have an image that could be painted quickly, so I started painting the fox. The character gave me freedom because it's an image that's not confined by race, religion or politics. You can do whatever you want with it, but it adds a sense of humour that brings a whole different element.

Original Trolley Hunters, London, 2004.

Brick Lane, London (Cyclops, Mau), 2008.

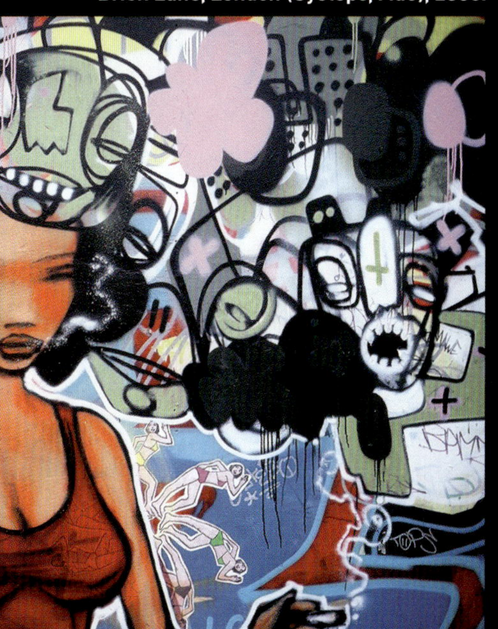

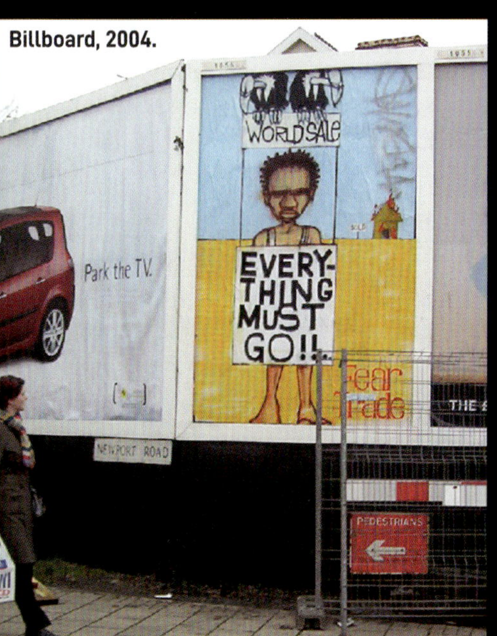

Billboard, 2004.

Why the fox? It's a country animal that has successfully adapted to urban life; always trespassing and hunted too...

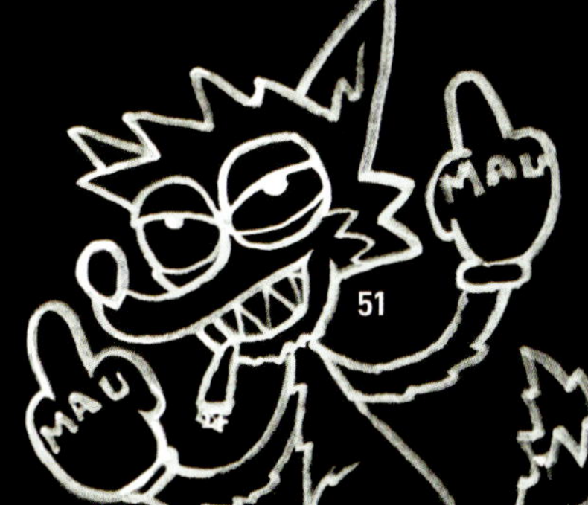

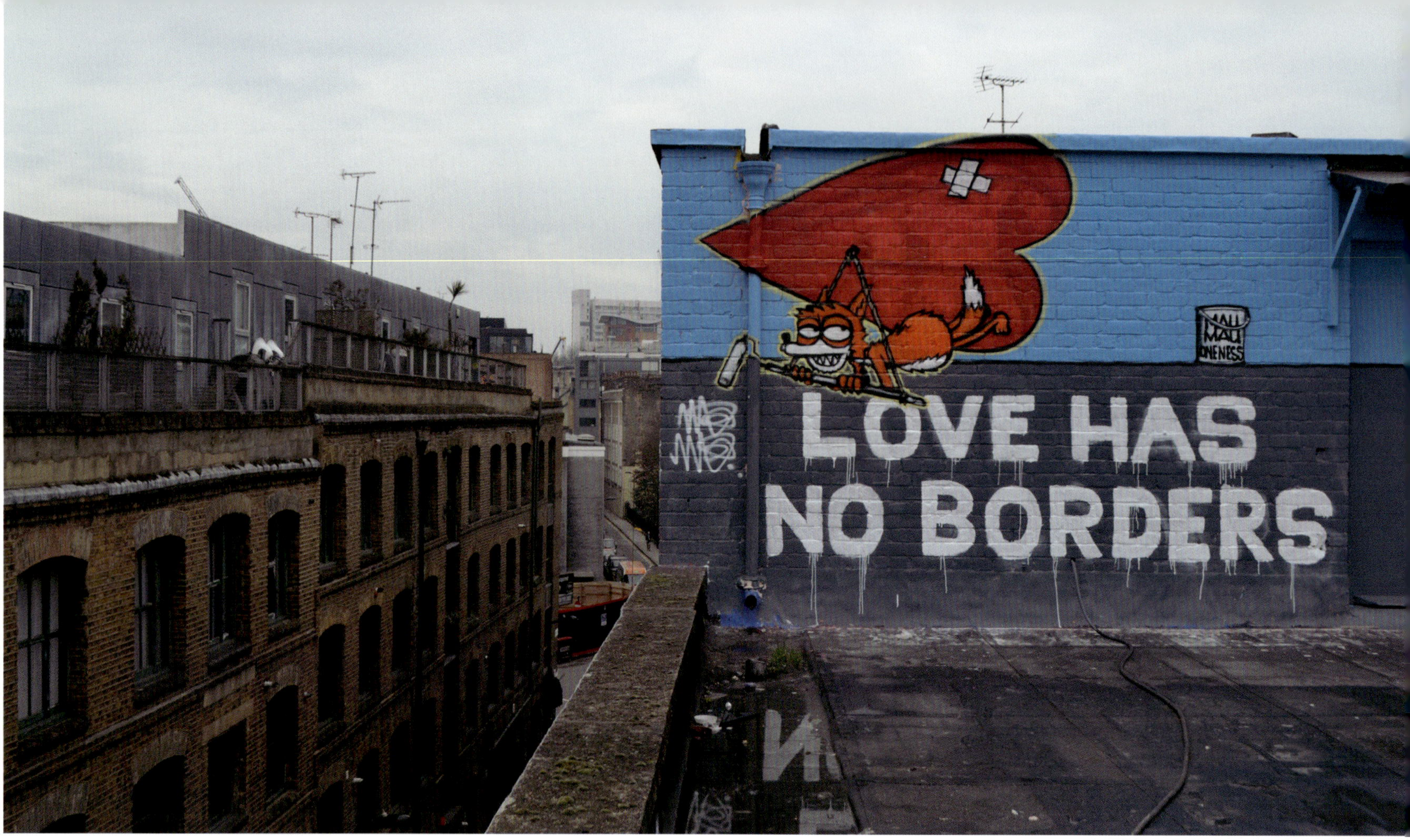

Love Has No Borders, London, 2017.

Street Foxes, London, 2000s.

Ain't Where You From, London, 2016.

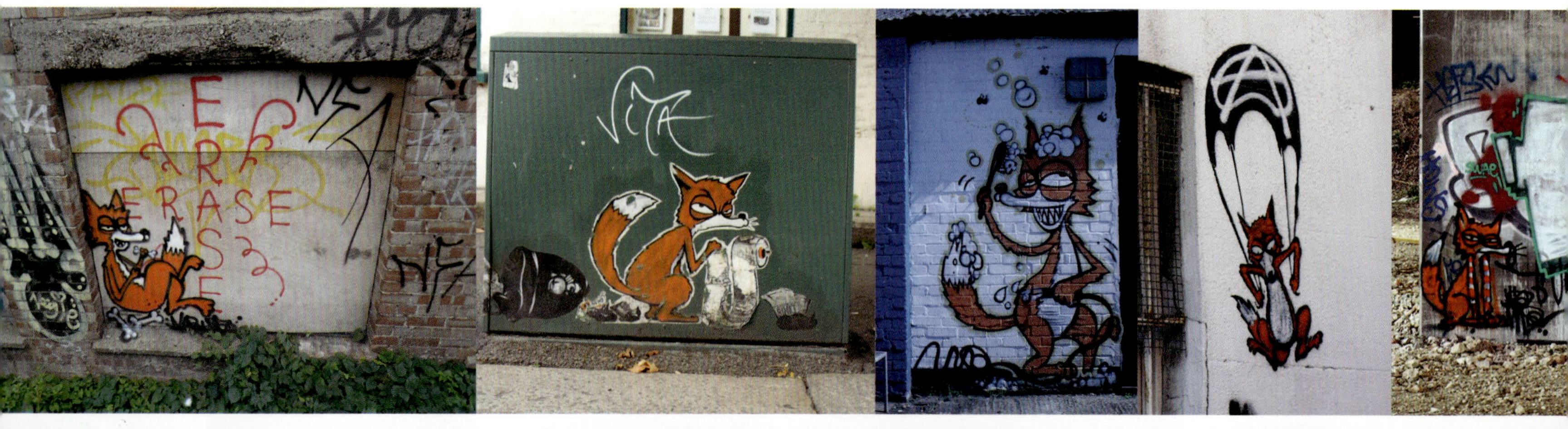

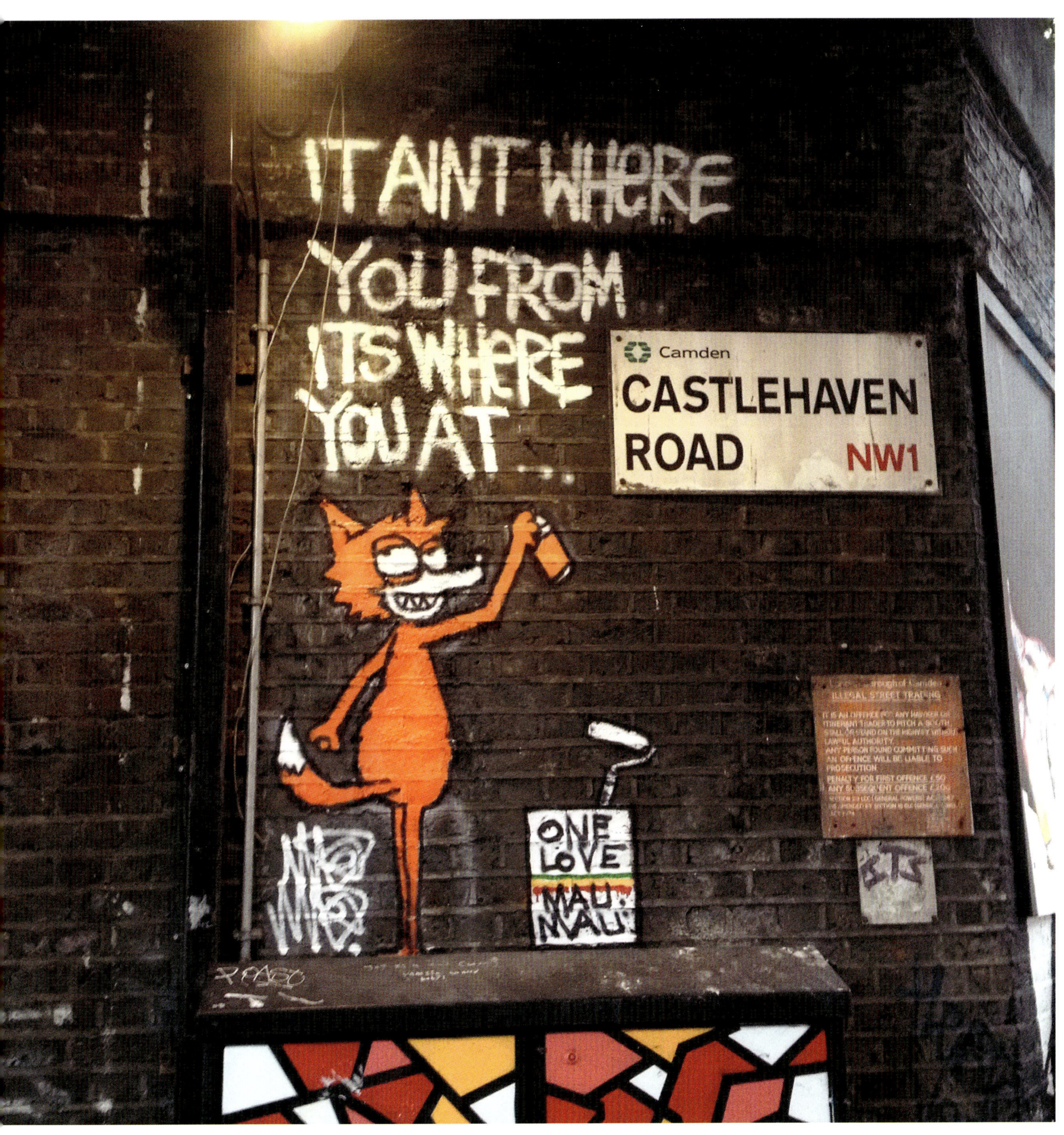
IT AINT WHERE
YOU FROM
ITS WHERE
YOU AT...
Camden
CASTLEHAVEN
ROAD
NW1
ILLEGAL STREET TRADING
ONE
LOVE
MAU
MAU

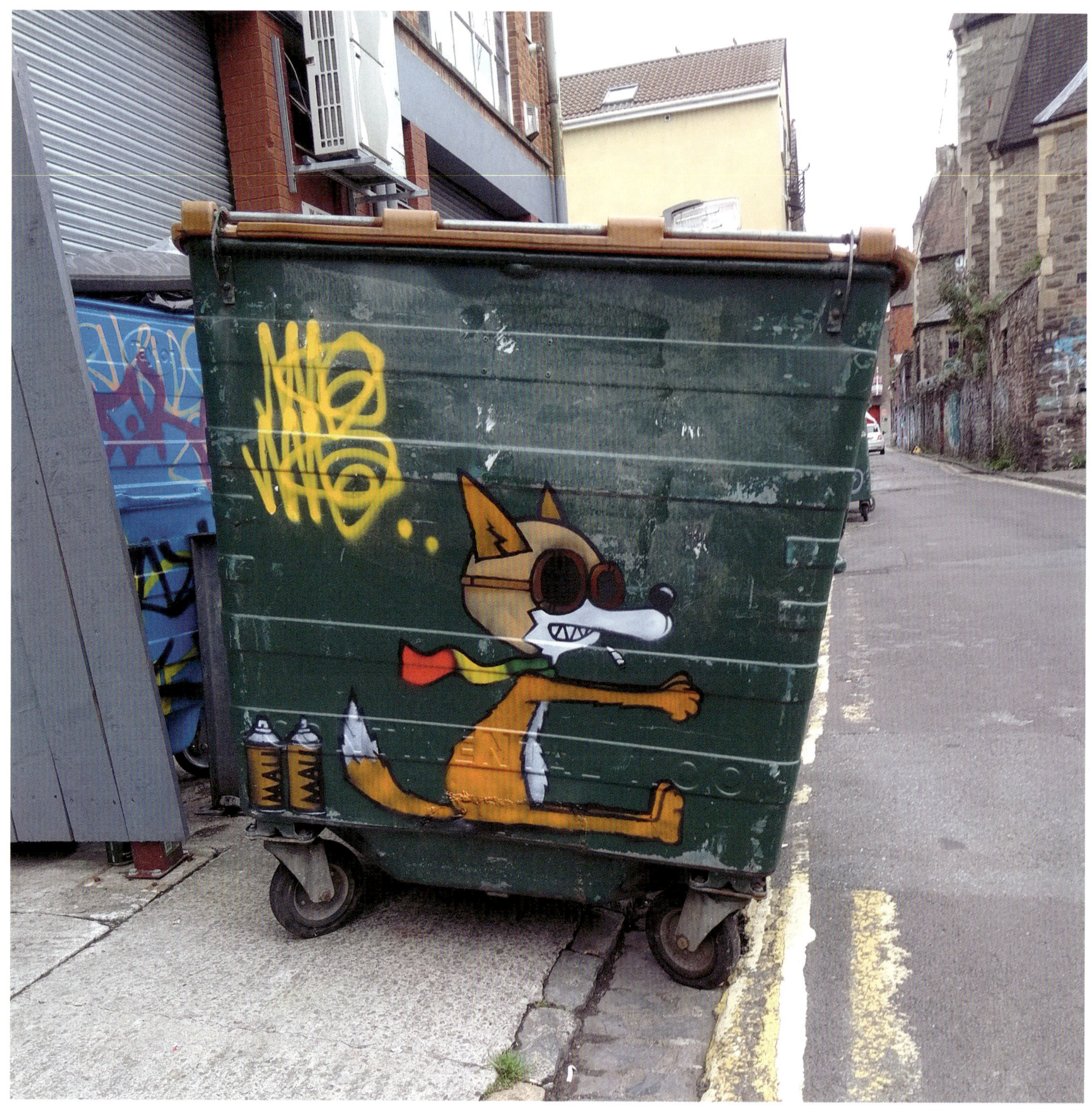

Baron Fox, Bristol, 2016.

Bite The Hand That Feeds You, Bristol, 2016.

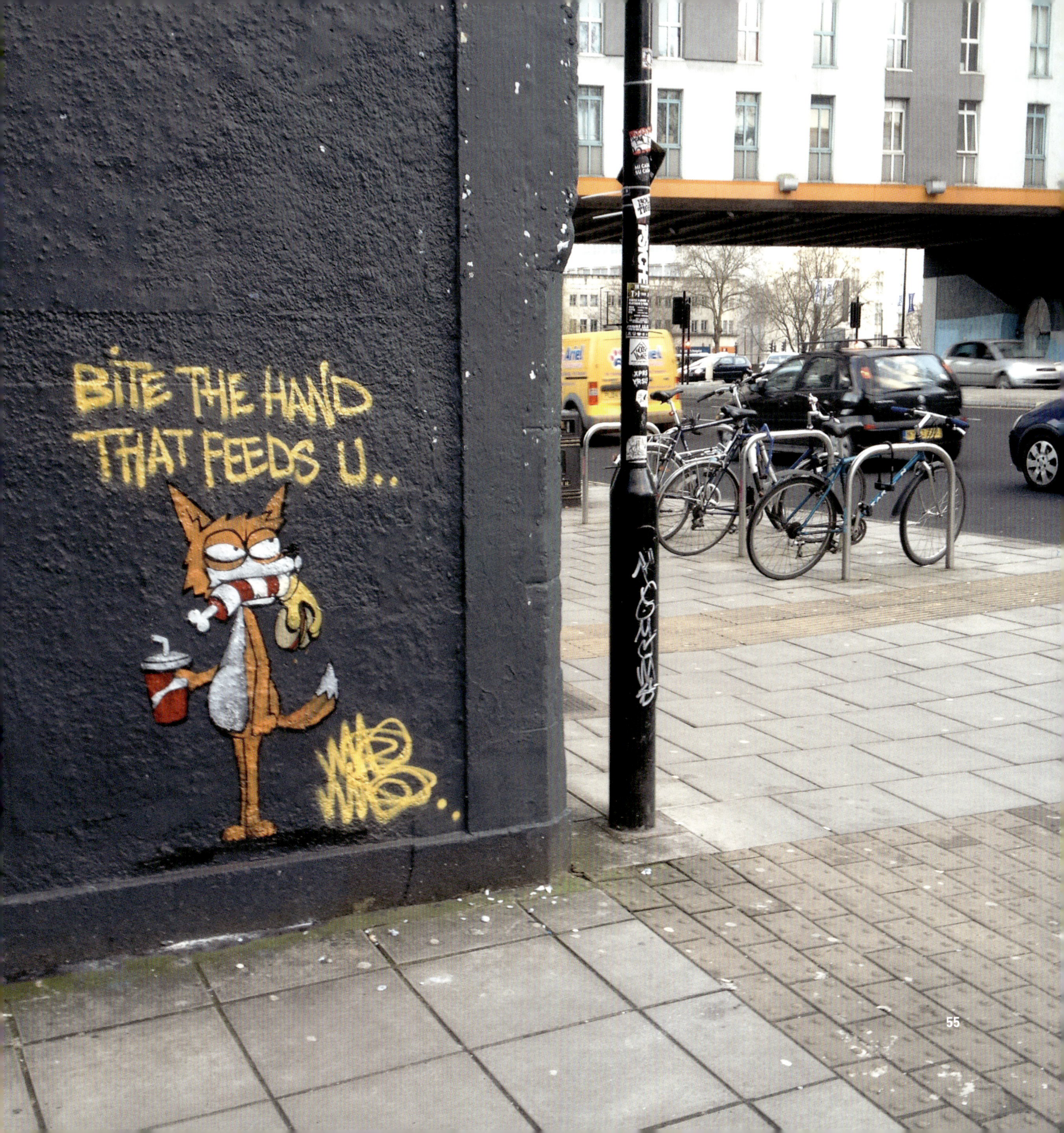
BITE THE HAND
THAT FEEDS U..

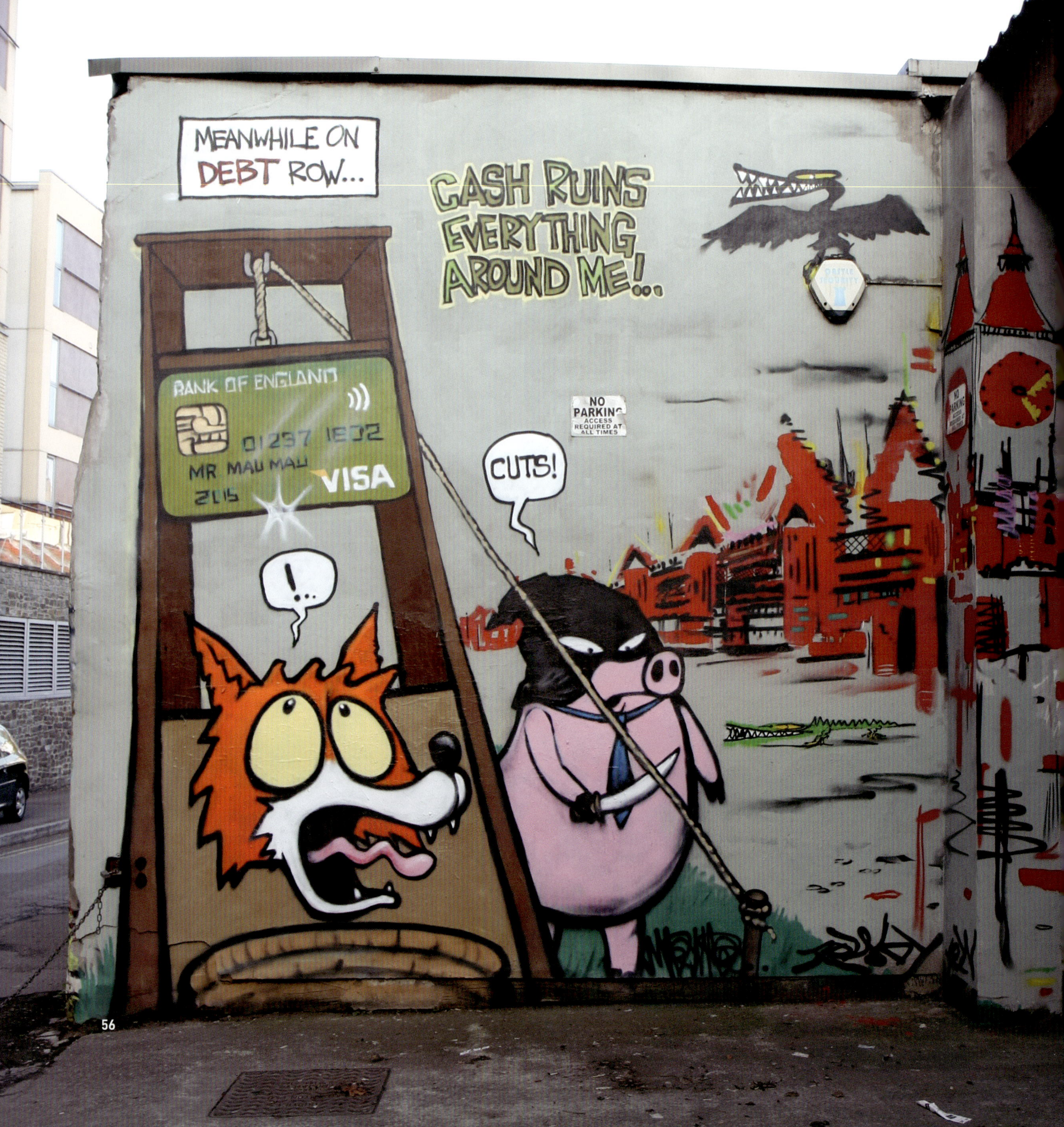
MEANWHILE ON DEBT ROW...
CASH RUINS EVERYTHING AROUND ME!...
RANK OF ENGLAND
01237
MR MAU MAU
VISA
NO PARKING ACCESS REQUIRED AT ALL TIMES
CUTS!
!...

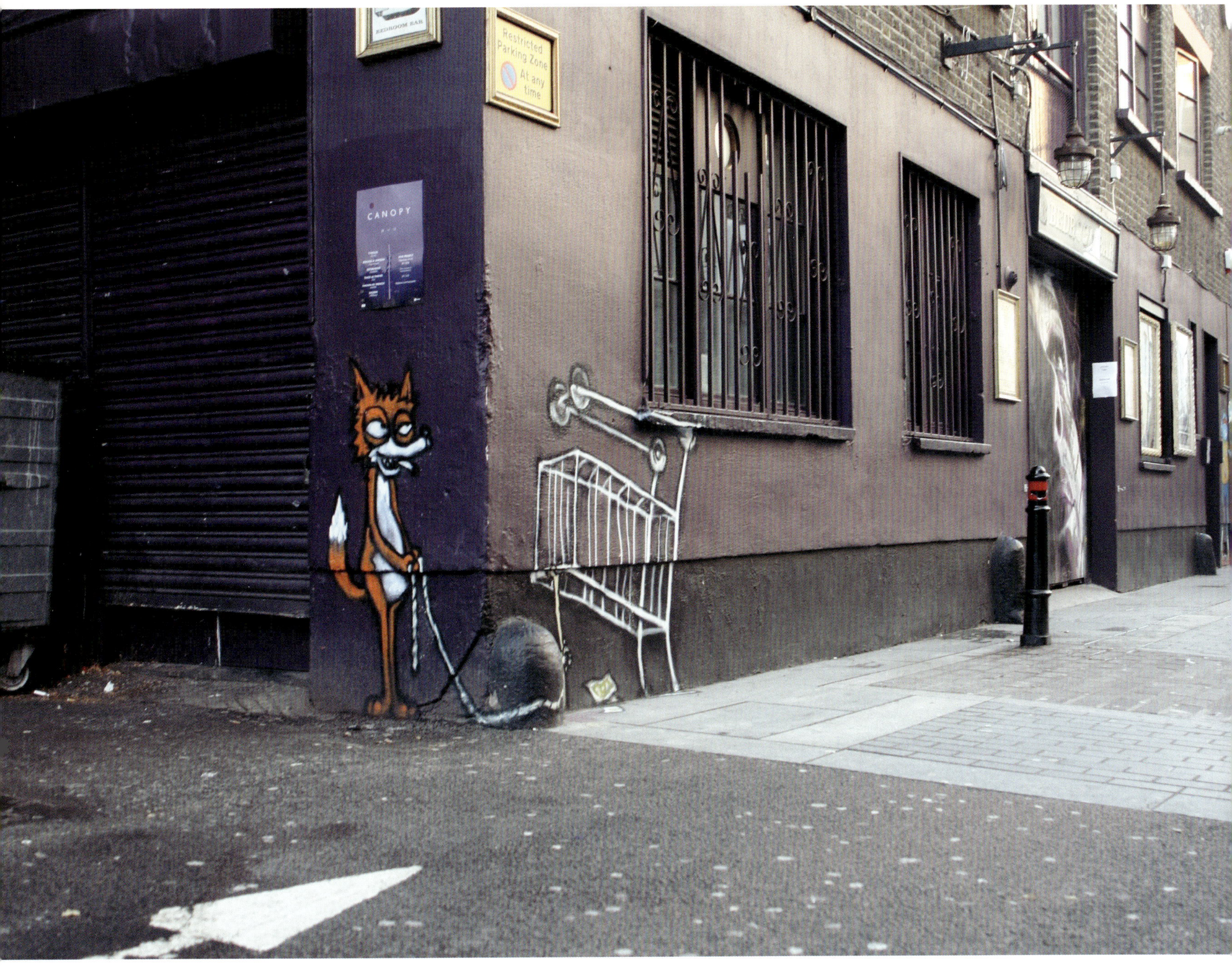

Debt Row, Bristol (Rowdy, Mau), 2015.

Money Trap, London, 2015.

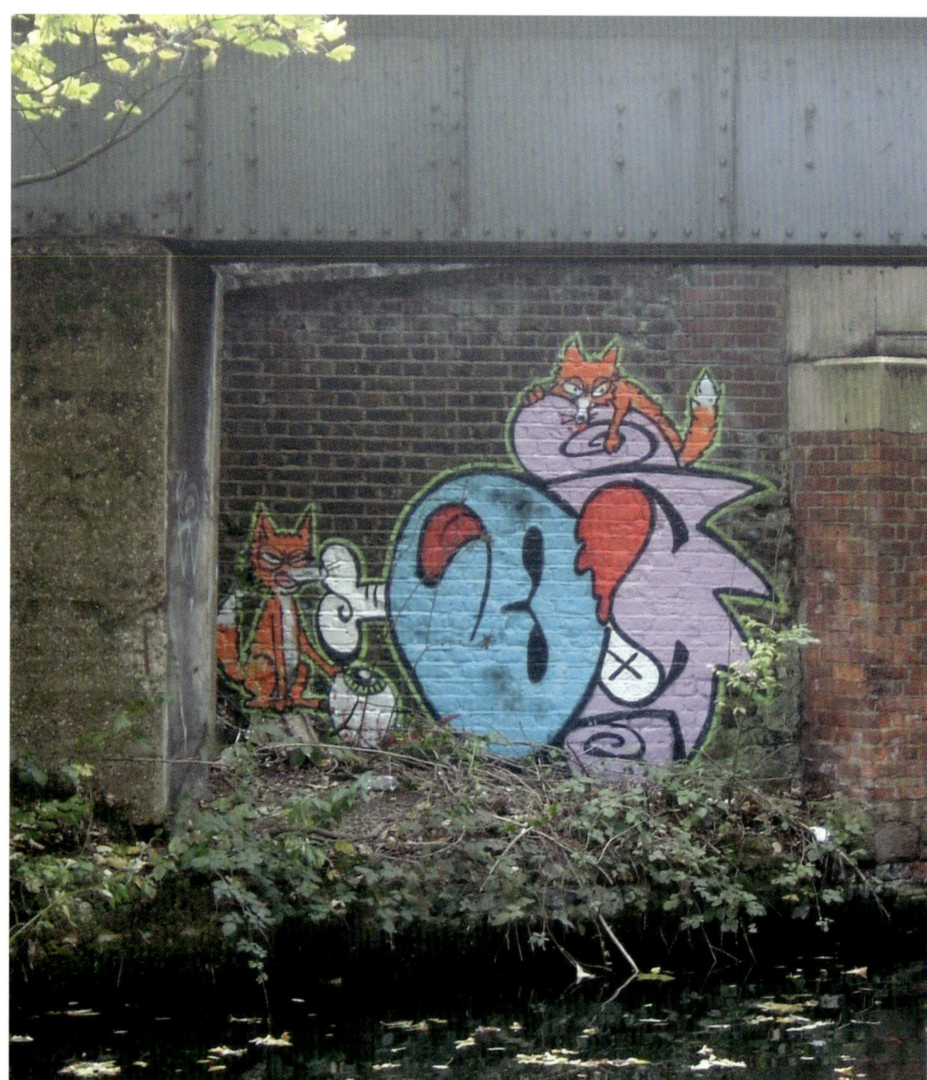

Hertford Union Canal (Mo, Mau), 2010.

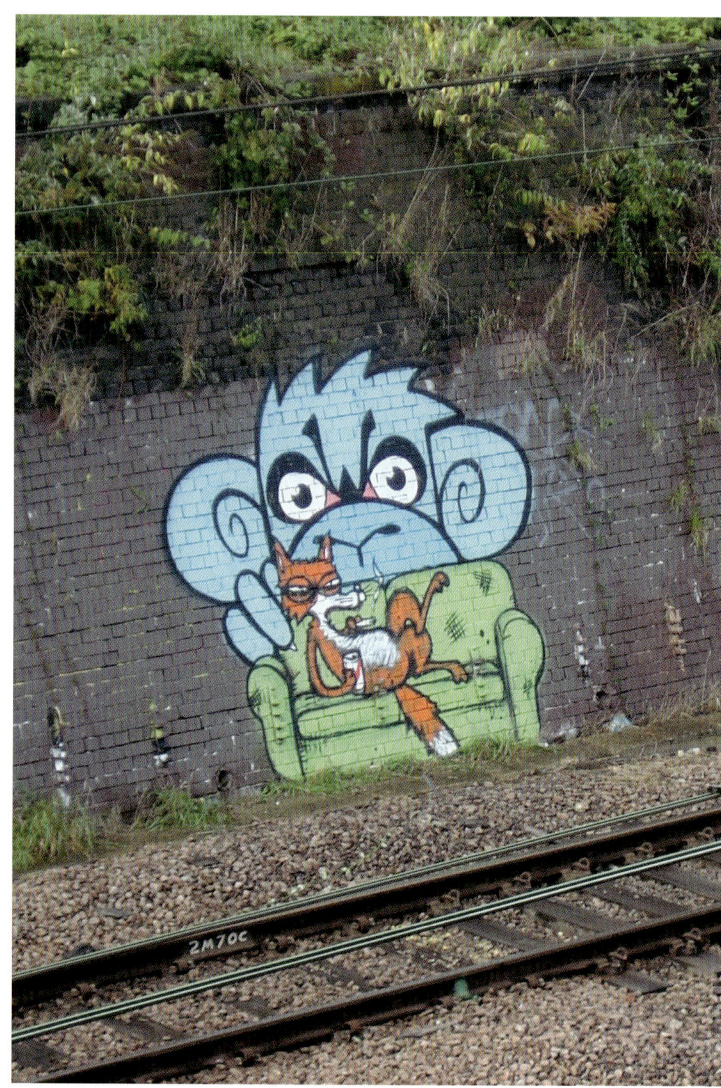

Finsbury Park, East Coast Mainline (Mo, Mau), 2010.

London studio

After a while I got a studio in Hackney Wick. The Olympic Village was being developed around the corner but for the time being rents were cheap so lots of artists were living and working there. I painted with Chu, Cyclops and Mighty Mo, who all had studios nearby. We went out painting a lot.

I had good times painting with Monkey. We'd cruise around on mash up old bikes looking for spots to paint. Monkey could climb, and he knew all the 'get-ons'- the places where you can get on the train tracks. The main risk of getting caught is getting on and off the tracks. Once you are down there, you feel pretty safe because the only people about are the 'trackies' – security guards and maintenance workers. They always have torches so you can see them coming from a mile away.

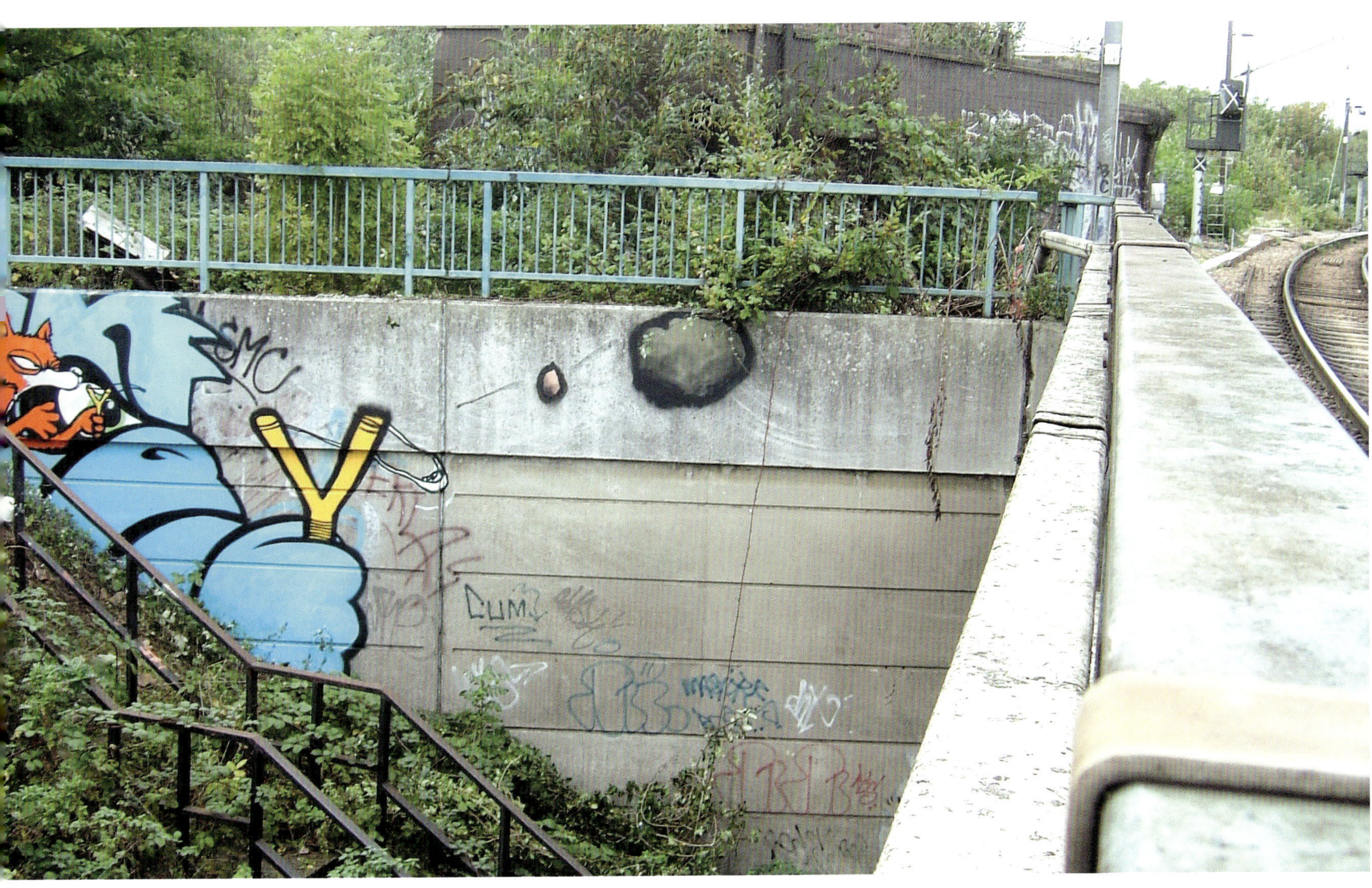

Hackney Wick, London Overground (Mo, Mau), circa 2010.

One time we did a Bomber piece outside Dalston Kingsland station. We initially painted two planes, but the next day we went to check out the piece and were disappointed when we realised how small it looked from the train. So that night, we went back and added a third bomber. Everyone could see it after that.

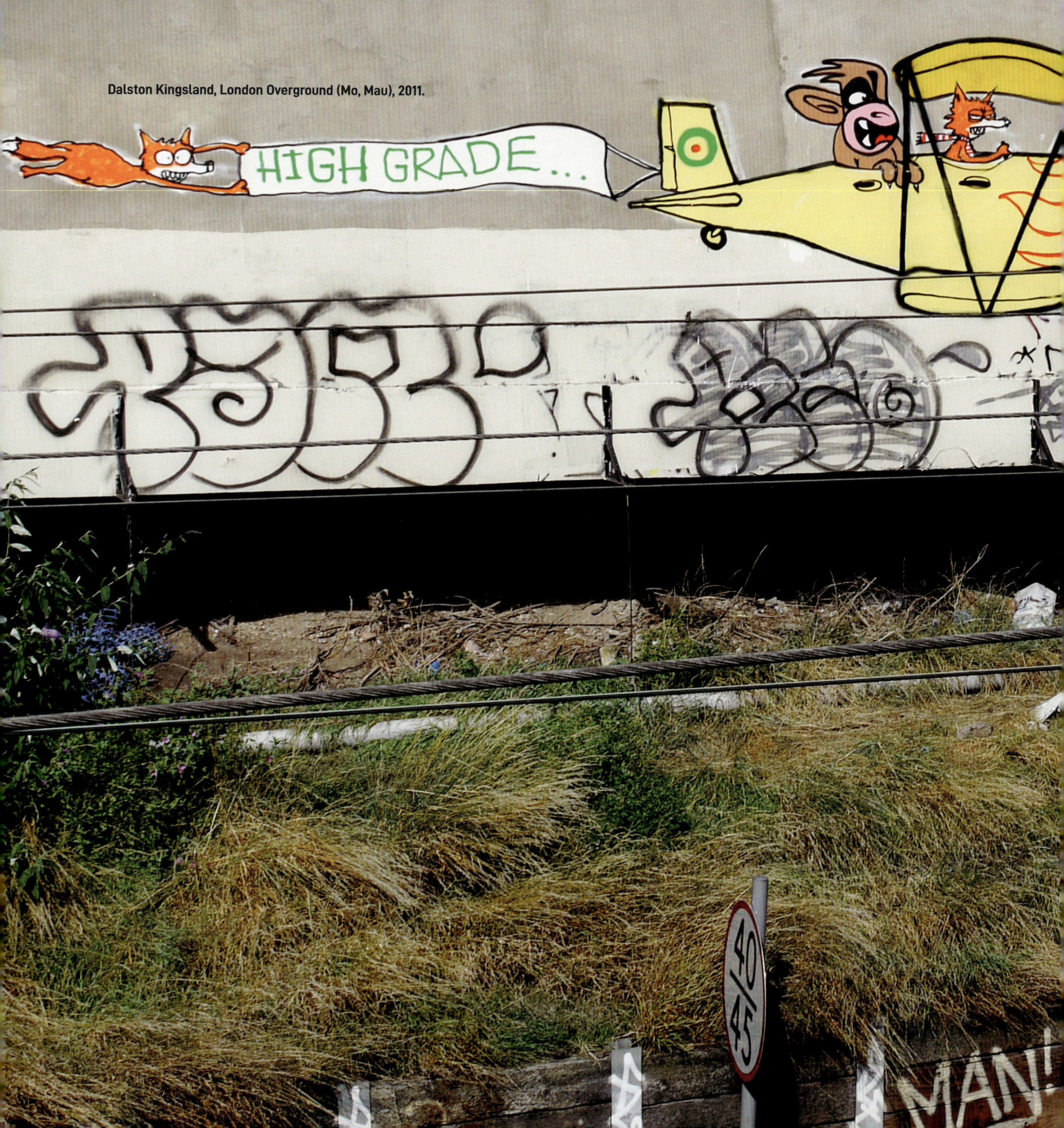

Dalston Kingsland, London Overground (Mo, Mau), 2011.

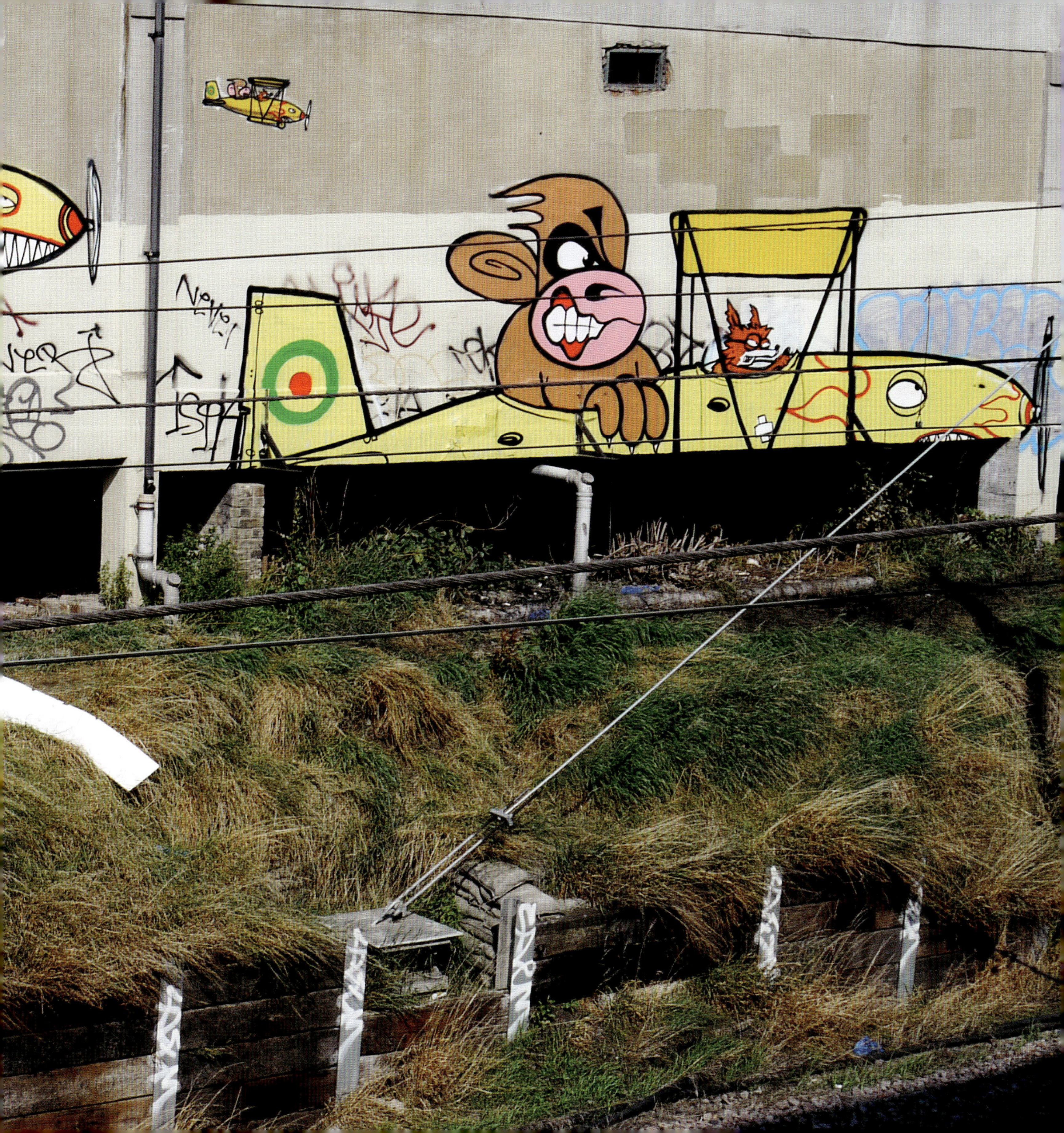

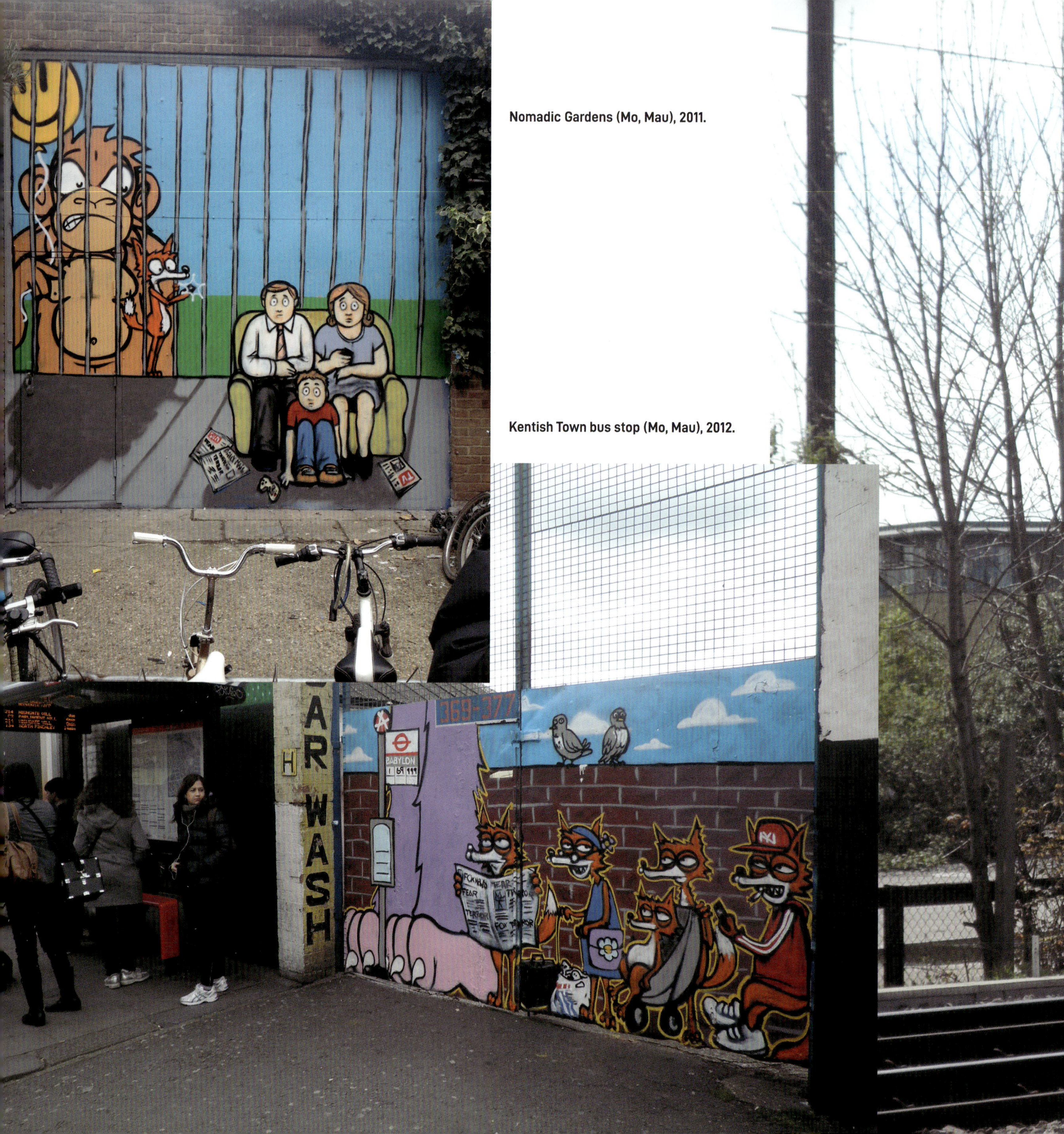

Nomadic Gardens (Mo, Mau), 2011.

Kentish Town bus stop (Mo, Mau), 2012.

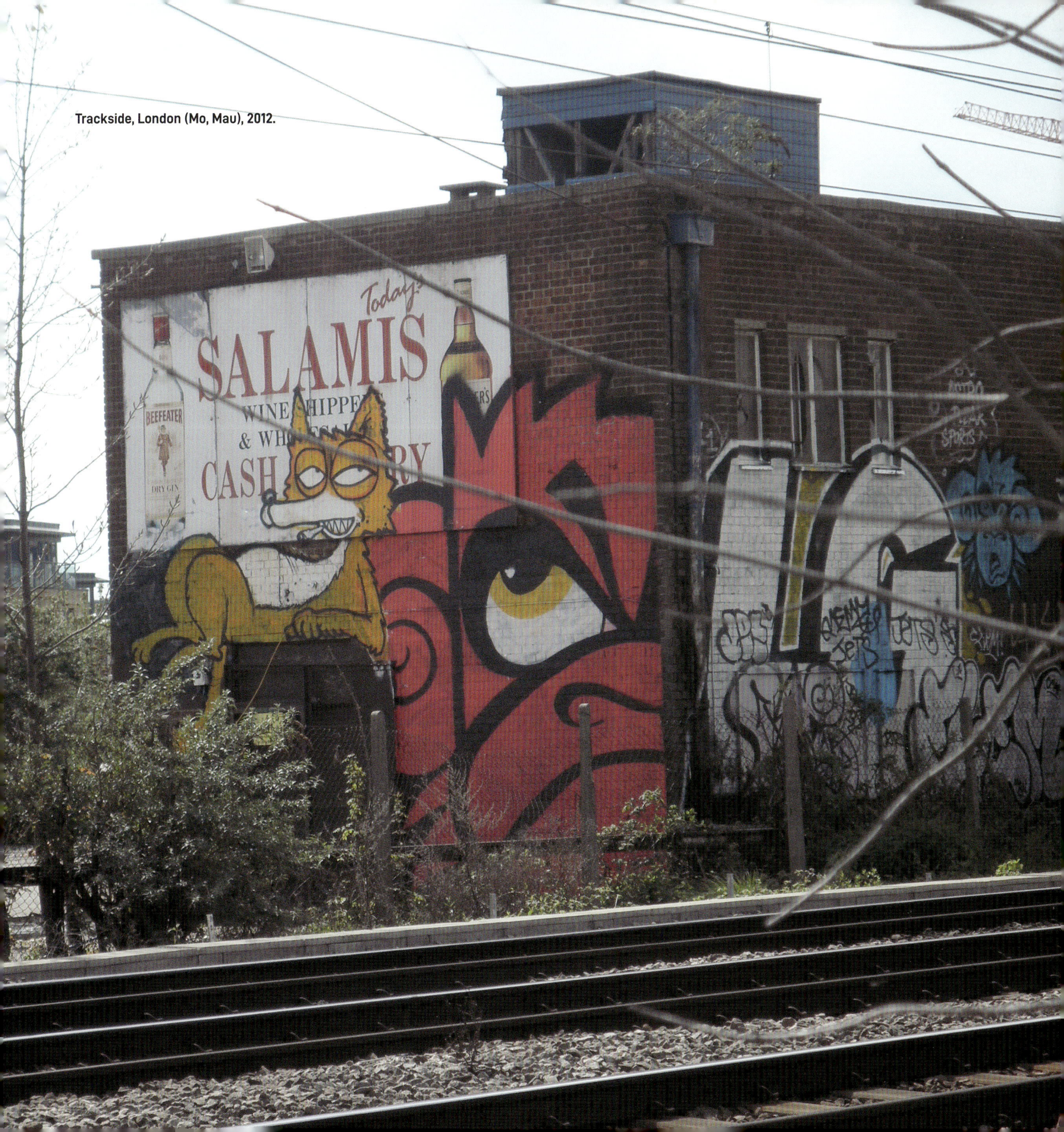

Trackside, London (Mo, Mau), 2012.

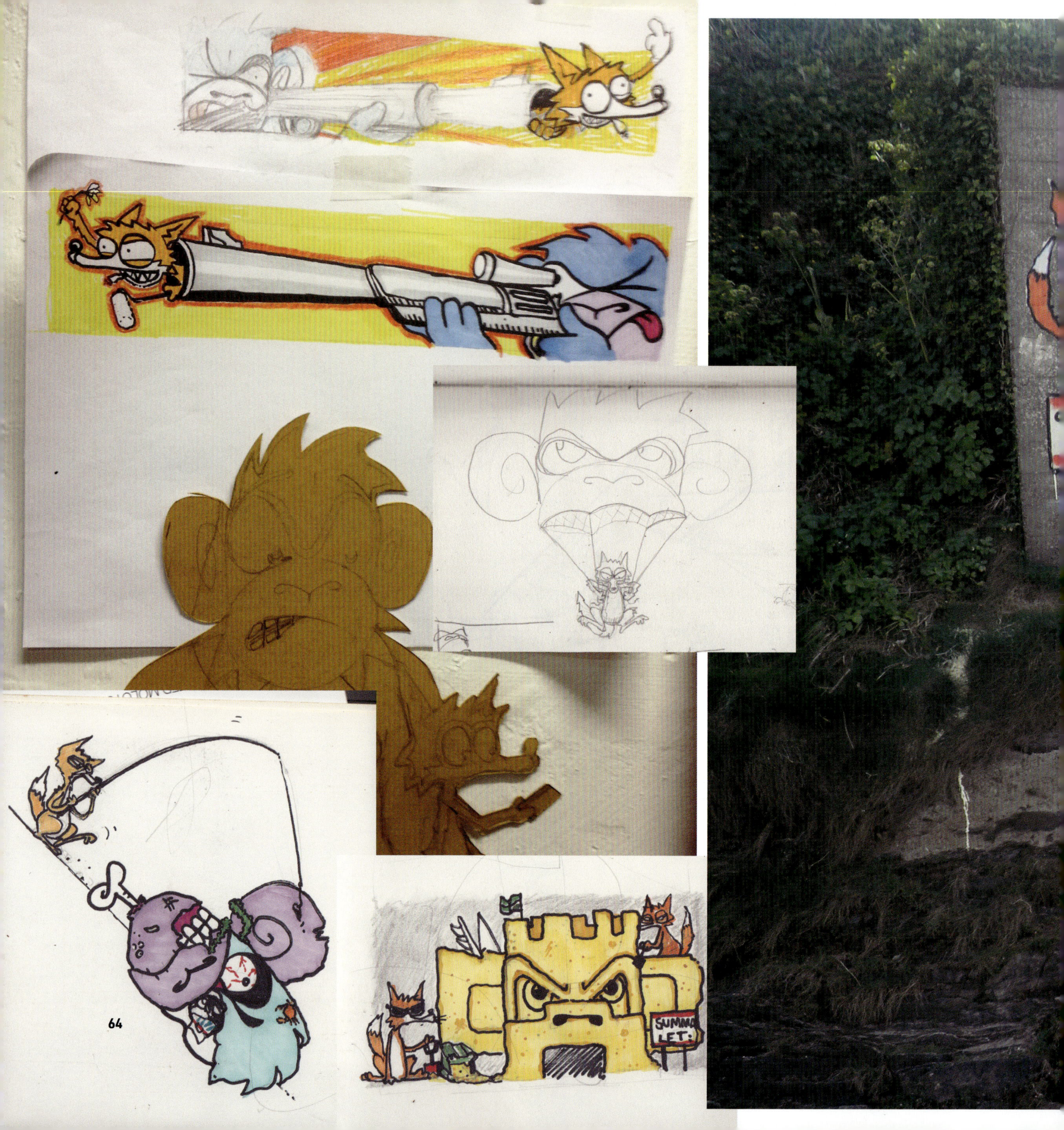
SUMMA
LET.

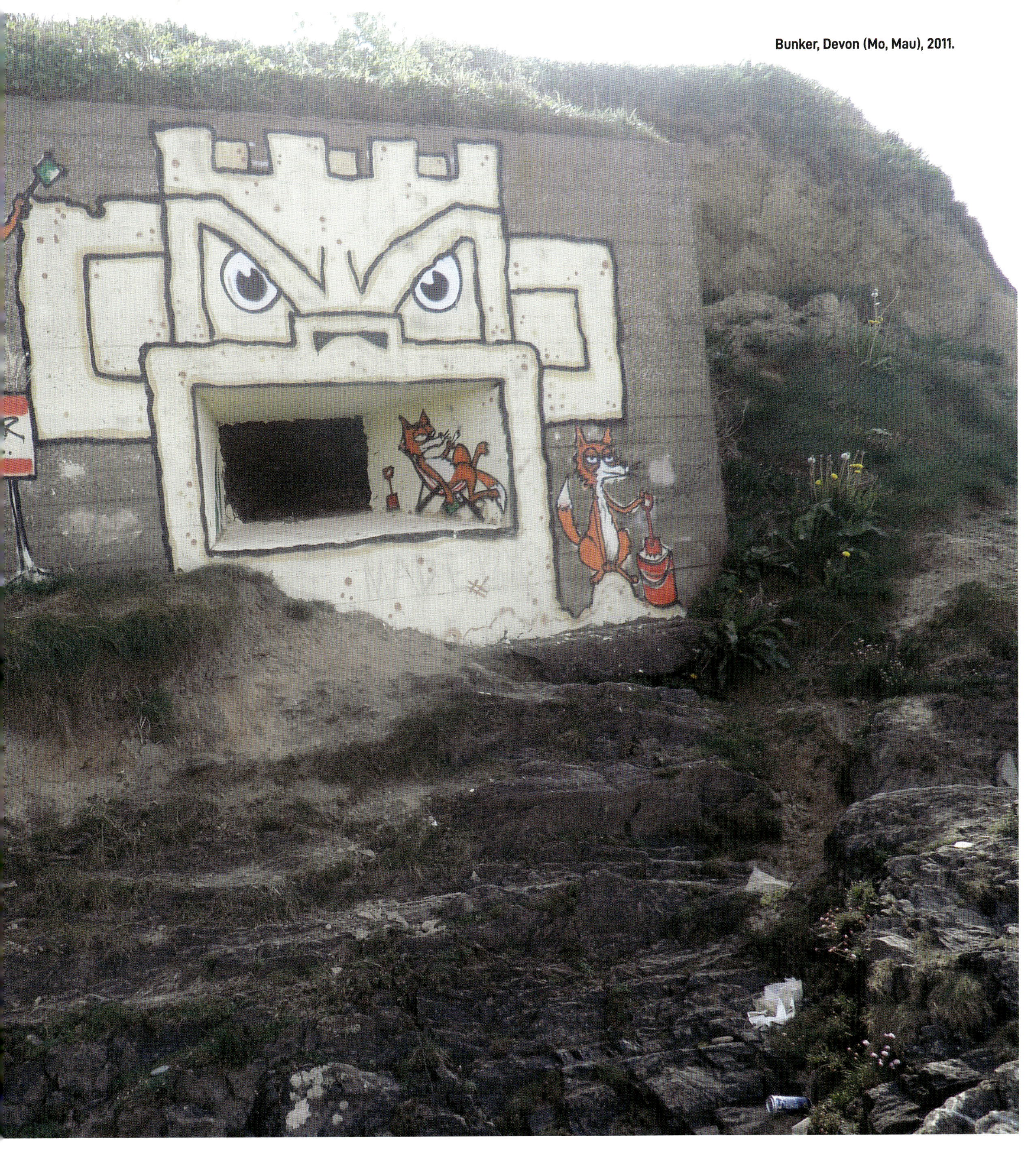

Bunker, Devon (Mo, Mau), 2011.

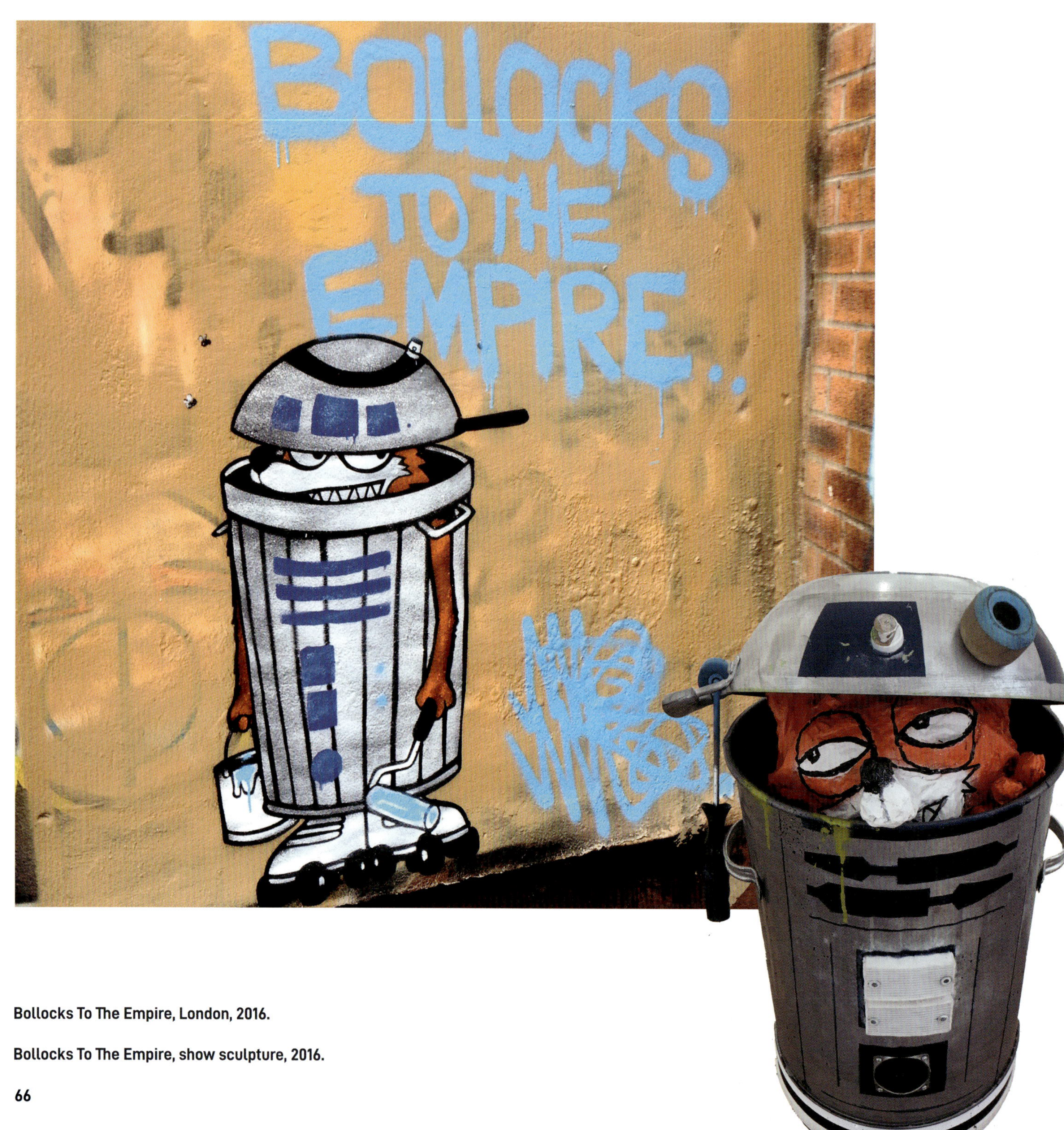

Bollocks To The Empire, London, 2016.

Bollocks To The Empire, show sculpture, 2016.

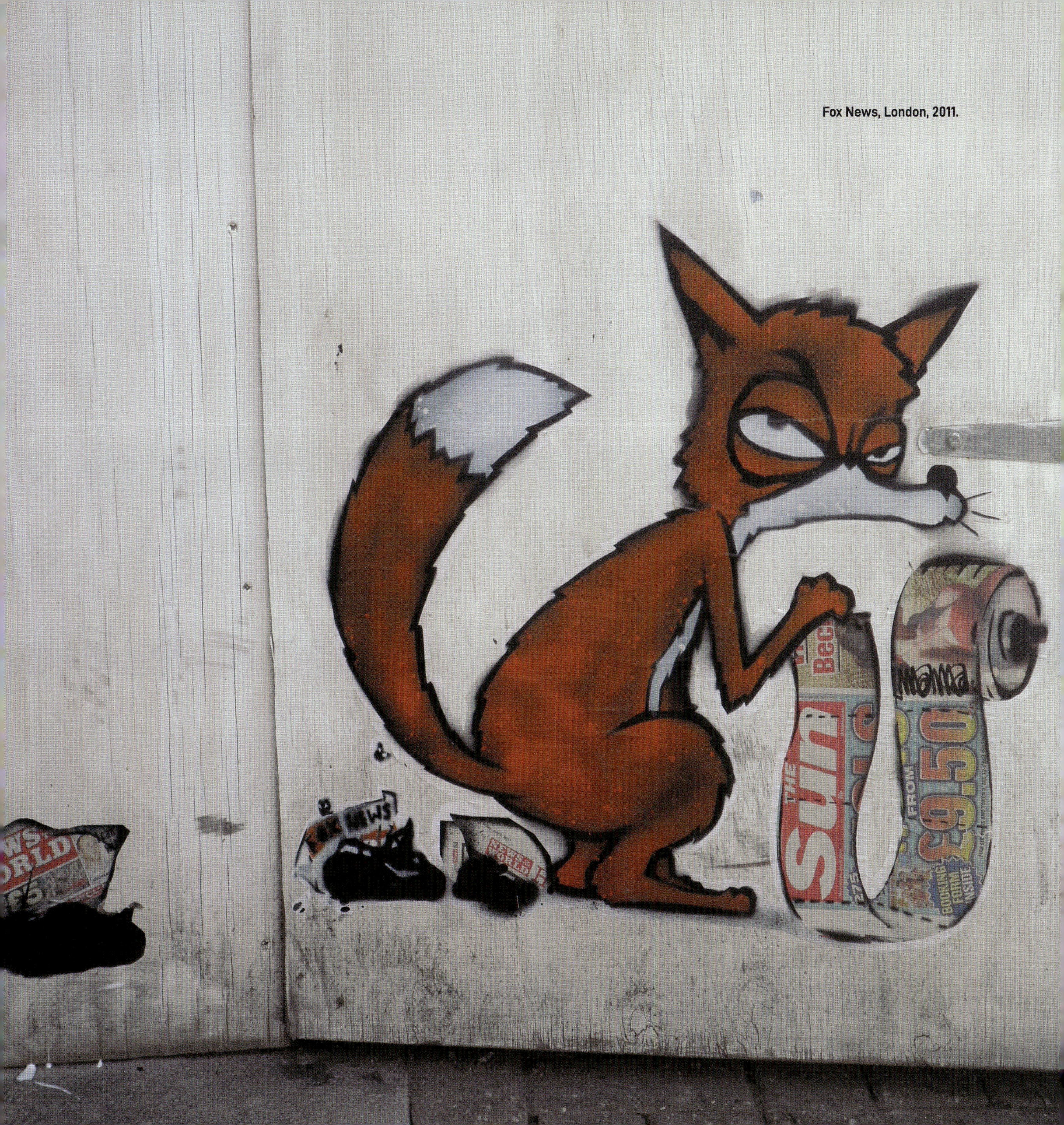

Fox News, London, 2011.

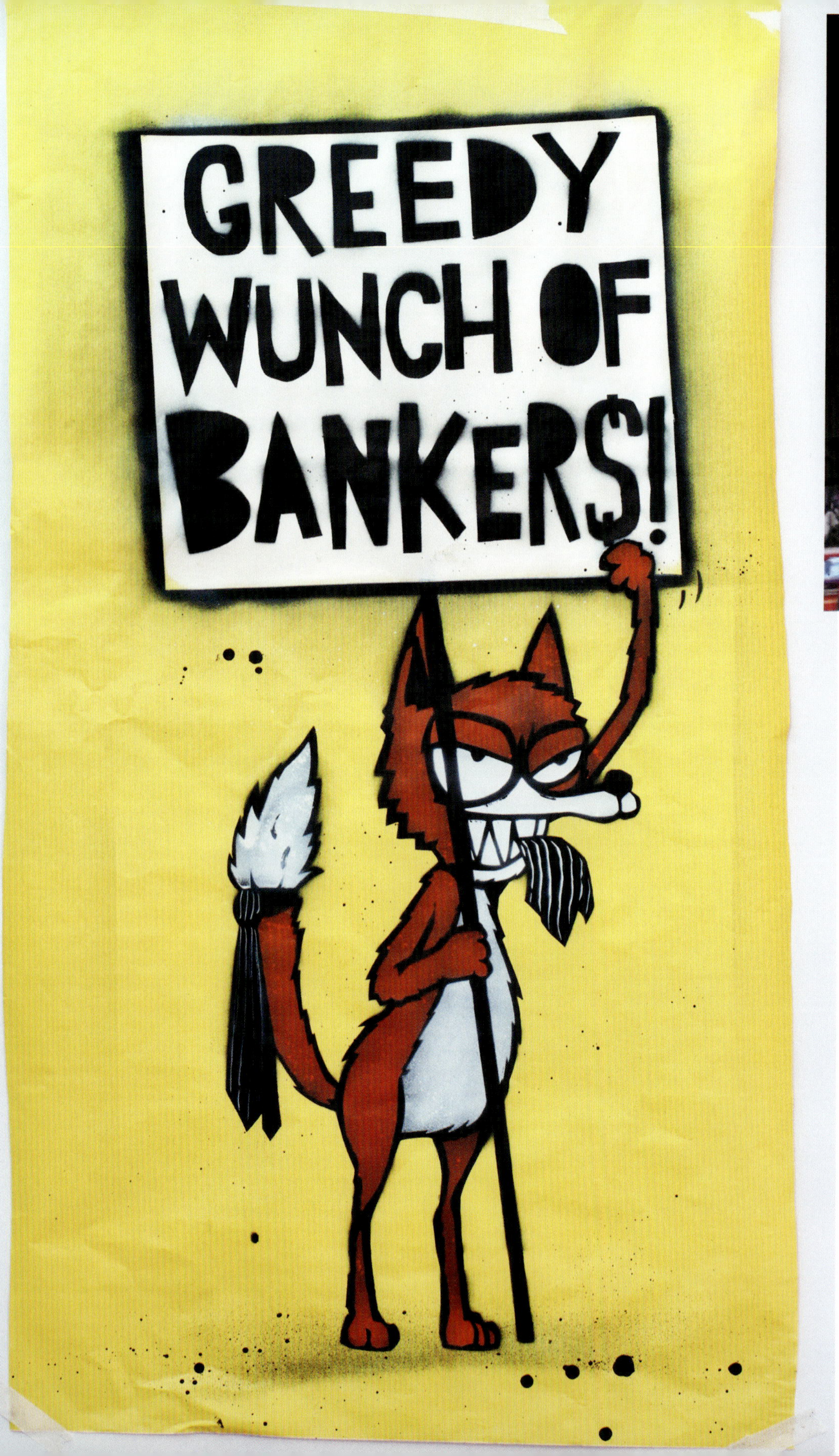

GREEDY WUNCH OF BANKER$!

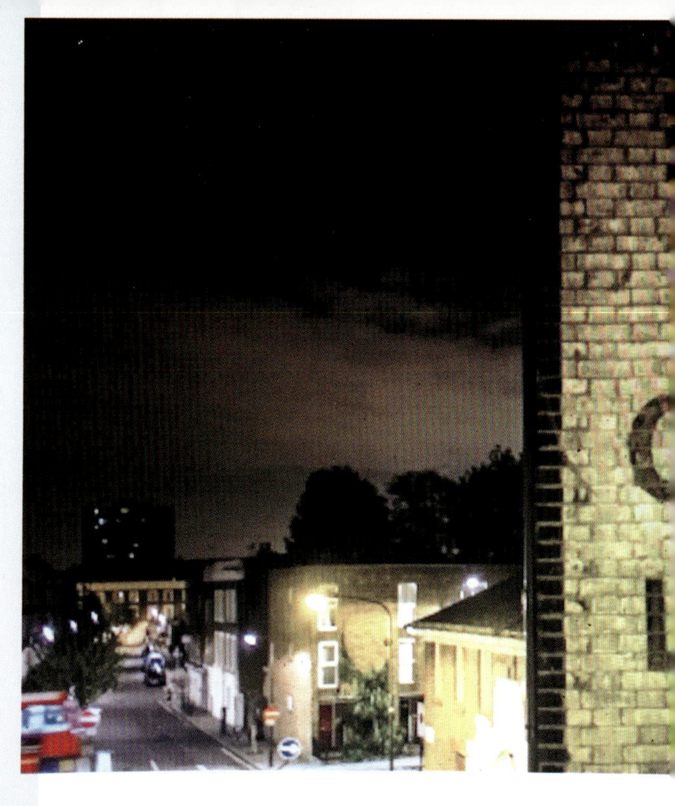

Camden, London

Occupy were doing a lot of protests in London and I was asked to do some artwork for them. Some of them had a squat up in Camden and they told me about a spot that could only be accessed from their building – the rooftop of a bank. It was a prime spot, right across the road from Camden tube station, but very on top in terms of risk as it was lit up under a streetlight in an area that's busy practically 24 hours a day. I spent most of the night waiting for it to quieten down, but it just didn't. Around 4am the streets below finally got quieter and I went for it. It was one of my favourite spots to have painted and, being central London, the piece has had loads of views.

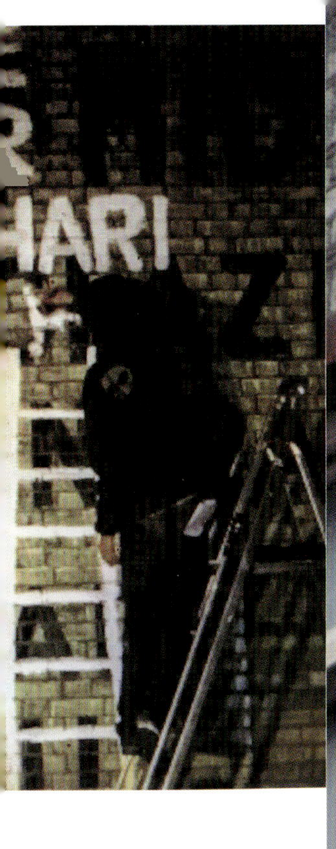

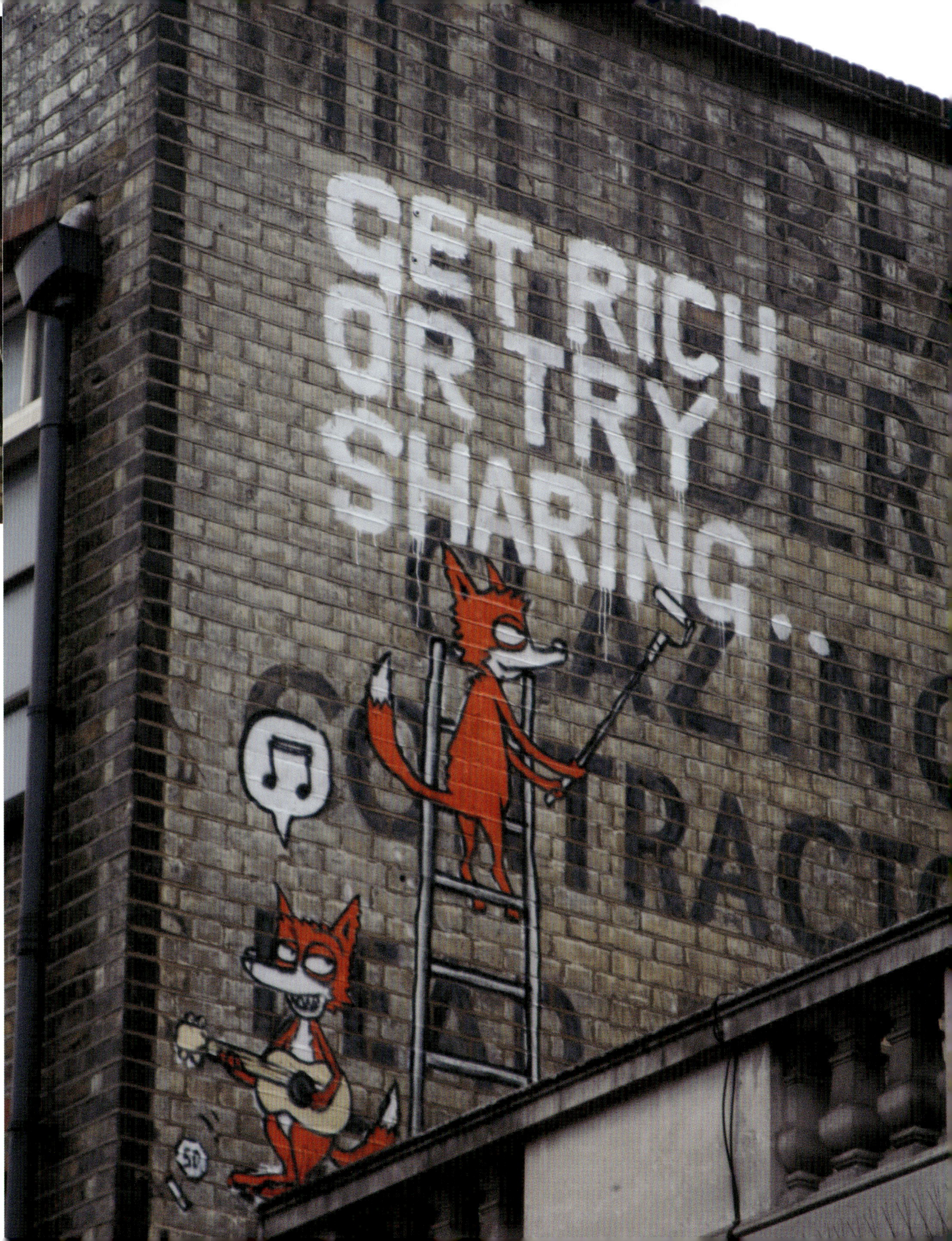

Get Rich Or Try Sharing, Camden, 2012.

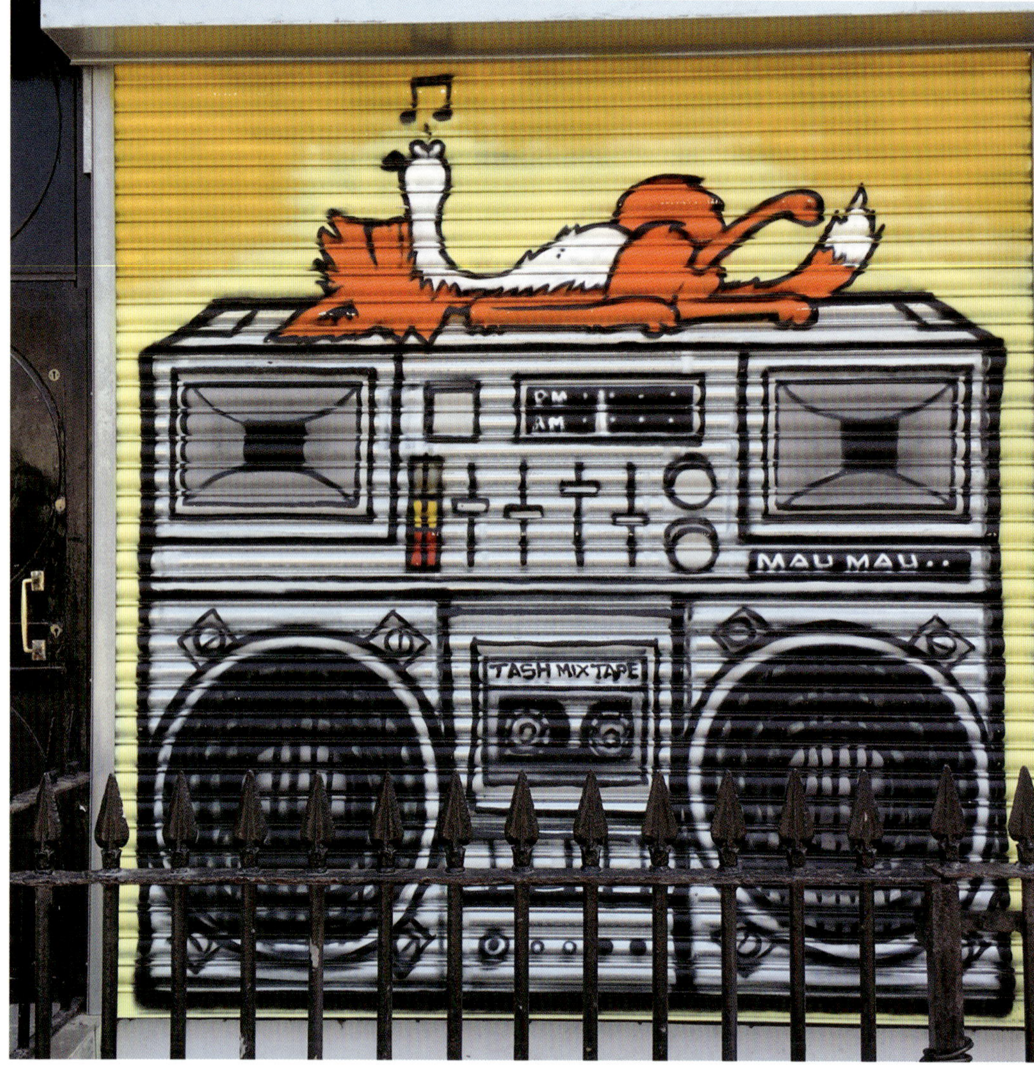

Boom Box, Brighton, 2017.

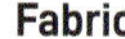

Fabric

In 2016 the legendary Fabric nightclub had its licence revoked - another club pushed aside in favour of gentrification. I painted the piece during the day pretending I had permission. It was my first 'pig' piece. I never want to get busted but getting busted by the pigs for painting pigs was another level... I'd met a couple of homeless guys who acted as lookouts, but as time went on they got more rowdy and started attracting attention. That day I did get busted - but for smoking weed not painting pigs!

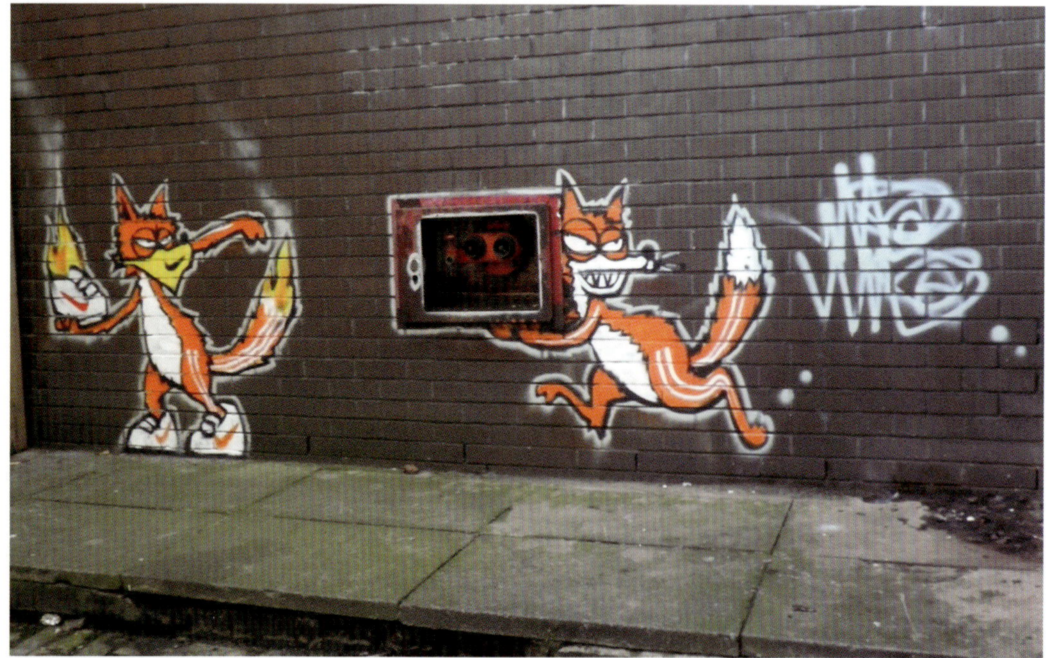

Riot Fox, Bristol, 2012.

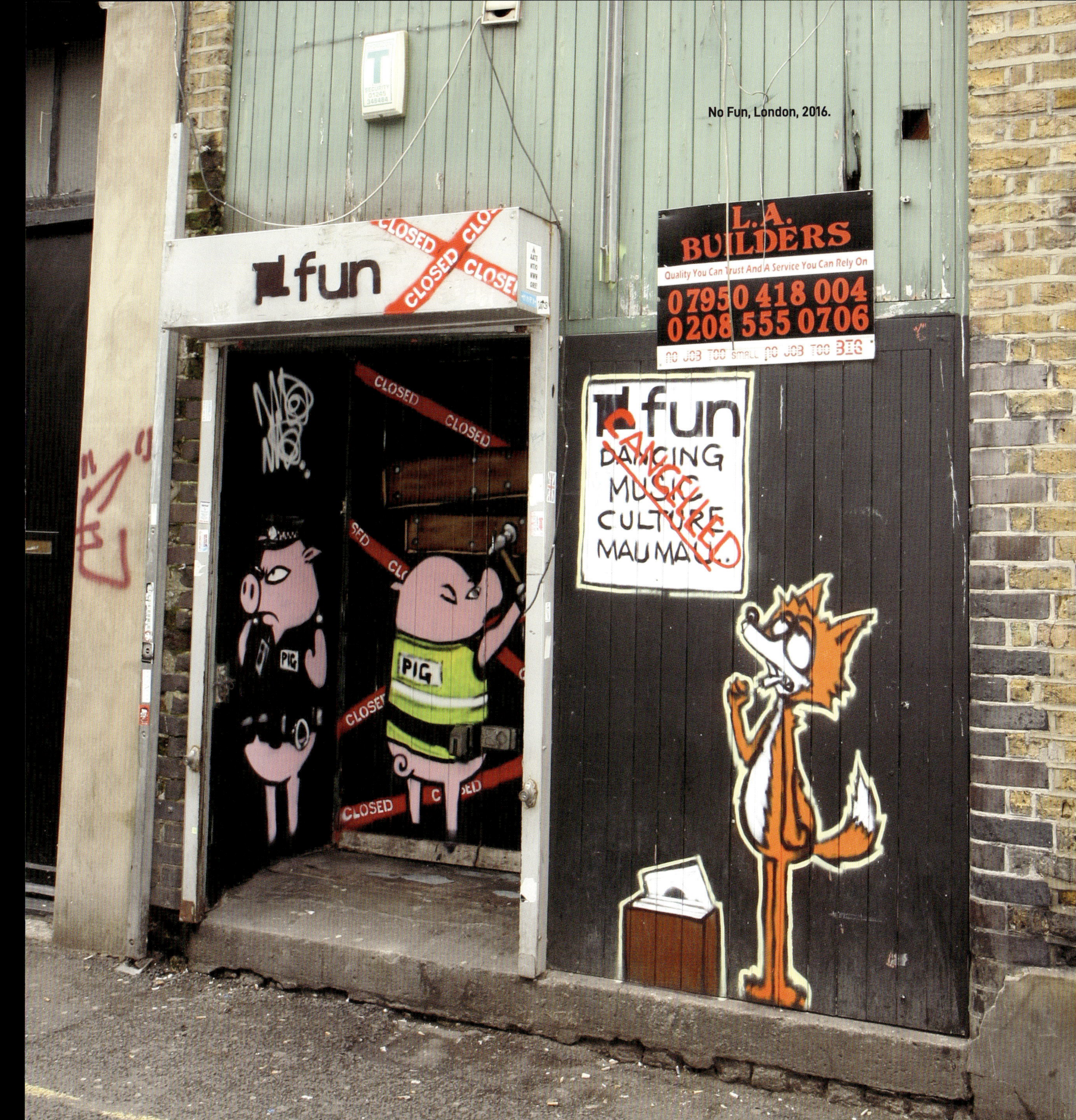

No Fun, London, 2016.

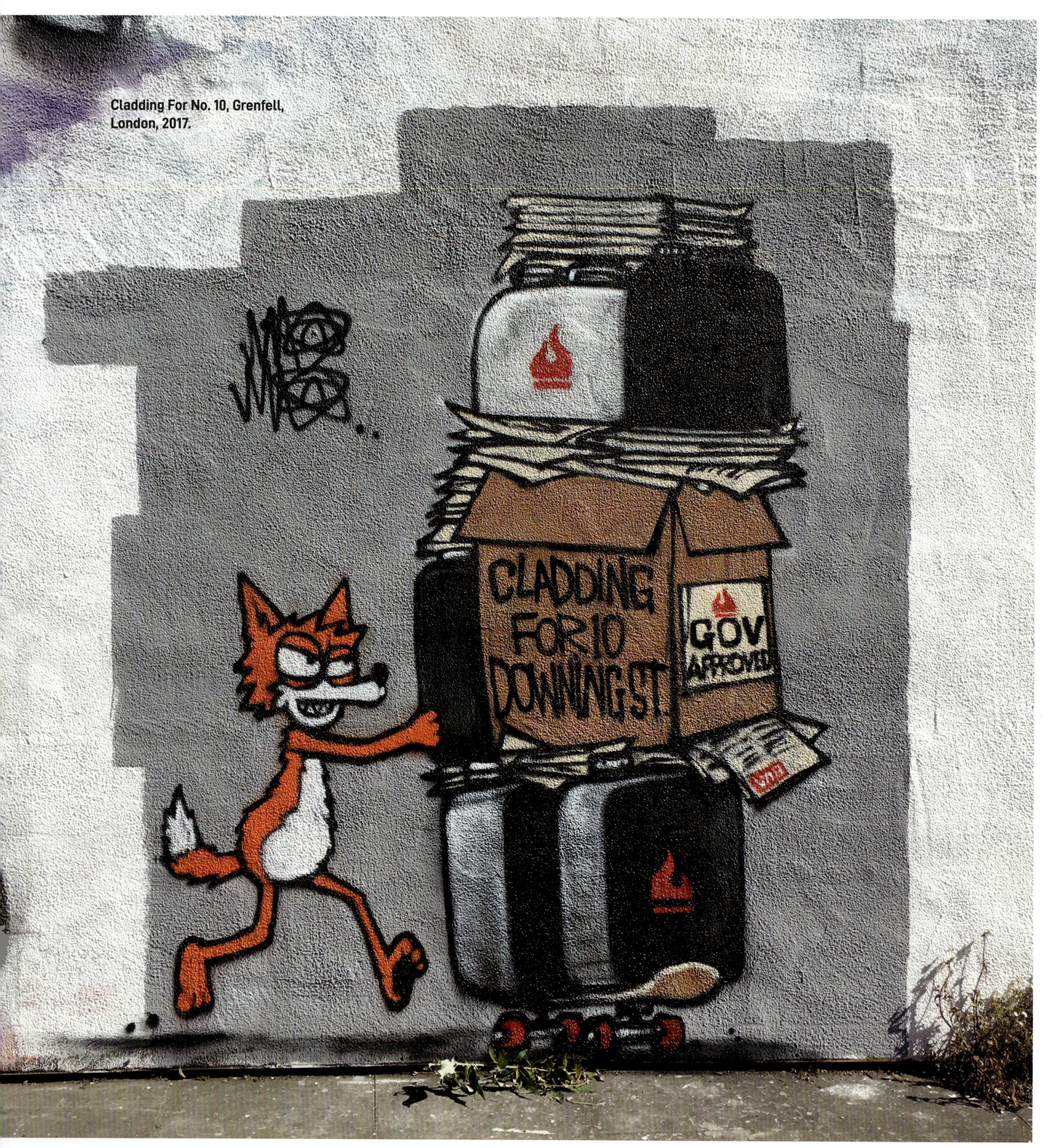

Cladding For No. 10, Grenfell, London, 2017.

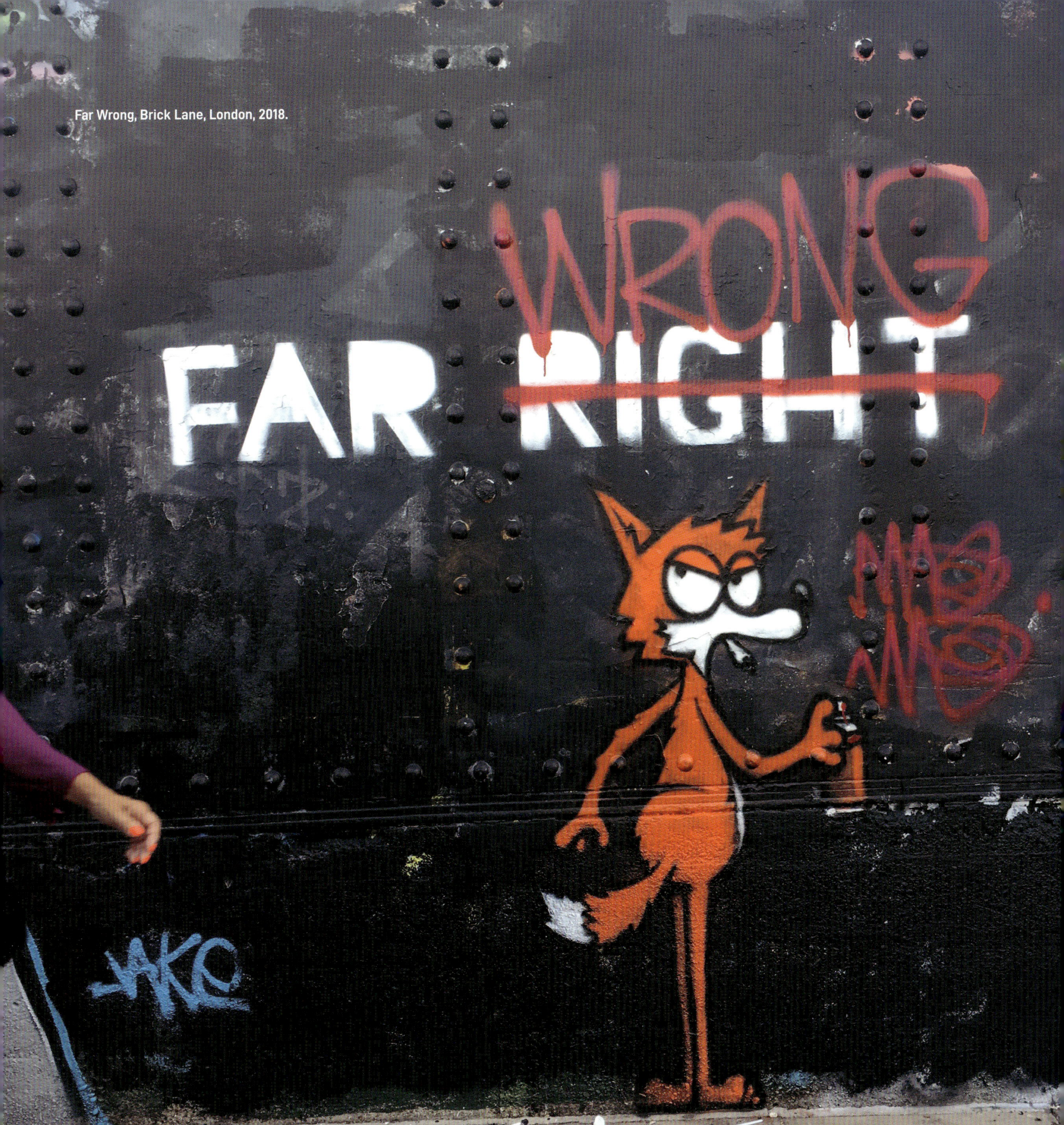

Far Wrong, Brick Lane, London, 2018.

In 2012, the Olympic torch made its way through the UK with heavy corporate sponsorship. I got a call from THTC clothing and they said they had a warehouse wall I could paint in West London so I painted the Clown Town piece. Within days the piece was painted over by the local council. The me picked up on the story as an example of London's zero tolerance to negative publicity towards the sponsors. The 'whitewashing' story was picked up Reuters and the Clown Town piece went around the world...

My Hackney days came to an end when the Olympics came to town. Rents rocketed, the area started getting gentrified and they began to target graffiti, with police busting artists and street pieces getting buffed.

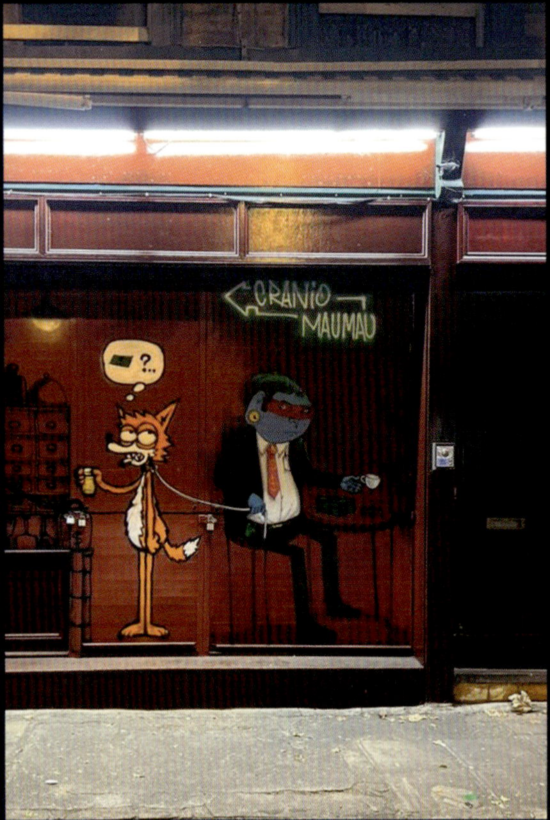

Cranio, Mau Mau, Dalston, London, 2022.

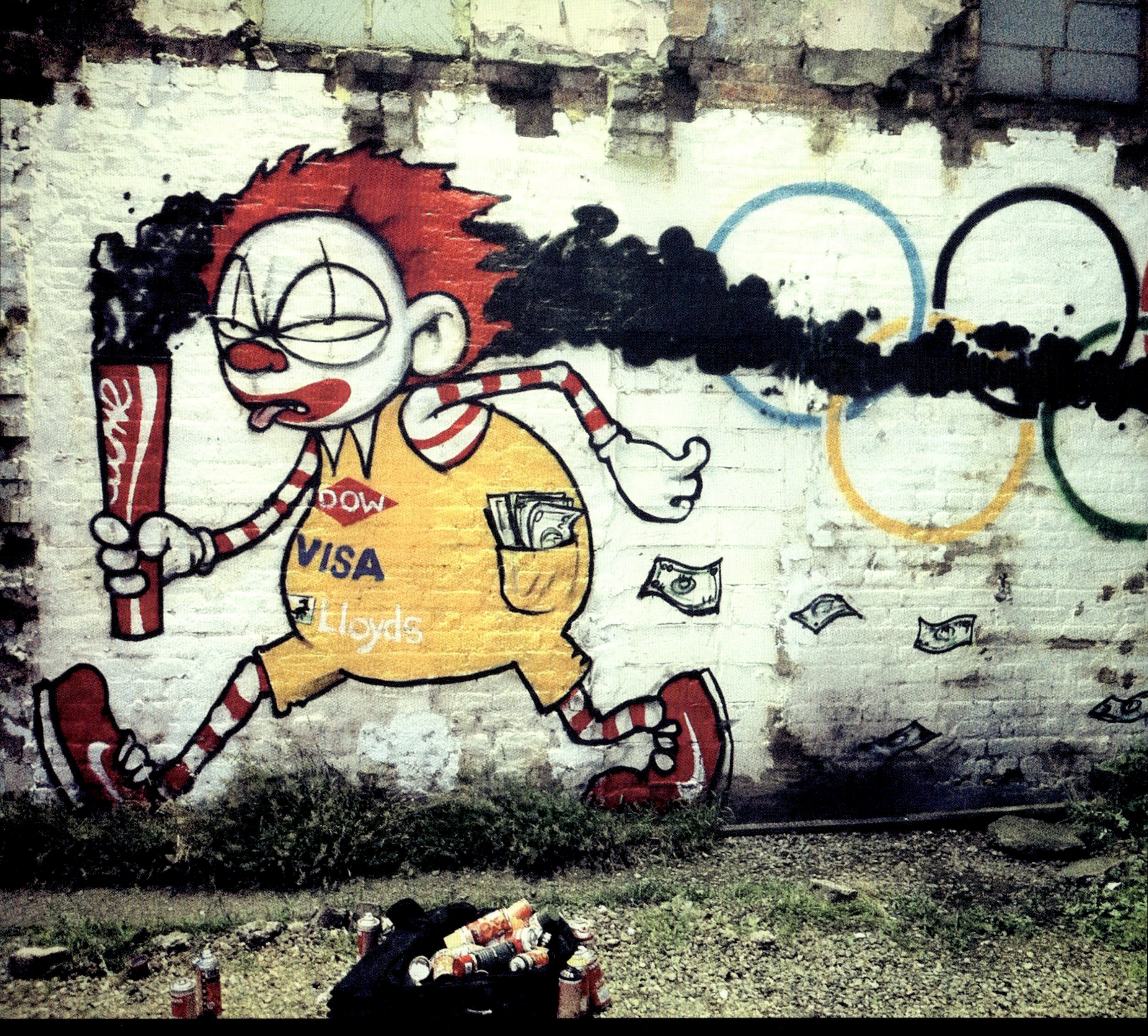

Clown Town, Ealing, London, 2012.

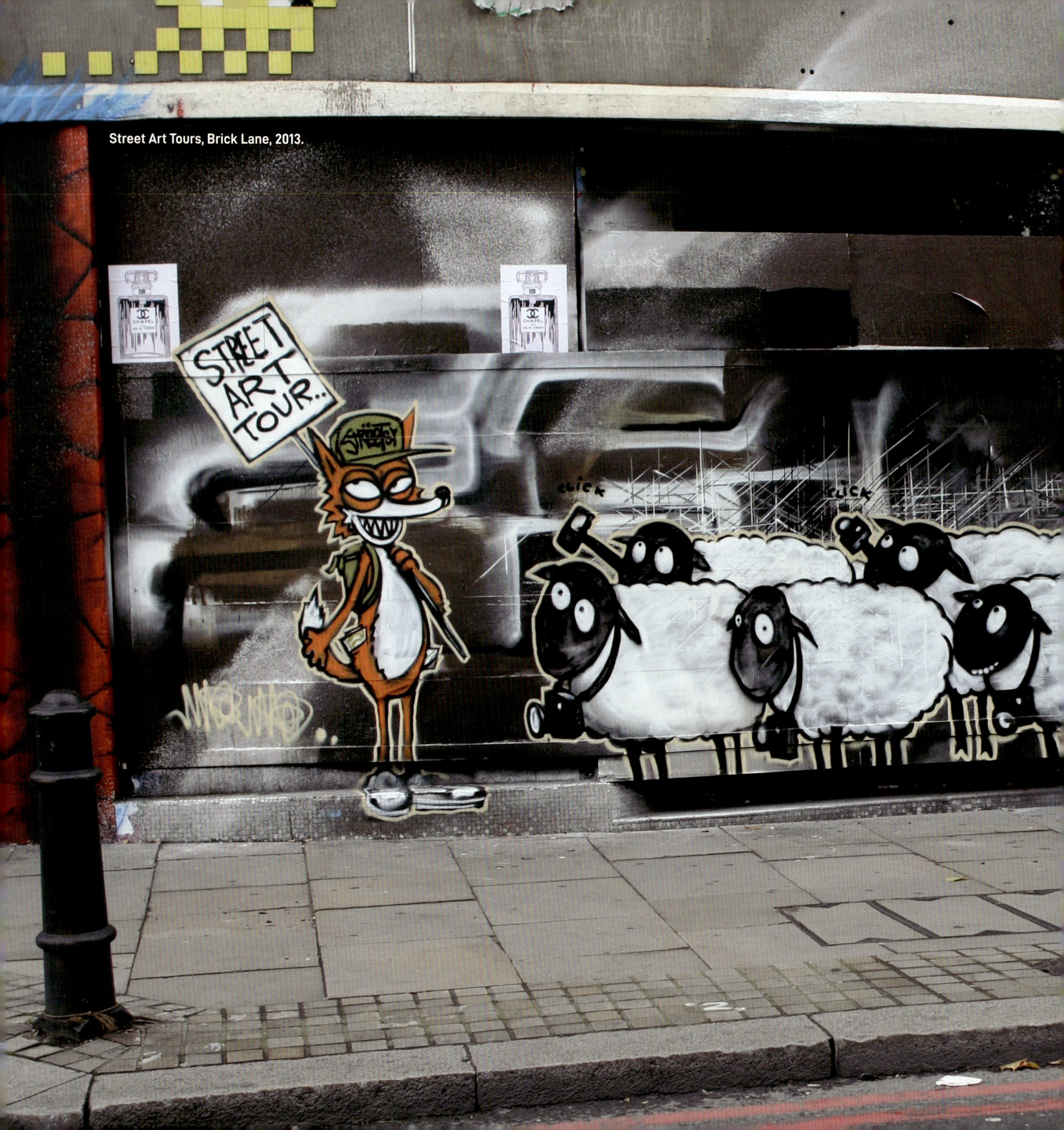

Street Art Tours, Brick Lane, 2013.

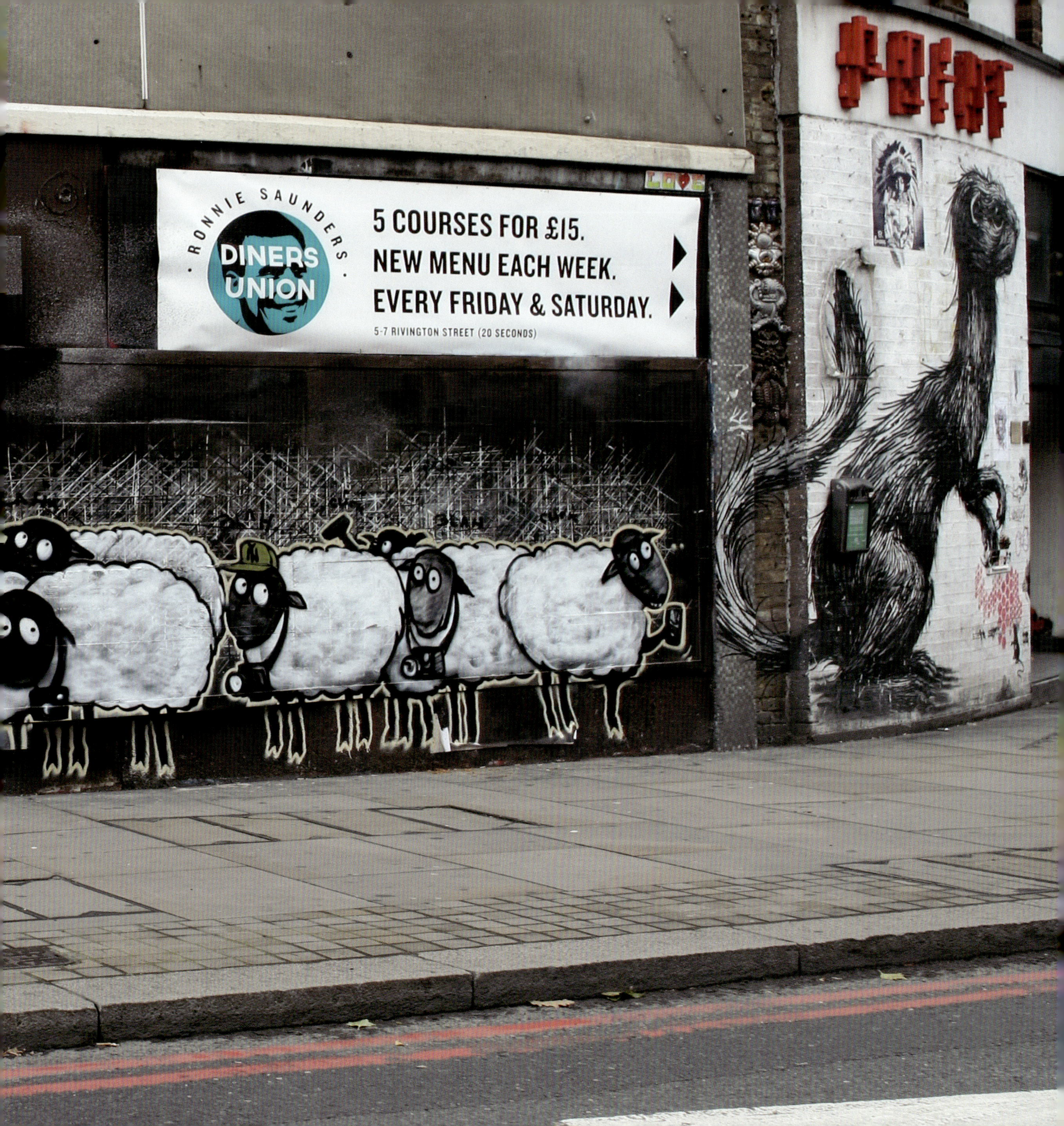
RONNIE SAUNDERS
DINERS UNION
5 COURSES FOR £15.
NEW MENU EACH WEEK.
EVERY FRIDAY & SATURDAY.
5-7 RIVINGTON STREET (20 SECONDS)

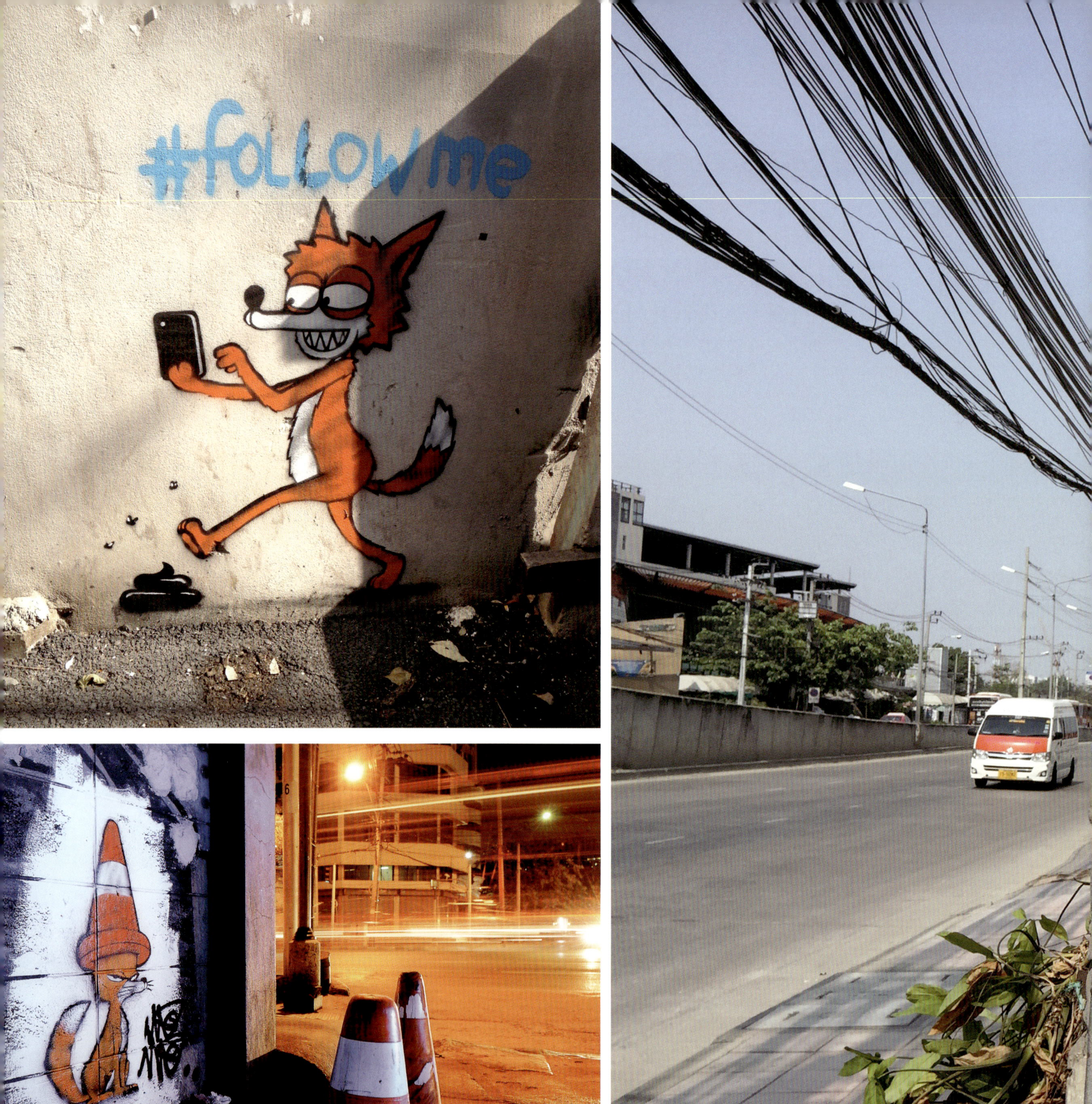
#follow me

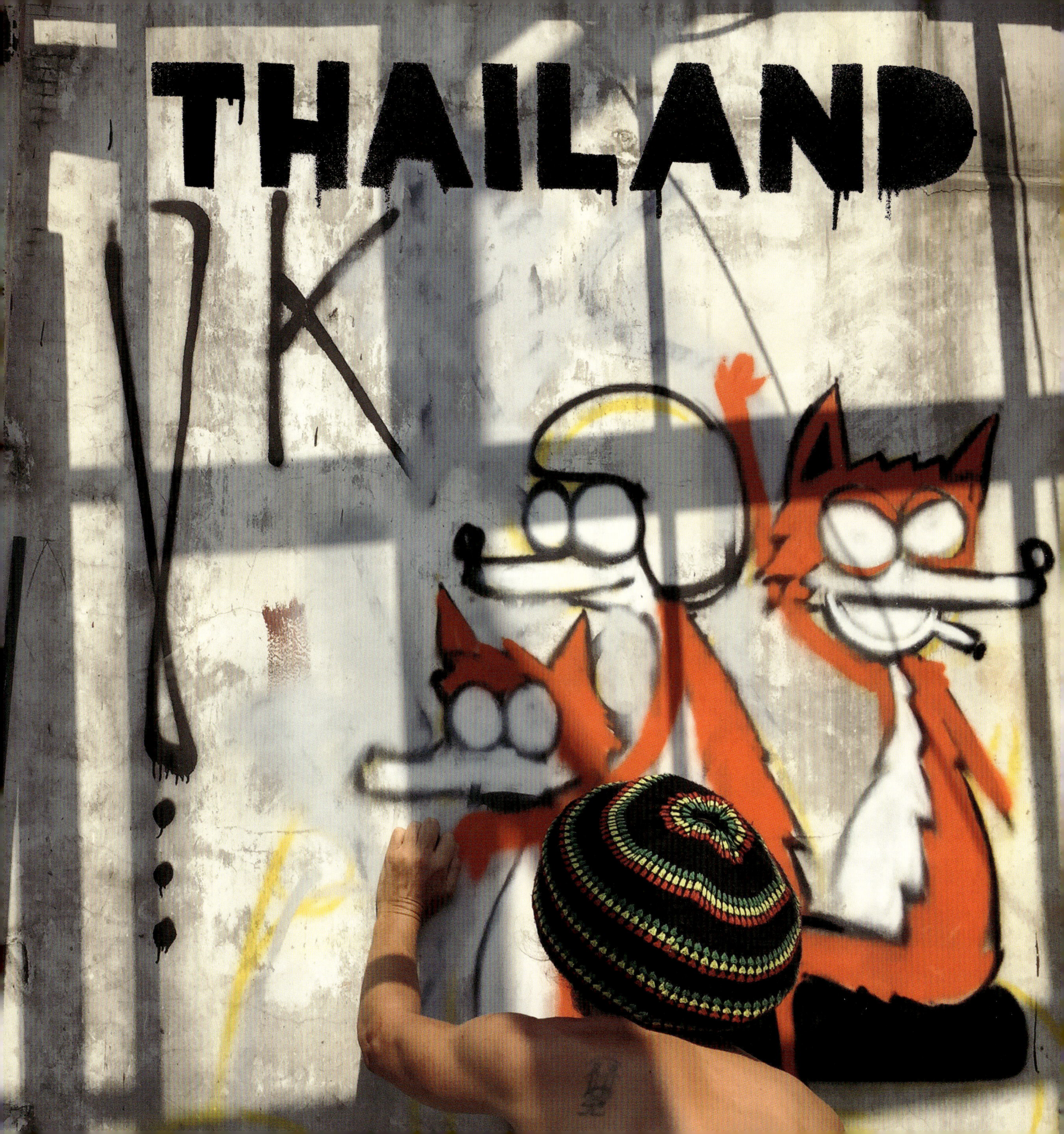

THAILAND

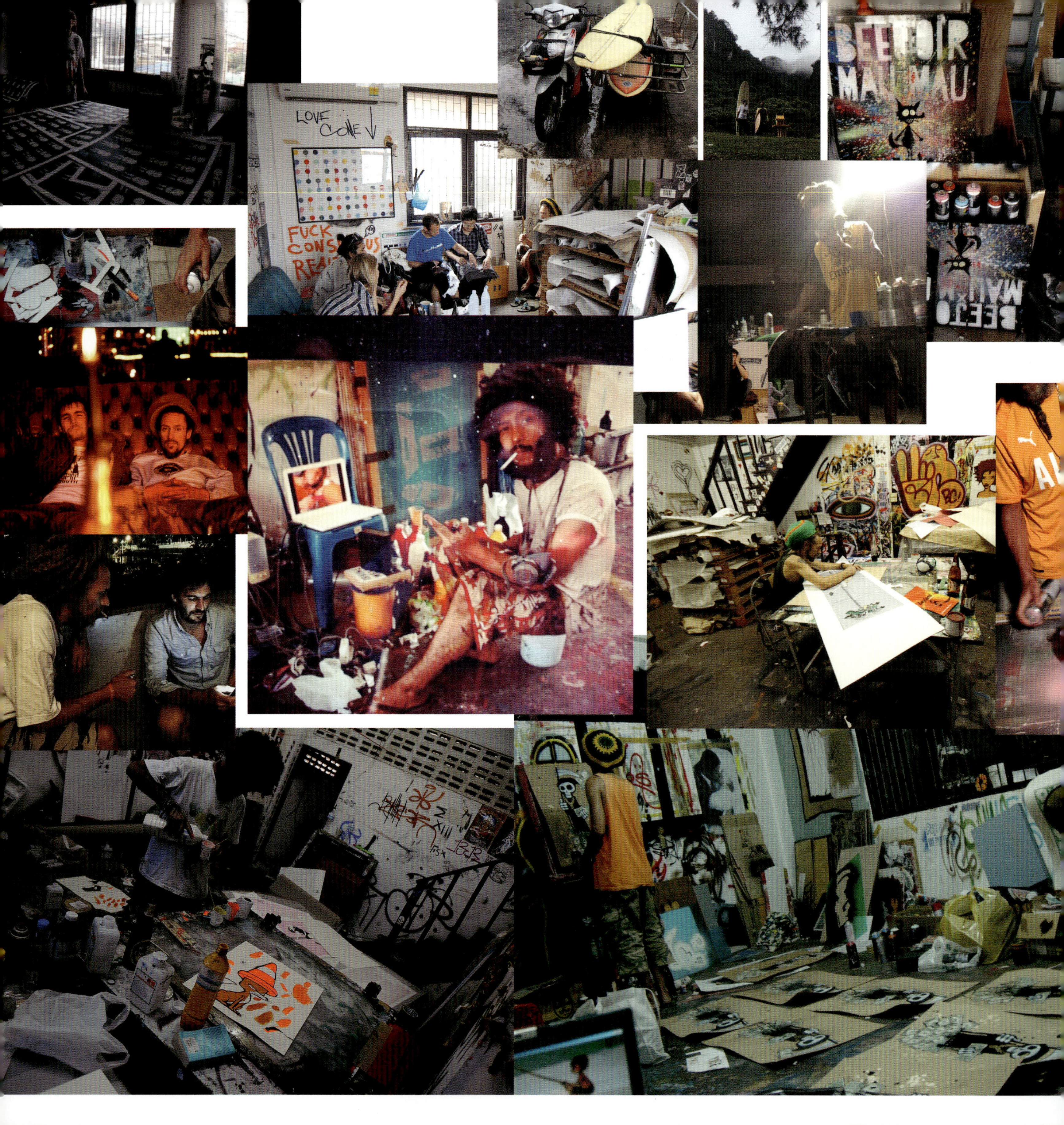
LOVE COME
FUCK

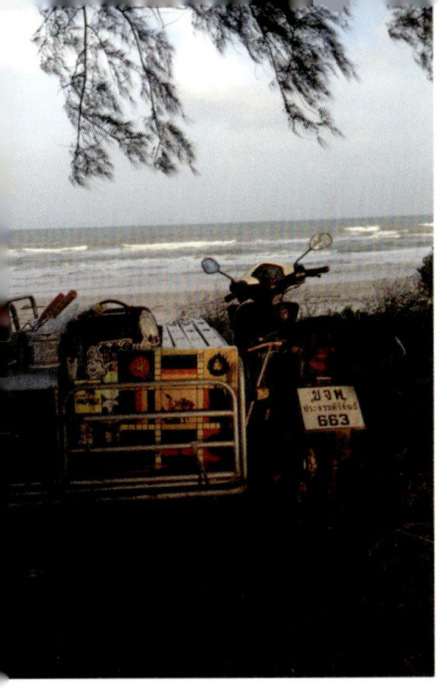

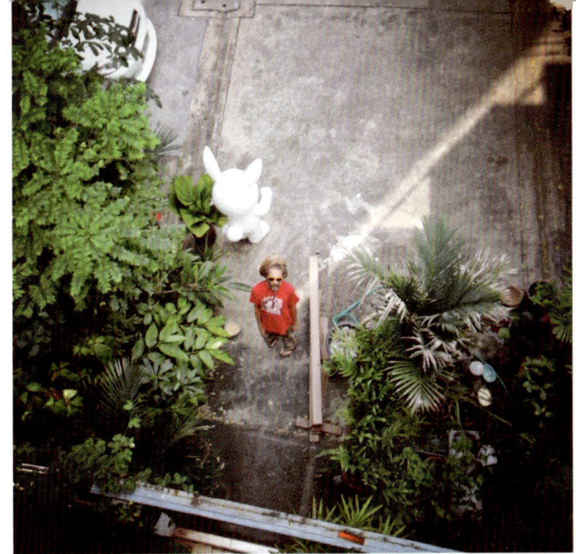

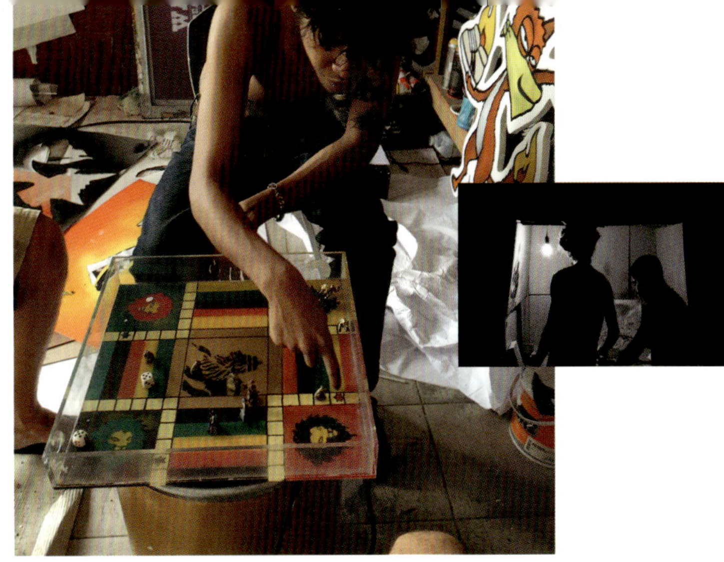

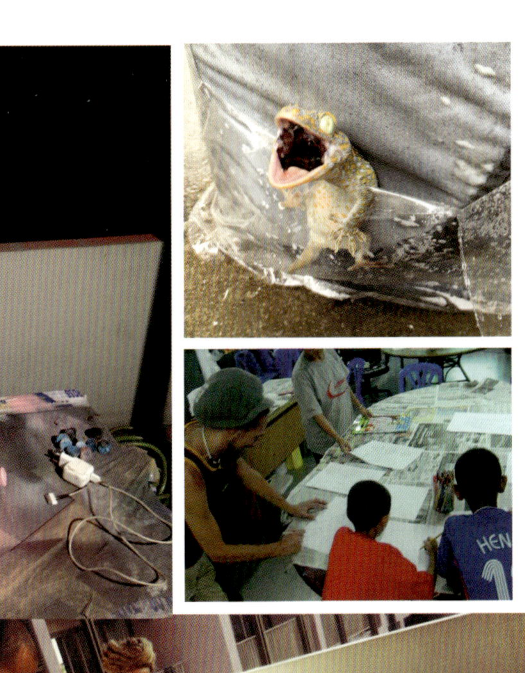

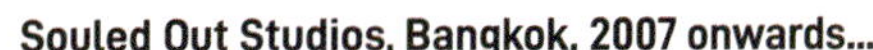

Souled Out Studios, Bangkok, 2007 onwards...

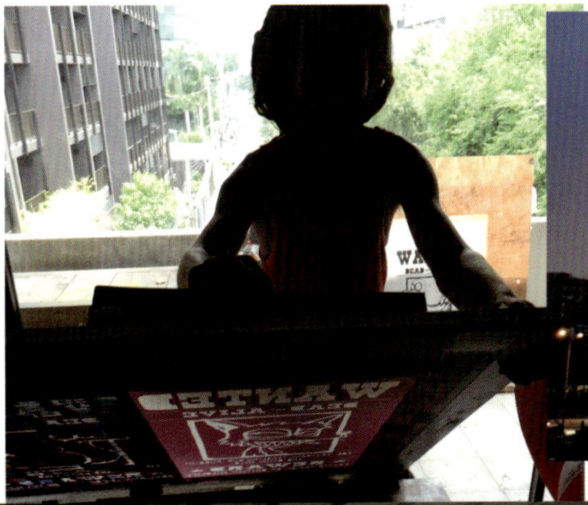

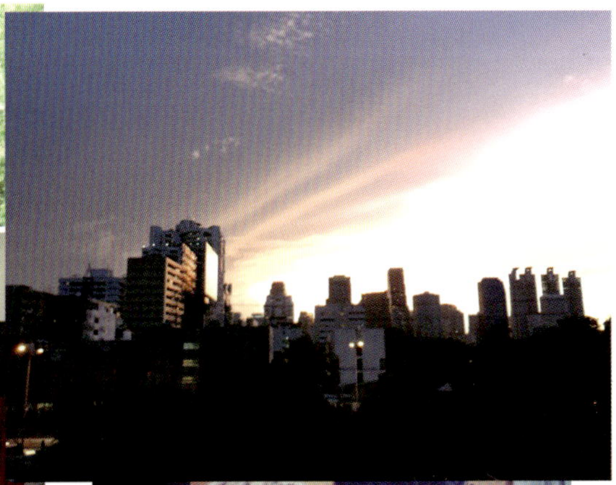

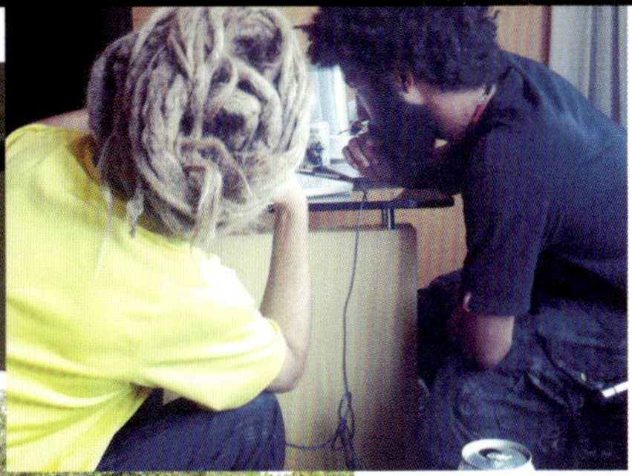

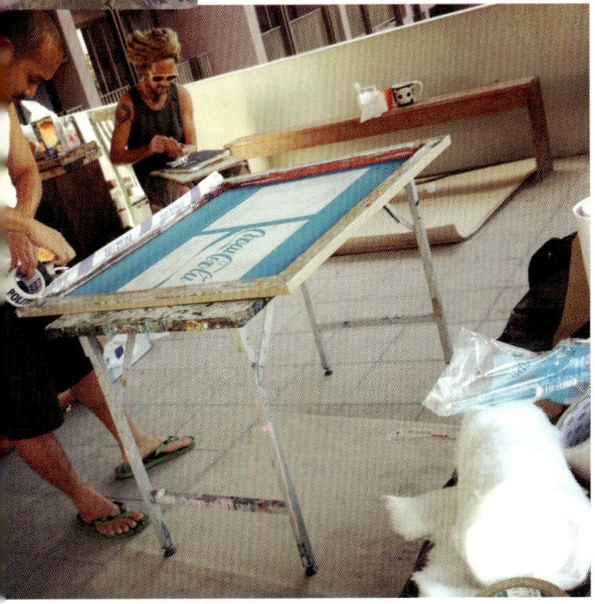

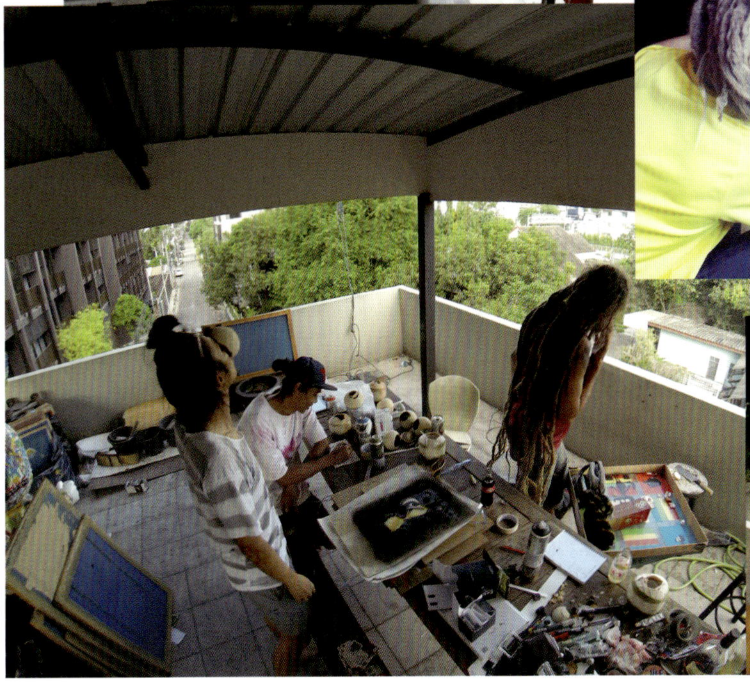

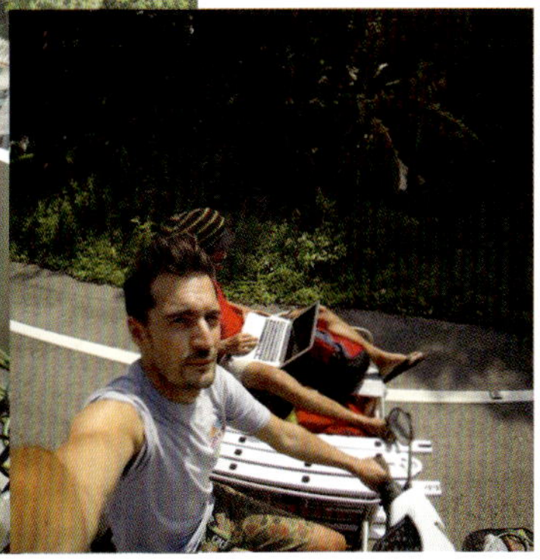

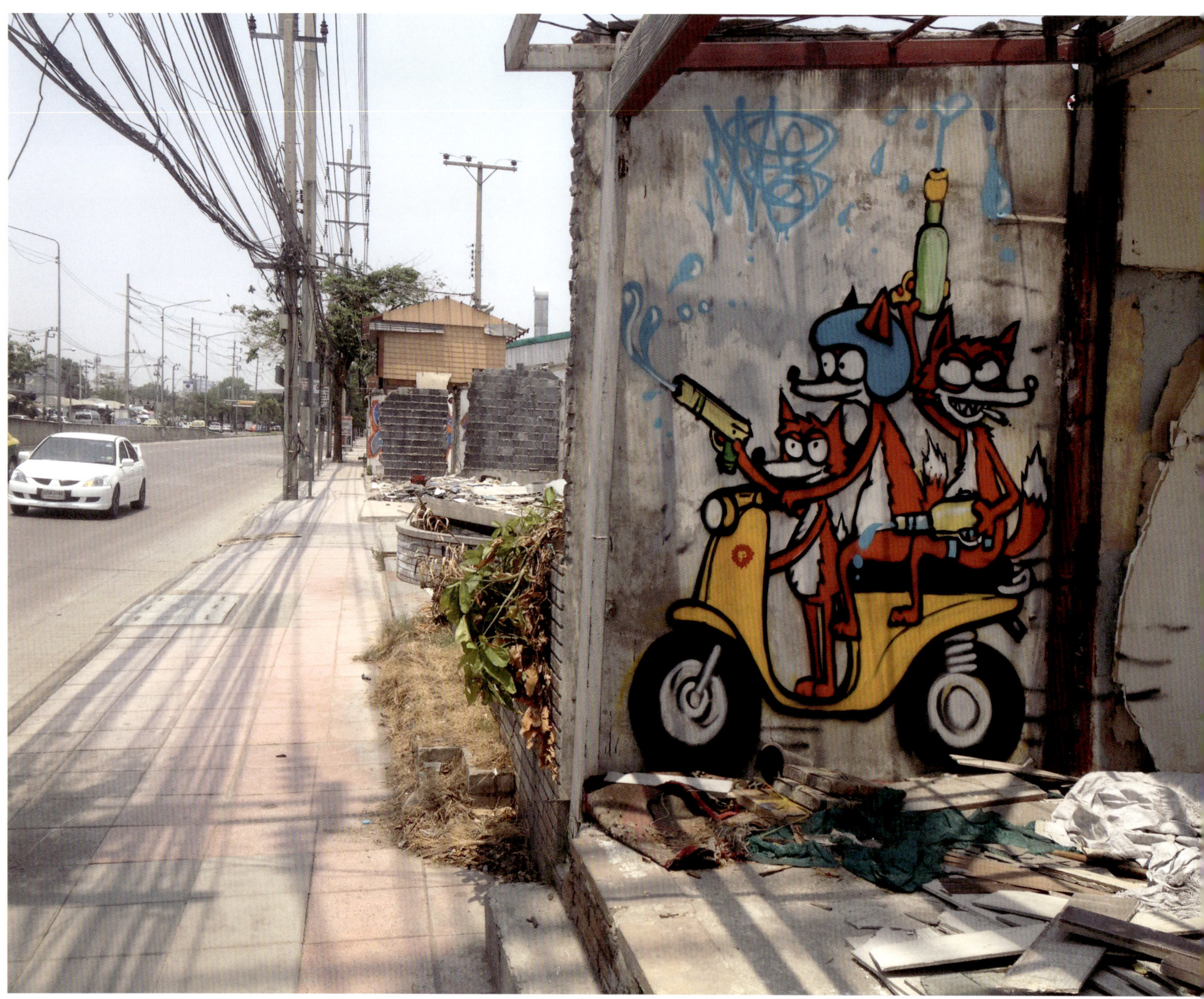

Songkran Fox, Bangkok, 2016.

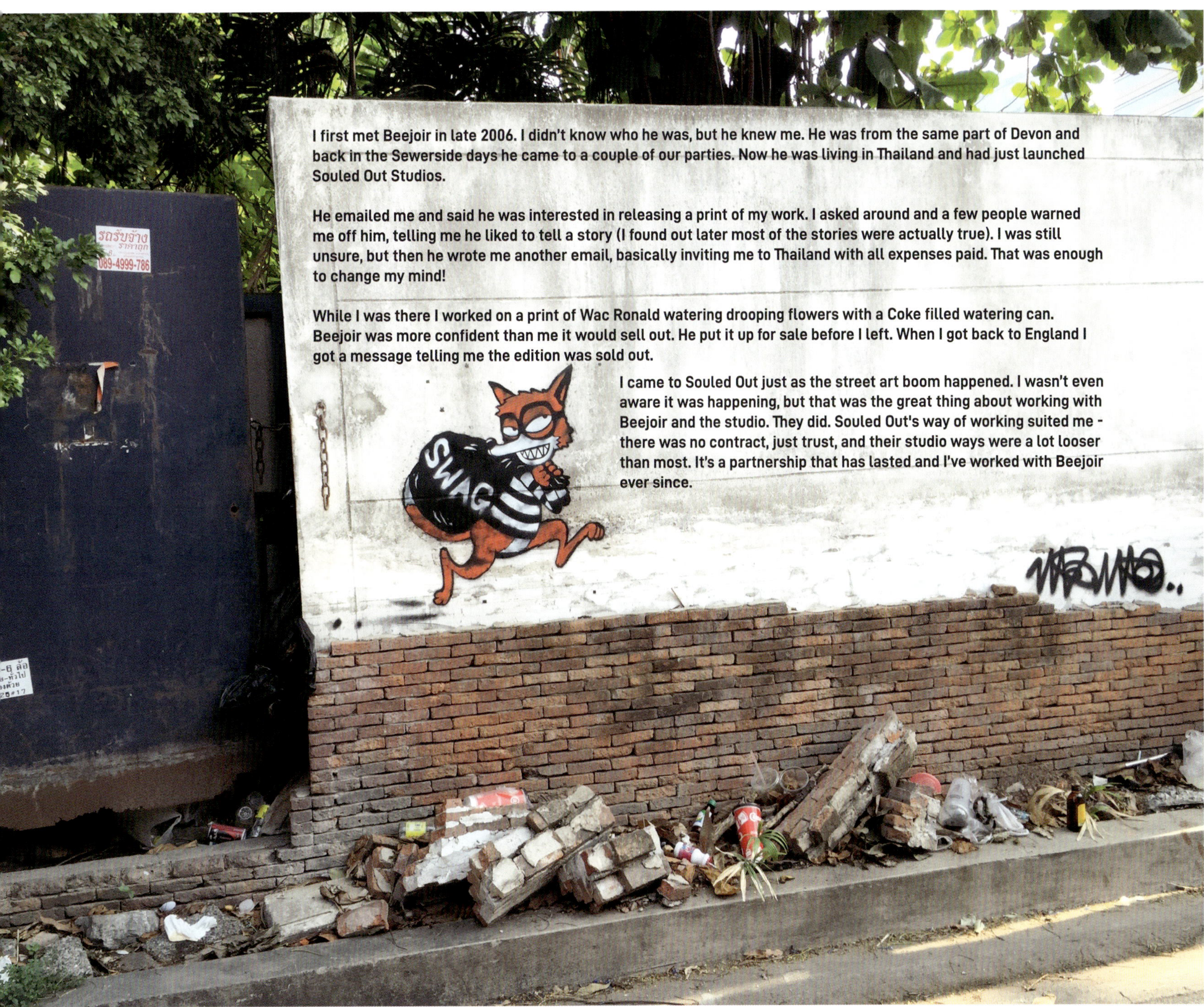

I first met Beejoir in late 2006. I didn't know who he was, but he knew me. He was from the same part of Devon and back in the Sewerside days he came to a couple of our parties. Now he was living in Thailand and had just launched Souled Out Studios.

He emailed me and said he was interested in releasing a print of my work. I asked around and a few people warned me off him, telling me he liked to tell a story (I found out later most of the stories were actually true). I was still unsure, but then he wrote me another email, basically inviting me to Thailand with all expenses paid. That was enough to change my mind!

While I was there I worked on a print of Wac Ronald watering drooping flowers with a Coke filled watering can. Beejoir was more confident than me it would sell out. He put it up for sale before I left. When I got back to England I got a message telling me the edition was sold out.

I came to Souled Out just as the street art boom happened. I wasn't even aware it was happening, but that was the great thing about working with Beejoir and the studio. They did. Souled Out's way of working suited me - there was no contract, just trust, and their studio ways were a lot looser than most. It's a partnership that has lasted and I've worked with Beejoir ever since.

Swag Fox, Bangkok, 2016.

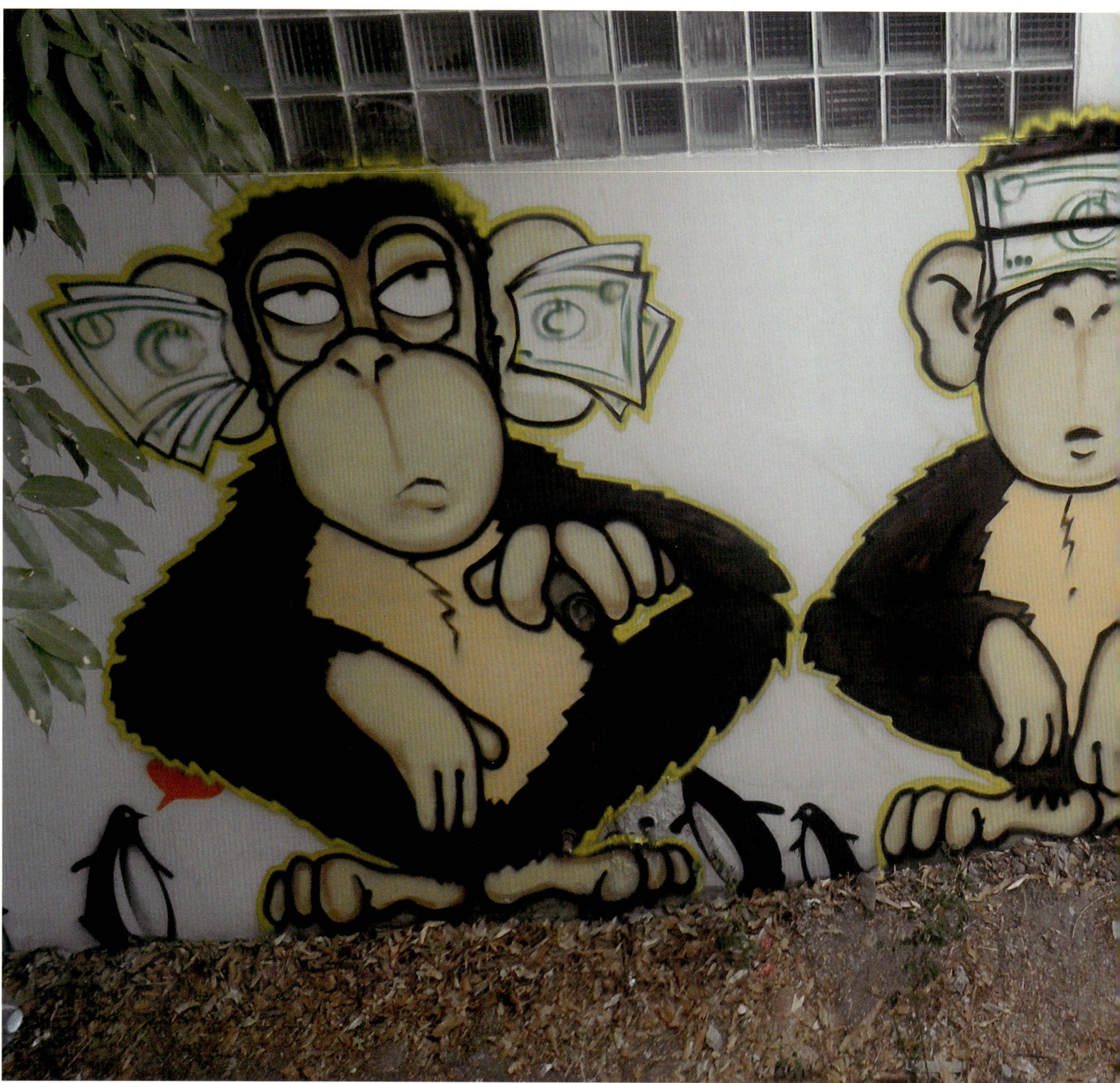

3 Monkeys, Wireless Road, Bangkok, 2011.

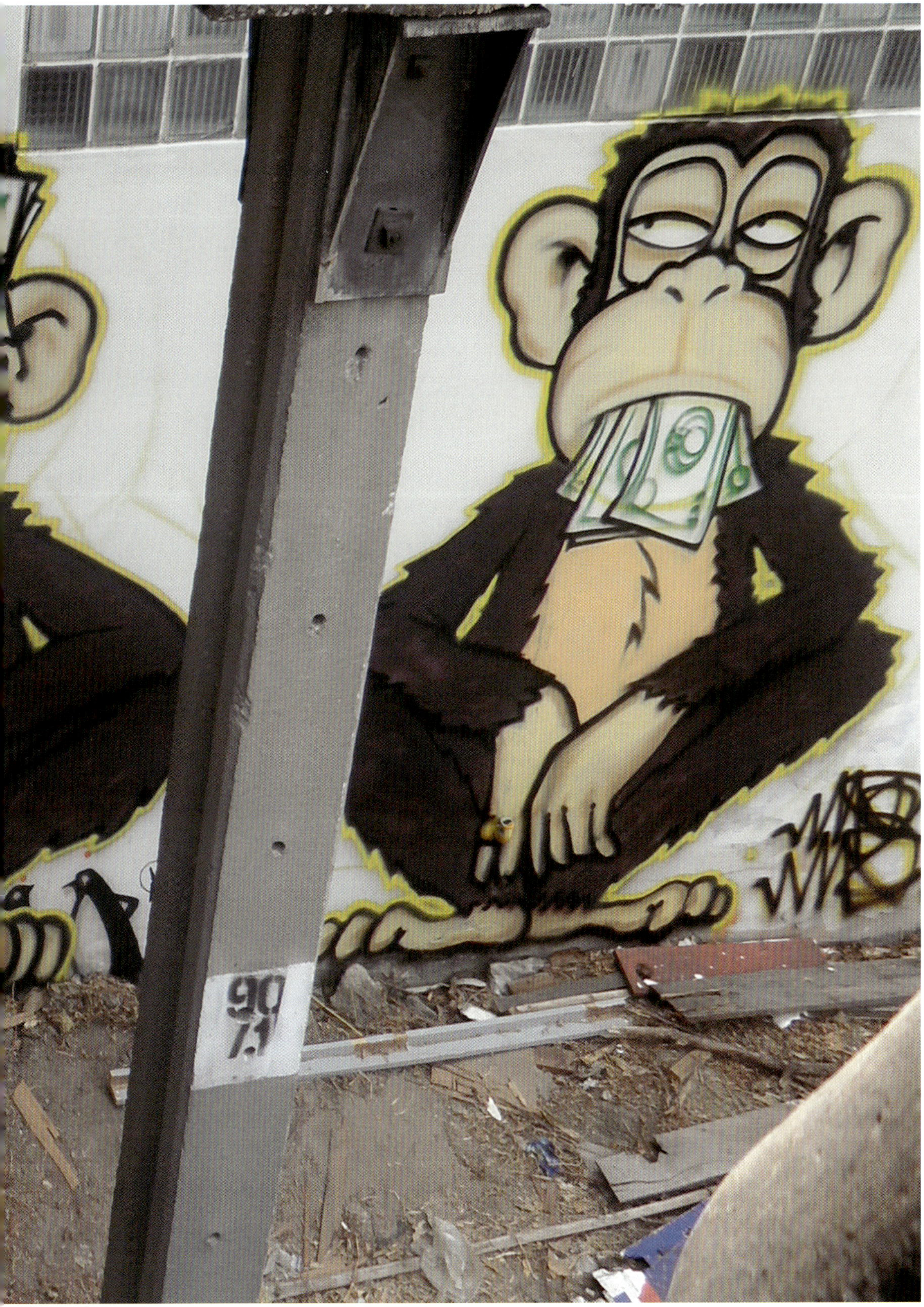

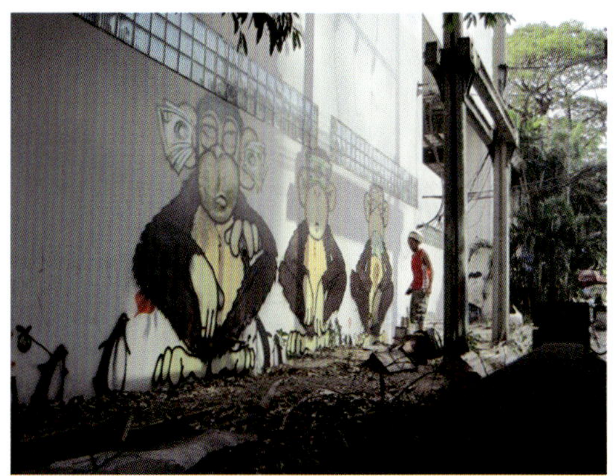

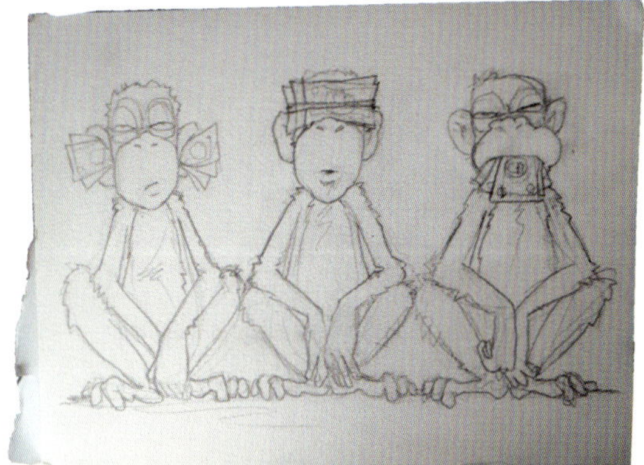

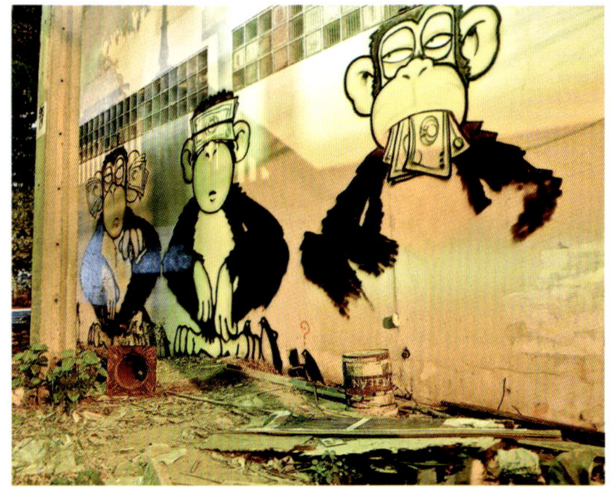

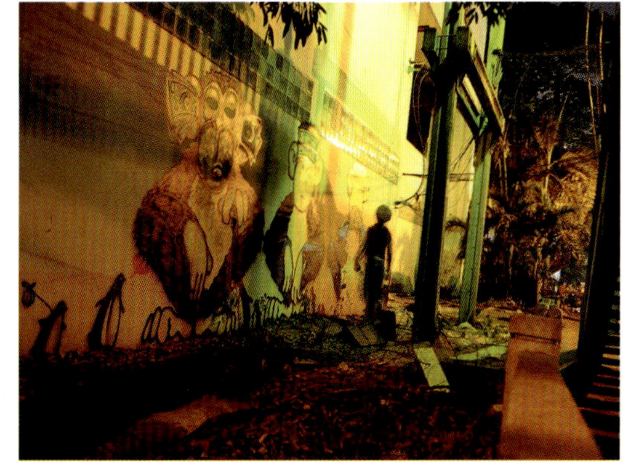

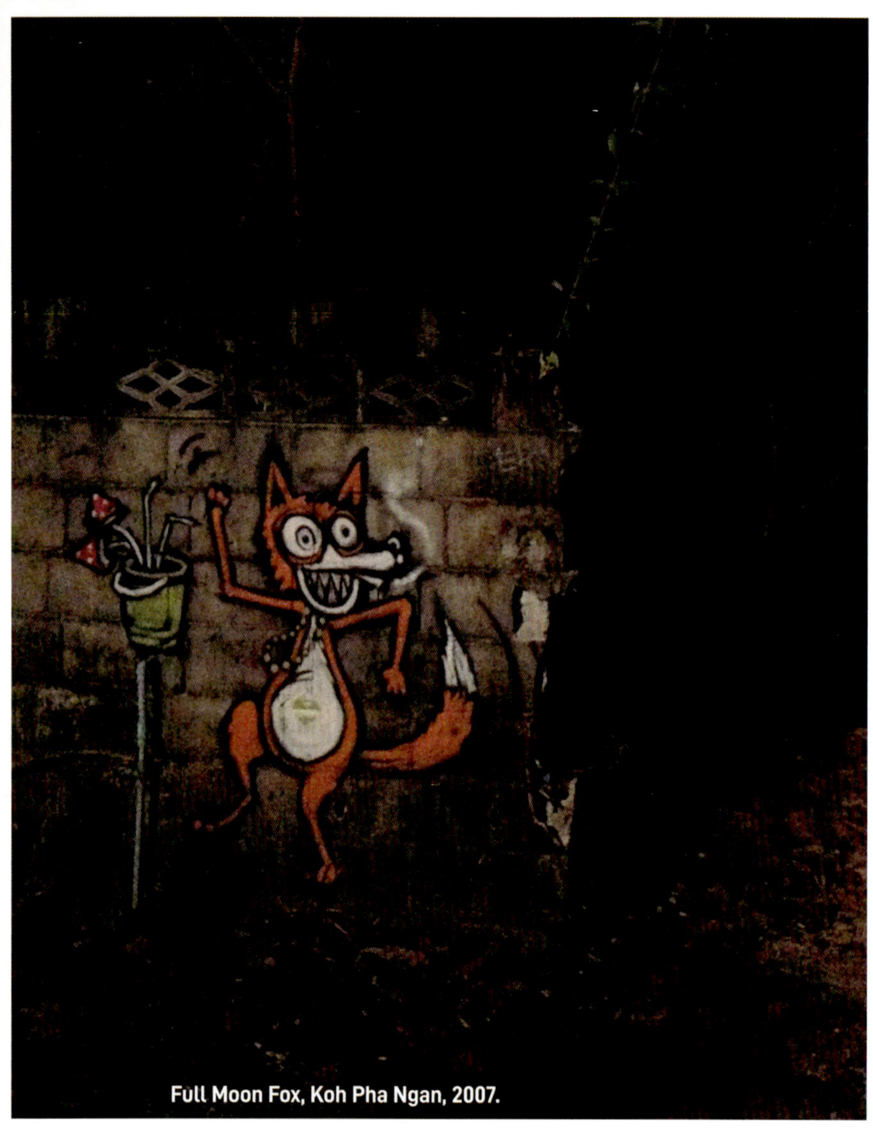

Full Moon Fox, Koh Pha Ngan, 2007.

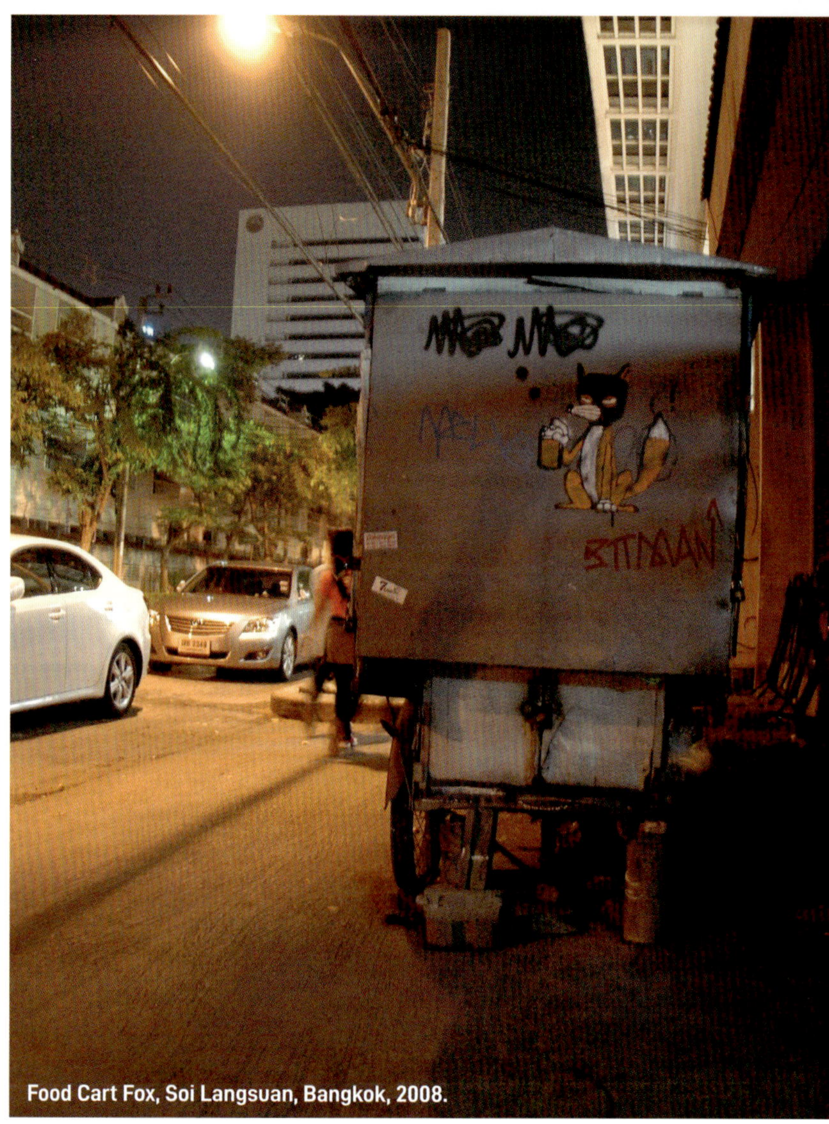

Food Cart Fox, Soi Langsuan, Bangkok, 2008.

Tantric Fox, Koh Pha Ngan, 2009.

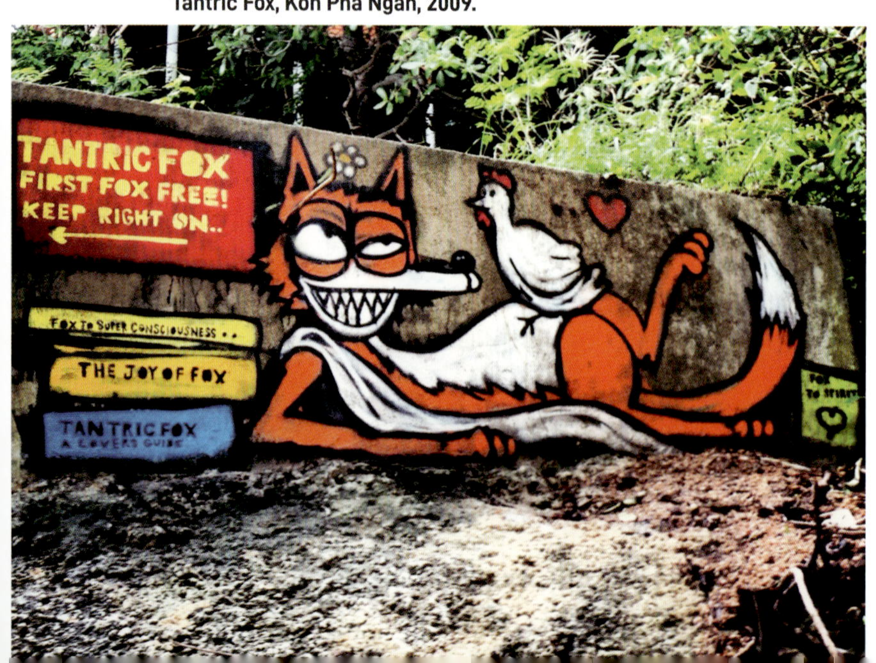

Selector Fox, Bangkok, 2014.

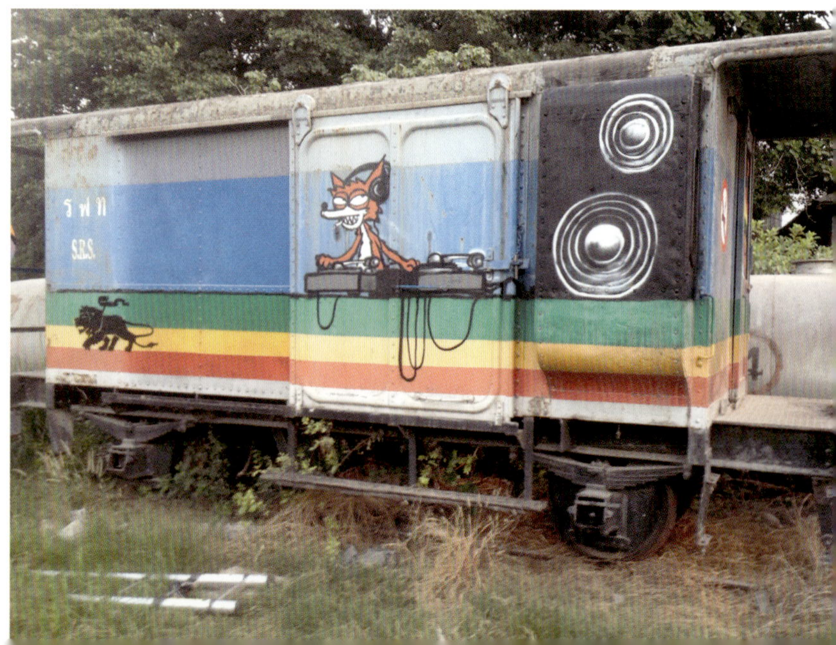

Peace Keeping, Bangkok, 2011.

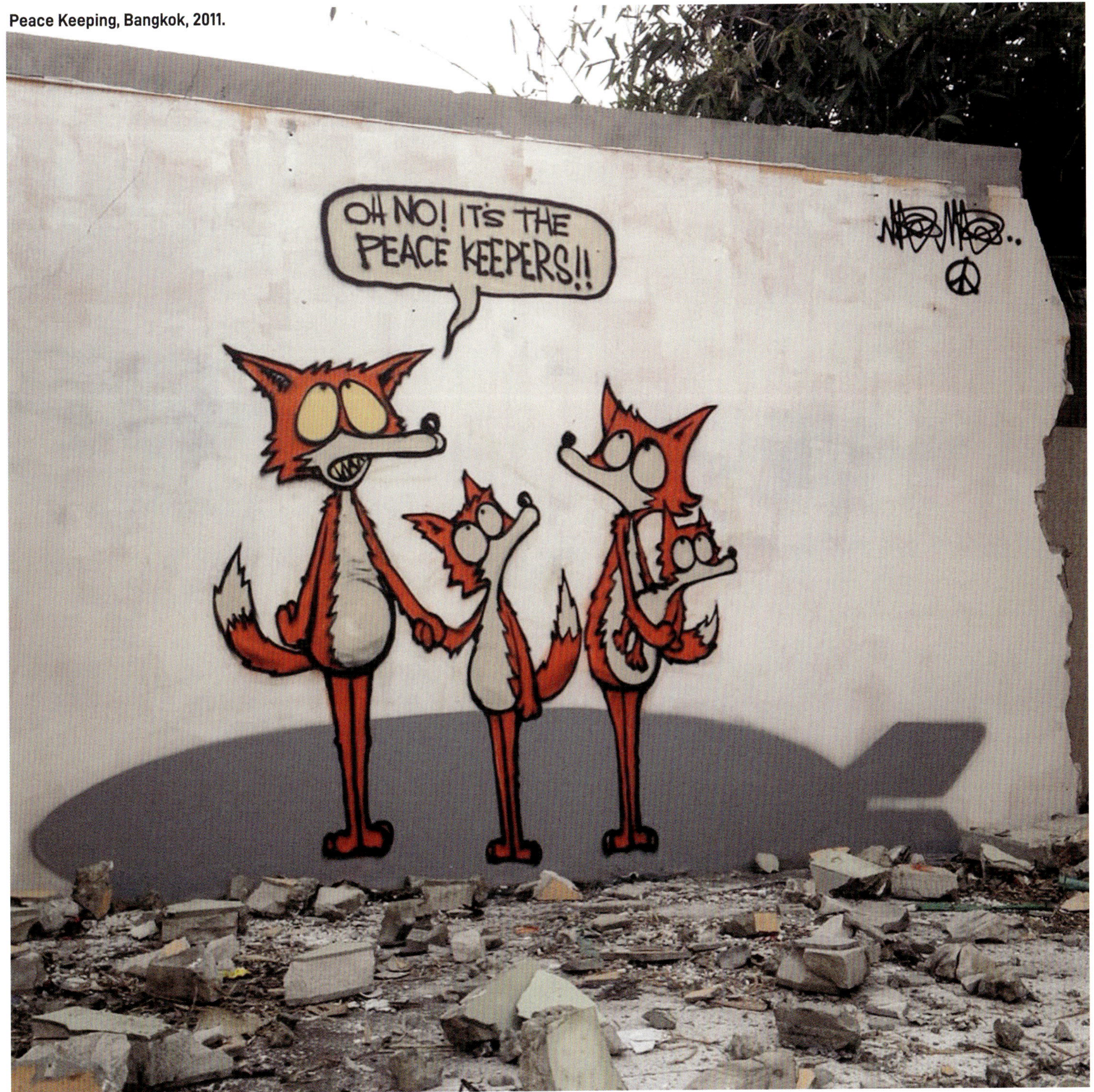

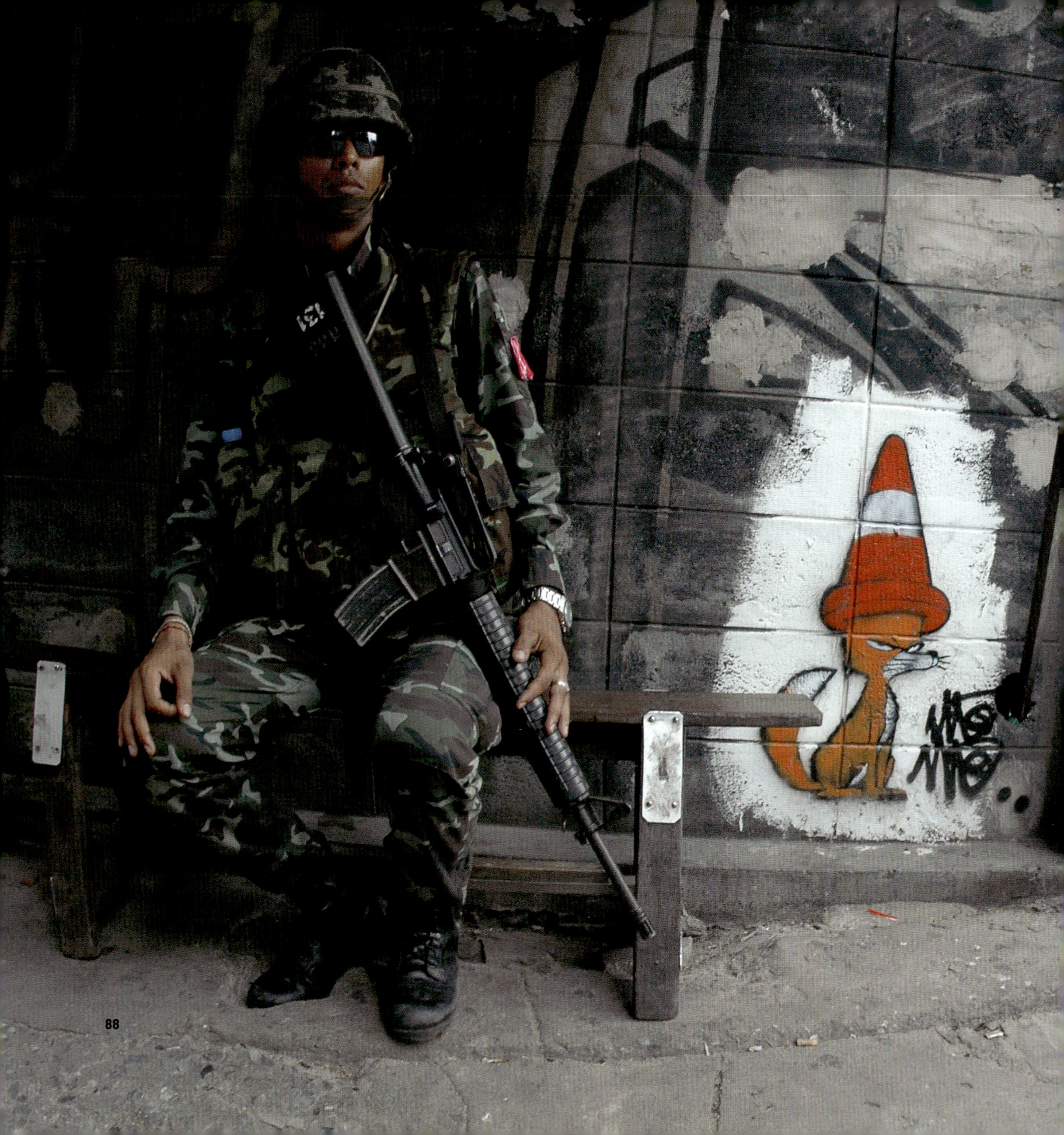

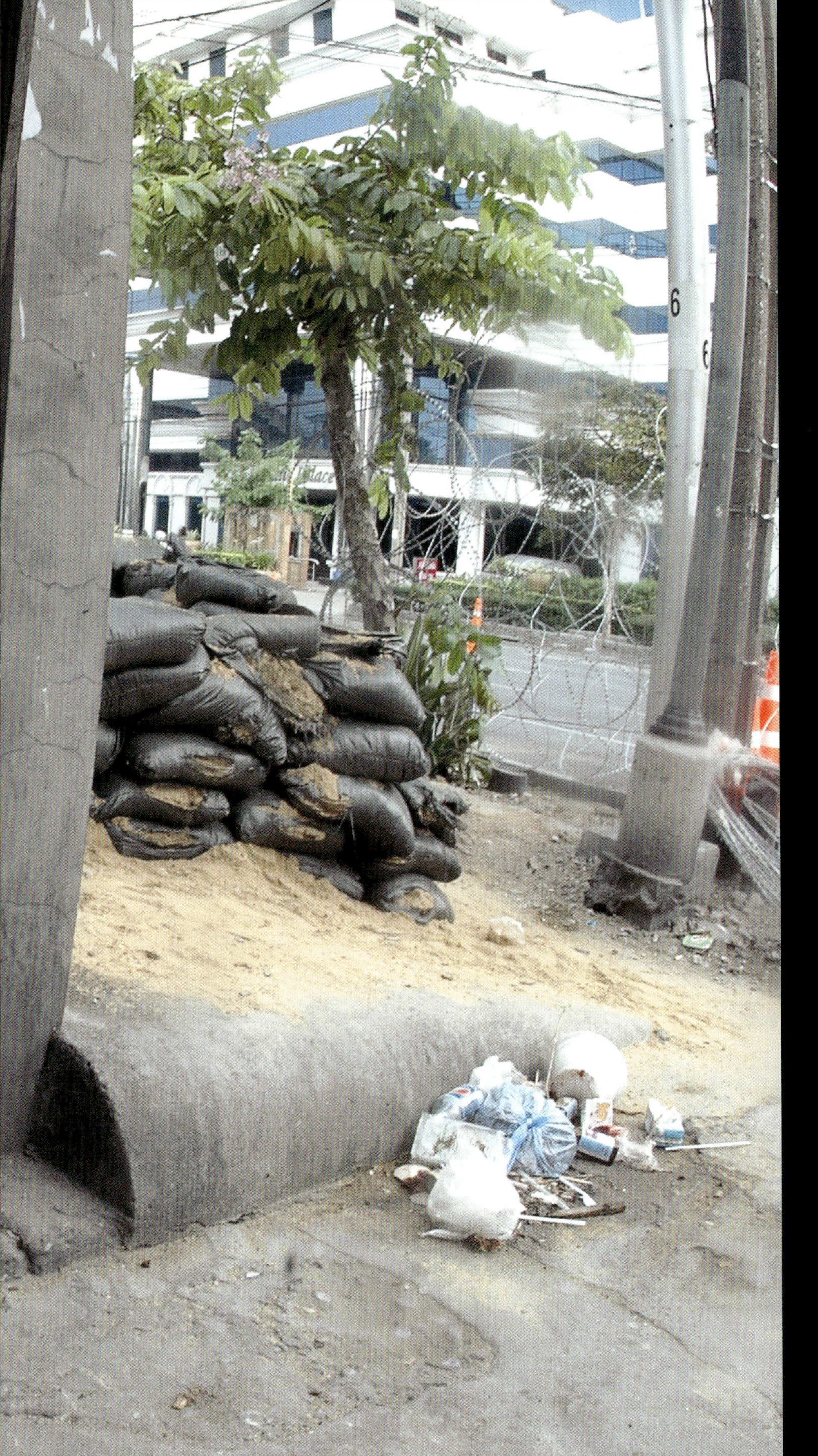

Traffic Fox, Bangkok road block, 2010.

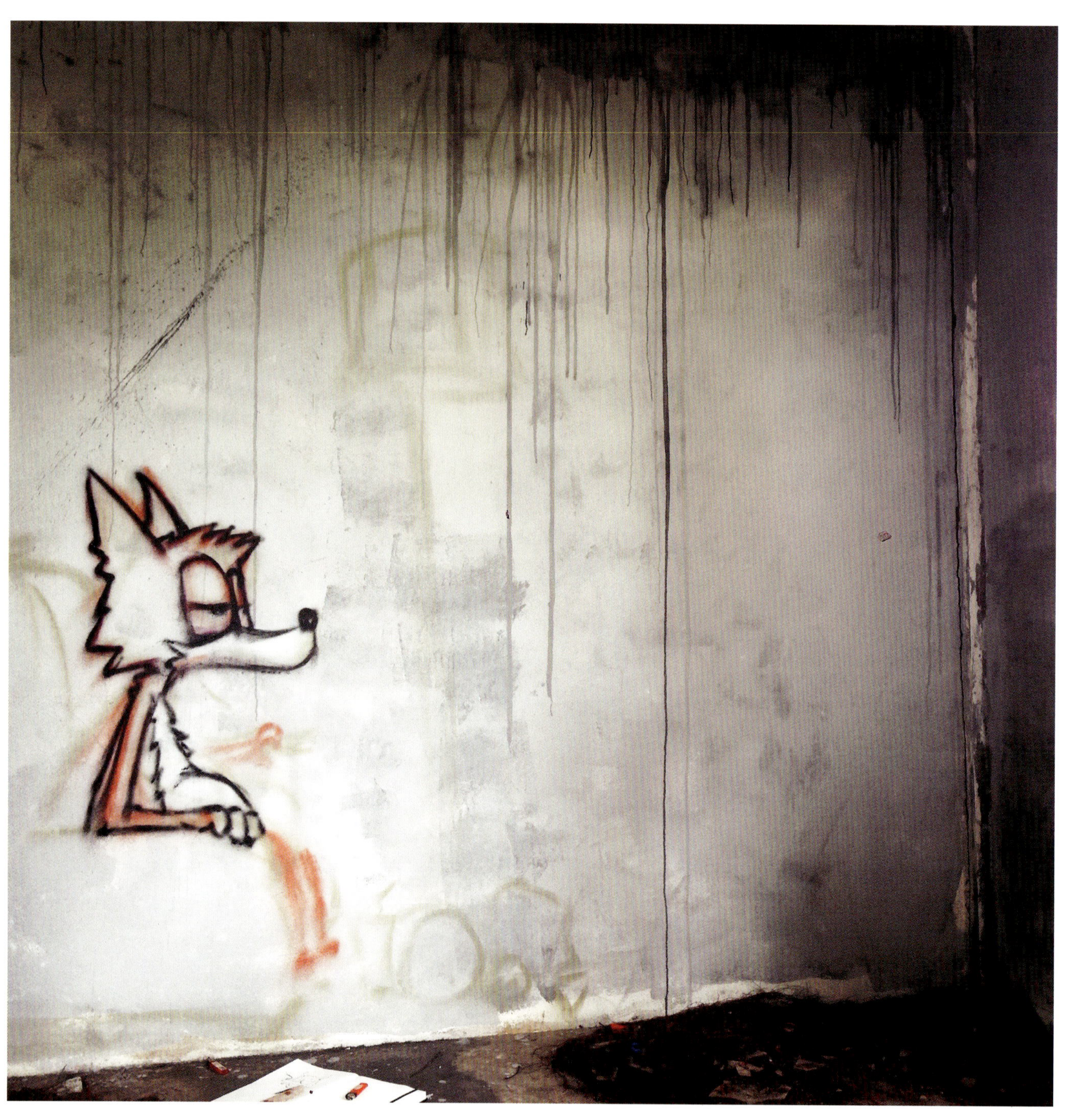

Goggle Fox, abandoned building, Bang Boet Beach, 2016.

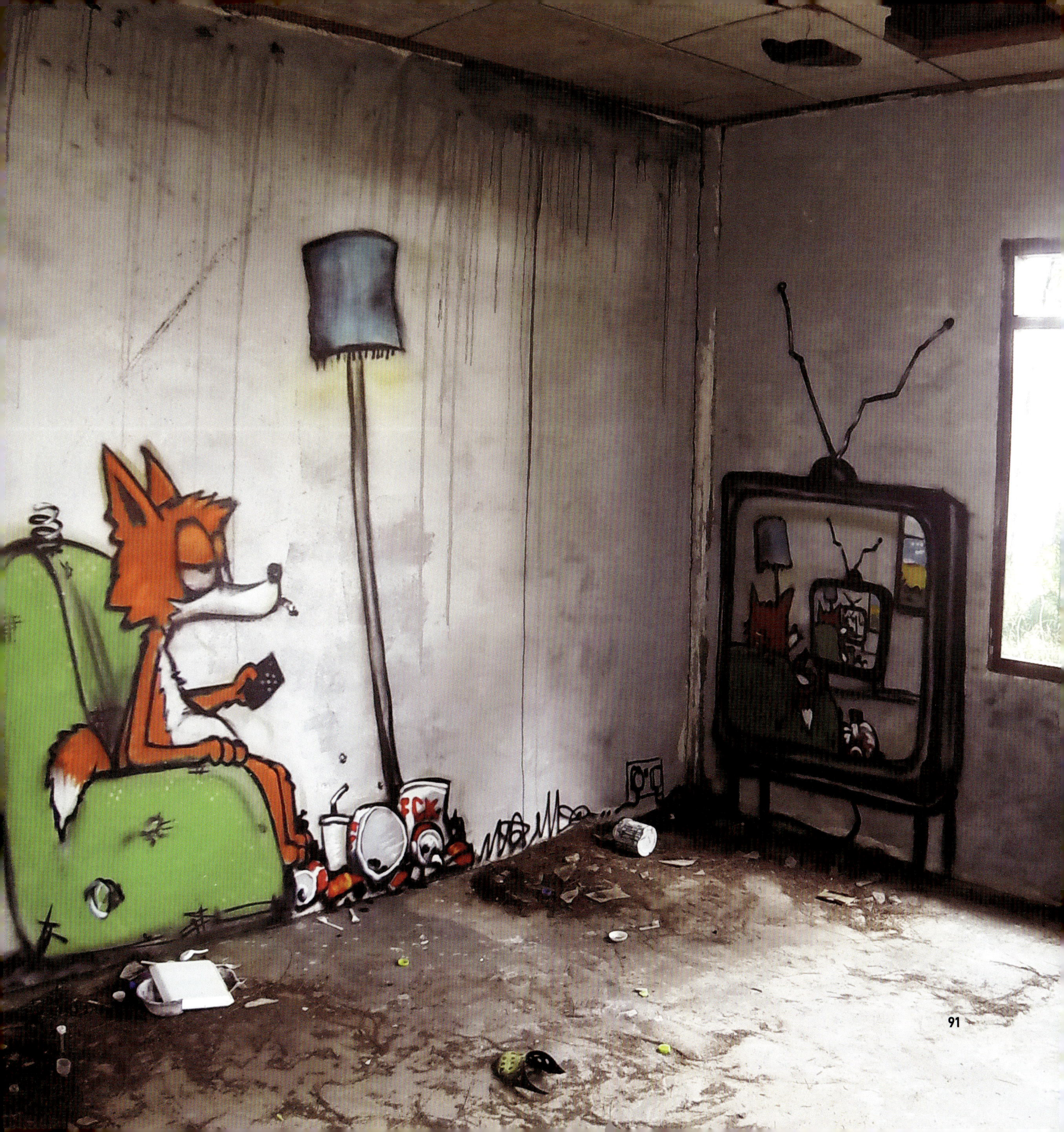
FCK

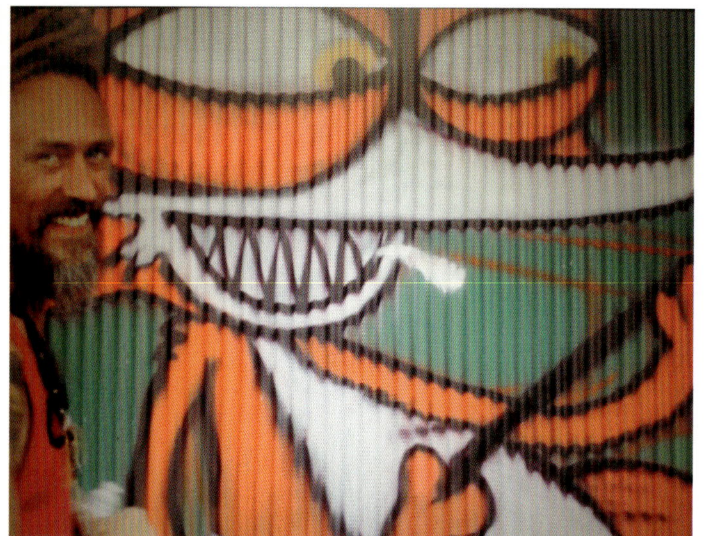

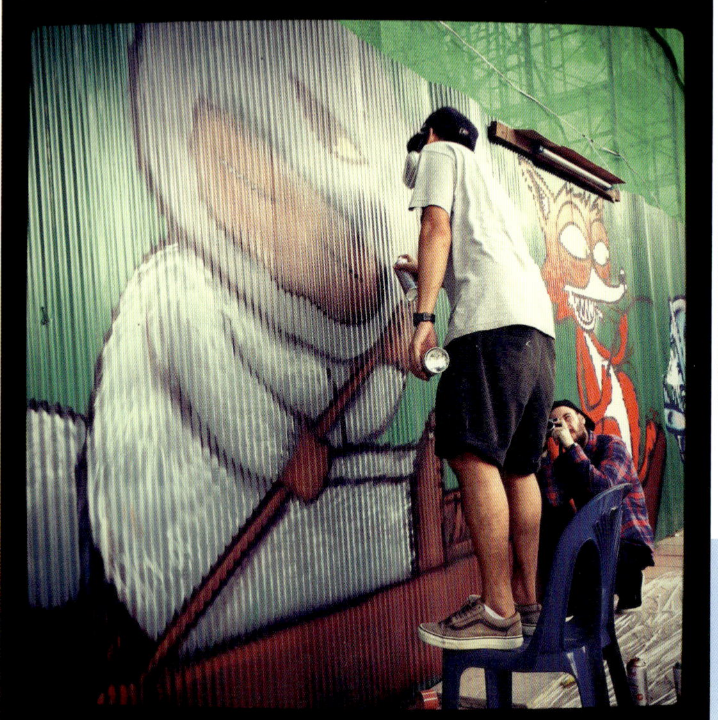

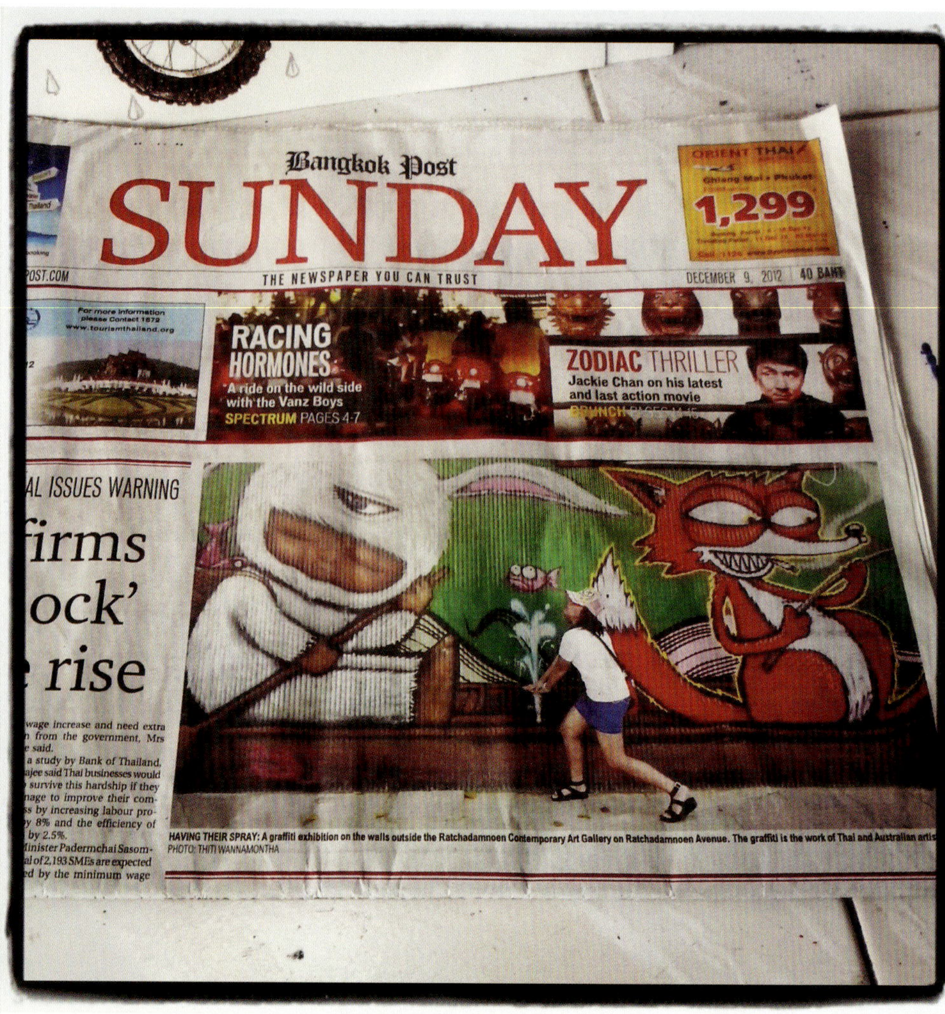

Soi Ratchadamnoen, Bangkok (Alex Face, Mau), 2012.

SOS Crew, Bangkok track side (Alex Face, Bon, Gong, Beejoir, Mau), 2016.

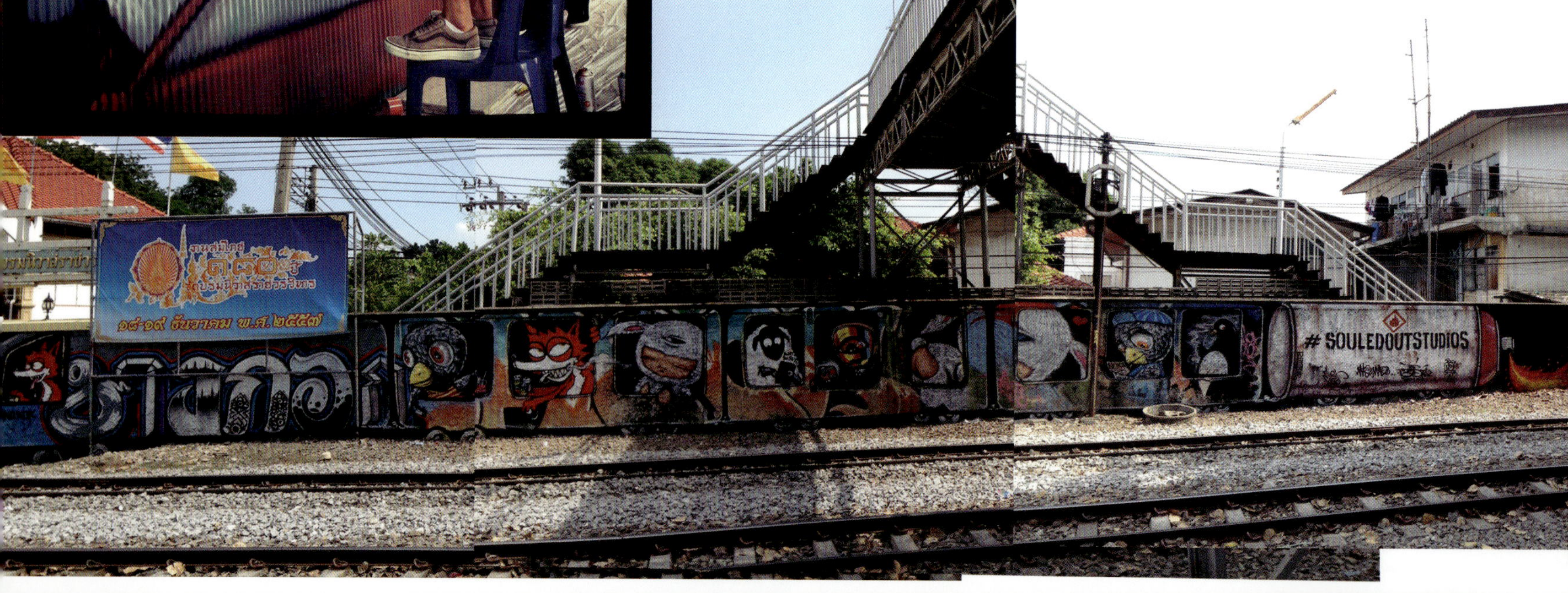

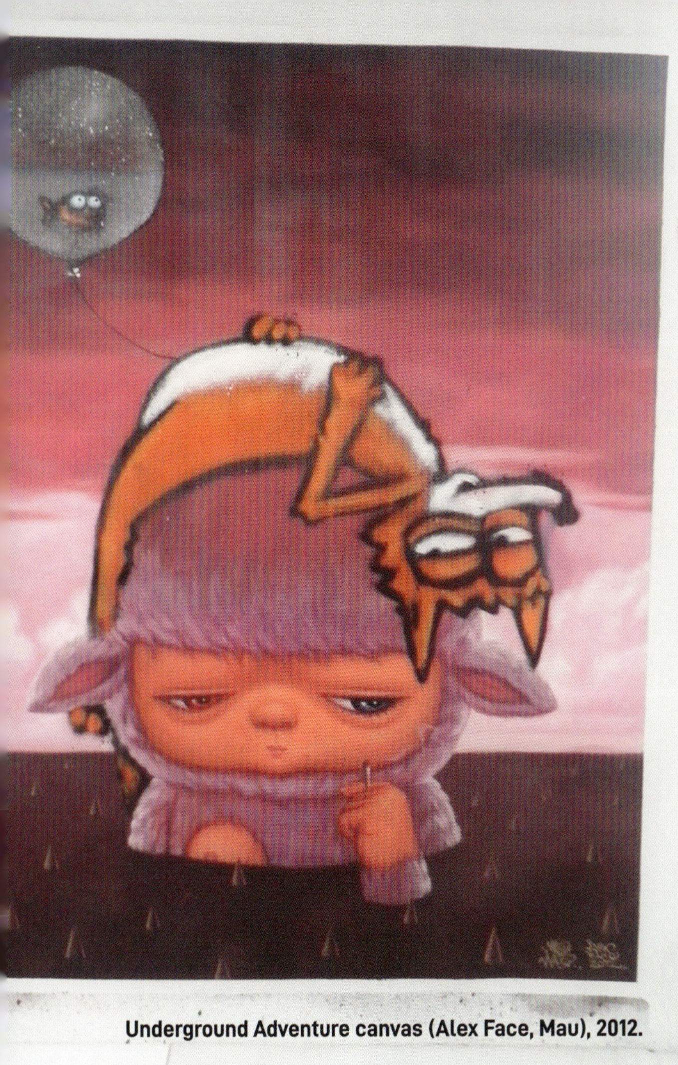

Underground Adventure canvas (Alex Face, Mau), 2012.

Souled Out Studios is based in Bangkok. The graffiti scene is big there now, but at the time there weren't many people painting on the street. I would often get local people thanking me for brightening up a wall, and they'd bring me food and drinks.

The 3 Monkeys piece went down really well with street vendors. They thought it referred to the police, known locally as monkeys due to their brown uniforms.

Through Souled Out and Beejoir I hooked up with local artists like Alex Face, AMP, Bon and Gong. Back then Bangkok wasn't so developed and there were lots of derelict buildings and unfinished car parks to paint. Basically, so long as you didn't paint on the King's walls it was all good.

Chatuchak, Bangkok (Alex Face, Mau), 2011.

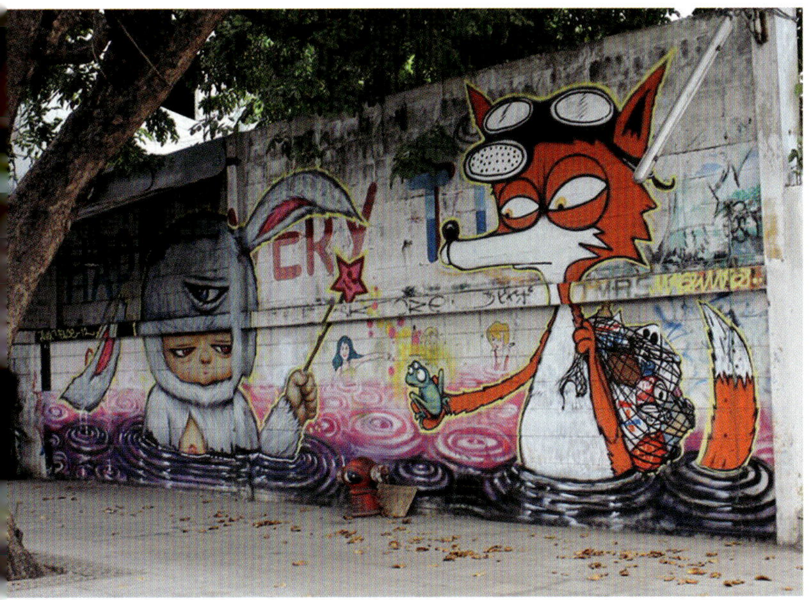

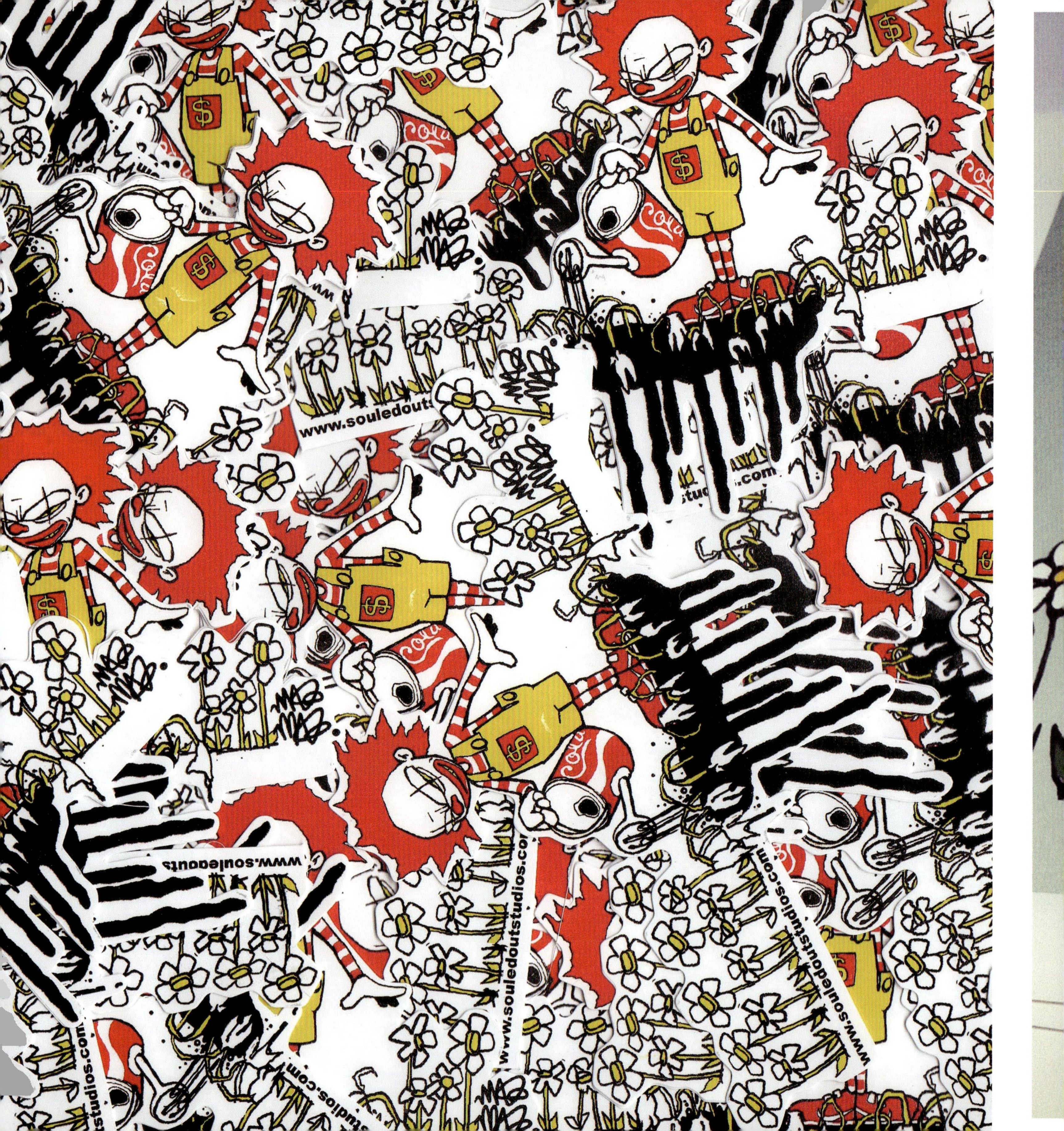
www.souledoutstudios.com
www.souledoutstudios.com
Cola

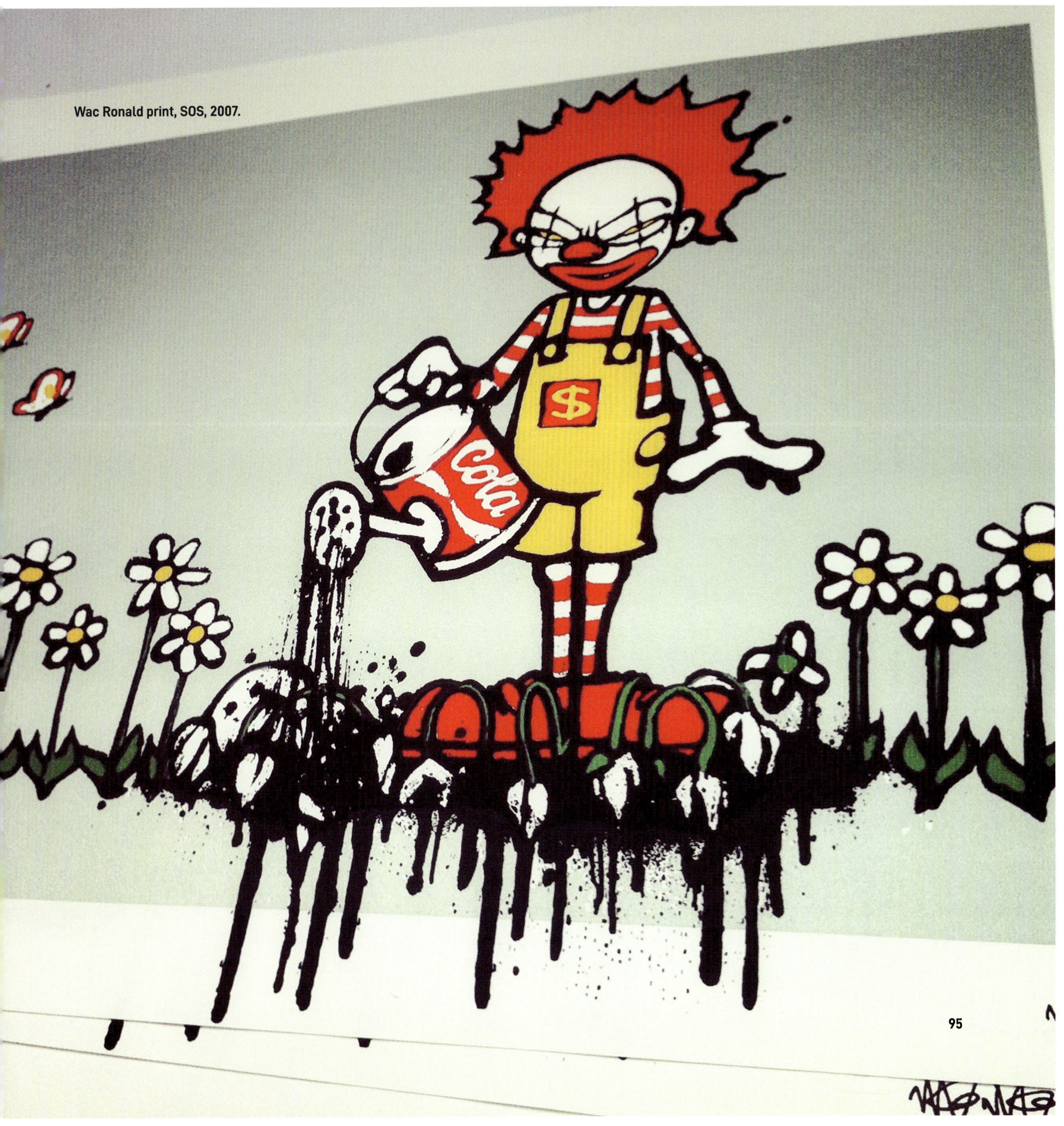

Wac Ronald print, SOS, 2007.

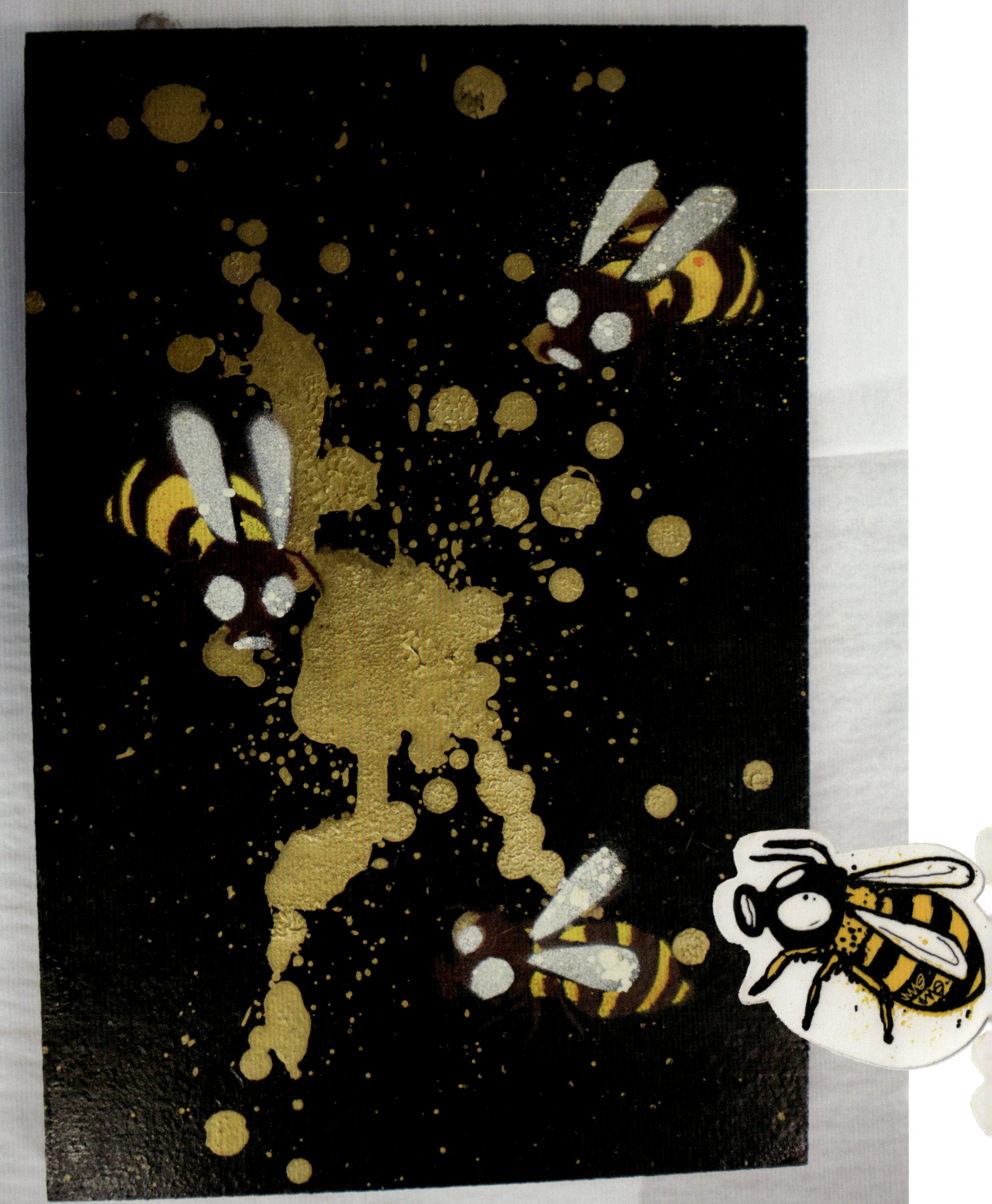

Money Bees, SOS edition, 2008.

Munney, Let Them Hang print, 2007.

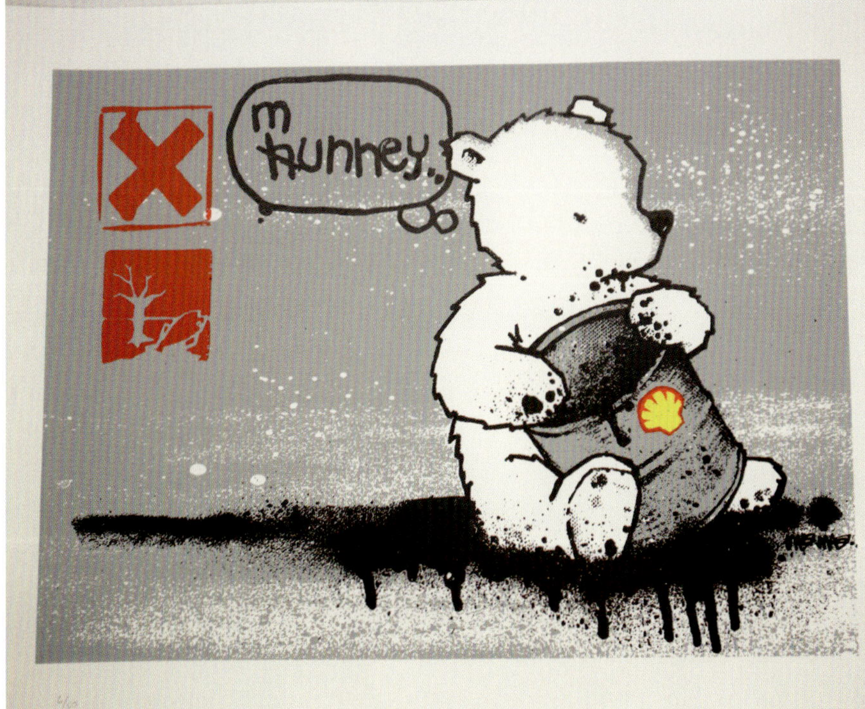

Don't Care Bear, SOS print, 2008.

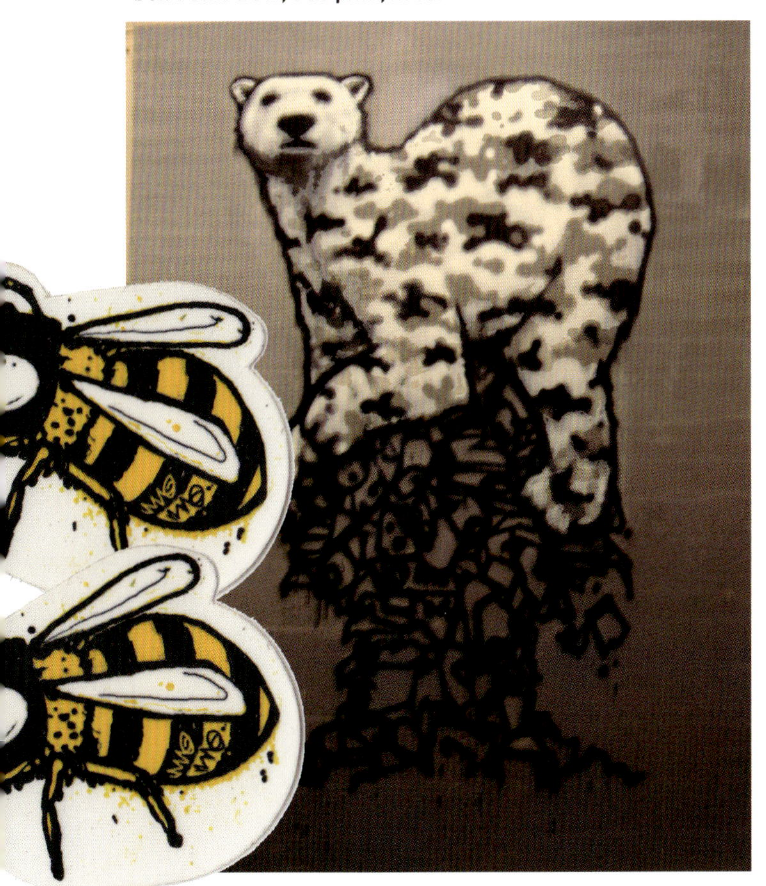

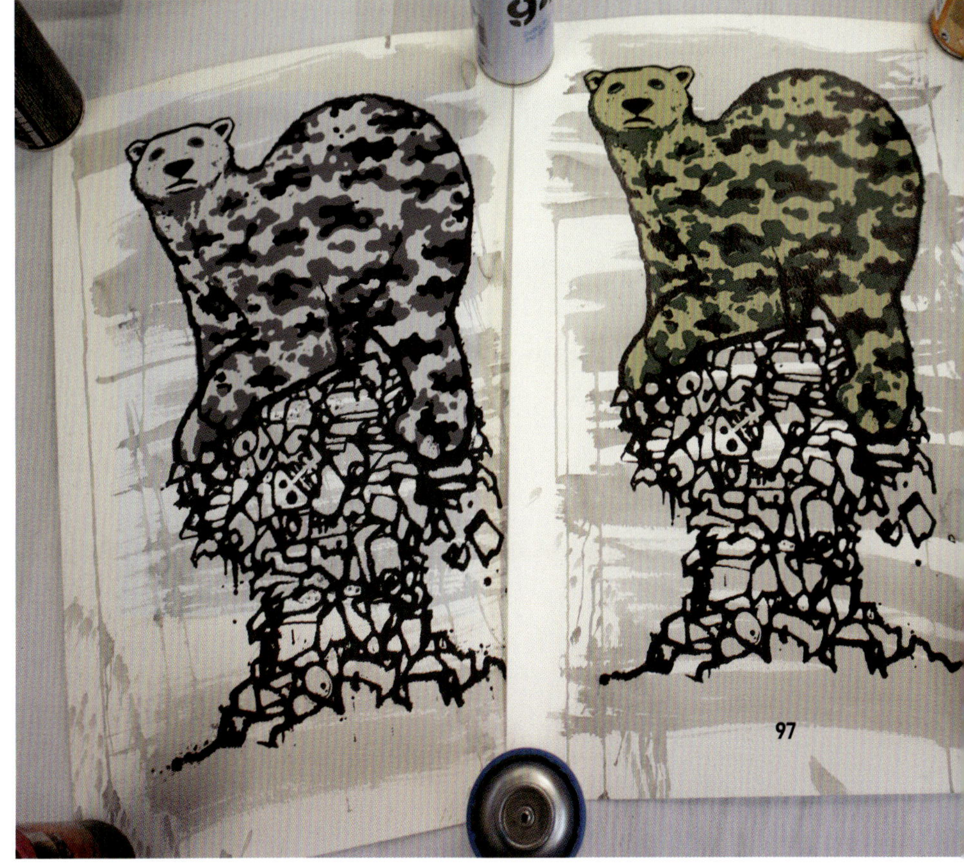

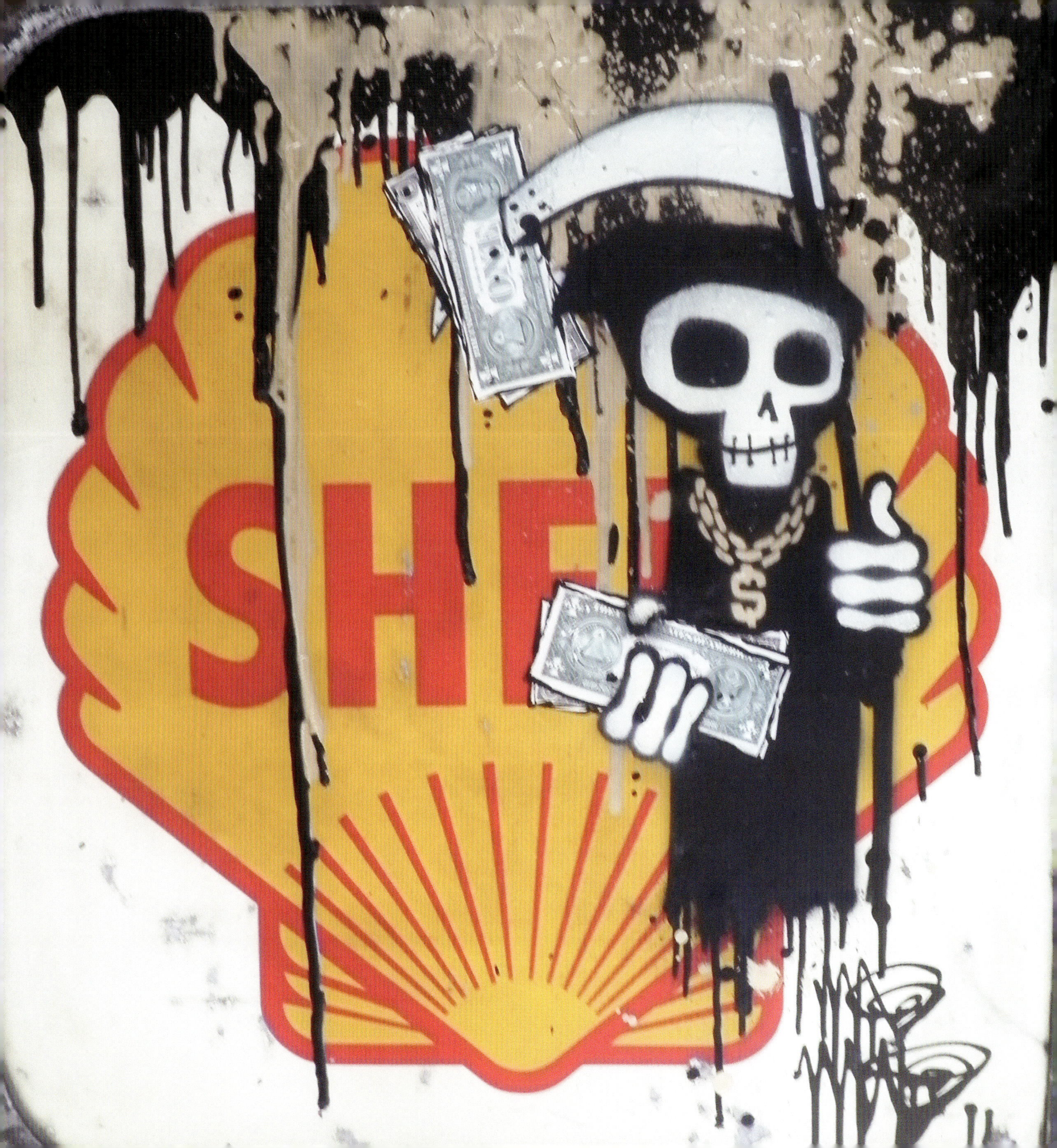

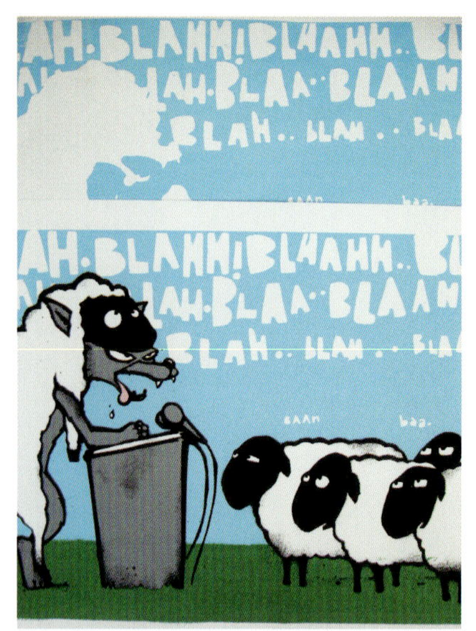

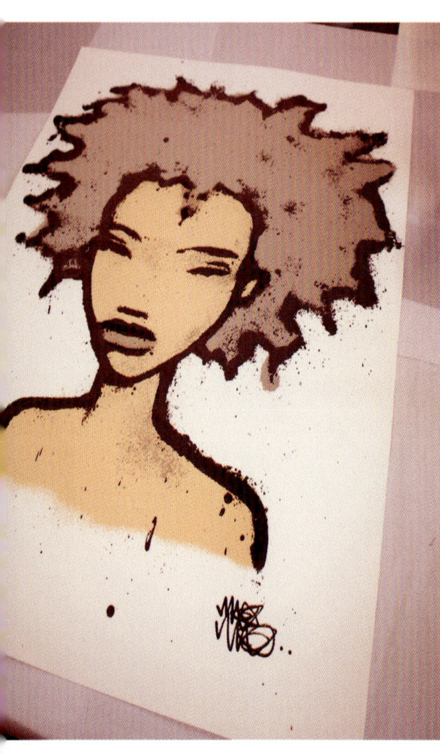

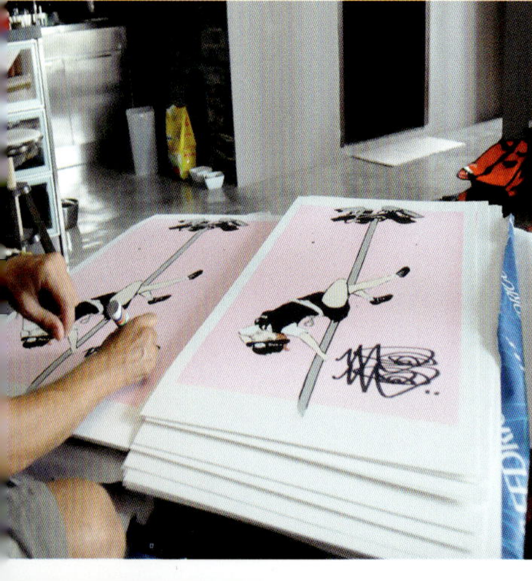

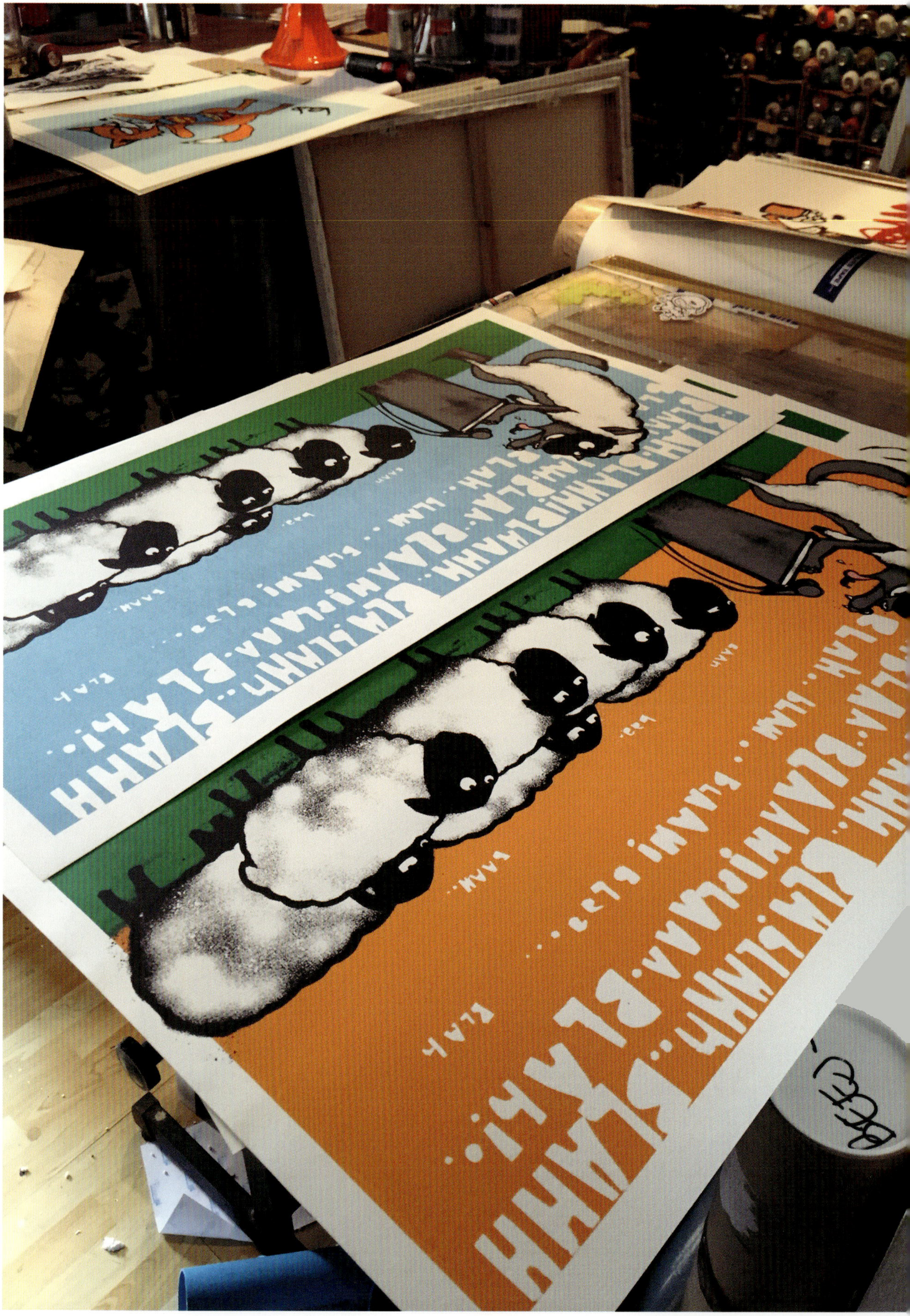

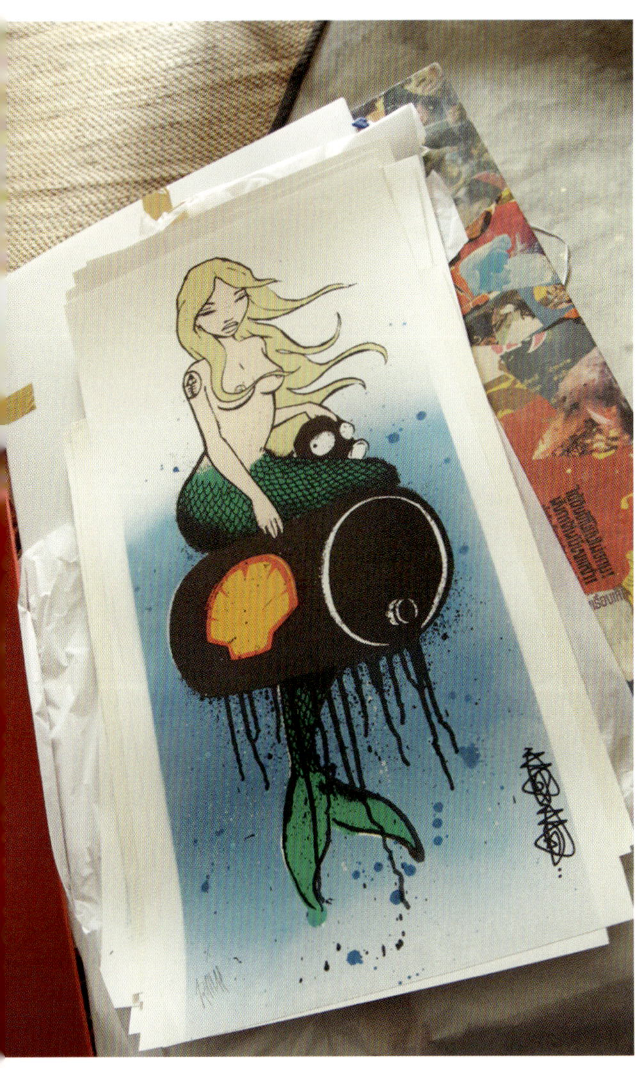

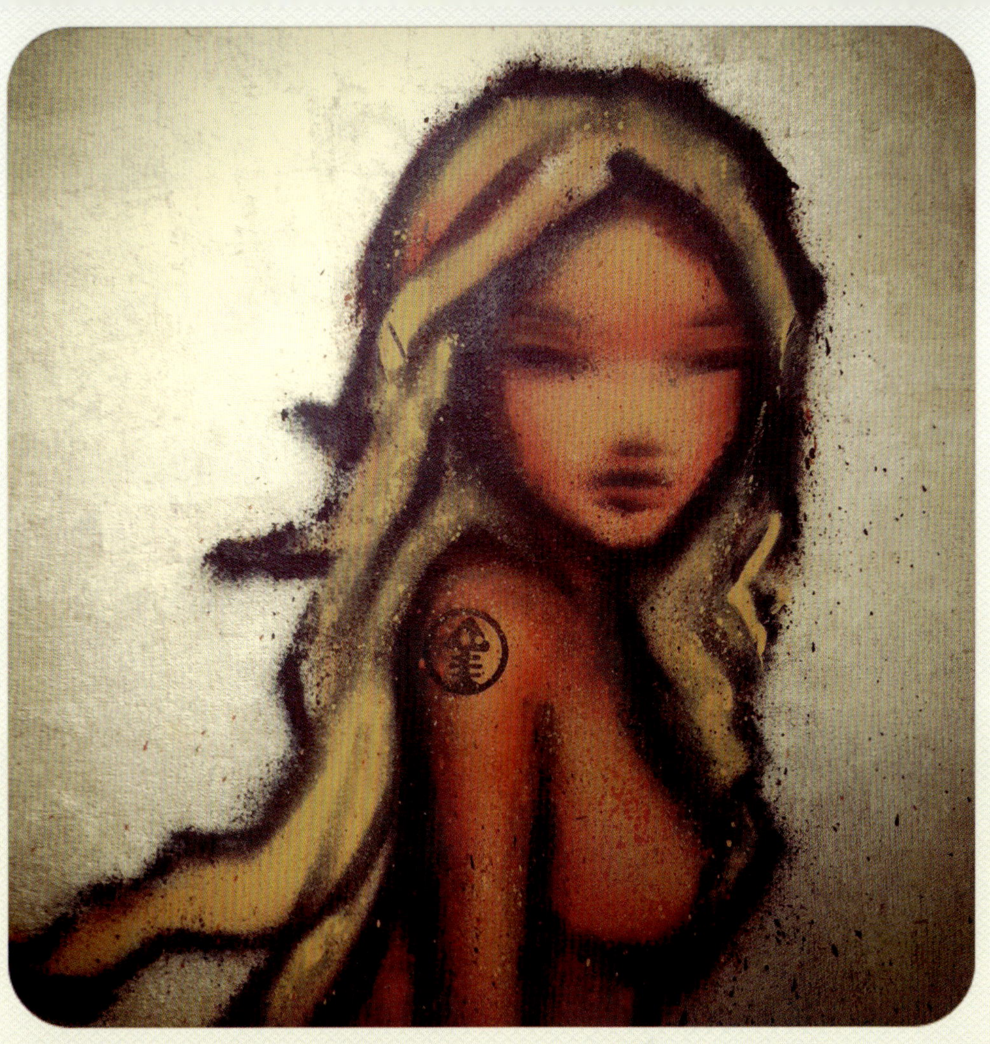

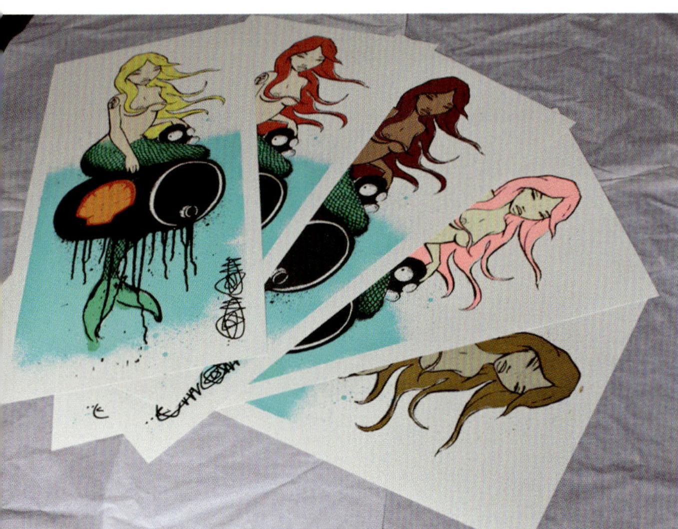

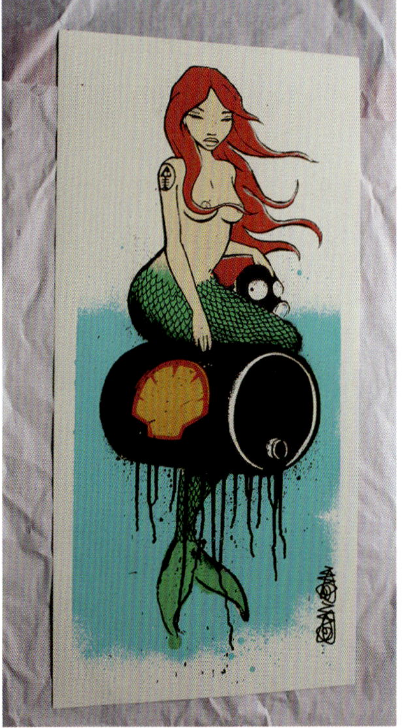

Above:
Mermaid in Oil print, SOS, 2009.

Portrait print, SOS, 2009.

Peep Show print, SOS, 2010.

Opposite page:
Wolf In Sheeple's Clothing print, SOS, 2011.

PREVIOUS PAGE:
Business Heads print, 2007.
Bling Reaper on reclaimed Shell sign, 2008.

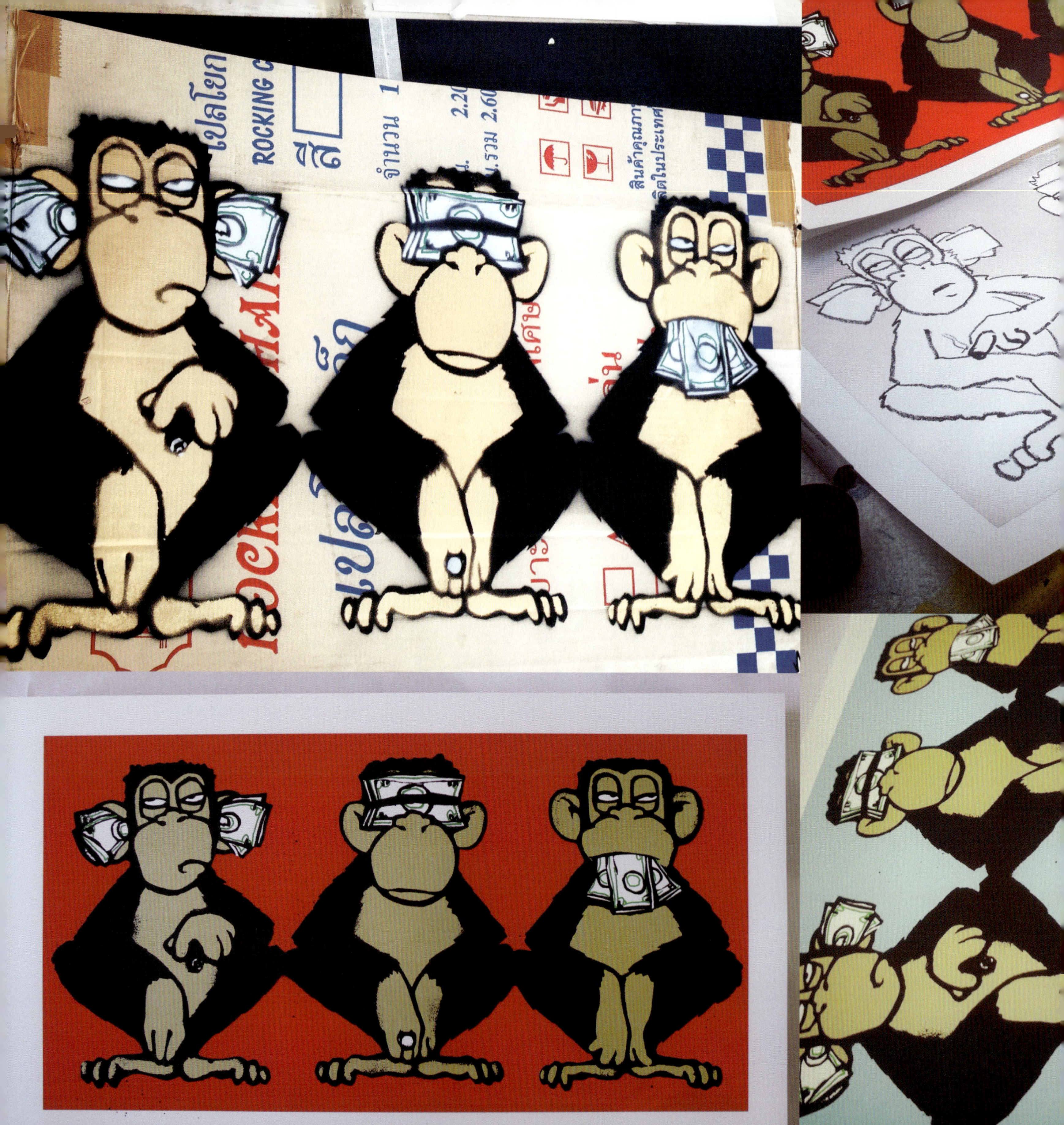

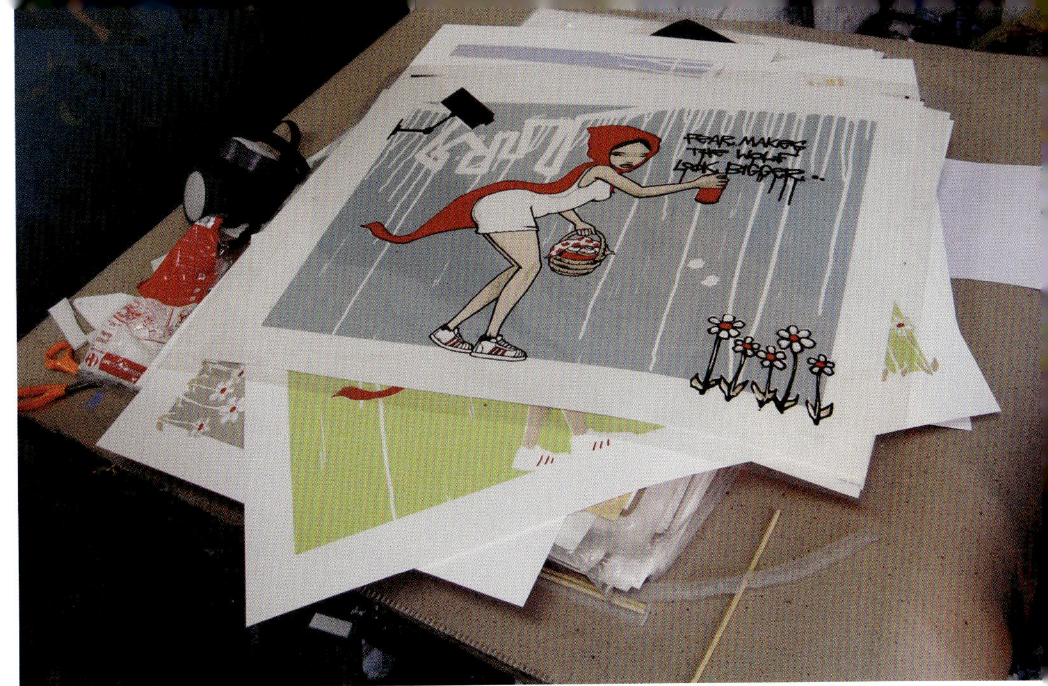

3 Monkeys print, SOS, 2012.

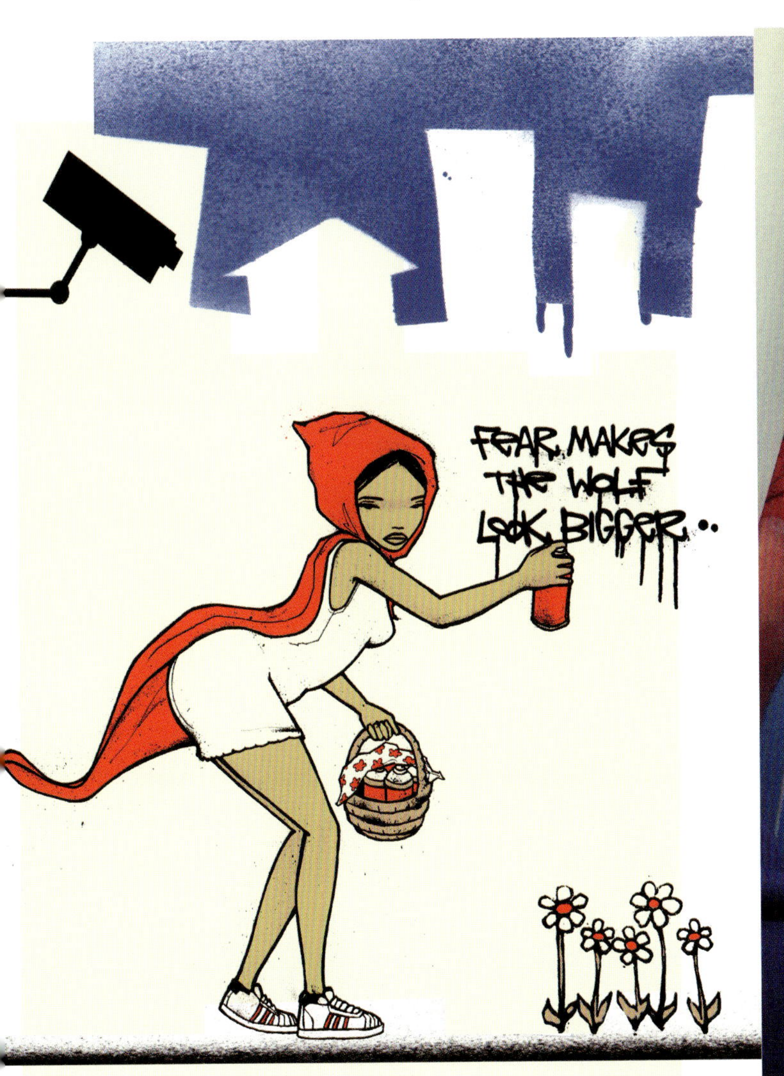

L'il Red print, SOS, 2008.

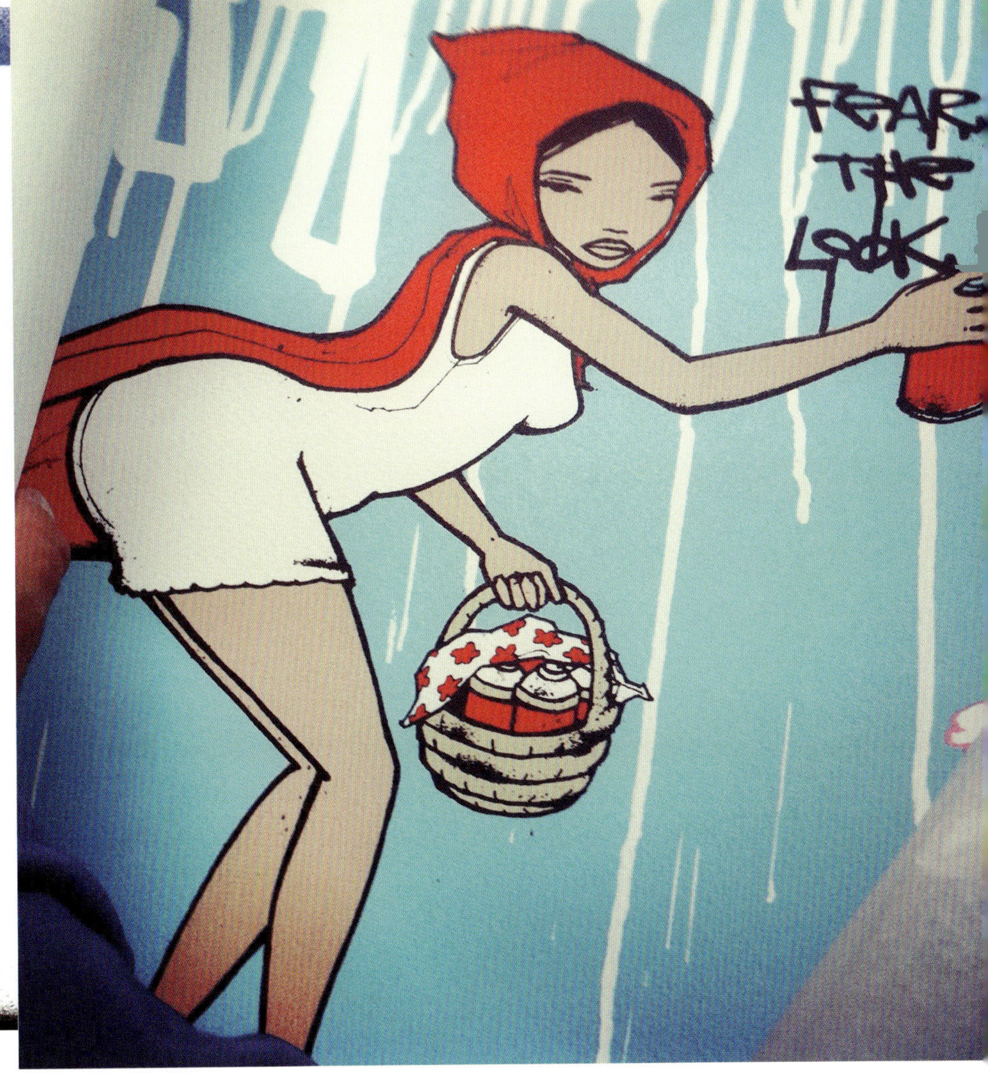

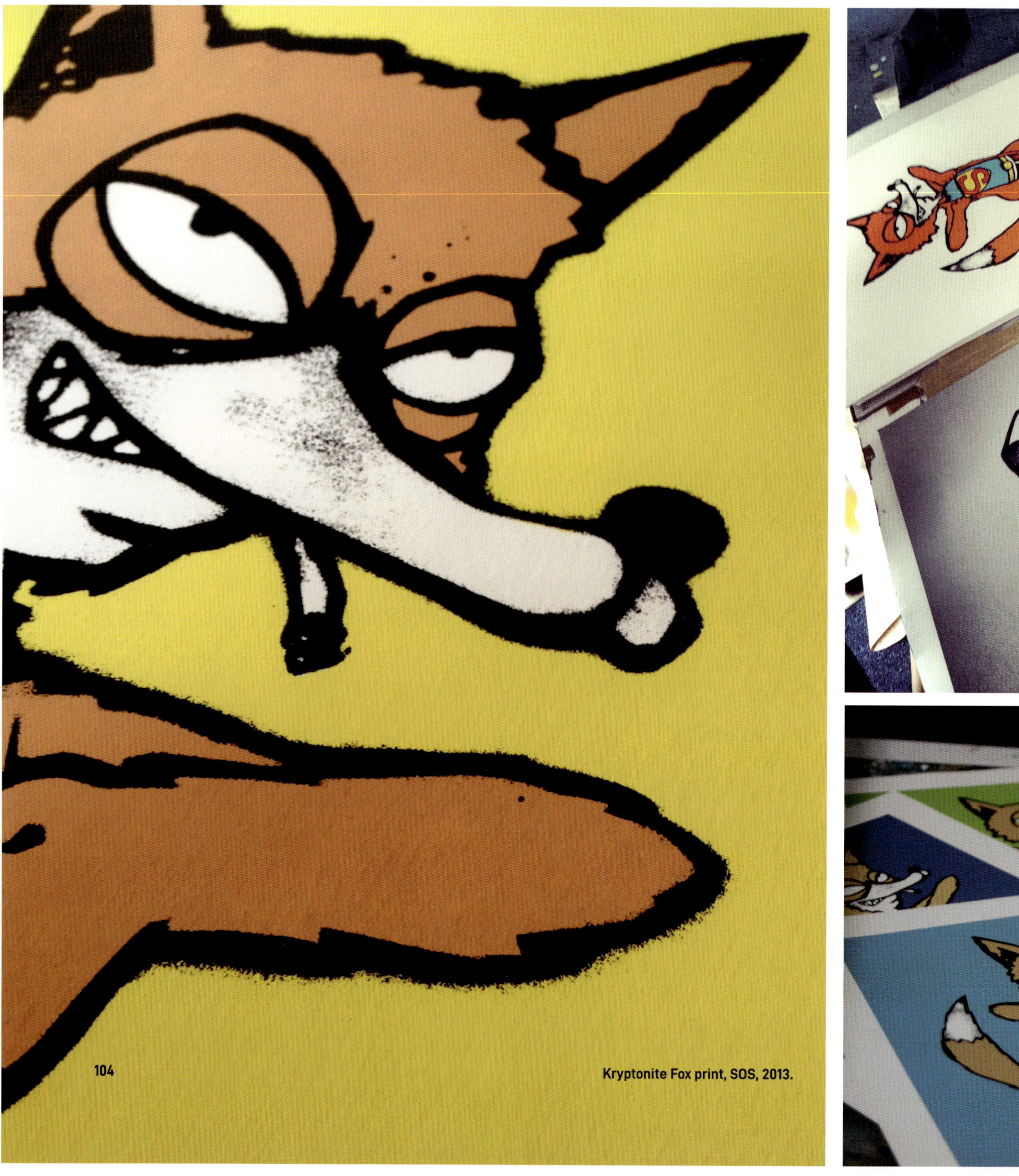

Kryptonite Fox print, SOS, 2013.

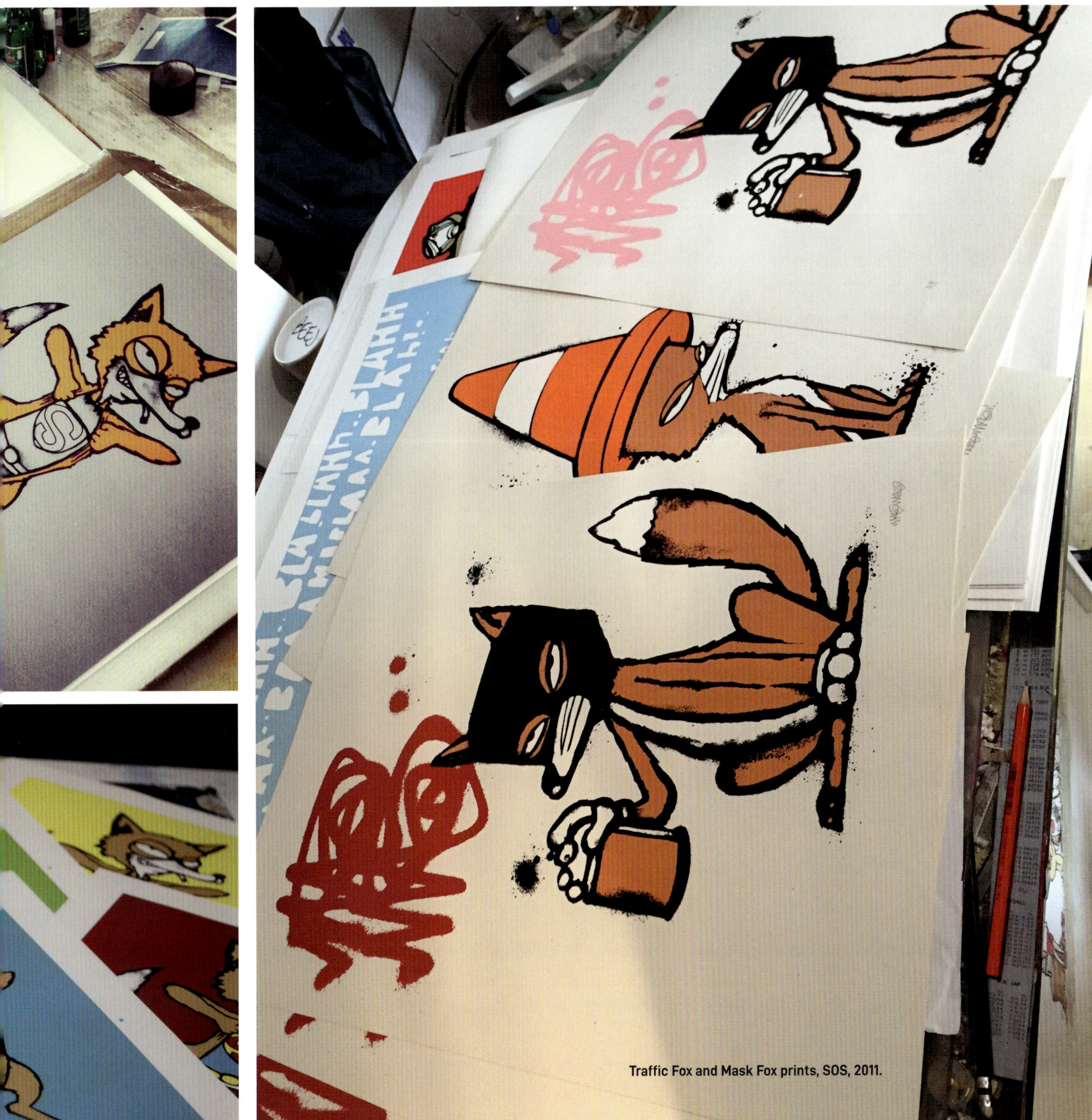

Traffic Fox and Mask Fox prints, SOS, 2011.

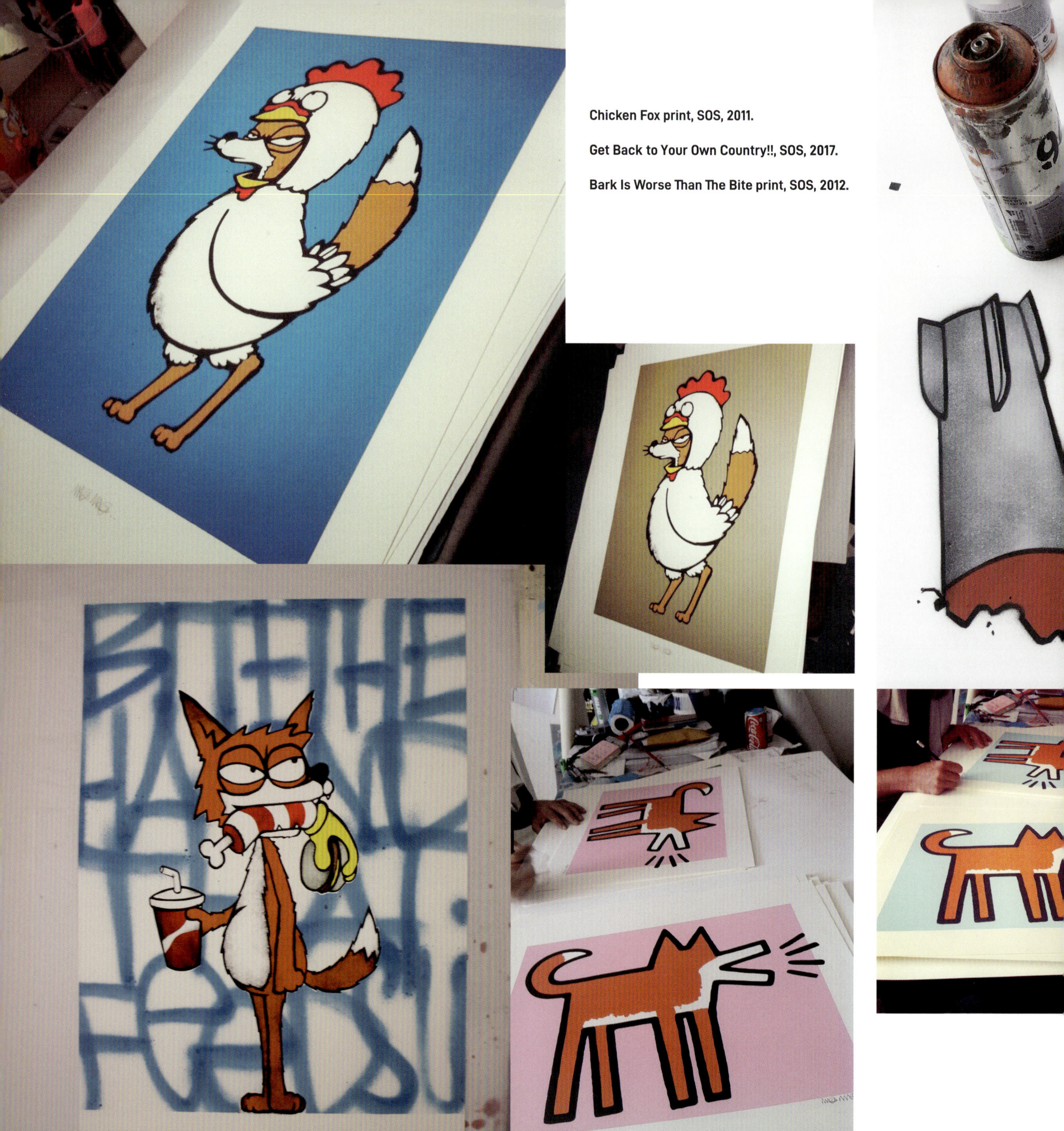

Chicken Fox print, SOS, 2011.

Get Back to Your Own Country!!, SOS, 2017.

Bark Is Worse Than The Bite print, SOS, 2012.

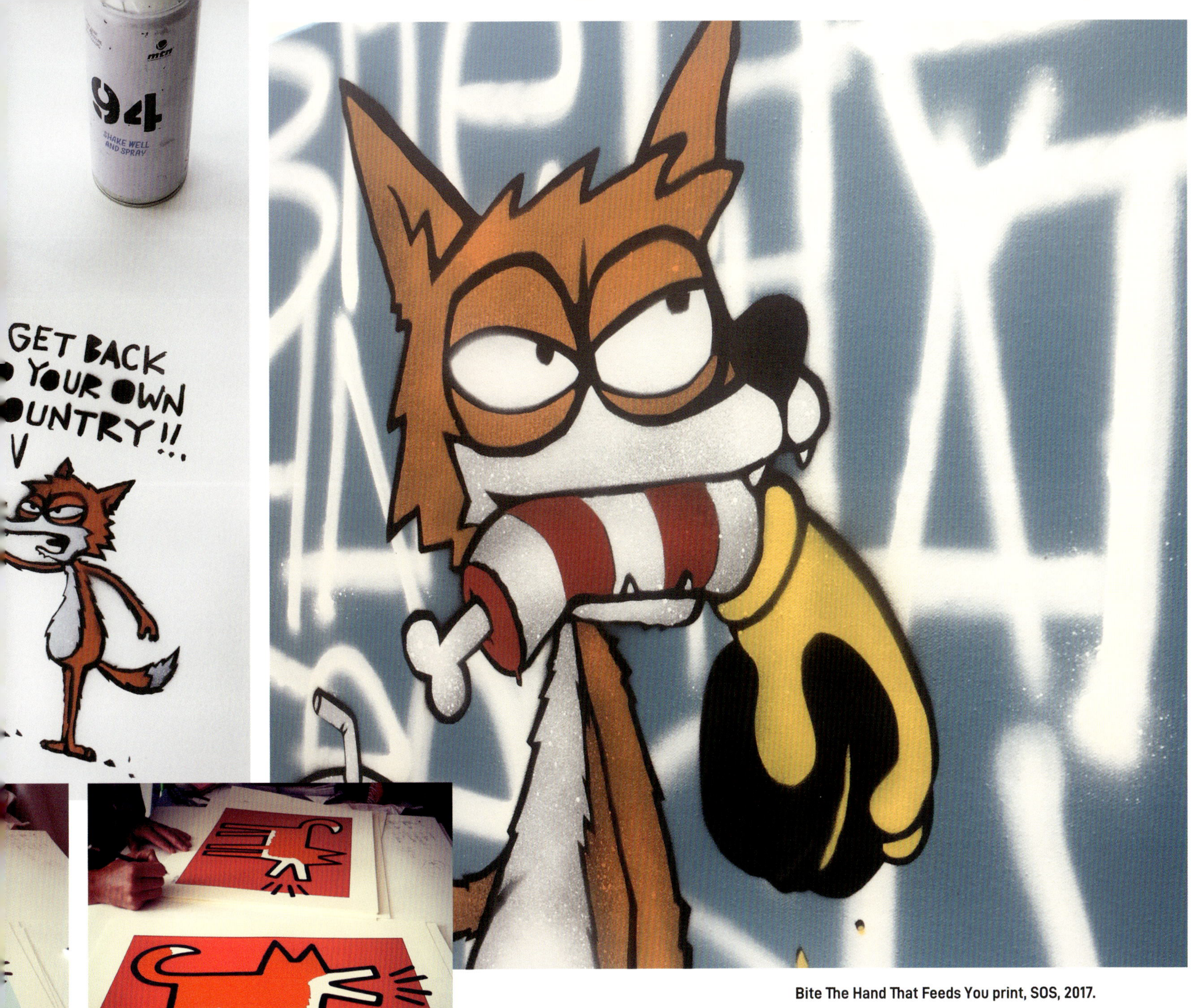

Bite The Hand That Feeds You print, SOS, 2017.

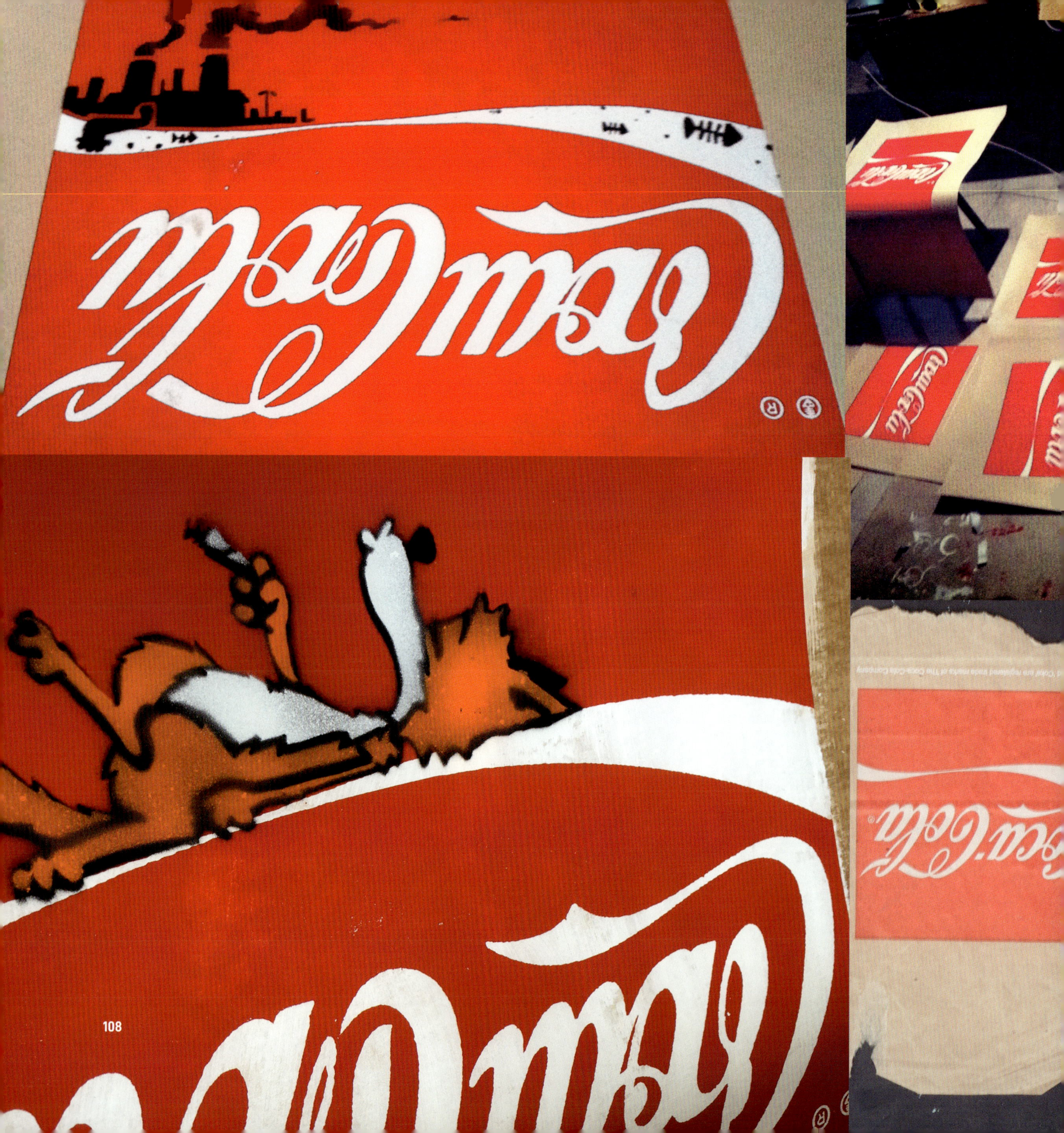

Enjoy Mau Mau, SOS editions, 2013.

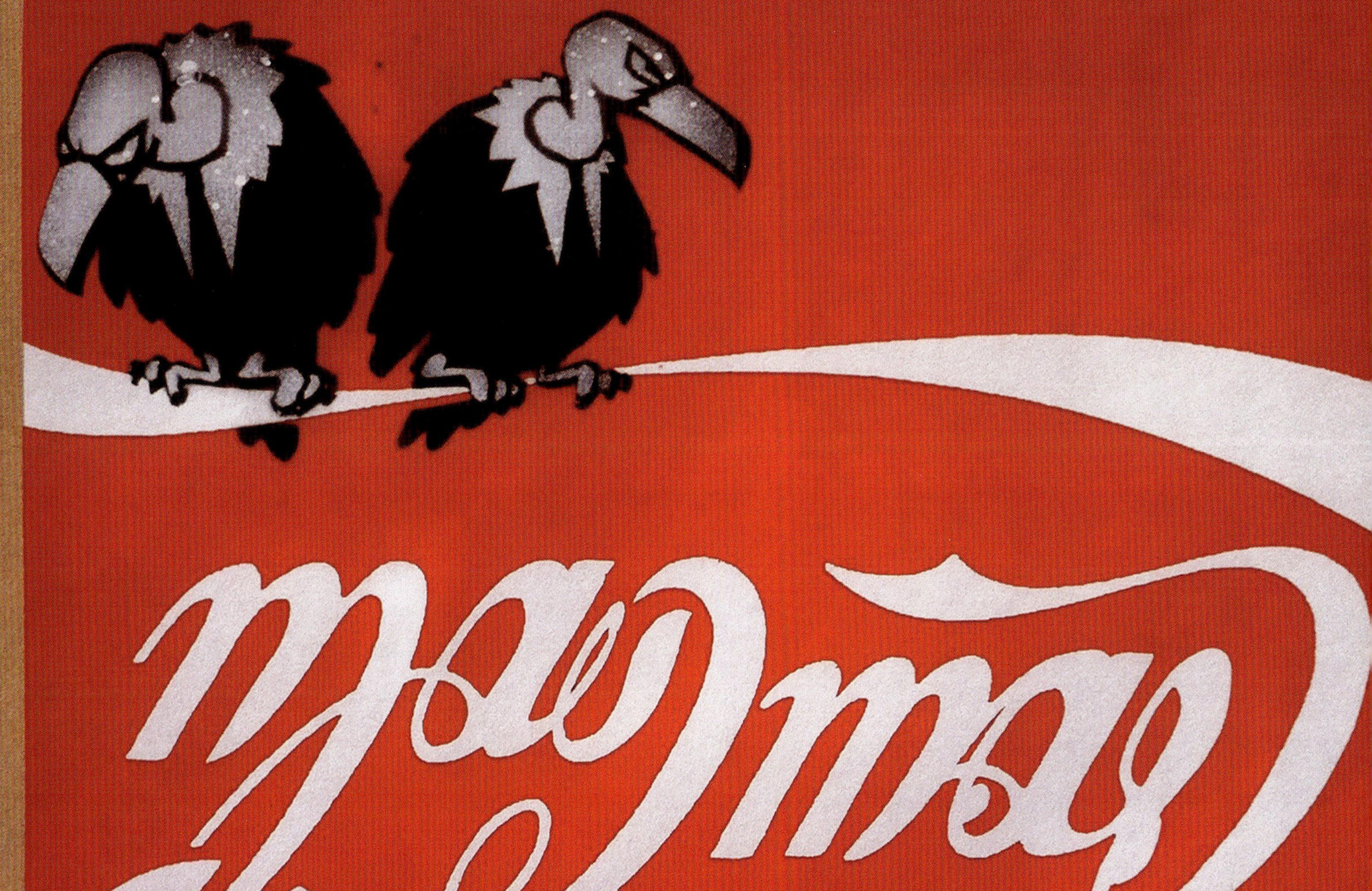

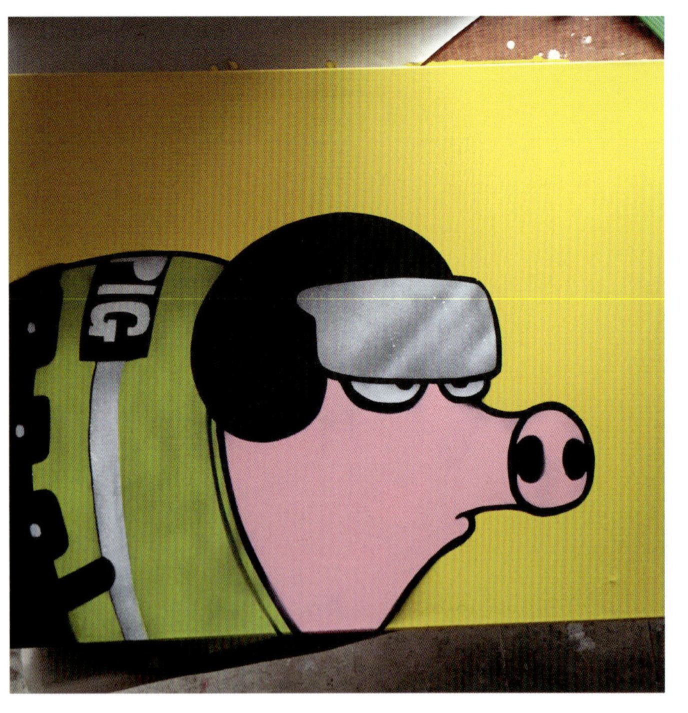

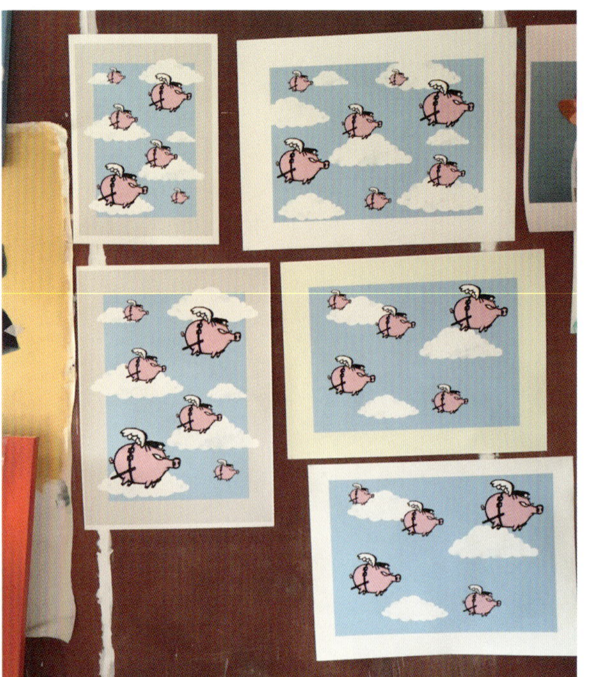

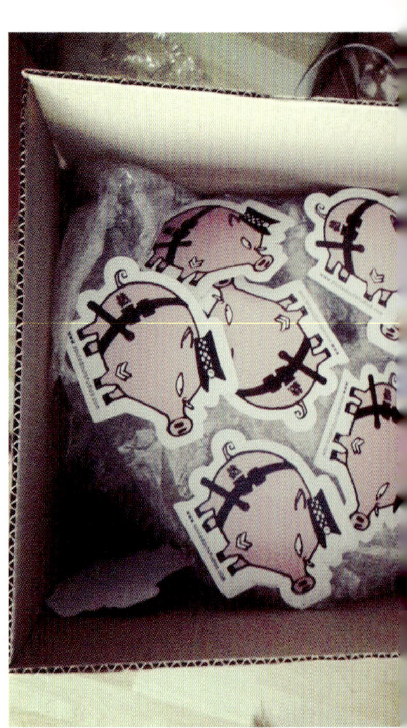

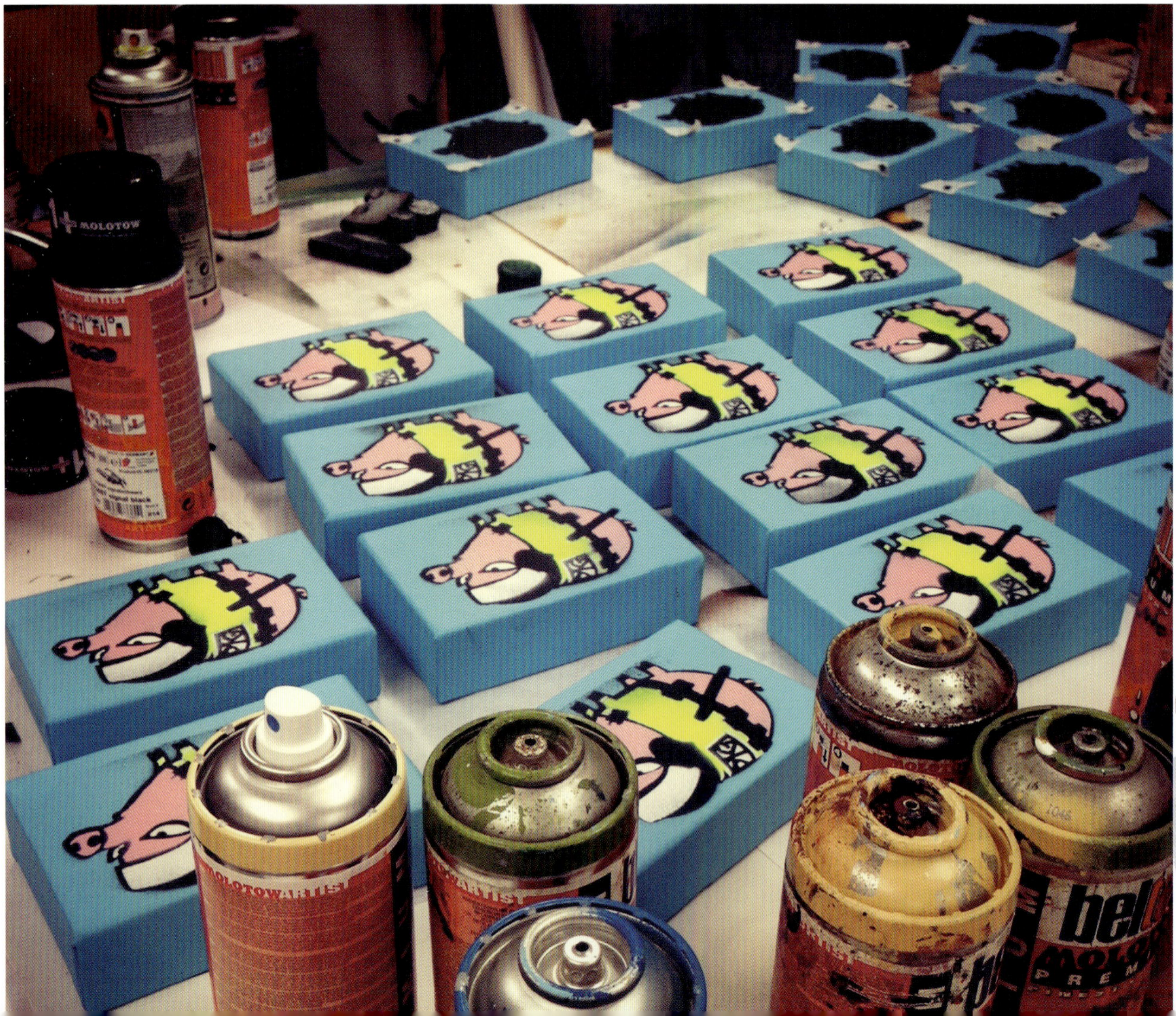

Thailand is a great country to create art in because you have access to so many different materials and skilled crafts people and you can get small runs made very easily. It allows a lot more creative freedom because you can try out different things relatively cheaply. For instance, you can take a sketch, or even a sticker, to a craftsman who will turn it into a three dimensional bronze.

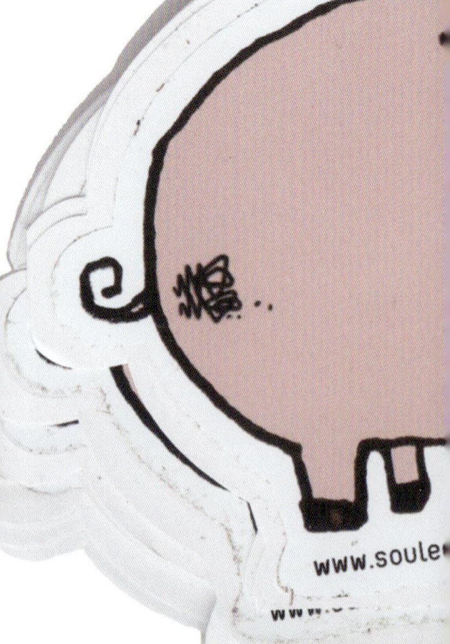

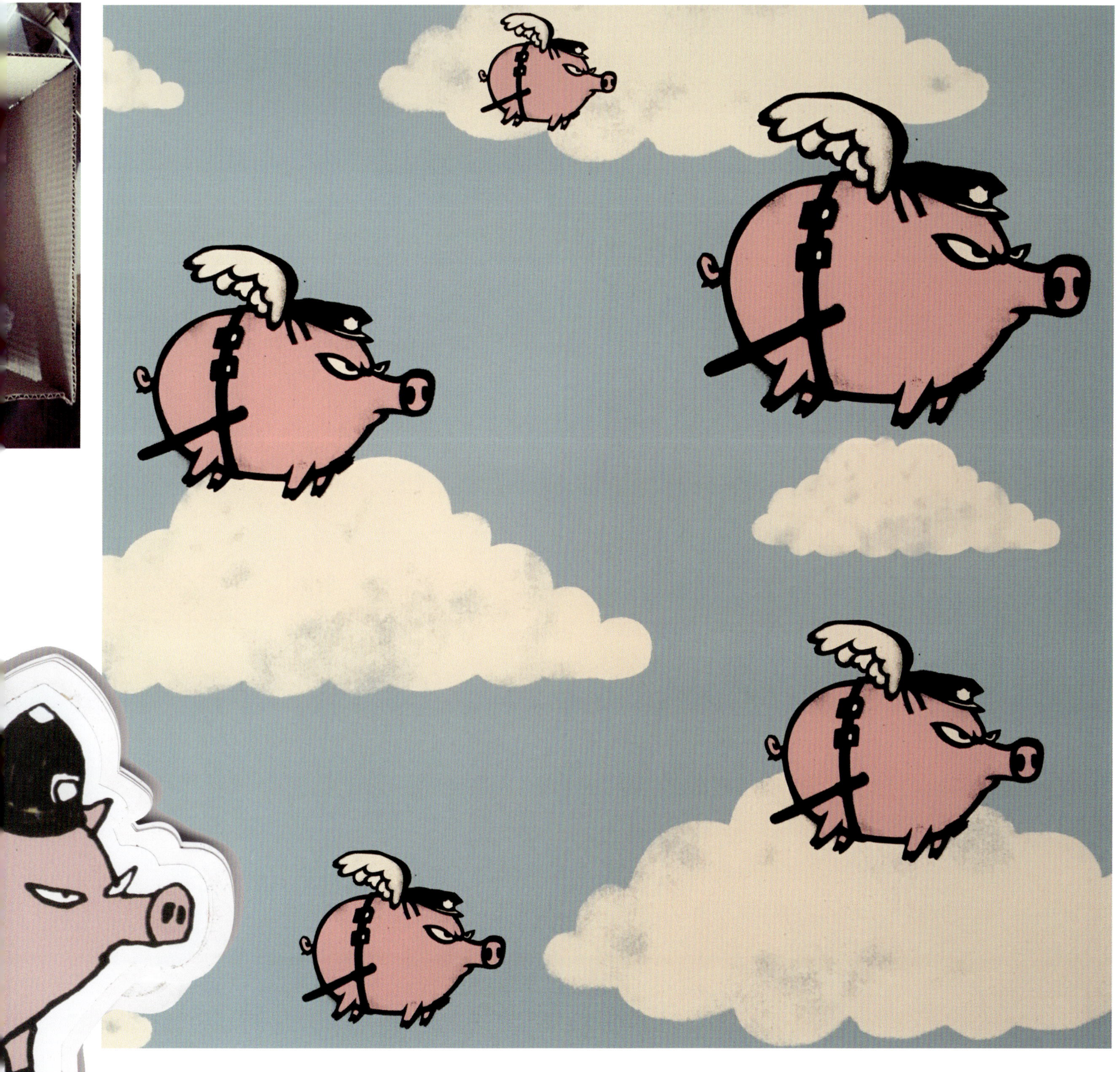

Bottom Left: Riot Pig mini canvas edition, SOS, 2013.

Flying Pigs print, SOS, 2013.

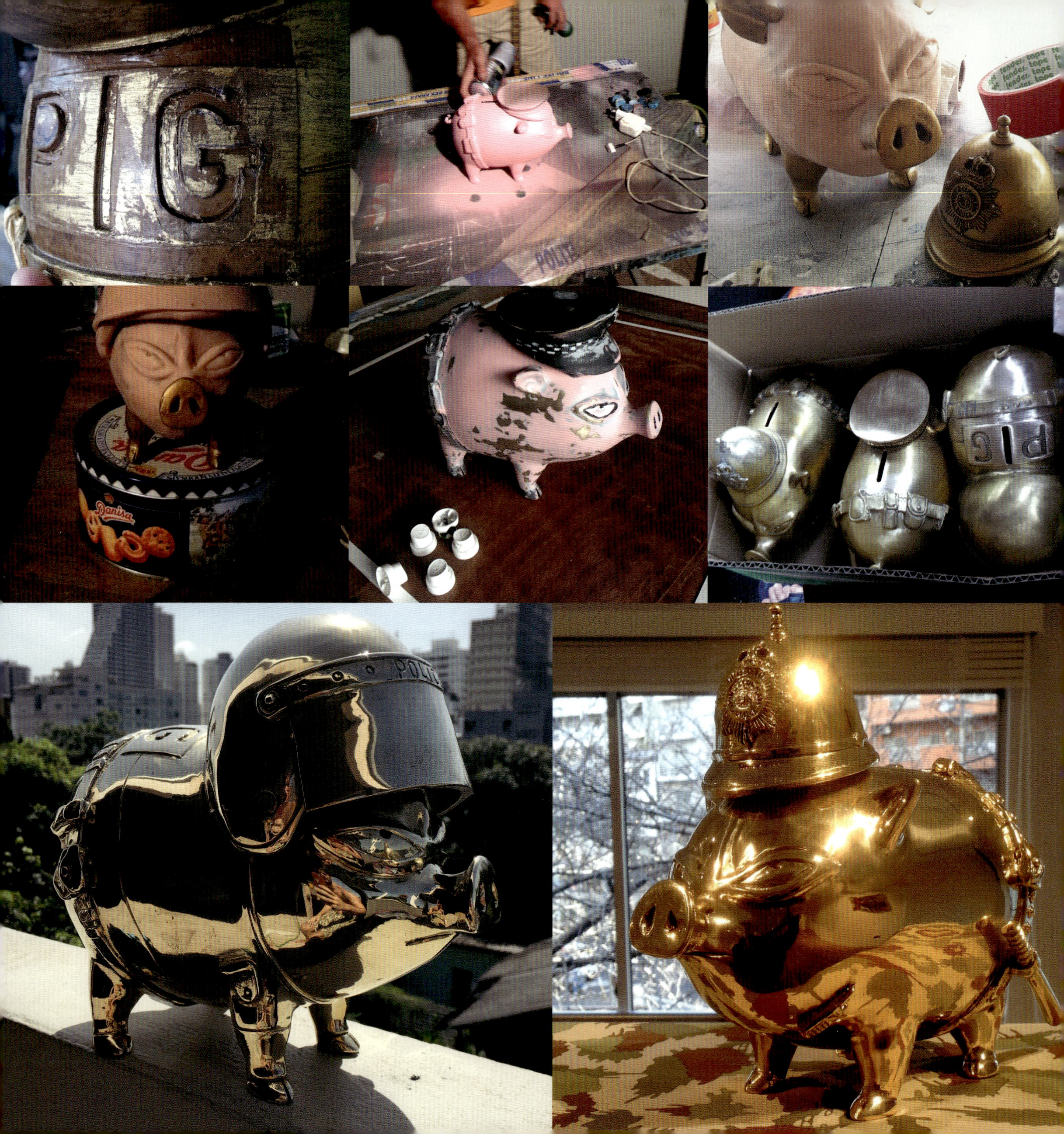
PIG
Danisa

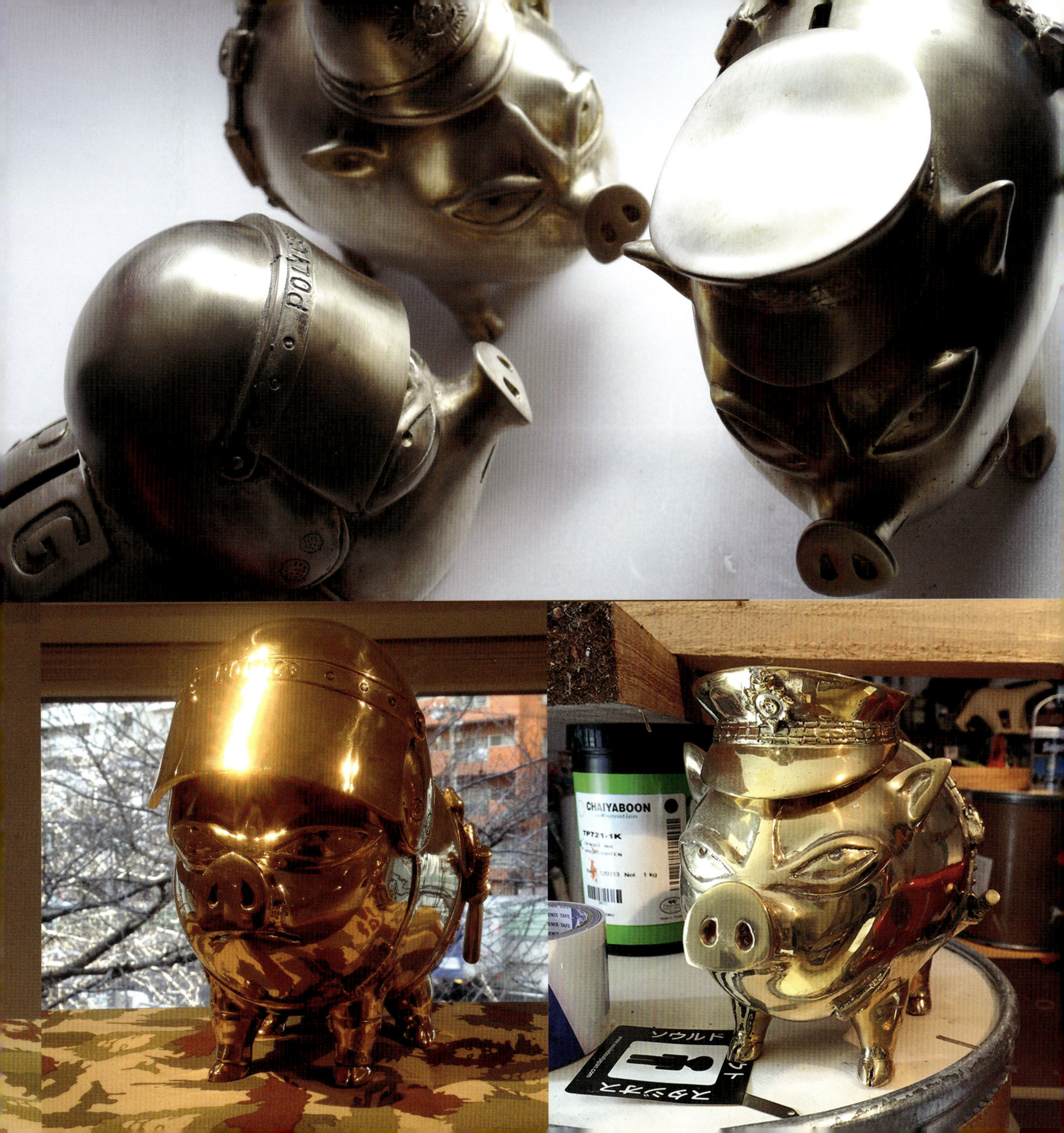
POLICE
CHAIYABOON
TP721-1K
ソウルド

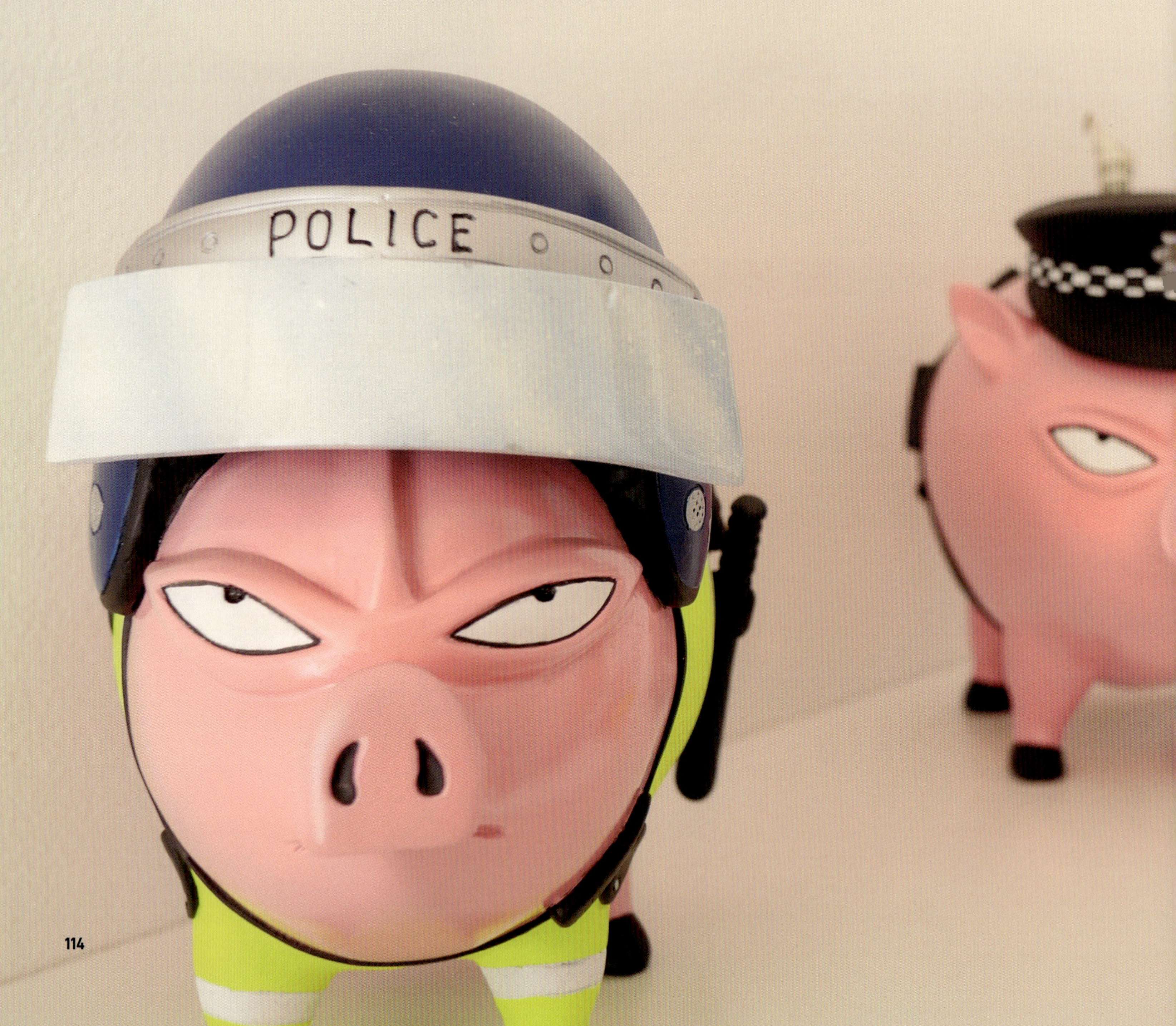
POLICE

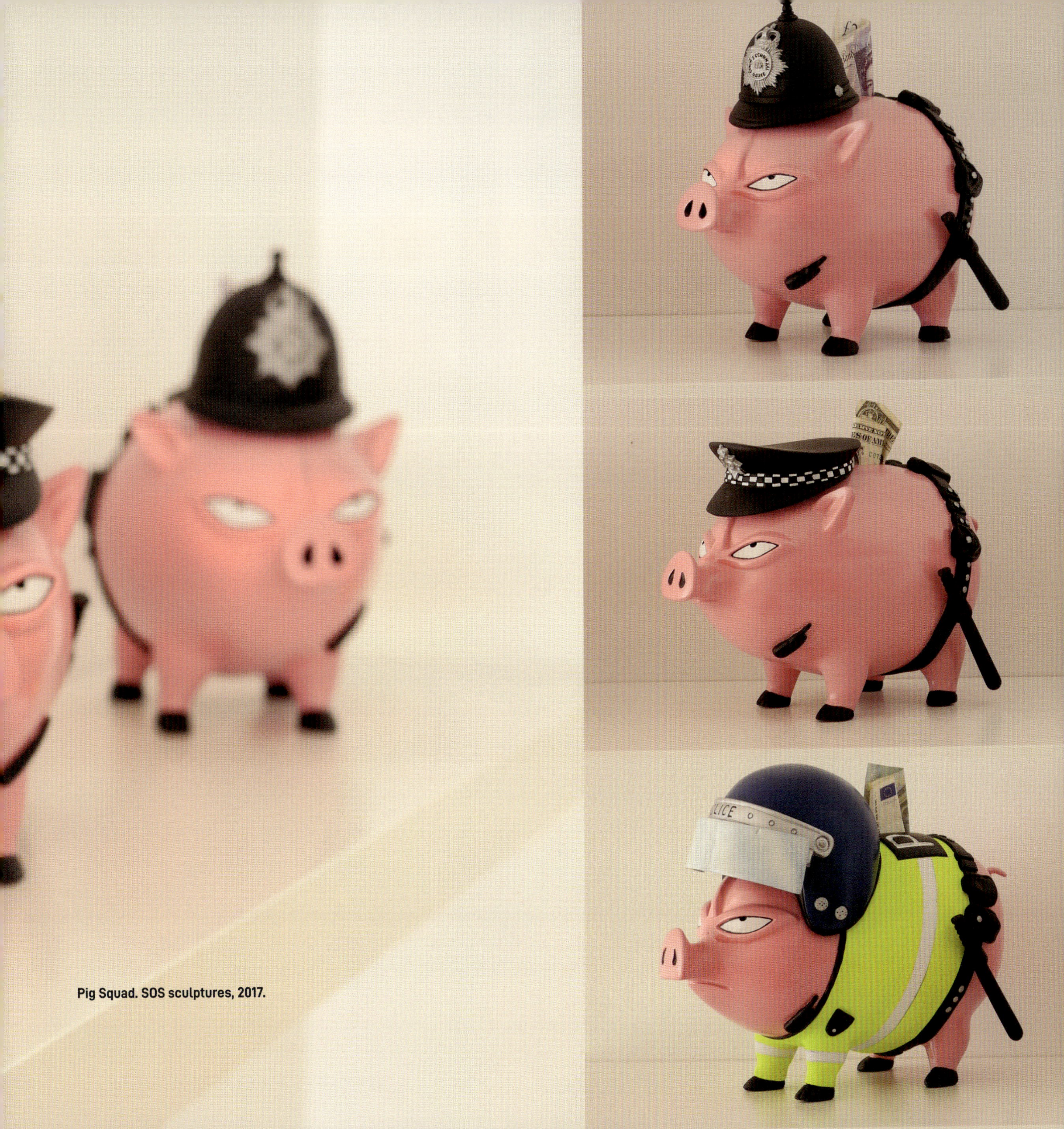

Pig Squad. SOS sculptures, 2017.

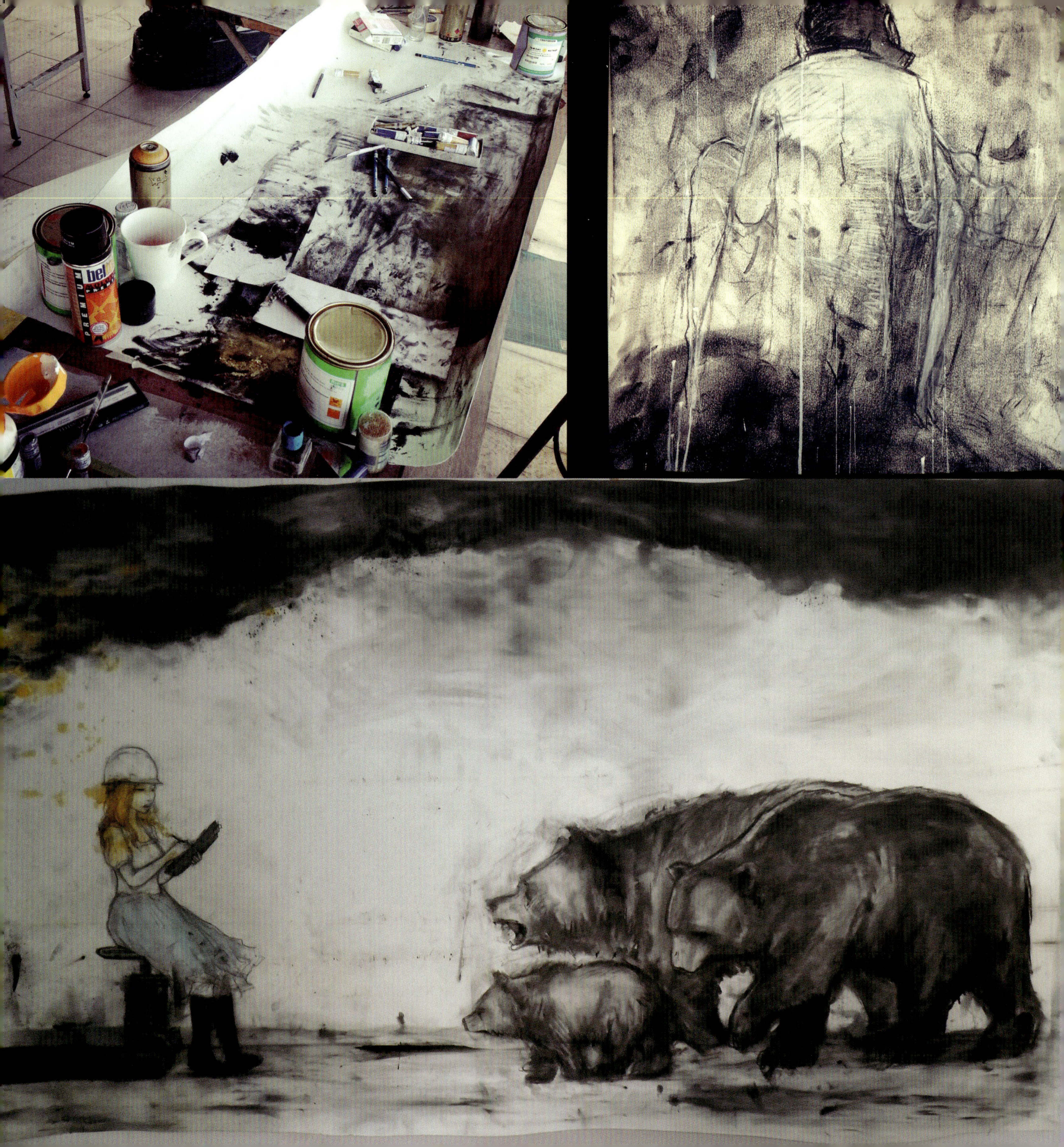
bel
PREMIUM

The Rescue, charcoal sketch, 2013.

Goldilocks, Guess Who's Coming To Dinner, charcoal sketch, 2013.

Cinderella 'n the Gold Sneaker, charcoal sketch, 2013.

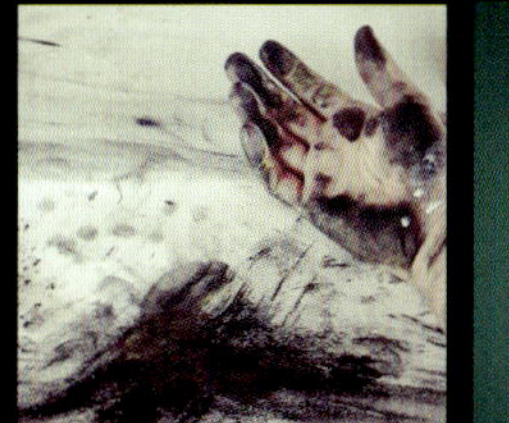

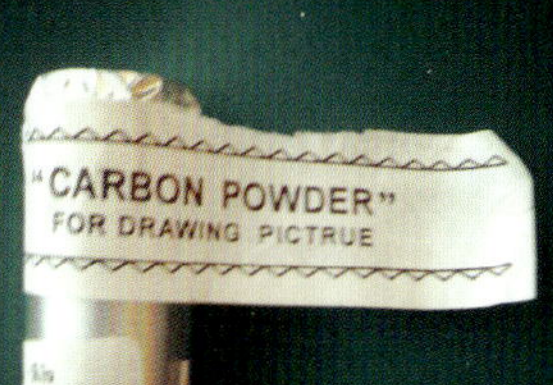

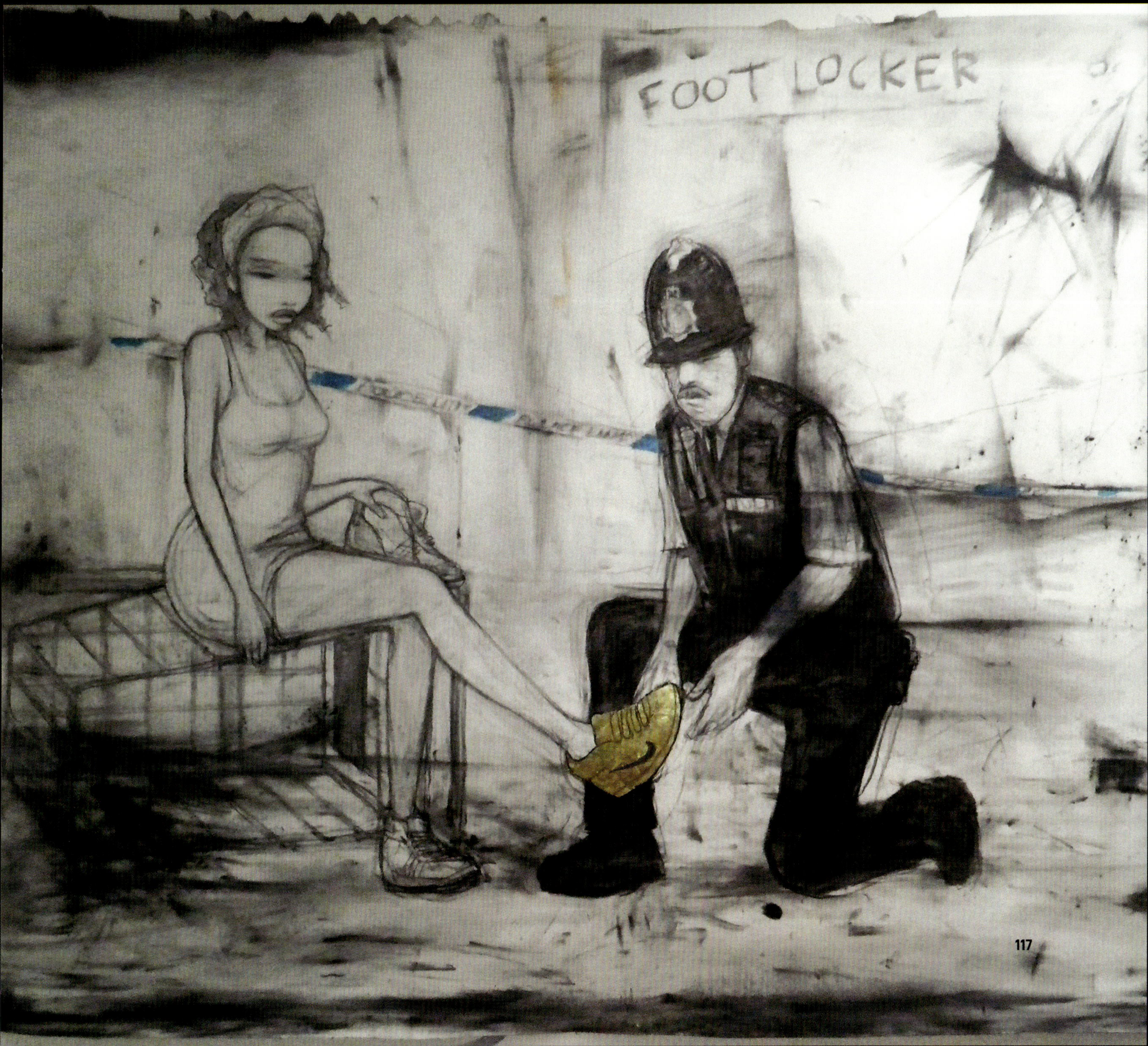

The Rescue, charcoal sketch, 2013.

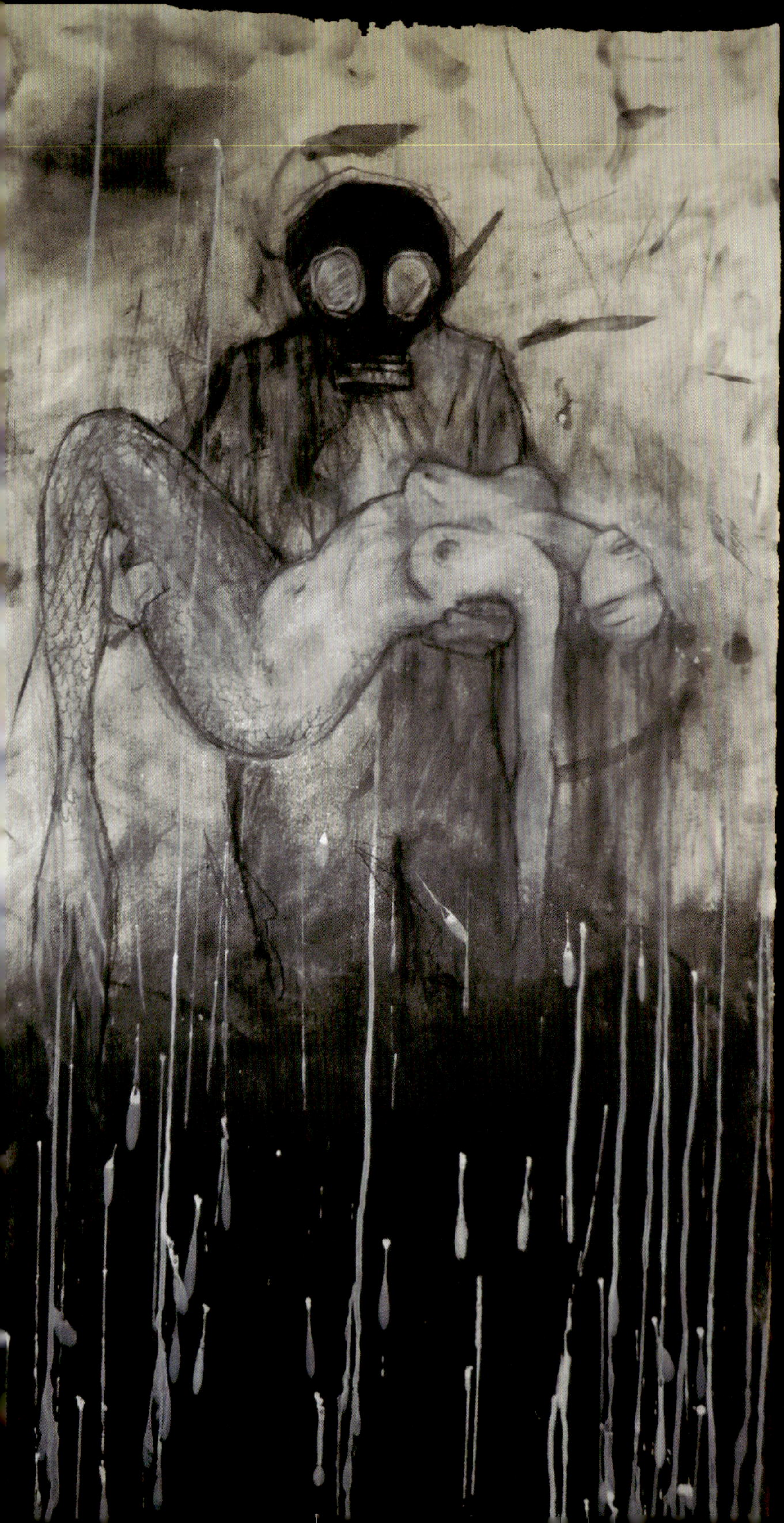

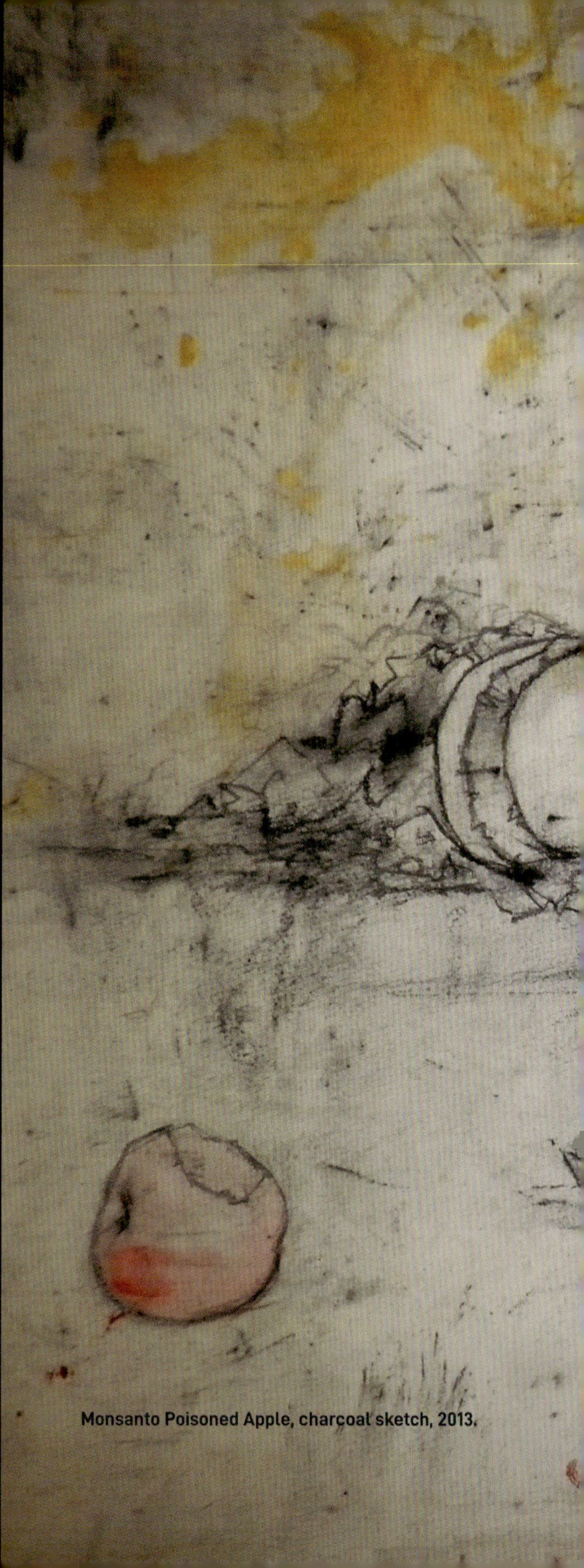

Monsanto Poisoned Apple, charcoal sketch, 2013.

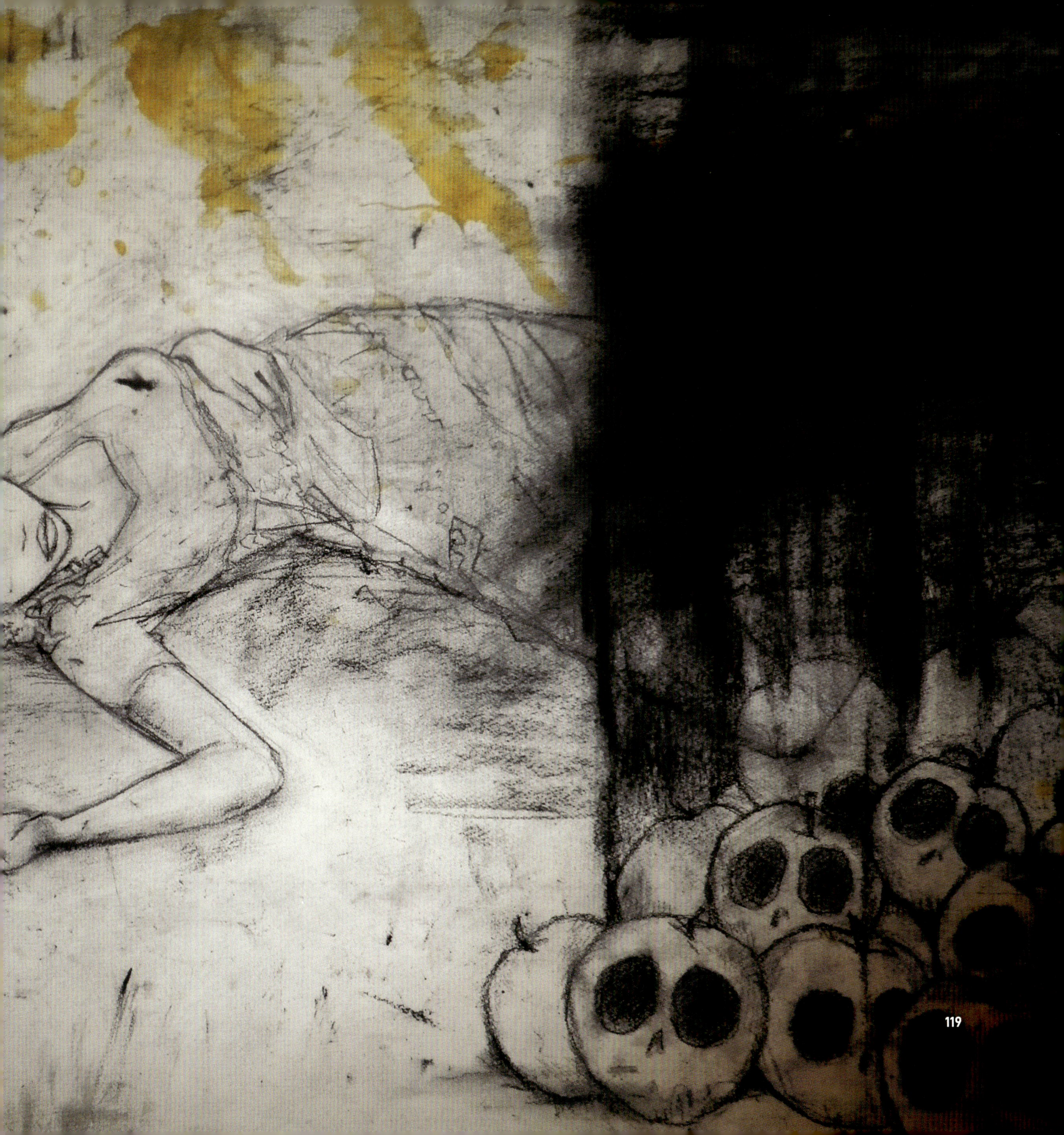

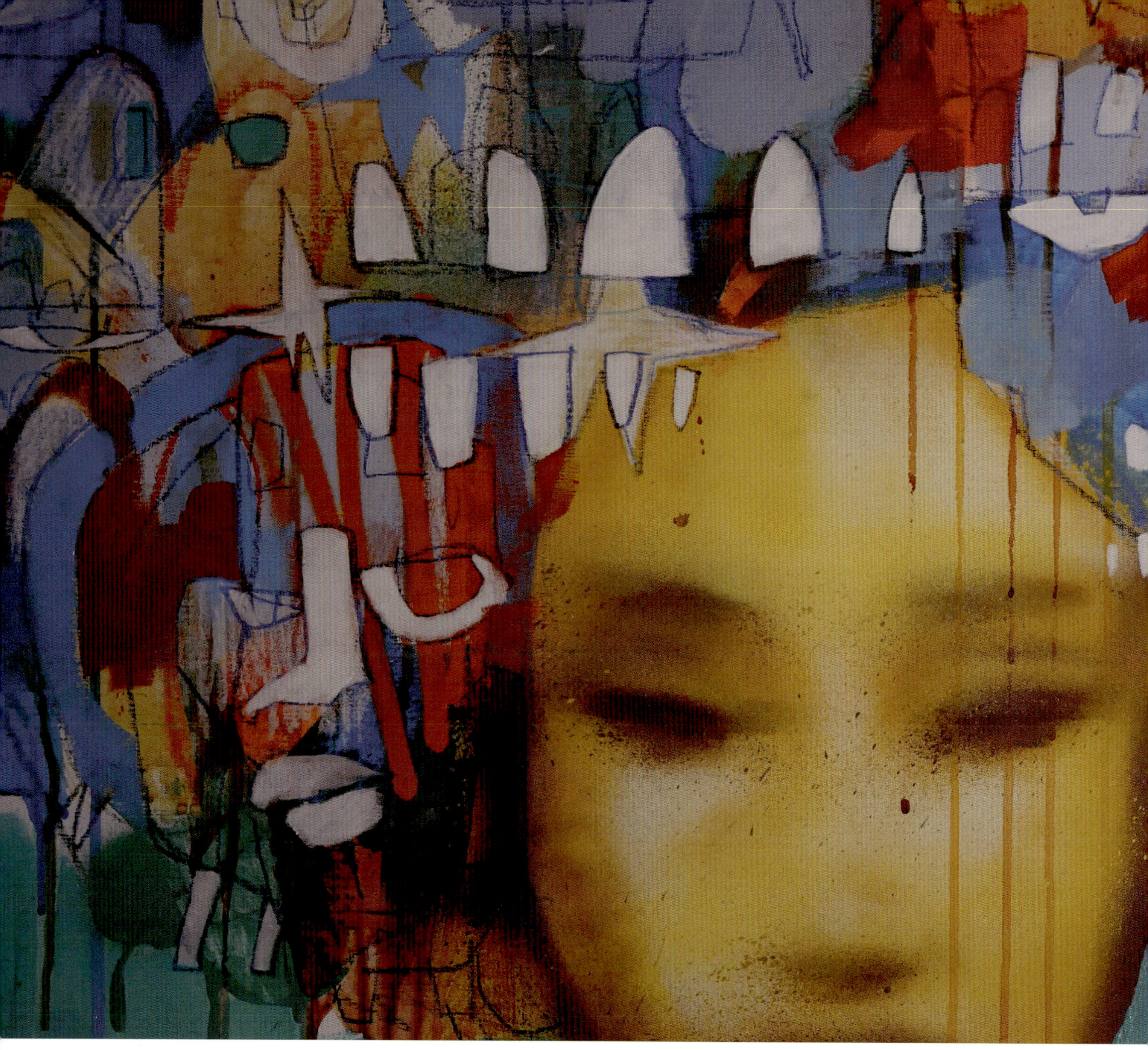

Portraits, SOS editions (Cyclops, Mau), 2018.

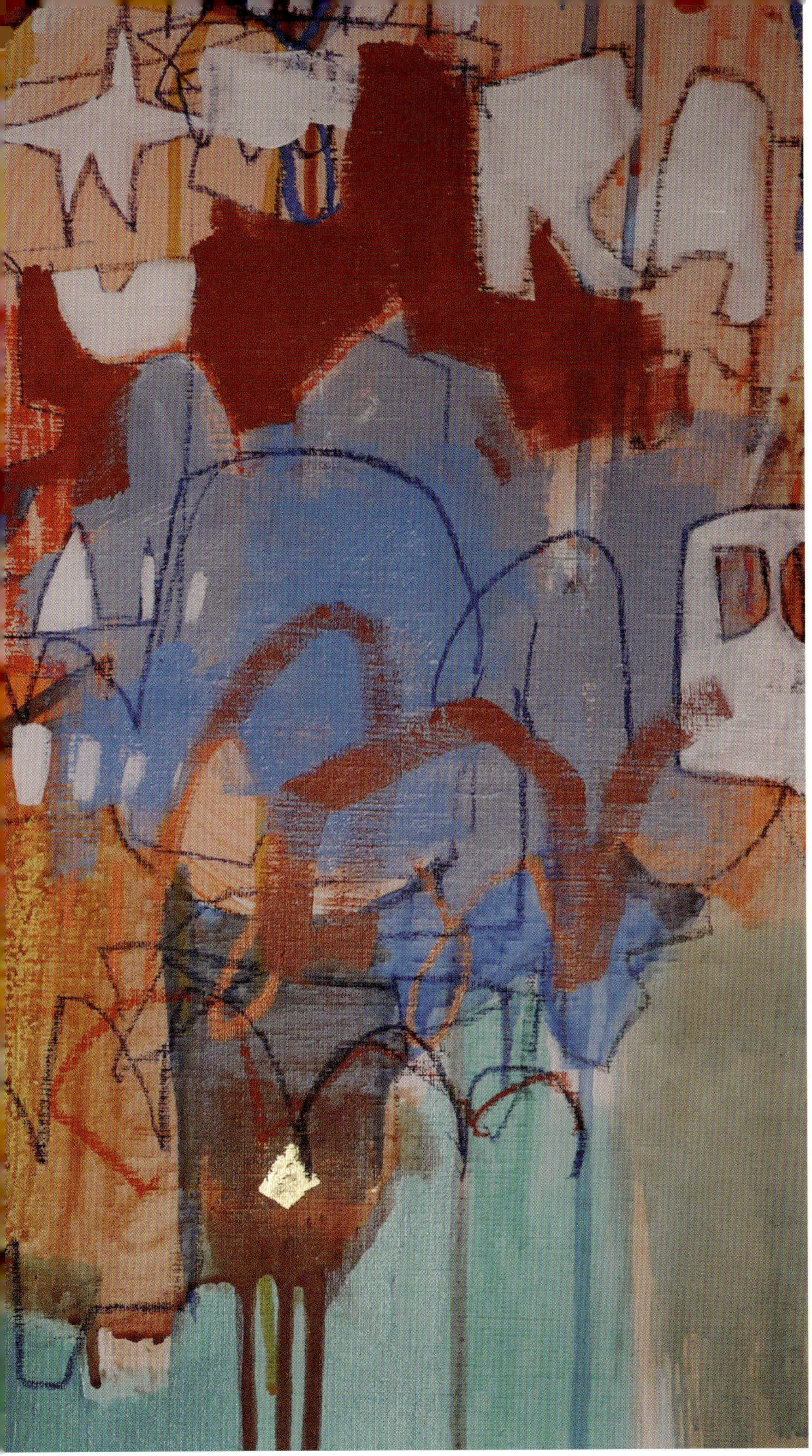

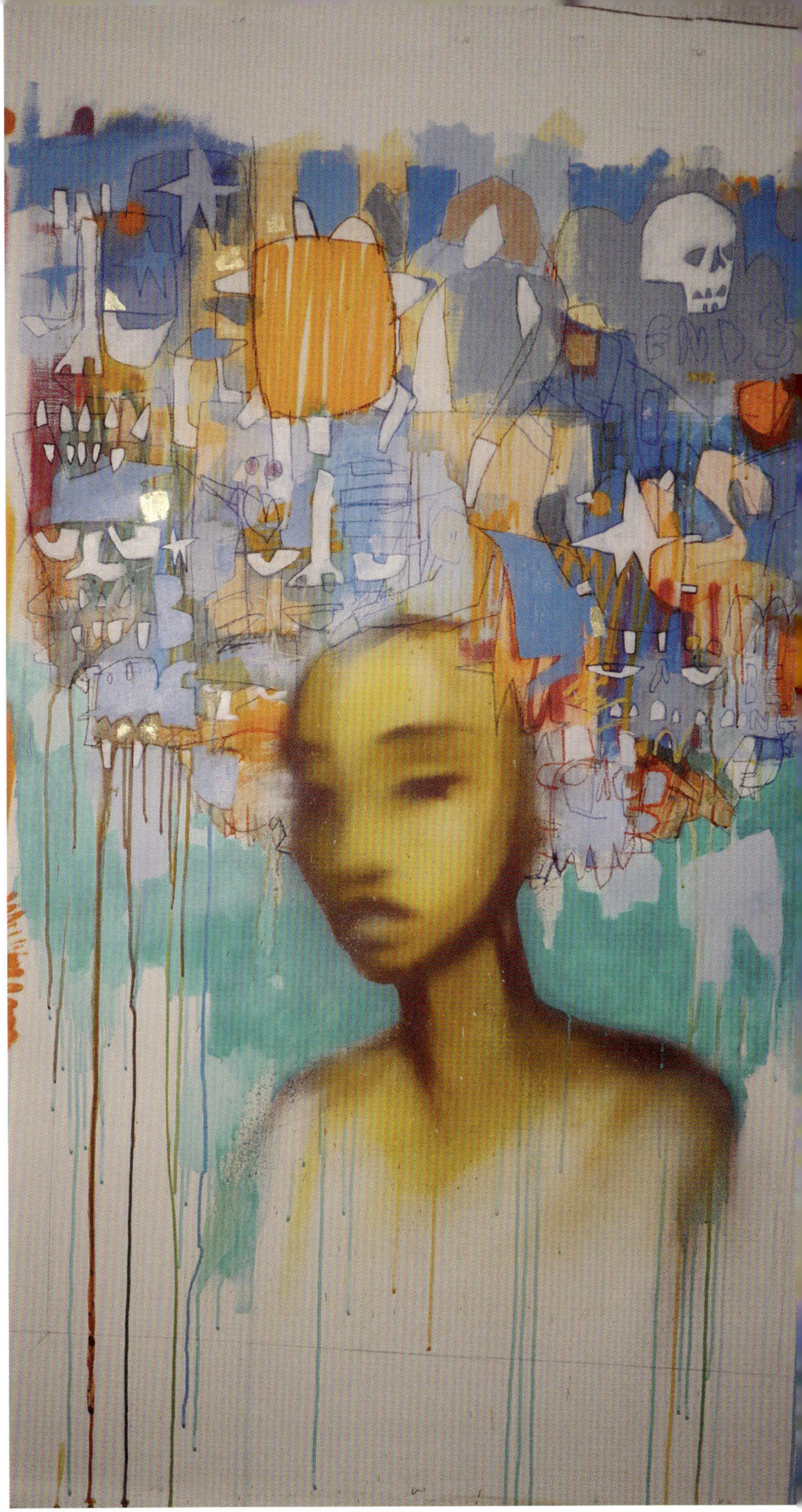

NEXT PAGE: Empress, SOS edition, 2020.

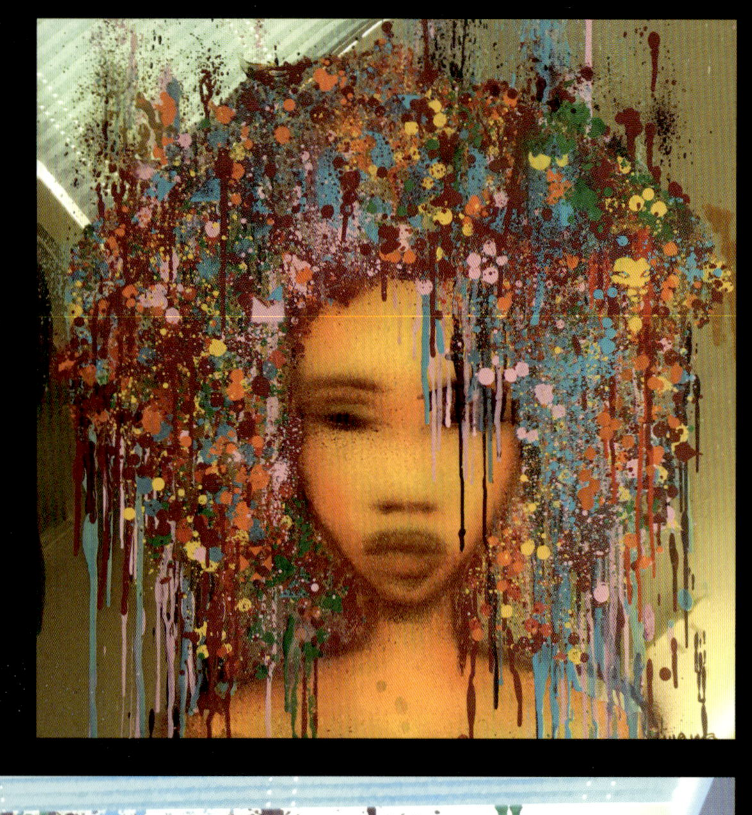

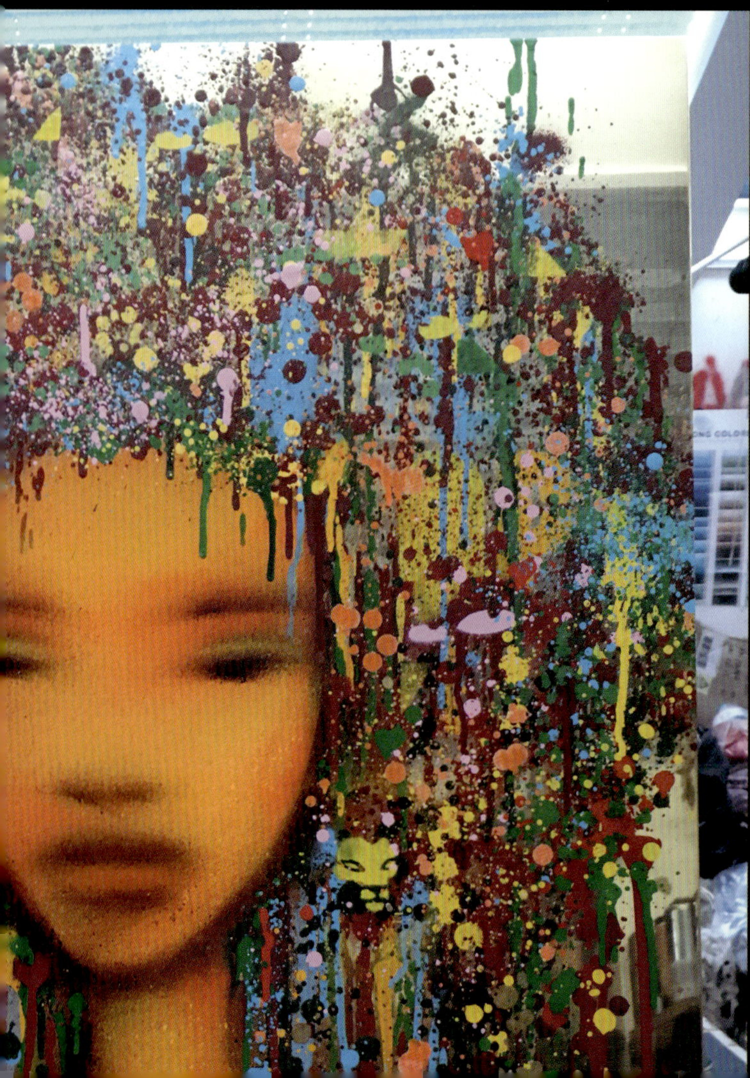

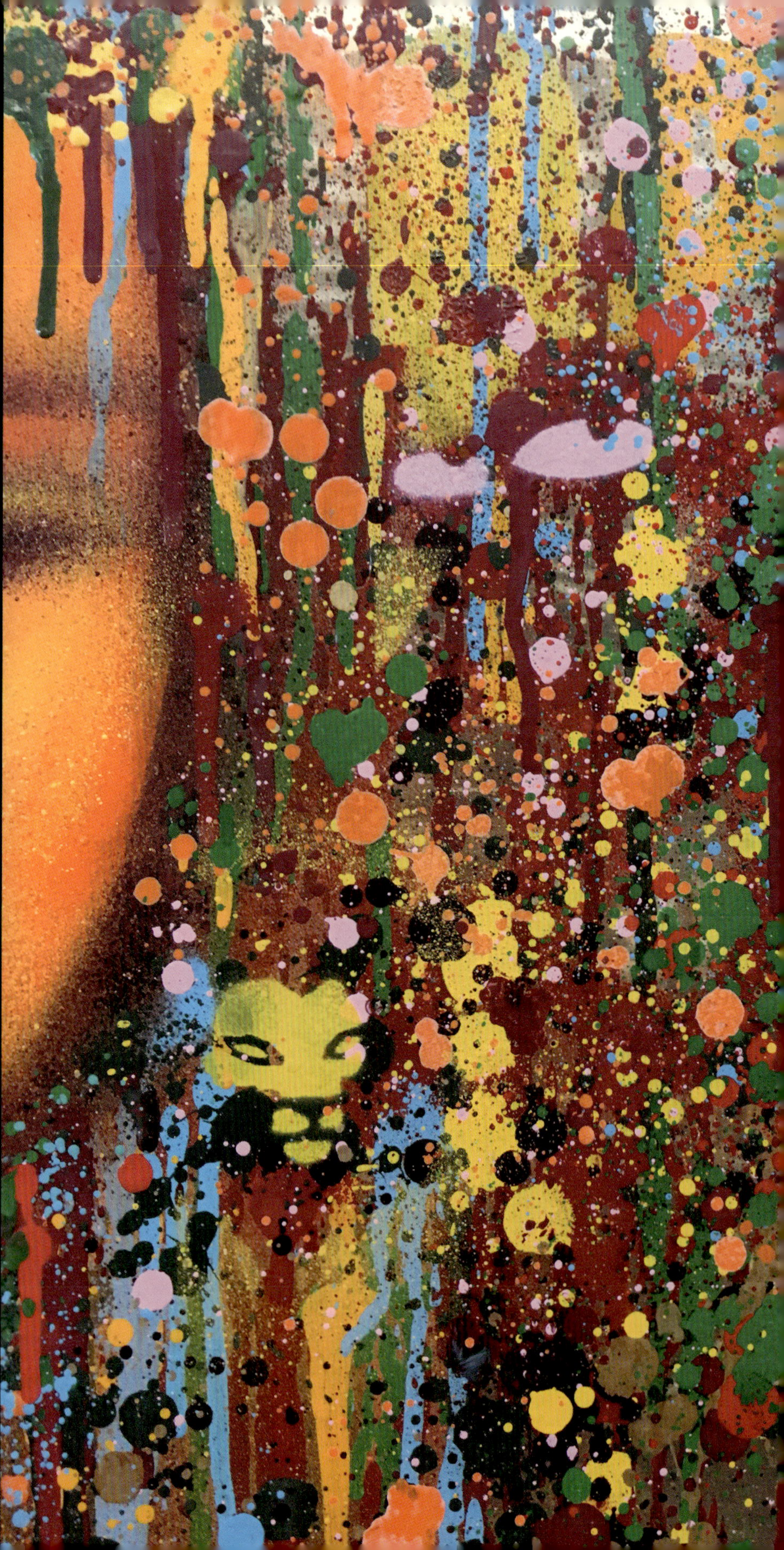

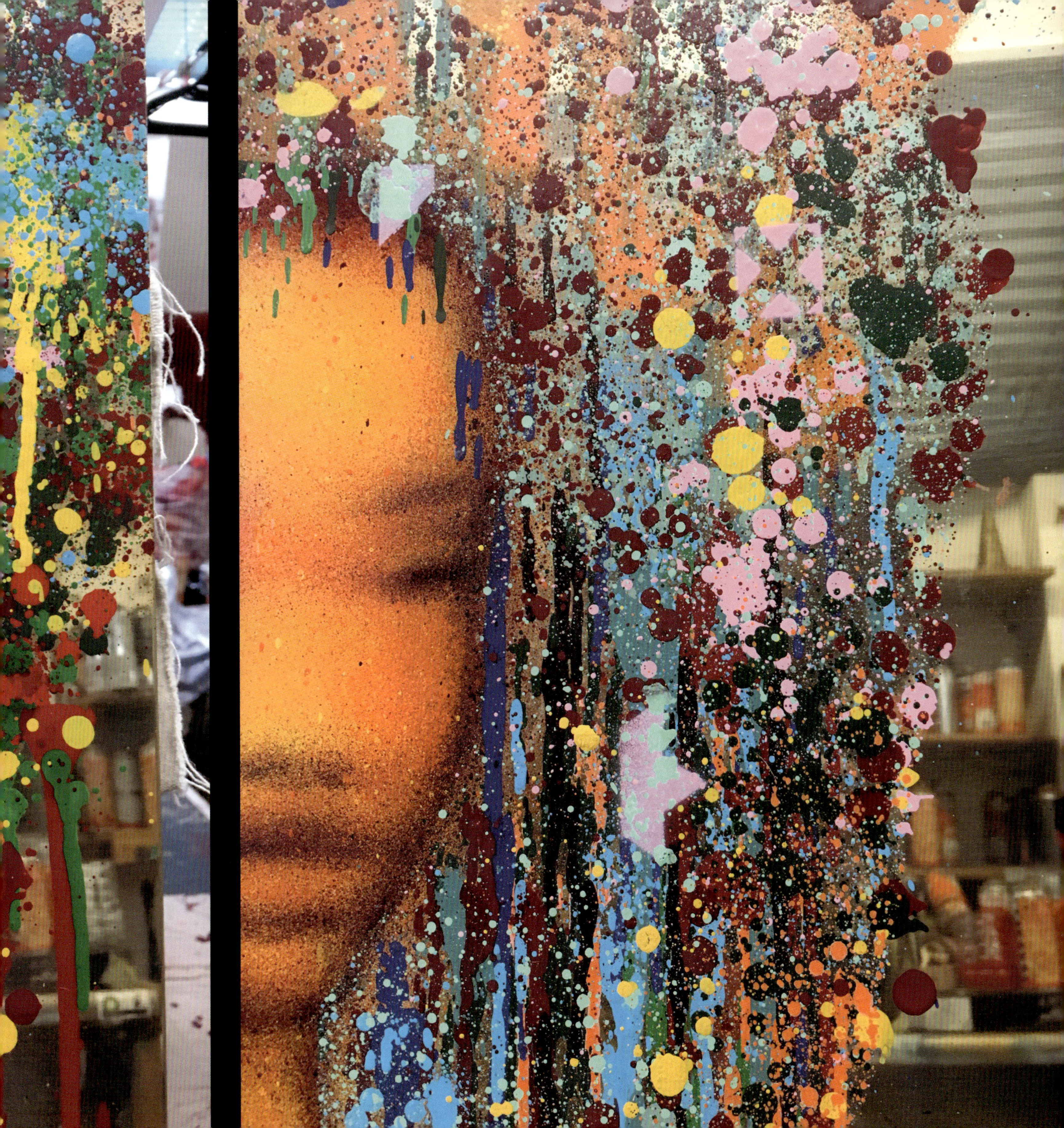

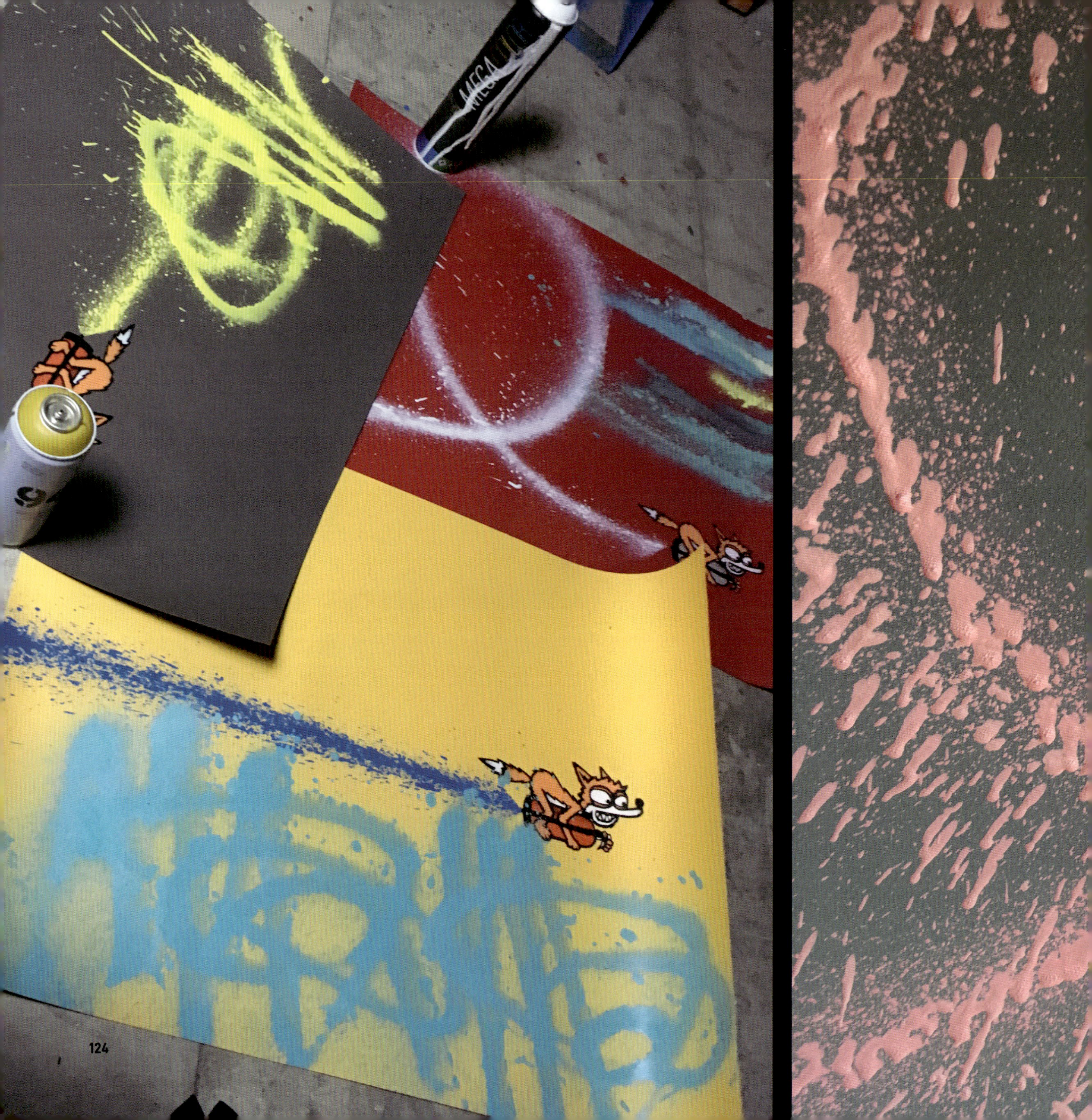

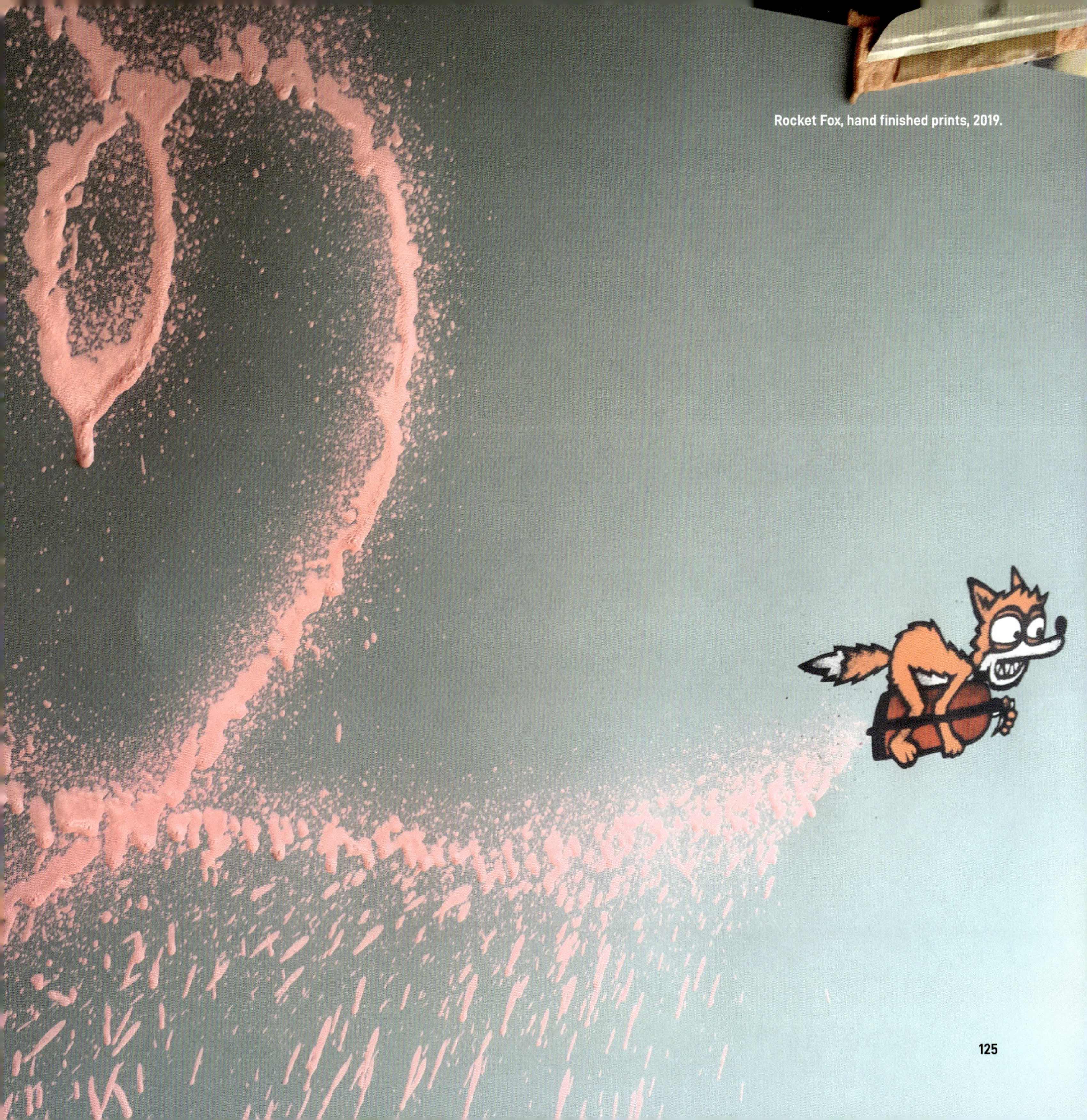

Rocket Fox, hand finished prints, 2019.

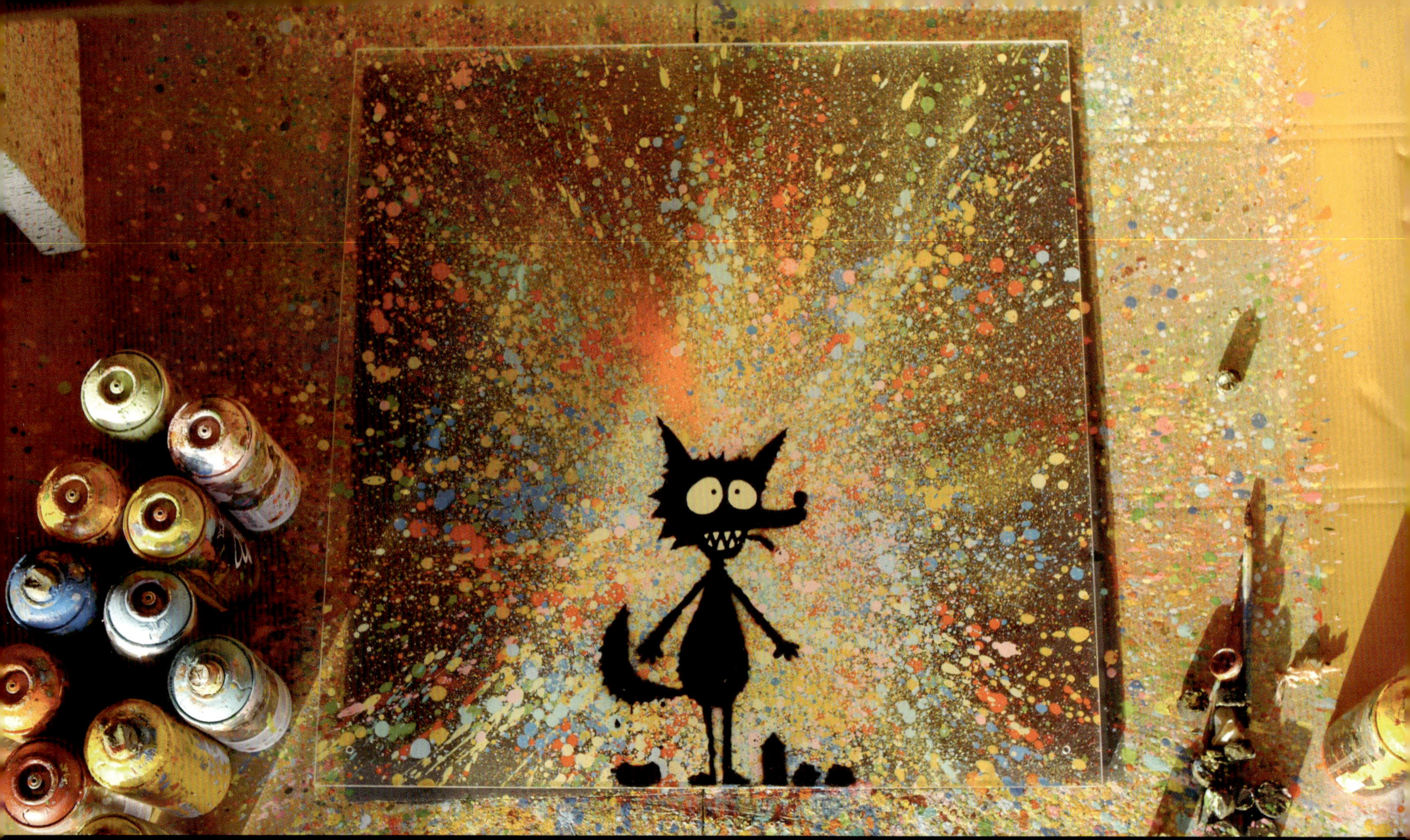

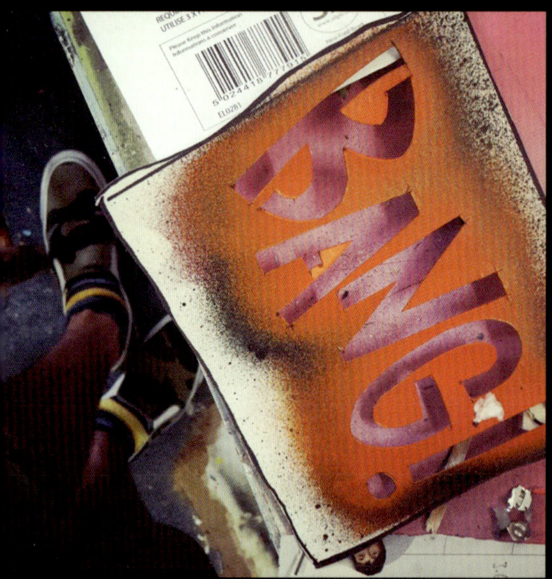

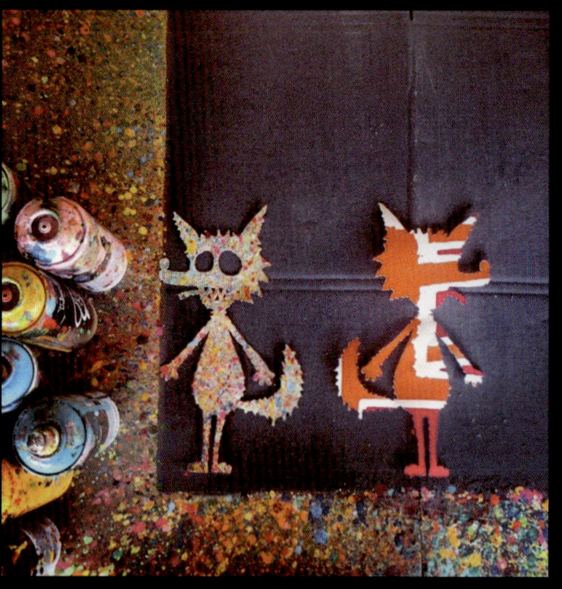

Paint Bomb Fox, SOS edition, 2014.

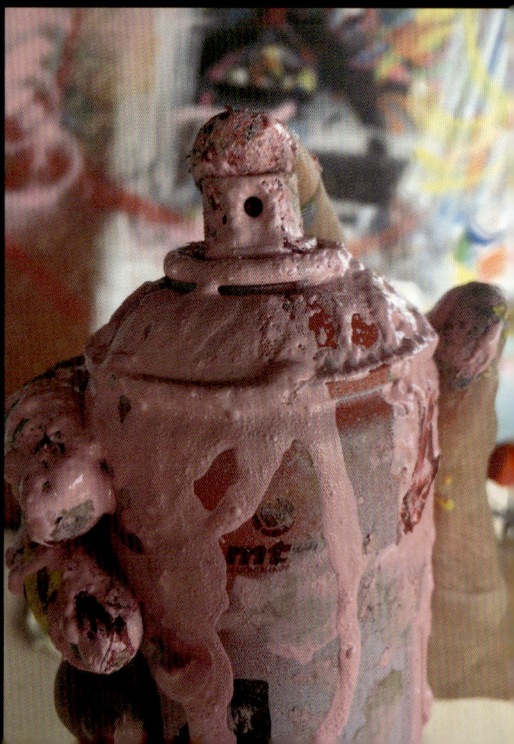

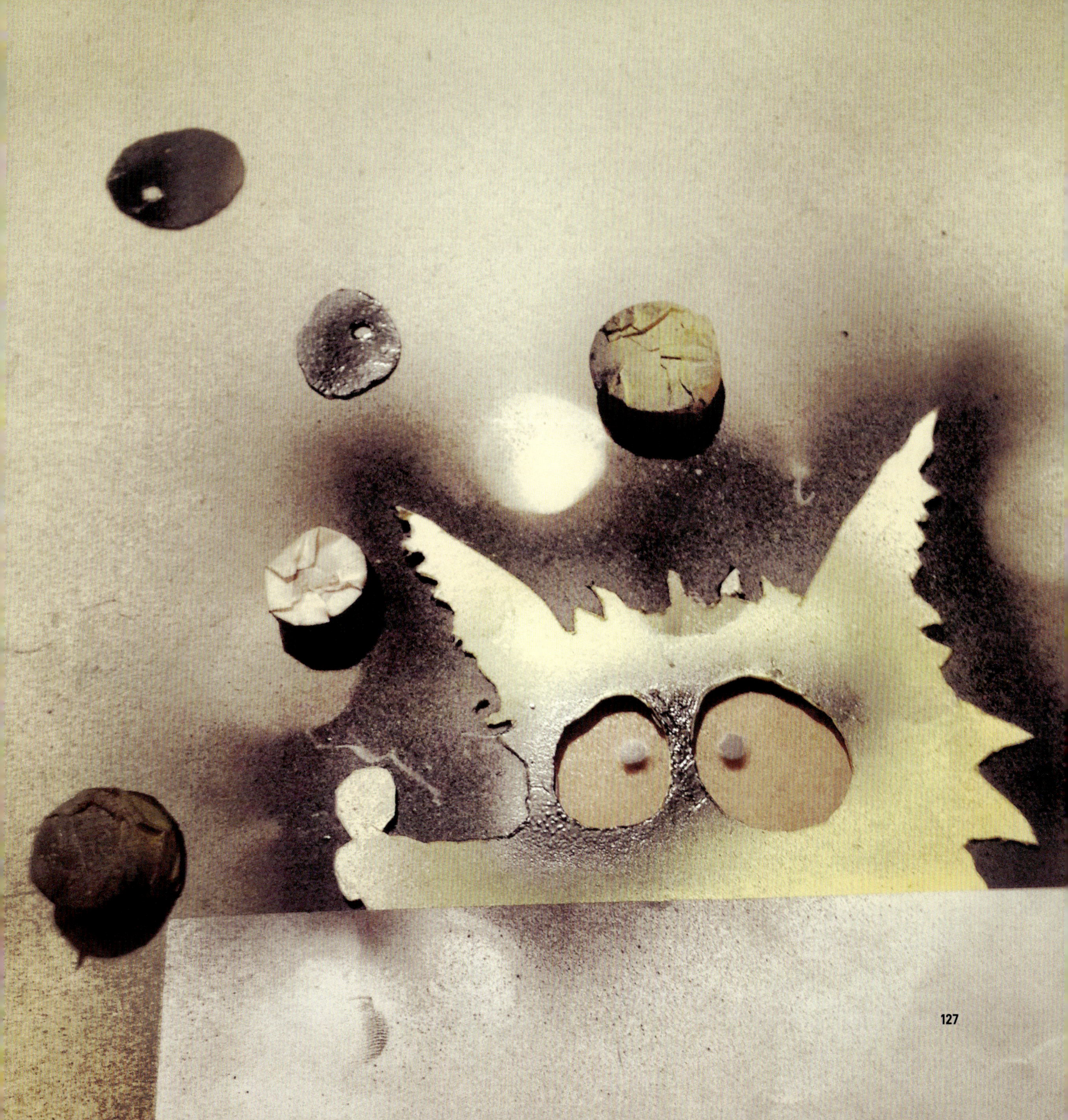

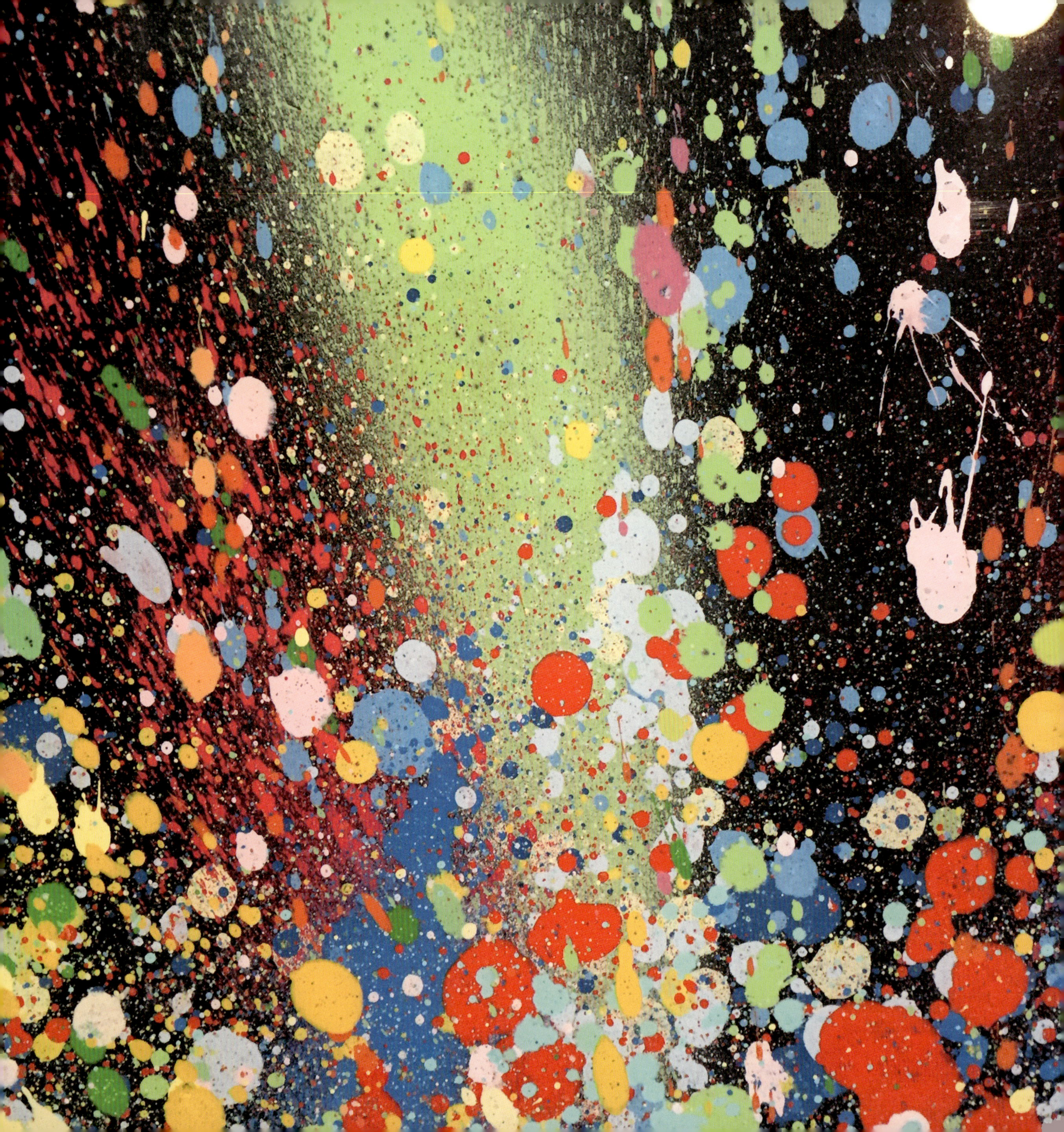

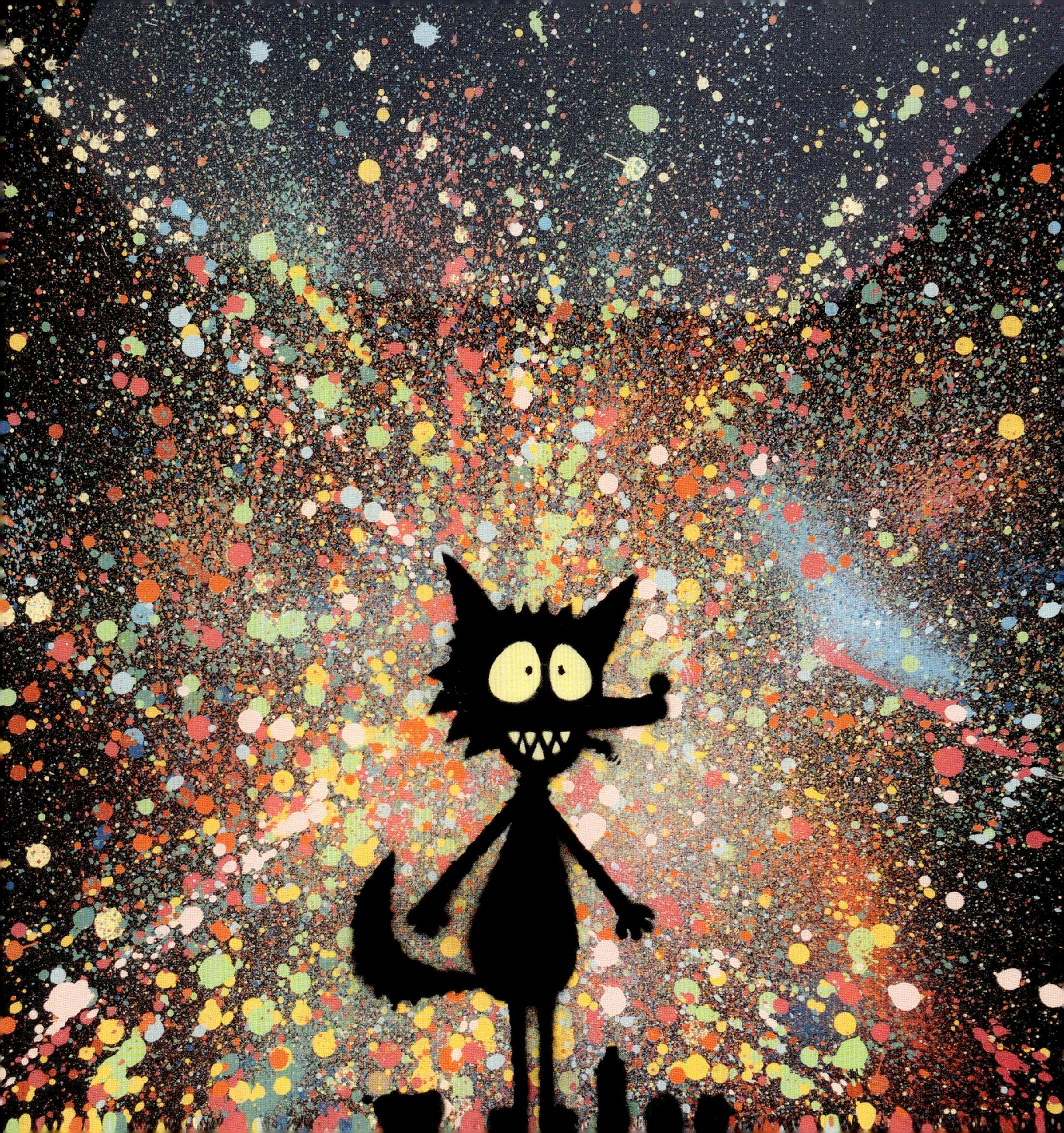

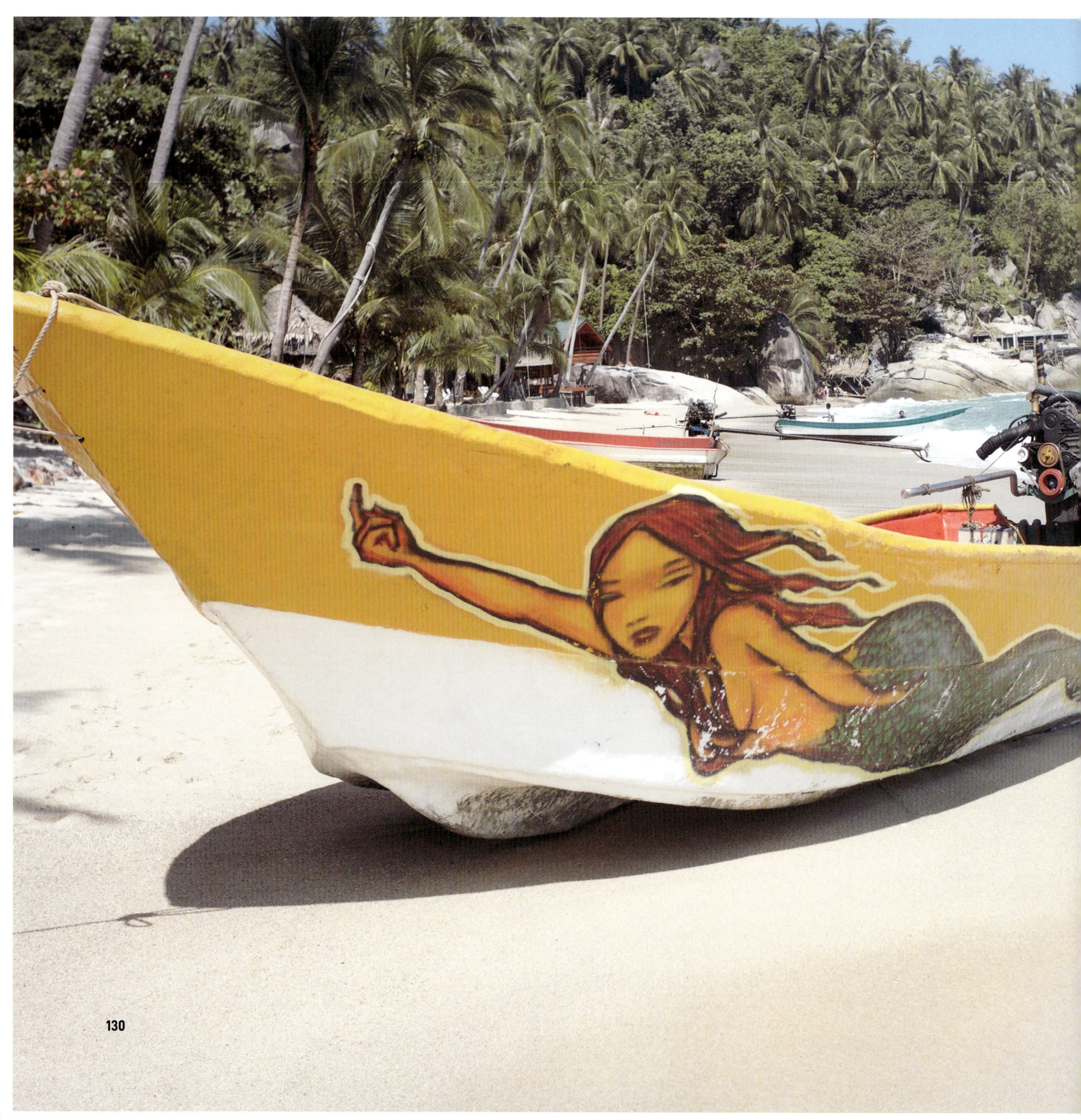

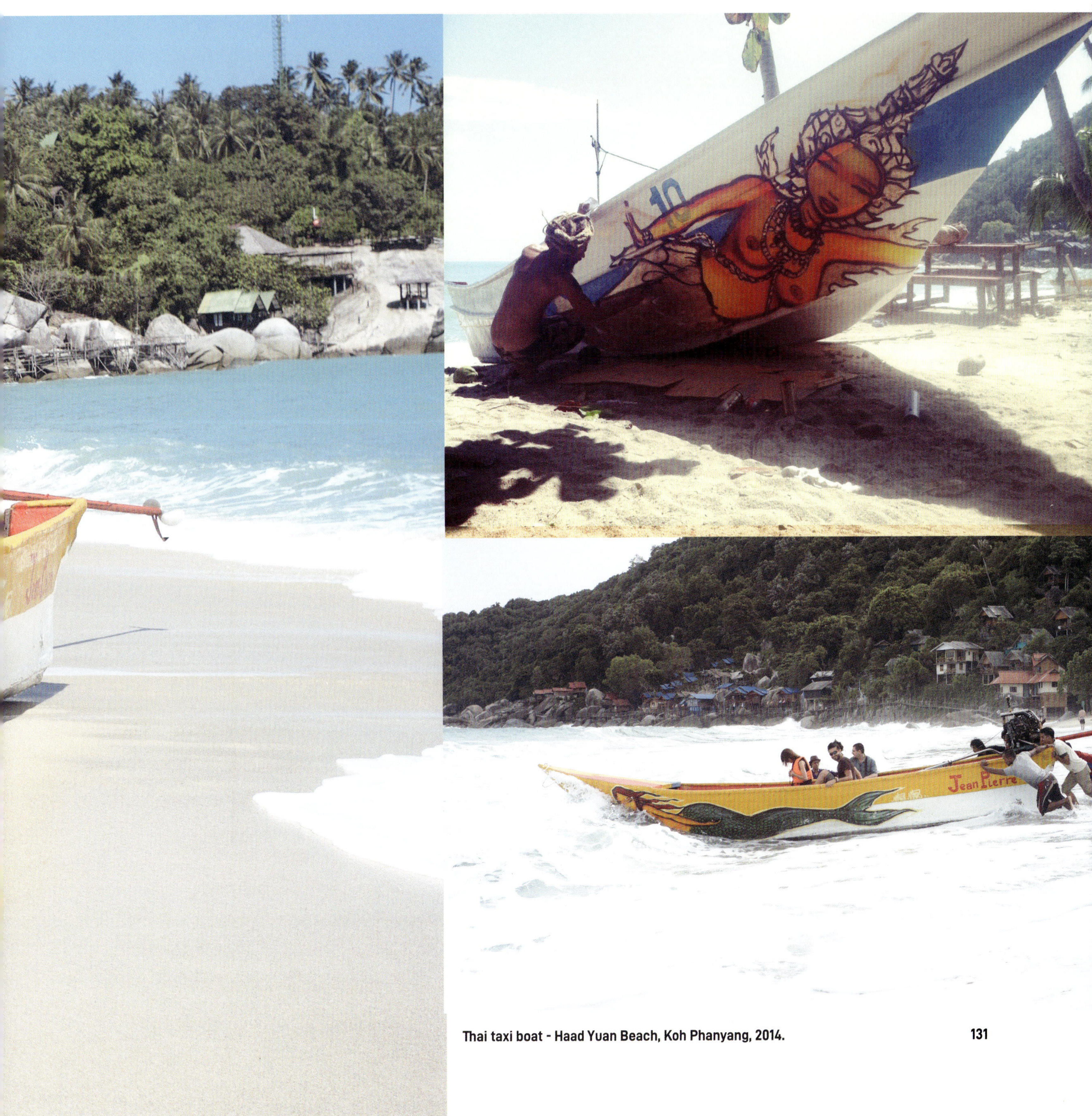

Thai taxi boat - Haad Yuan Beach, Koh Phanyang, 2014.

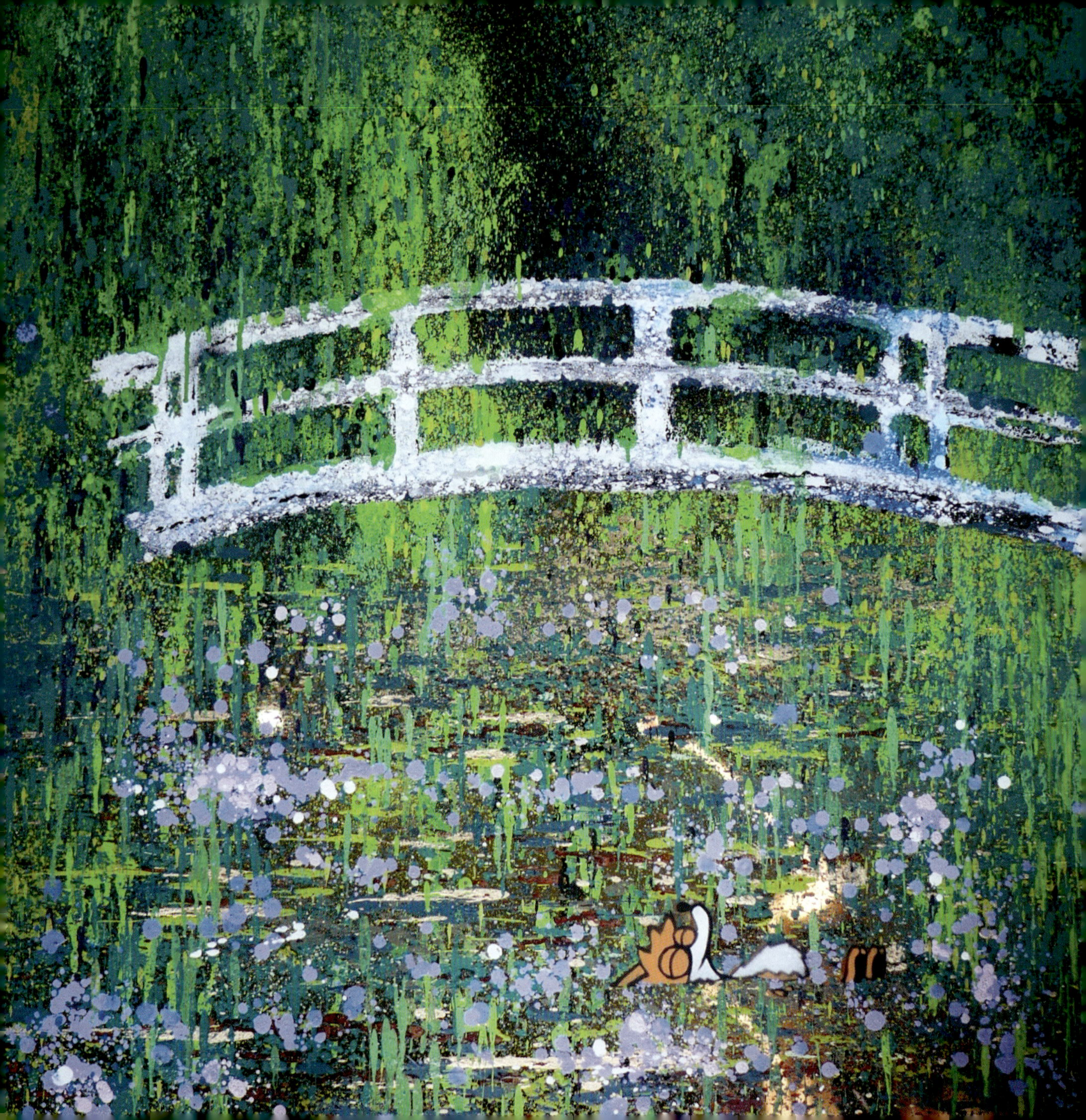

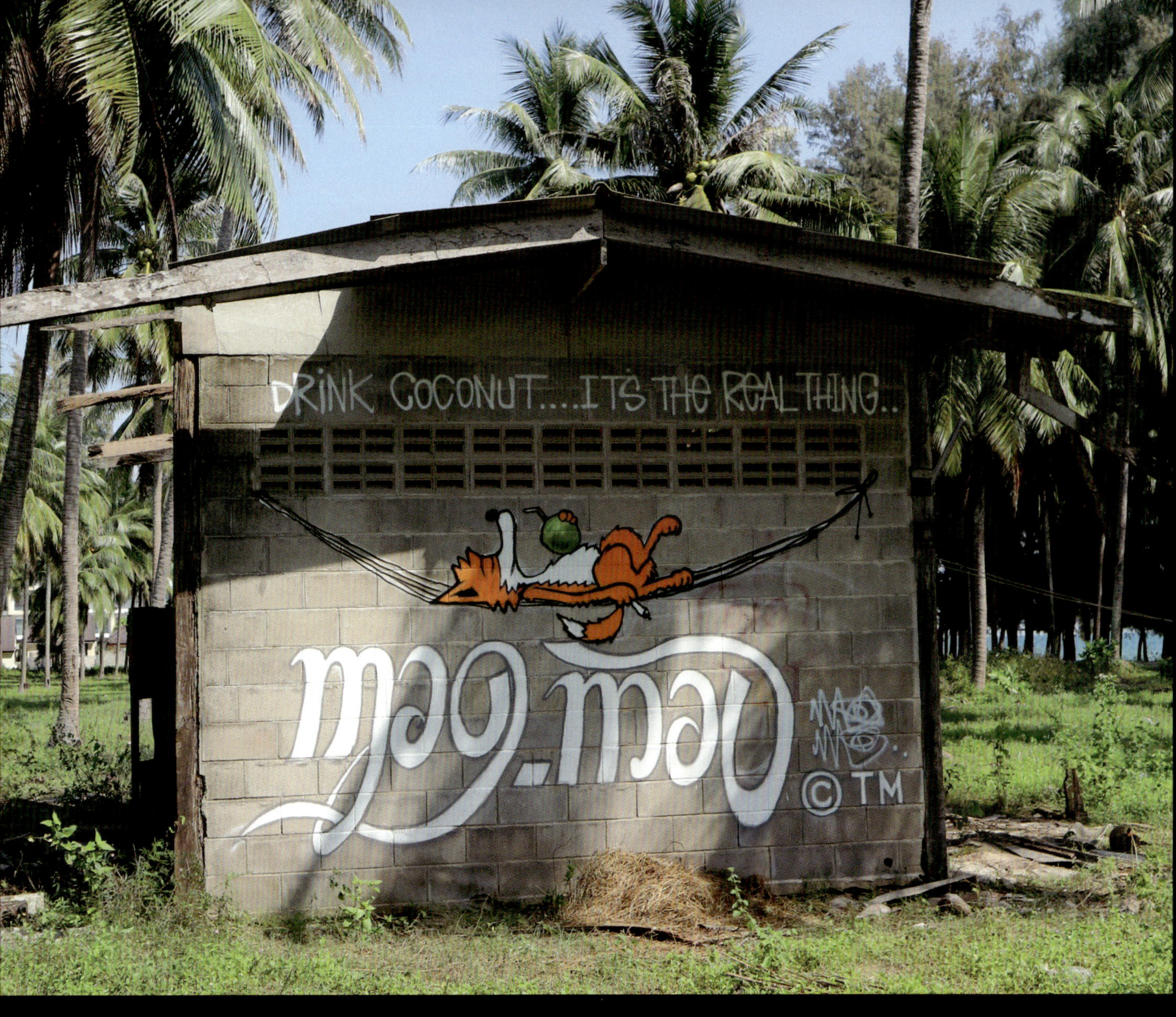

Drink coconut, its the real thing..Bang Saphan, 2022.

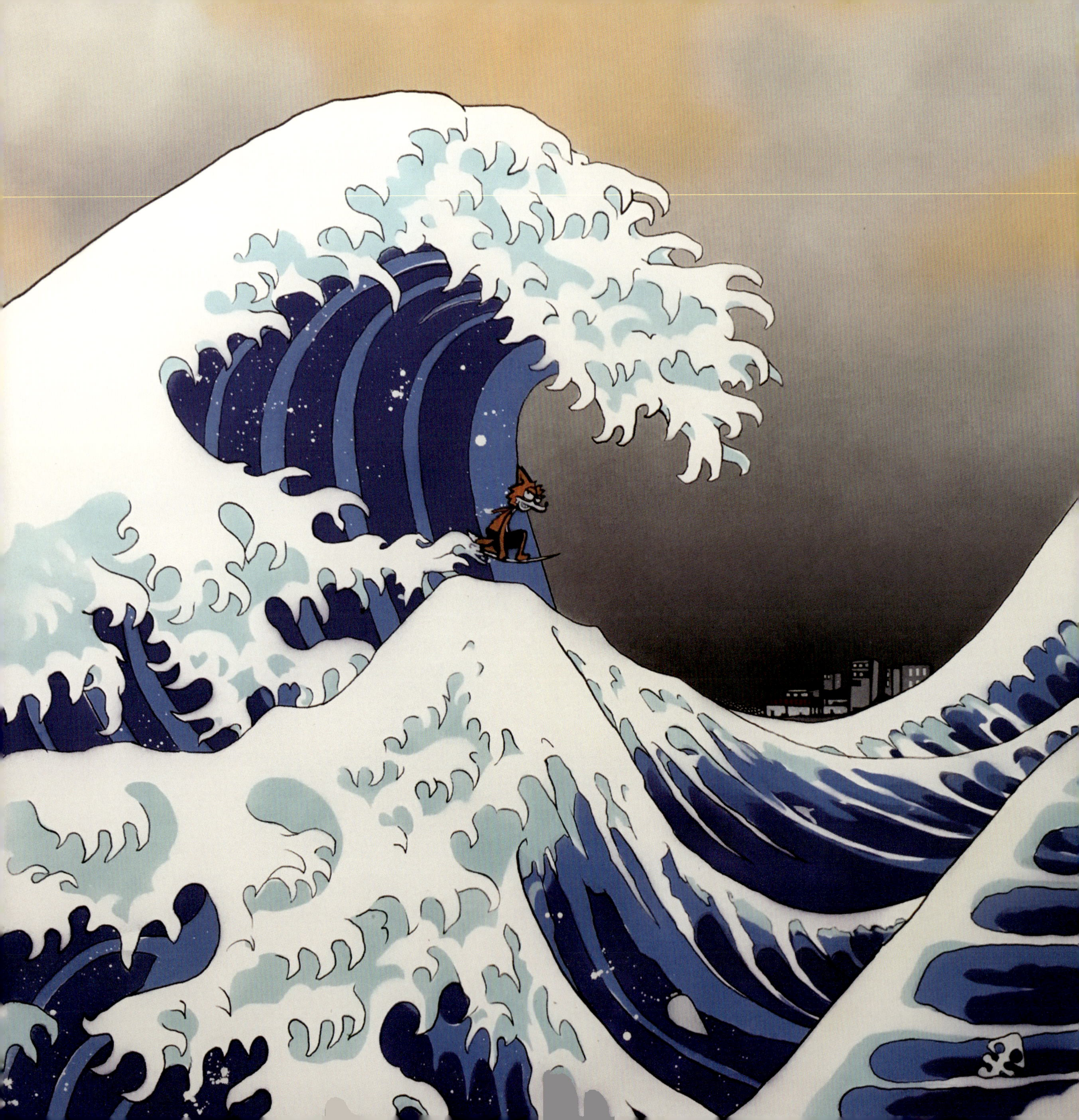

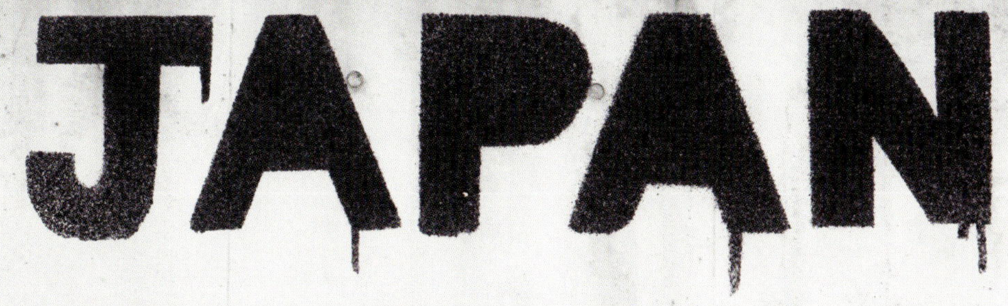

JAPAN

The first time I met Seigo, he arrived at Bangkok airport wearing a hat with the word 'FUCK' on it so we would be able to recognise him. Seigo is a street art dealer who is not your traditional Japanese businessman. When protestors shut down the same airport a few days later he ended up crashing on the couch in my hotel room and we hung out at the Souled Out studio working on an edition.

A year later he invited me out to do a show in Tokyo. That first trip I ended up in a huge theatre in the middle of Tokyo being called up on stage to be applauded by the cast of a musical because the director had used one of my images in the show's promotional material. I didn't have a clue what was going on. But that's been my experience of Japan, it's always filled with random encounters.

At the first show I met some TV producers who said they liked my art. We had a conversation about work, but something must have got lost in translation. When I went back the following year, this time with Beejoir, I was told they had used some of my images on a TV Soap they were making.

I assumed it would just be in the background of a street scene or something. We arrived on set and were introduced to 'Mau Mau Town'. They'd reproduced my pieces everywhere – copying them on walls, drinks machines and even road signs.

I love Japan but it took me a few trips to get my head around the cultural difference and the Japanese way of doing things; right down to the way the Japanese consume my art. The image is often more important than the sentiment or messaging behind the work. Often it's more about enjoying the cartoon character style of the image rather than the message.

On the street things are different. Japan is a very orderly culture and painting illegal spots is all the more risky as a result. Whenever I paint, on legal walls or as part of a show, I always attract a crowd and there is real interest and awe in the art making process.

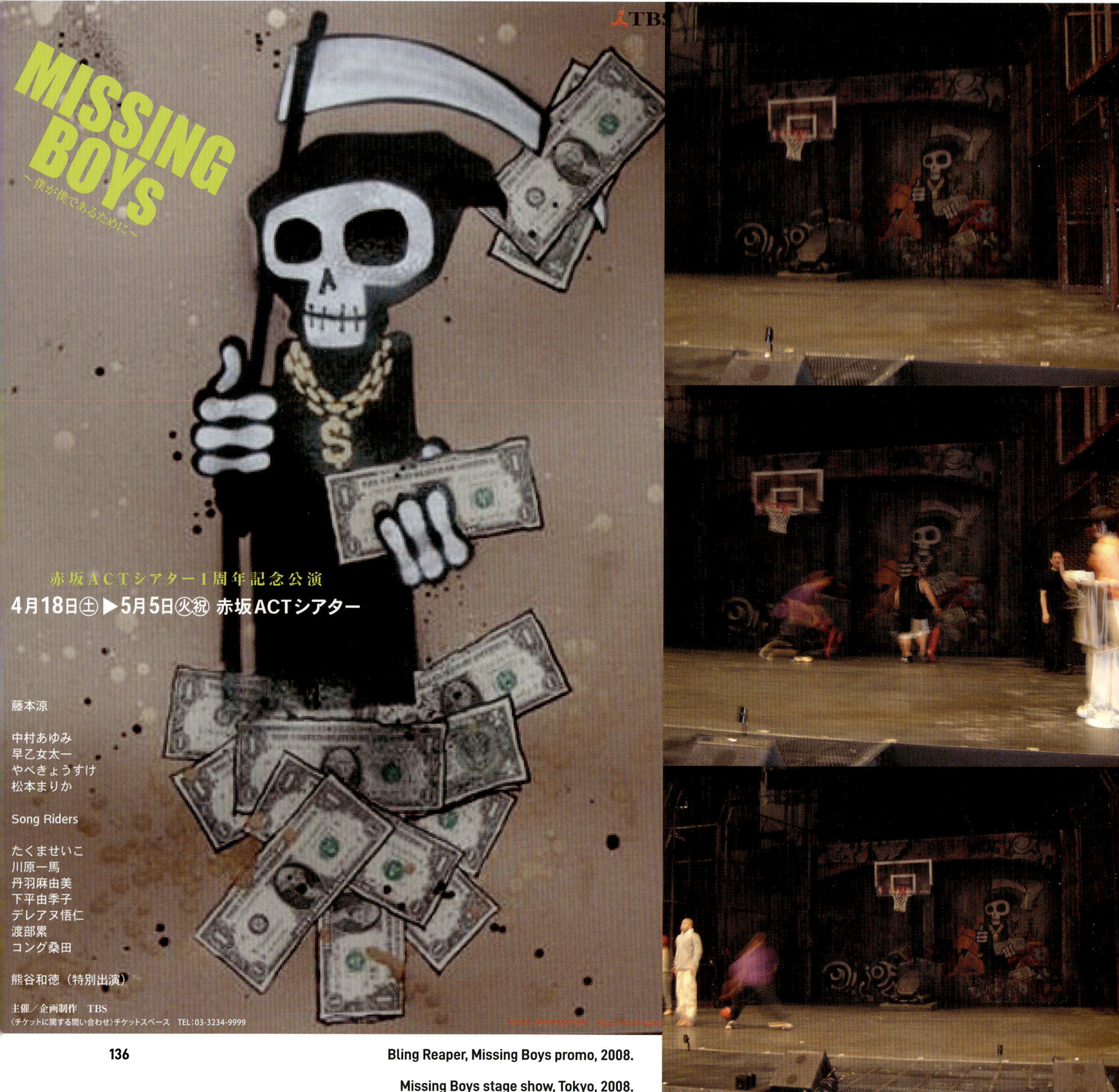

Bling Reaper, Missing Boys promo, 2008.

Missing Boys stage show, Tokyo, 2008.

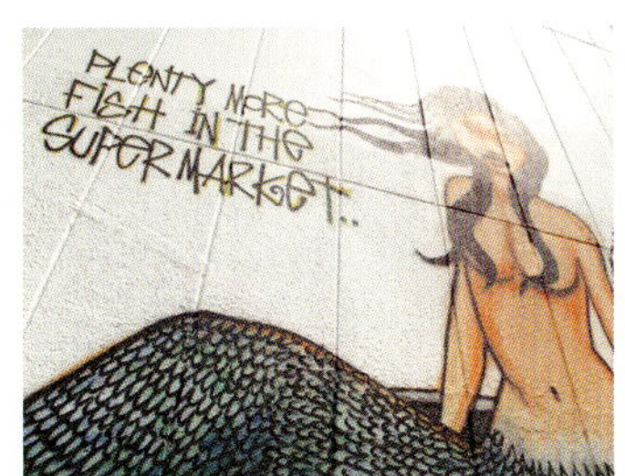

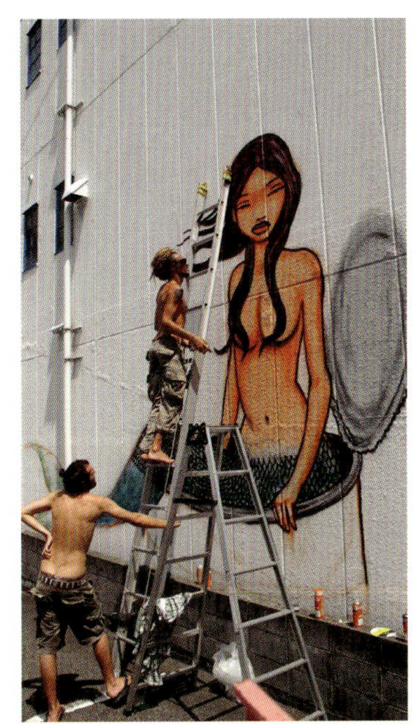

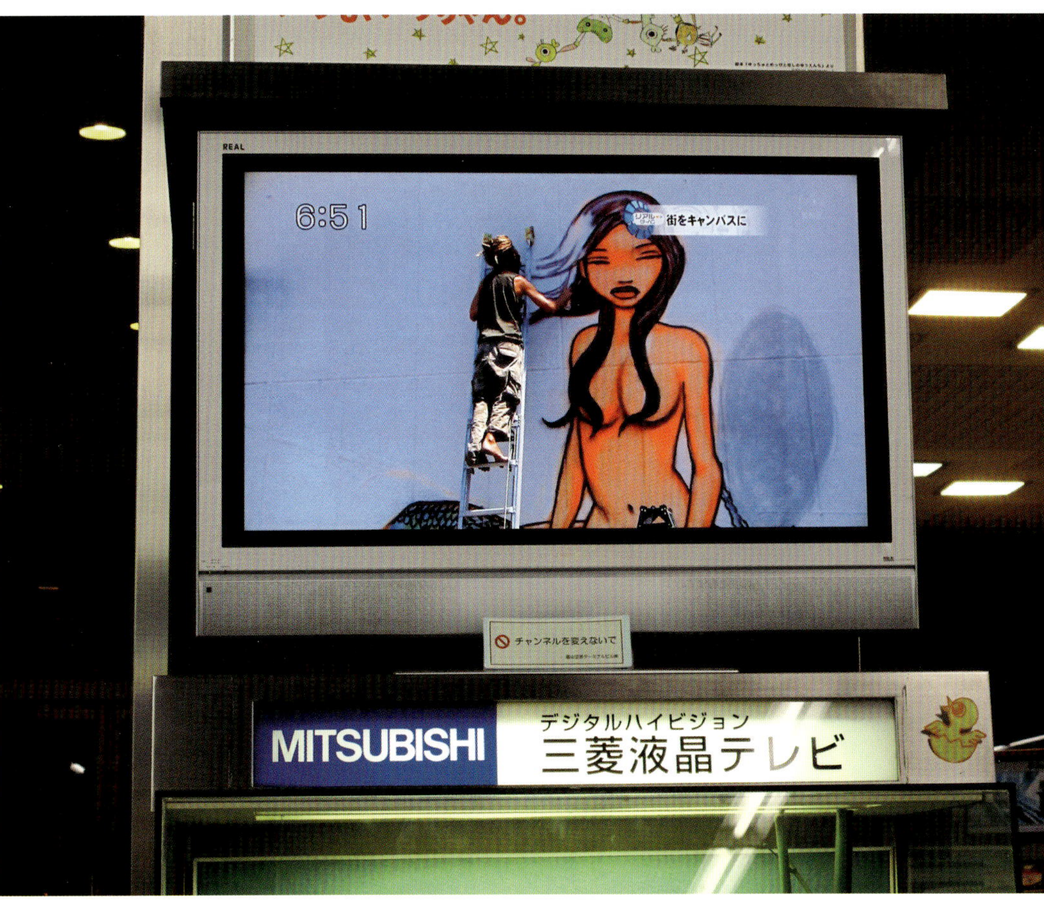

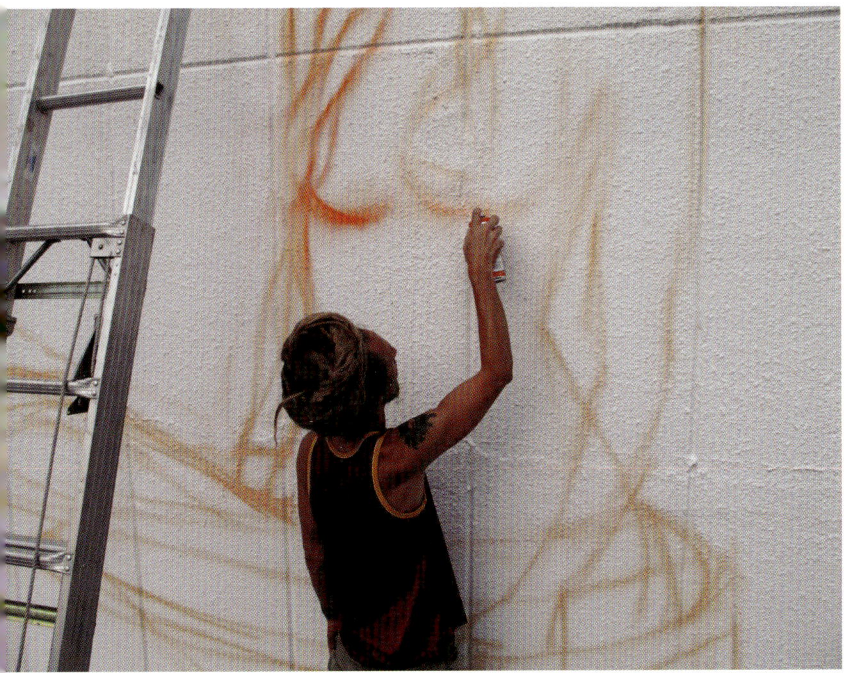

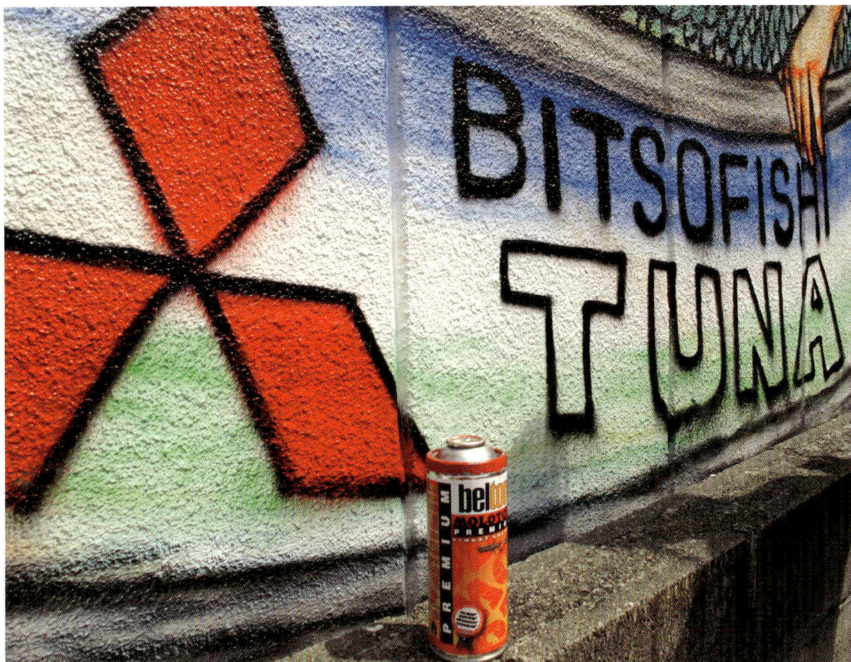

Plenty More Fish in the Factory, Toyama, 2009.

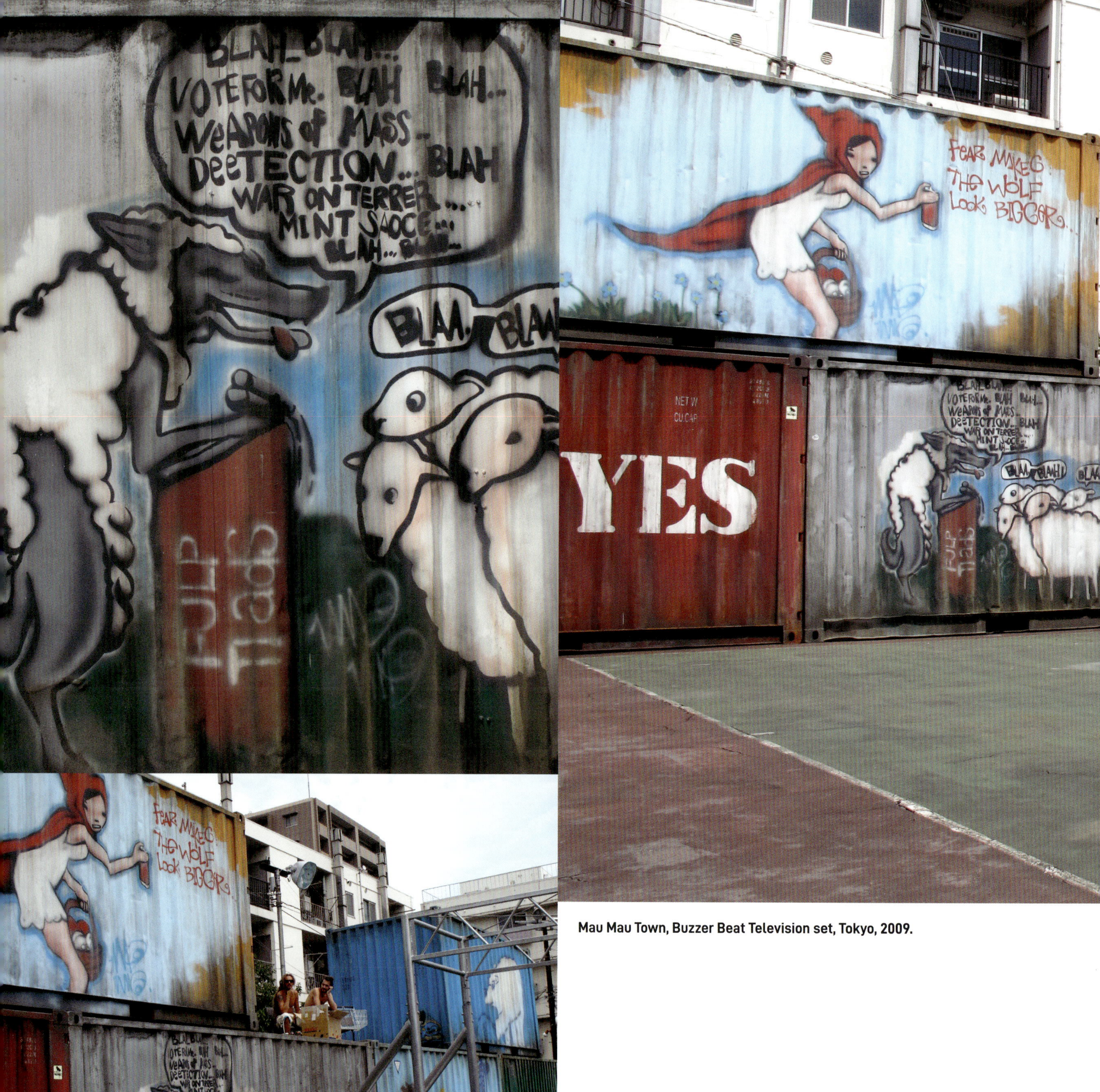

Mau Mau Town, Buzzer Beat Television set, Tokyo, 2009.

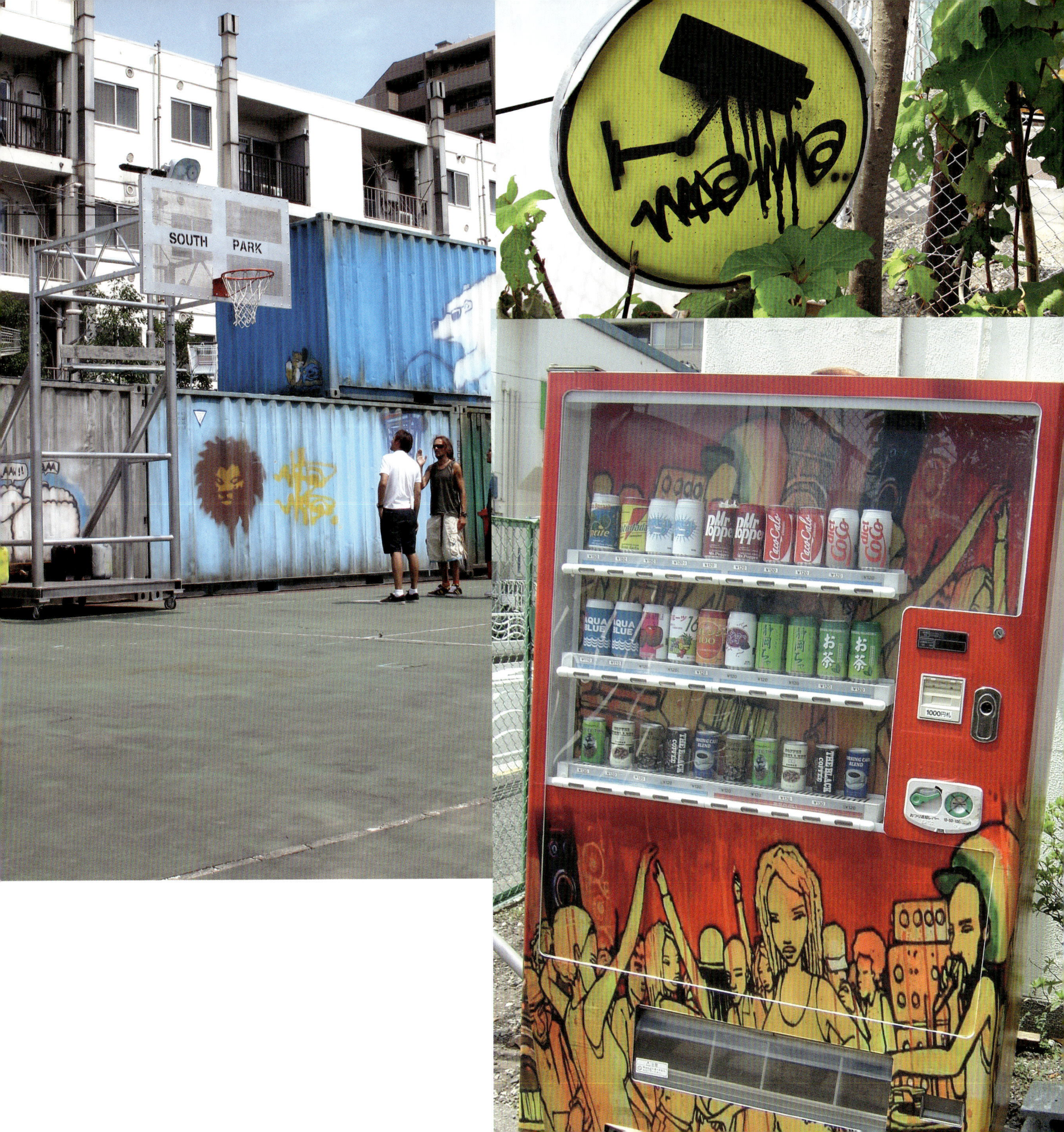
SOUTH PARK

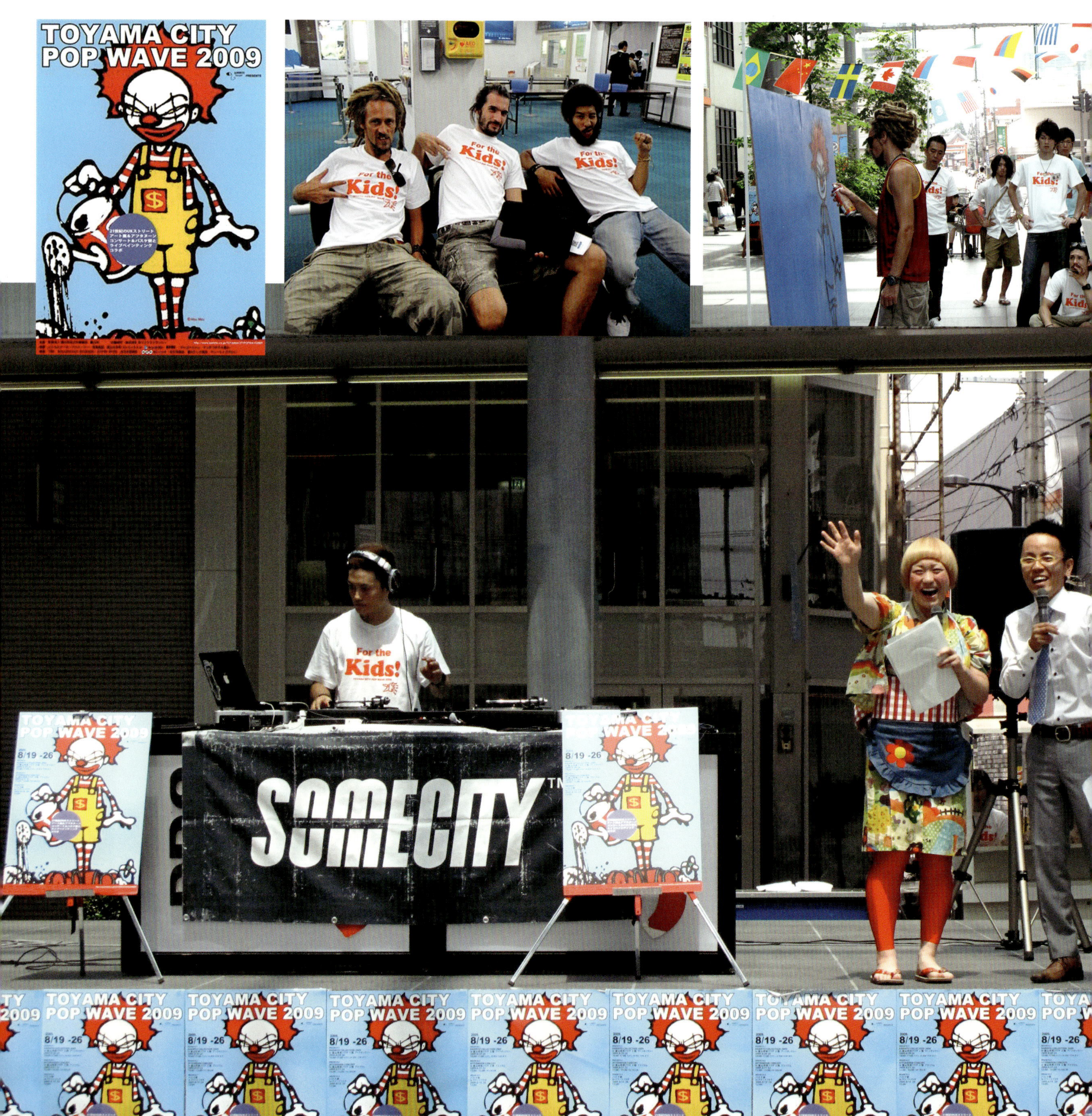

TOYAMA CITY
POP WAVE 2009
For the
Kids!
SOMECITY
8/19 -26

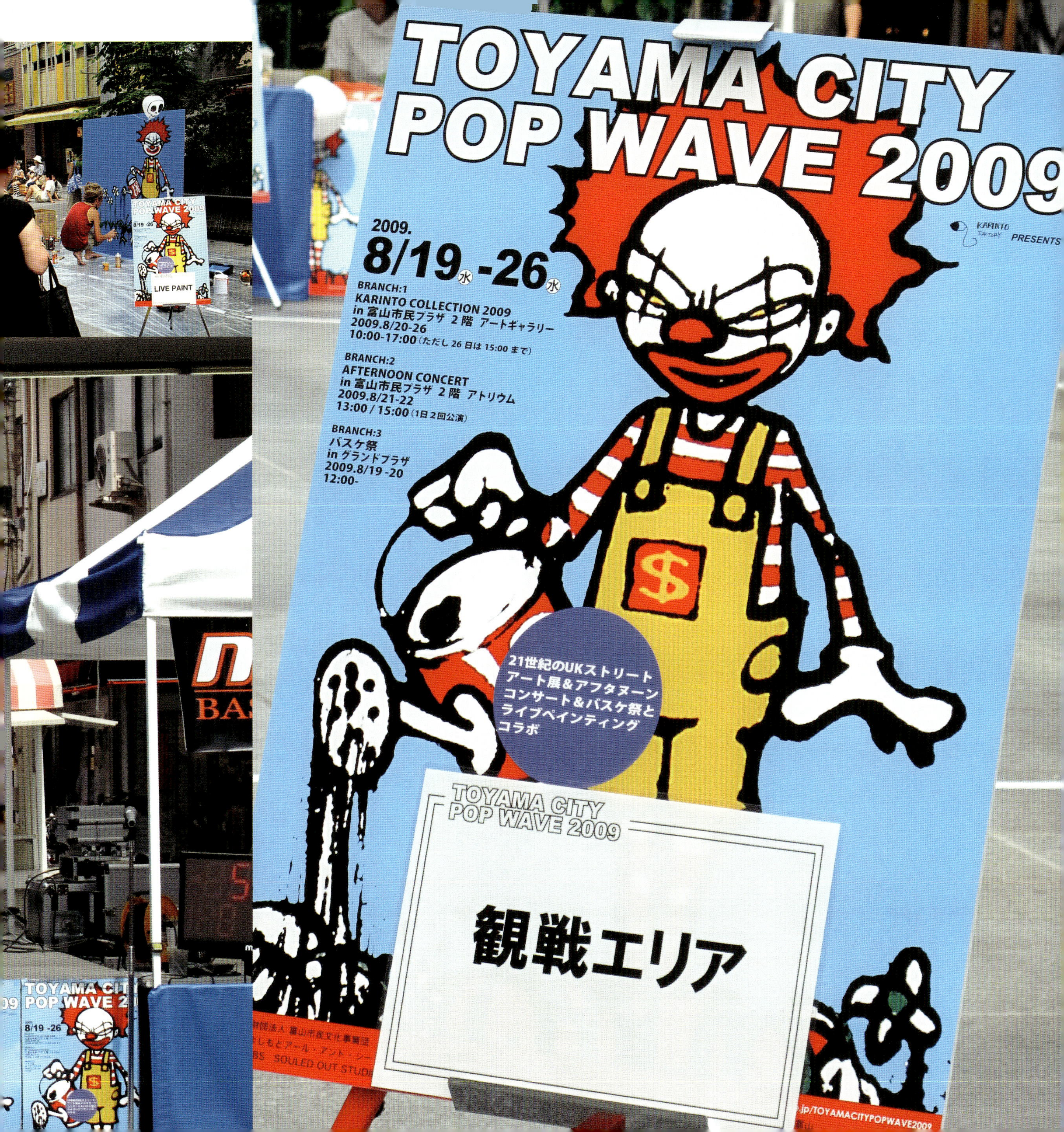

LIVE PAINT
TOYAMA CITY
POP WAVE 2009
KARINTO FACTORY PRESENTS
2009.
8/19(水)-26(水)
BRANCH:1
KARINTO COLLECTION 2009
in 富山市民プラザ 2階 アートギャラリー
2009.8/20-26
10:00-17:00（ただし 26 日は 15:00 まで）
BRANCH:2
AFTERNOON CONCERT
in 富山市民プラザ 2階 アトリウム
2009.8/21-22
13:00 / 15:00（1日 2回公演）
BRANCH:3
バスケ祭
in グランドプラザ
2009.8/19 -20
12:00-
21世紀のUKストリートアート展＆アフタヌーンコンサート＆バスケ祭とライブペインティングコラボ
TOYAMA CITY
POP WAVE 2009
観戦エリア
.jp/TOYAMACITYPOPWAVE2009

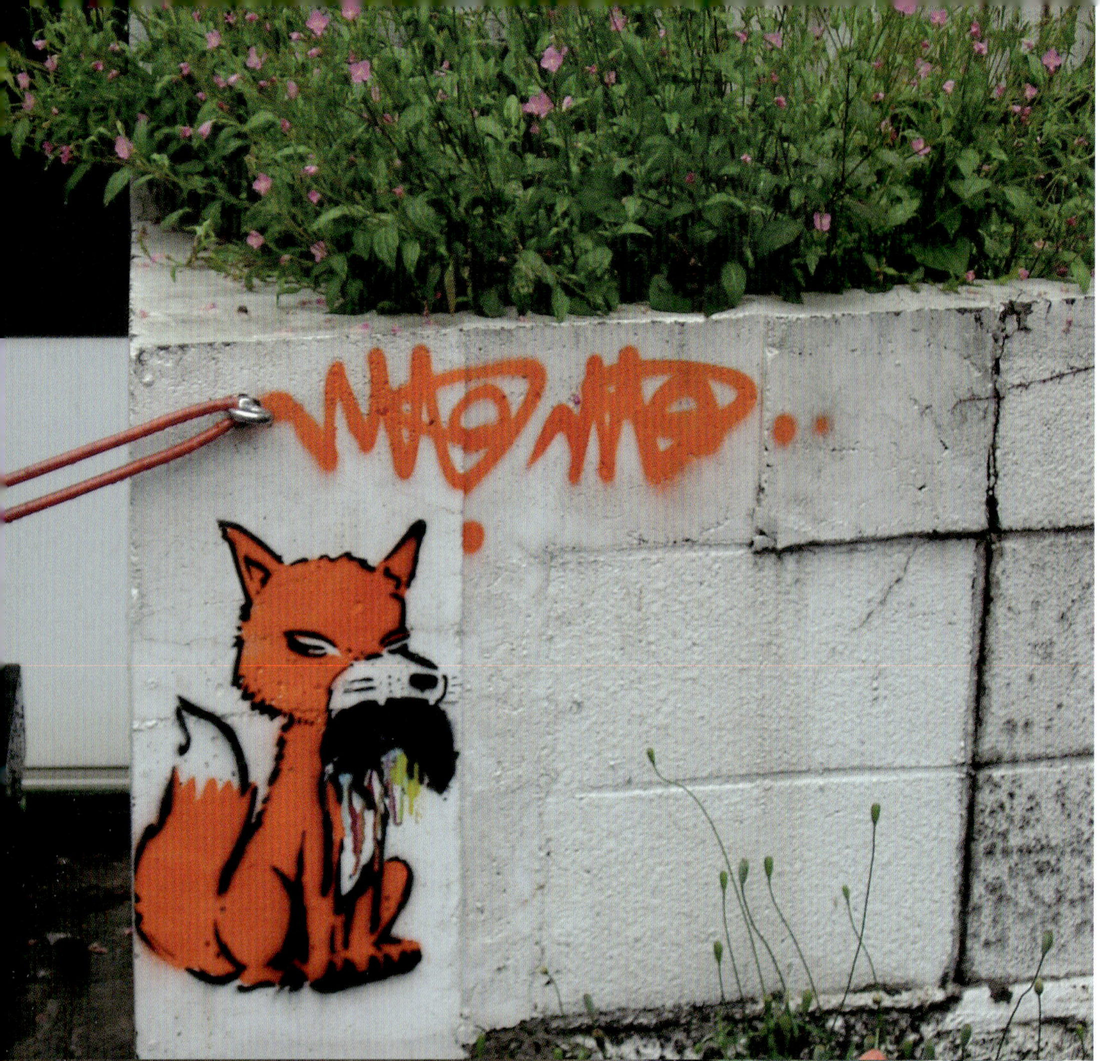

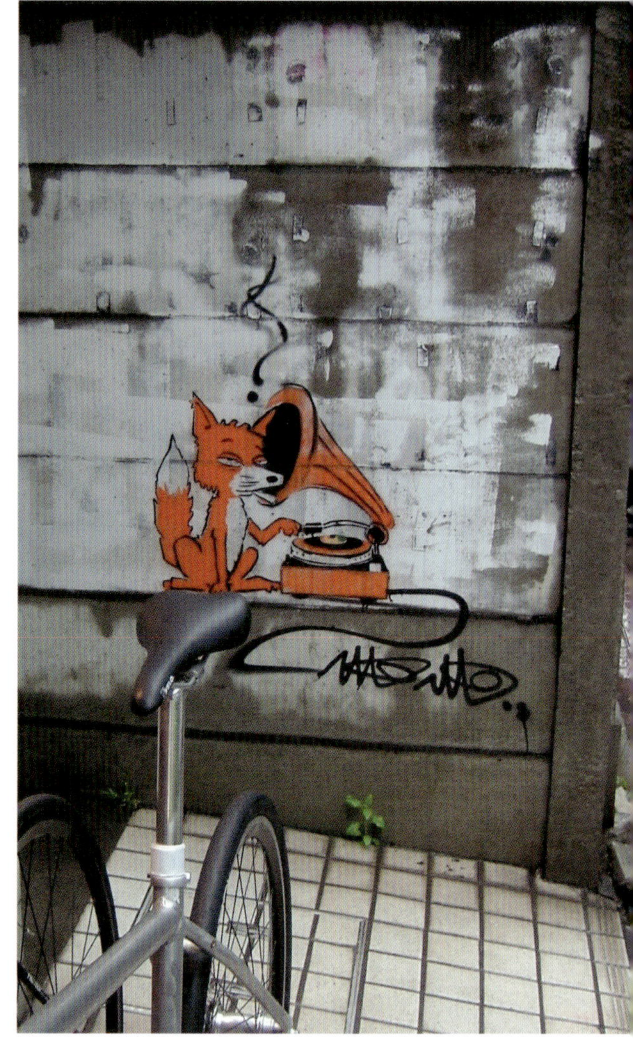

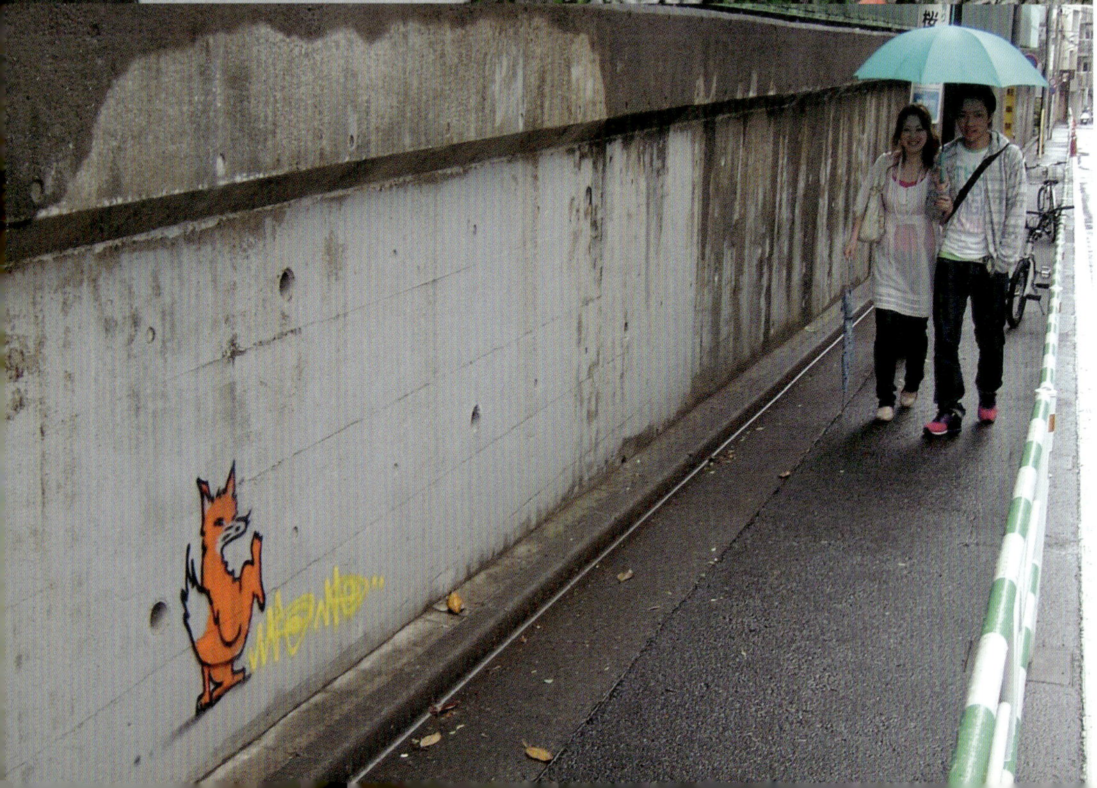

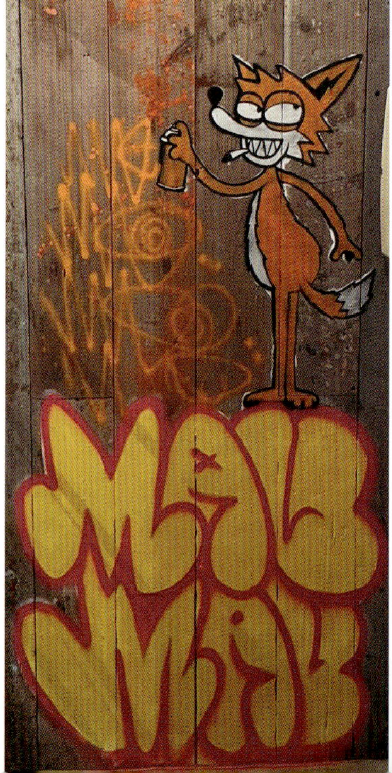

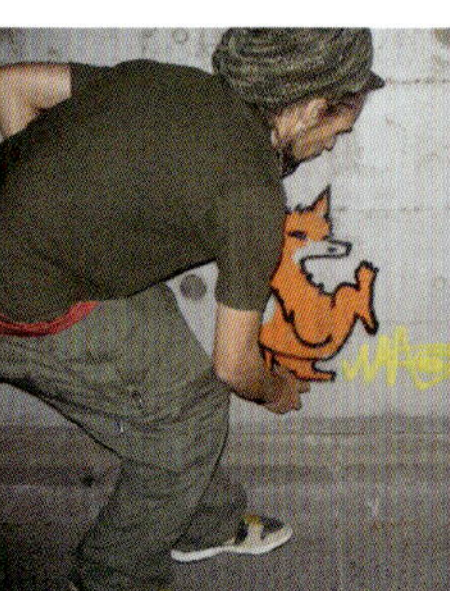

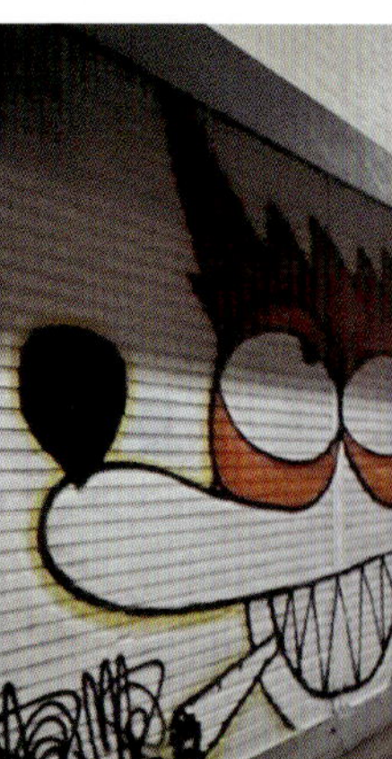

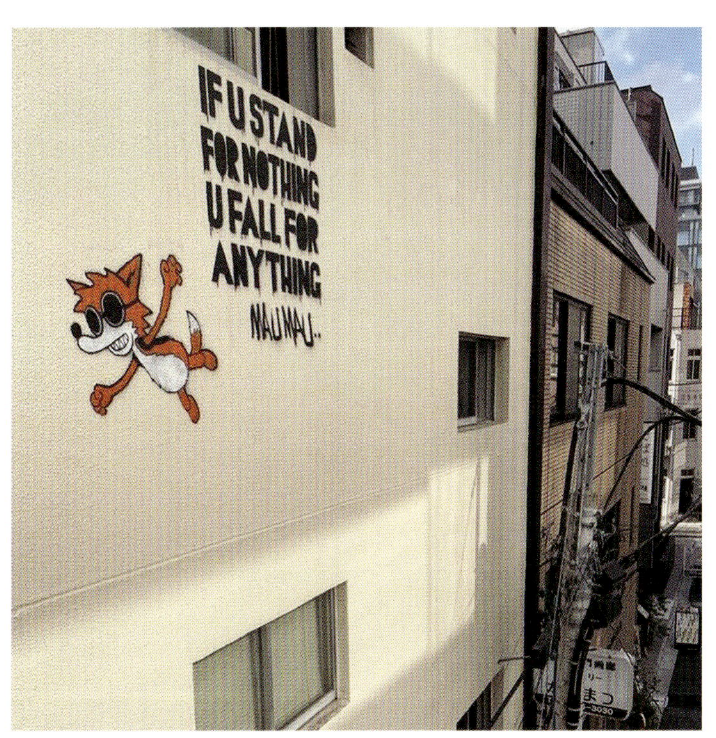

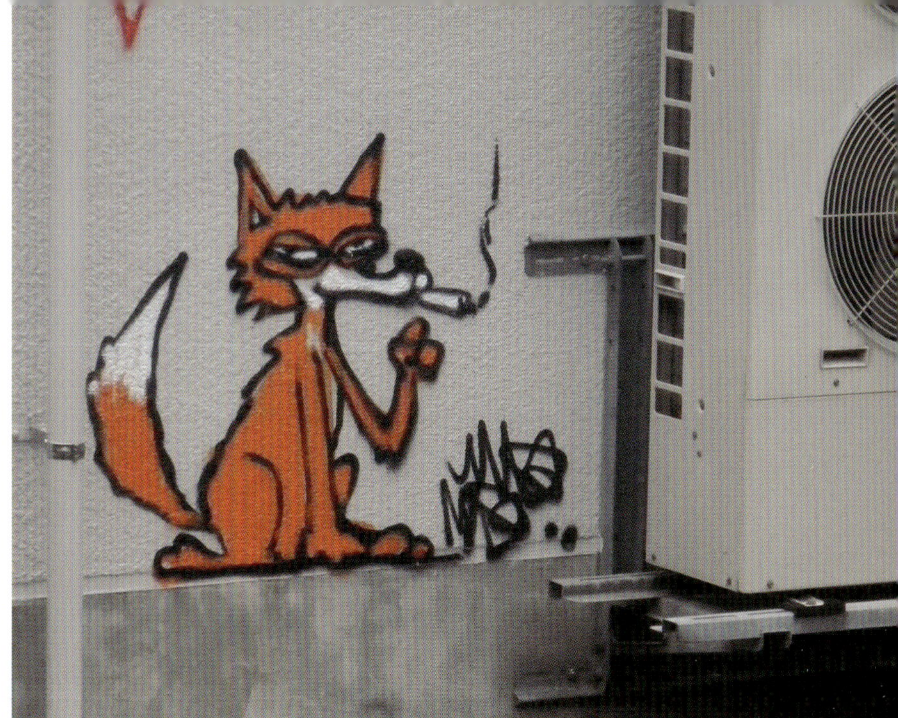

Original Street Foxes, Tokyo, 2008 to 2022

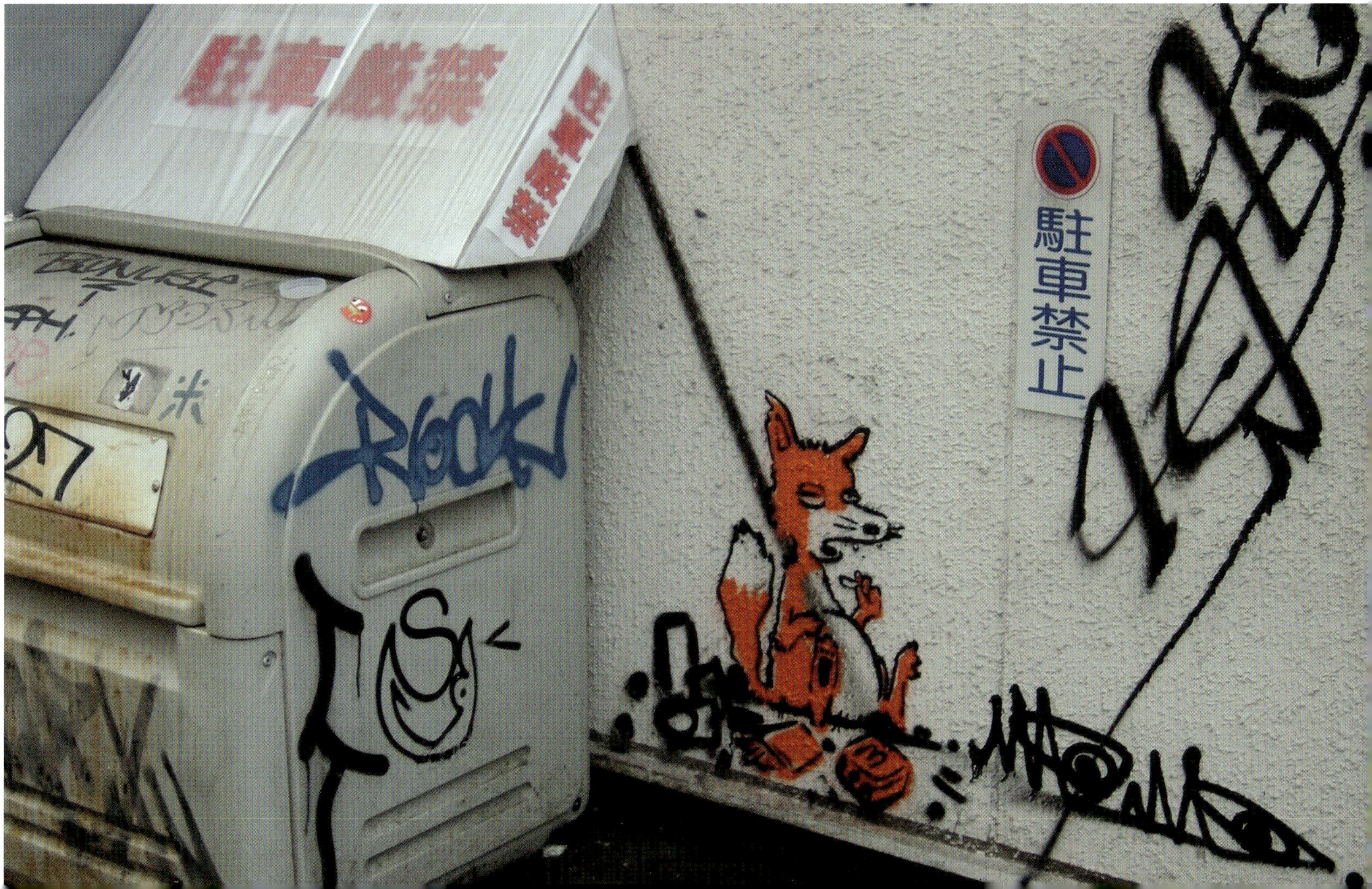

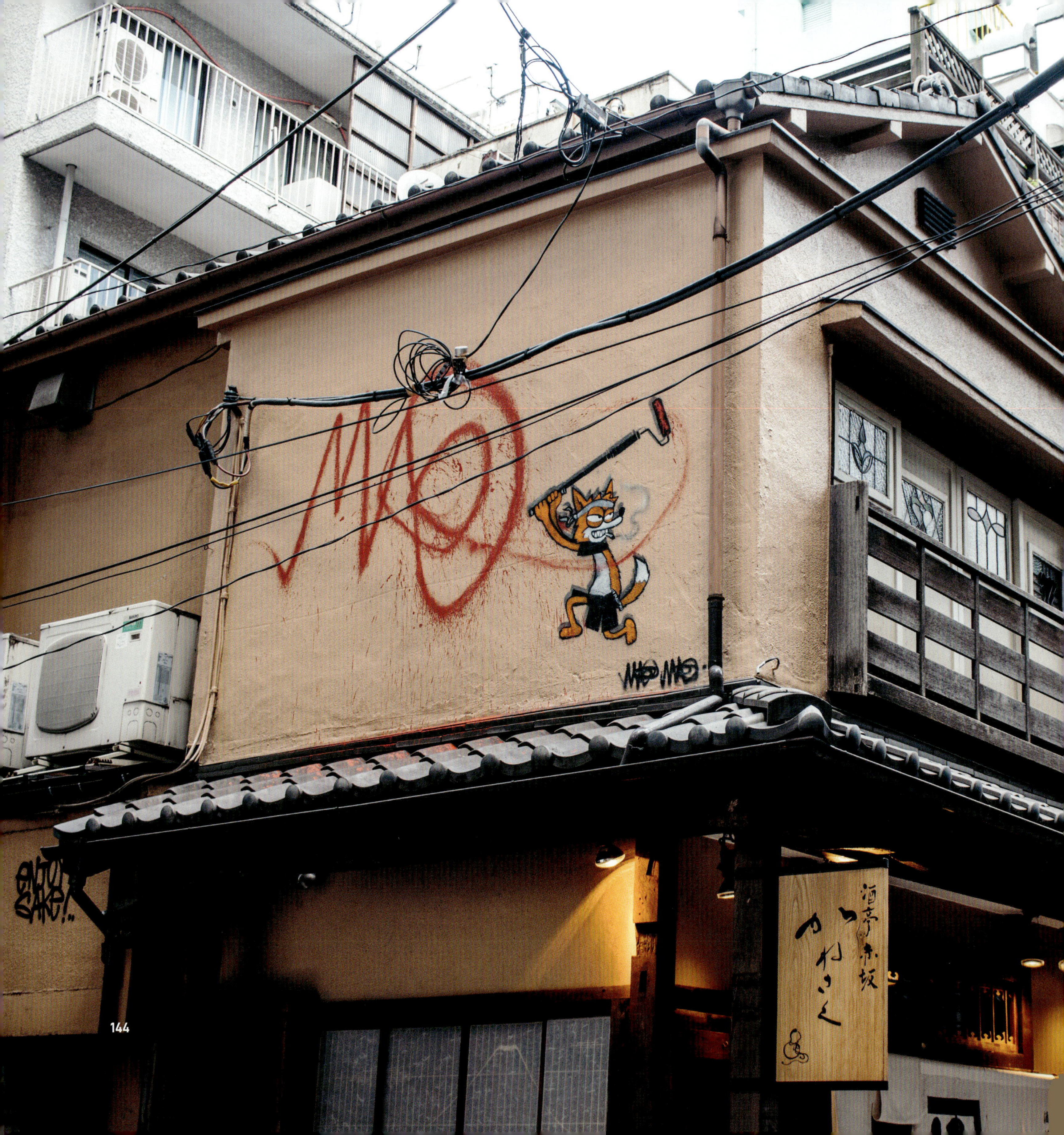
酒亭赤坂

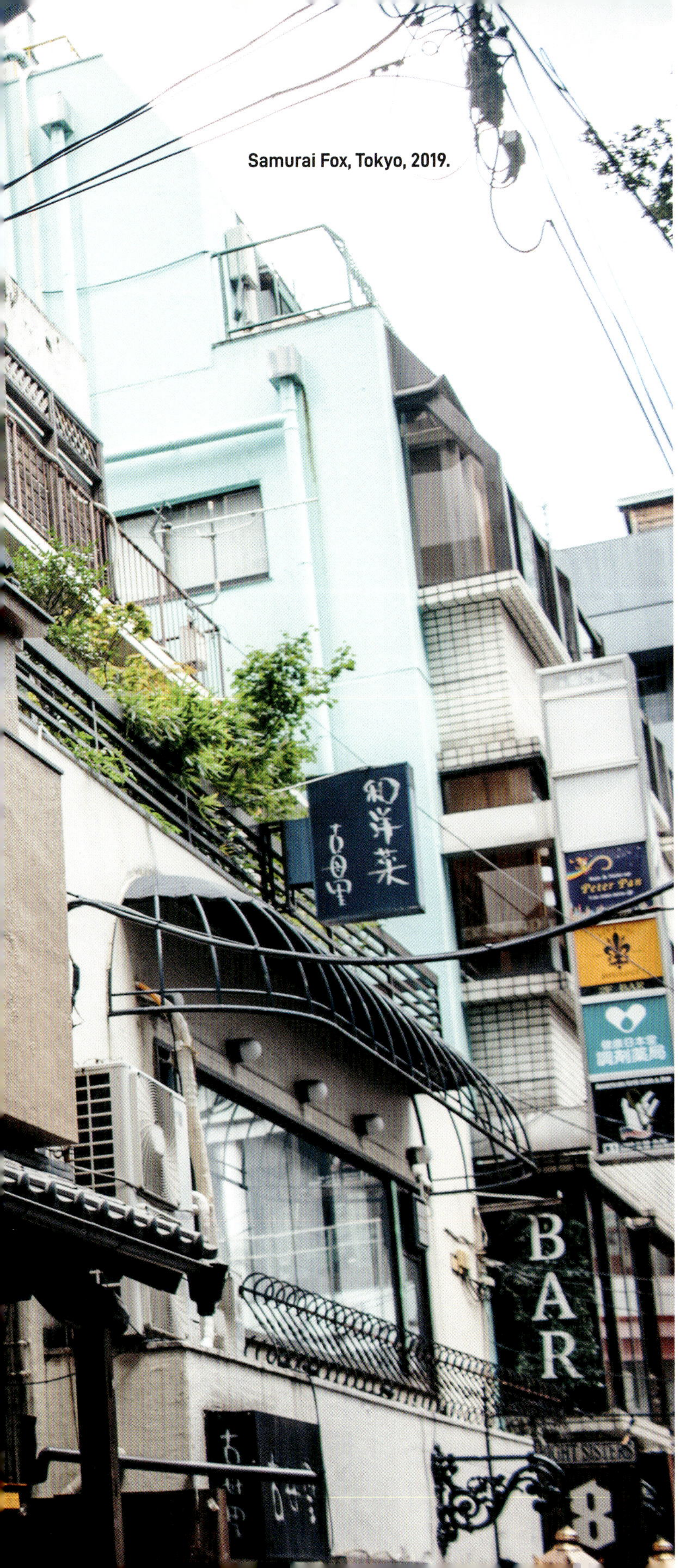

Samurai Fox, Tokyo, 2019.

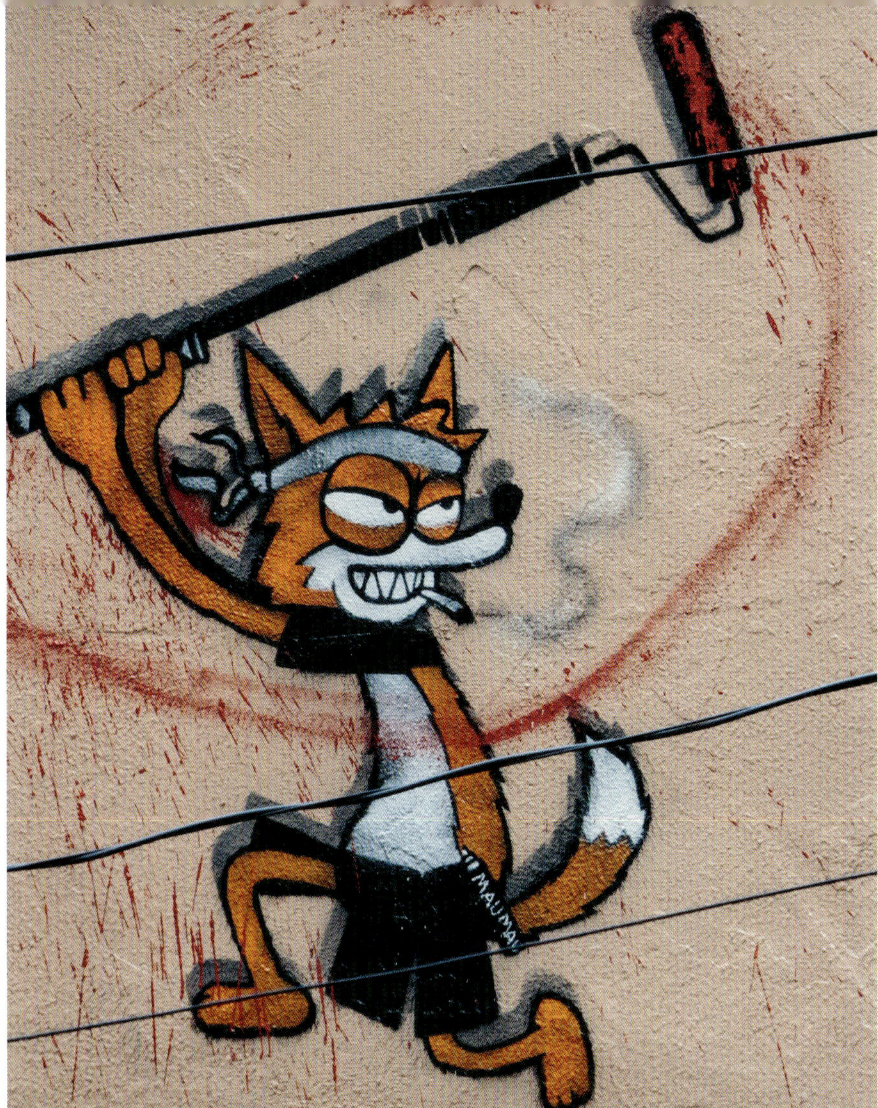

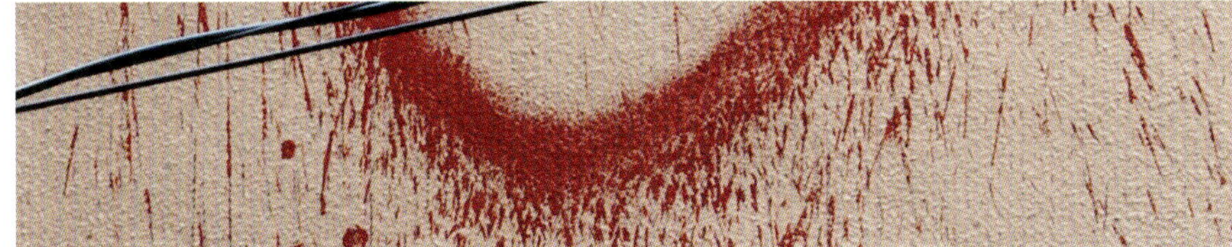

Japanese shows are very different too. I always end up signing a lot of autographs and many buyers will want the work signed and personalised to them. This desire to 'own' the work is really refreshing compared to the norm in other countries where my art is often seen as a commodity with clean signatures and edition numbers giving it resale value.

In Japan loyalty to the work goes to whole new levels. When I'm doing a show I will have people who have previously bought my work come to see the exhibition and bring me gifts. I don't get that anywhere else in the world...

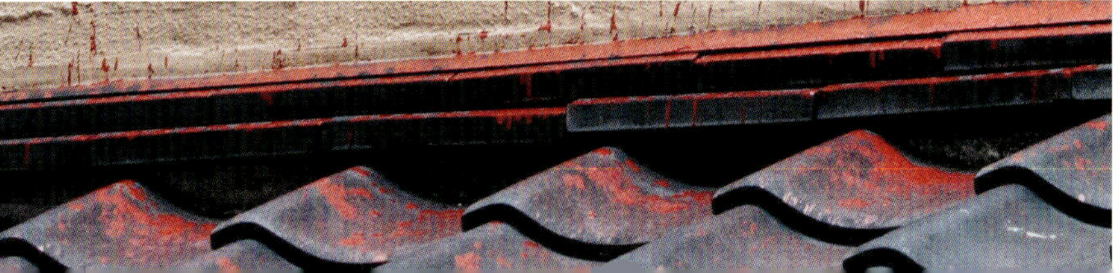

6:50
ストリートアーティスト
Mr.MAUMAU(ロンドン出身)
MITSUBISHI
デジタルハイビジョン
三菱液晶テレビ

SOULED OUT... GALLERY SHOW!
KIRISHI 6-10
OPEN TONIGHT
スケートボード禁止
NO Skateboarding

MISSING BOYS

BURNIN' AND ROOTIN'
MAU MAU SOLO EXHIBITION

BEEJOIR
MAU MAU
AT STALL BAGGAGE OPENING 6PM 12 DEC 2014
"2F 3-18-3 Aobadai Meguroku Tokyo 153-0042 JAPAN"

30%~80% OFF SALE

Dear Mau
Gift from
Aiko

MAUMAU

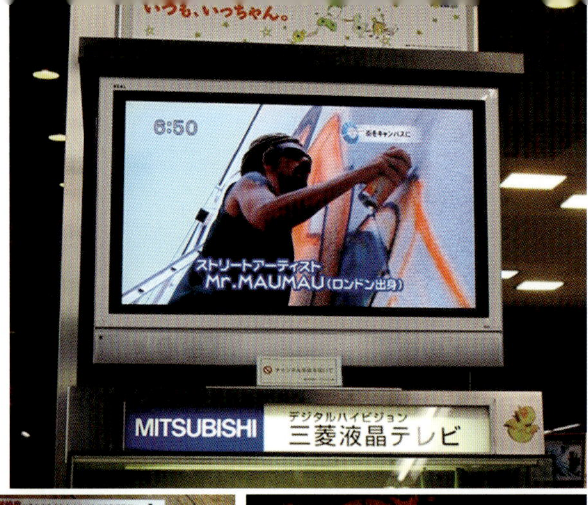

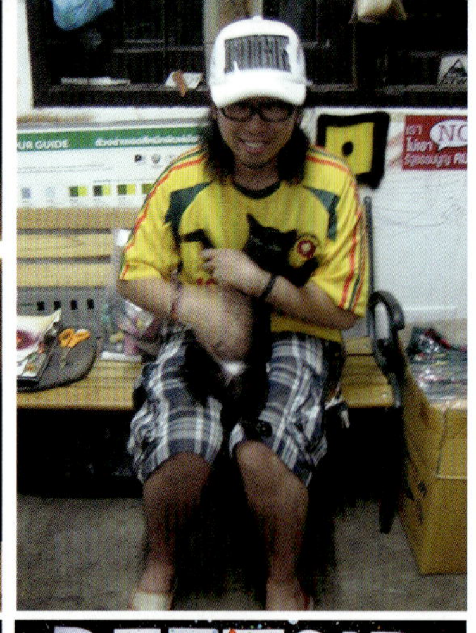

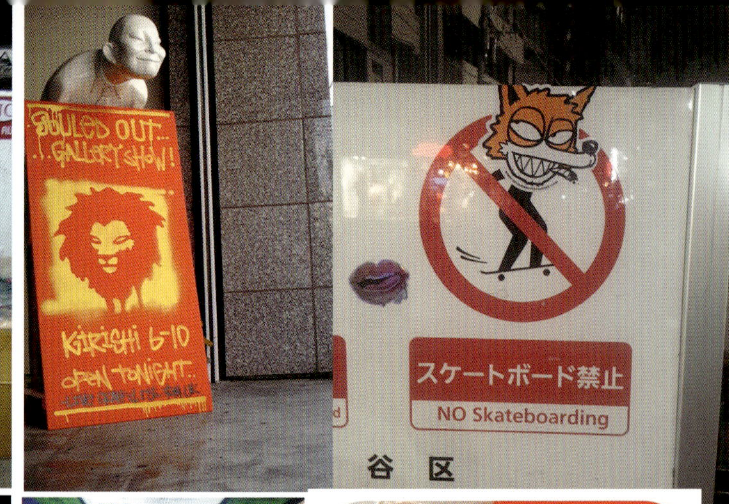

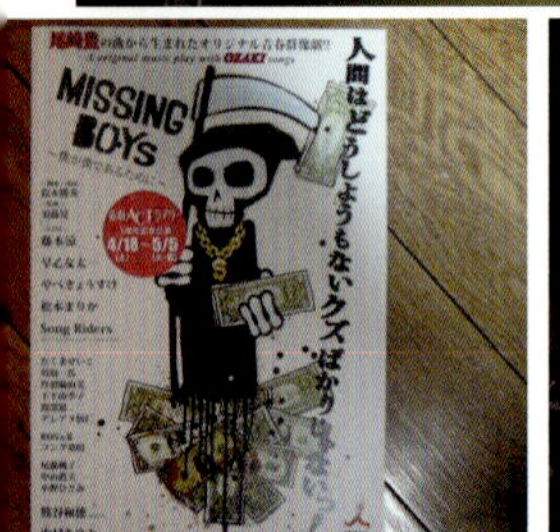

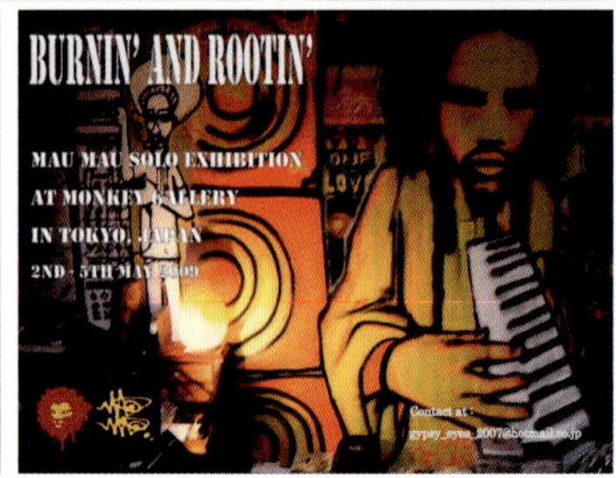

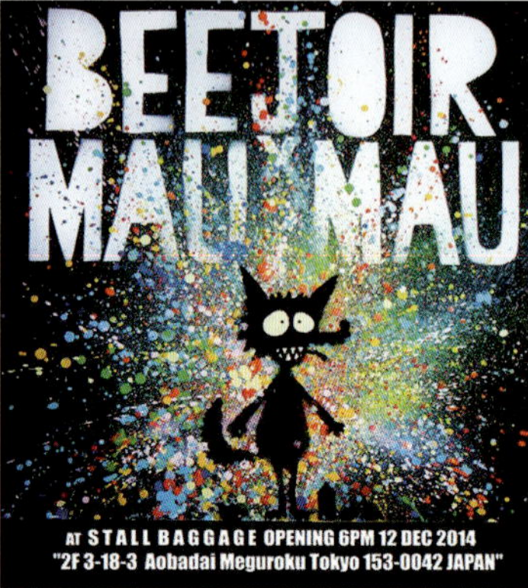

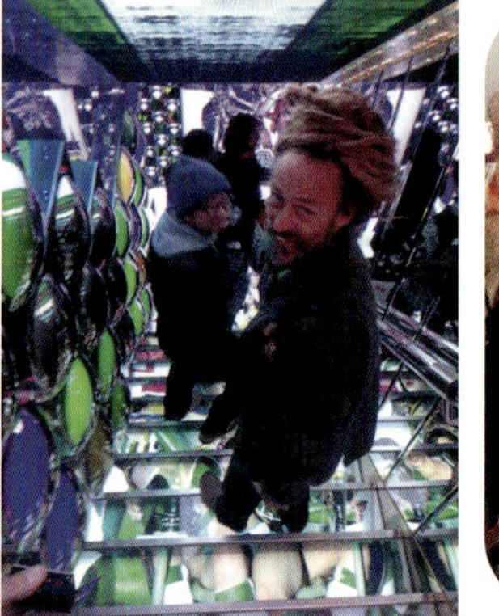

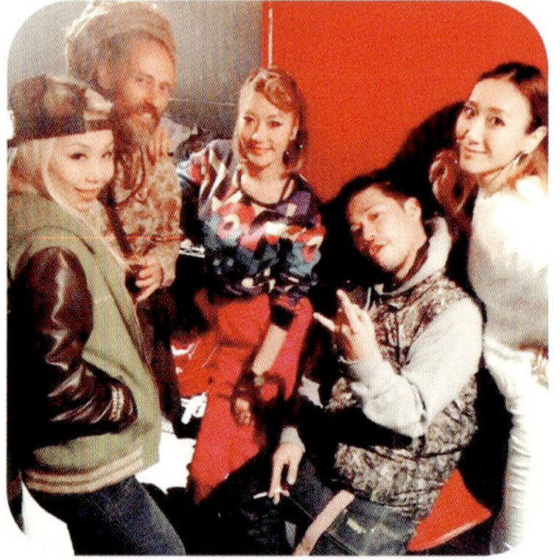

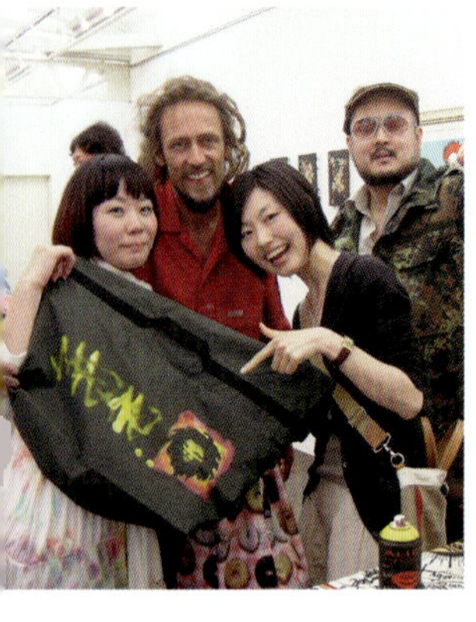

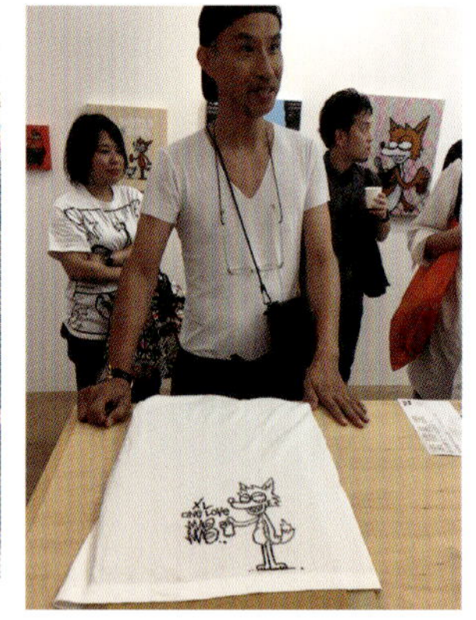

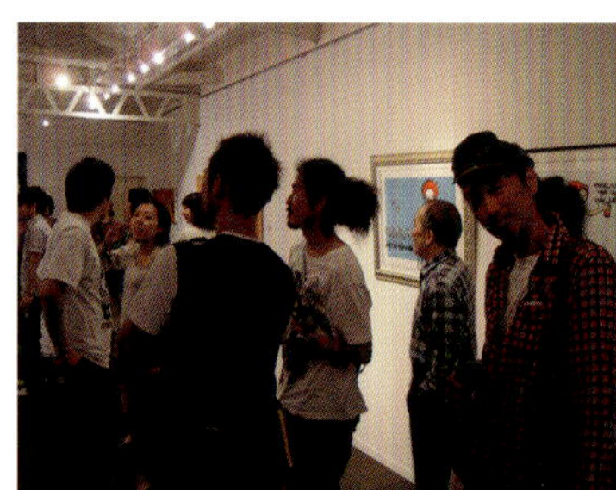

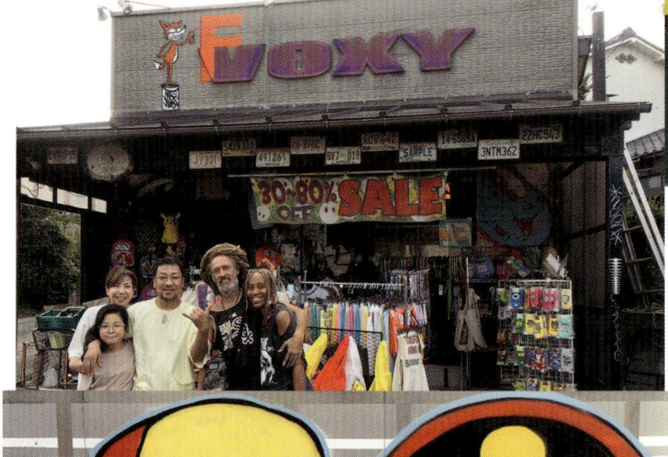

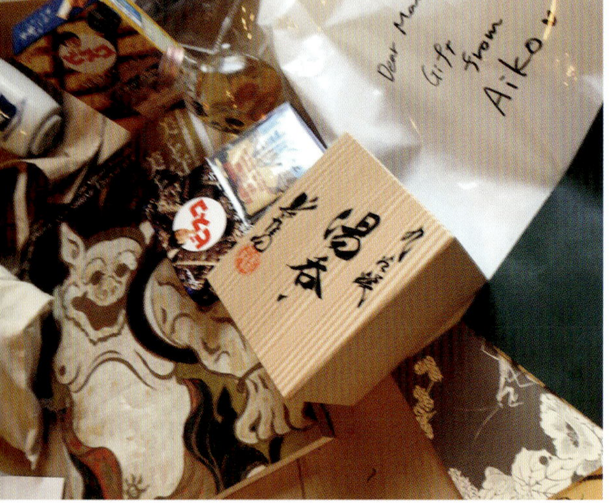

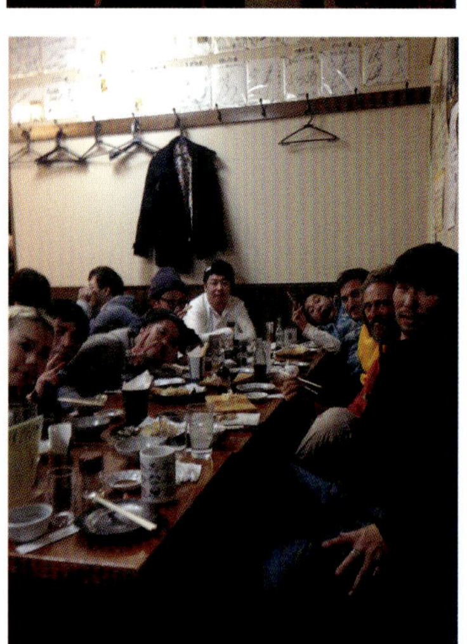

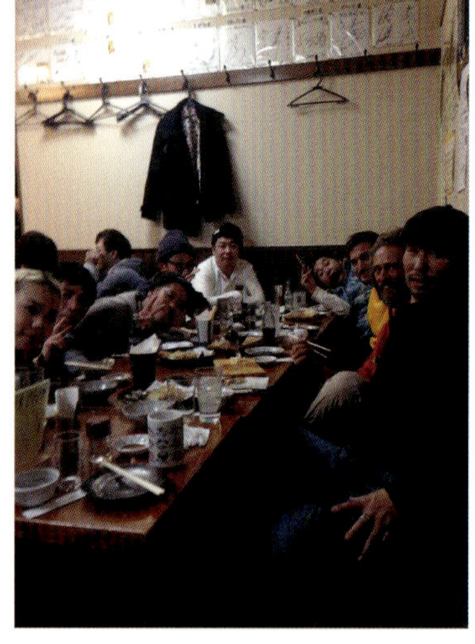

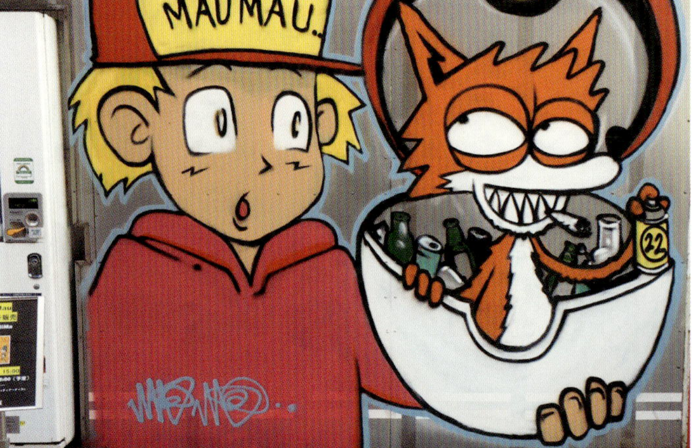

Tokyo, 2019.

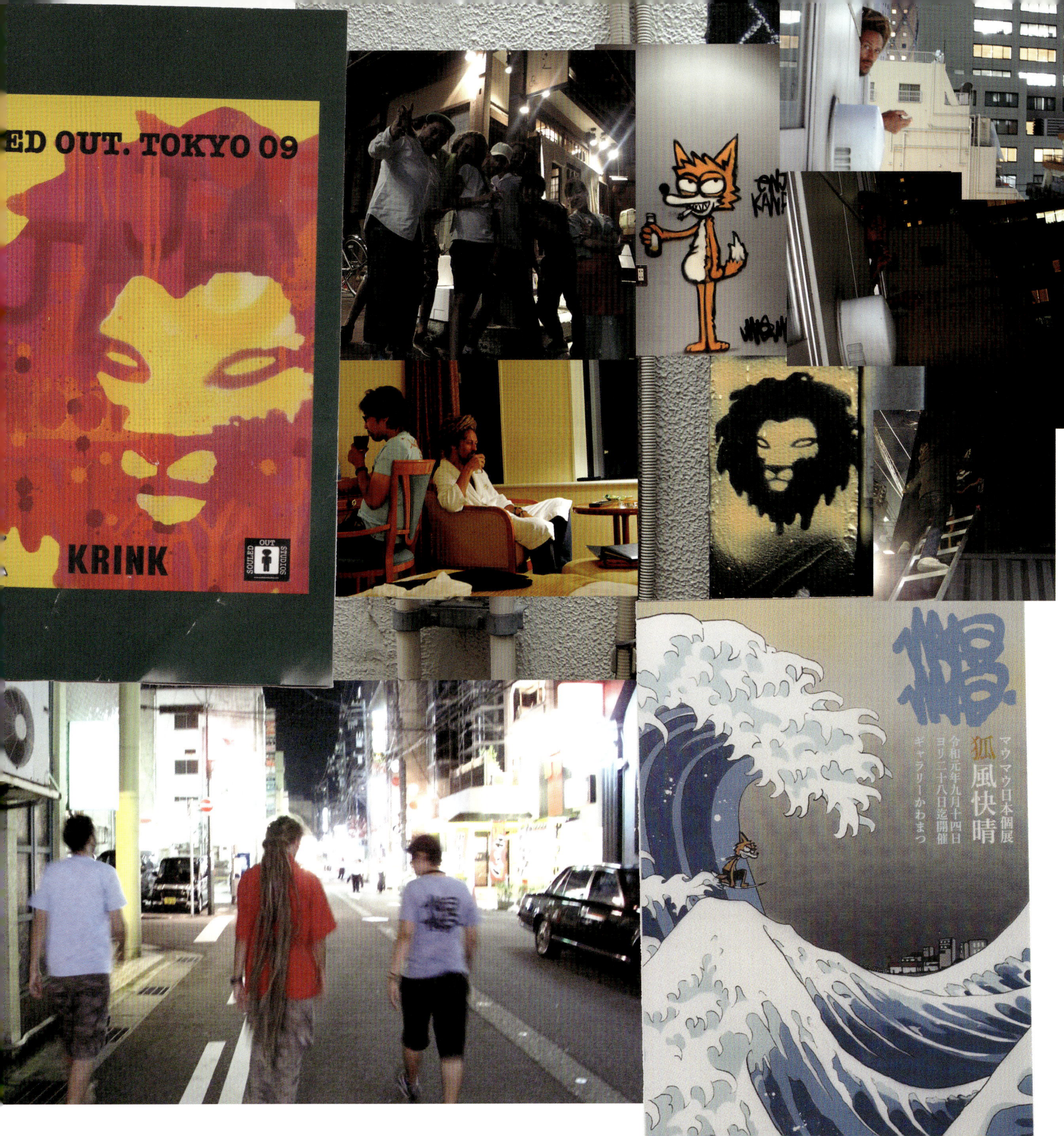
ED OUT. TOKYO 09
KRINK
SOULED OUT STUDIOS
マウマウ日本個展
狐風快晴
令和元年九月十四日
ヨリ二十八日迄開催
ギャラリーかわまつ

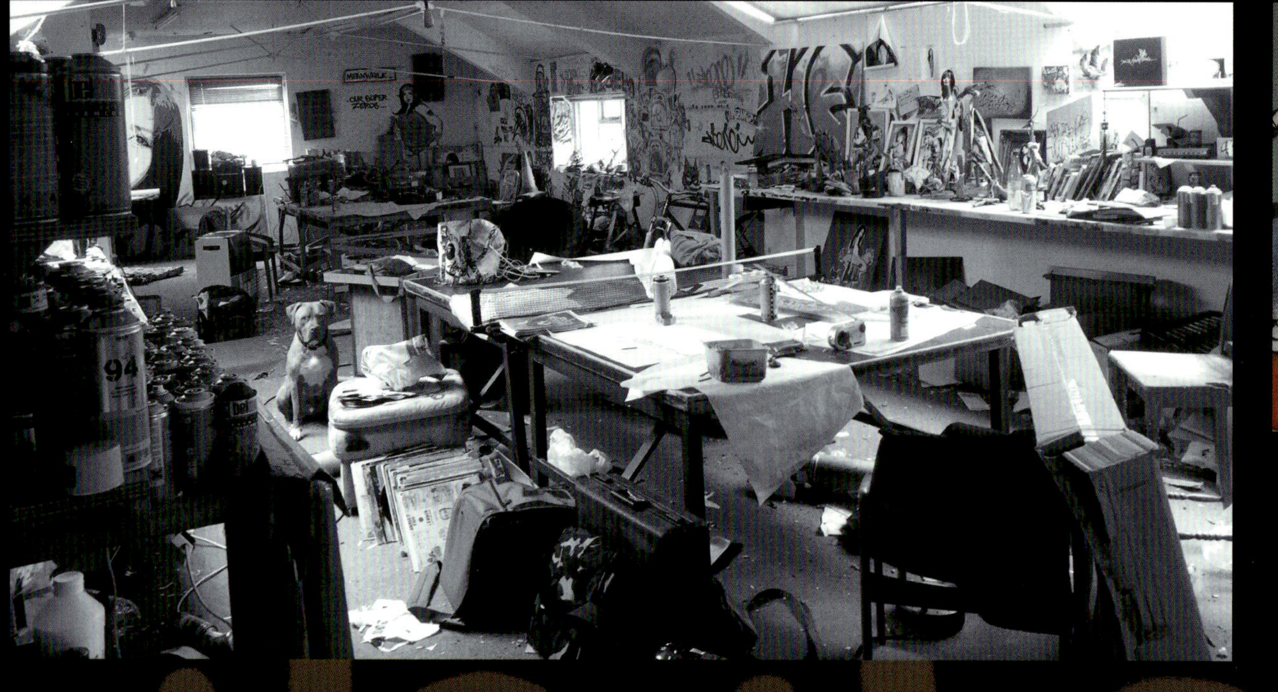

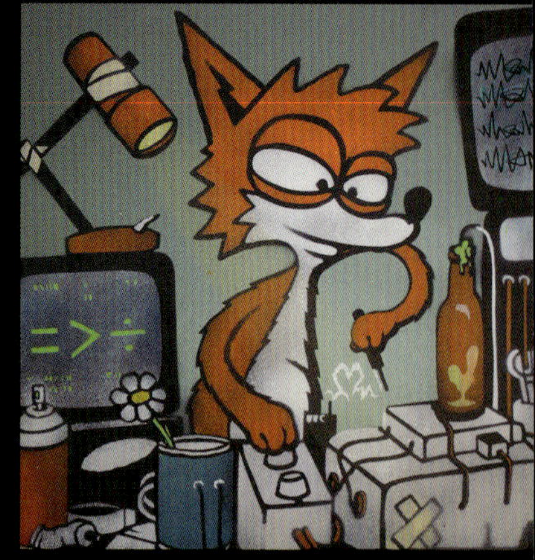

ADOX

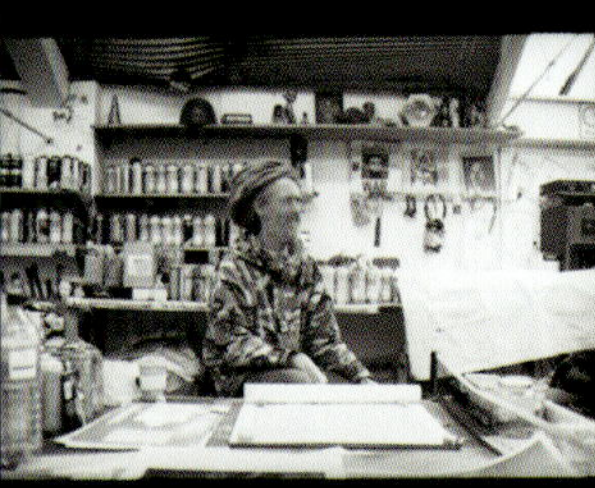

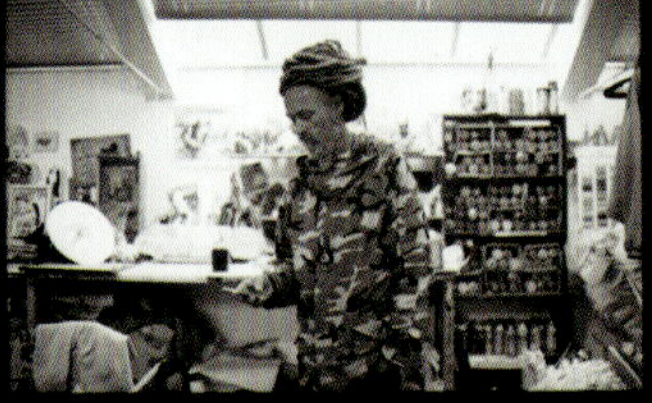

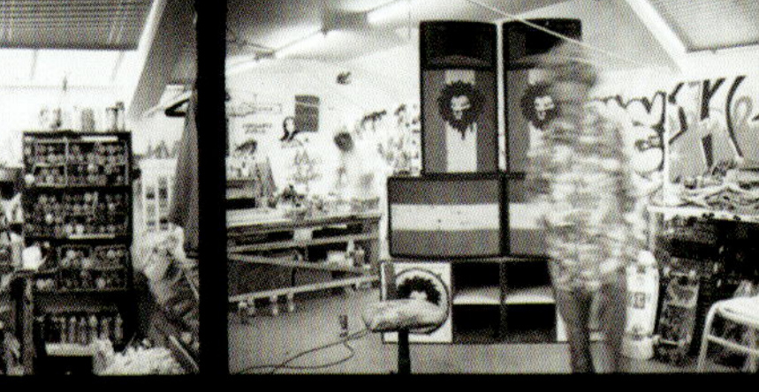

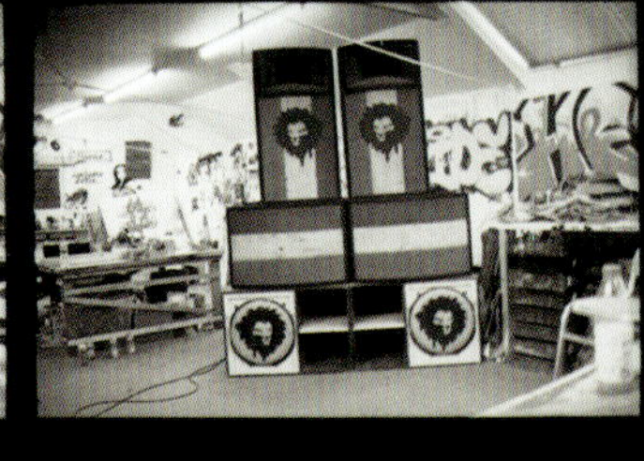

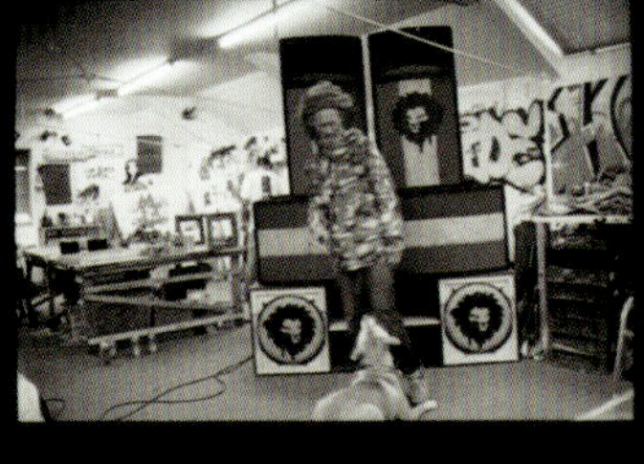

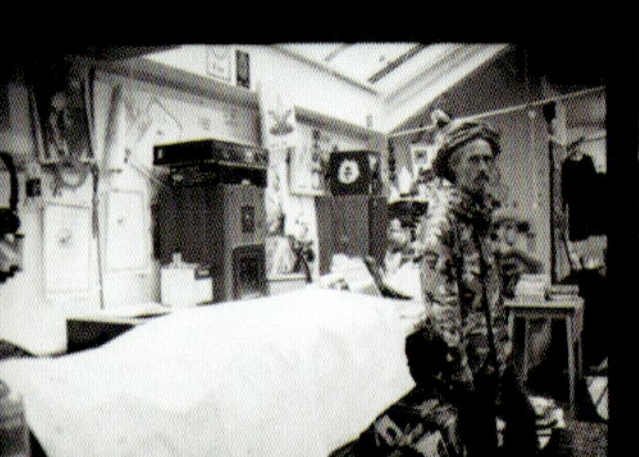

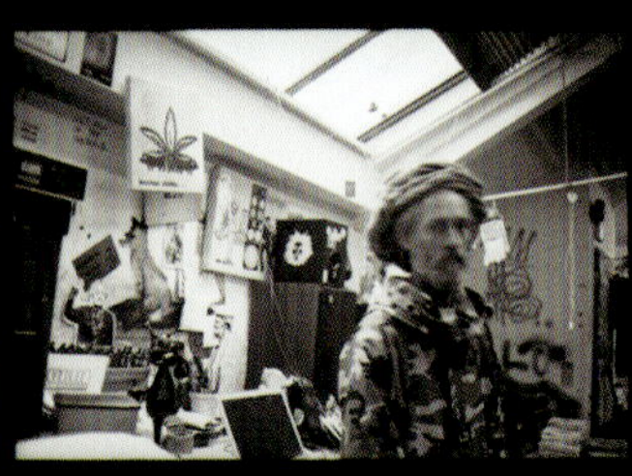

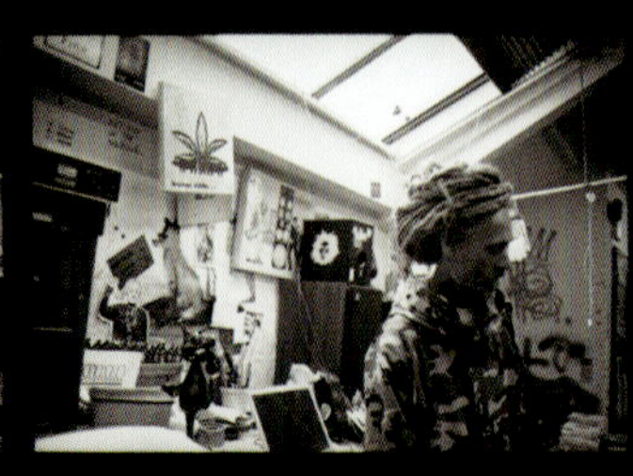

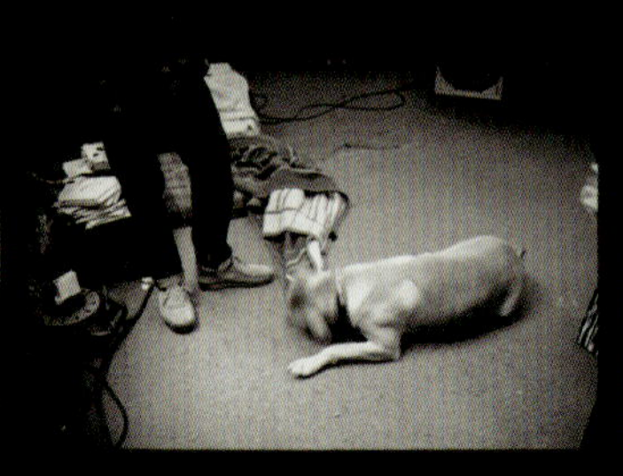

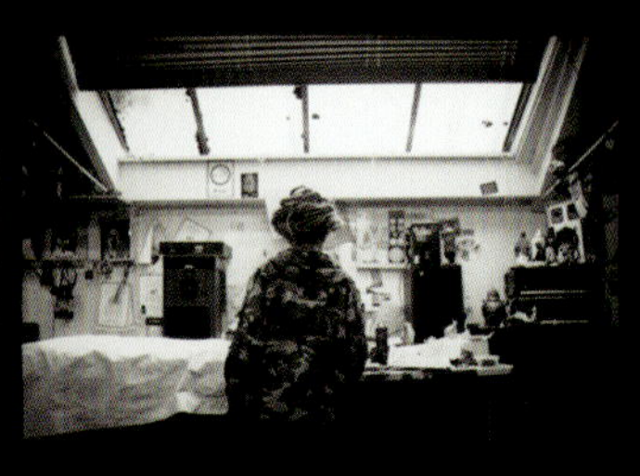

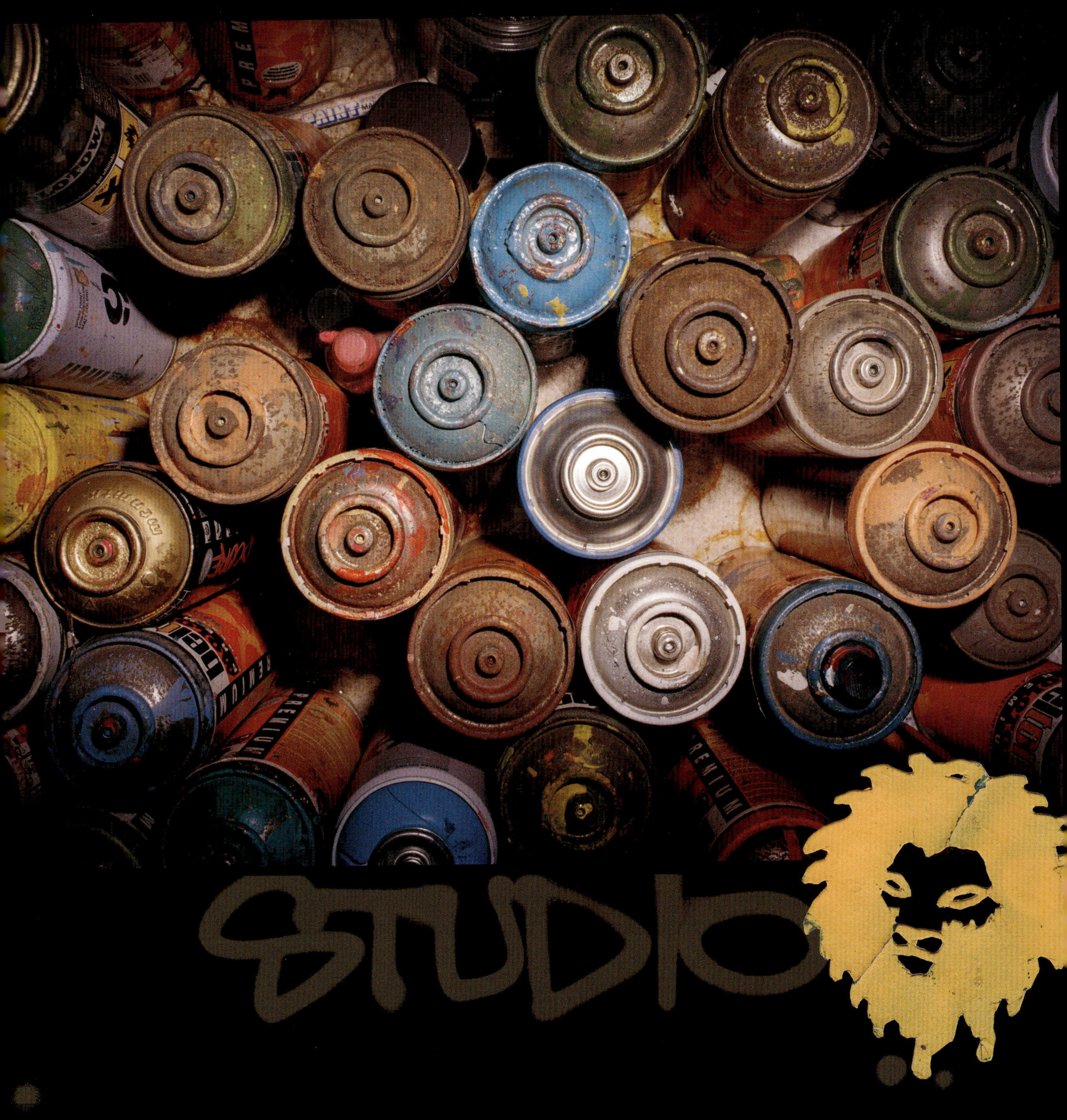
STUDIO

Monsanto Poison Apples, 2013.

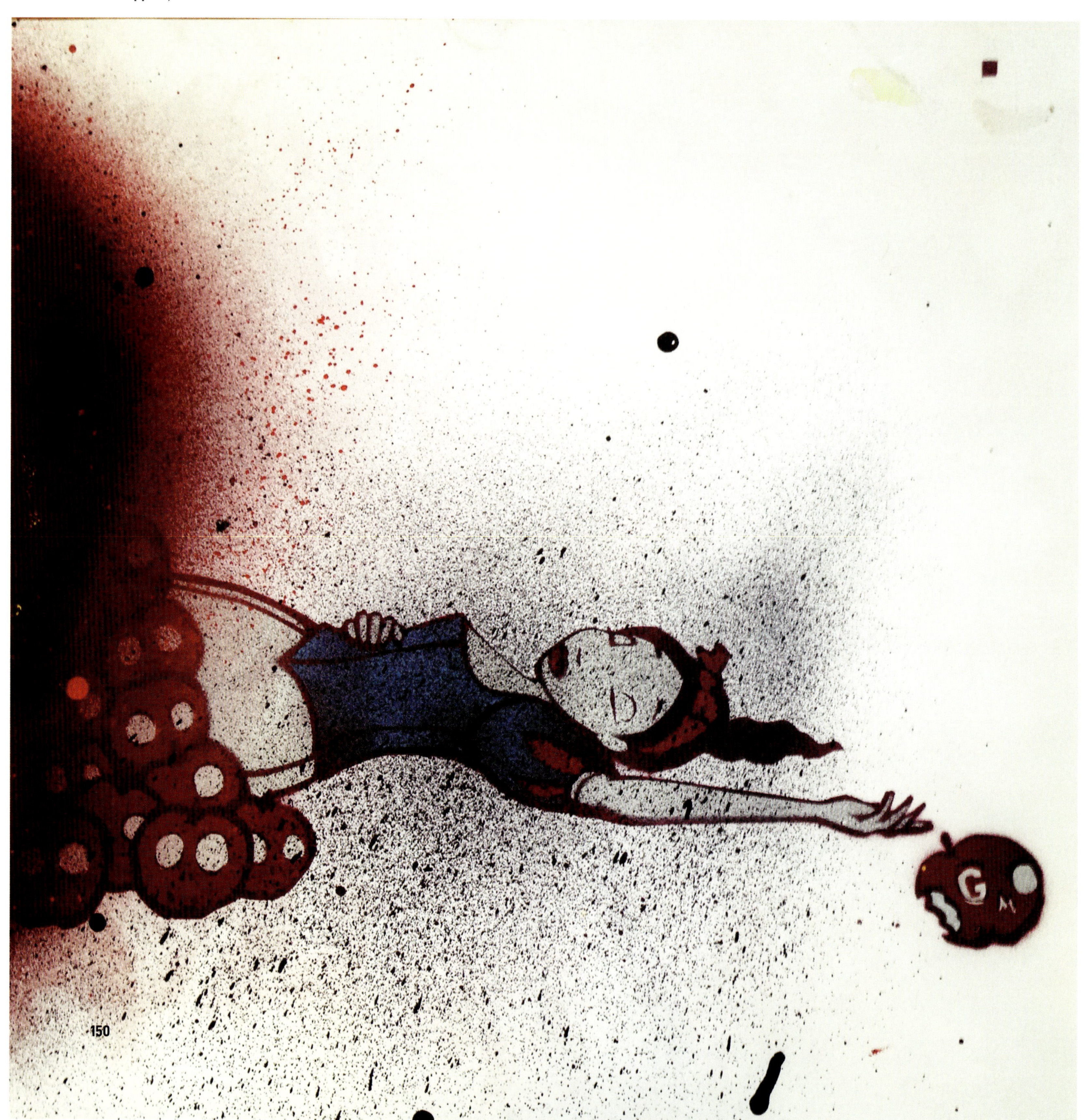

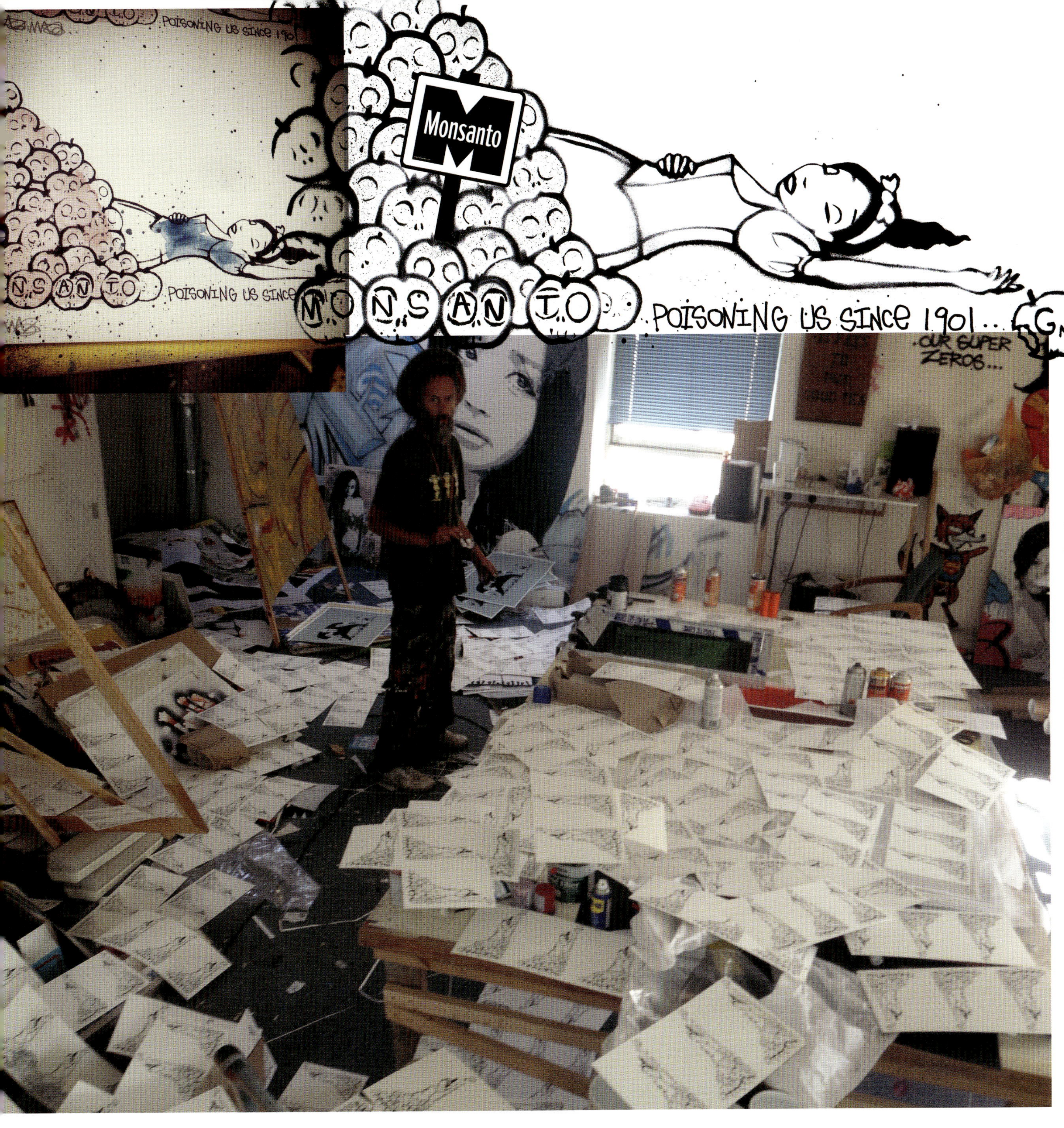
POISONING US SINCE 190
Monsanto
MONSANTO
POISONING US SINCE 1901...
OUR SUPER ZEROS...

AMAZON 20% OF

WORLD'S OXYGEN, PLANTS, ANIMALS

EVERYTHING MU$T GO!

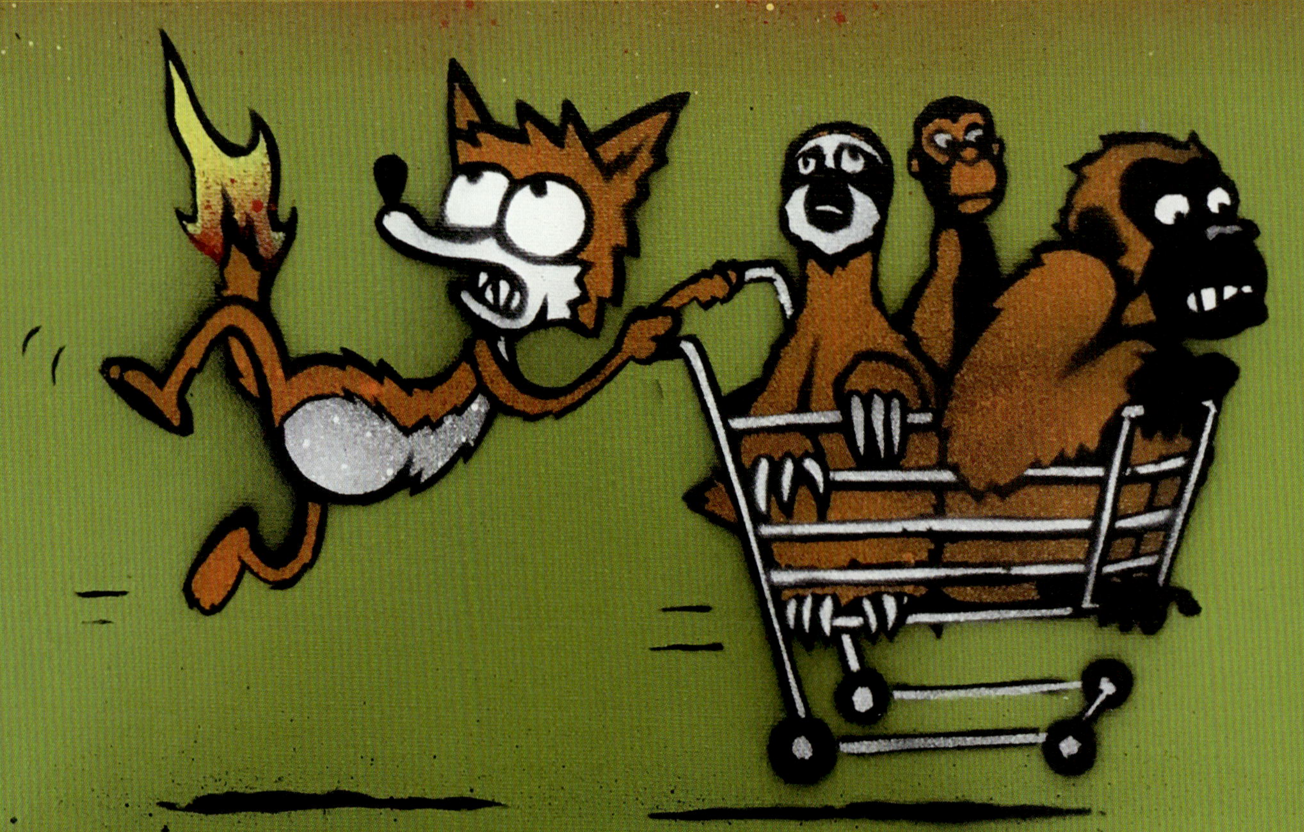

Opposite: Amazon 20% canvas, 2020.

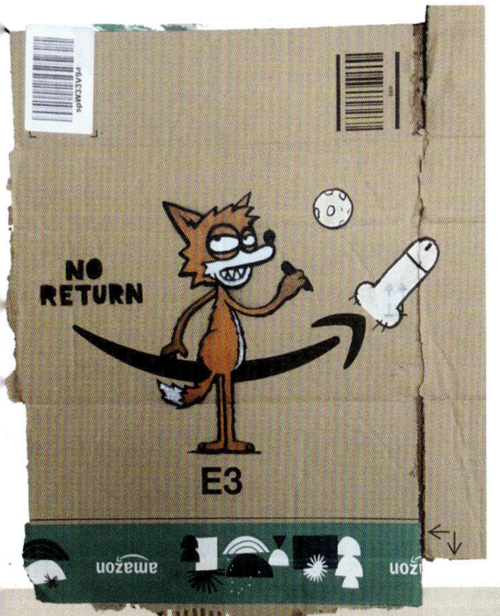

Amazon No Return, 2021.

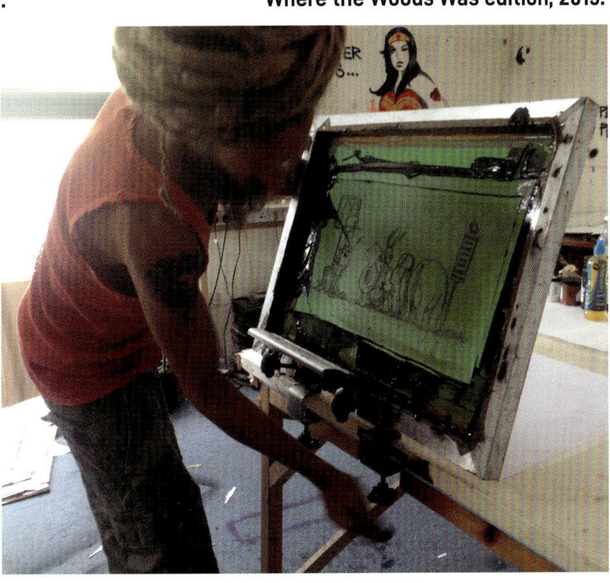

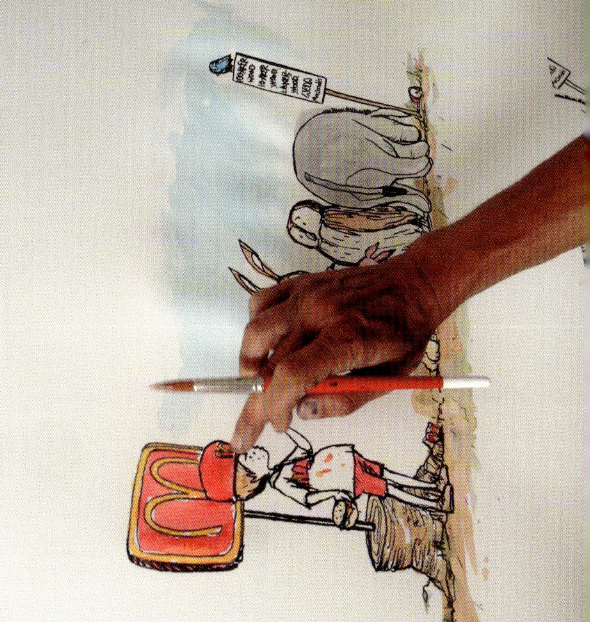

Where the Woods Was edition, 2013.

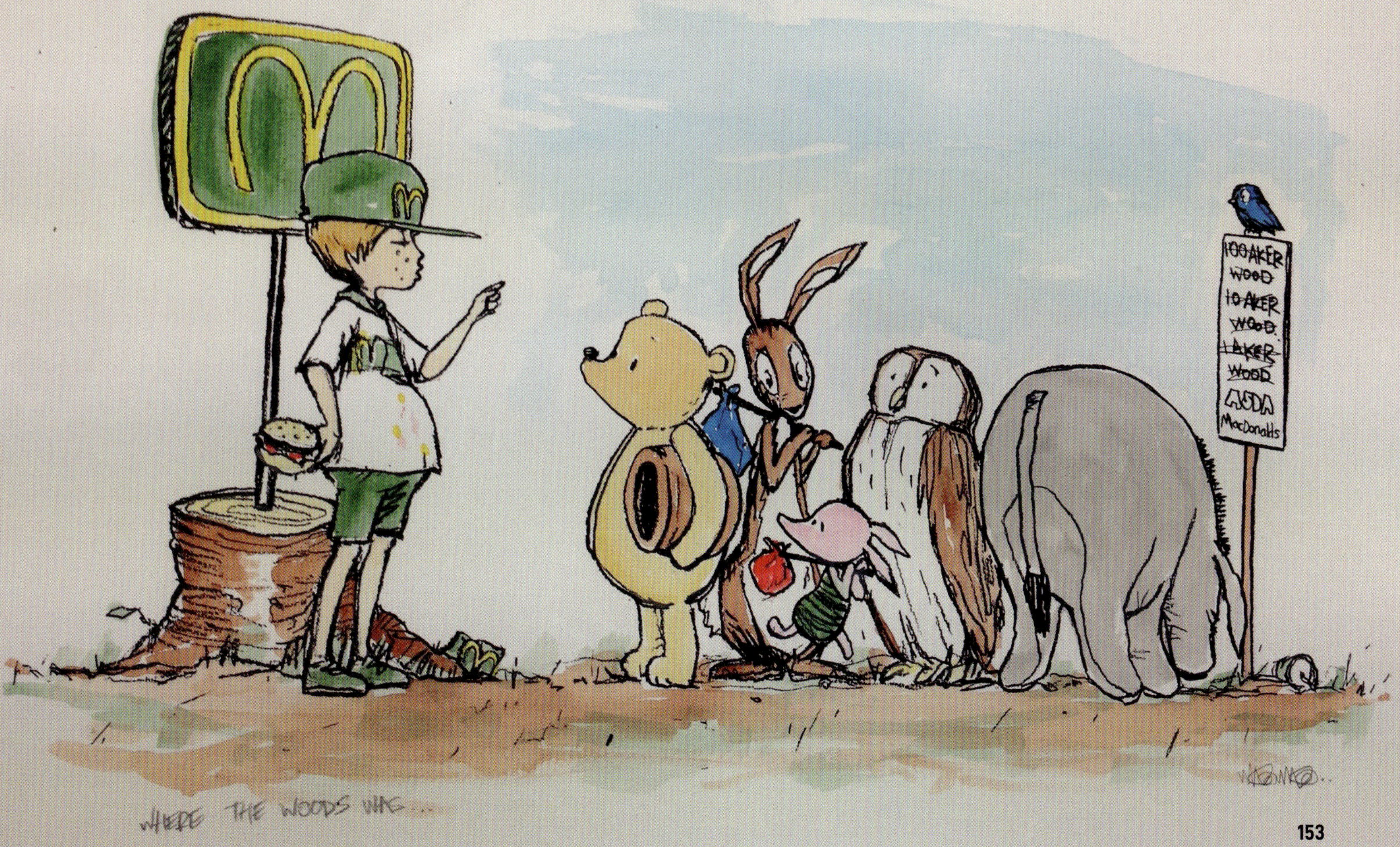

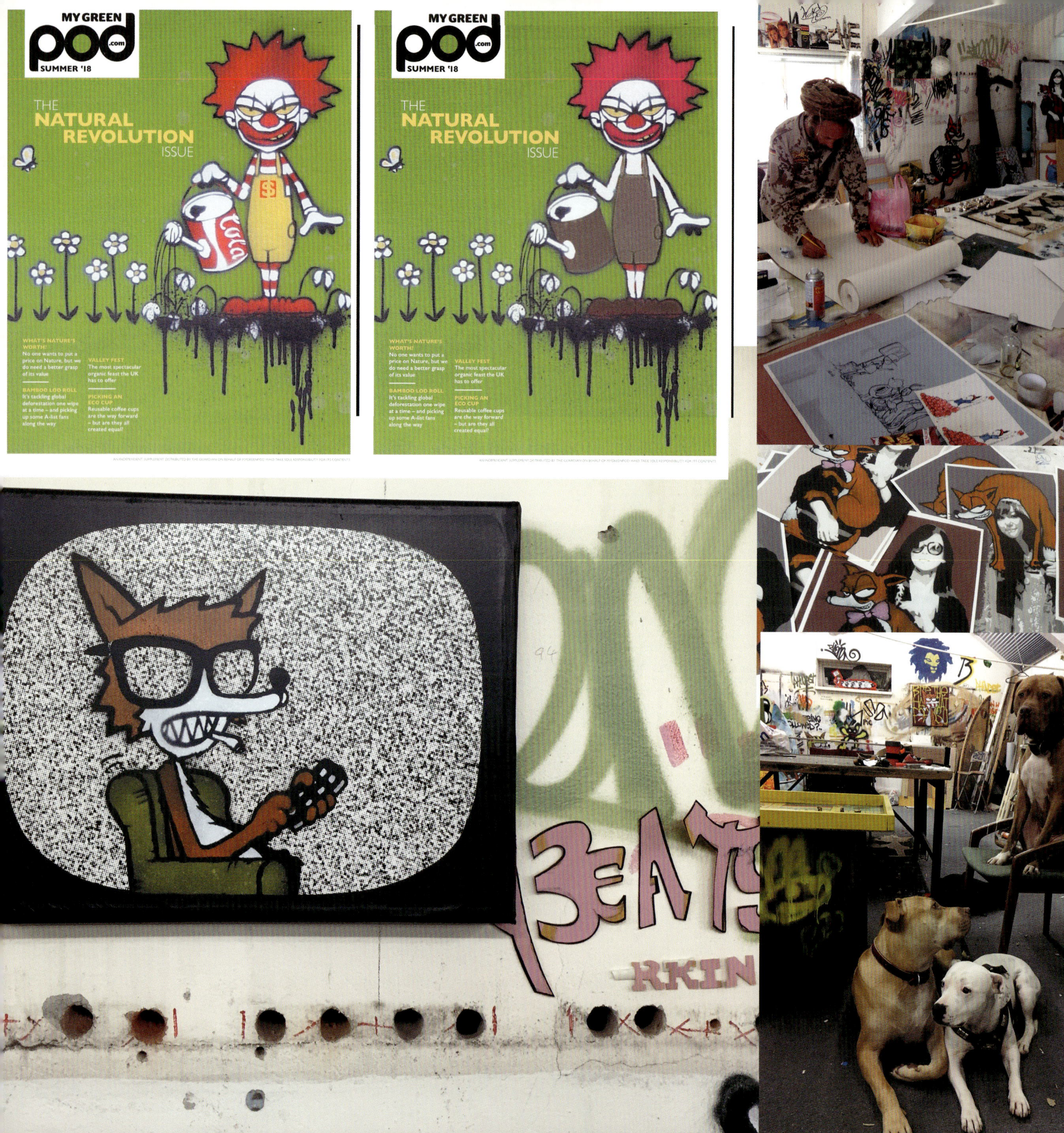
MY GREEN
pod
.com
SUMMER '18
THE
NATURAL
REVOLUTION
ISSUE
WHAT'S NATURE'S WORTH?
No one wants to put a price on Nature, but we do need a better grasp of its value
BAMBOO LOO ROLL
It's tackling global deforestation one wipe at a time – and picking up some A-list fans along the way
VALLEY FEST
The most spectacular organic feast the UK has to offer
PICKING AN ECO CUP
Reusable coffee cups are the way forward – but are they all created equal?

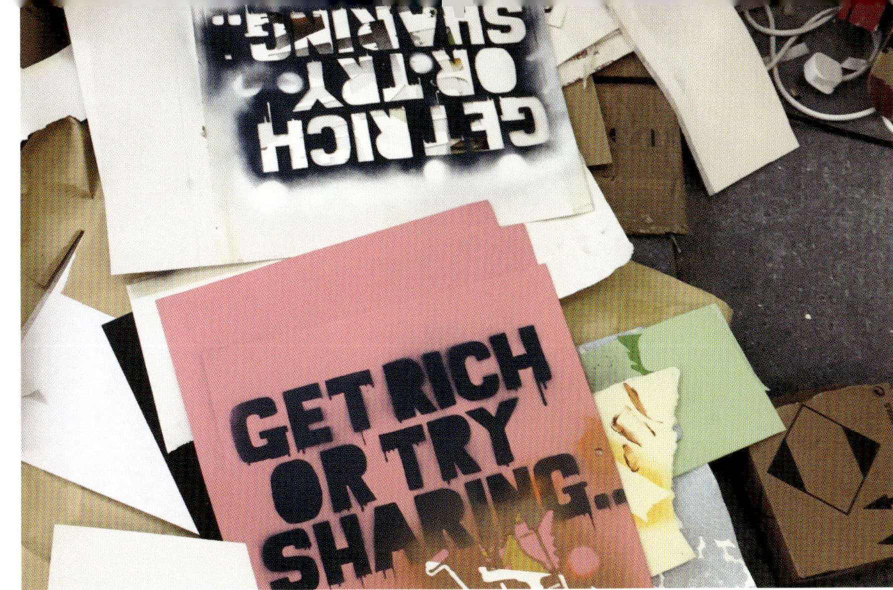

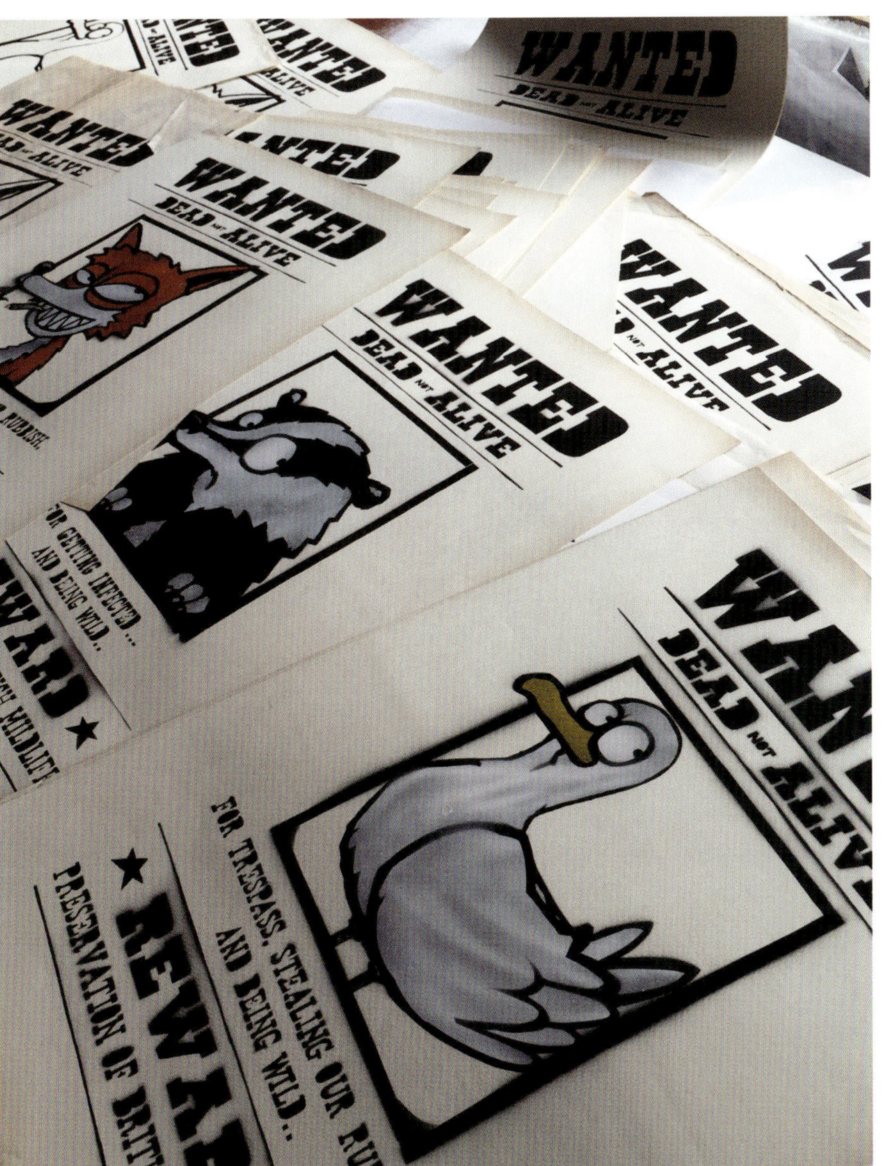

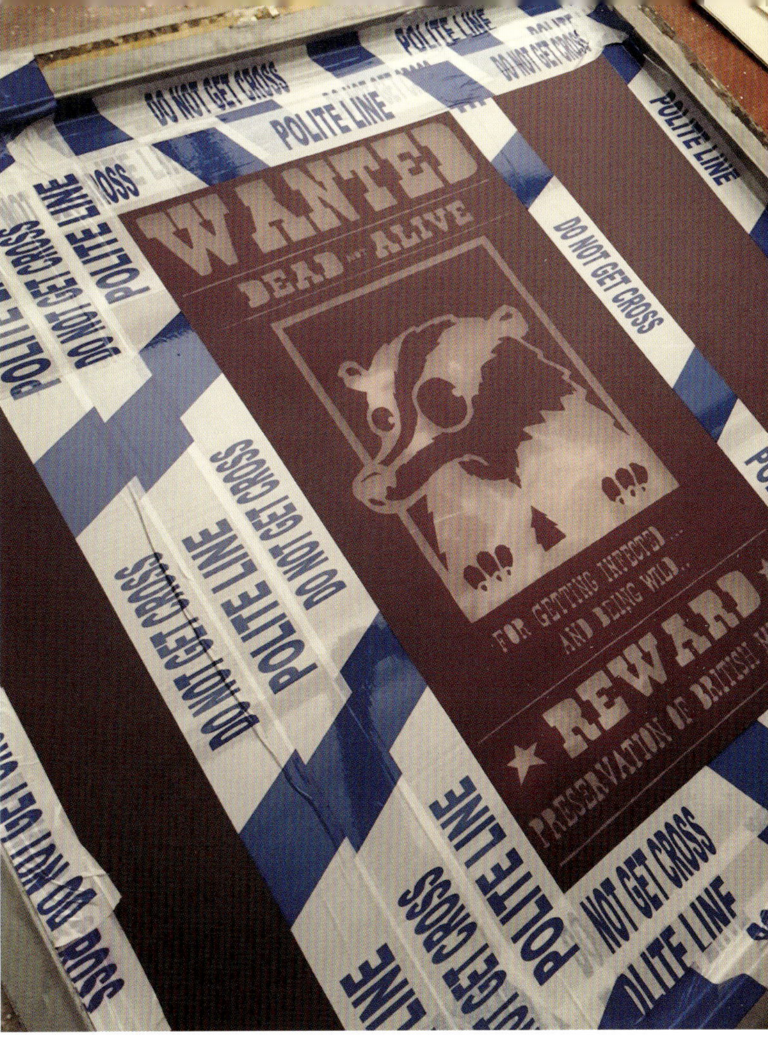

Top left: Cover illustration: Guardian supplement (original & buffed version), Summer 2018.

Too Much White Noise edition, 2015.

Lap Fox edition (Zhe, Mau), 2014.

Dogtown Studio Gang.

Wanted posters, Gully, Badger and Fox, 2019.

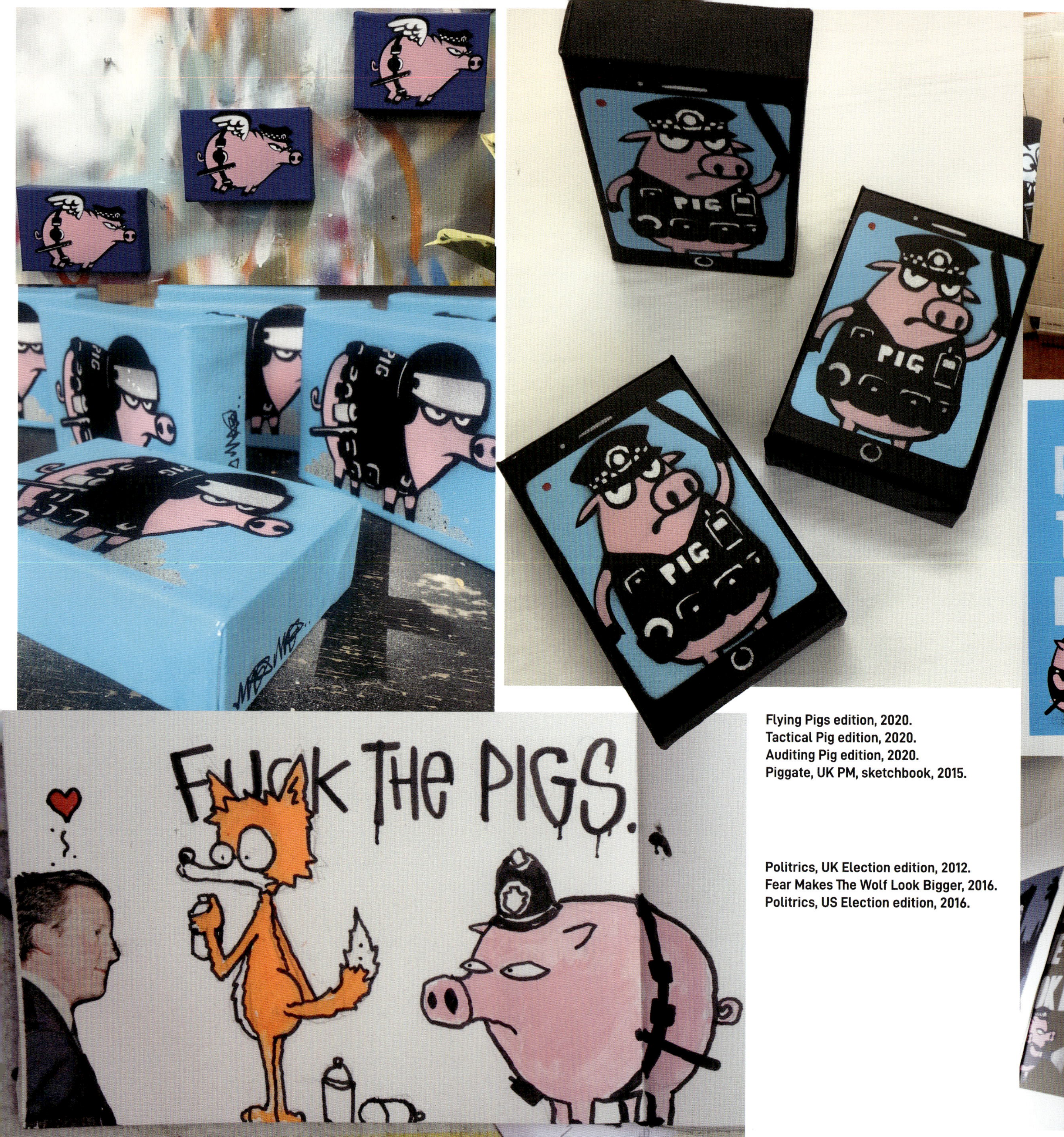

Flying Pigs edition, 2020.
Tactical Pig edition, 2020.
Auditing Pig edition, 2020.
Piggate, UK PM, sketchbook, 2015.

Politrics, UK Election edition, 2012.
Fear Makes The Wolf Look Bigger, 2016.
Politrics, US Election edition, 2016.

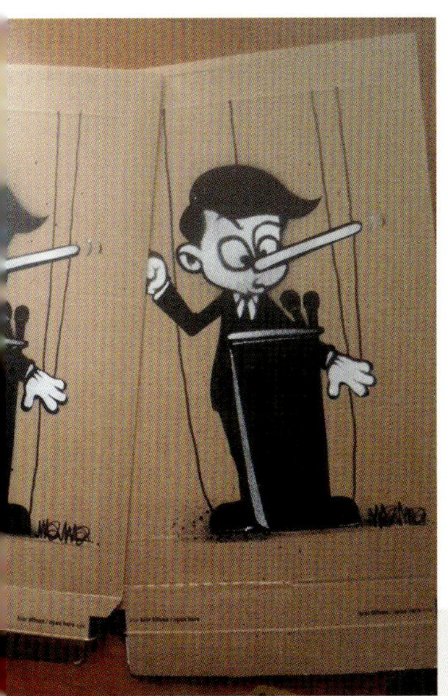

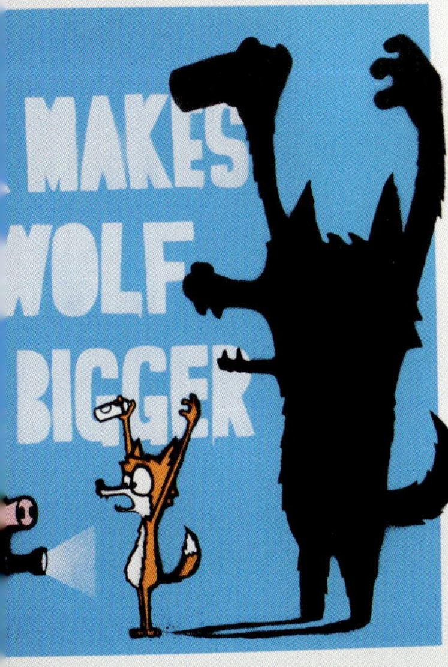
MAKES
WOLF
BIGGER

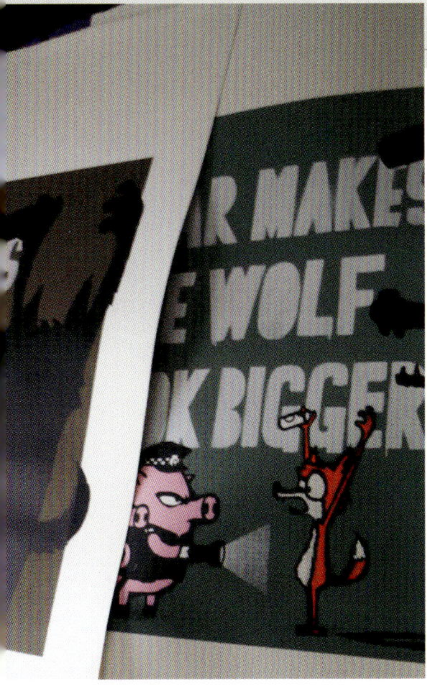
MAKES
WOLF
BIGGER

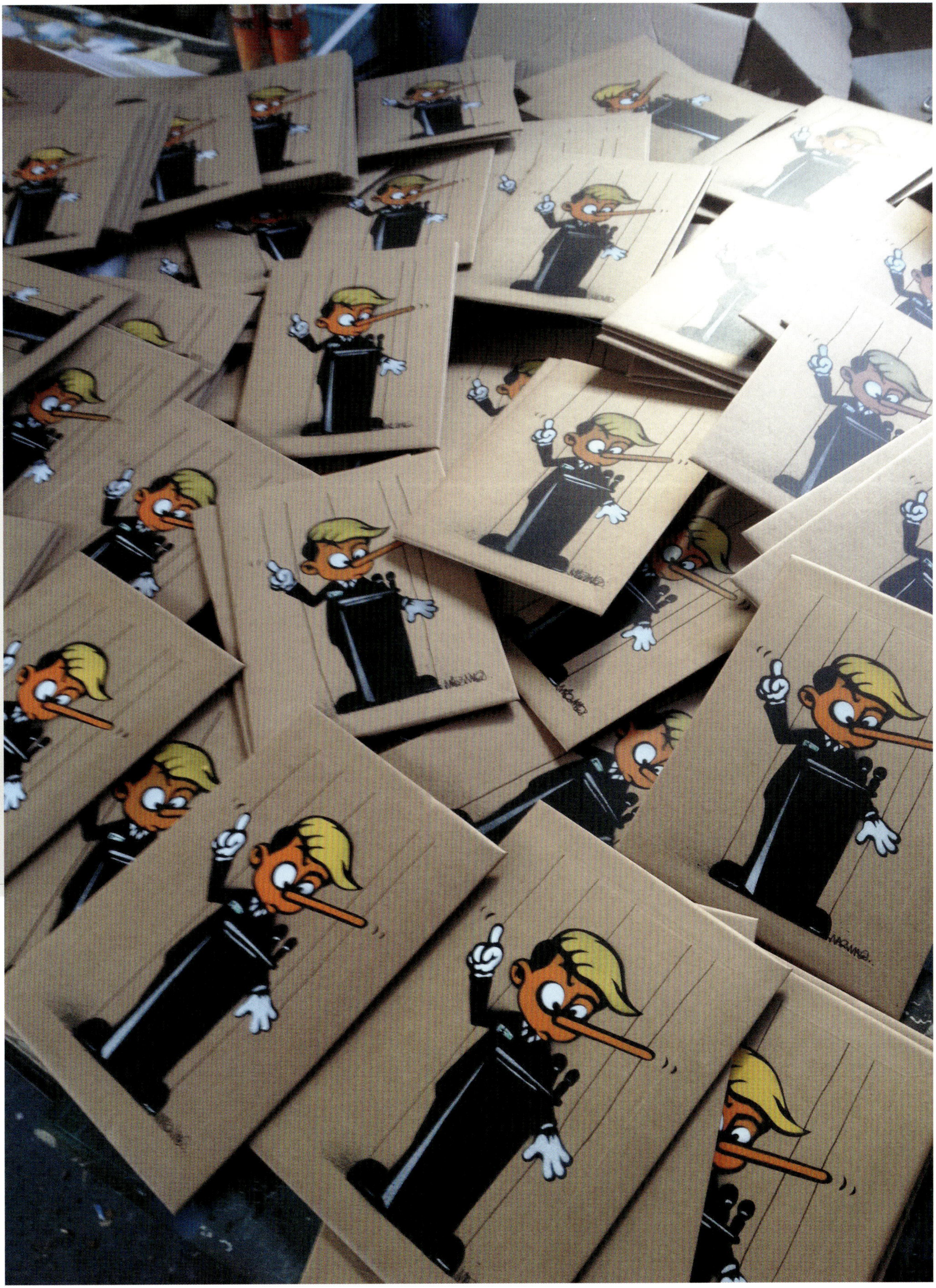

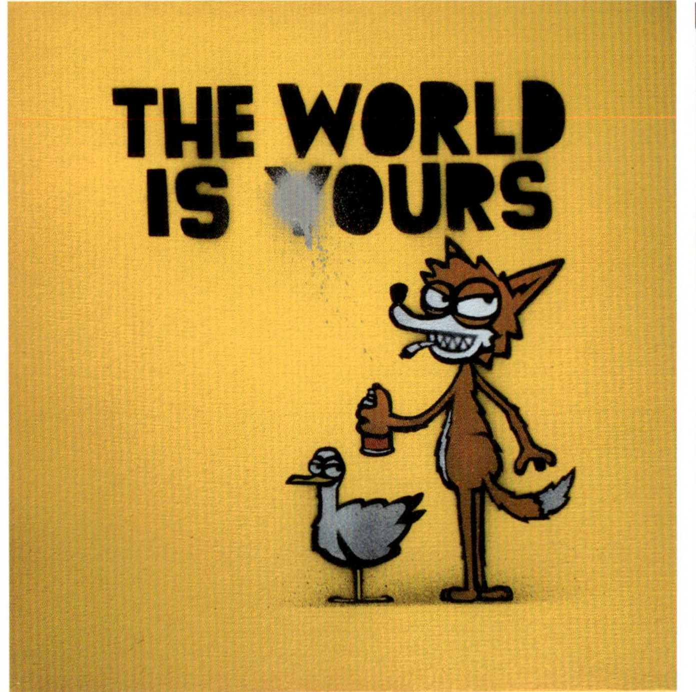

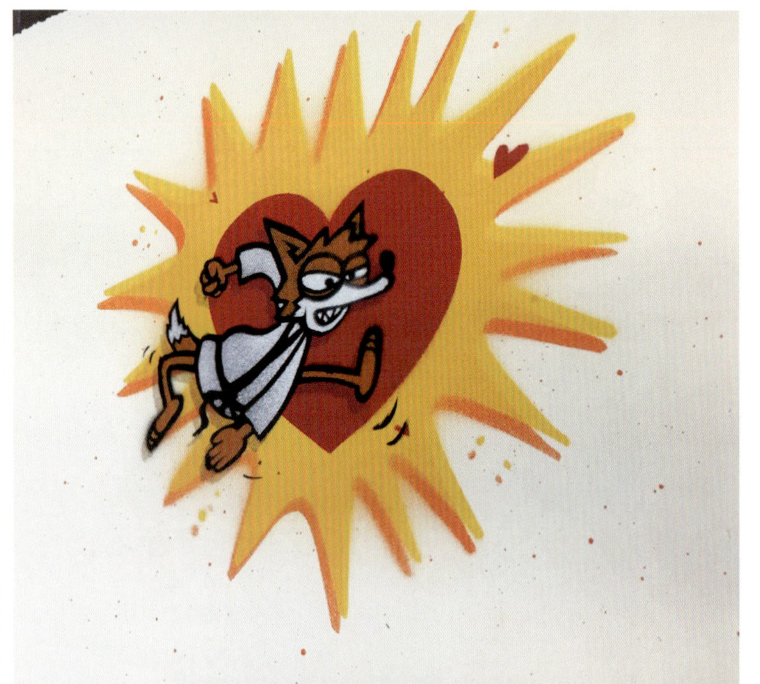

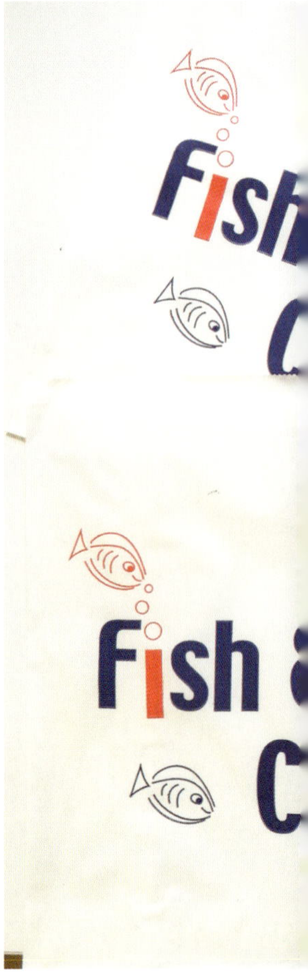

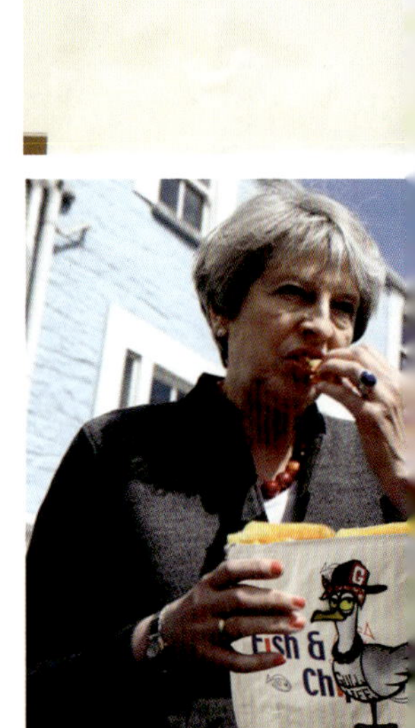

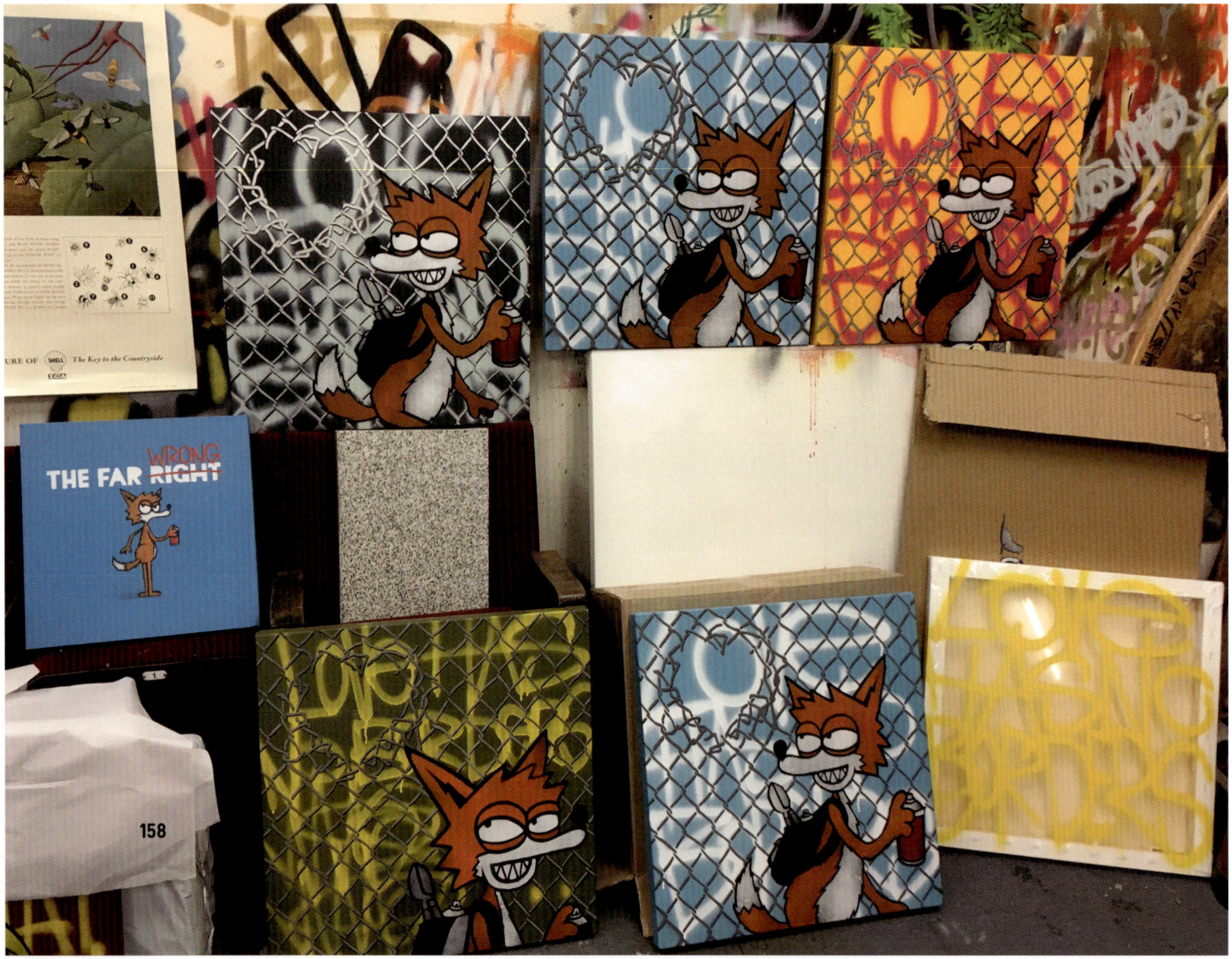

The World is Ours edition, 2018.
Phooey Fox, 2019.
Love Has No Borders, 2017.
Gull Life, 2017.

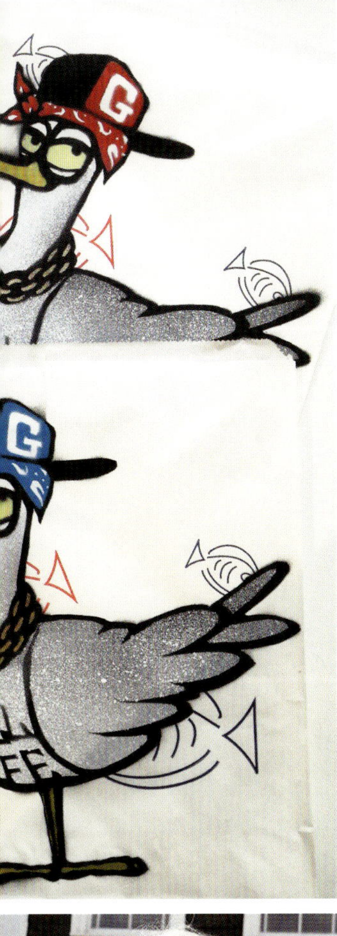

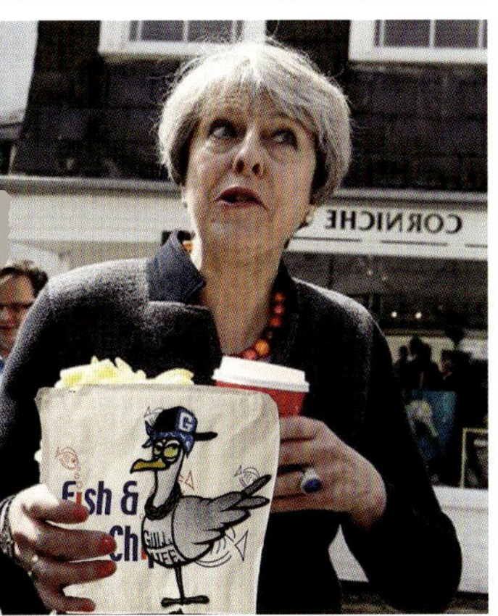

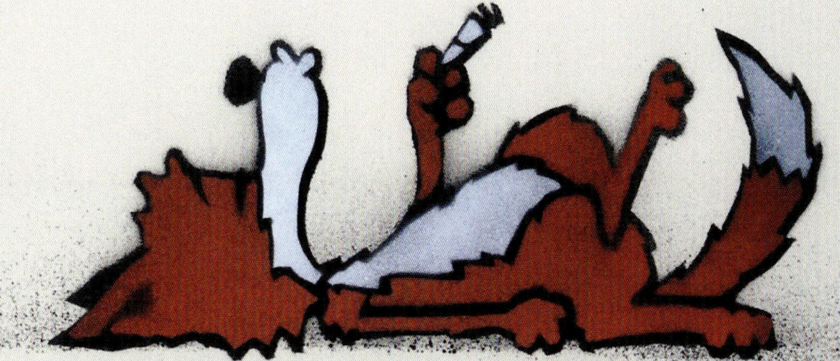

High Times Fox, 2014

Plan B edition, 2019.

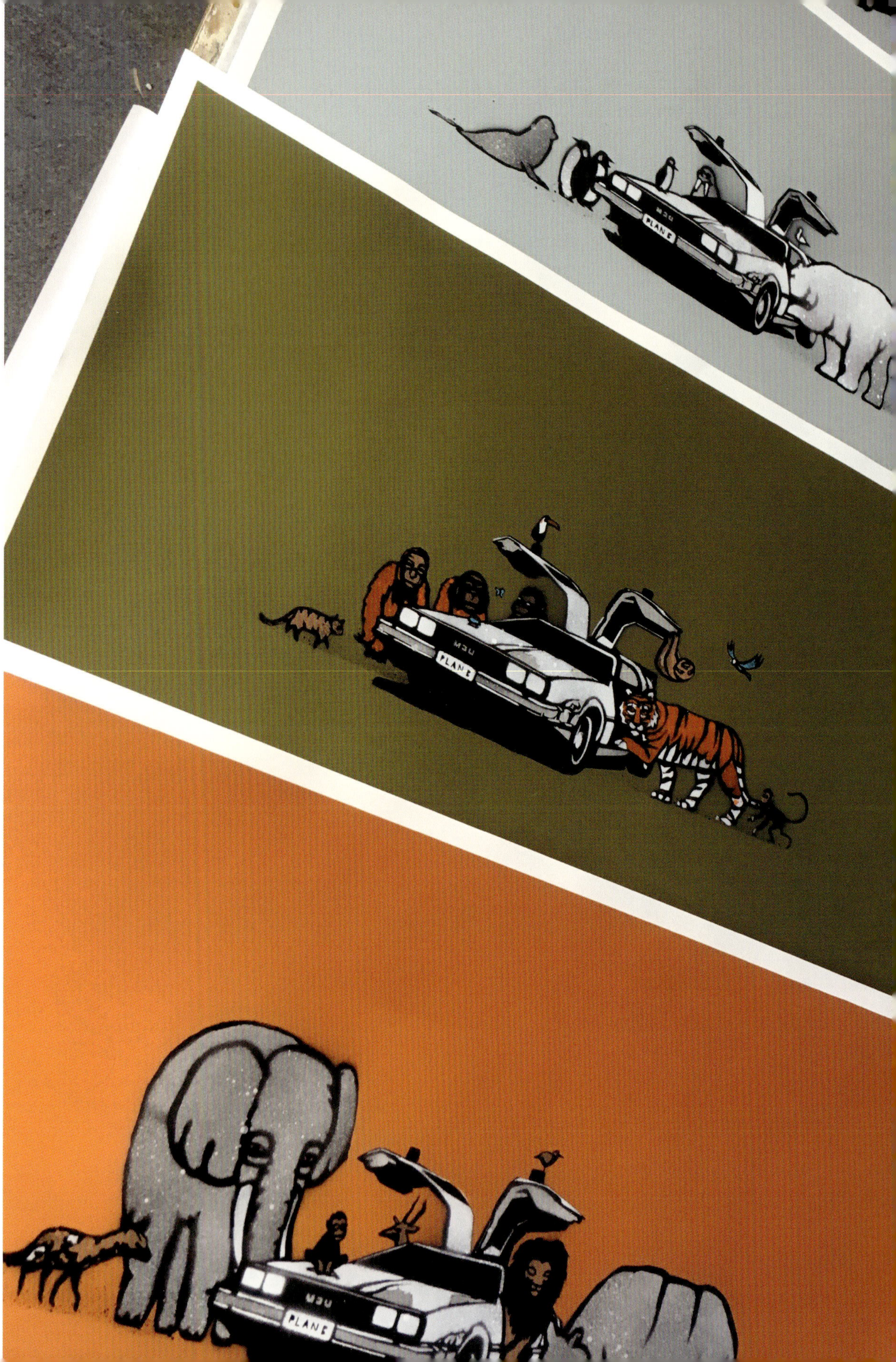

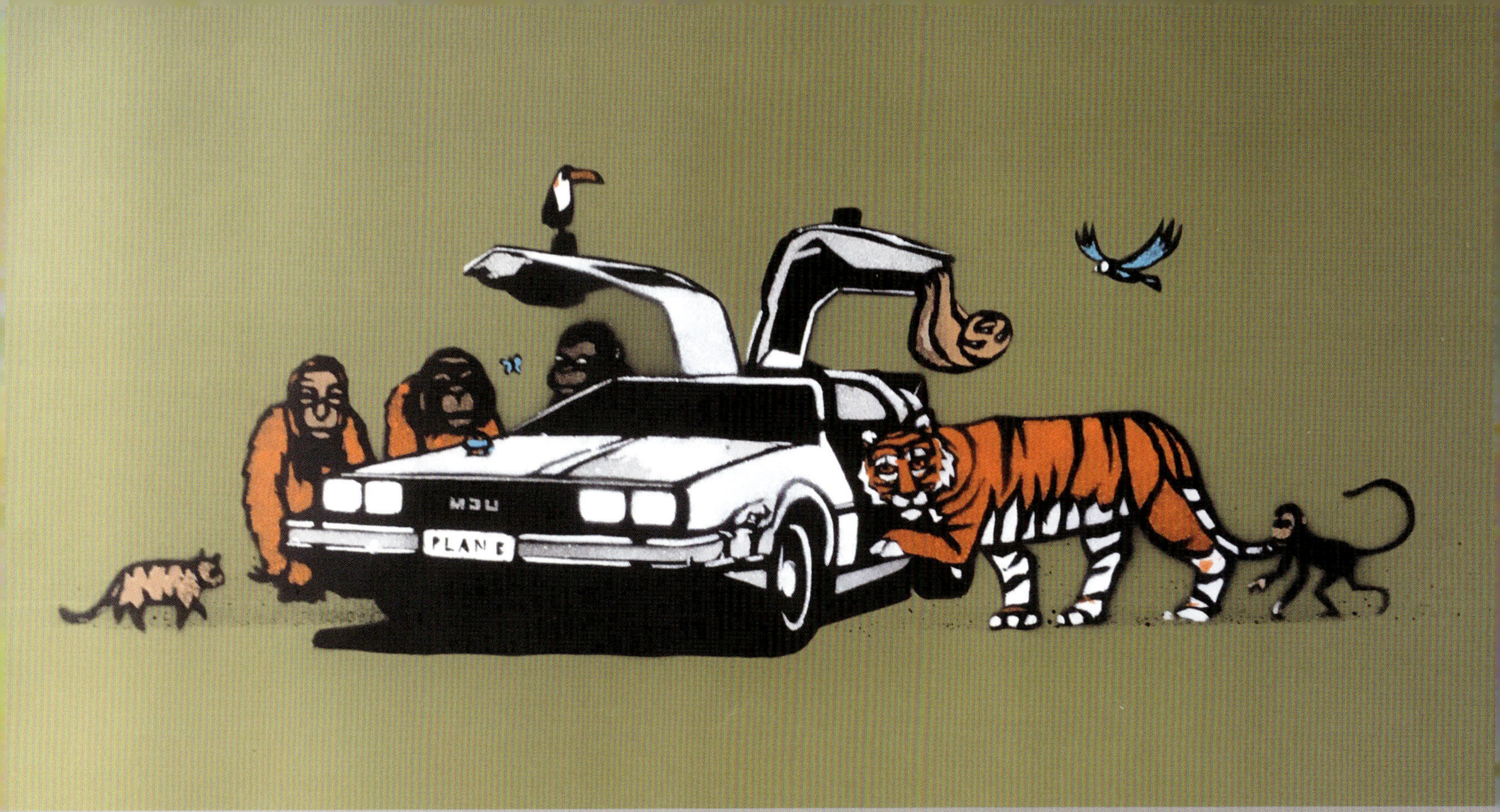

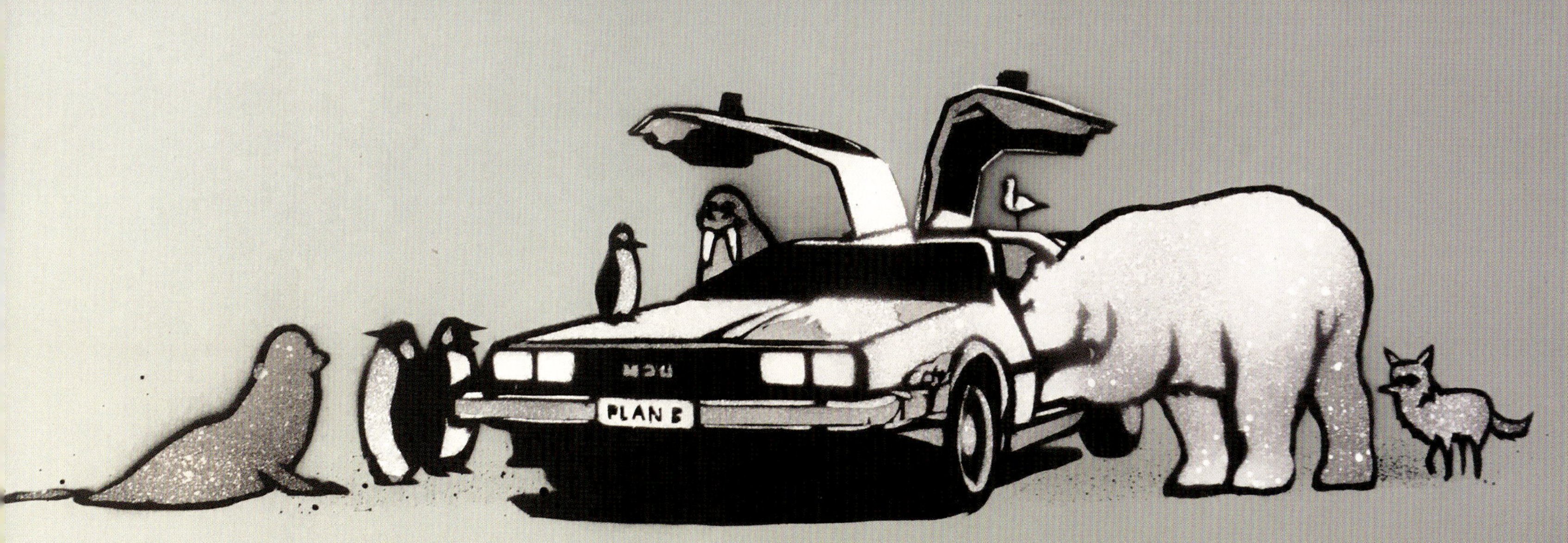
PLAN B

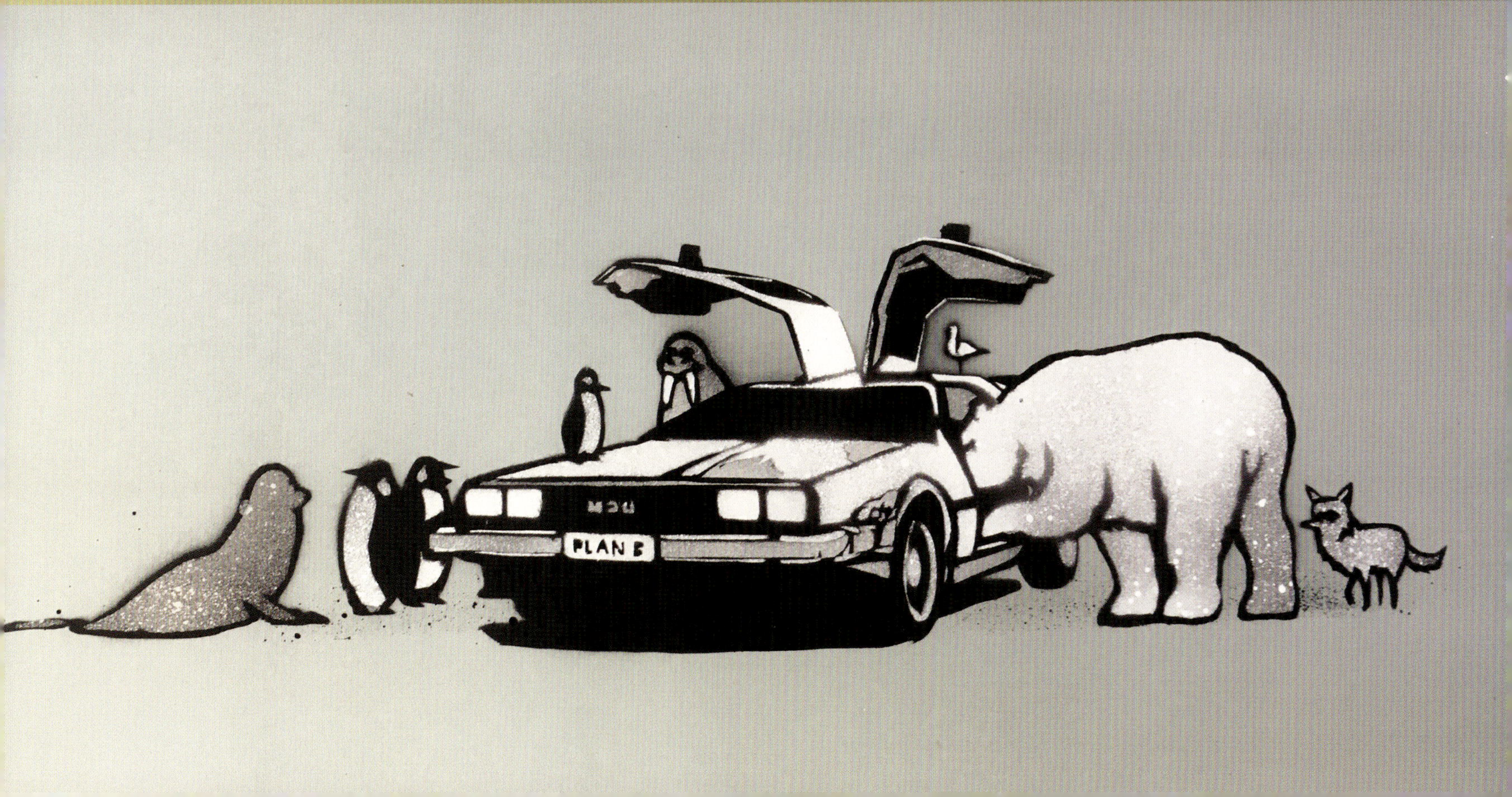

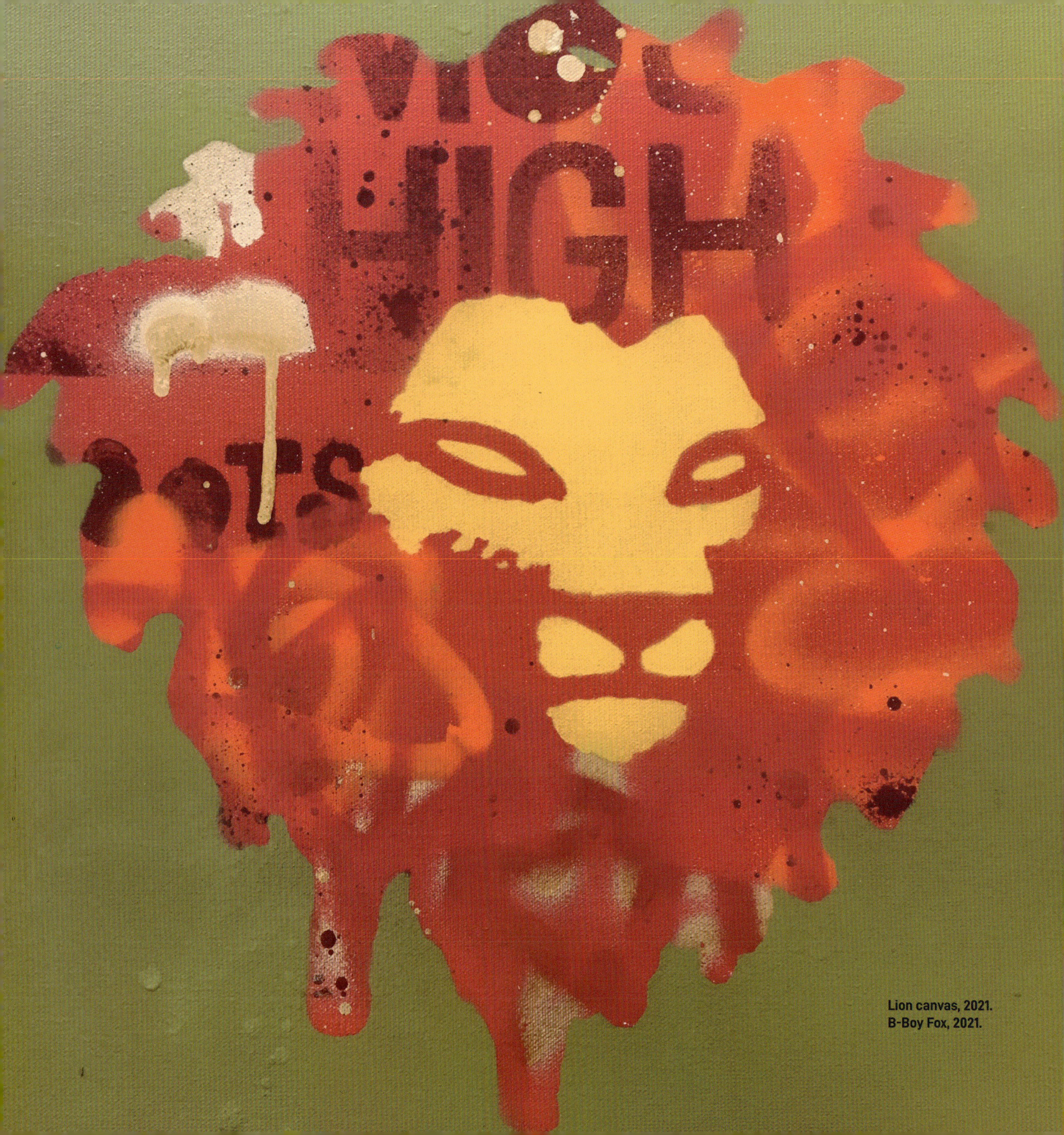

Lion canvas, 2021.
B-Boy Fox, 2021.

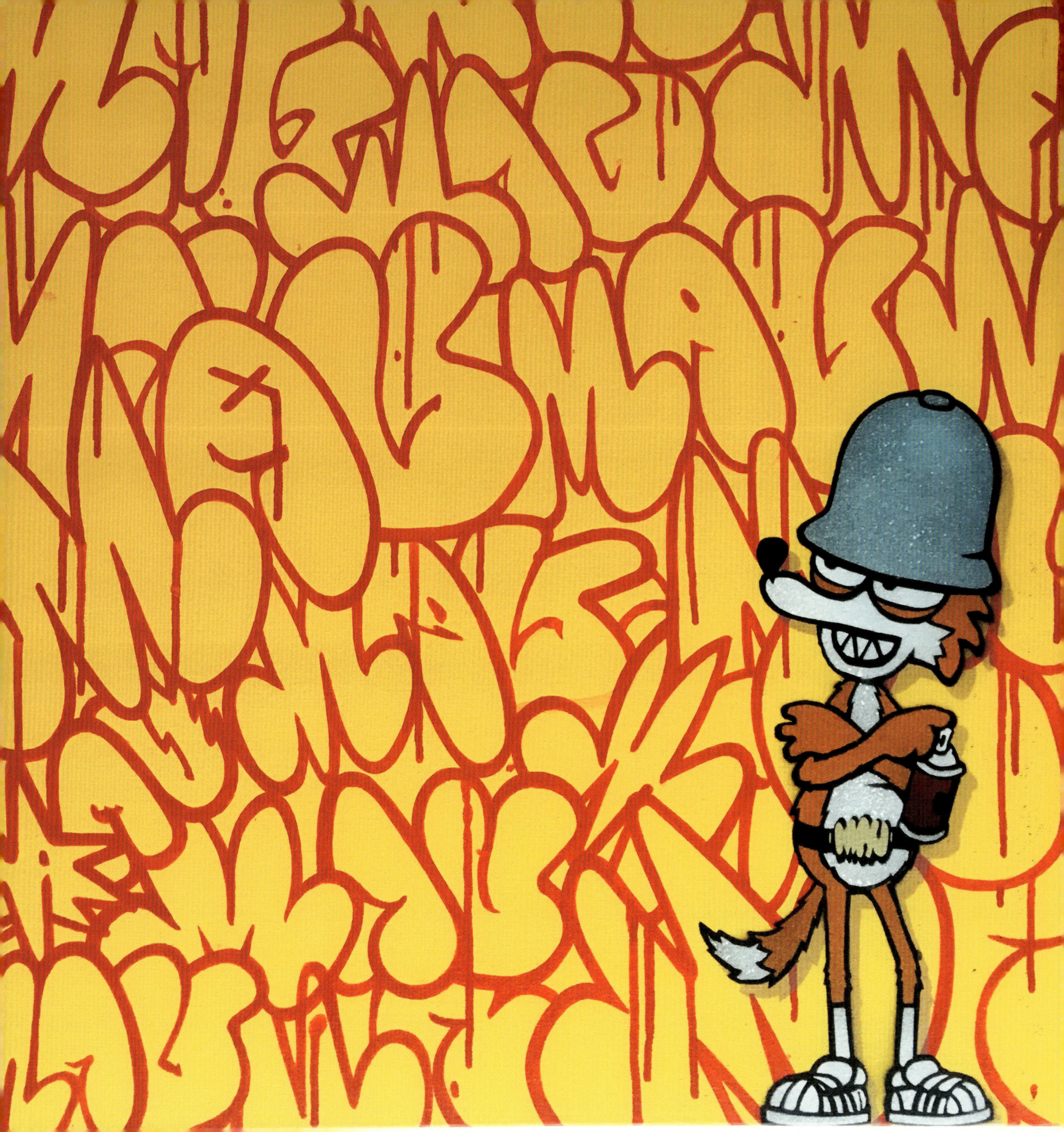

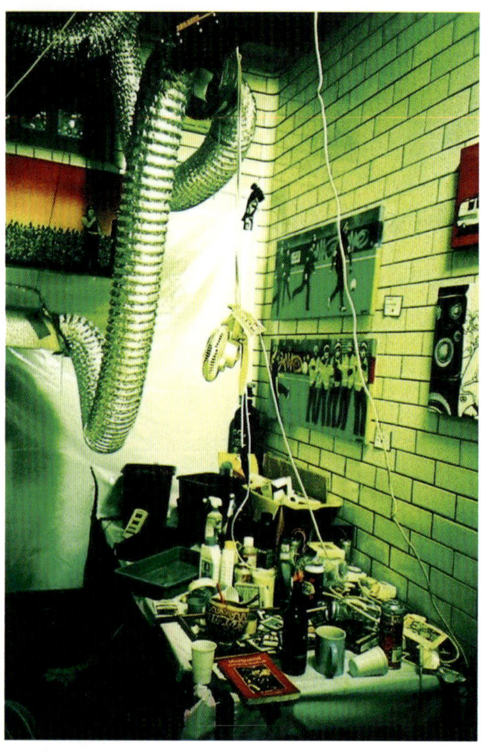

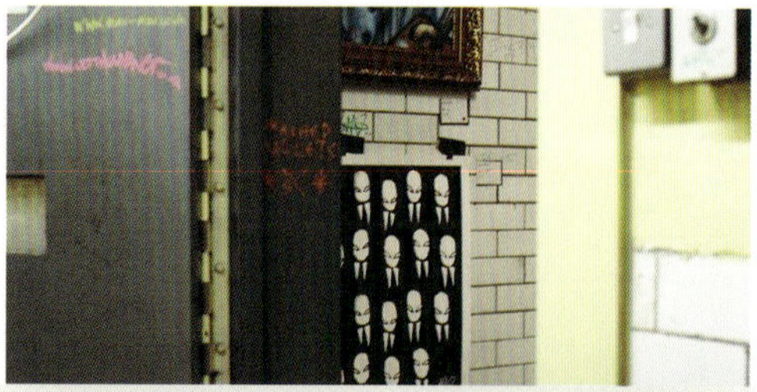

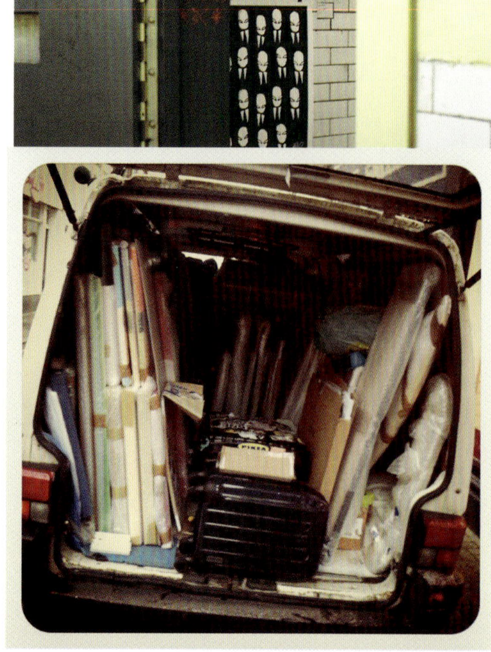

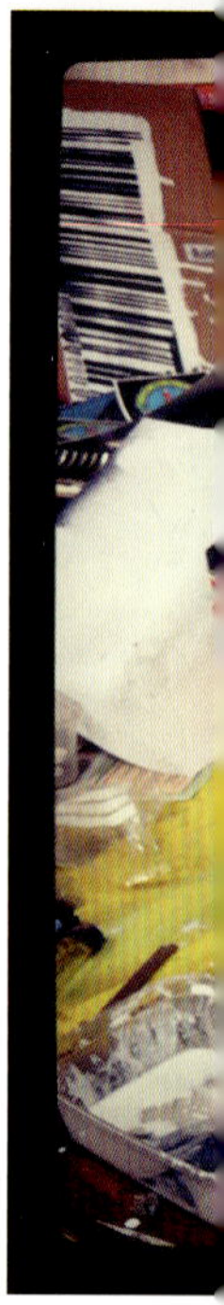

12 Days Before Christmas, Bristol (2007)

The first show I sold a decent amount of work I did an installation. It was a group show in an old police station and I had one of the holding cells. I decided to turn it into a cannabis grow room that had been busted. I borrowed a load of grow kit, set up pots with chopped stalks in them and put in a small sound system playing ganja tunes on repeat. It was the middle of December, so the building was freezing, but in my cell it was warm from the grow-light and packed full of people smoking weed.

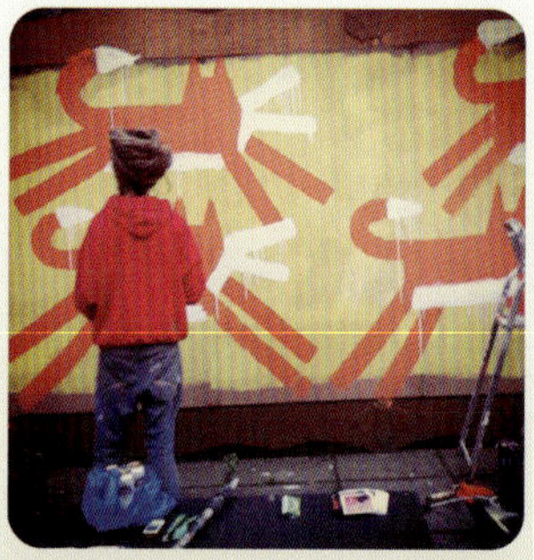

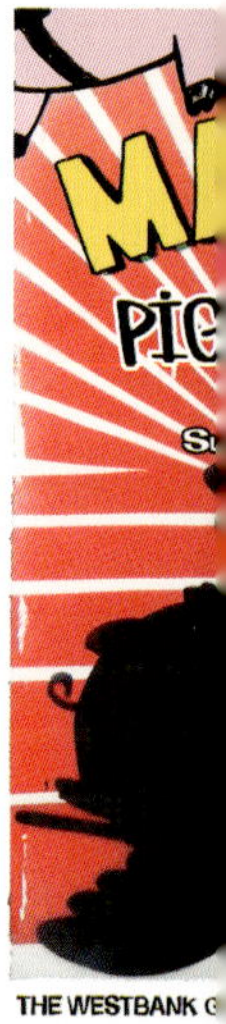

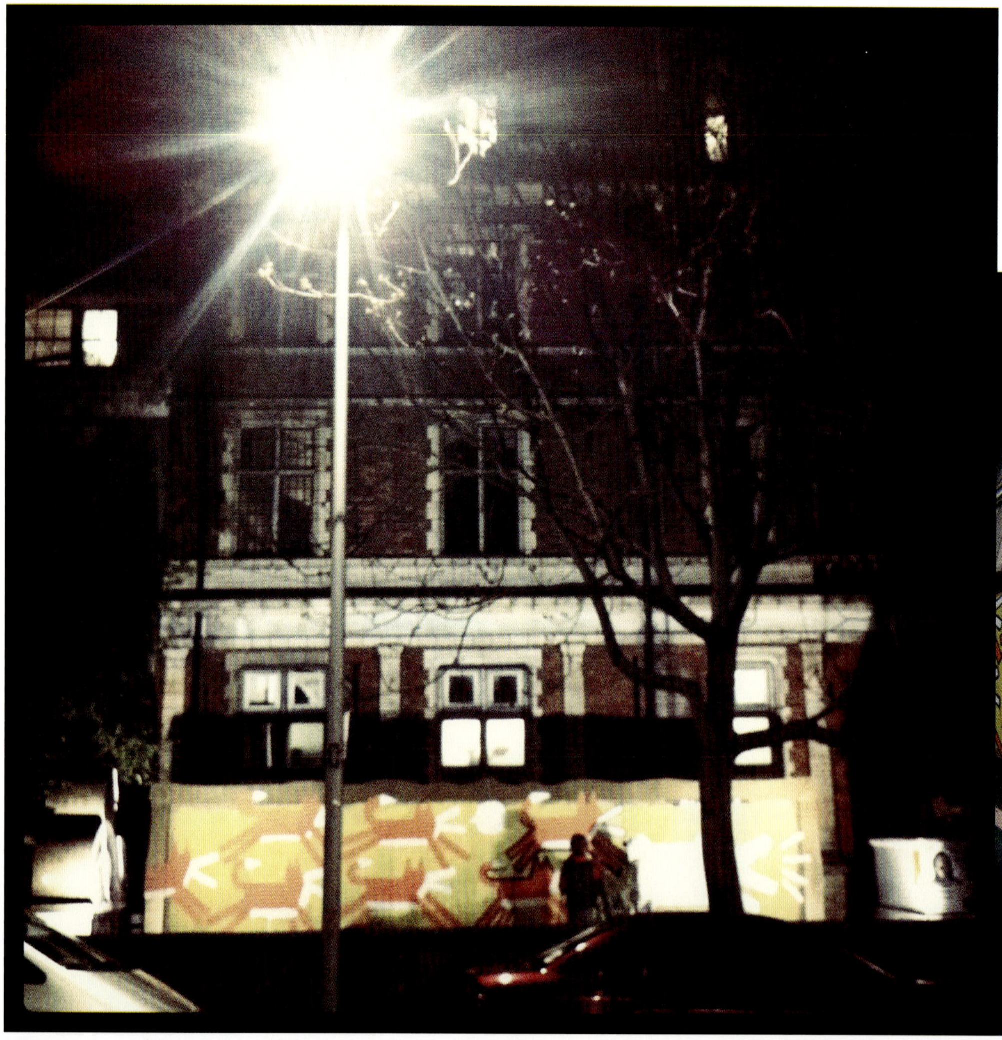

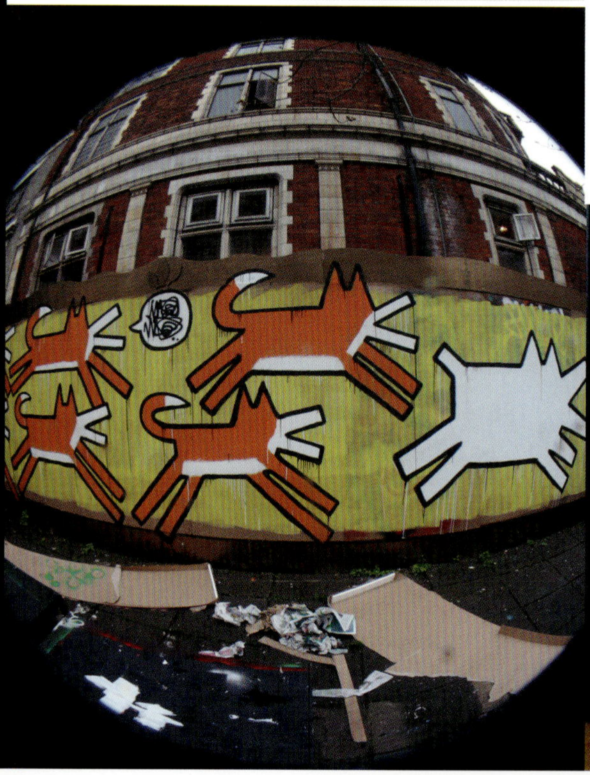

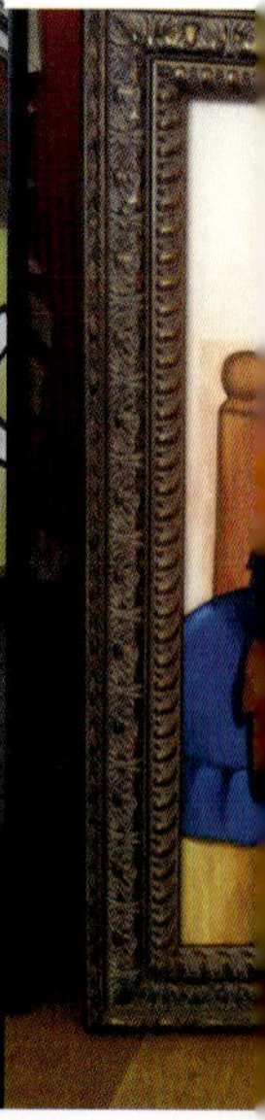

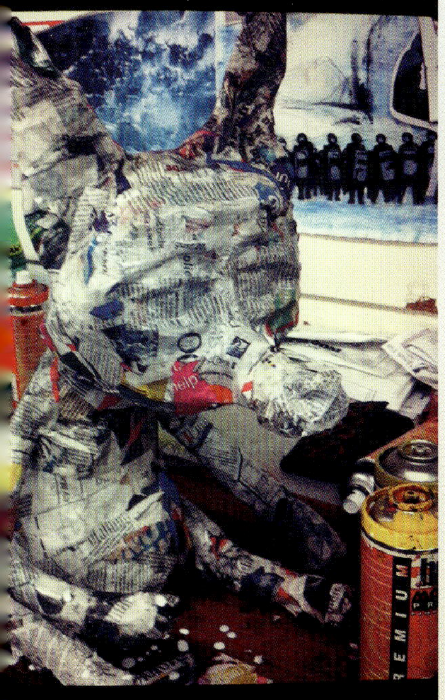

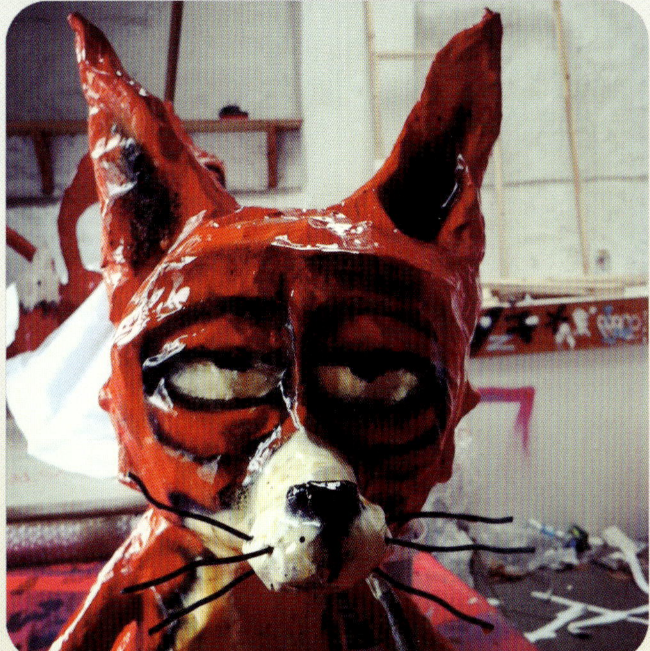

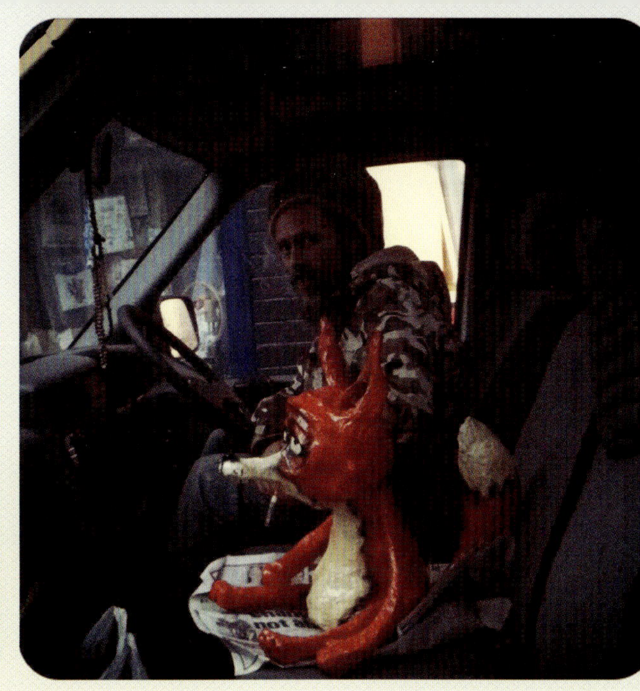

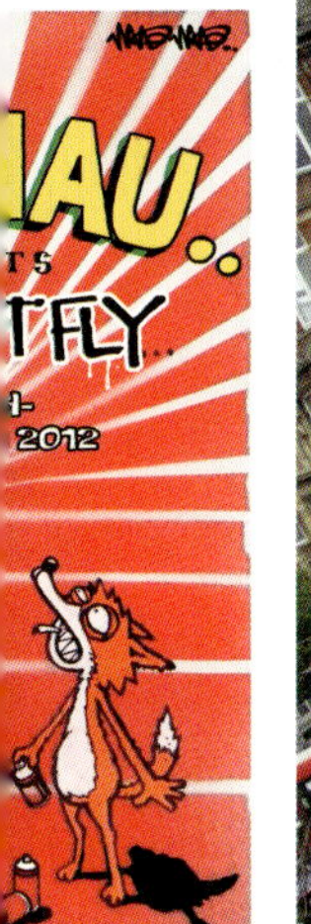

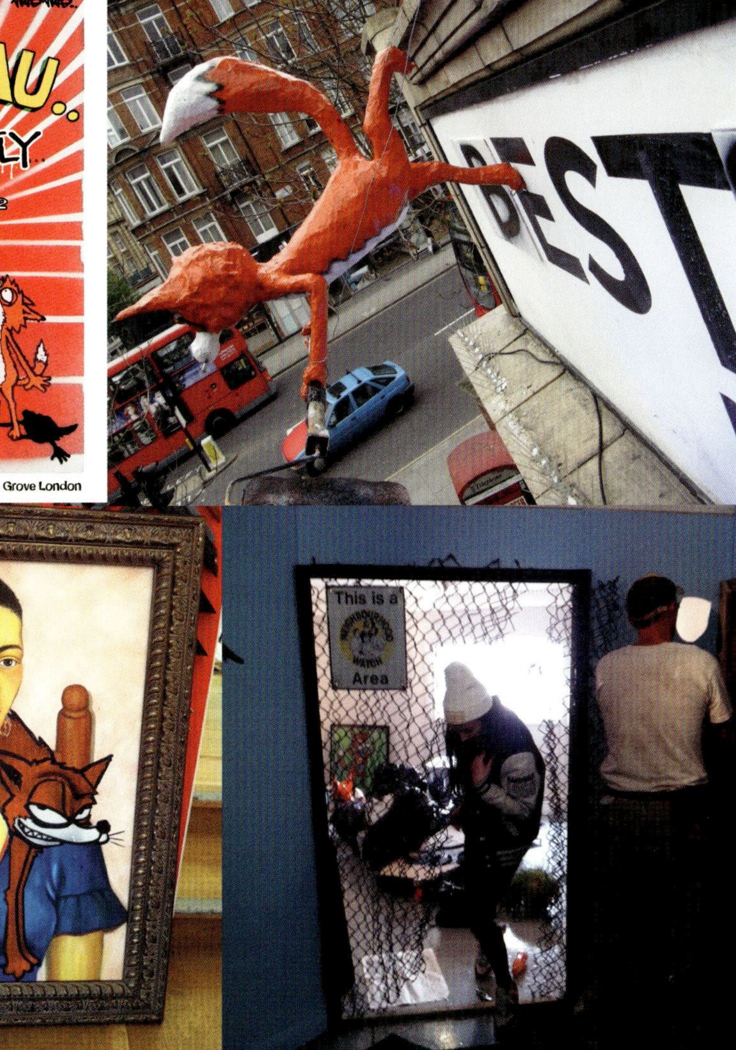

Pigs Might Fly, London (2012)

For Pigs Might Fly, my first solo show, I decided to do another installation. I put together a crew to help me prepare for the show - Beejoir and a few of the Devon crew with a selection of skills. The owners said we could do what we liked with the space so we spent a few days transforming the gallery. We built new walls and secret rooms that you entered through wardrobes, and made the props from papier-mâché and upcycled junk.

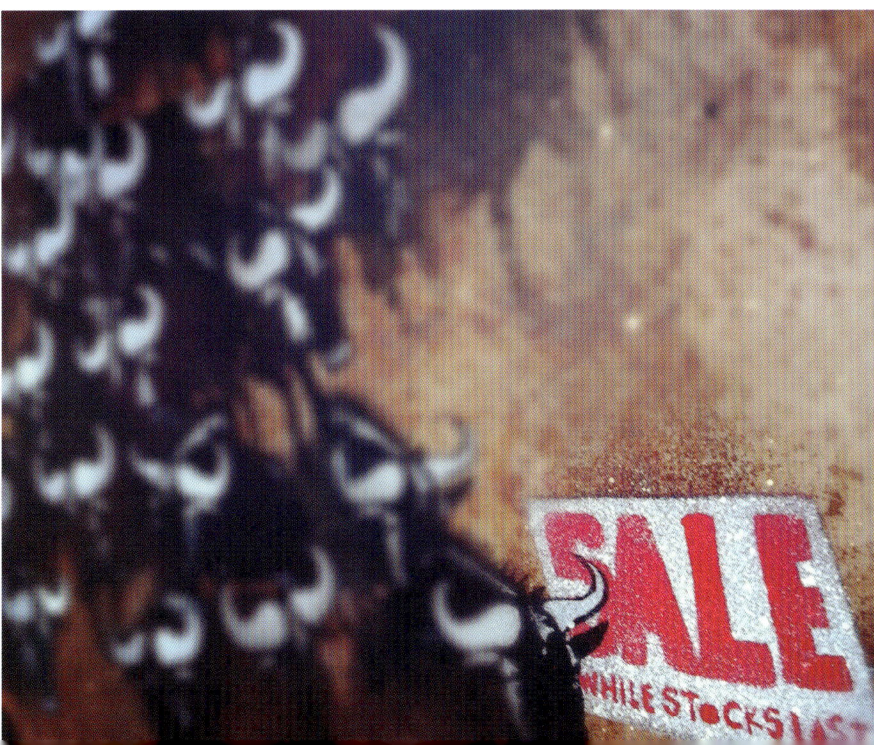

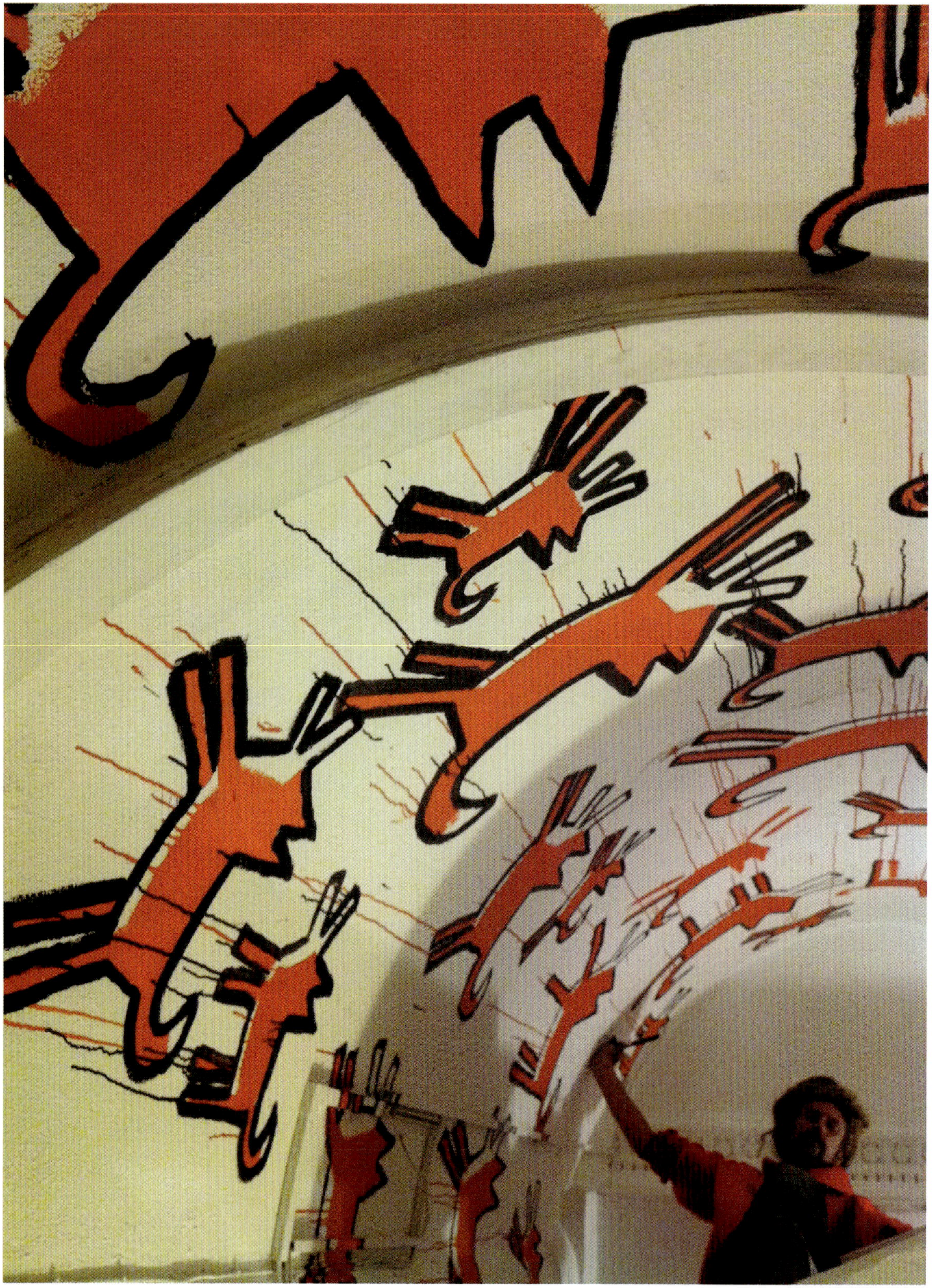

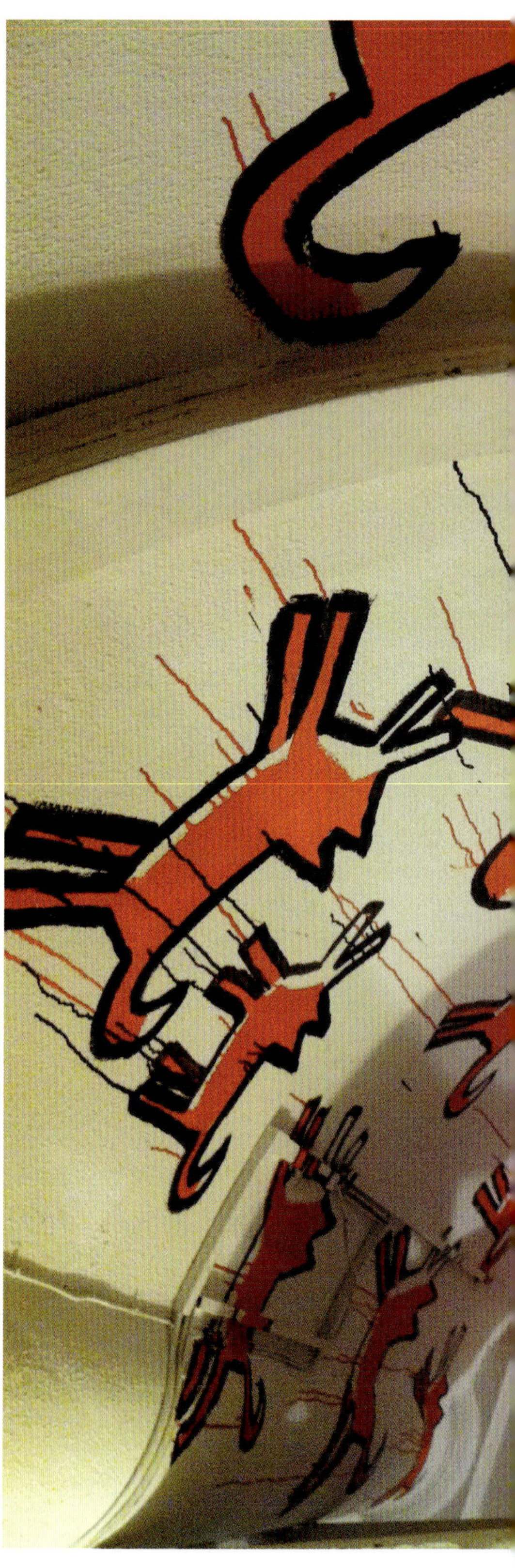

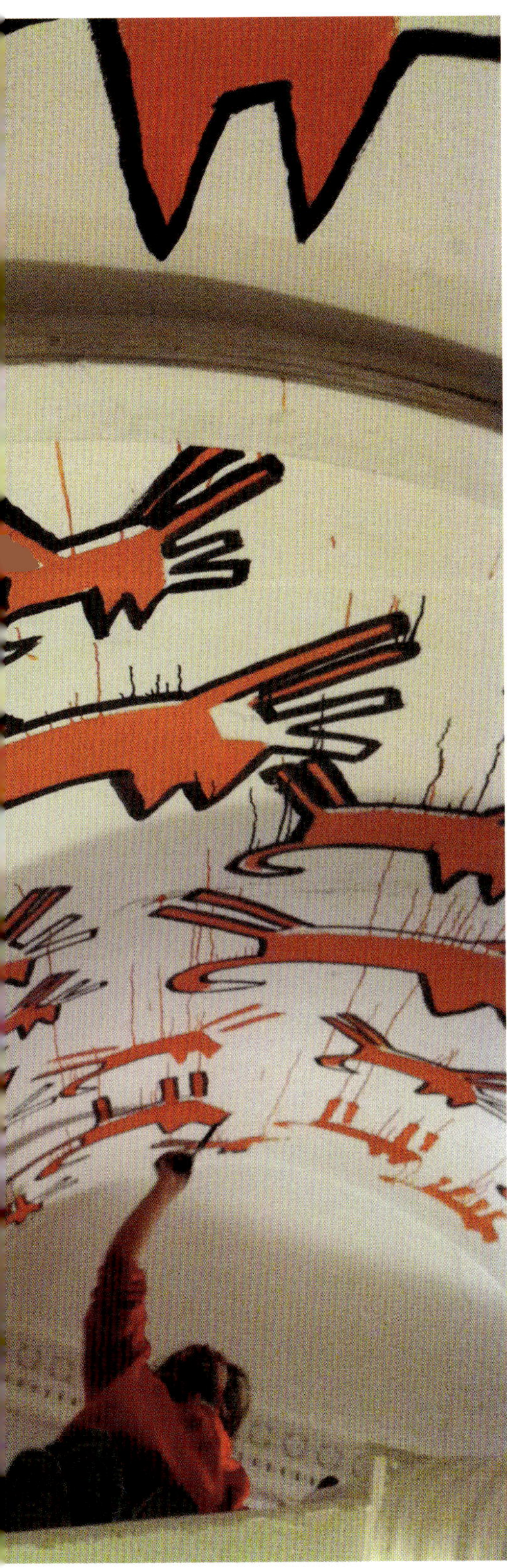

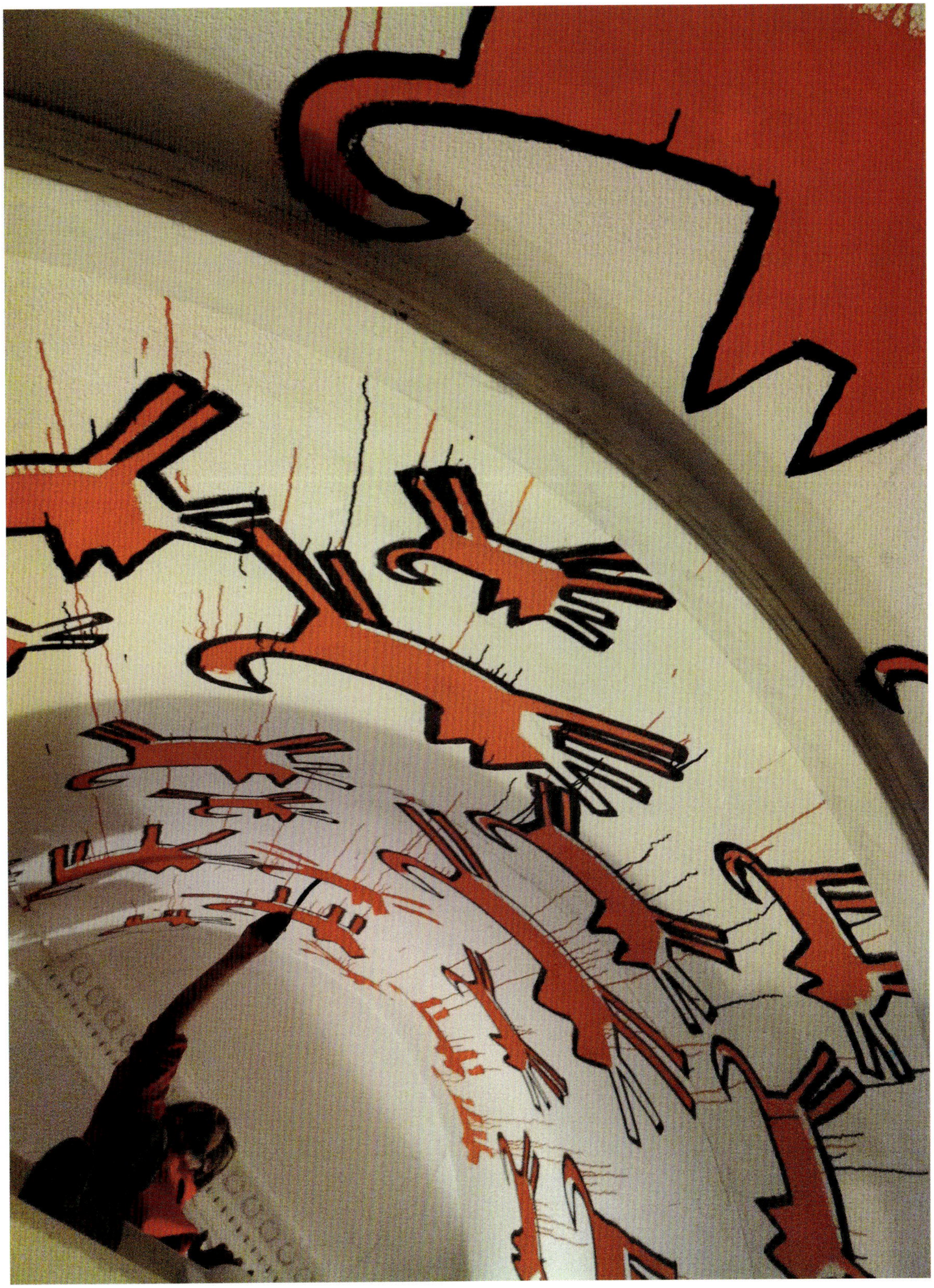

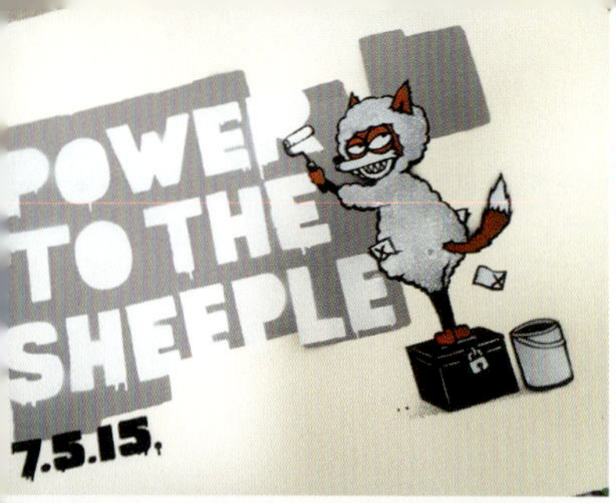

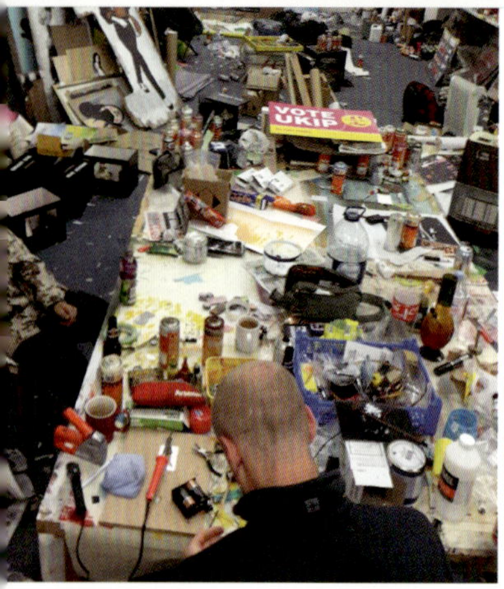

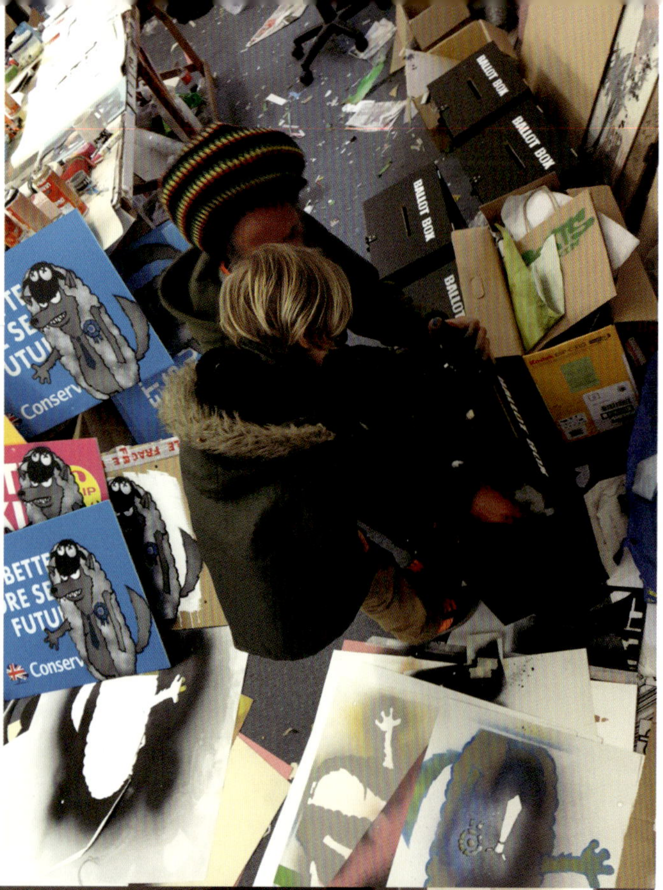

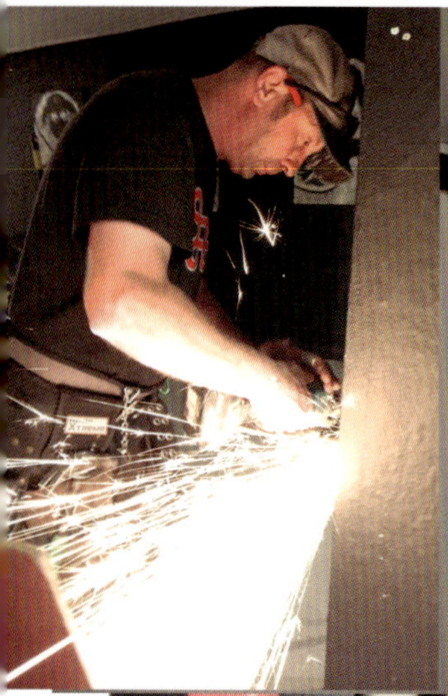

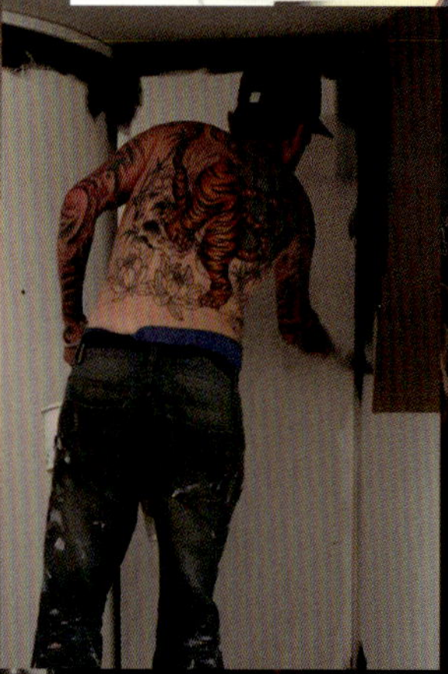

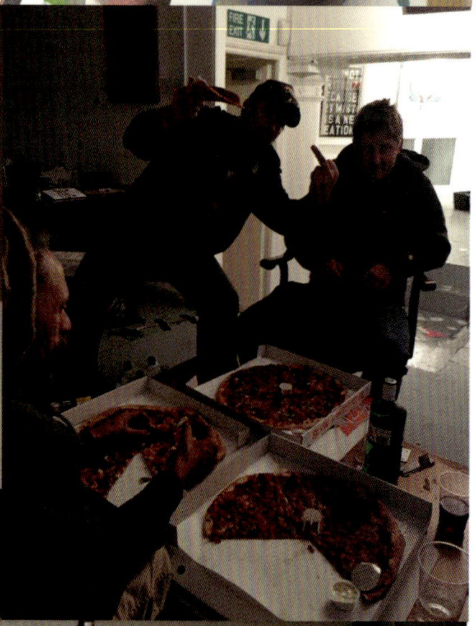

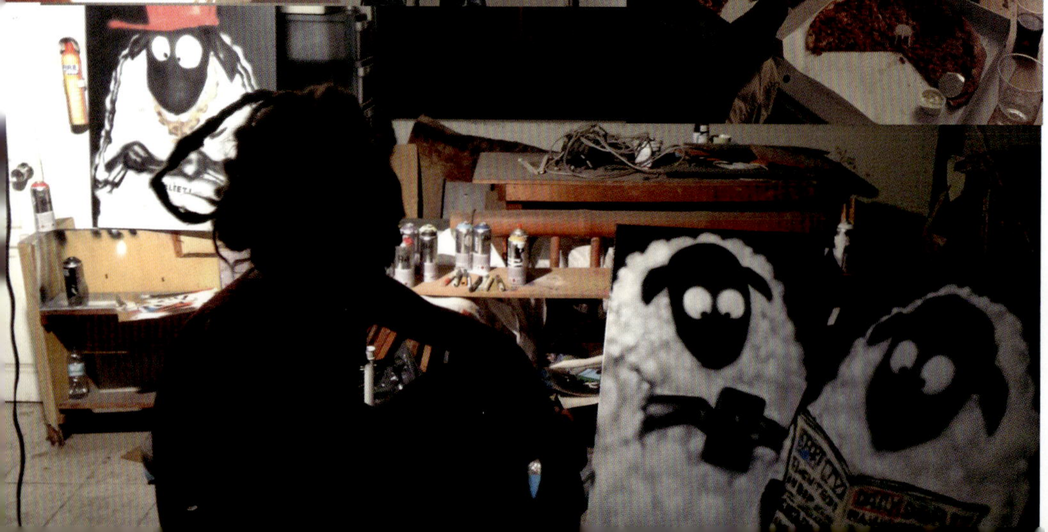

Power To The Sheeple, London (2015)

A couple of years later we returned to the Westbank to do a show that coincided with the 2015 UK election. We installed ballot boxes, 'rolling' booths and put wolf billboards outside using the colours and symbols of the political parties. On the day of the show we had to turn some confused people away who had turned up to vote, mistaking it for a real polling station!

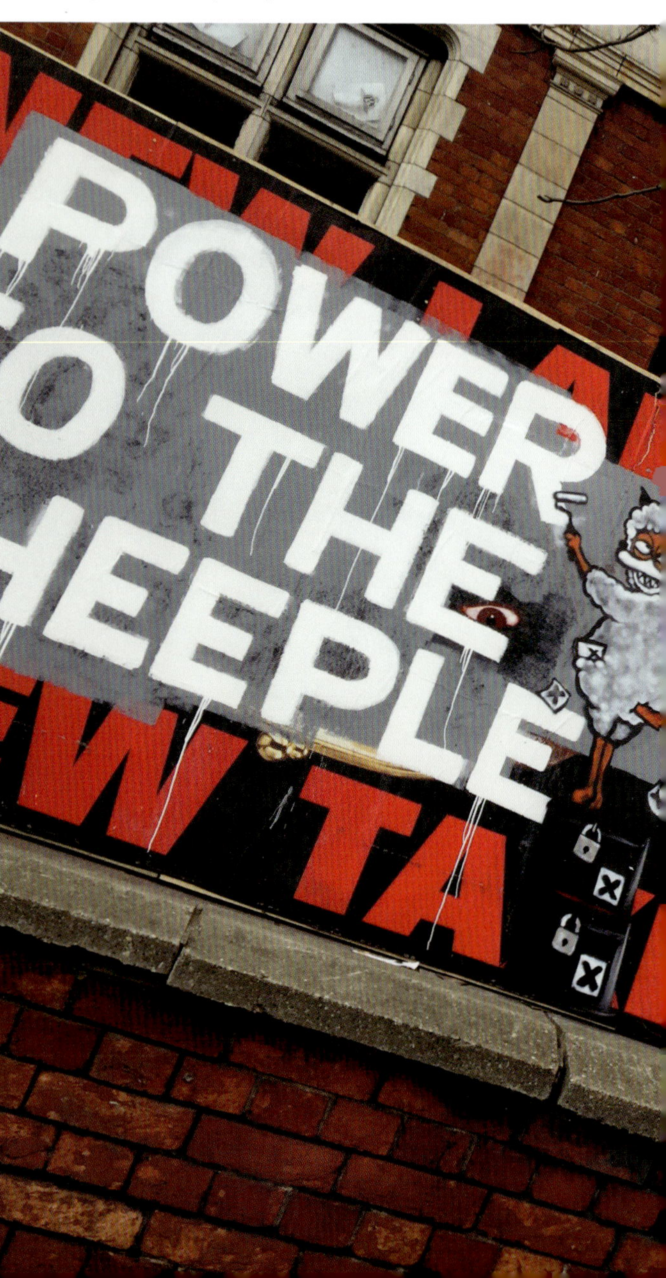

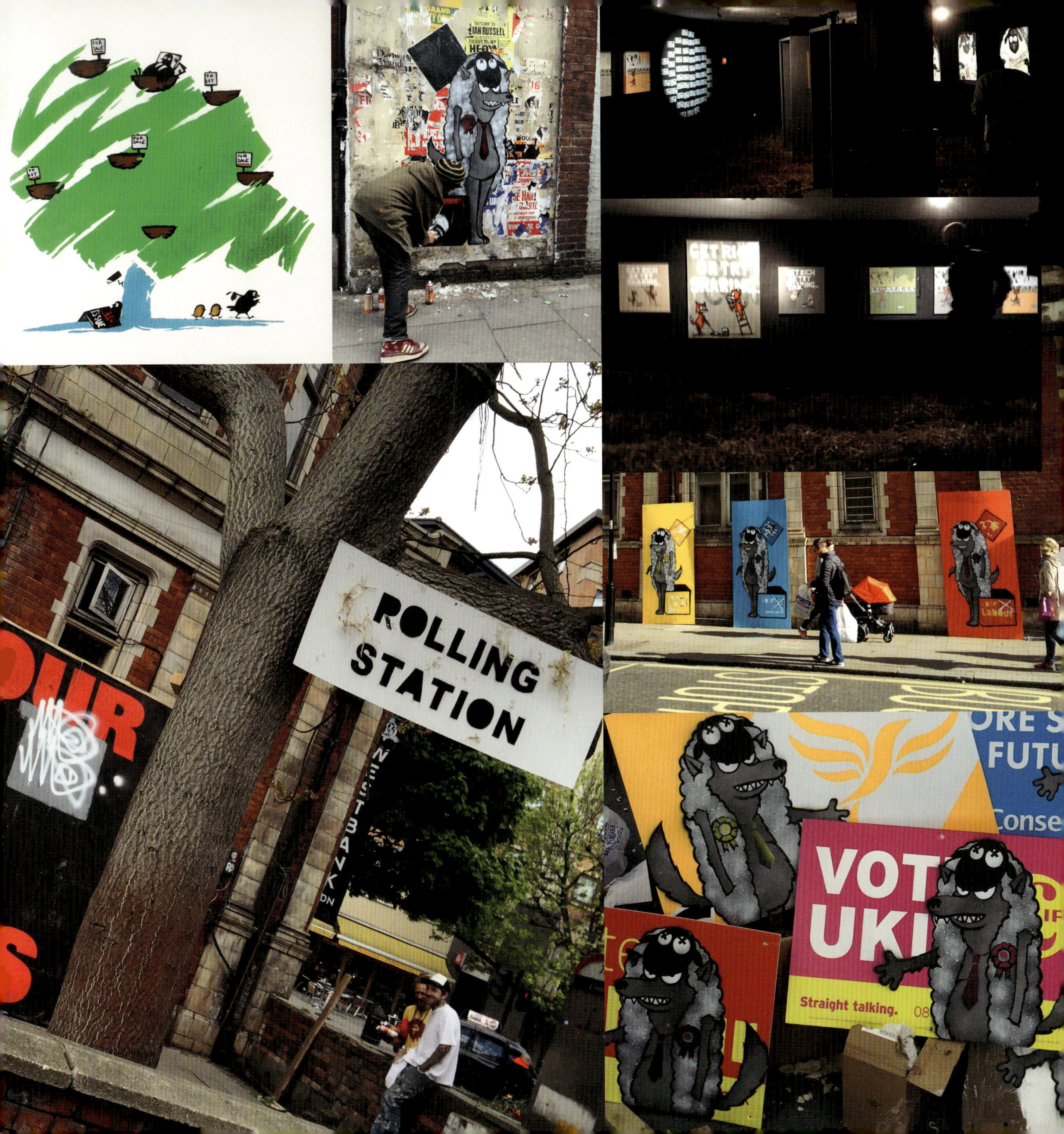
ROLLING
STATION
Straight talking.

Souled Out Studios group show, Bangkok (2018)

The nice thing about becoming better known is getting invites to show your work in different countries.
I've been lucky to have the experience of visiting some great cities around the world and meeting many interesting people.

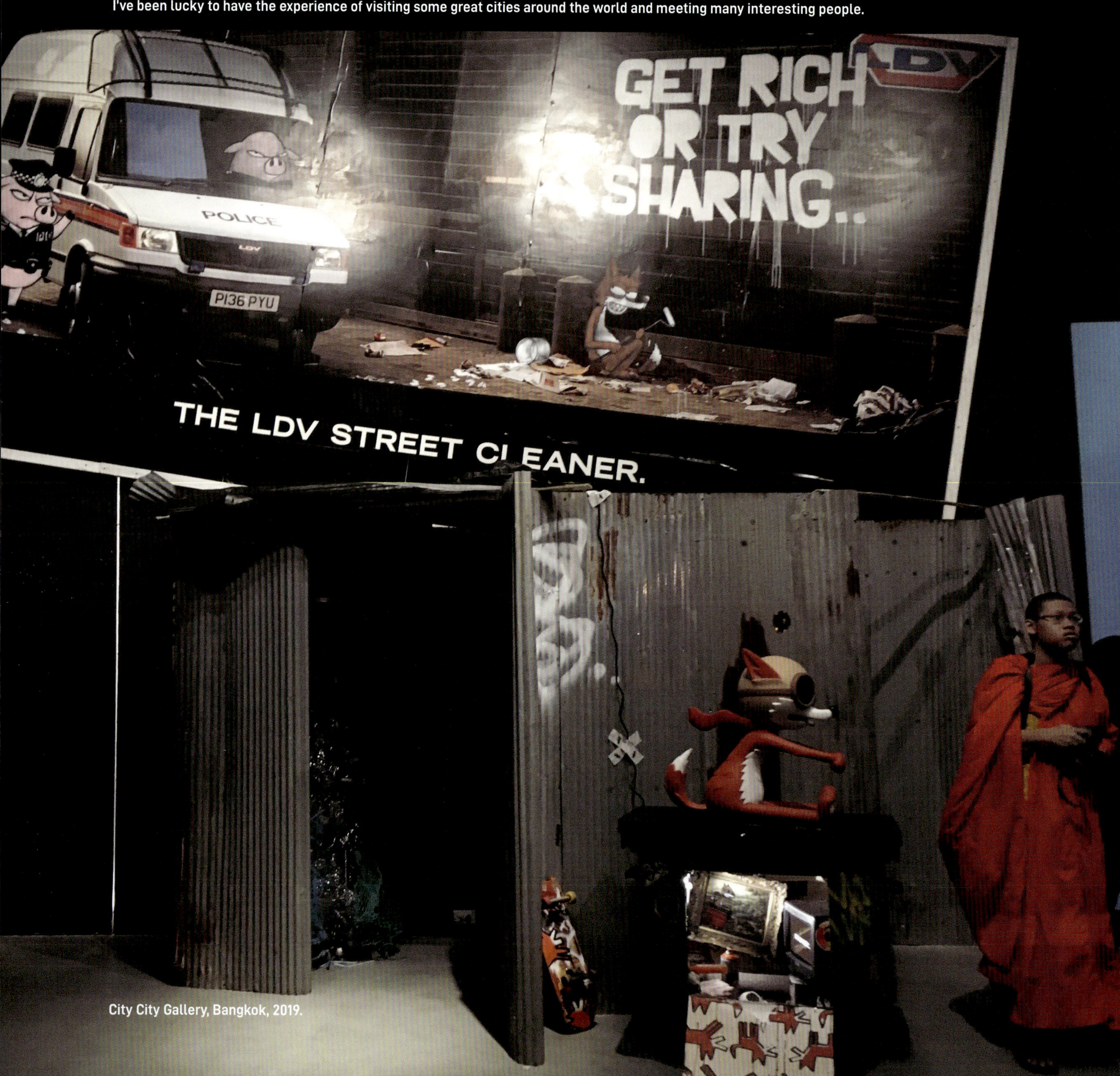

City City Gallery, Bangkok, 2019.

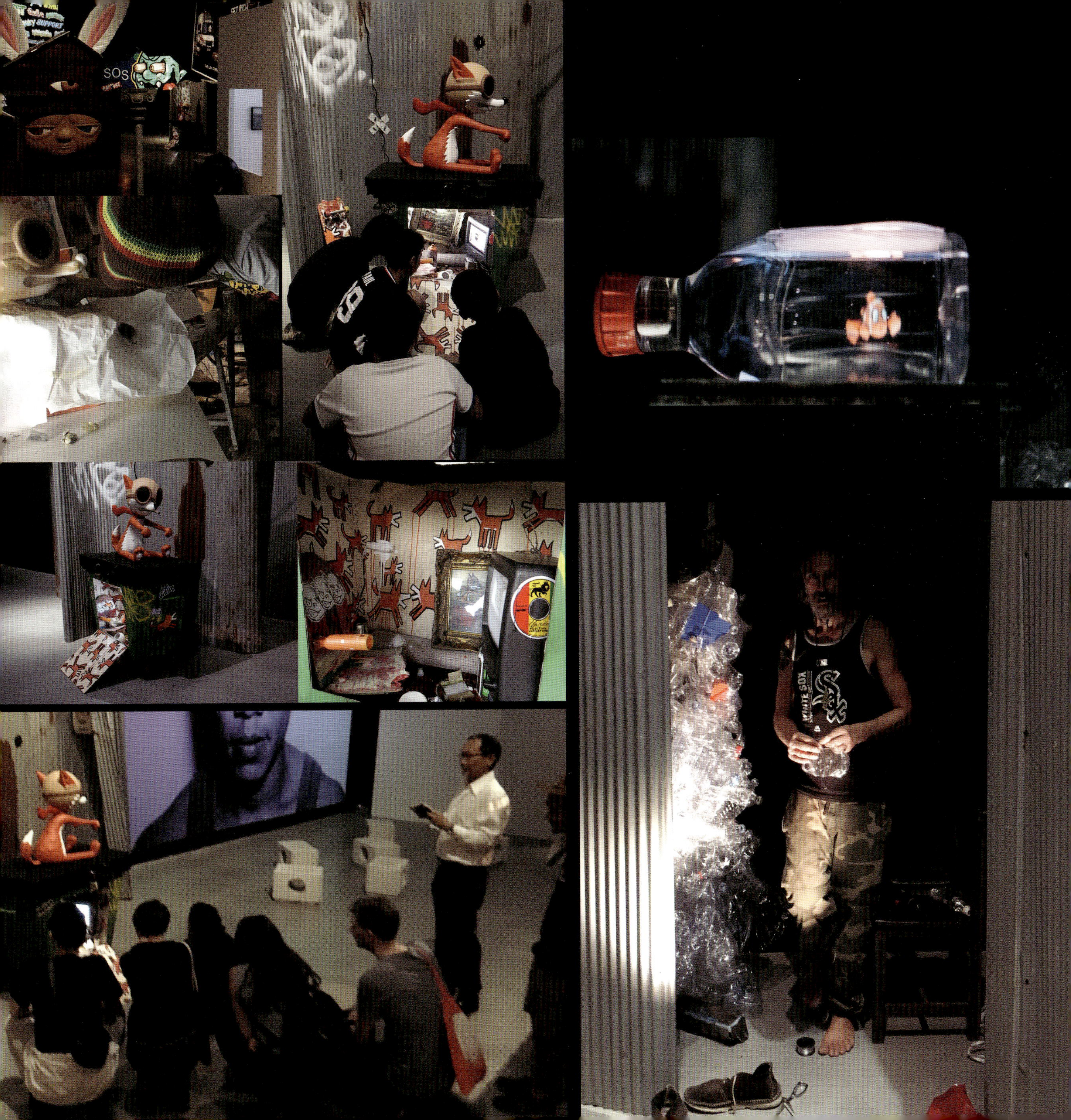
SOS
WHITE SOX

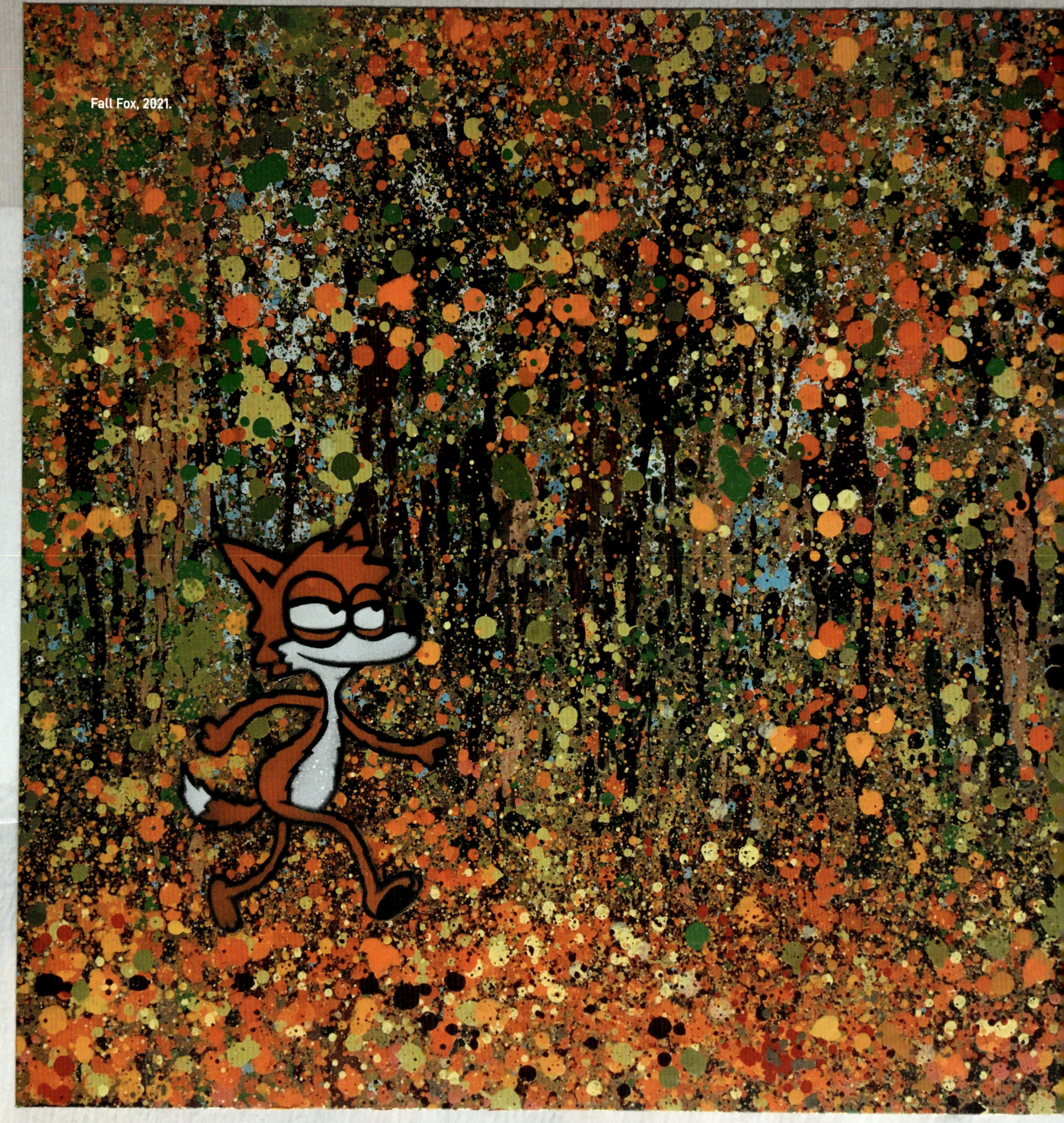

Fall Fox, 2021.

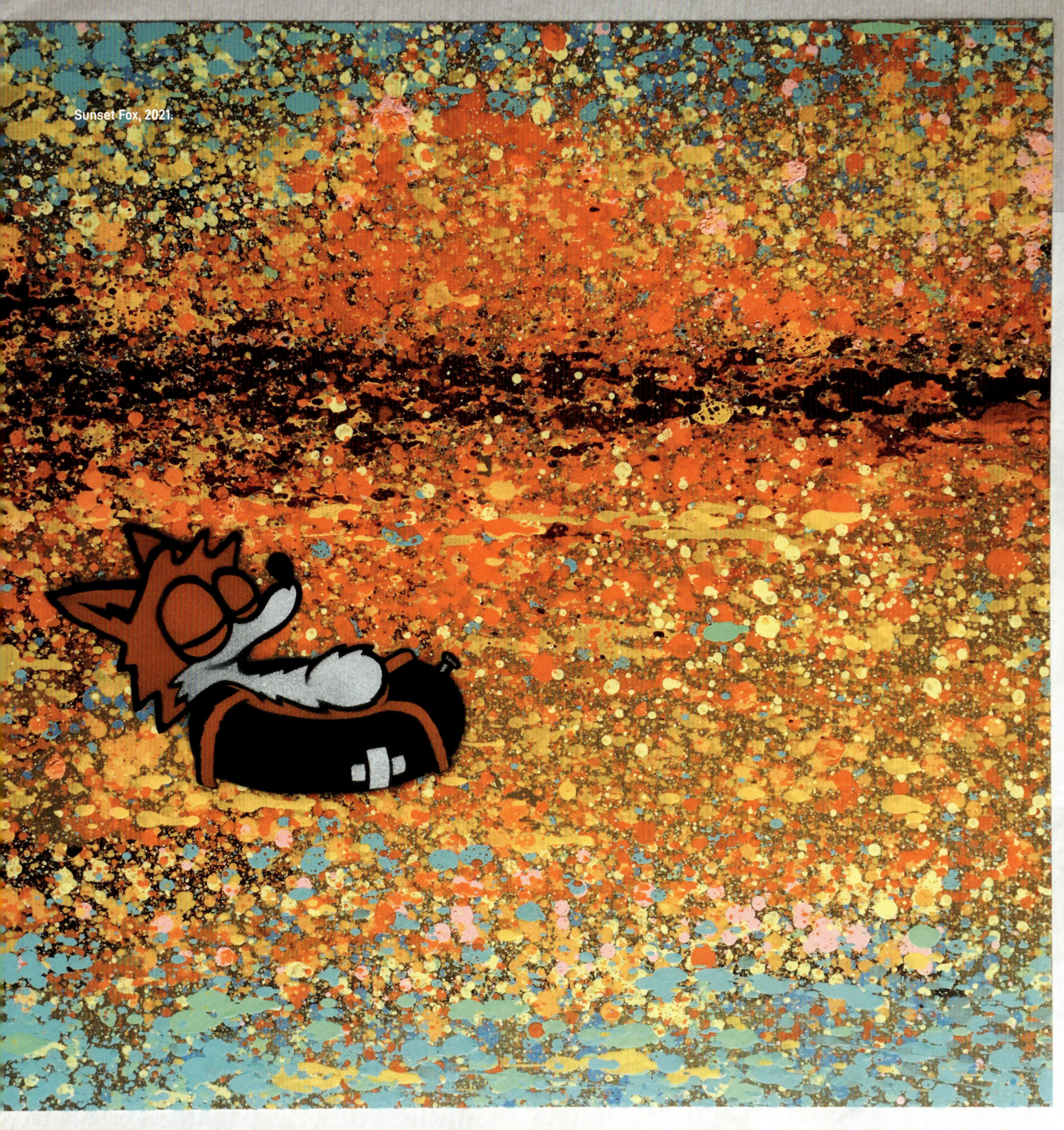
Sunset Fox, 2021.

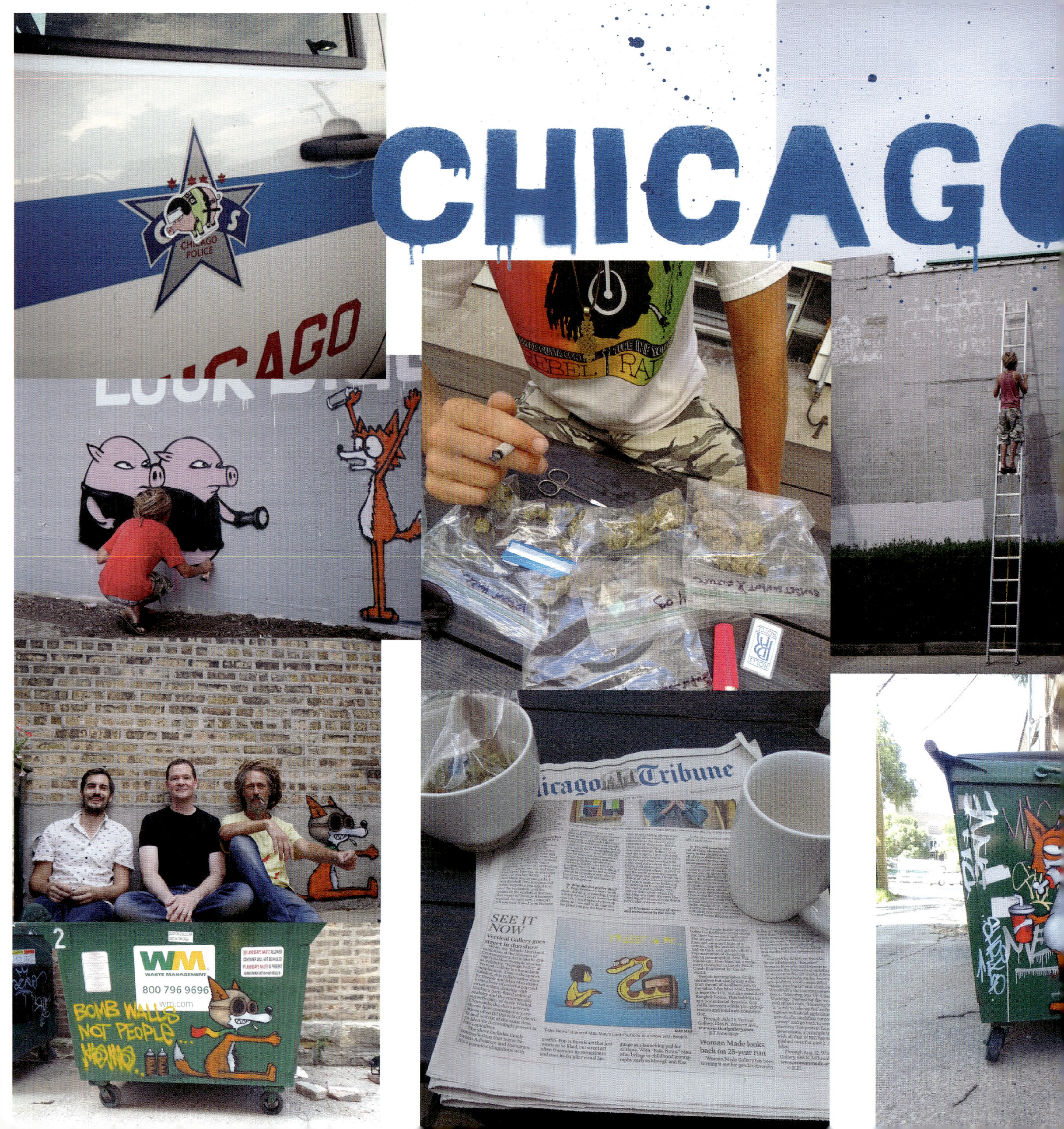
CHICAGO
CHICAGO POLICE
CHICAGO
WM
WASTE MANAGEMENT
800 796 9696
wm.com
BOMB WALLS
NOT PEOPLE
Chicago Tribune
SEE IT NOW
Vertical Gallery goes street in duo show
Woman Made looks back on 25-year run

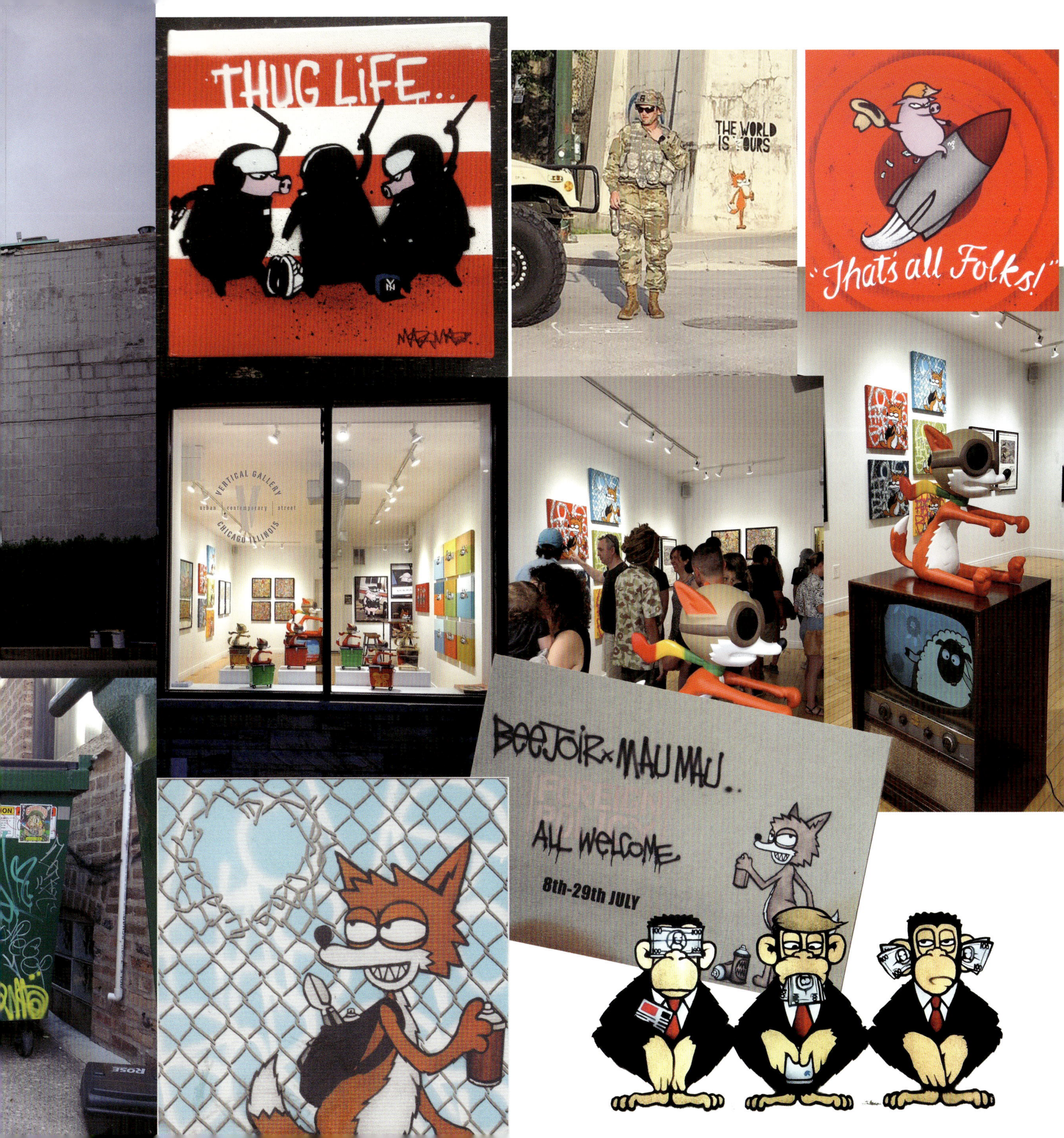
THUG LiFE..
MAU MAU
THE WORLD IS OURS
"That's all Folks!"
VERTICAL GALLERY
urban contemporary street
CHICAGO ILLINOIS
BEEJOIR x MAU MAU..
ALL WELCOME
8th-29th JULY

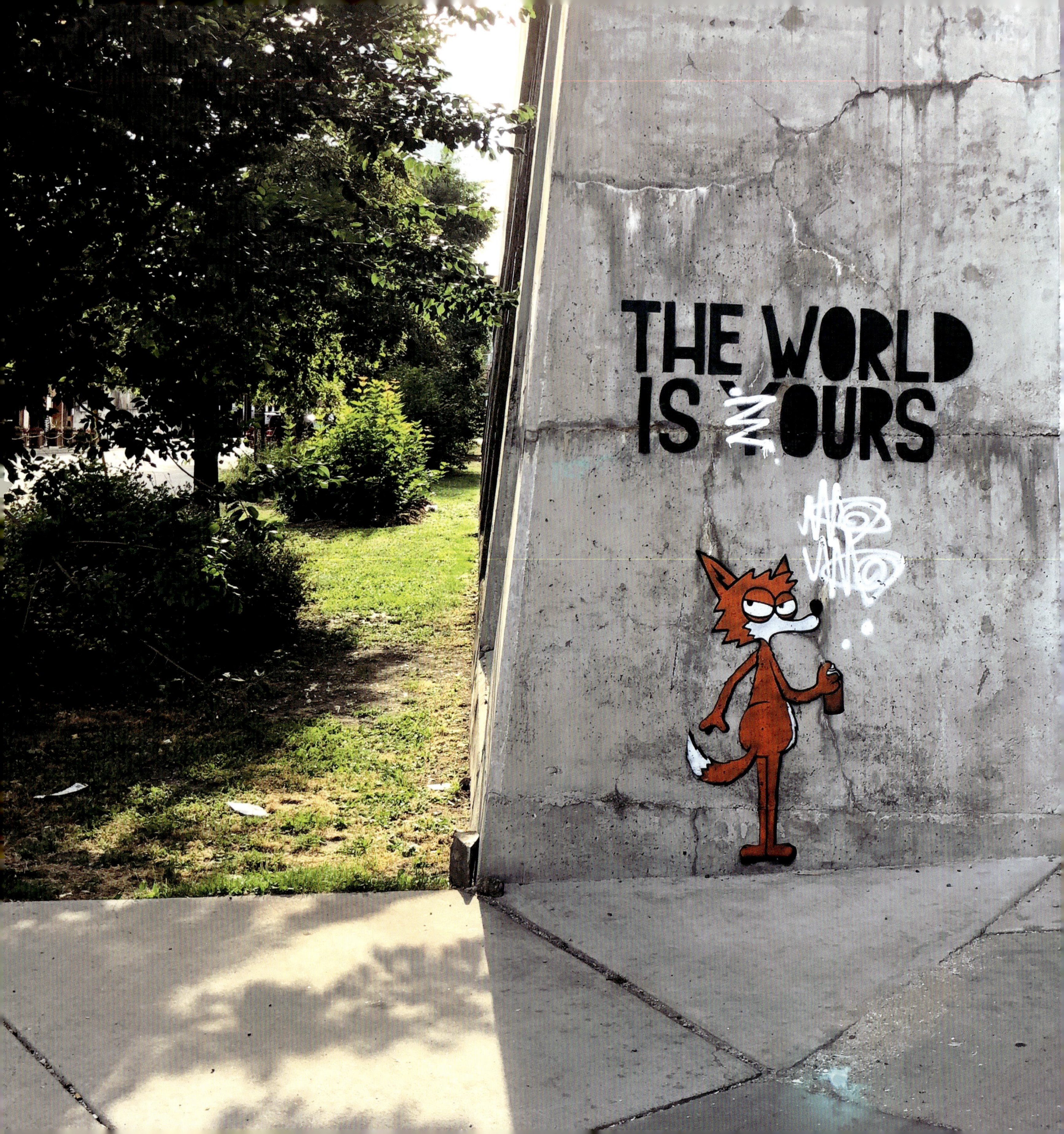
THE WORLD
IS YOURS

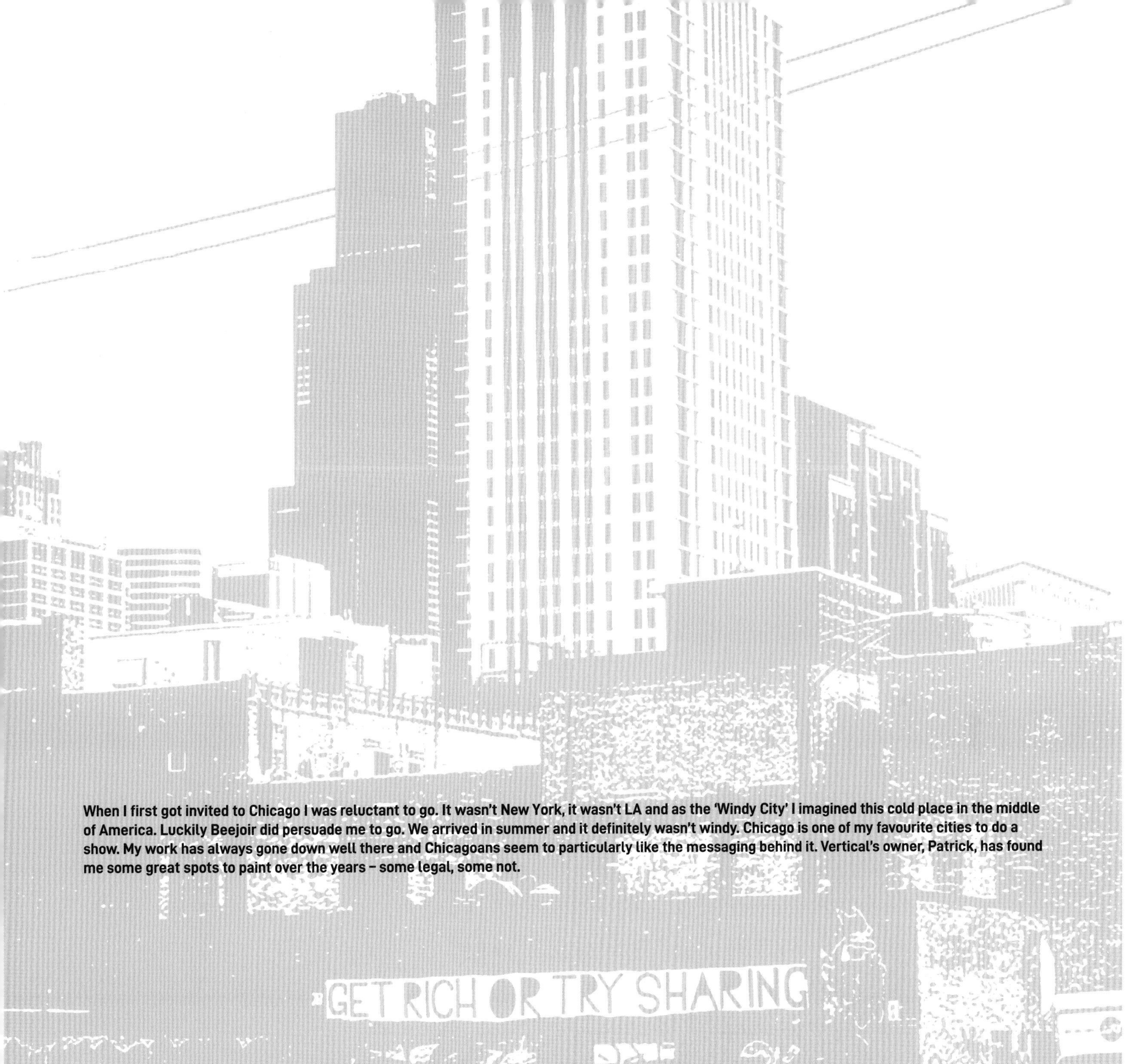

When I first got invited to Chicago I was reluctant to go. It wasn't New York, it wasn't LA and as the 'Windy City' I imagined this cold place in the middle of America. Luckily Beejoir did persuade me to go. We arrived in summer and it definitely wasn't windy. Chicago is one of my favourite cities to do a show. My work has always gone down well there and Chicagoans seem to particularly like the messaging behind it. Vertical's owner, Patrick, has found me some great spots to paint over the years – some legal, some not.

The World is Ours, Corner of N. Milwaukee St & W. Hubbard St, 2019.

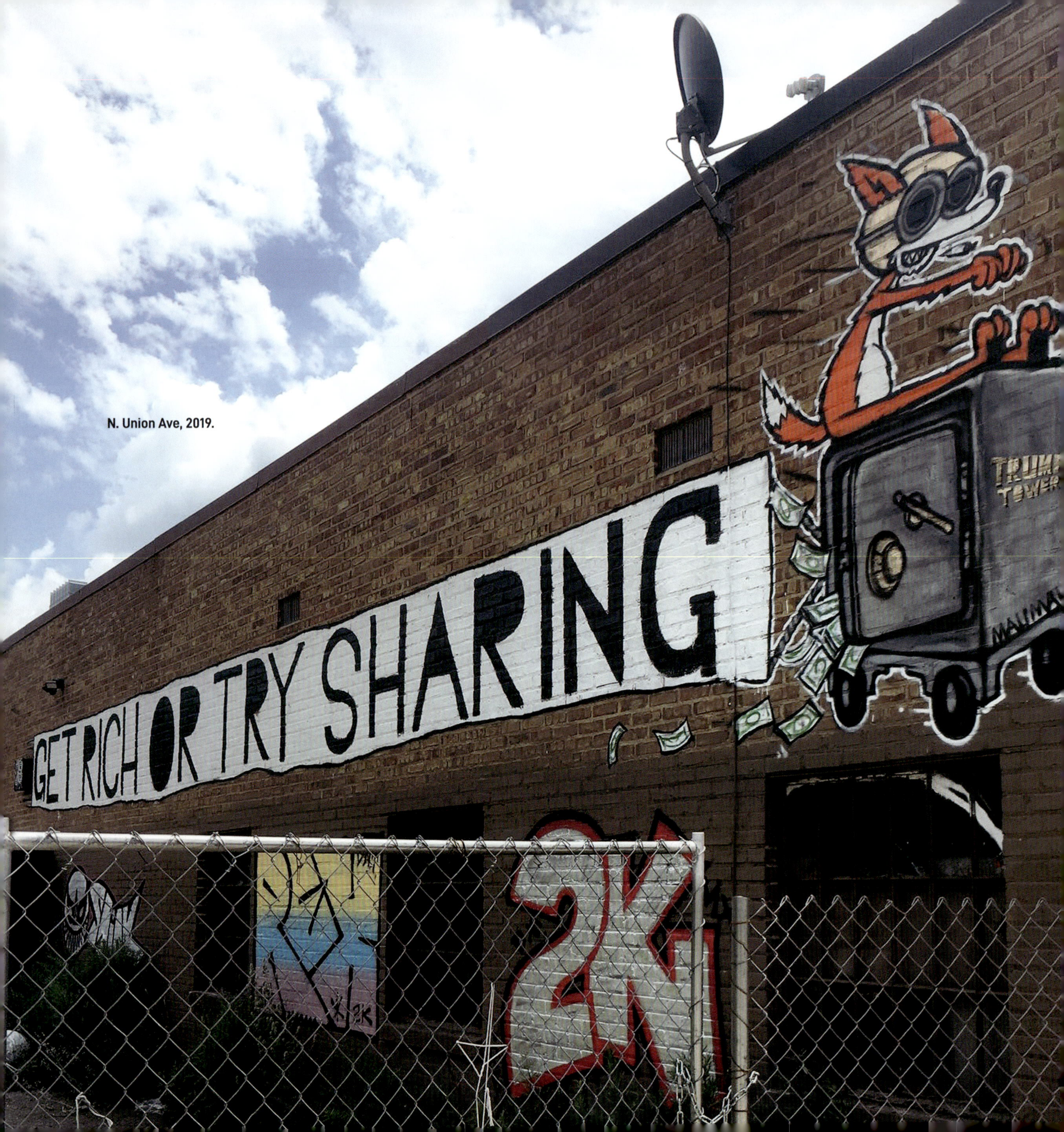

N. Union Ave, 2019.

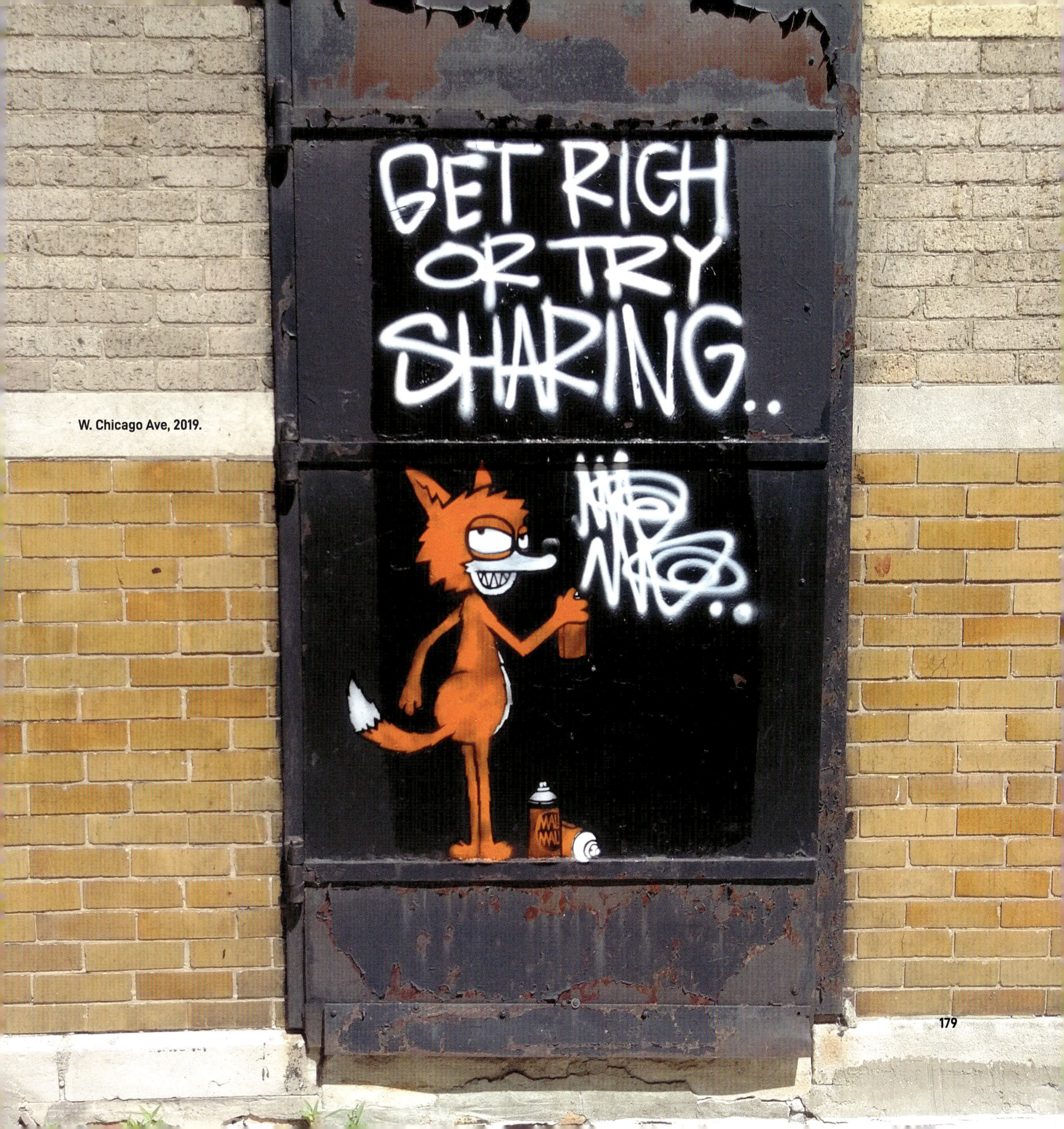

W. Chicago Ave, 2019.

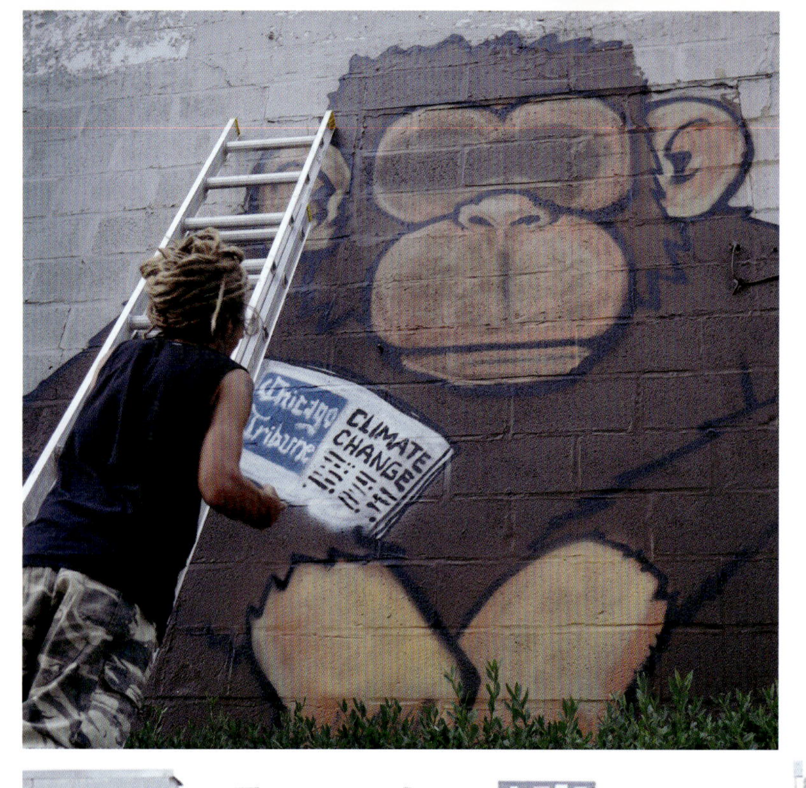

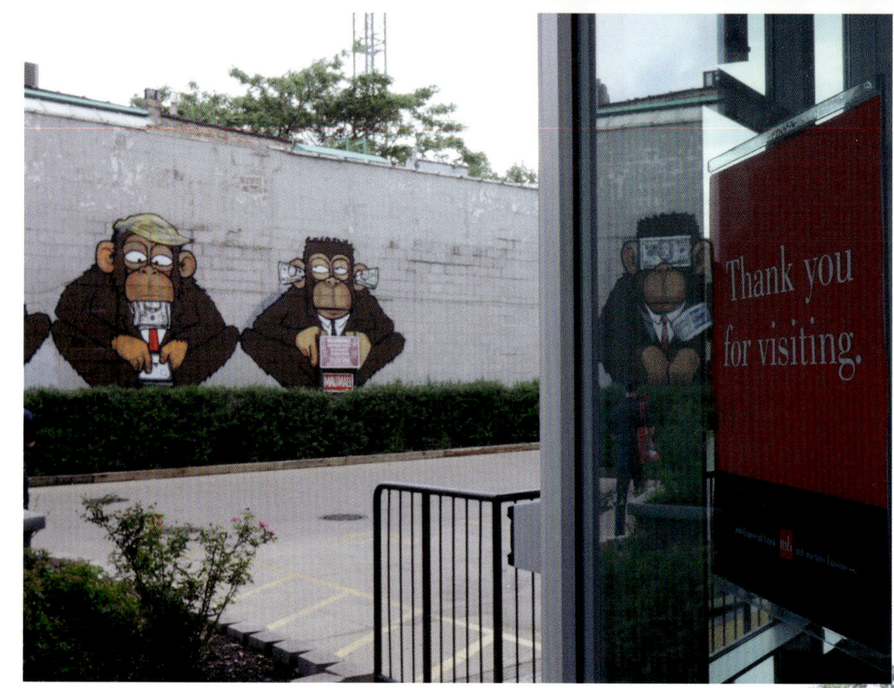

3 Monkeys Trump, W. Division St, 2017.

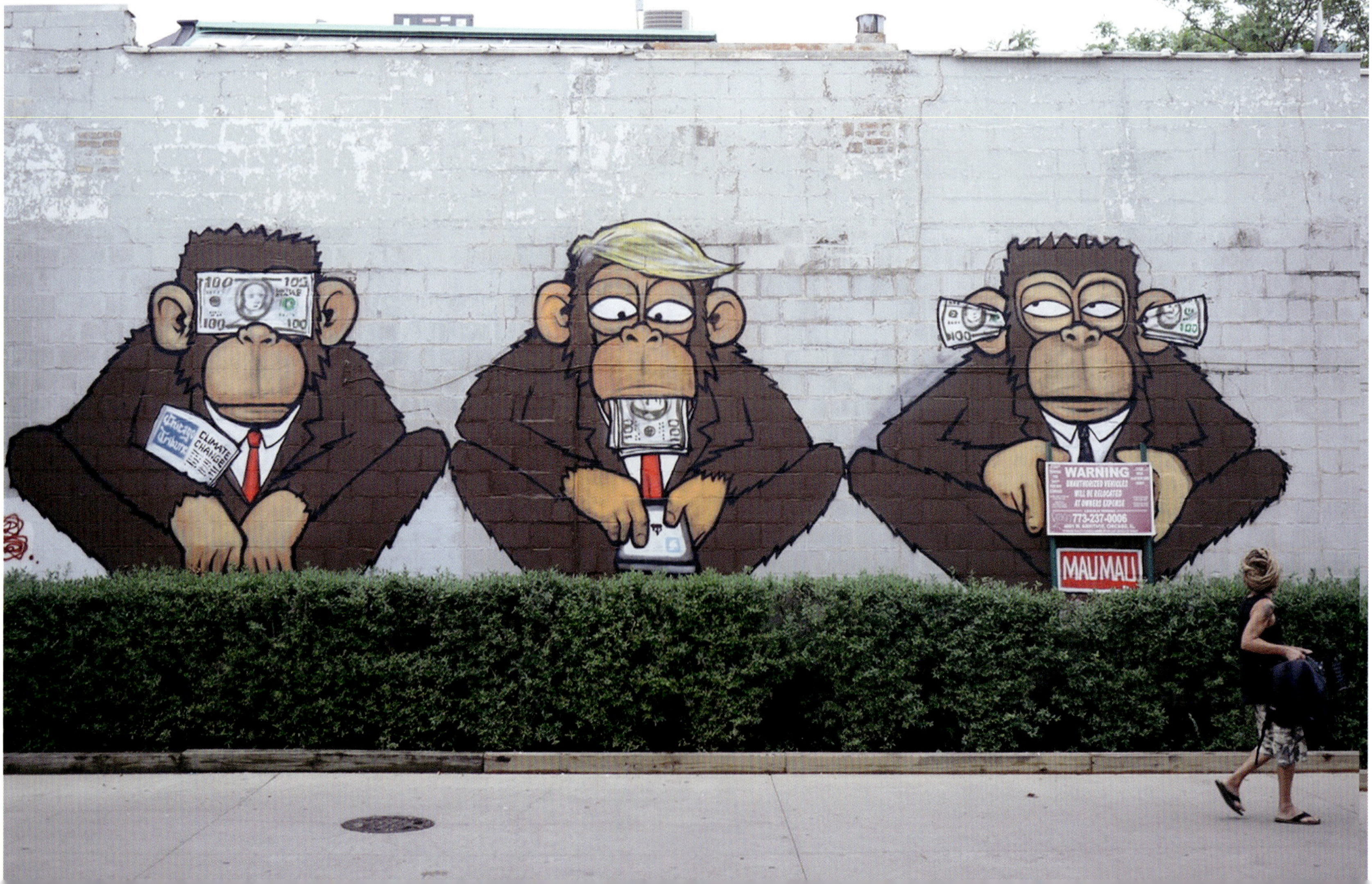

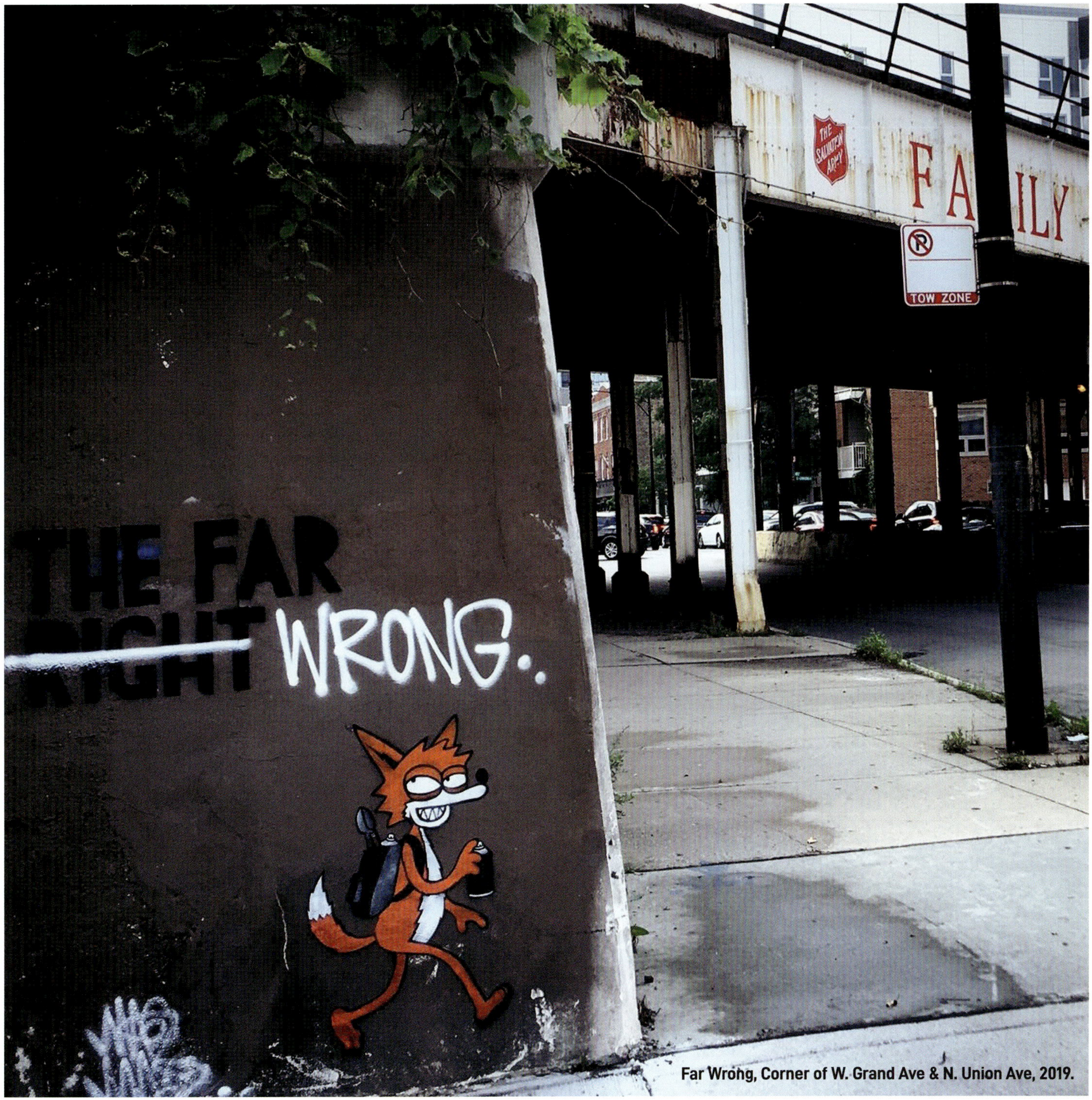

Far Wrong, Corner of W. Grand Ave & N. Union Ave, 2019.

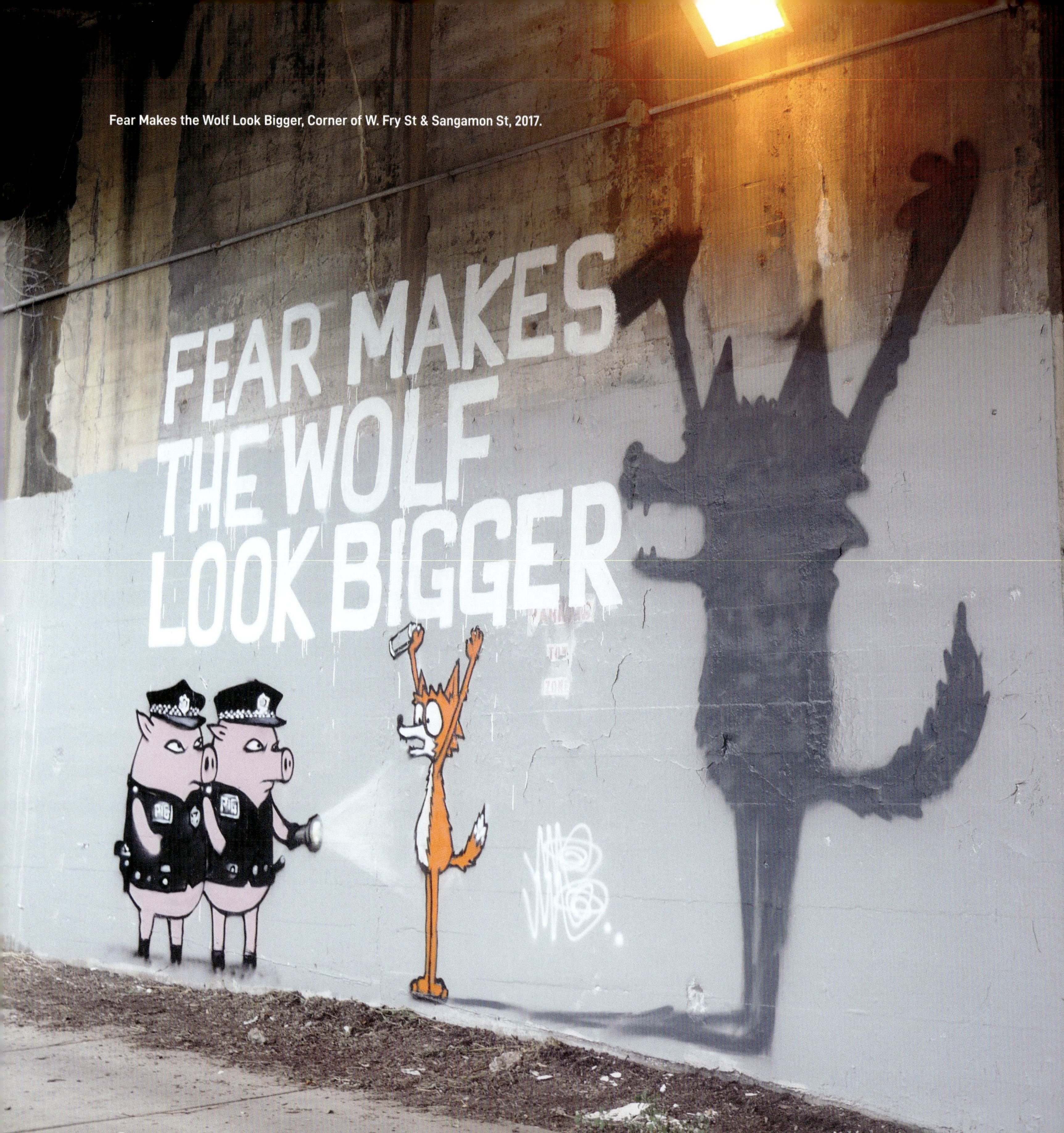

Fear Makes the Wolf Look Bigger, Corner of W. Fry St & Sangamon St, 2017.

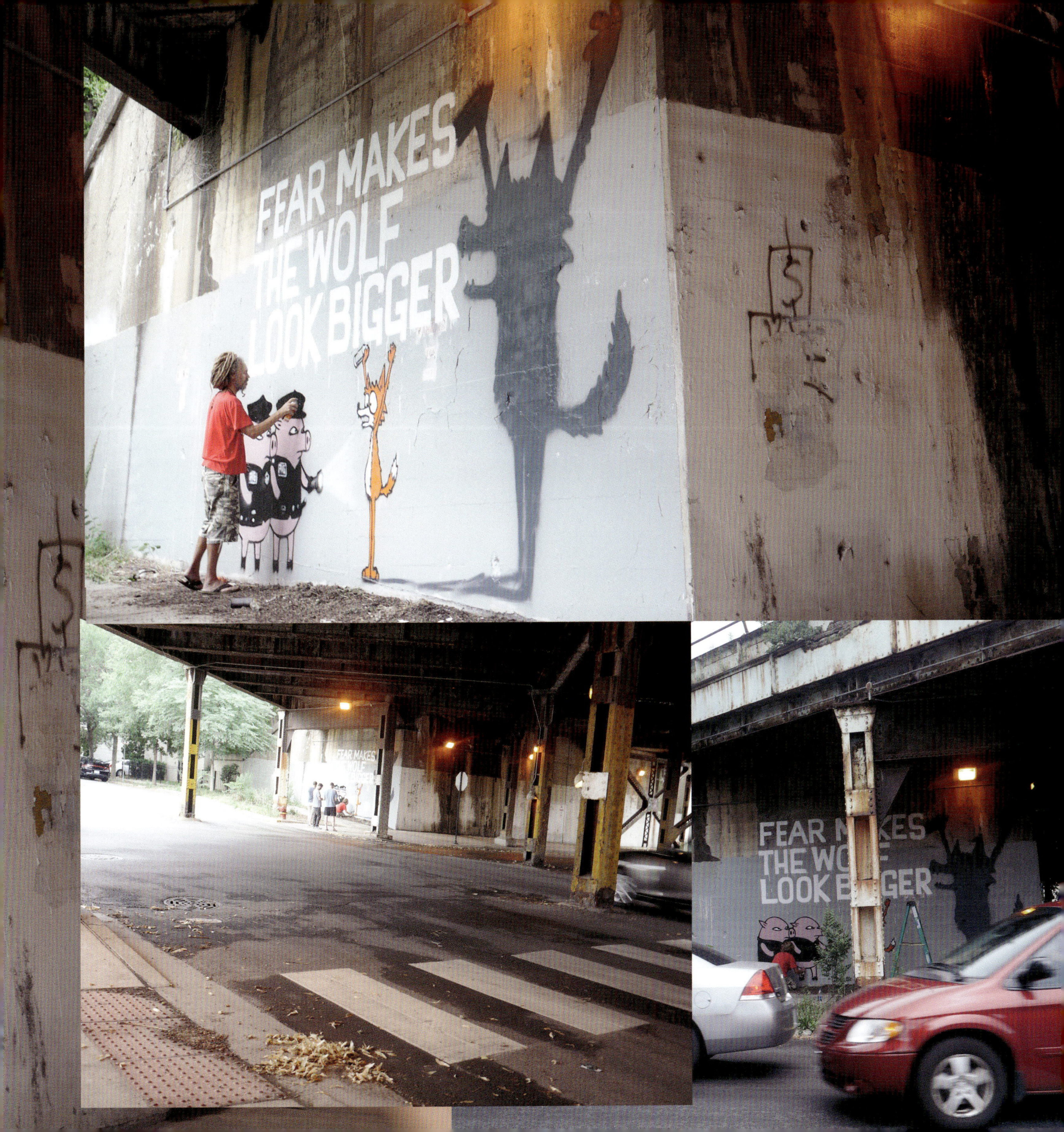
FEAR MAKES
THE WOLF
LOOK BIGGER

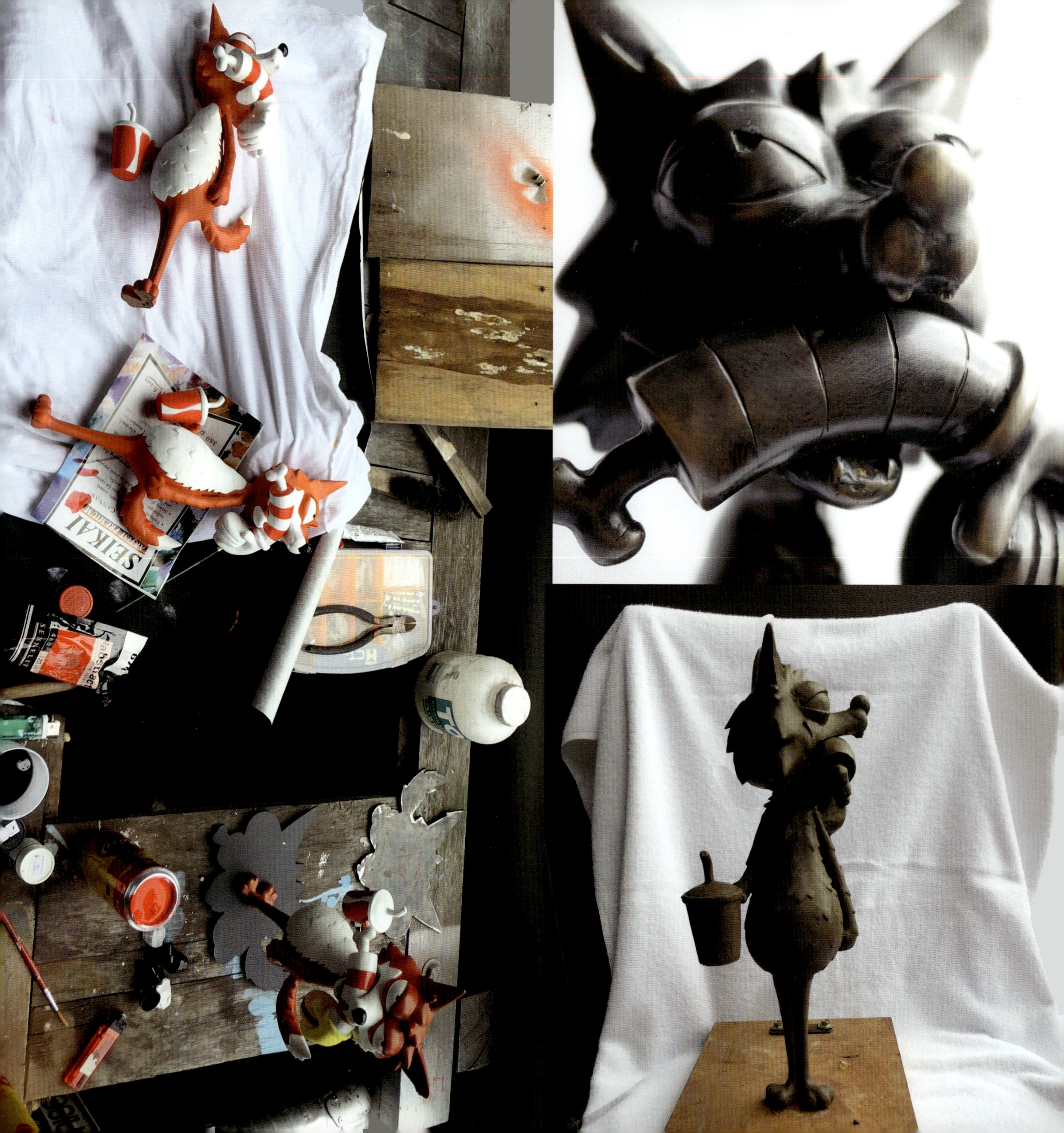
SEIKAI

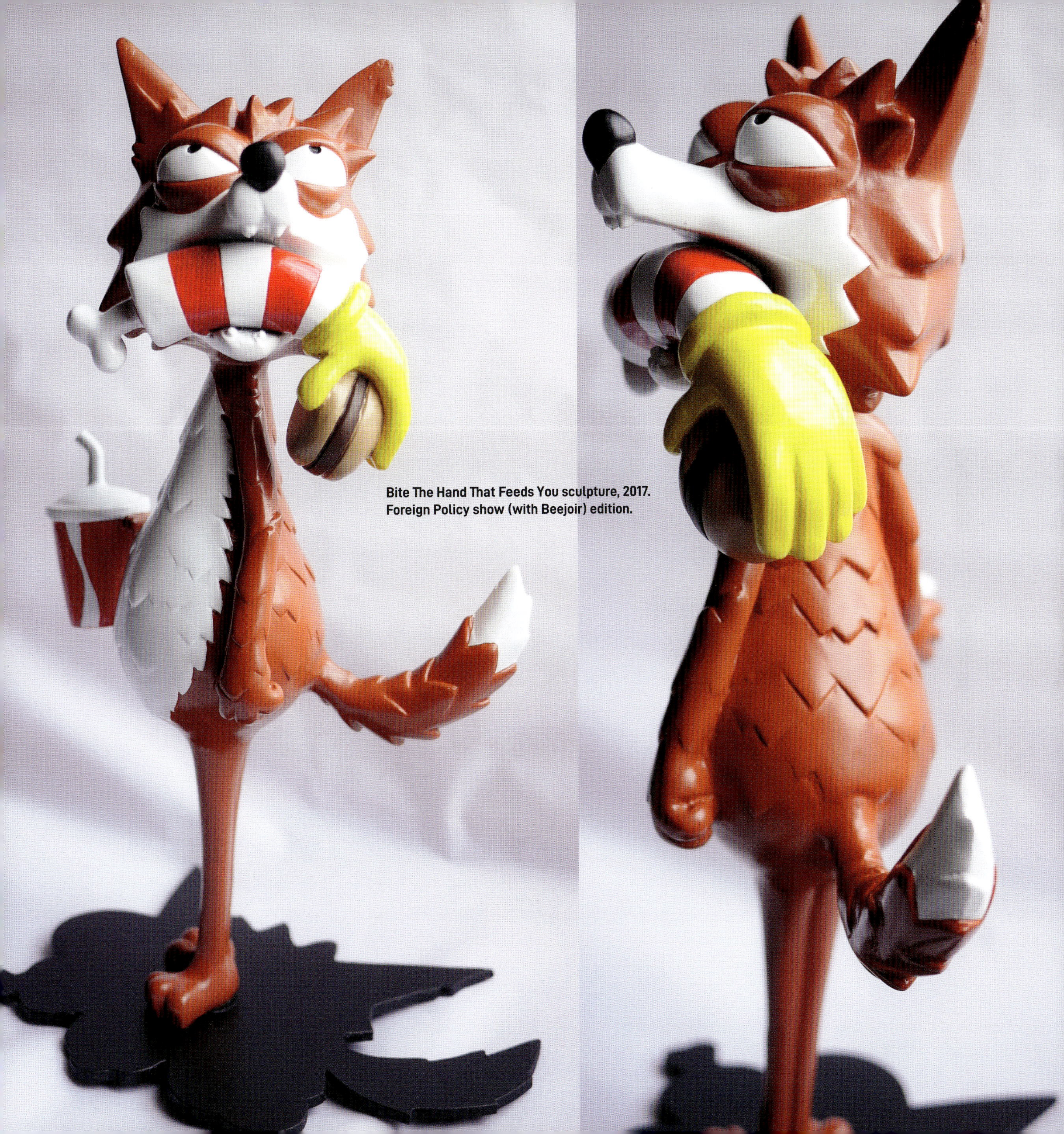

Bite The Hand That Feeds You sculpture, 2017.
Foreign Policy show (with Beejoir) edition.

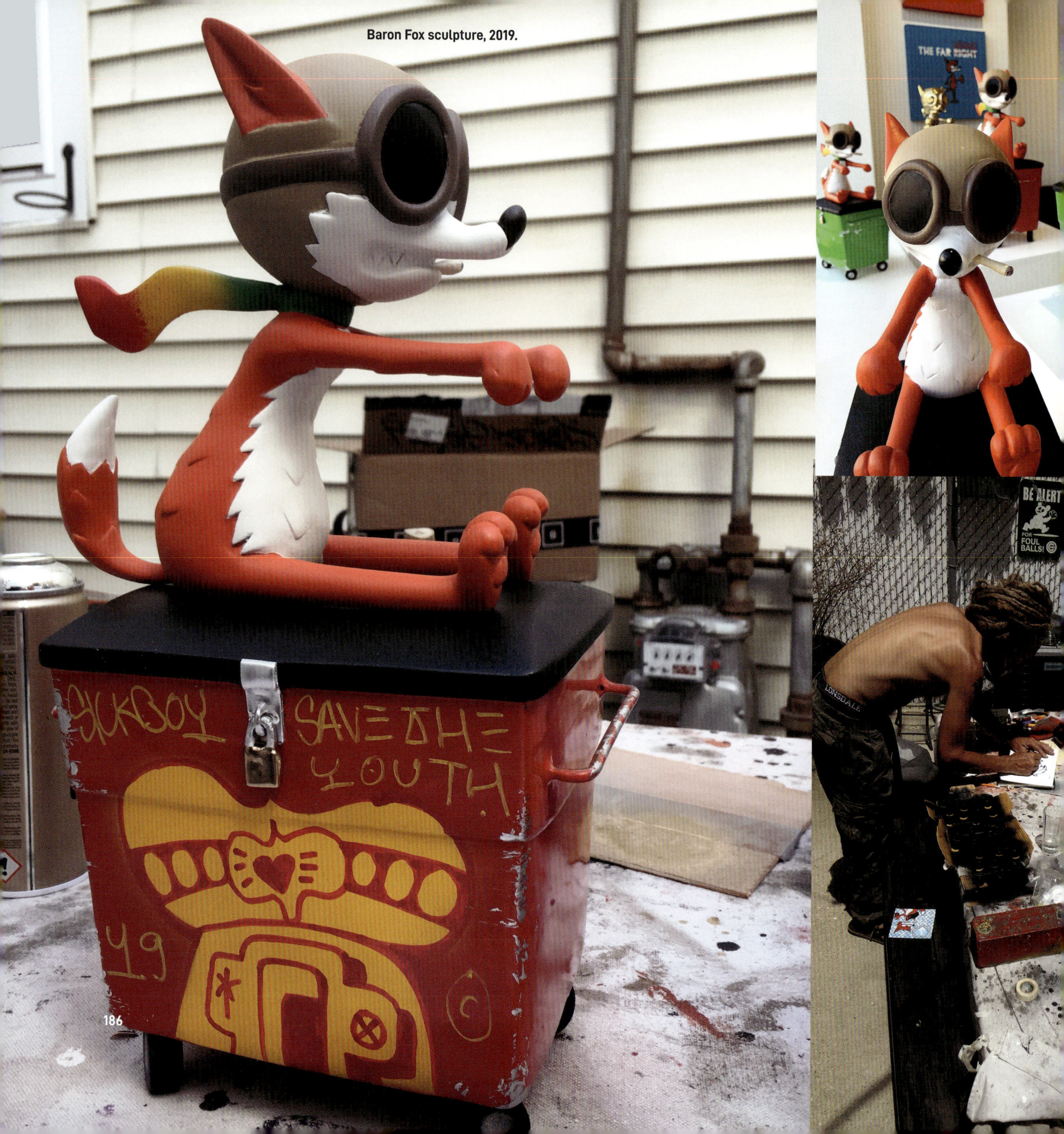

Baron Fox sculpture, 2019.

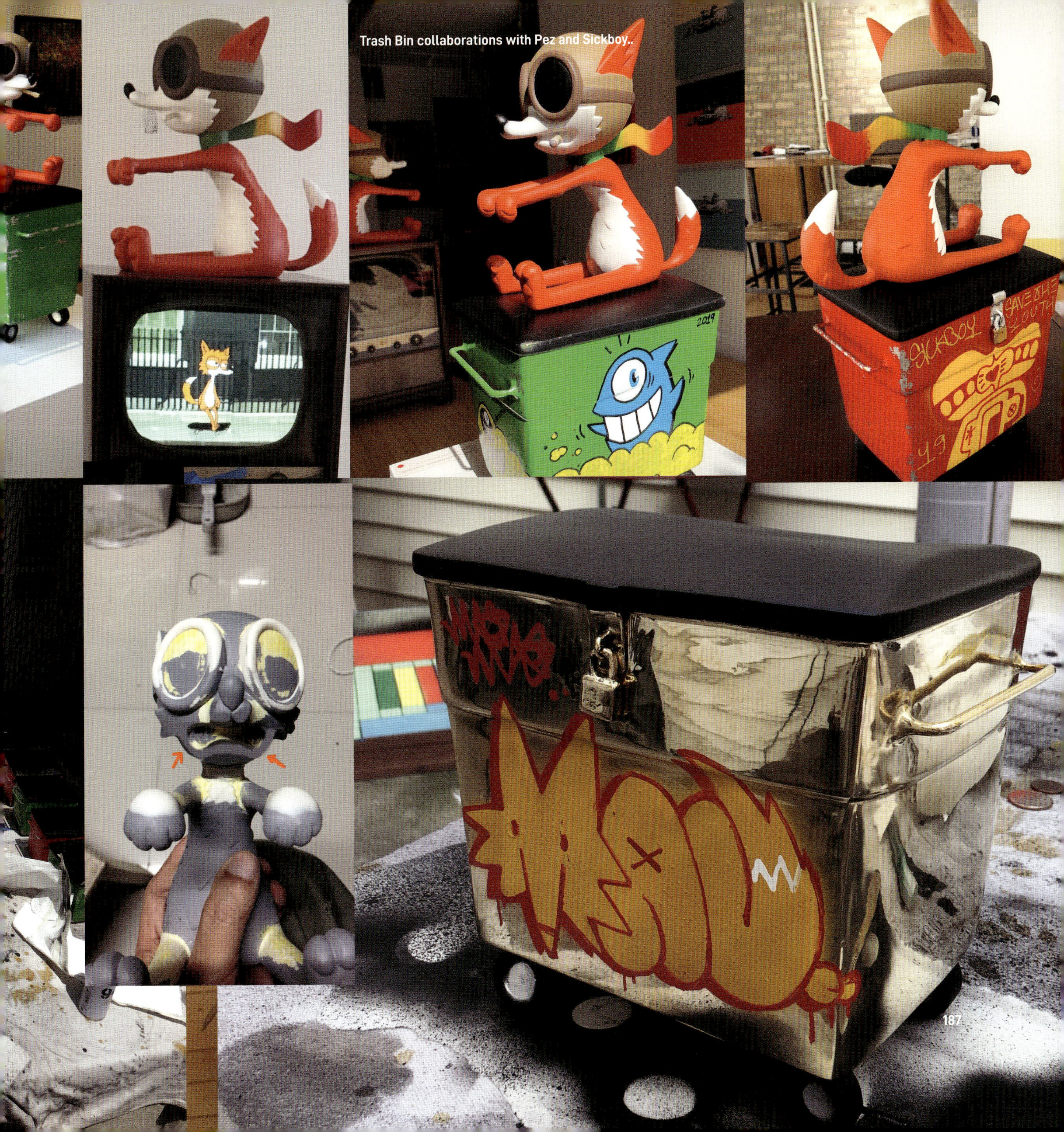

Trash Bin collaborations with Pez and Sickboy..

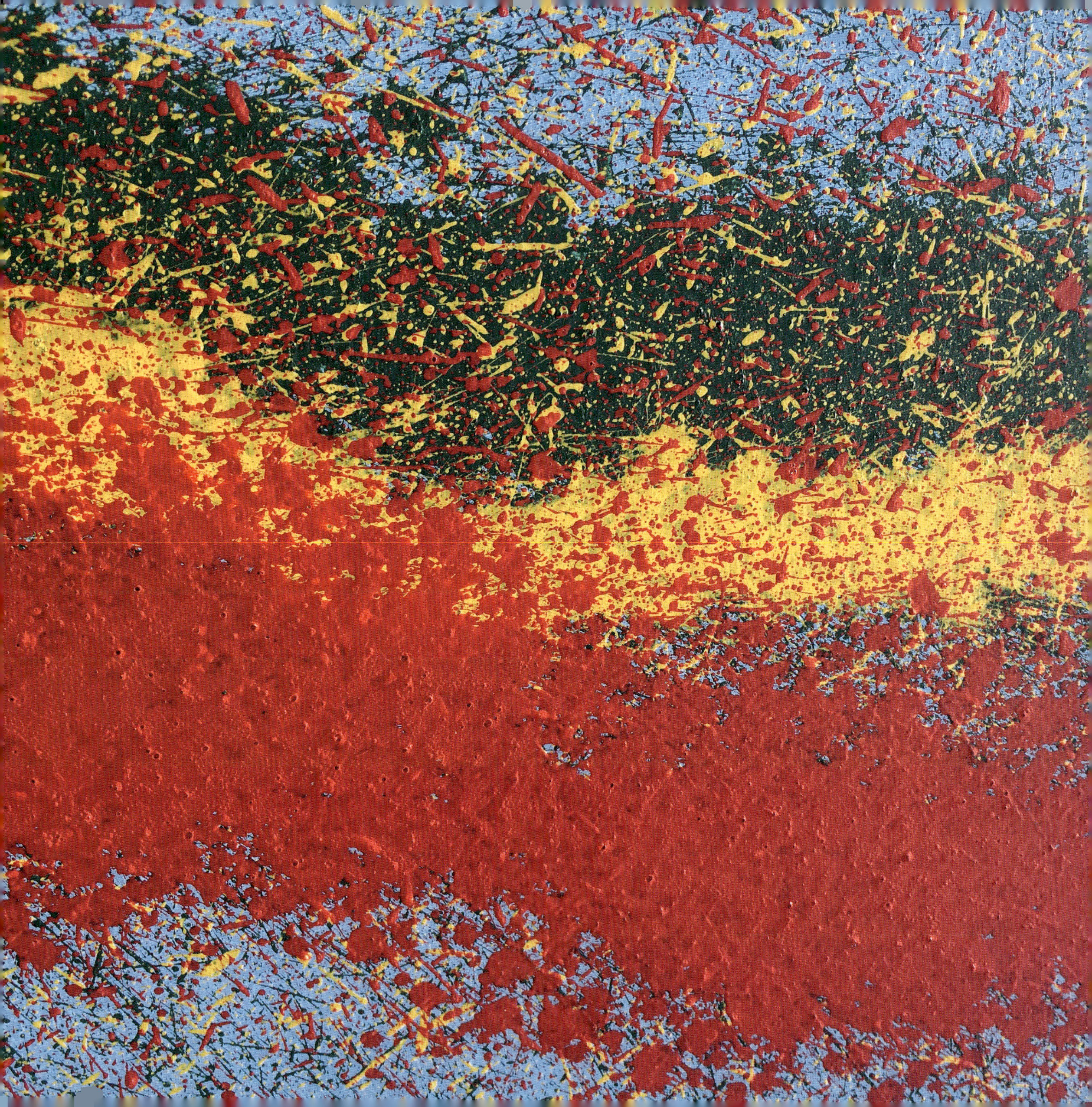

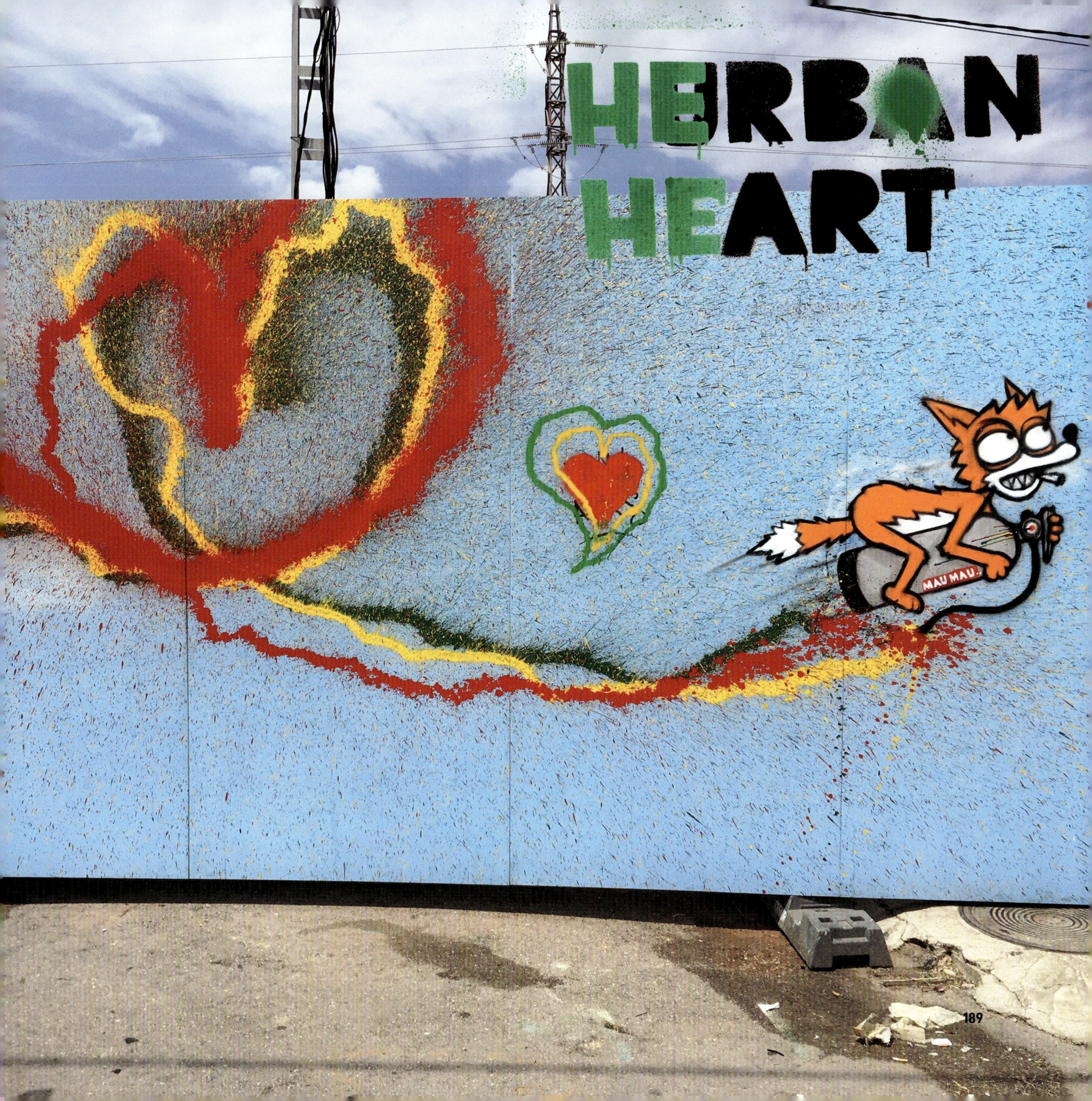
HERBAN
HEART
MAU MAU

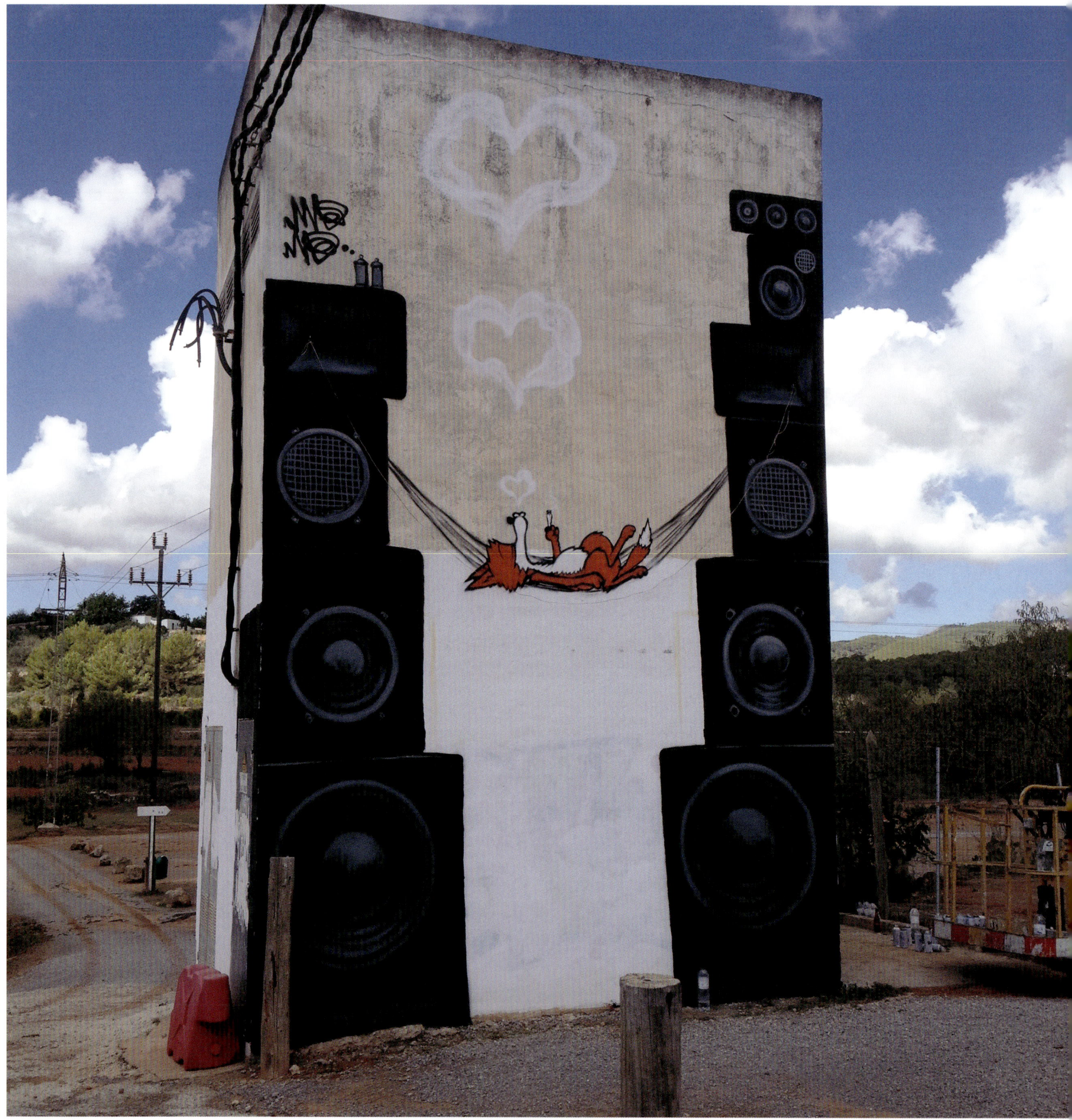

Stringin' Up a Sound, Ibiza, 2016.
Barcelona trackside, 2014.
Spannabis, Barcelona, 2014.

PREVIOUS PAGE: Rototom Festival, Spain, 2018.

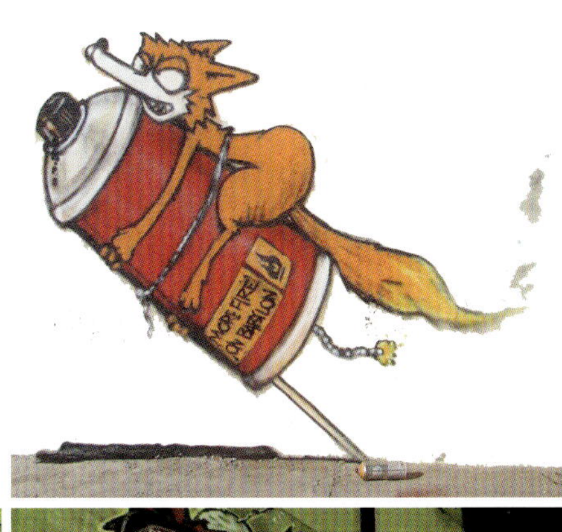

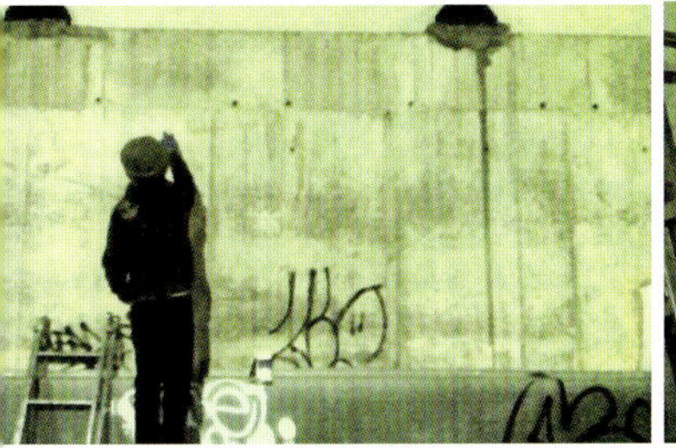

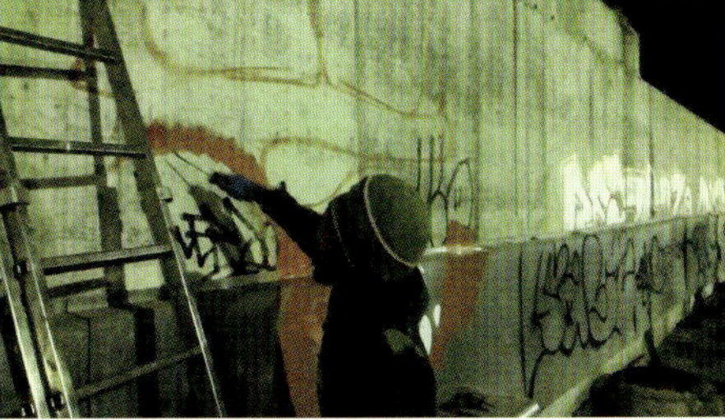

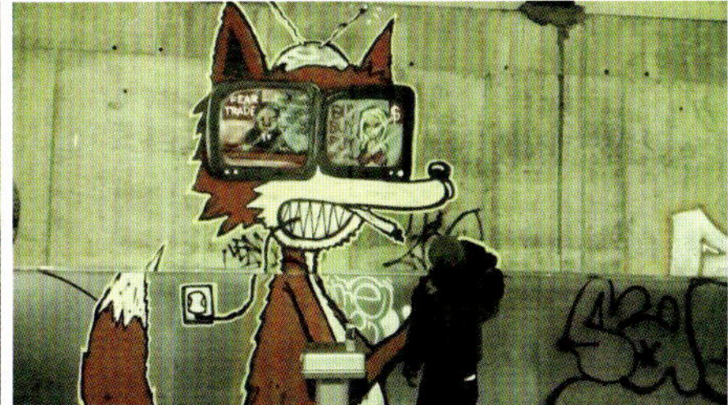

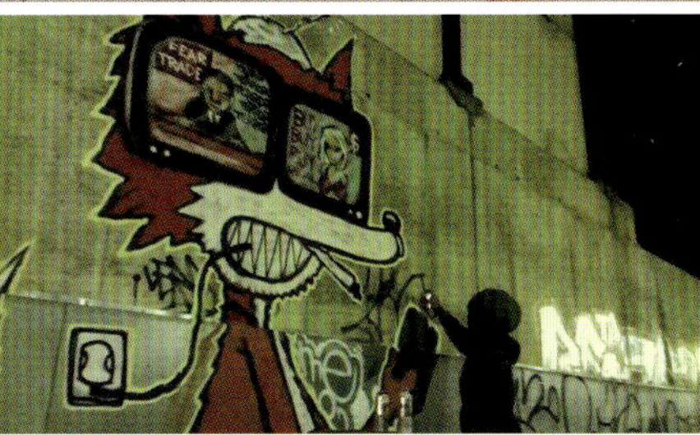

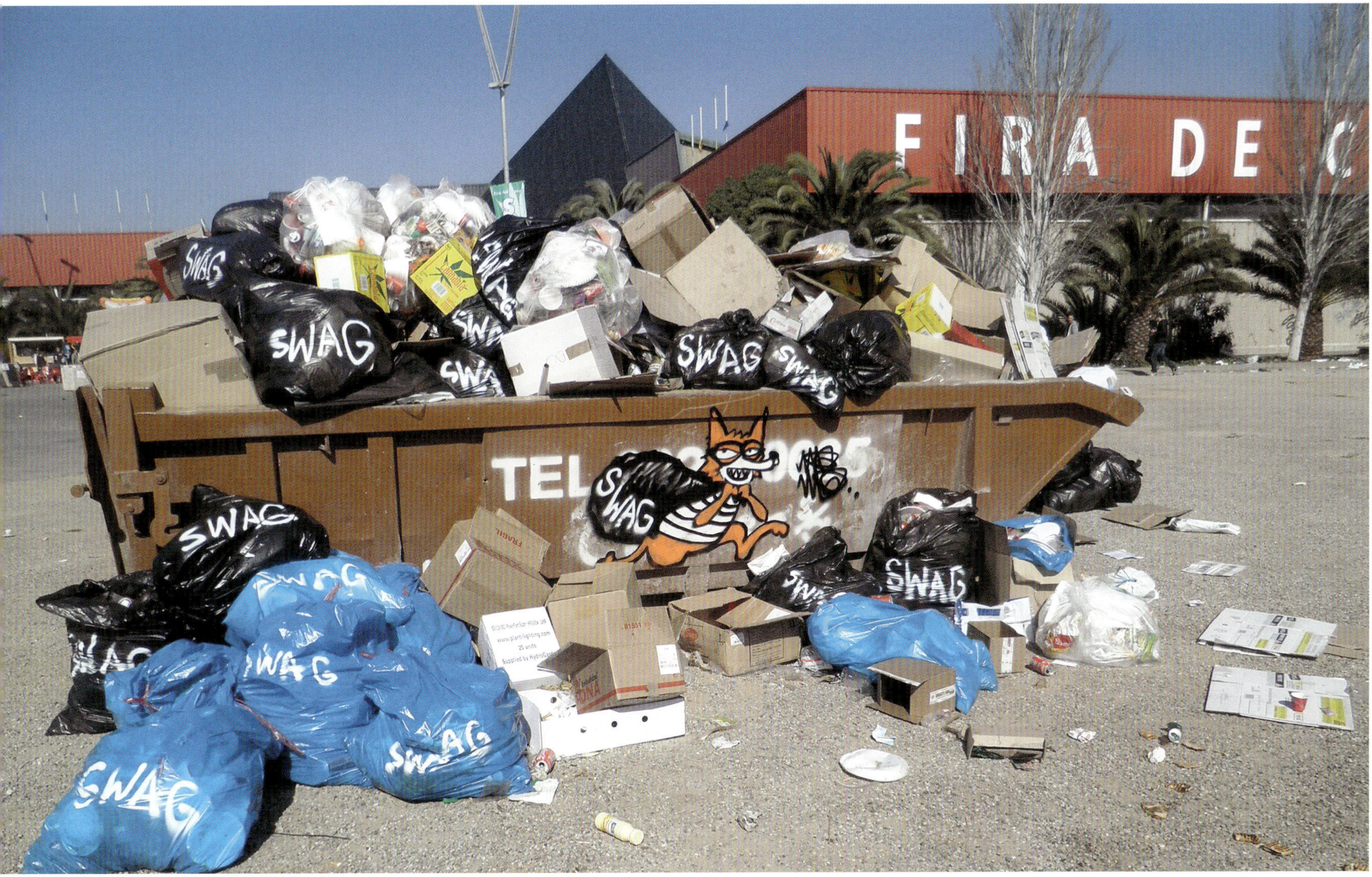

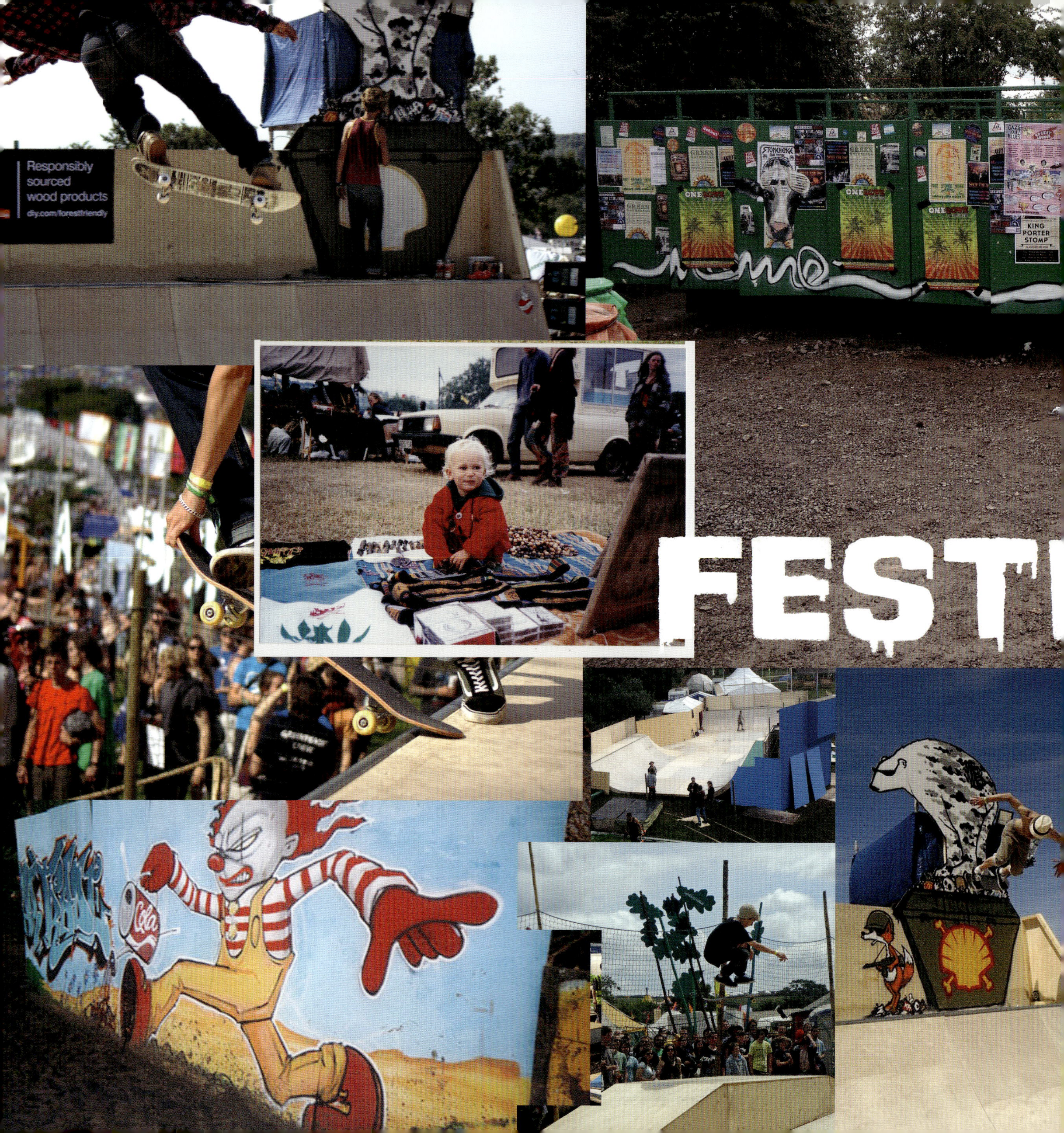
Responsibly
sourced
wood products
diy.com/forestfriendly
KING
PORTER
STOMP
Cola
FESTI

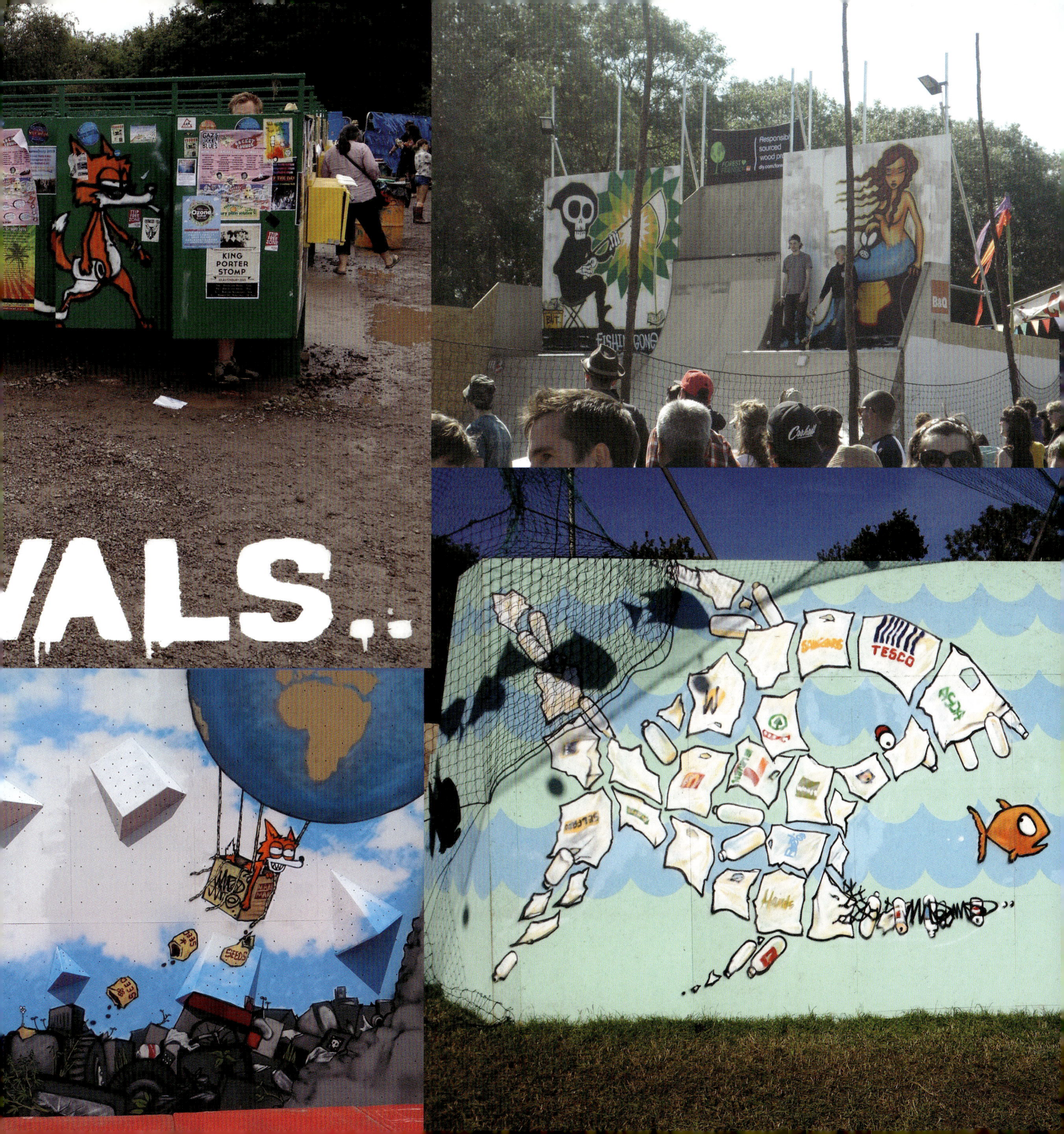
VALS..
KING
PORTER
STOMP
TESCO
ASDA
SEEDS

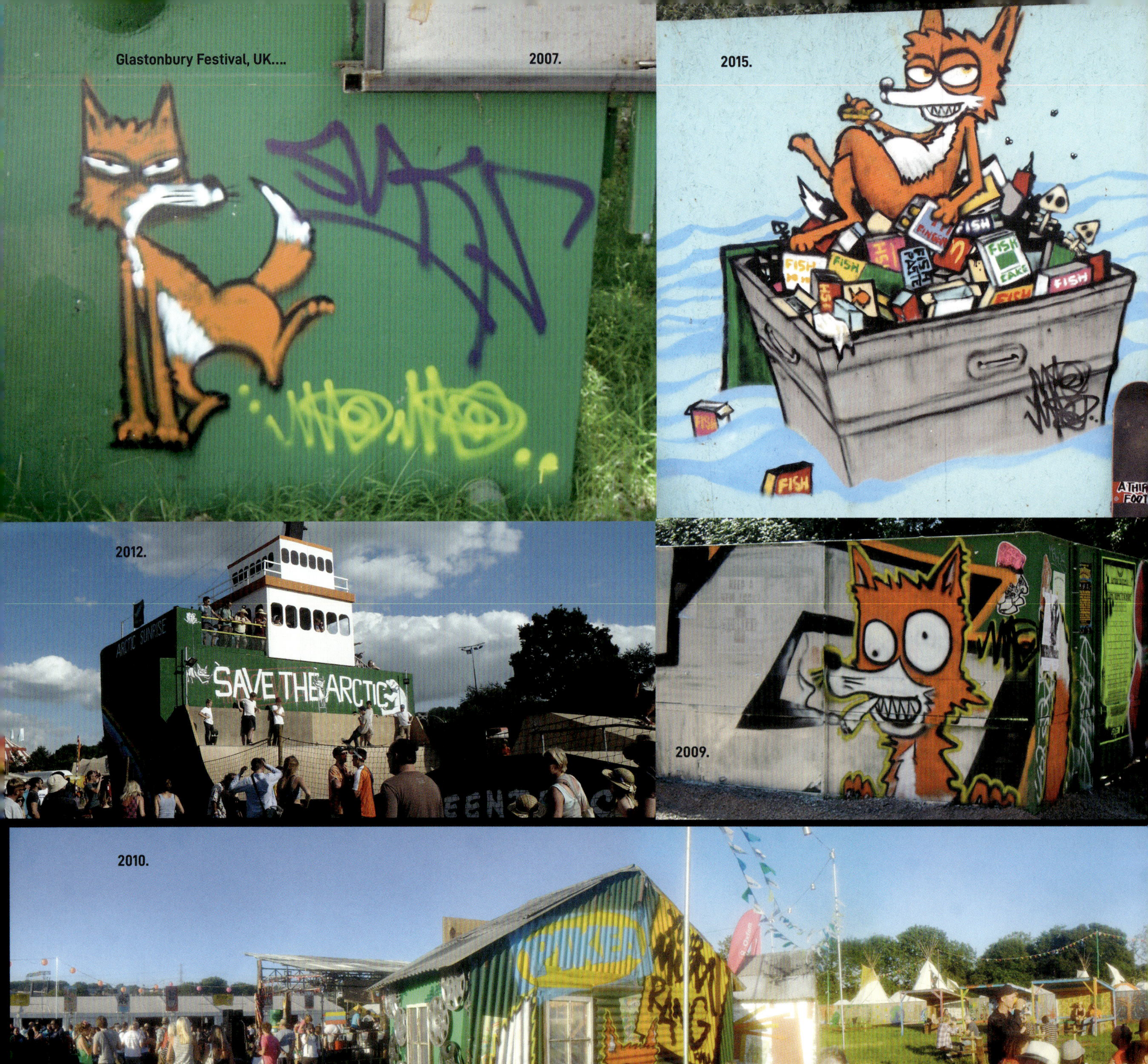

Glastonbury Festival, UK.... 2007.

2015.

2012.

2009.

2010.

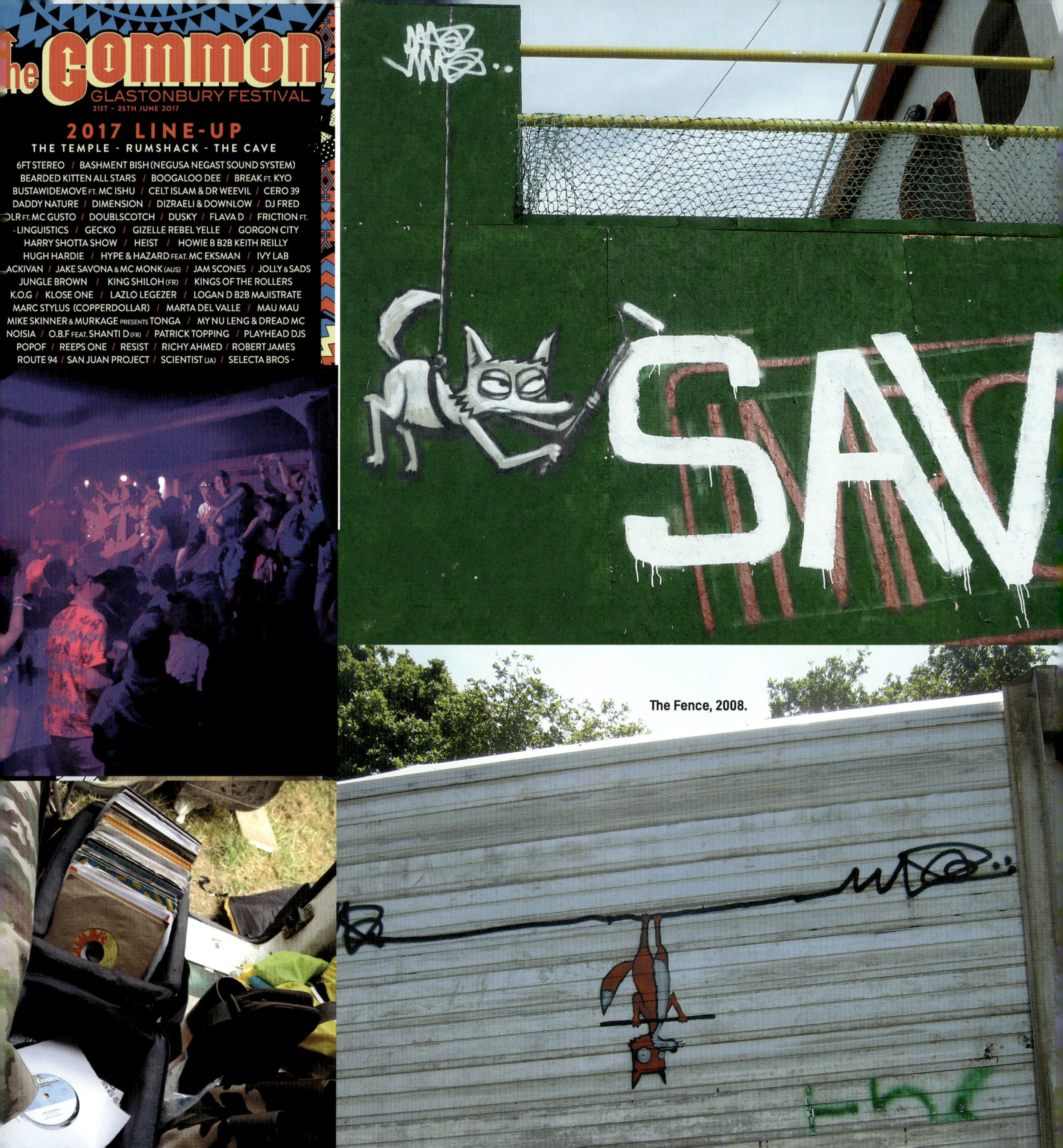

The Fence, 2008.

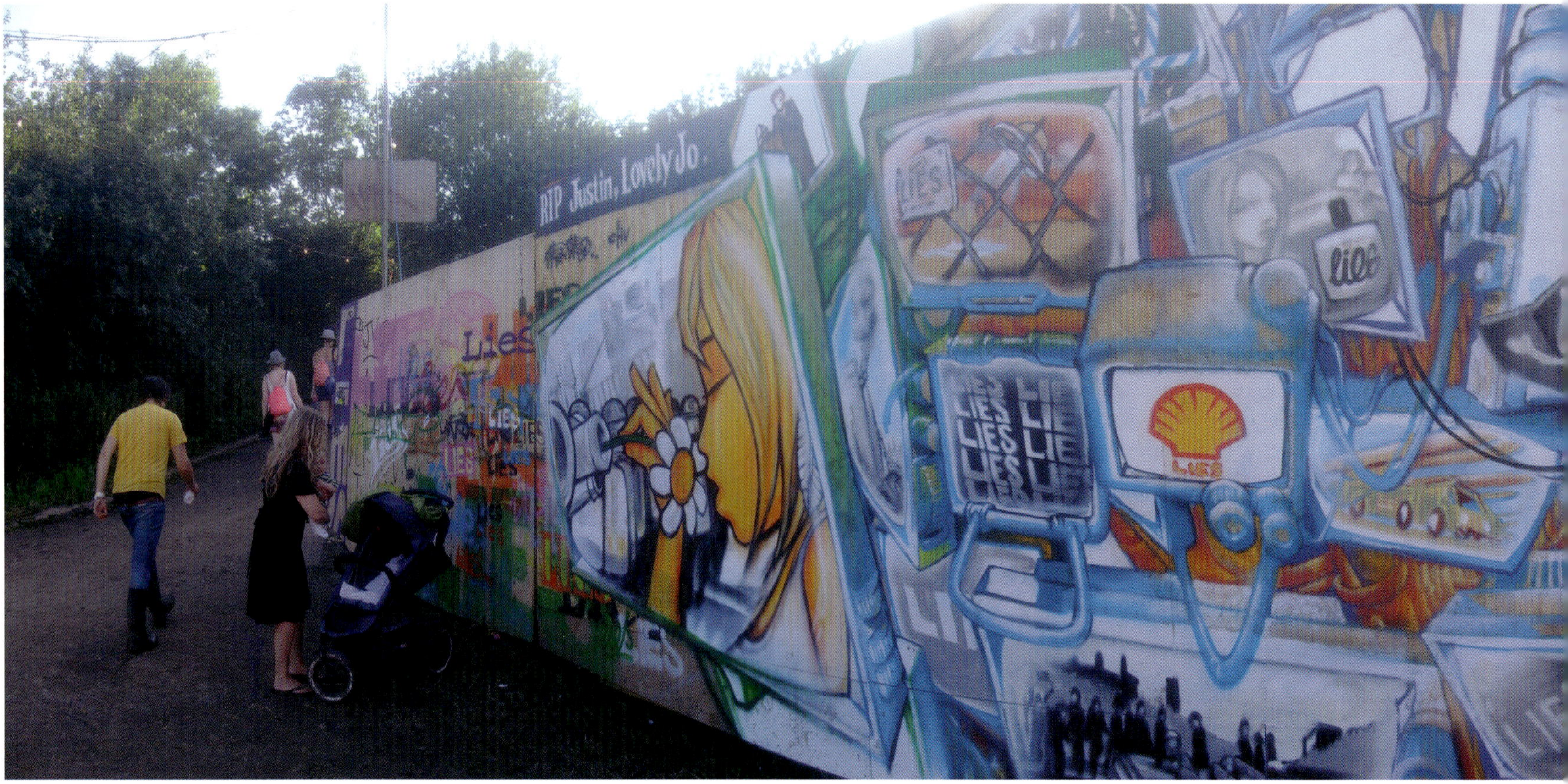
RIP Justin, Lovely Jo.
LIES

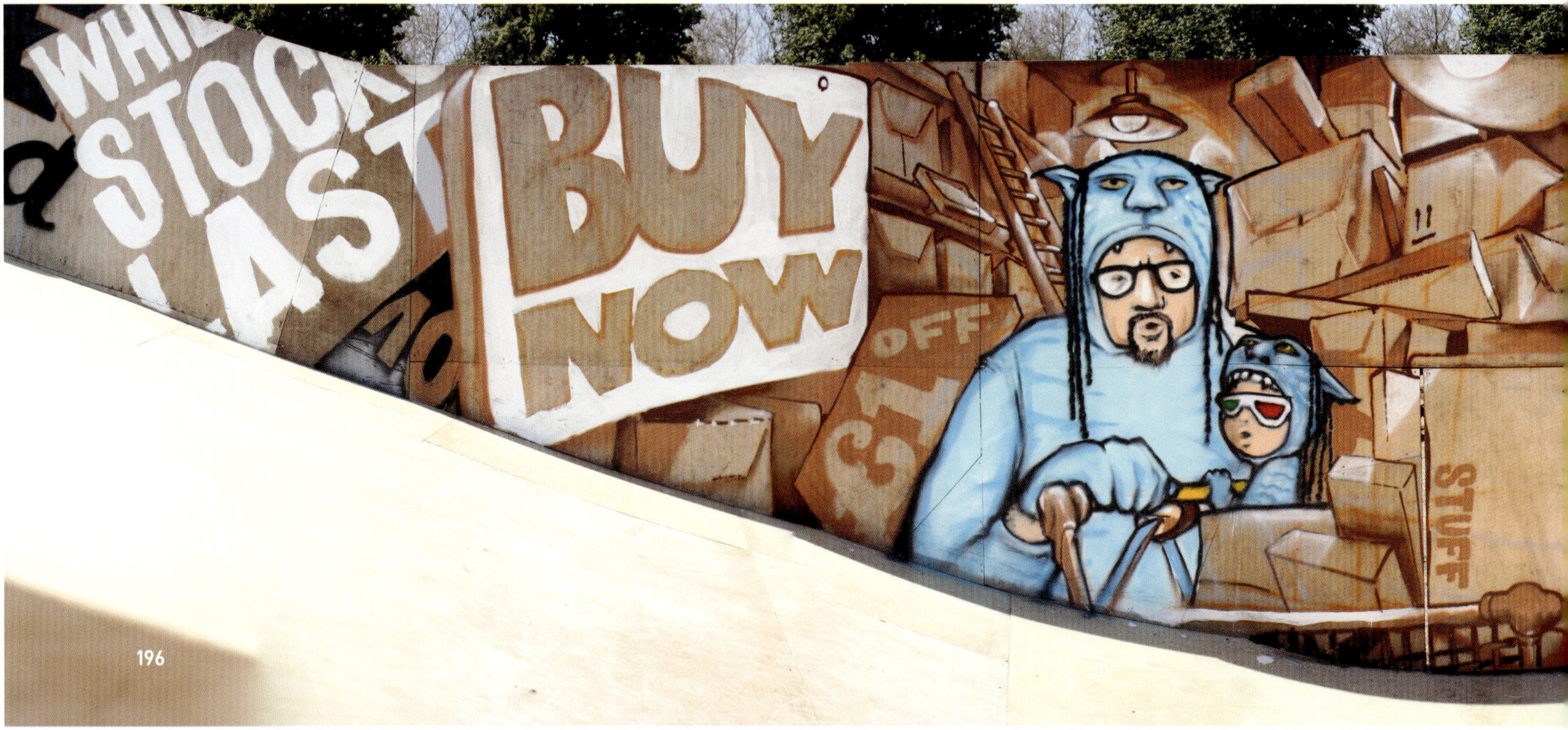
BUY NOW
OFF
STUFF

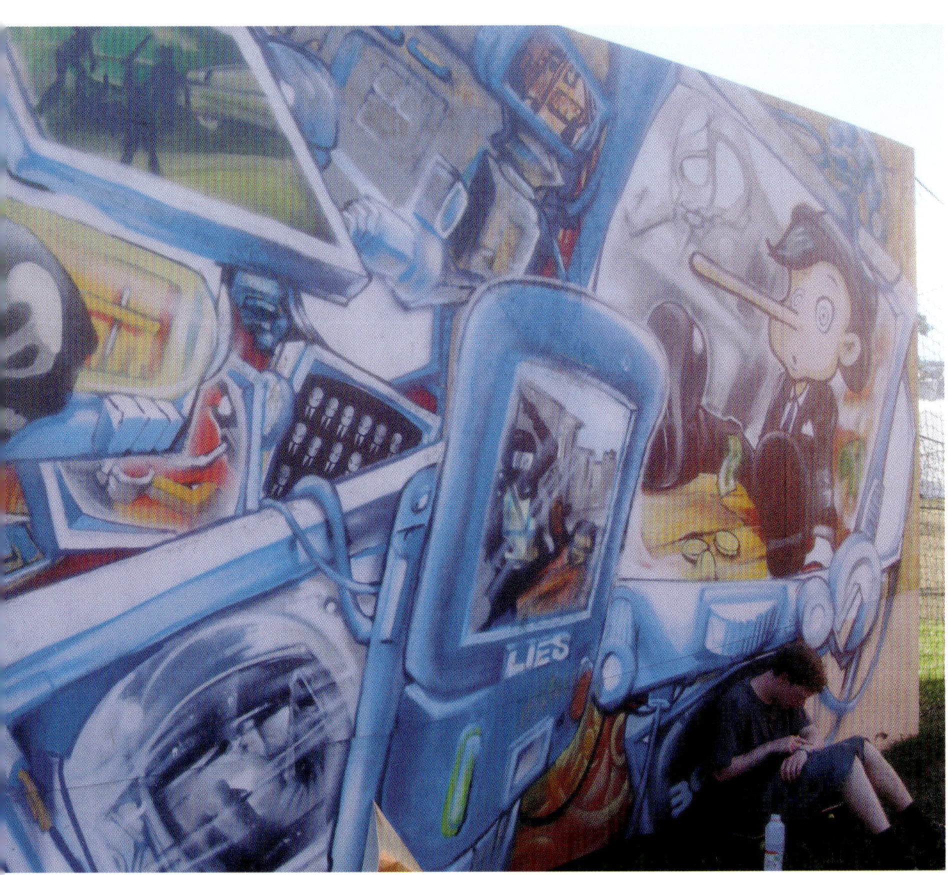

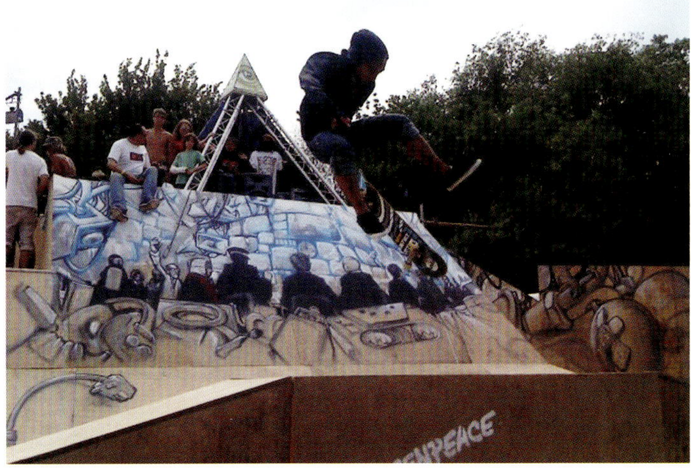

Glastonbury Skate Park (Chu, Mau).
Top: Lies
Bottom: While Stocks Last

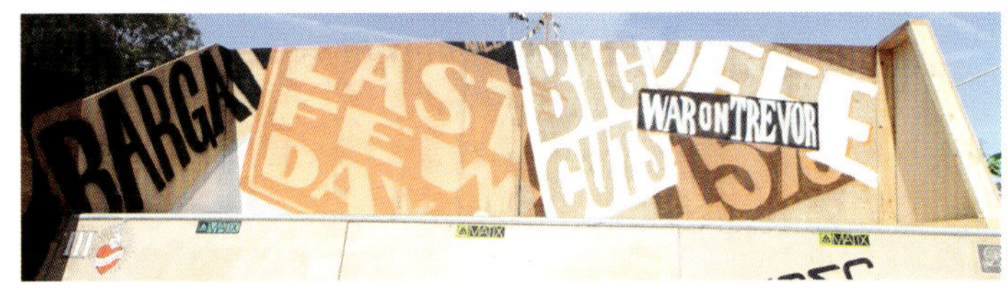

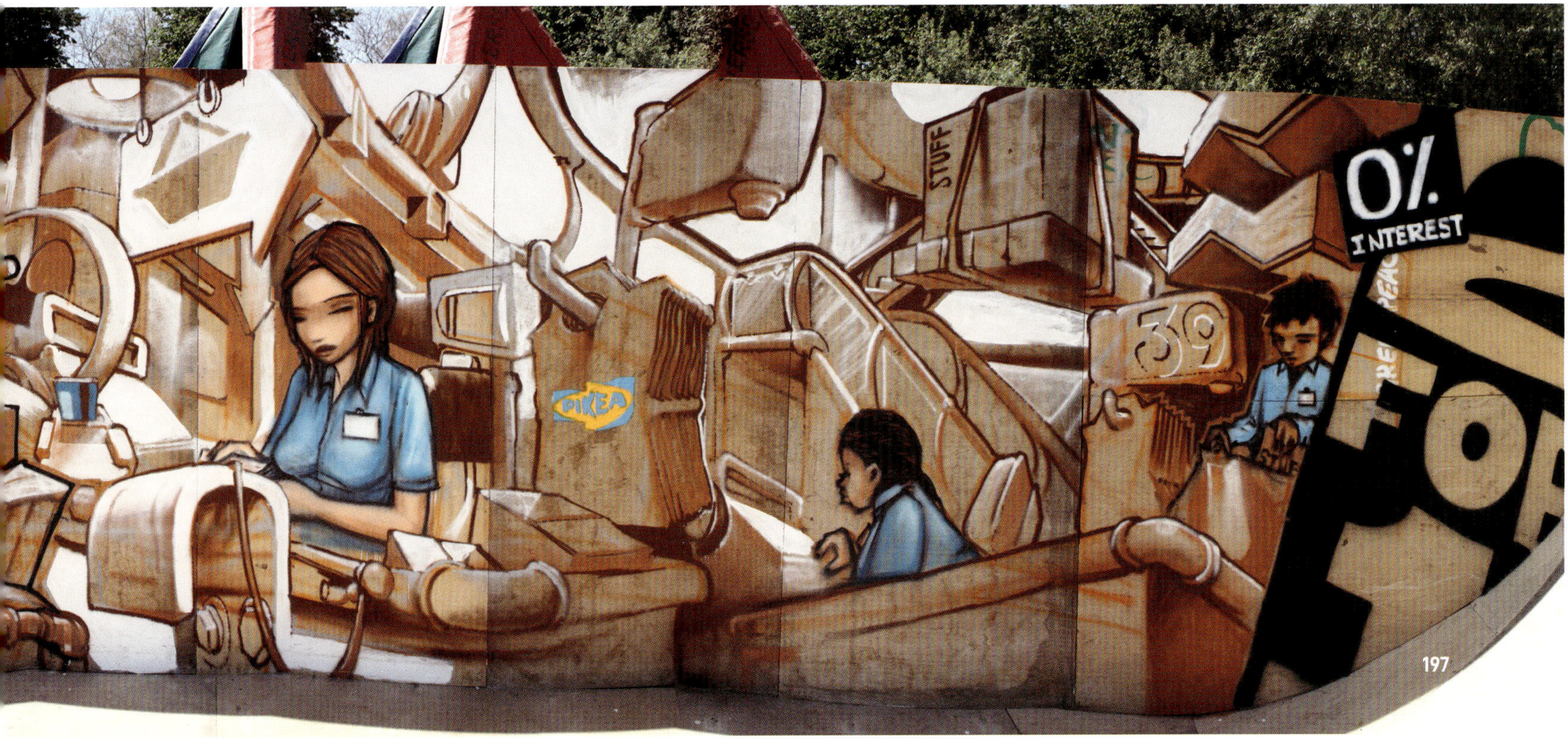

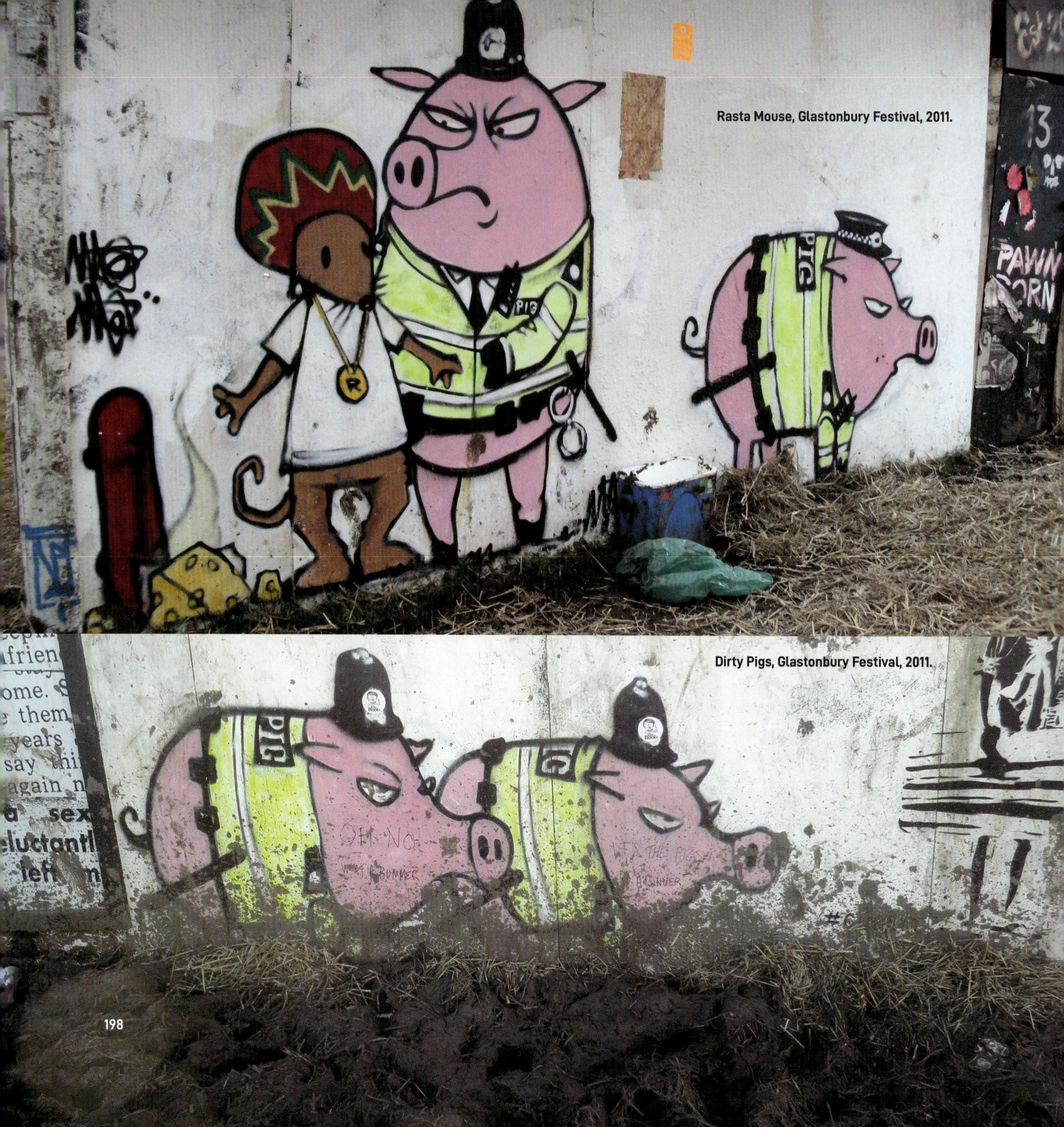

Rasta Mouse, Glastonbury Festival, 2011.

Dirty Pigs, Glastonbury Festival, 2011.

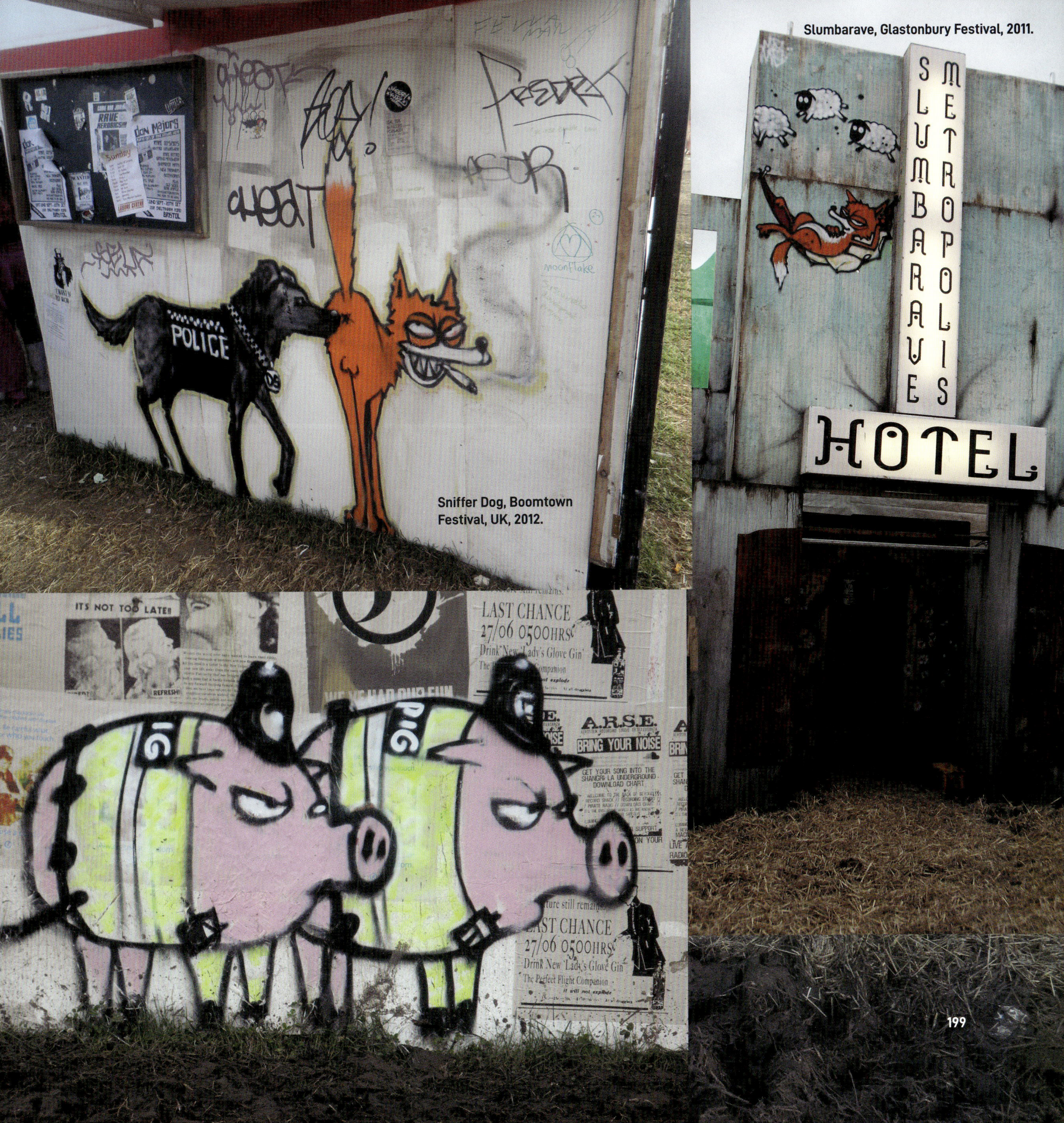

Sniffer Dog, Boomtown Festival, UK, 2012.

Slumbarave, Glastonbury Festival, 2011.

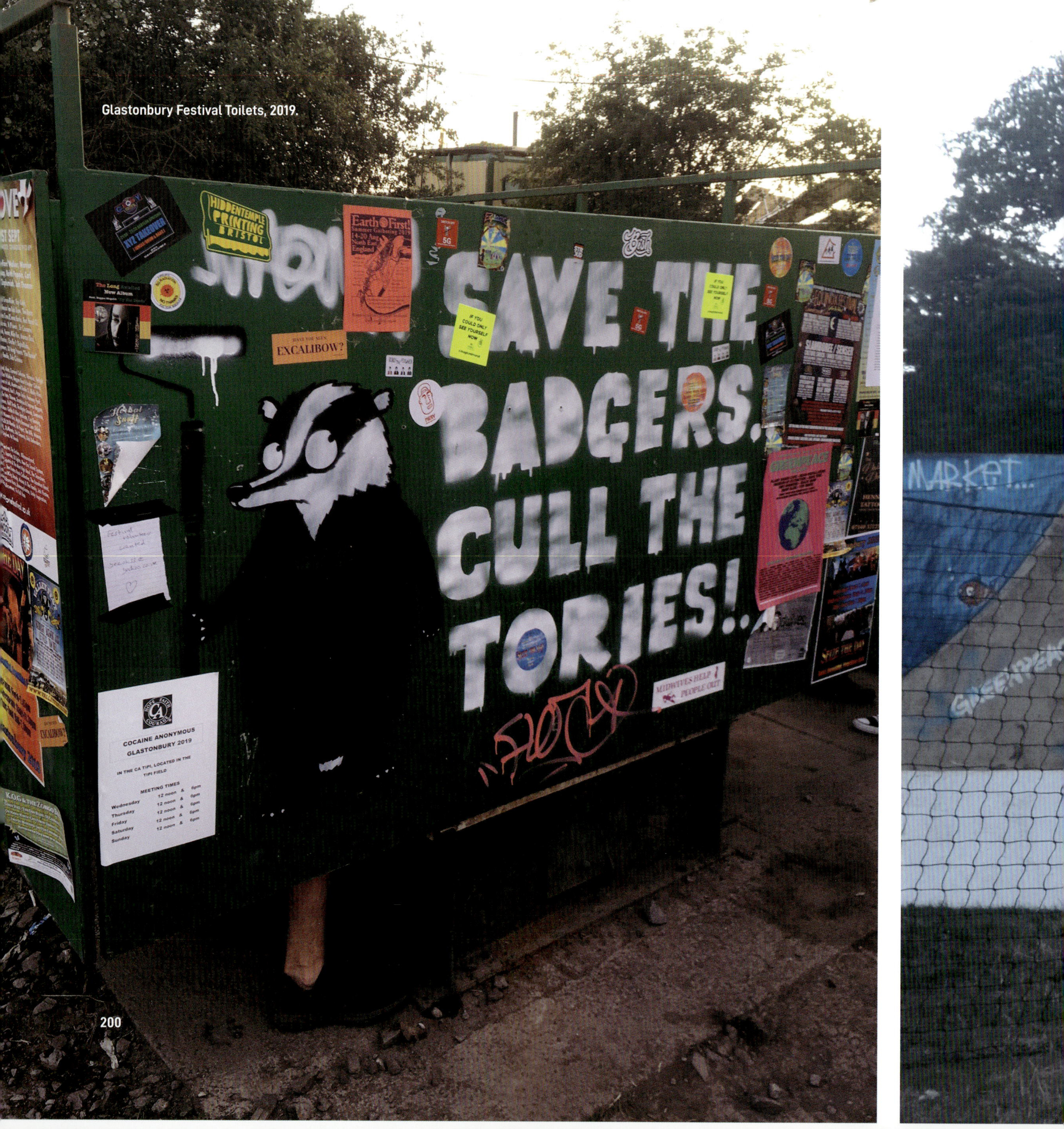

Glastonbury Festival Toilets, 2019.

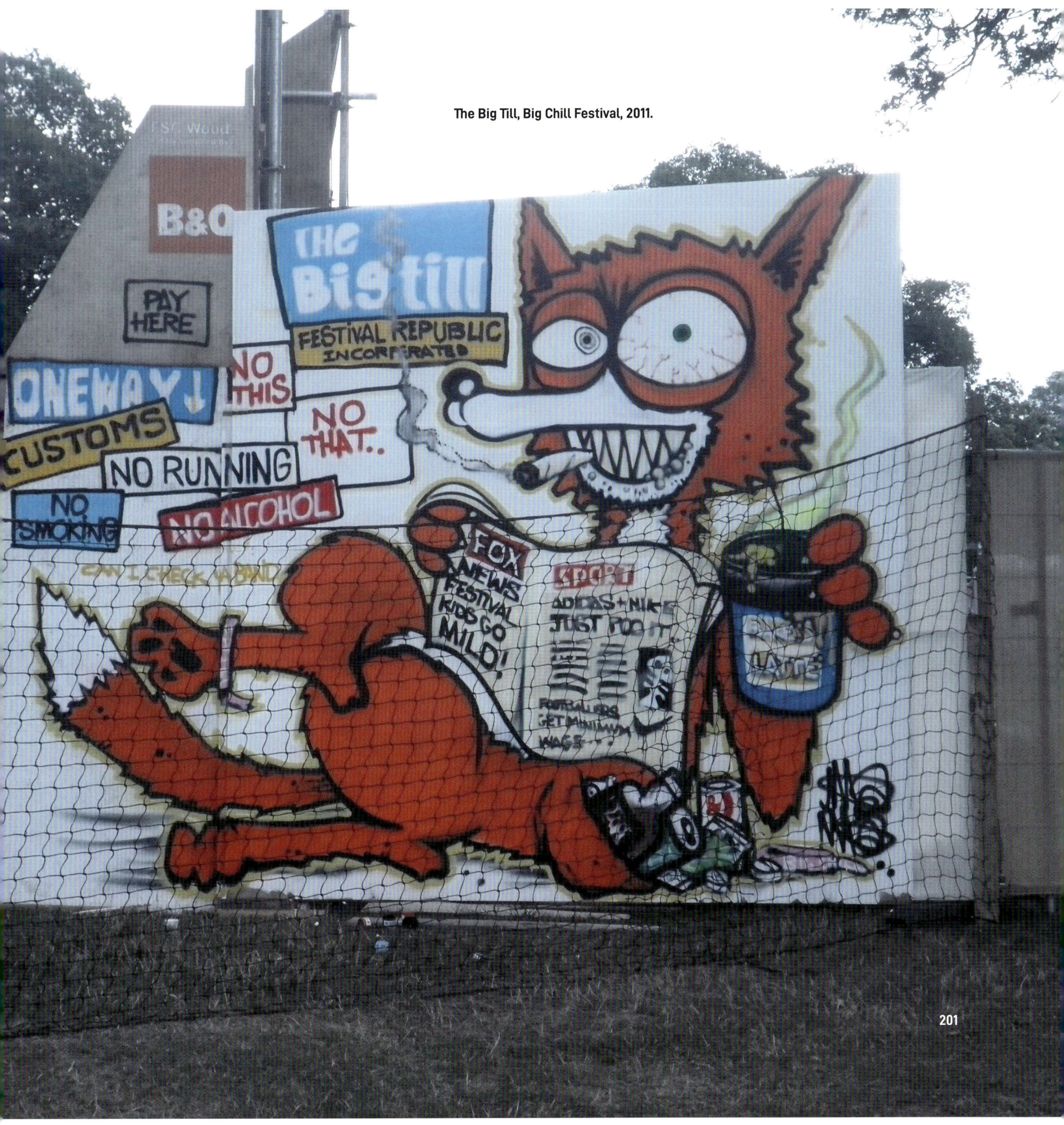

The Big Till, Big Chill Festival, 2011.

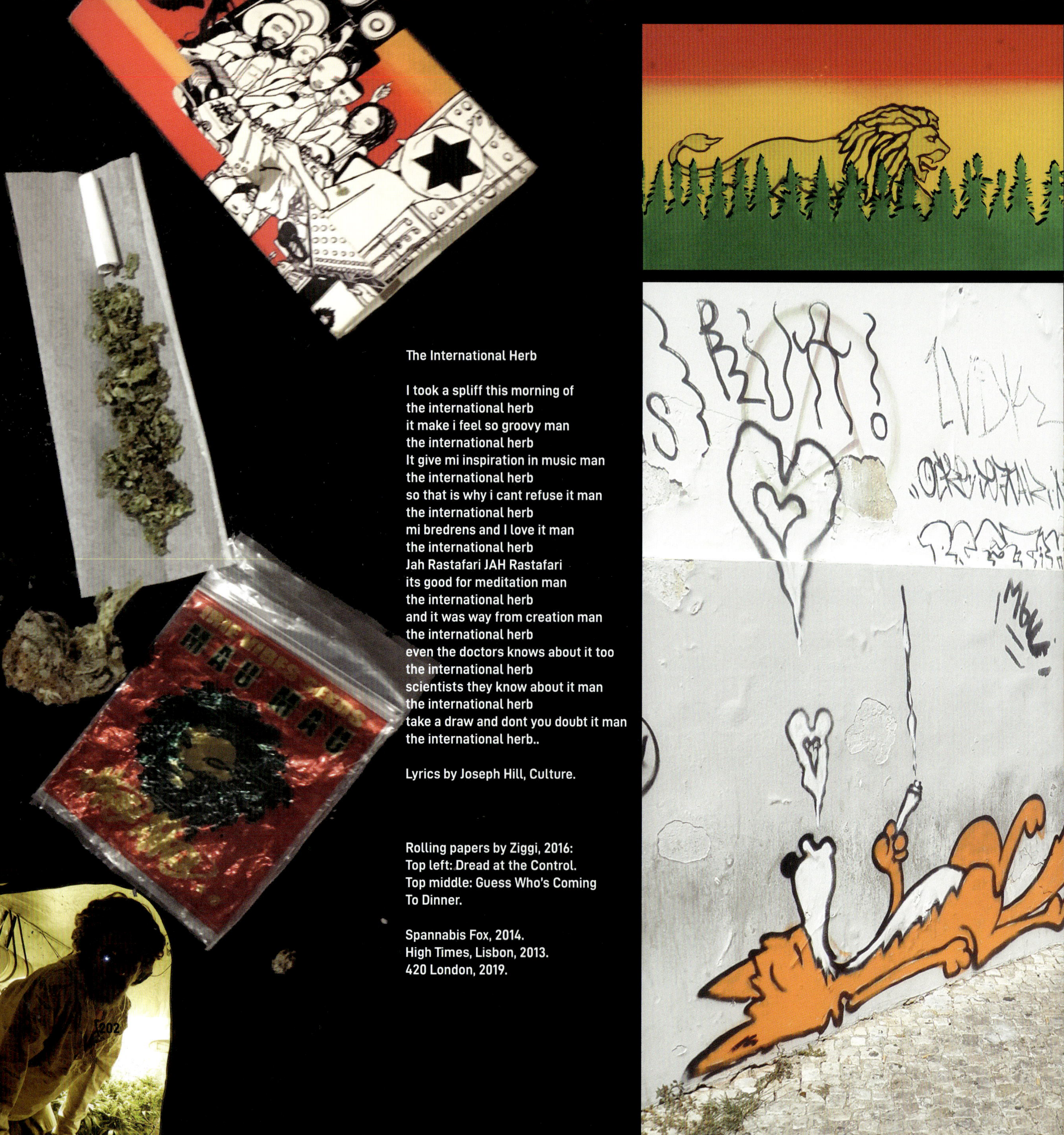

The International Herb

I took a spliff this morning of
the international herb
it make i feel so groovy man
the international herb
It give mi inspiration in music man
the international herb
so that is why i cant refuse it man
the international herb
mi bredrens and I love it man
the international herb
Jah Rastafari JAH Rastafari
its good for meditation man
the international herb
and it was way from creation man
the international herb
even the doctors knows about it too
the international herb
scientists they know about it man
the international herb
take a draw and dont you doubt it man
the international herb..

Lyrics by Joseph Hill, Culture.

Rolling papers by Ziggi, 2016:
Top left: Dread at the Control.
Top middle: Guess Who's Coming
To Dinner.

Spannabis Fox, 2014.
High Times, Lisbon, 2013.
420 London, 2019.

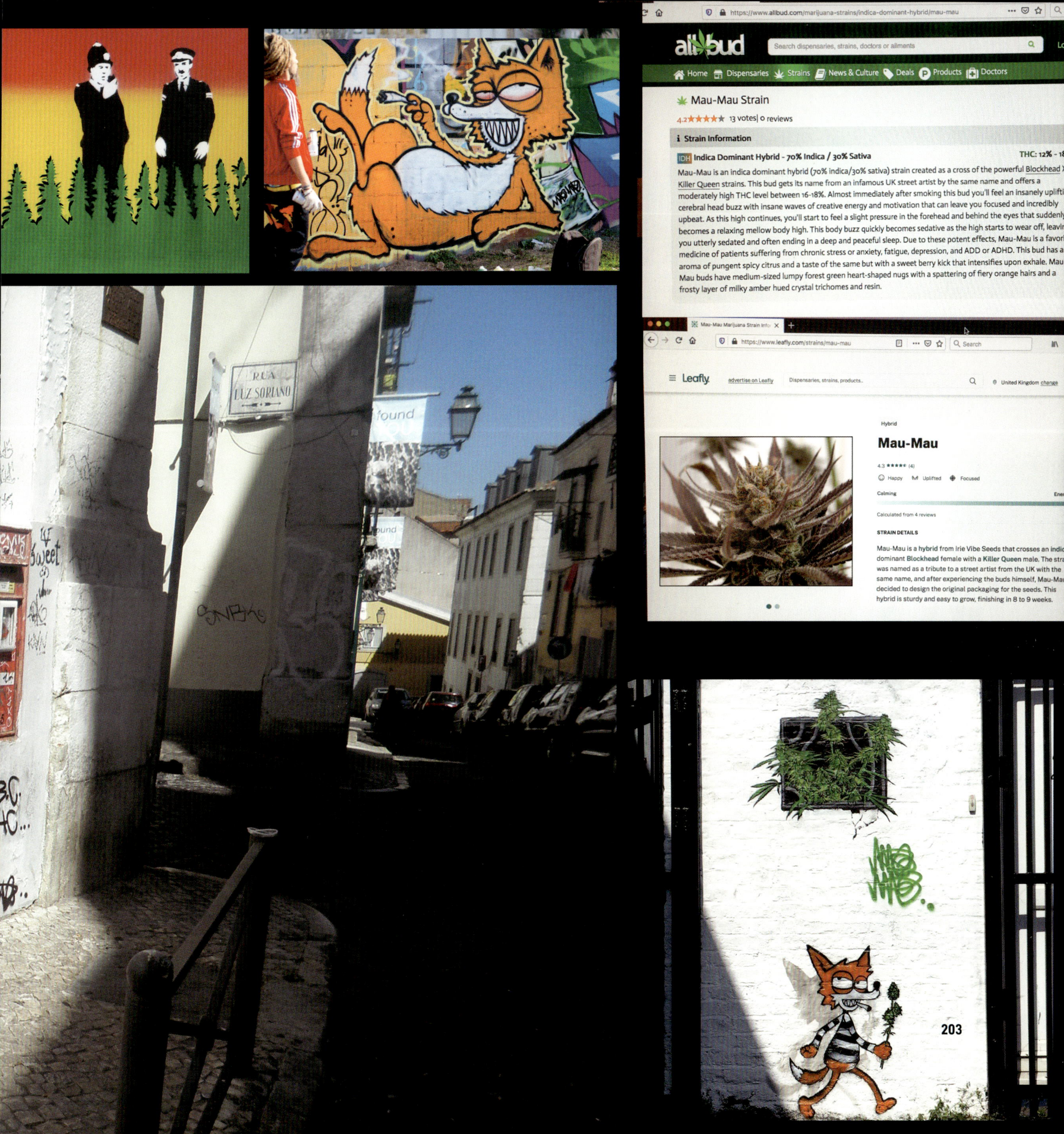

https://www.allbud.com/marijuana-strains/indica-dominant-hybrid/mau-mau
allbud
Search dispensaries, strains, doctors or ailments
Home
Dispensaries
Strains
News & Culture
Deals
Products
Doctors
Mau-Mau Strain
4.2 13 votes| 0 reviews
Strain Information
IDH Indica Dominant Hybrid - 70% Indica / 30% Sativa
Mau-Mau is an indica dominant hybrid (70% indica/30% sativa) strain created as a cross of the powerful Blockhead X Killer Queen strains. This bud gets its name from an infamous UK street artist by the same name and offers a moderately high THC level between 16-18%. Almost immediately after smoking this bud you'll feel an insanely uplifting cerebral head buzz with insane waves of creative energy and motivation that can leave you focused and incredibly upbeat. As this high continues, you'll start to feel a slight pressure in the forehead and behind the eyes that suddenly becomes a relaxing mellow body high. This body buzz quickly becomes sedative as the high starts to wear off, leaving you utterly sedated and often ending in a deep and peaceful sleep. Due to these potent effects, Mau-Mau is a favorite medicine of patients suffering from chronic stress or anxiety, fatigue, depression, and ADD or ADHD. This bud has an aroma of pungent spicy citrus and a taste of the same but with a sweet berry kick that intensifies upon exhale. Mau-Mau buds have medium-sized lumpy forest green heart-shaped nugs with a spattering of fiery orange hairs and a frosty layer of milky amber hued crystal trichomes and resin.
https://www.leafly.com/strains/mau-mau
Leafly
advertise on Leafly
Dispensaries, strains, products...
United Kingdom change
Hybrid
Mau-Mau
4.3 (4)
Happy
Uplifted
Focused
Calming
Calculated from 4 reviews
STRAIN DETAILS
Mau-Mau is a hybrid from Irie Vibe Seeds that crosses an indica dominant Blockhead female with a Killer Queen male. The strain was named as a tribute to a street artist from the UK with the same name, and after experiencing the buds himself, Mau-Mau decided to design the original packaging for the seeds. This hybrid is sturdy and easy to grow, finishing in 8 to 9 weeks.
RUA
LUZ SORIANO

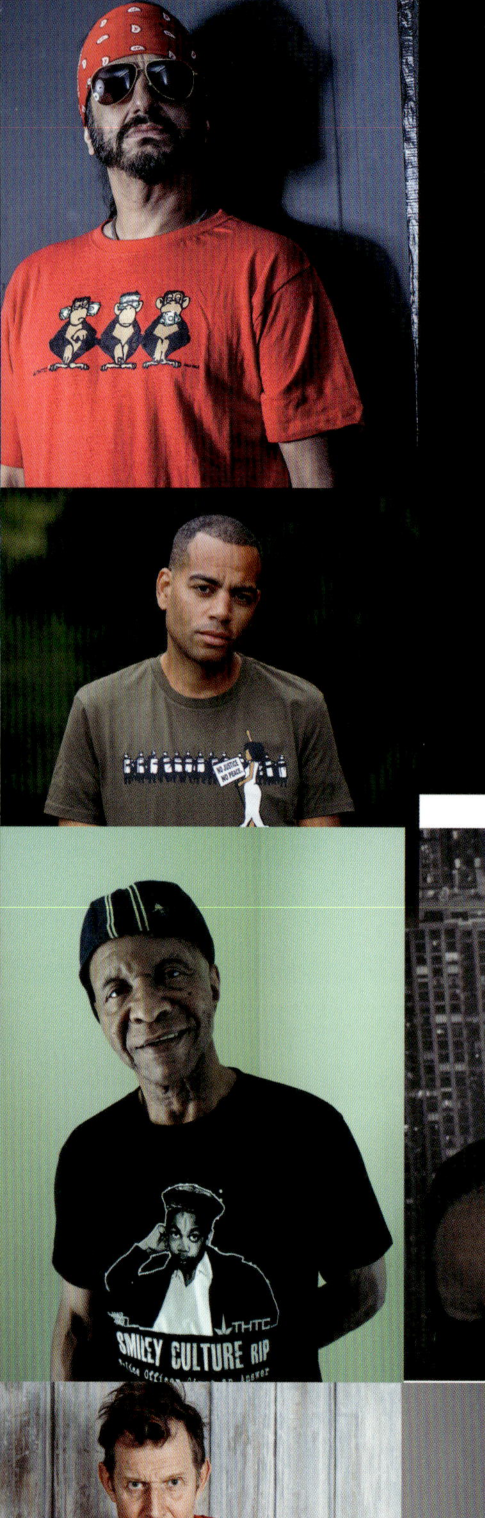

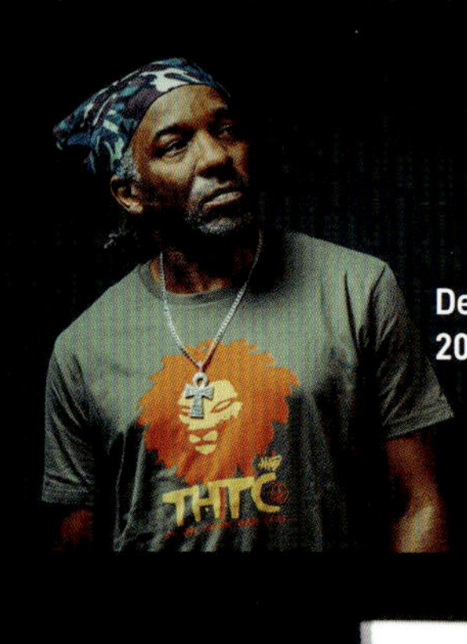

Designs for THTC clothing company, 2001 to present day.

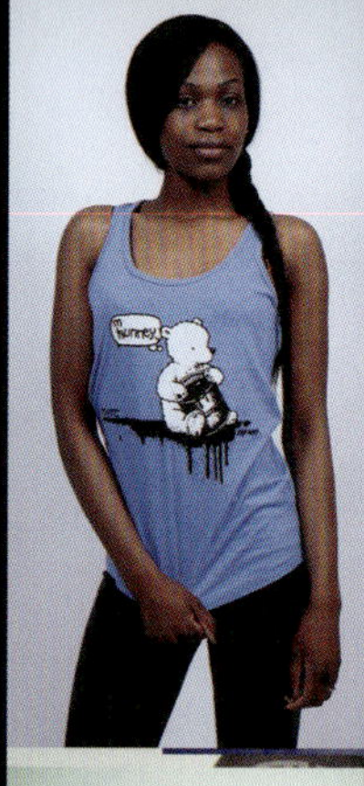
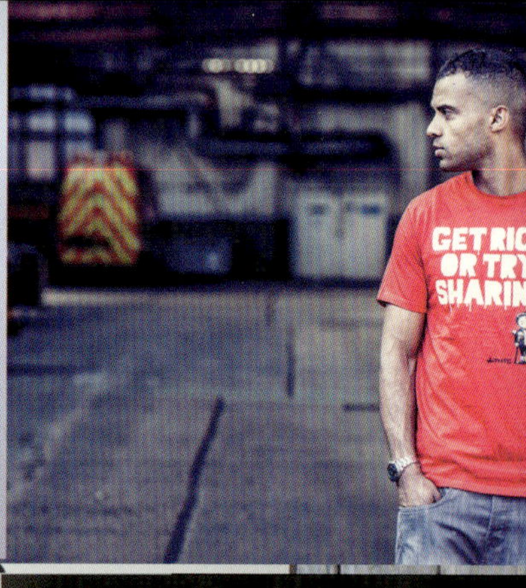
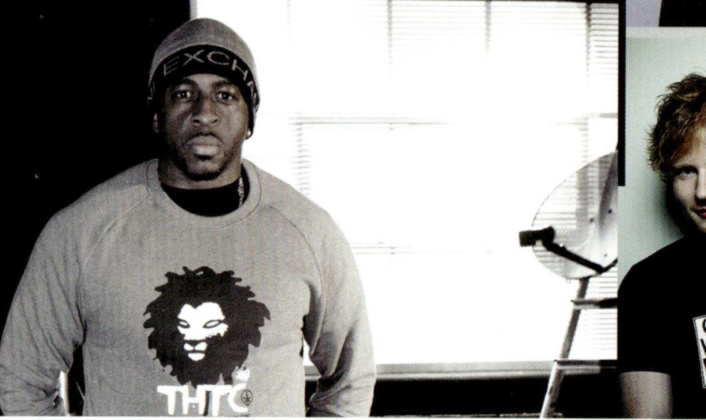

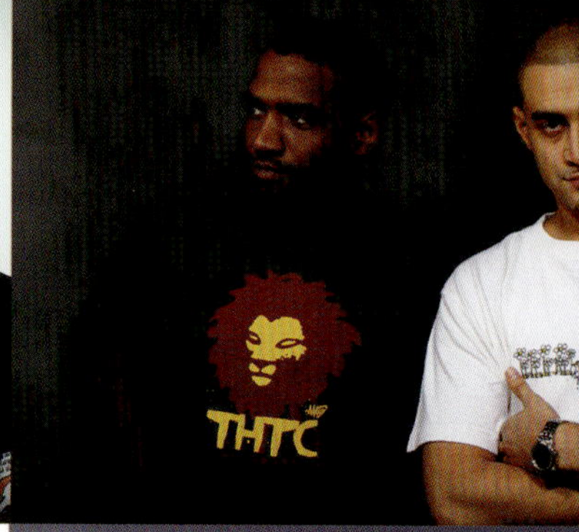

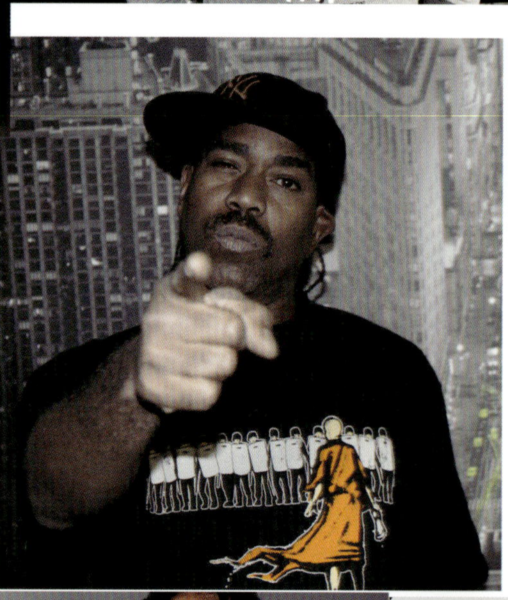
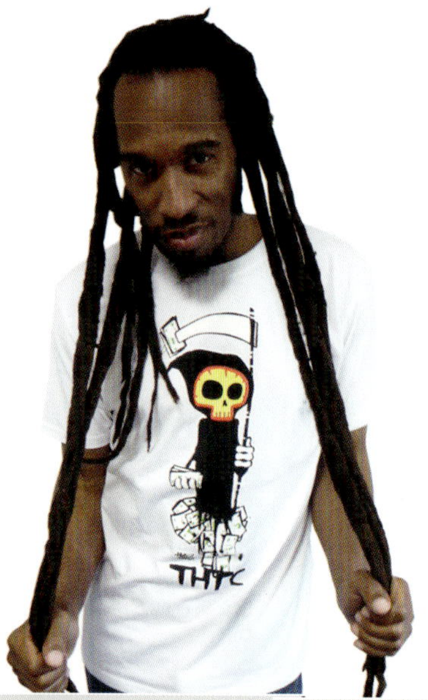

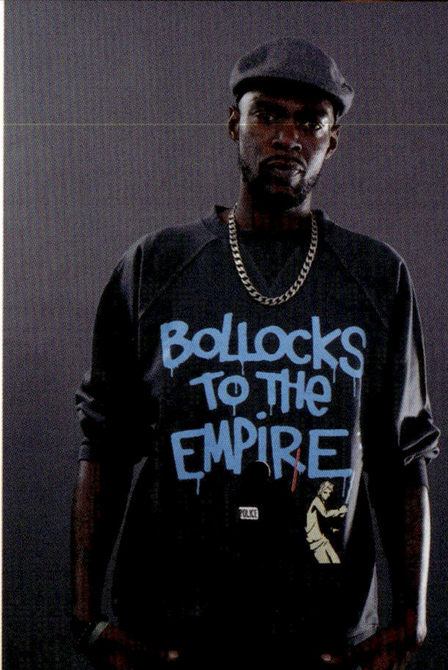

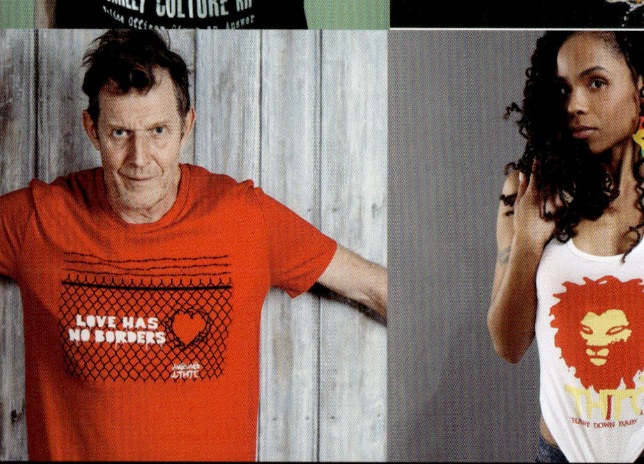

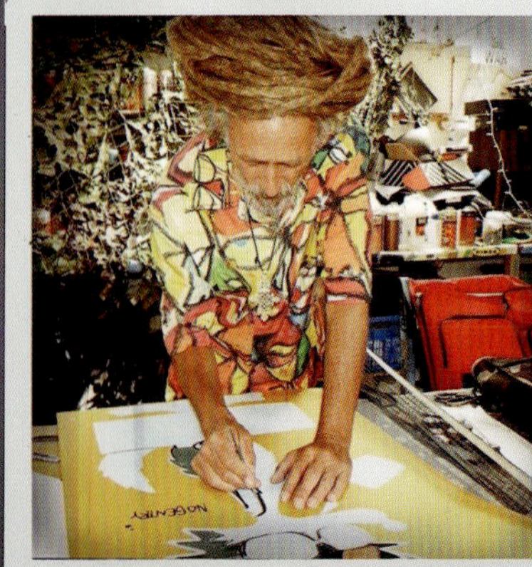
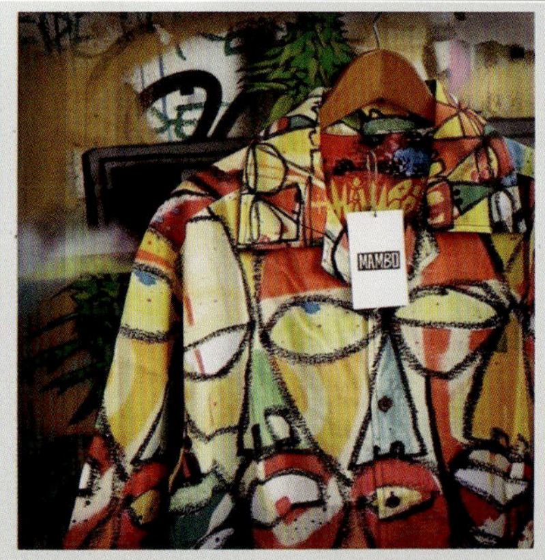

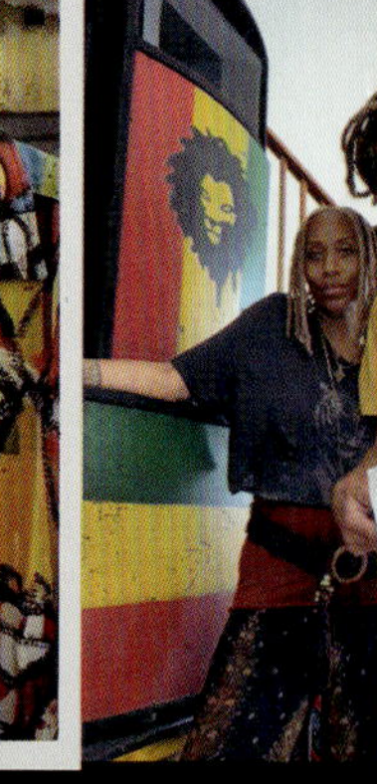

ANIMATION

Animation Projects - (co-produced with Dunk).
Skitz, Domestic Science, 2001,
Rodney P, Riddim Killa, 2002,
The Herbalizer, Something Wicked This Way Comes, 2002.
The Mildlife Show, 2016.

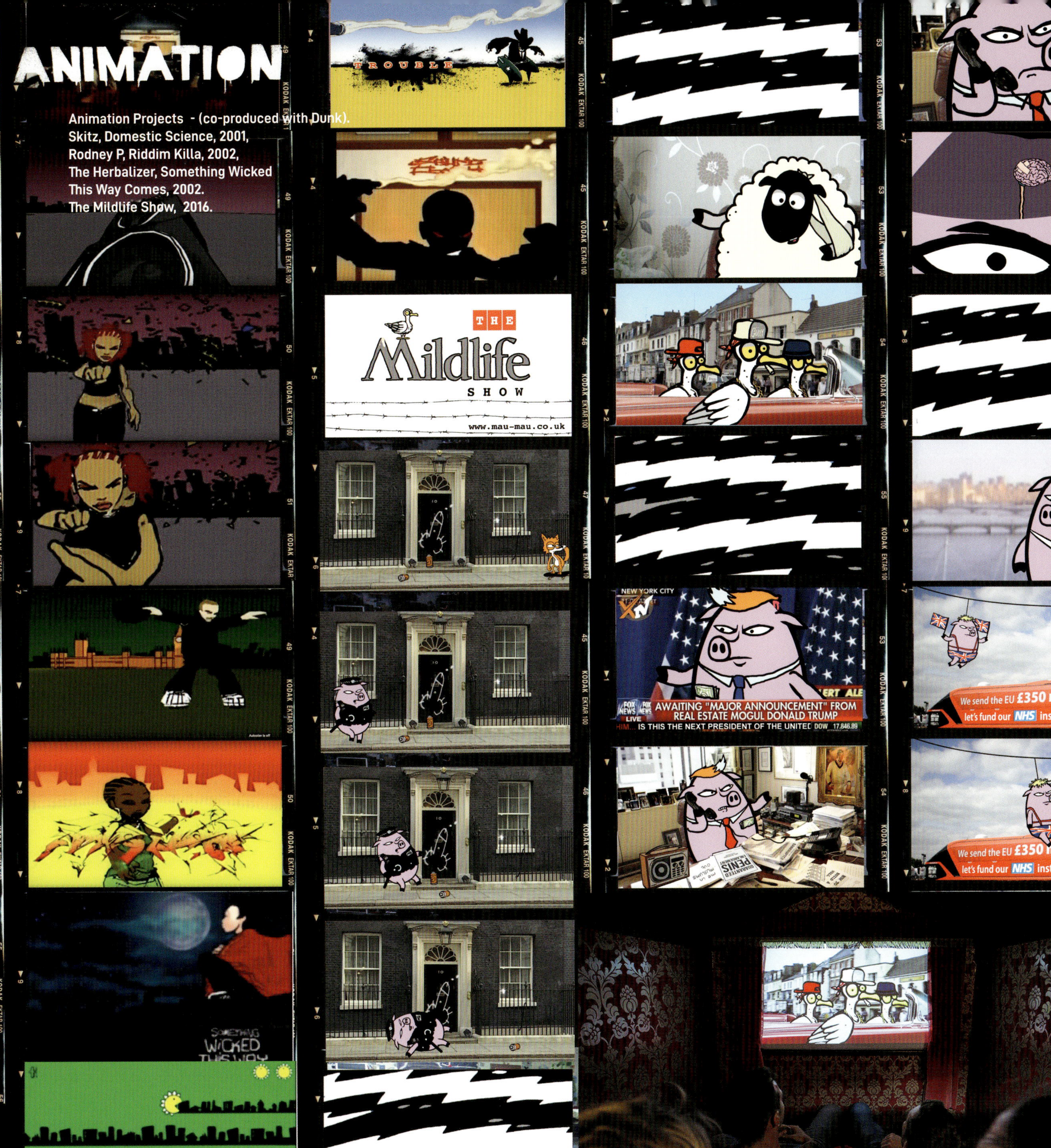

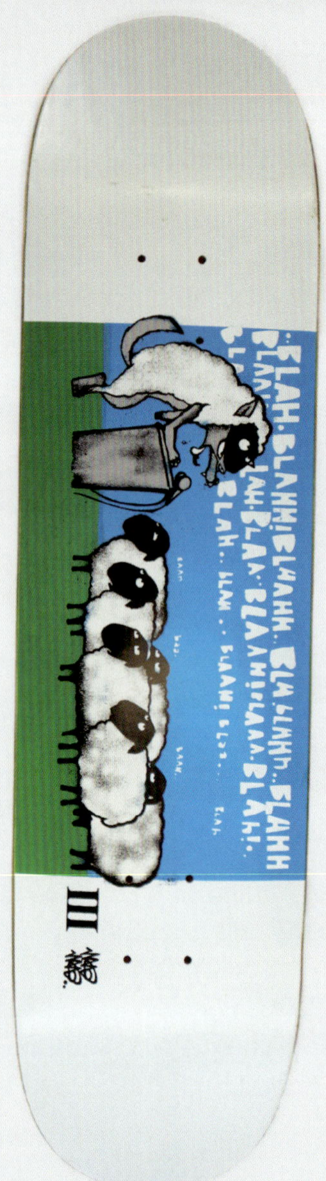

Wolf in Sheeples Clothing, A Third Foot, 2011.

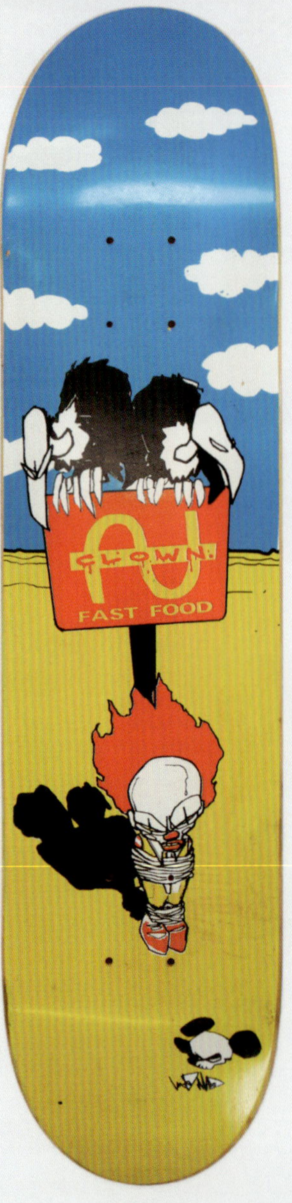

Fast Food, Clown Skateboards, 2005.

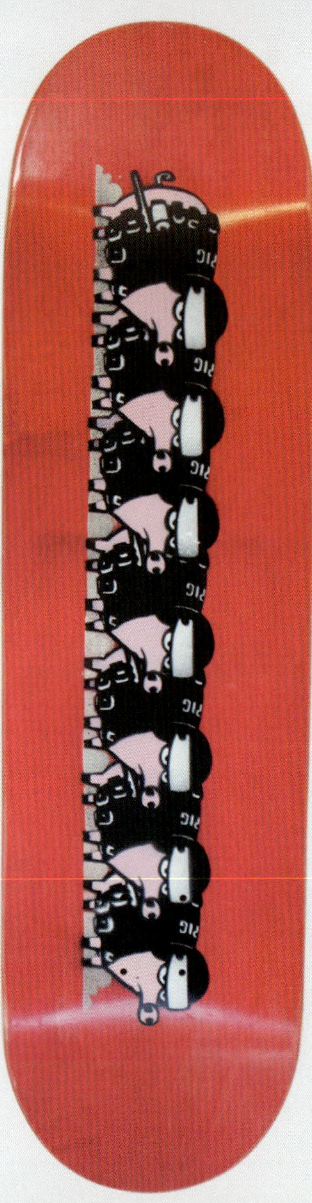

Riot Pig stencil on A Third Foot Blank, 2017.

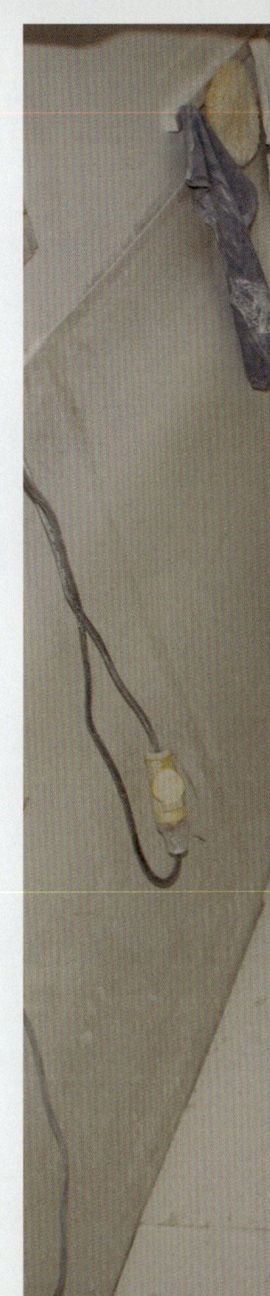

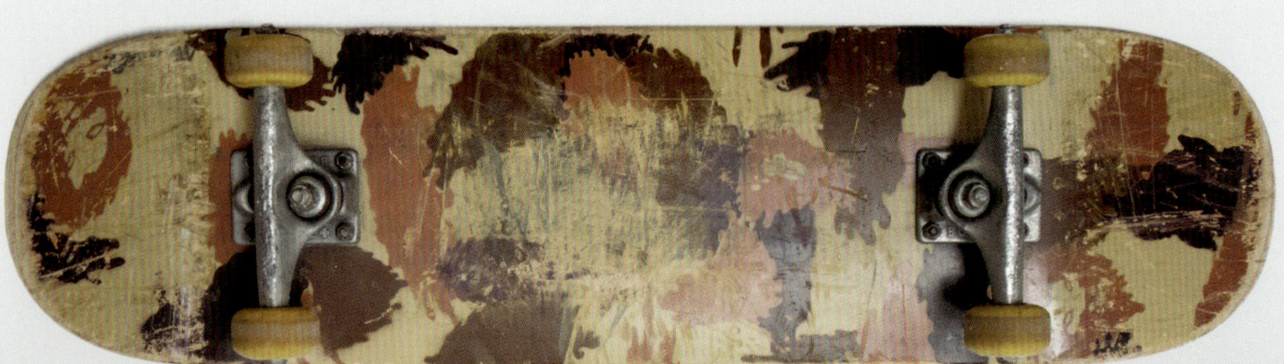

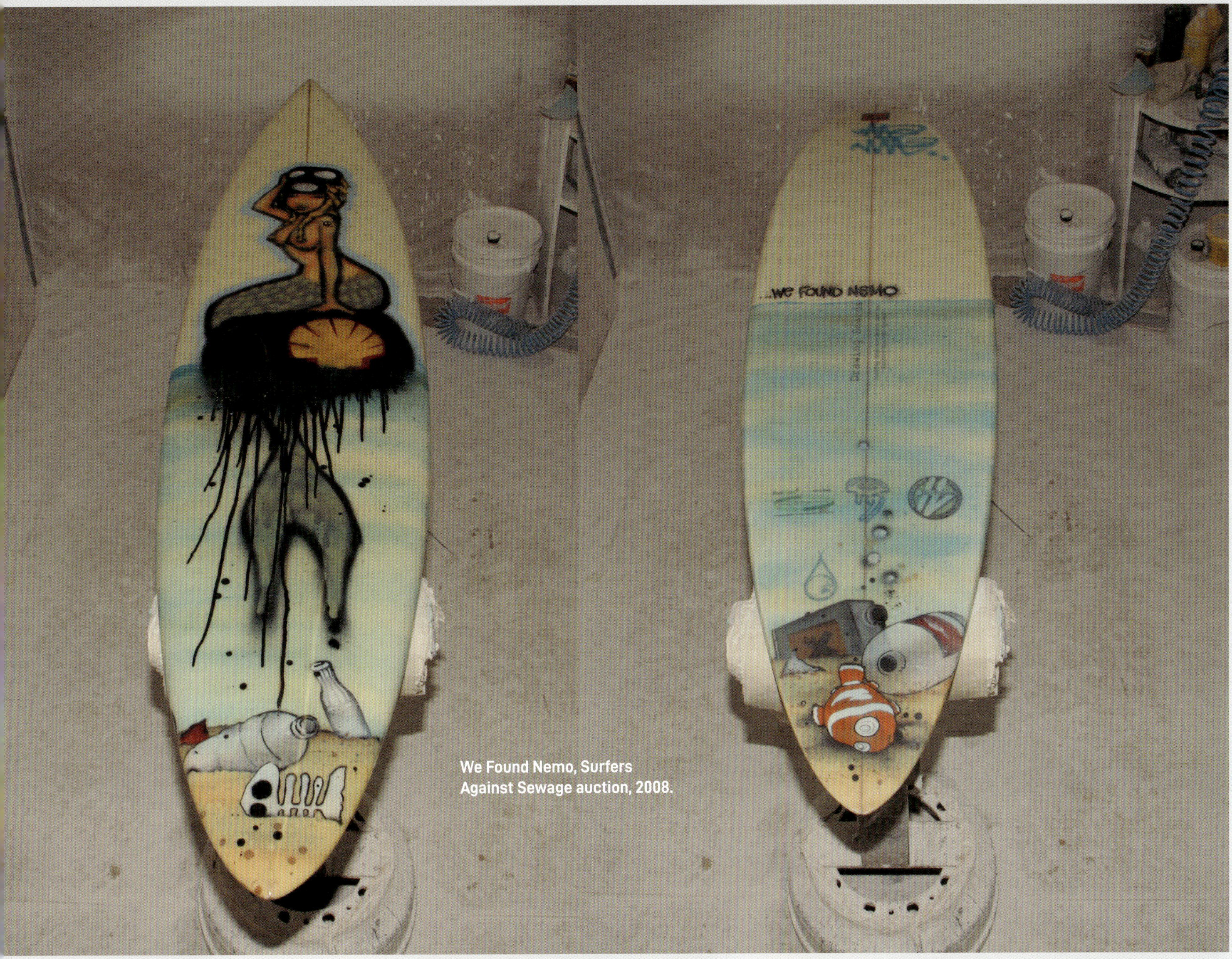

We Found Nemo, Surfers Against Sewage auction, 2008.

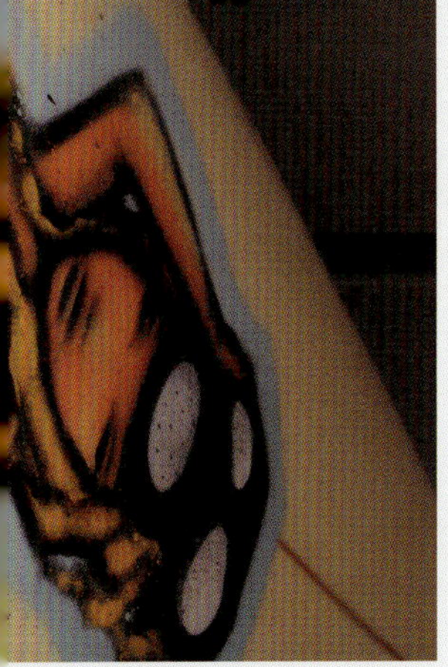

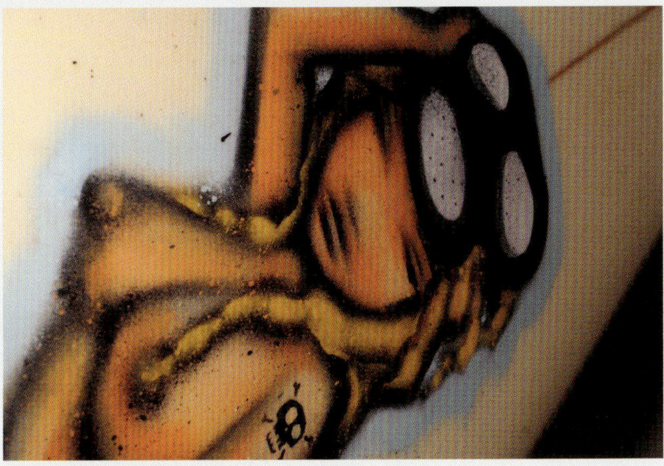

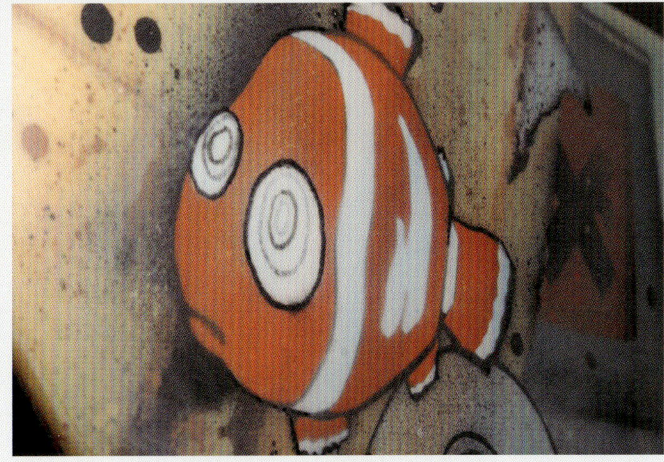

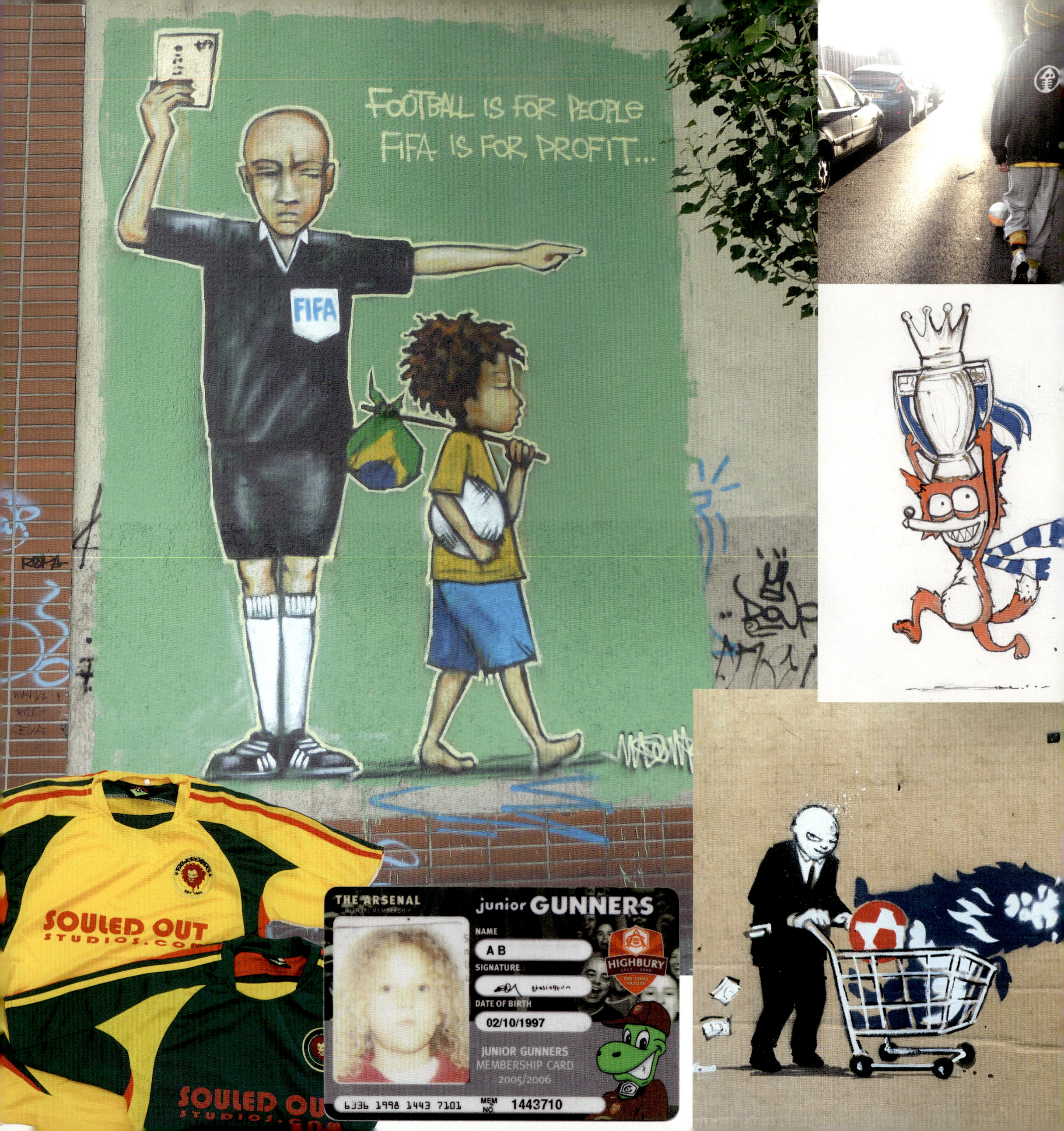

FOOTBALL IS FOR PEOPLE
FIFA IS FOR PROFIT...
FIFA
SOULED OUT
STUDIOS.COM
THE ARSENAL
junior GUNNERS
NAME
A B
SIGNATURE
DATE OF BIRTH
02/10/1997
HIGHBURY
JUNIOR GUNNERS
MEMBERSHIP CARD
2005/2006
6336 1998 1443 7101
MEM NO.
1443710
SOULED OUT

The beautiful game, sometimes...

Left to right:
FIFA Gold Card, Slovakia, 2014.
Leicester (Foxes) Champions, 2016.
Souled Out Studios football shirts, 2007.
Junior Gunners membership.
Not So Super League, 2021.

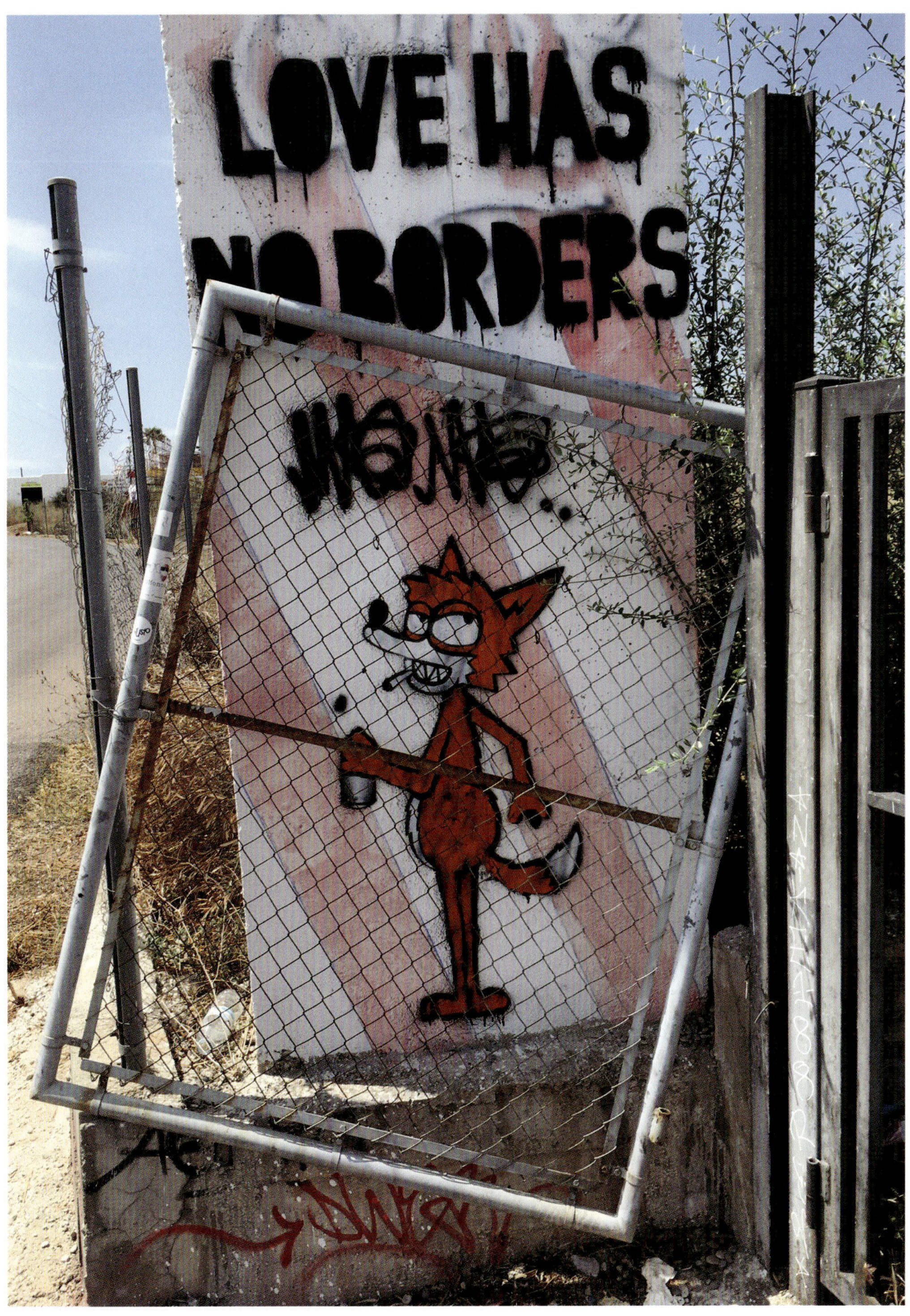

Love Has No Borders, Benicàssim, Spain, 2018.

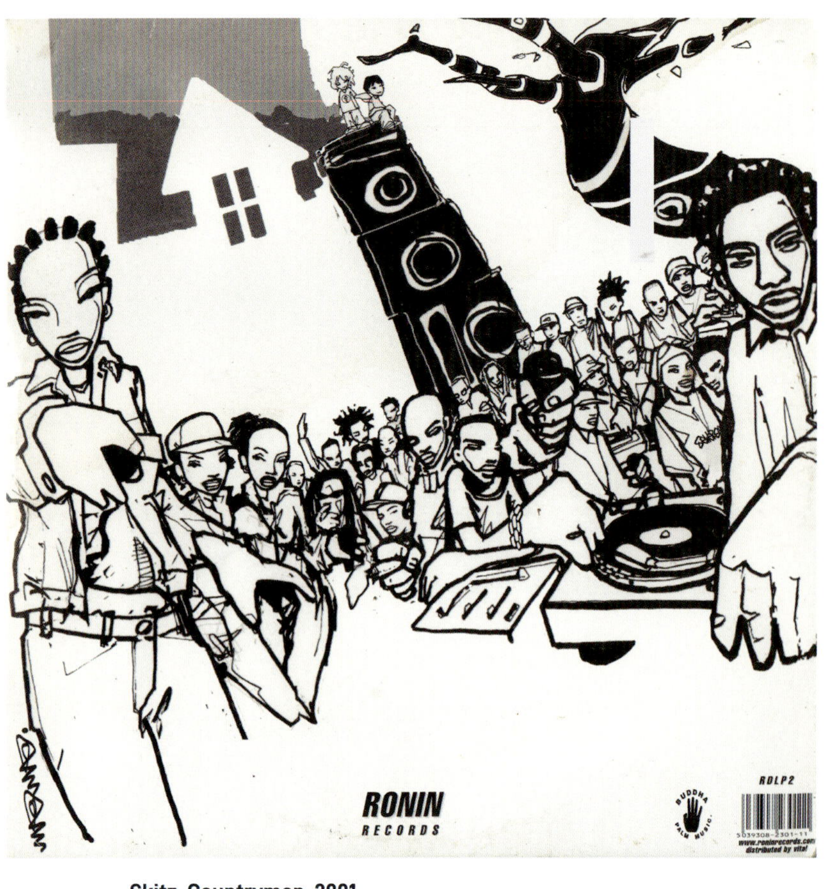

Skitz, Countryman, 2001.

Joe Burn, Spark it Up, 2014.

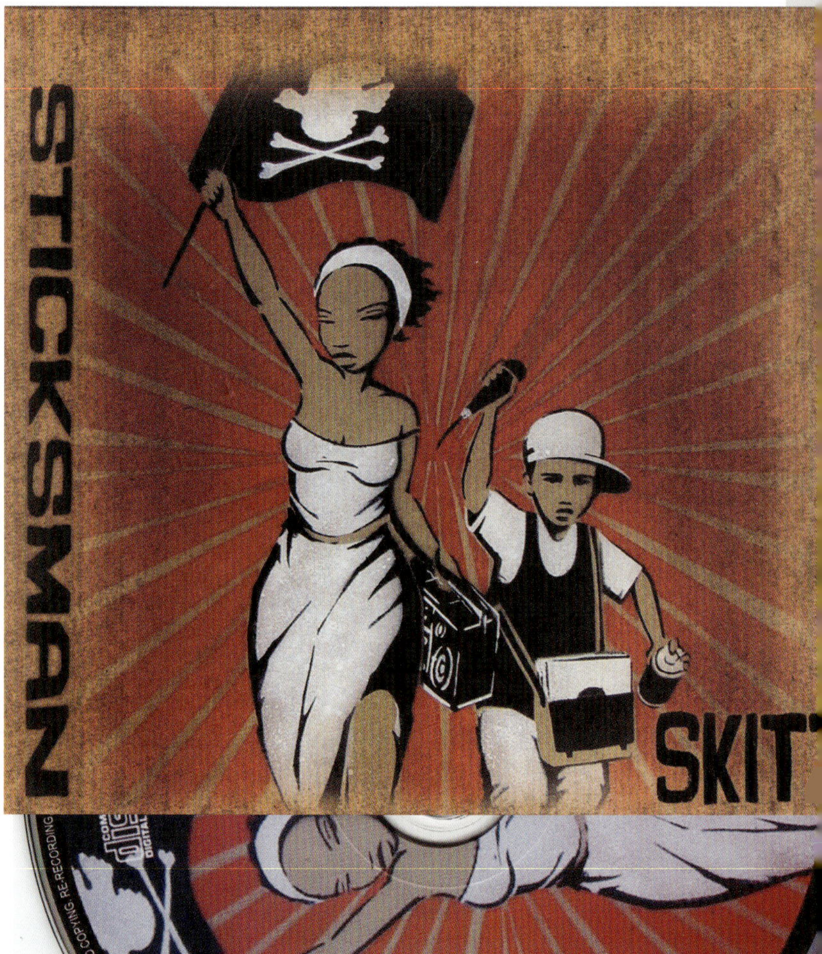

Skitz, Sticksman, 2010.

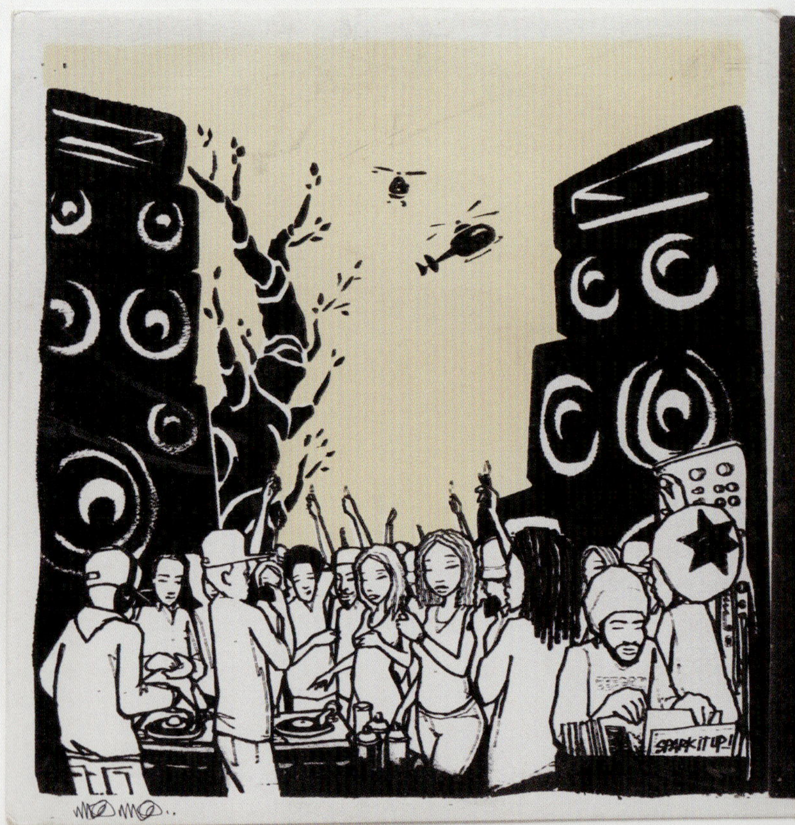

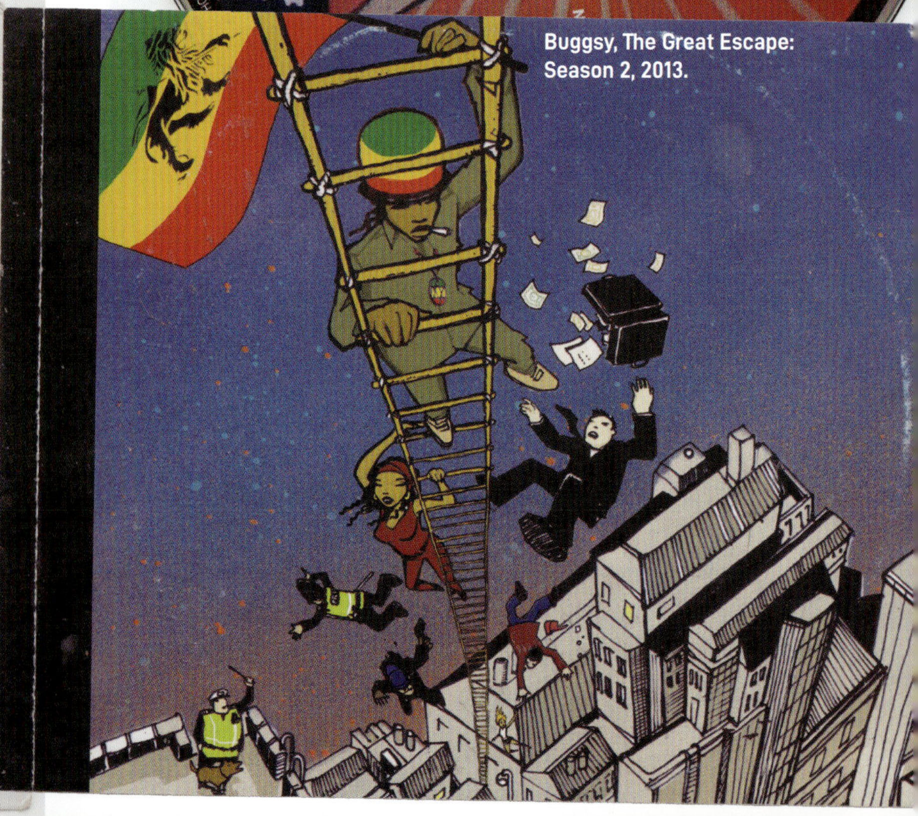

Buggsy, The Great Escape: Season 2, 2013.

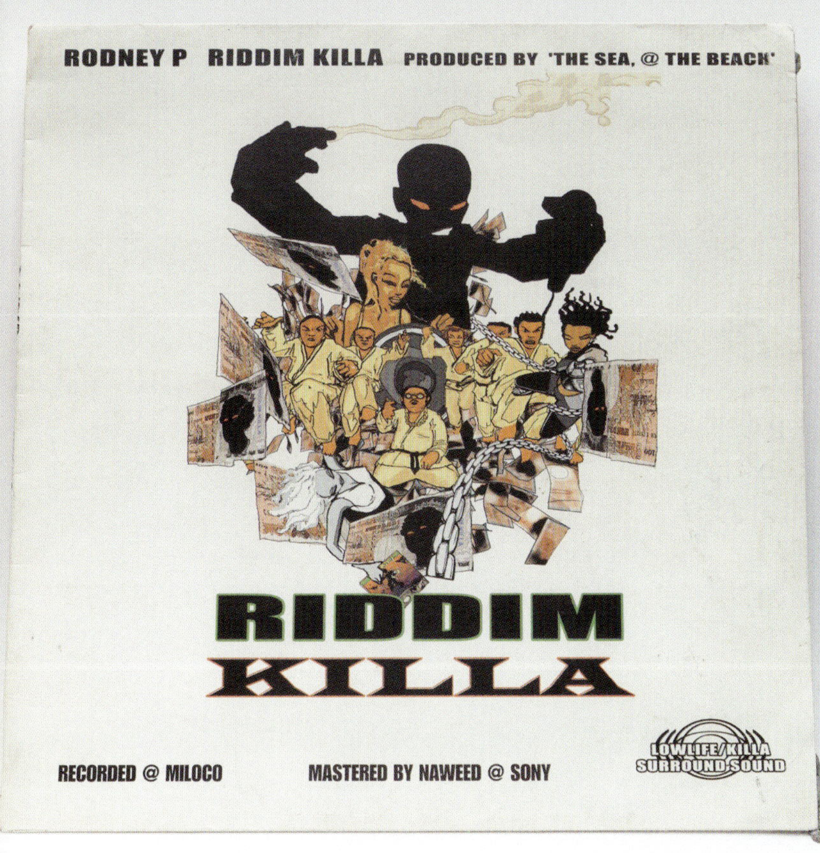

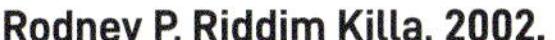
Rodney P, Riddim Killa, 2002.

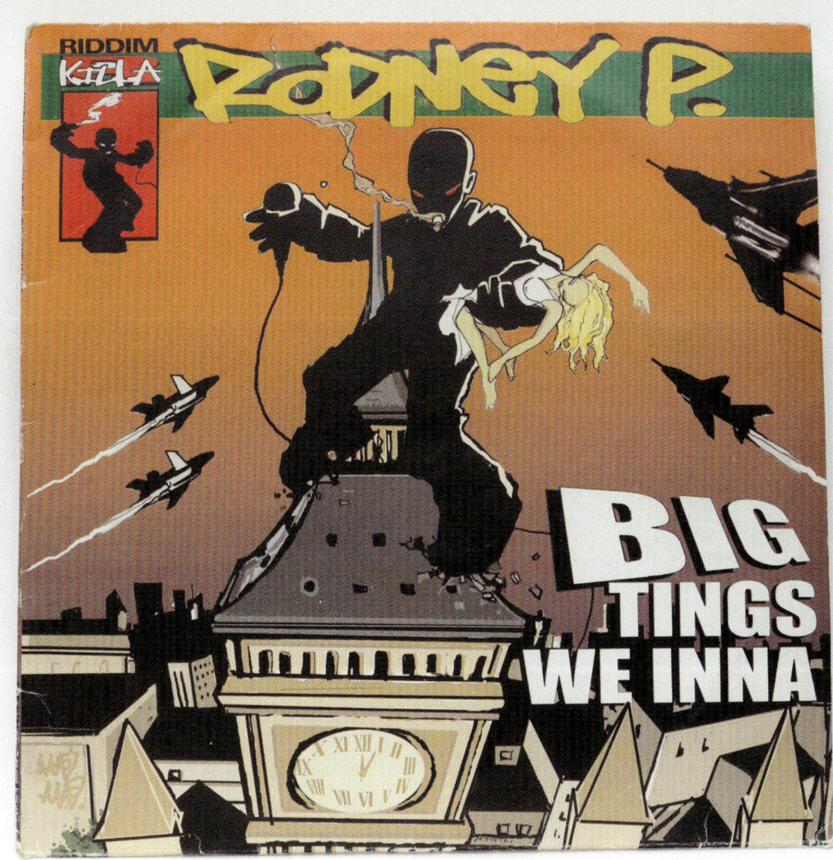

Rodney P, Big Tings We Inna, 2001.

Sizzla, Without Jah Jah, 2018.

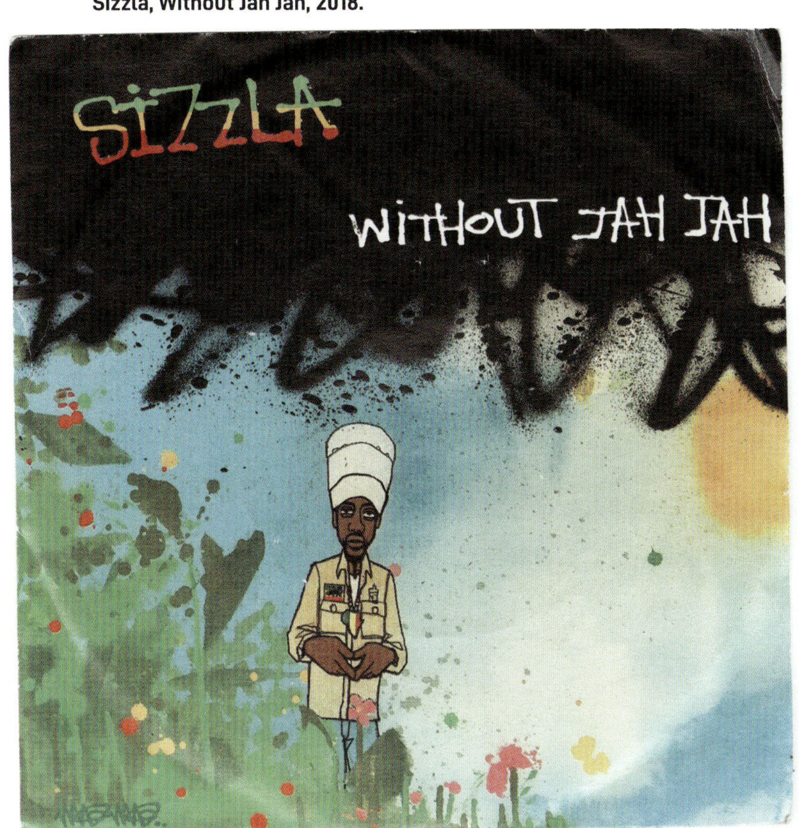

Micah Shemaiah, Original Dread, 2015.

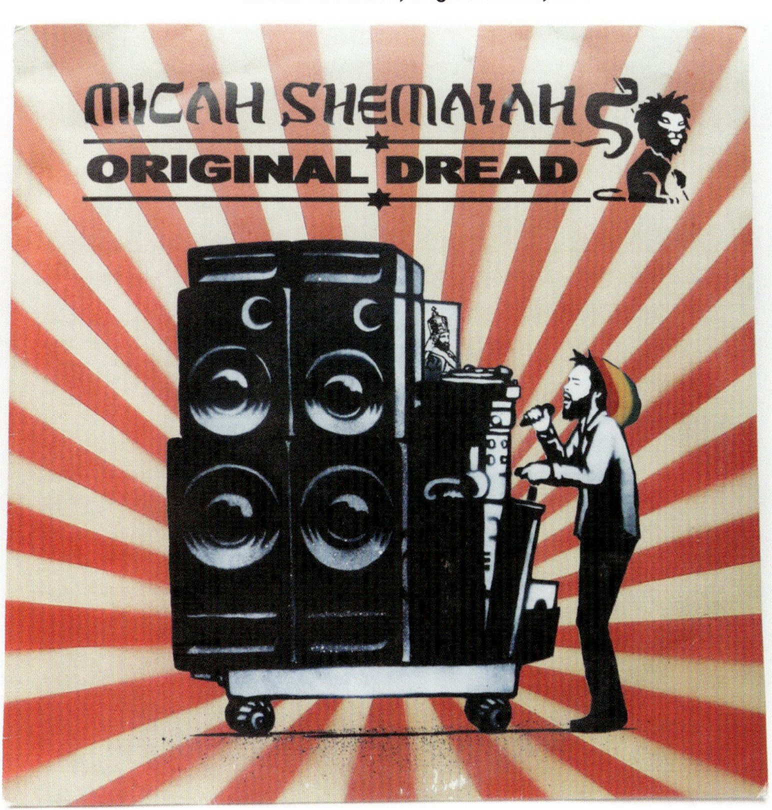

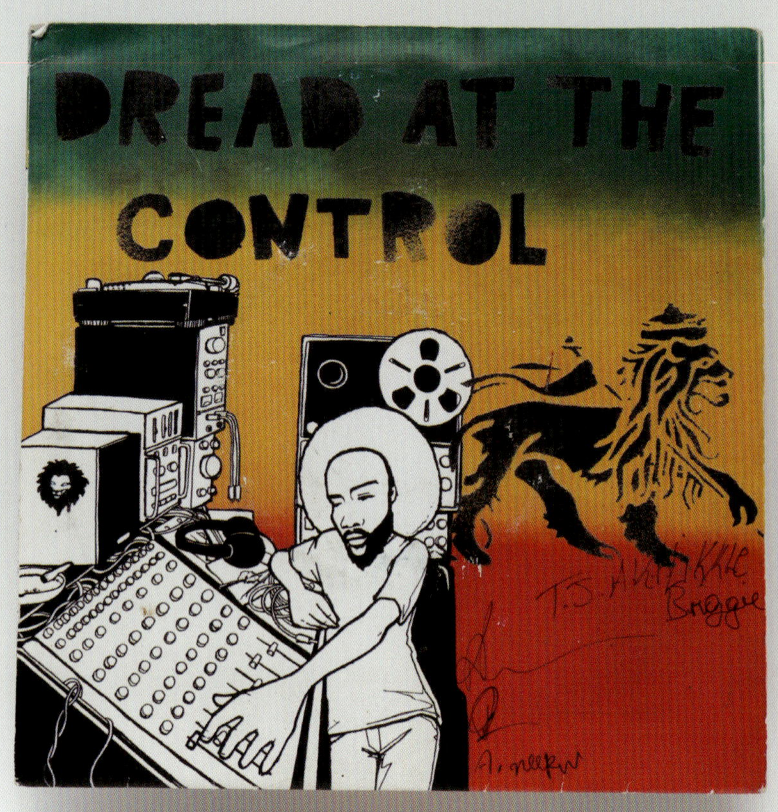

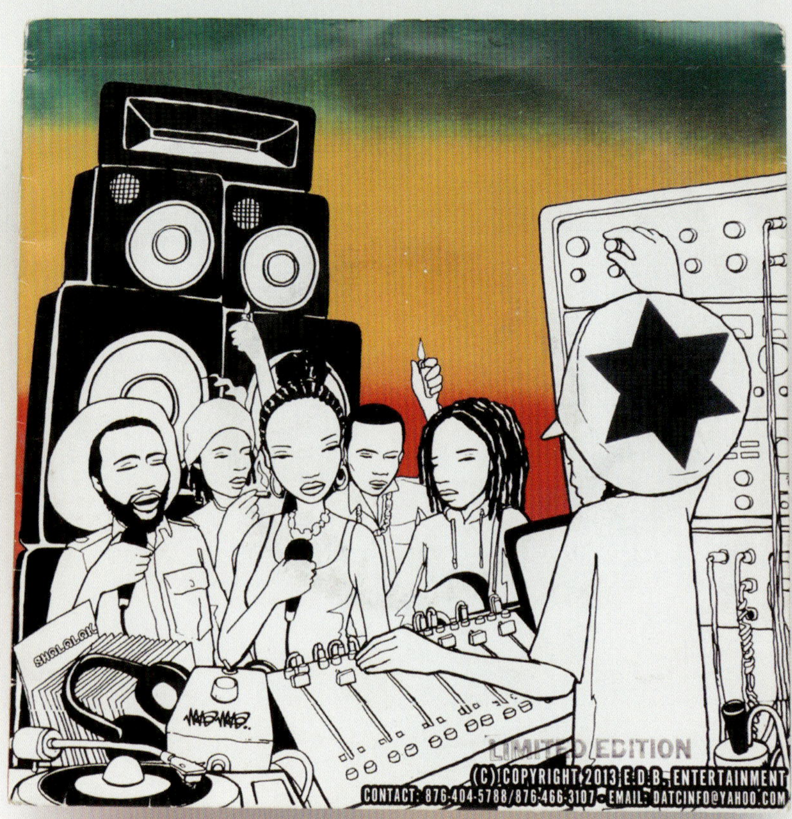

Micah Shemaiah, Dread At The Control, 2013 - Front/Back cover.

Micah Shemaiah, Rockers Party, 2015 - Front/Back cover.

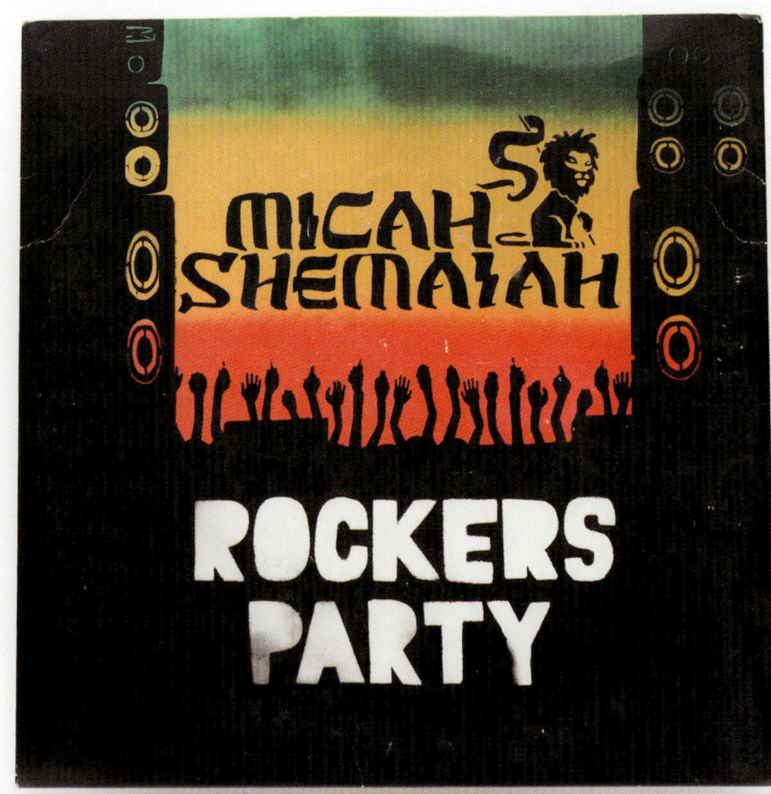

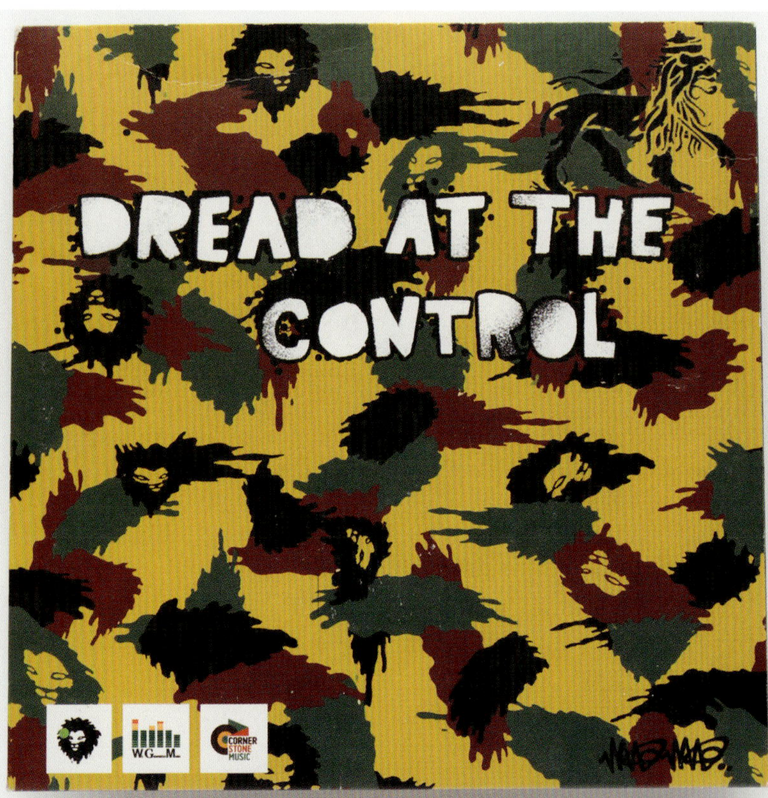

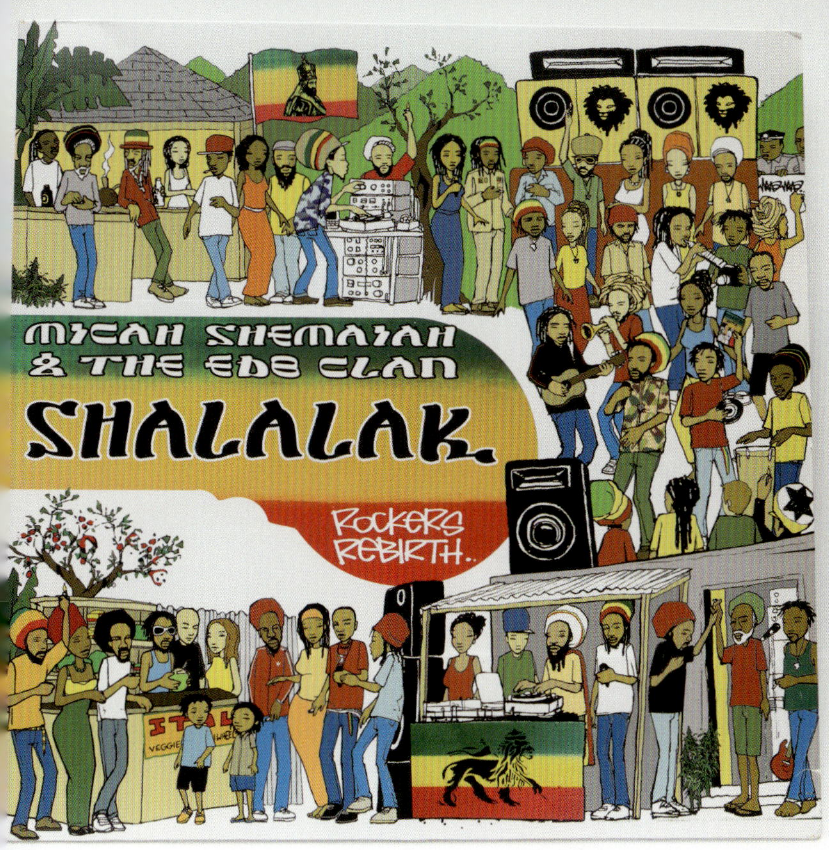

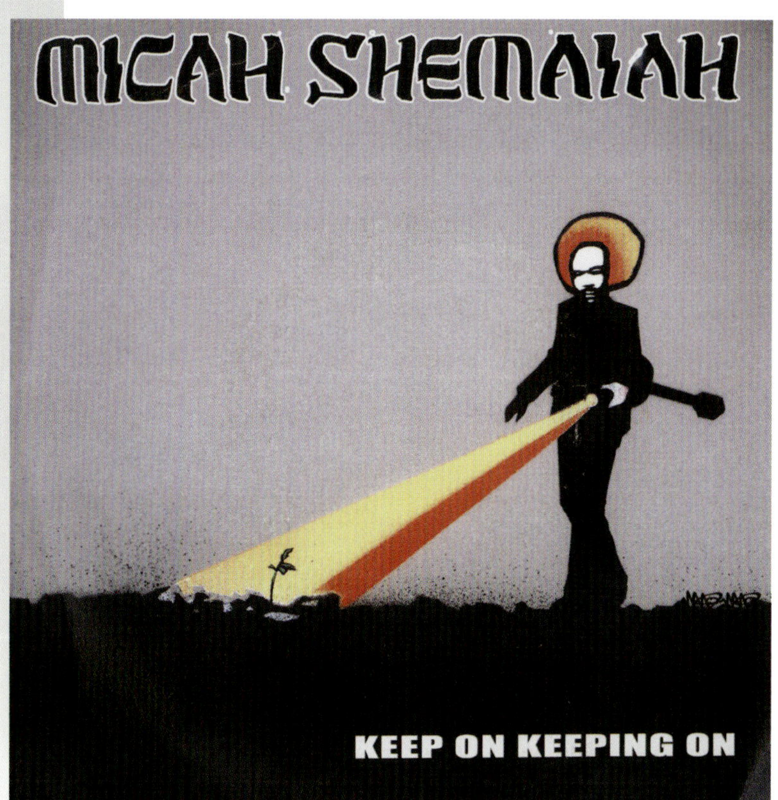

Micah Shemaiah & The EDB Clan, Shalalak, 2015.

Micah Shemaiah, Keep On Keeping On, 2017.

Micah Shemaiah, Reggae Rockit, 2014, Back/Front cover.

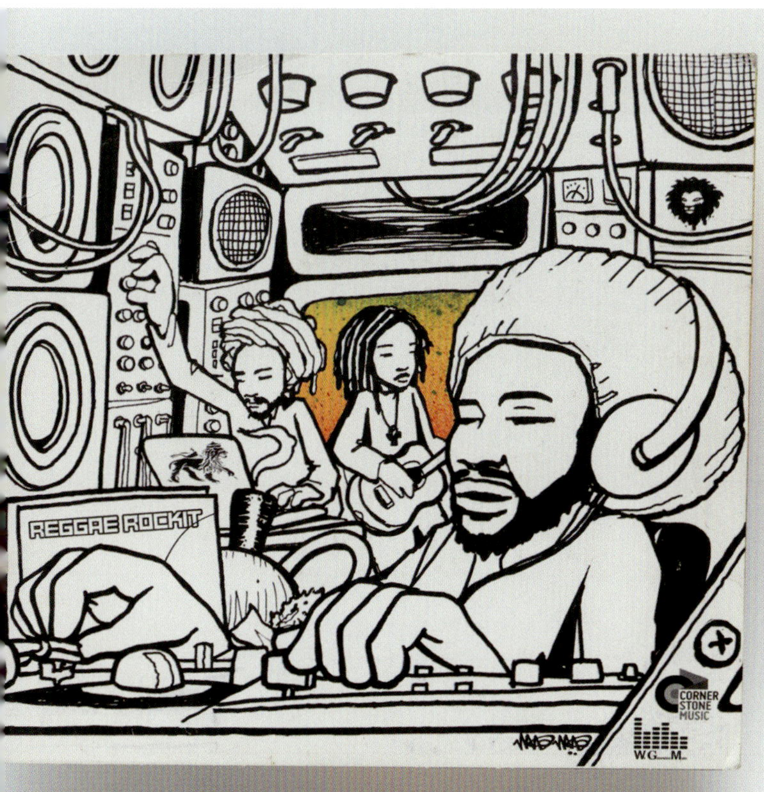

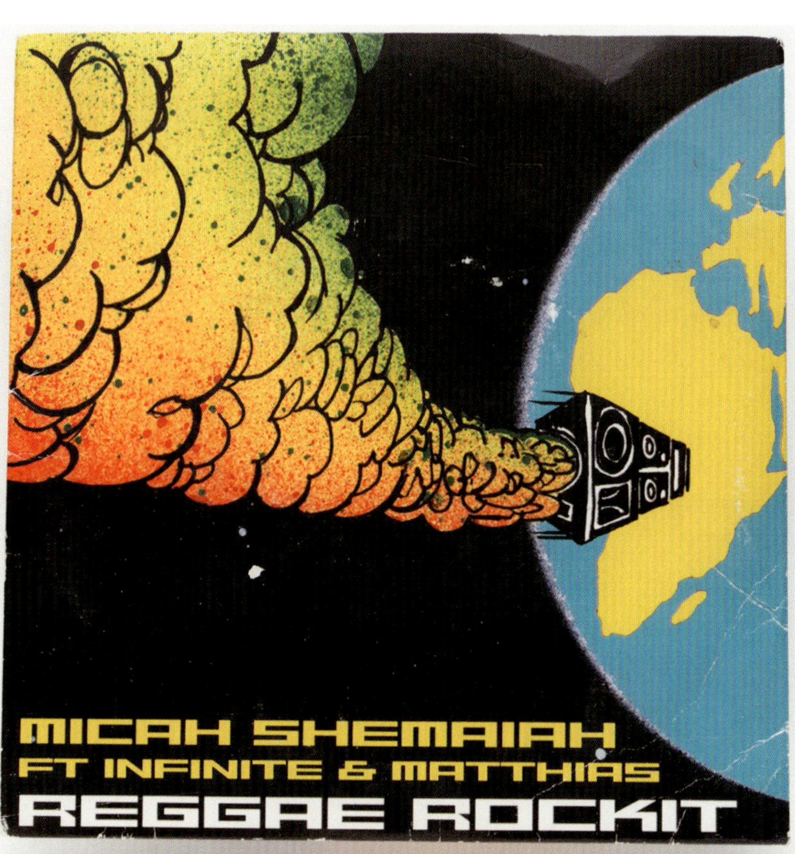

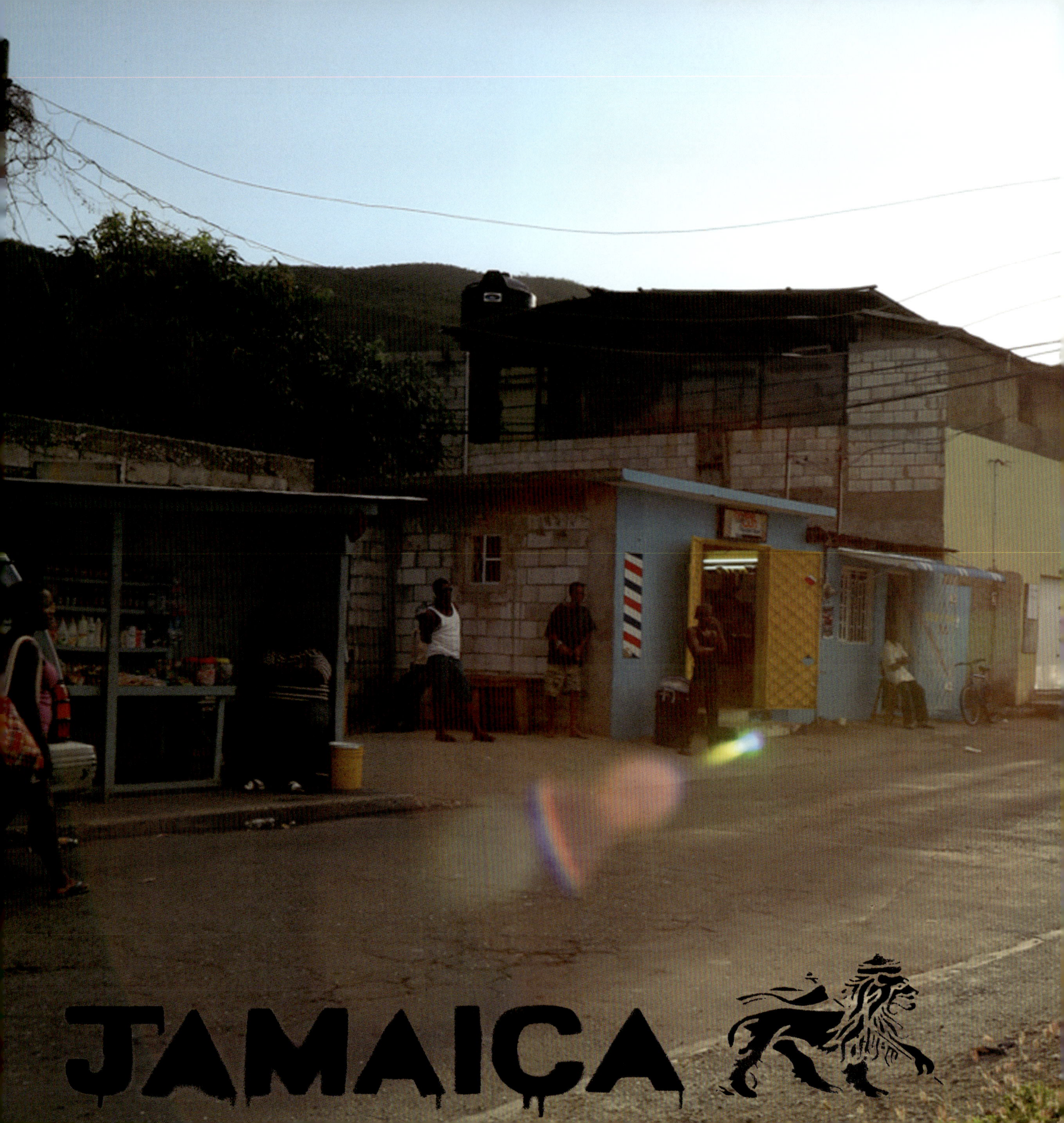
JAMAICA

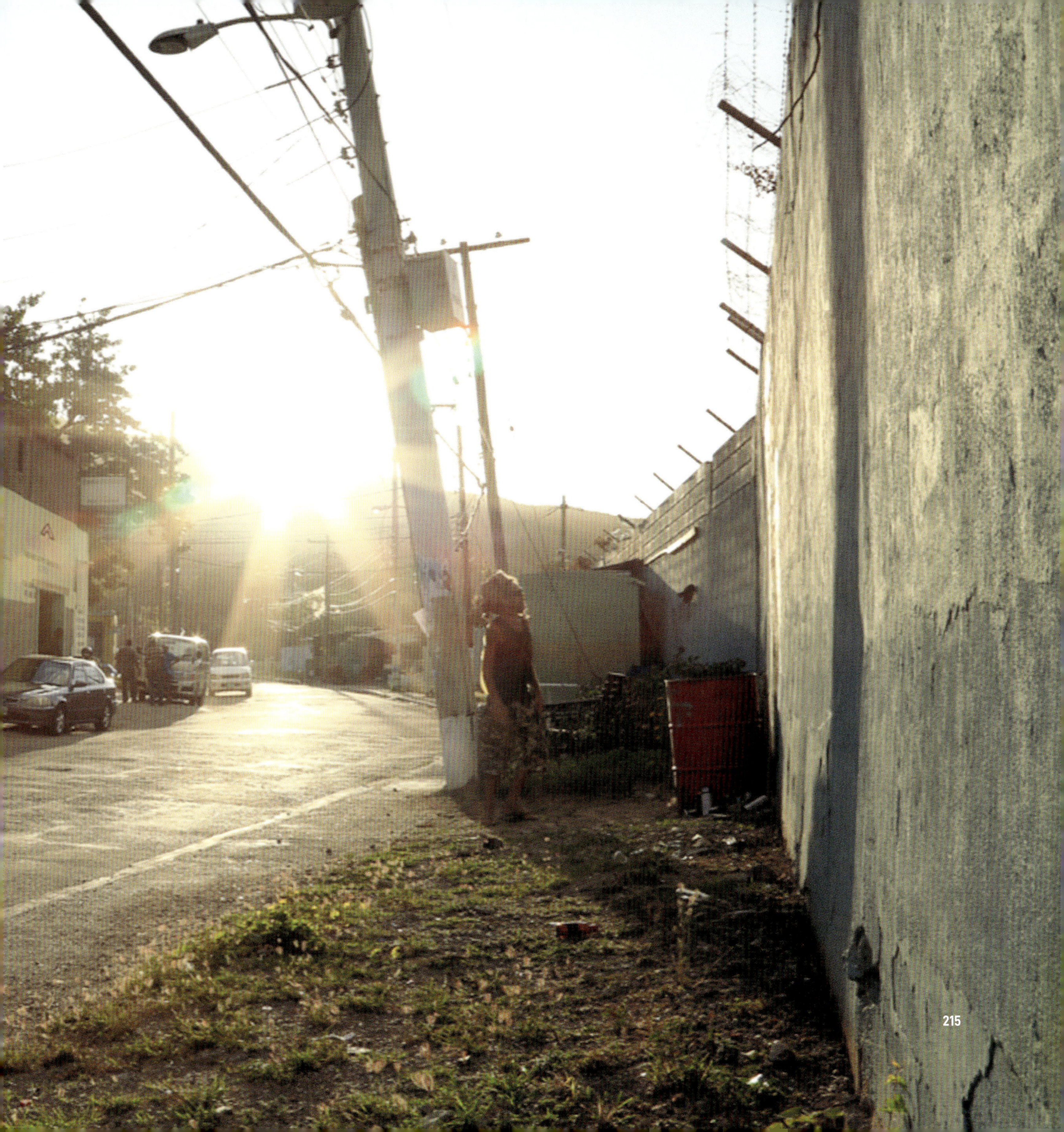

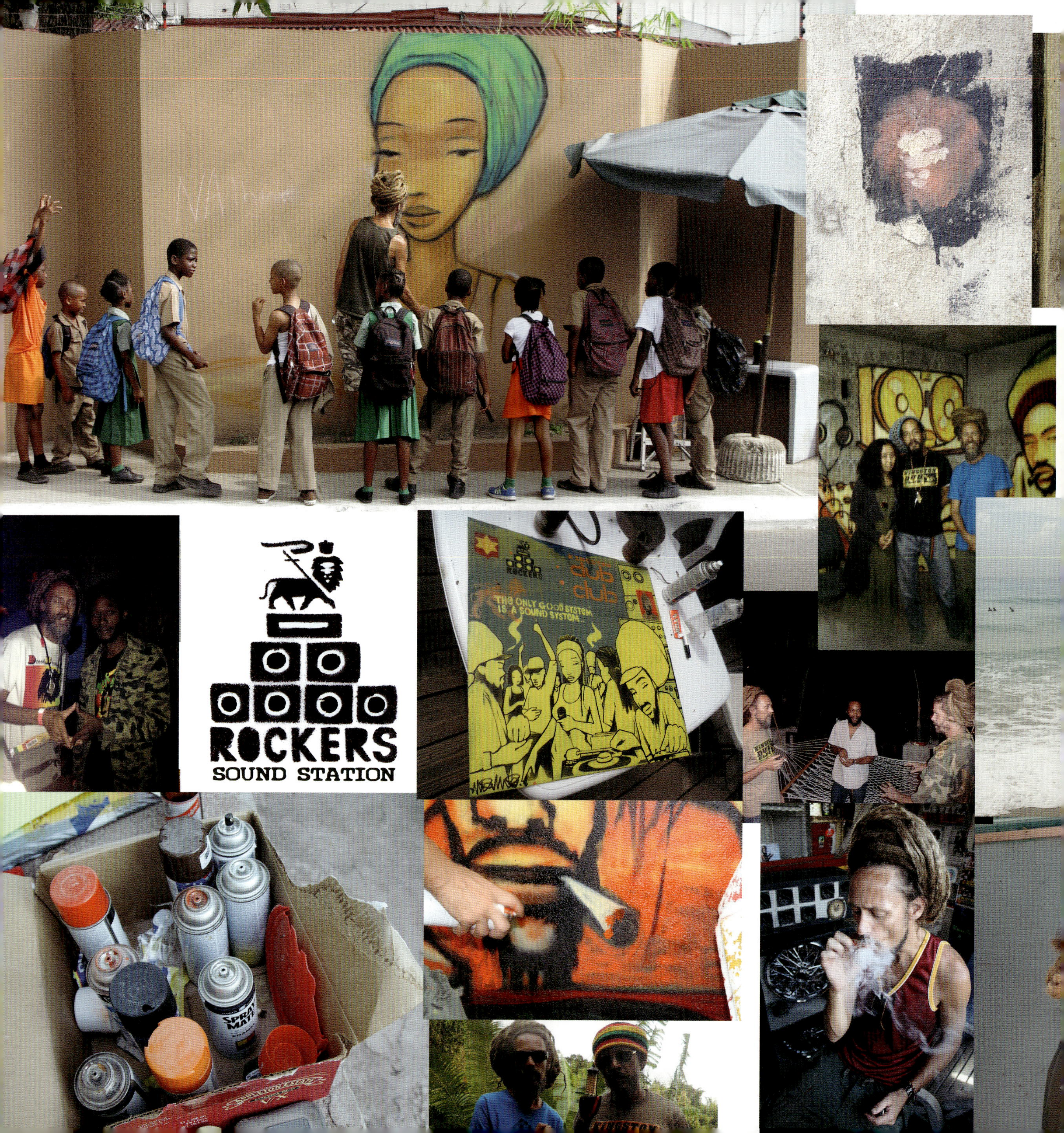

ROCKERS
SOUND STATION
dub club
THE ONLY GOOD SYSTEM IS A SOUND SYSTEM...

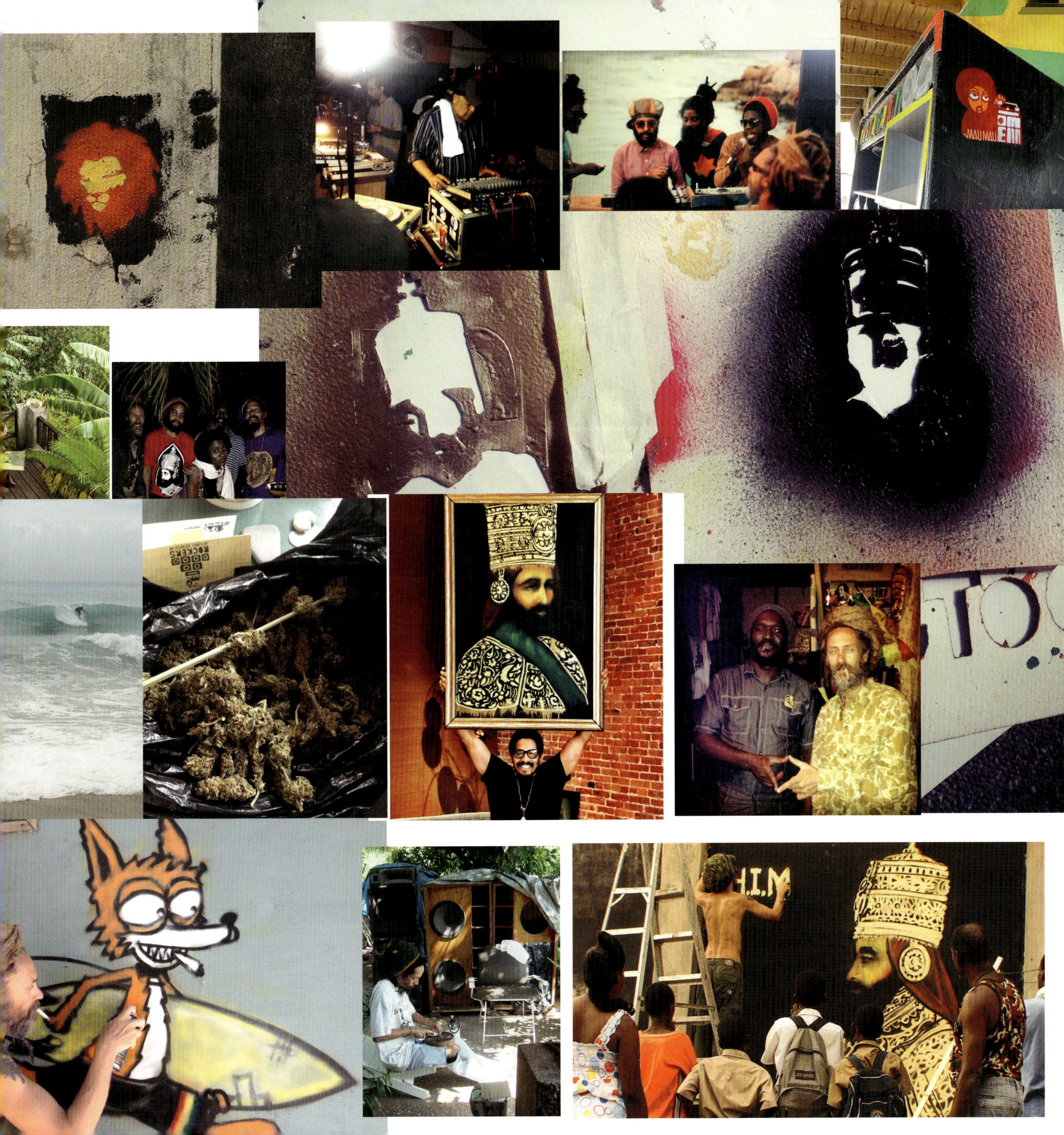
H.I.M

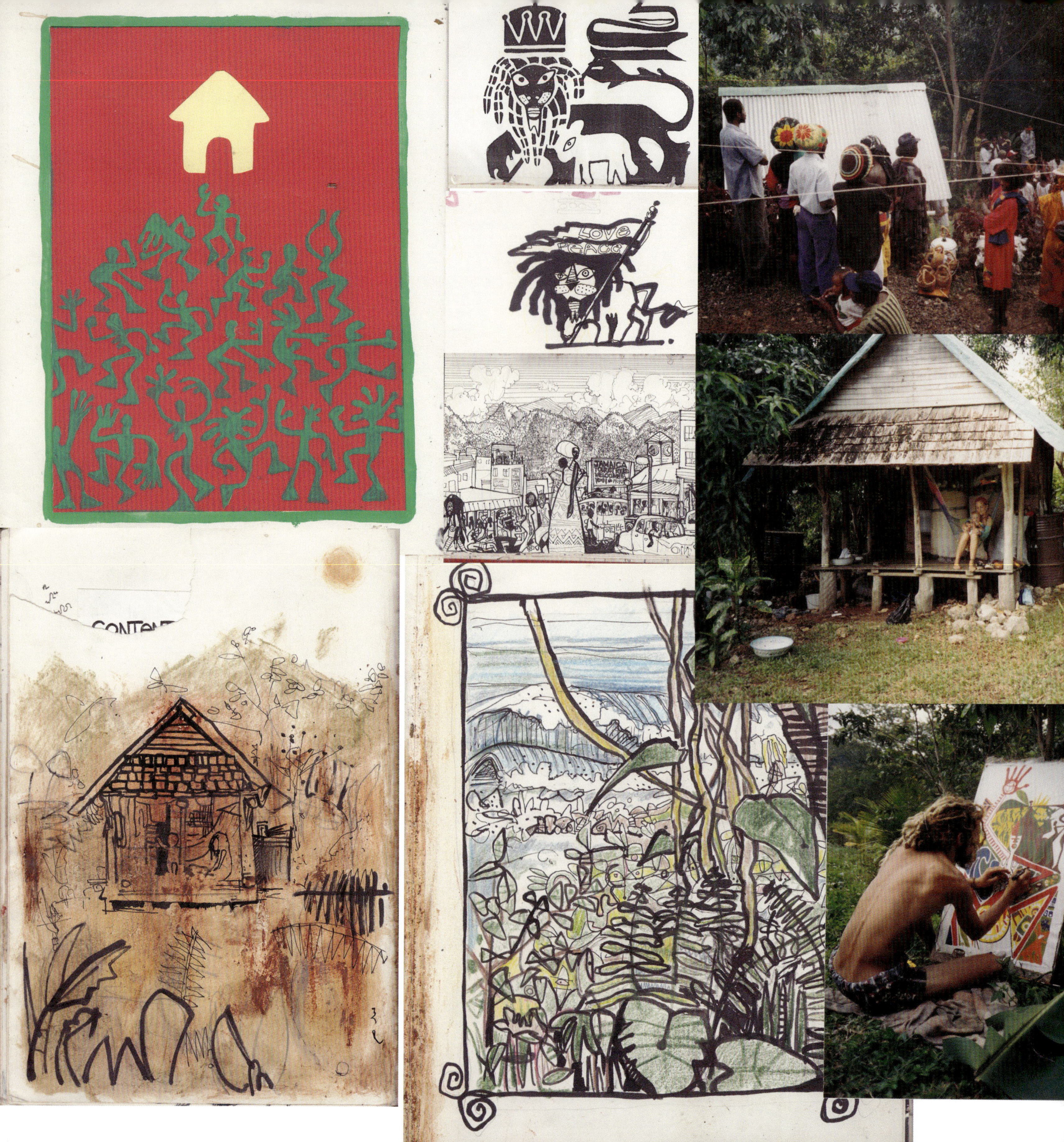
LOVE

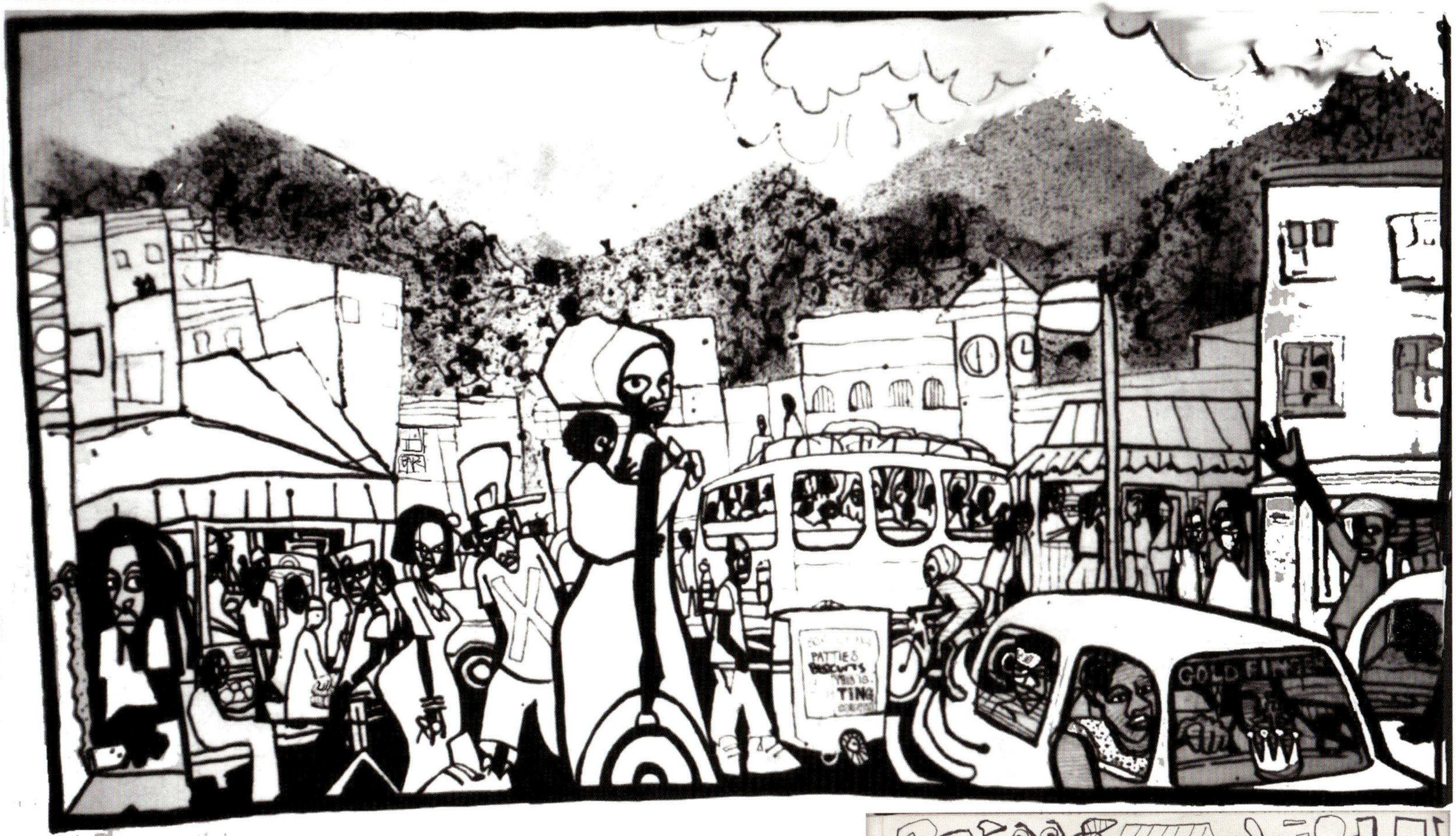

It was in the early 1990s that I first went to Jamaica. At the time I was trying to make a living doing graphics, mainly club flyers and logos. Money was tight, we'd just had a baby and the lease was up on our place. I managed to get the cash together for plane tickets, without much money to spend once we got there.

Landing in Montego Bay we saw that most tourists were on private beaches behind fences. It wasn't the Jamaica I was hoping to find. Running out of money, we were offered a place to stay in the hills in return for helping out at a school run by the inspirational Sister P. It was a completely different vibe from what I'd seen up to that point. I ended up staying on for about six months travelling the whole island.

At that time there was no street art in Jamaica, apart from memorial pieces of Jamaican heroes. Jamaica, and especially Kingston had quite a rough edge to it, but I soon found a lot of love for the artwork and this led to more walls to paint. Over the years I've been lucky to have the opportunity to paint in parts of Kingston that would be out of bounds to most, thanks to the friends I've got there.

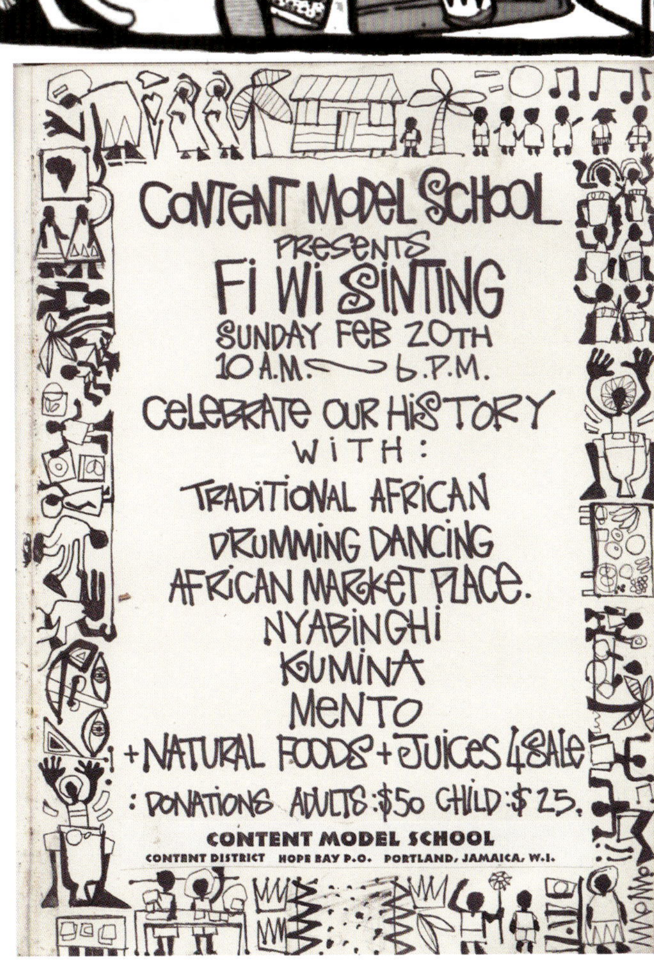

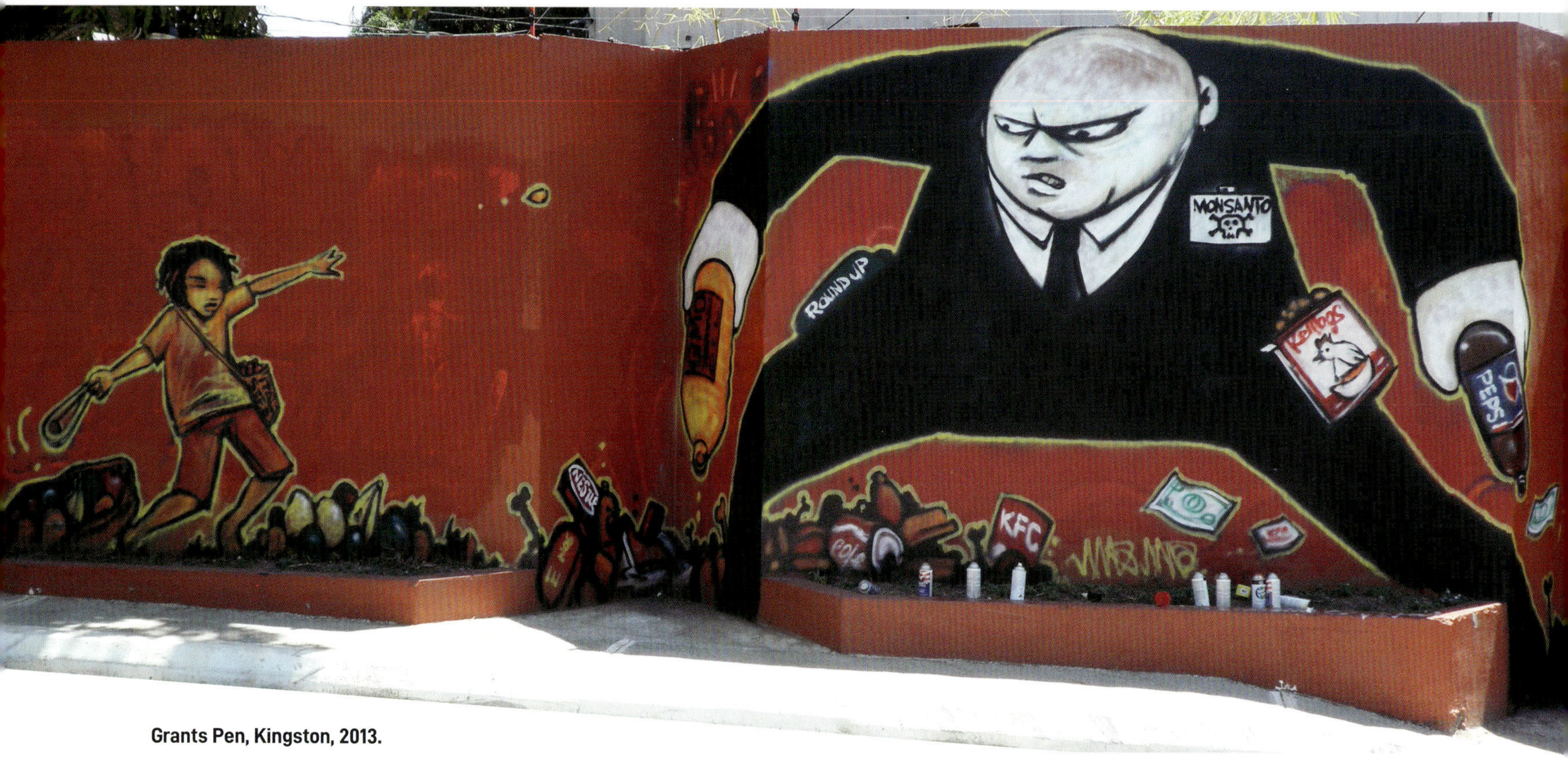

Grants Pen, Kingston, 2013.

August Town, Kingston, 2014.

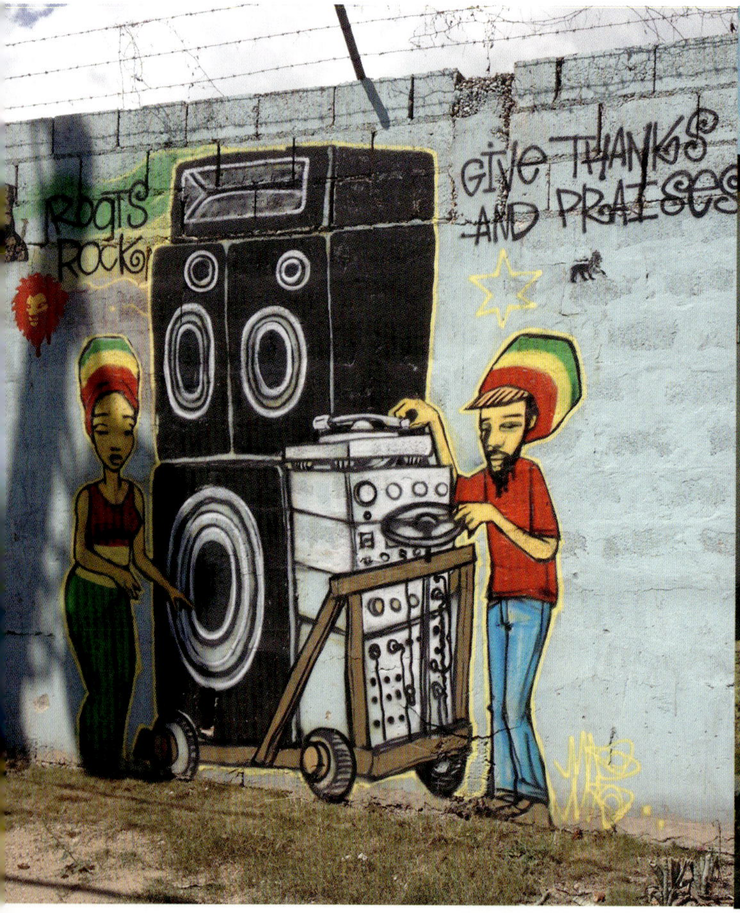

King Jammy's Studio, Waterhouse, Kingston, 2014.

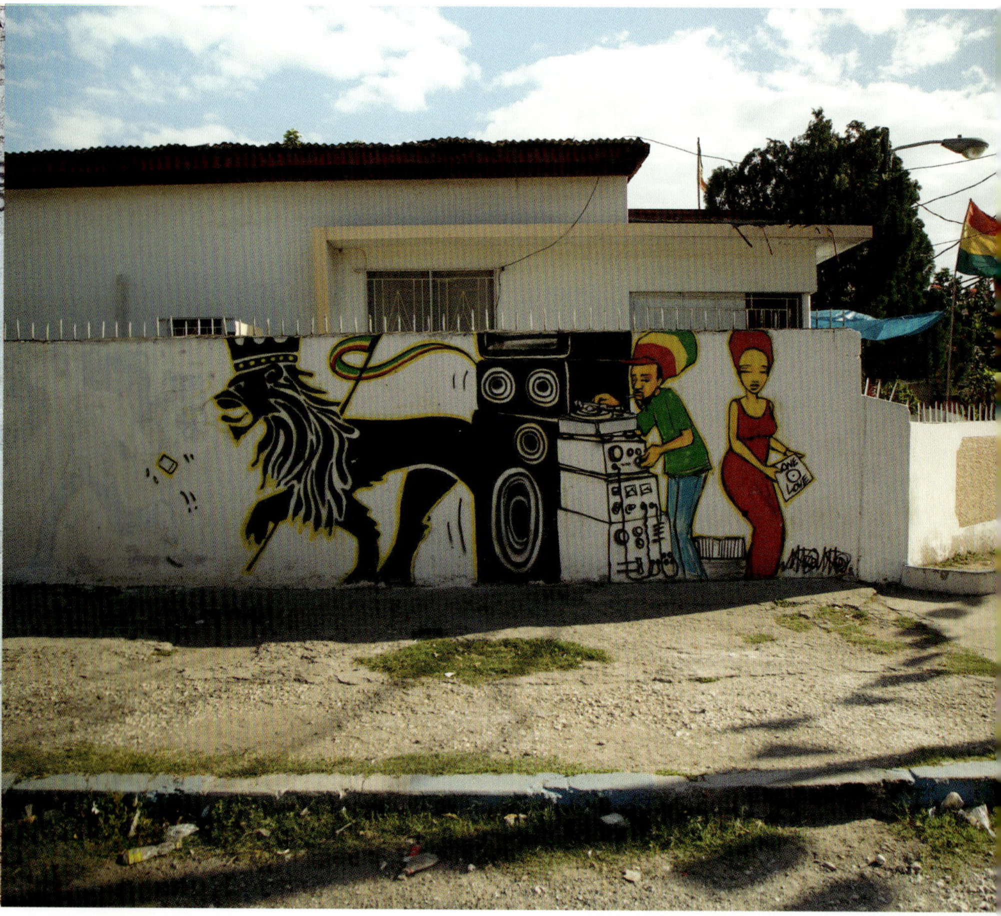

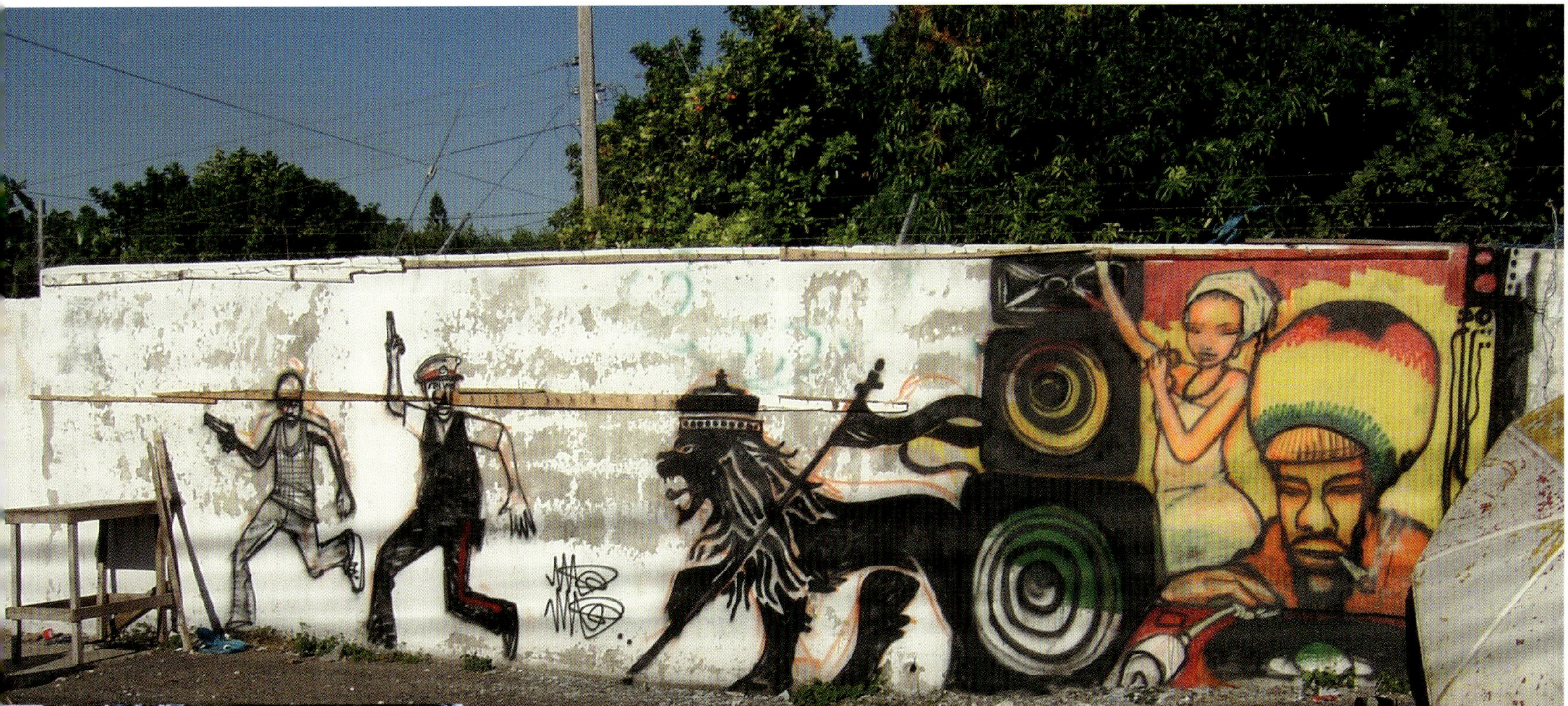

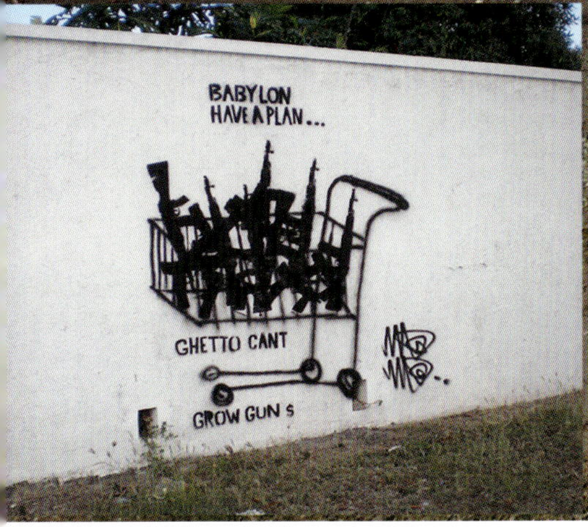

Russell Heights, Kingston, 2009.

Manor Park, Gullyside, Kingston, 2009.

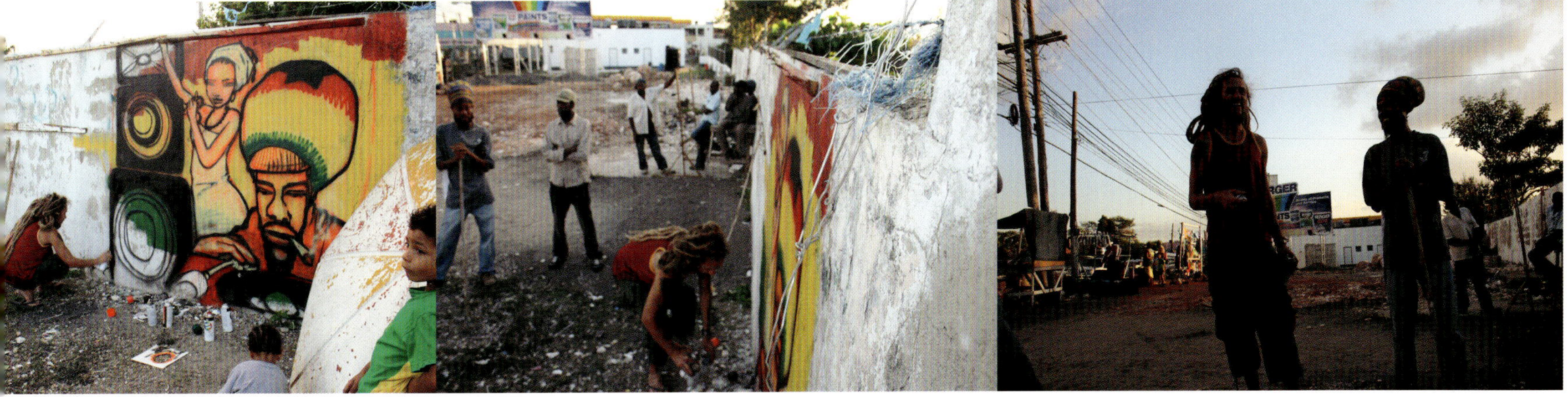

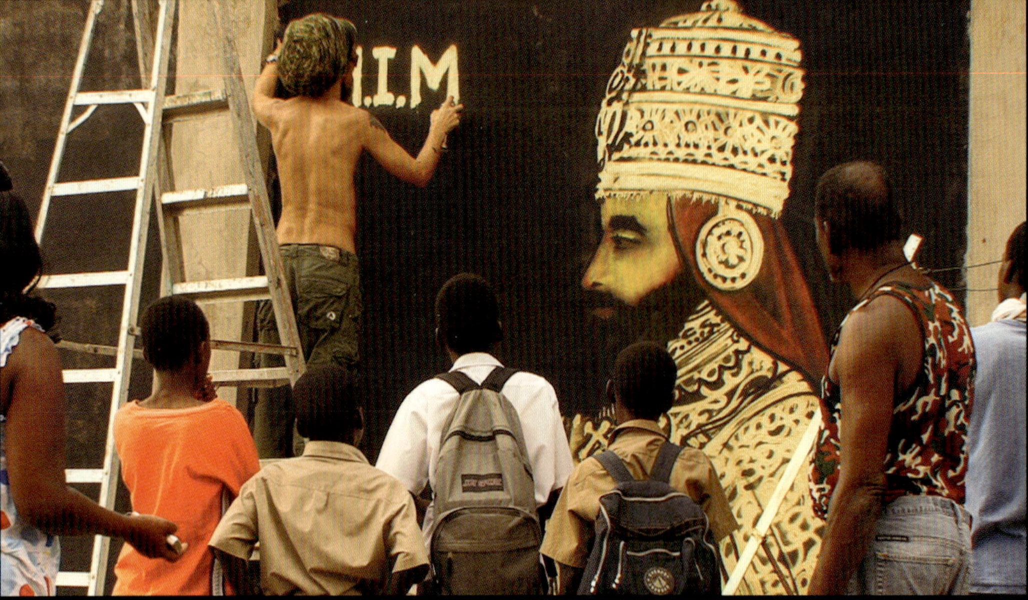

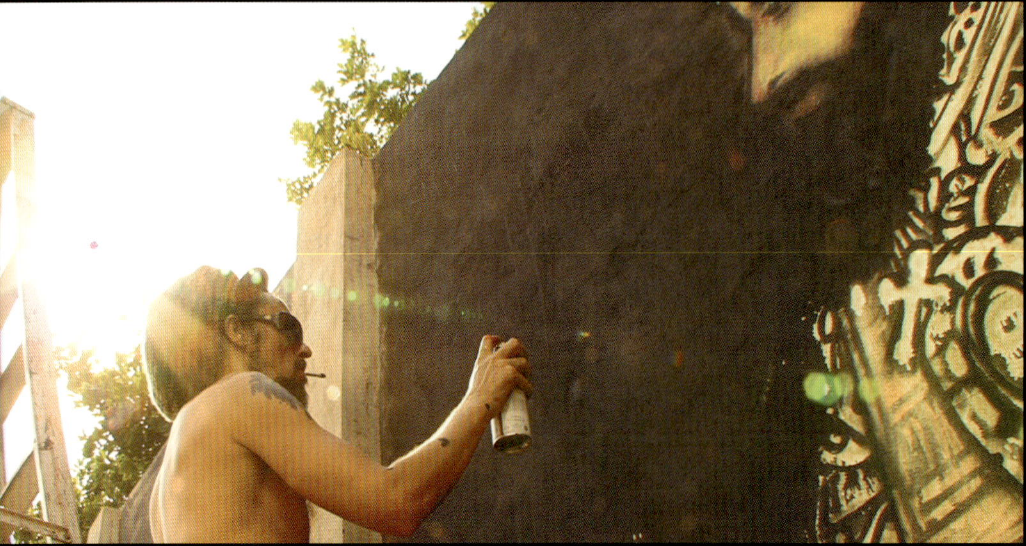

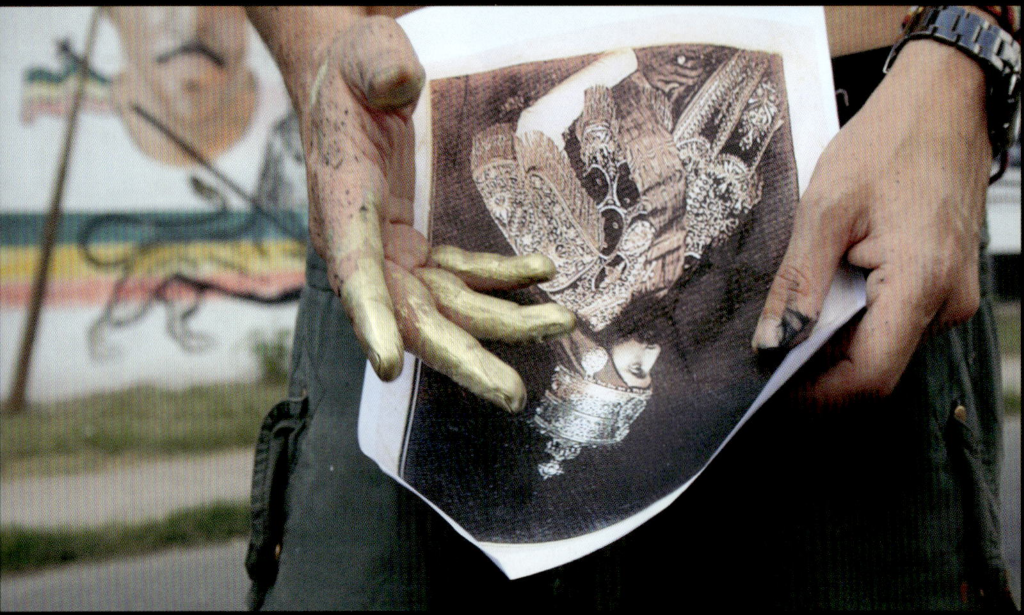

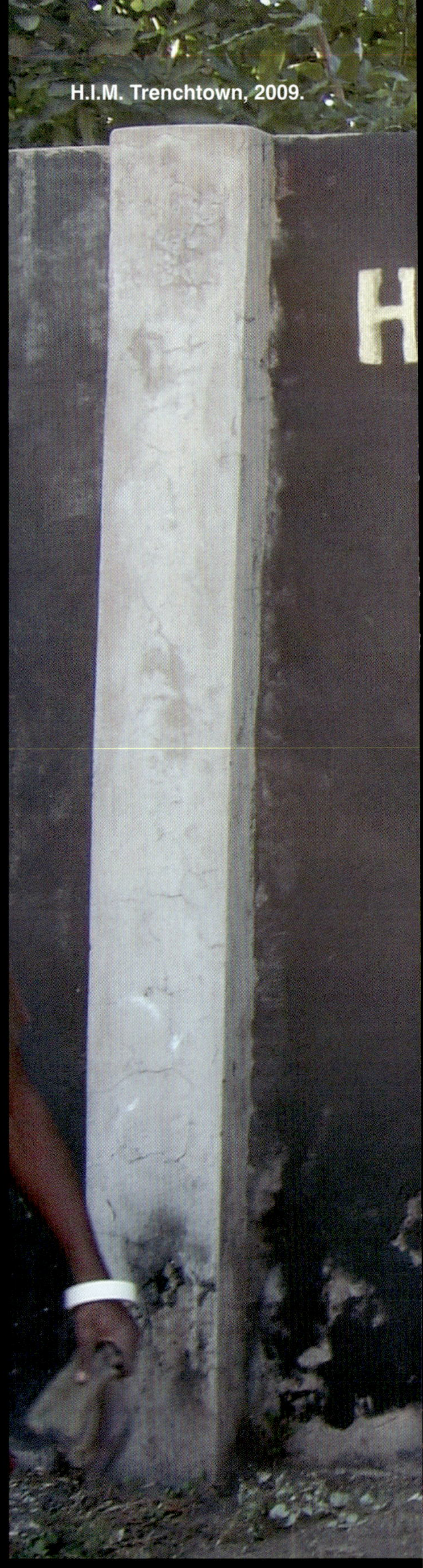

H.I.M. Trenchtown, 2009.

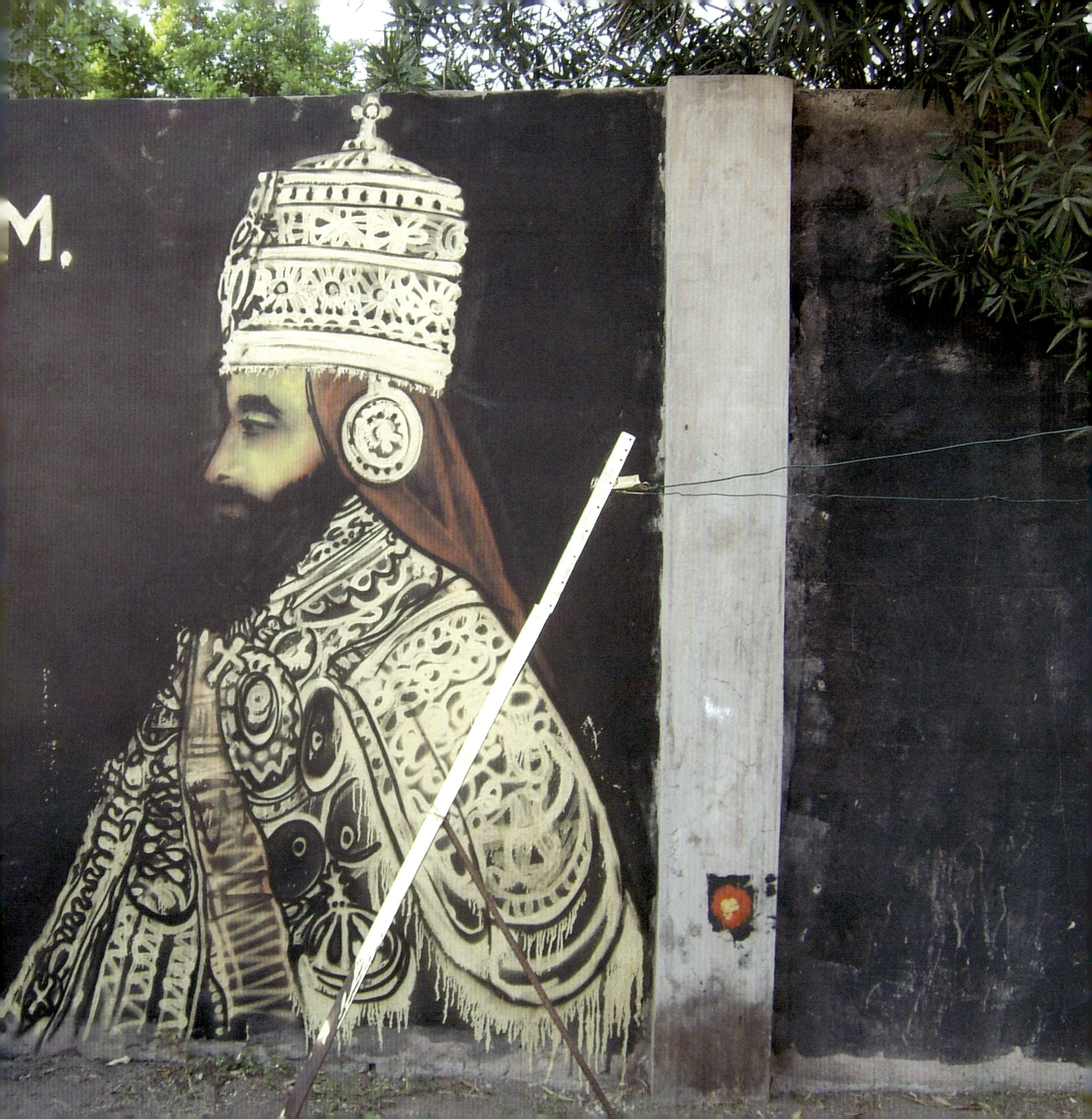
M.

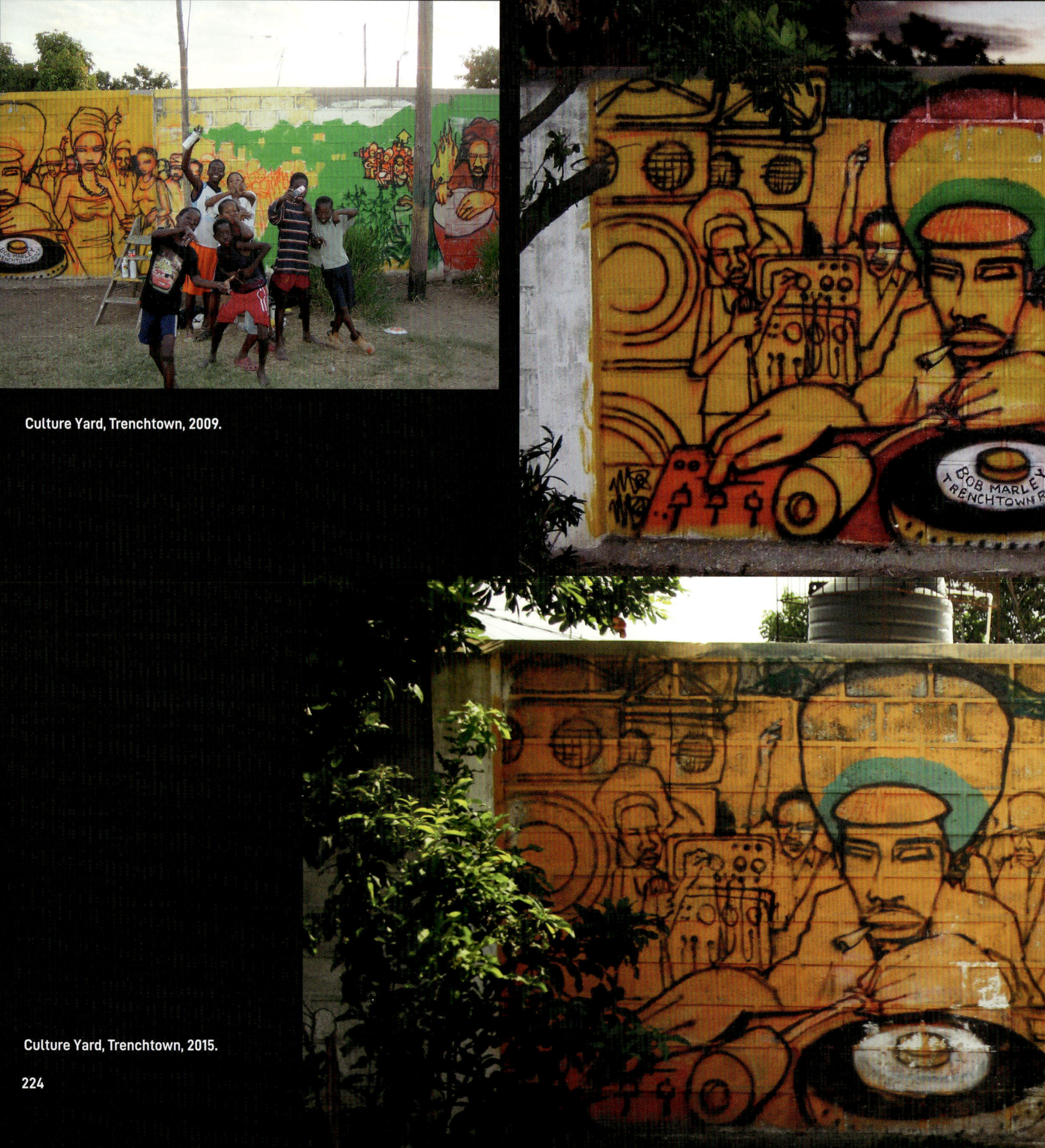

Culture Yard, Trenchtown, 2009.

Culture Yard, Trenchtown, 2015.

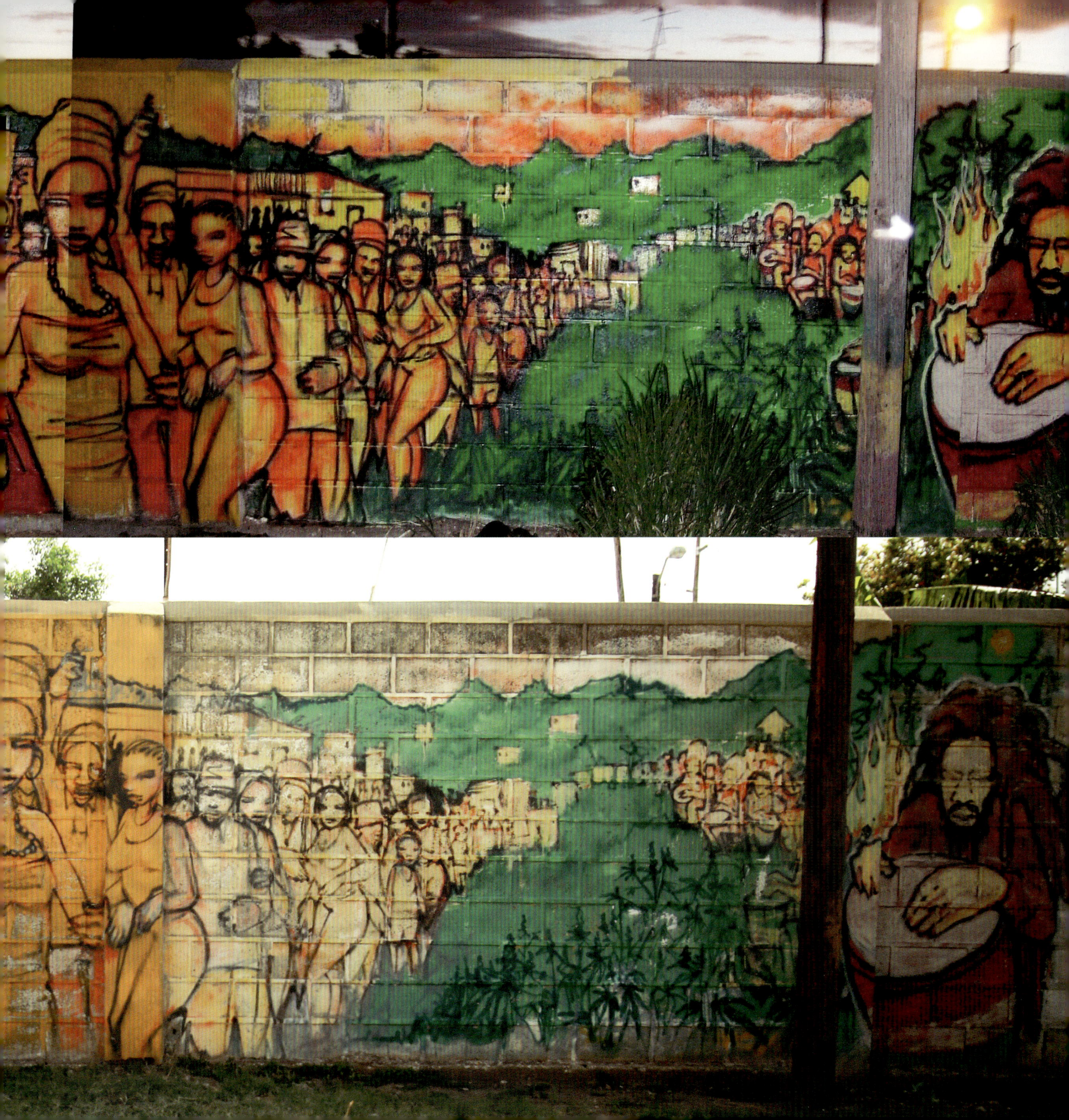

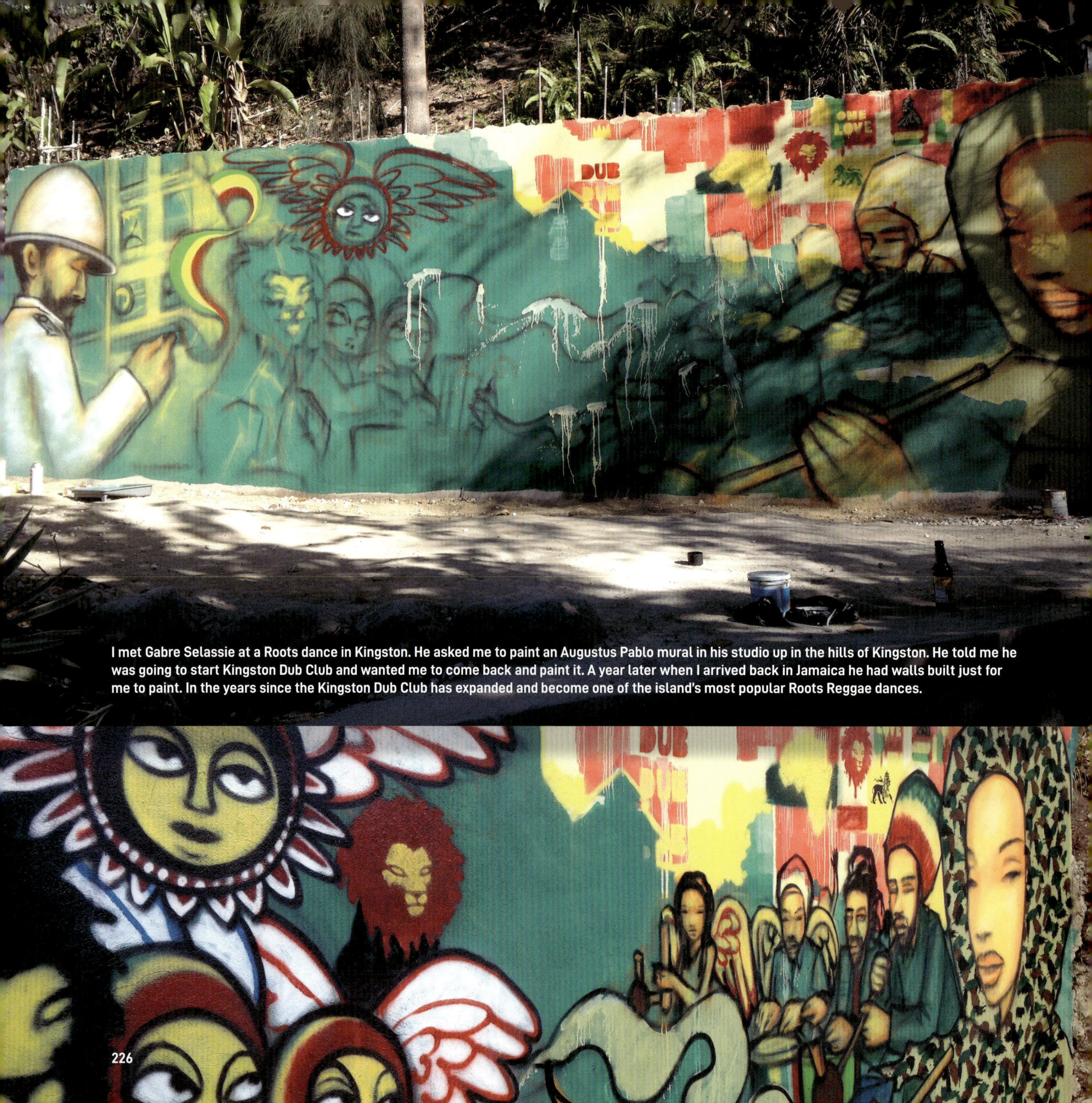

I met Gabre Selassie at a Roots dance in Kingston. He asked me to paint an Augustus Pablo mural in his studio up in the hills of Kingston. He told me he was going to start Kingston Dub Club and wanted me to come back and paint it. A year later when I arrived back in Jamaica he had walls built just for me to paint. In the years since the Kingston Dub Club has expanded and become one of the island's most popular Roots Reggae dances.

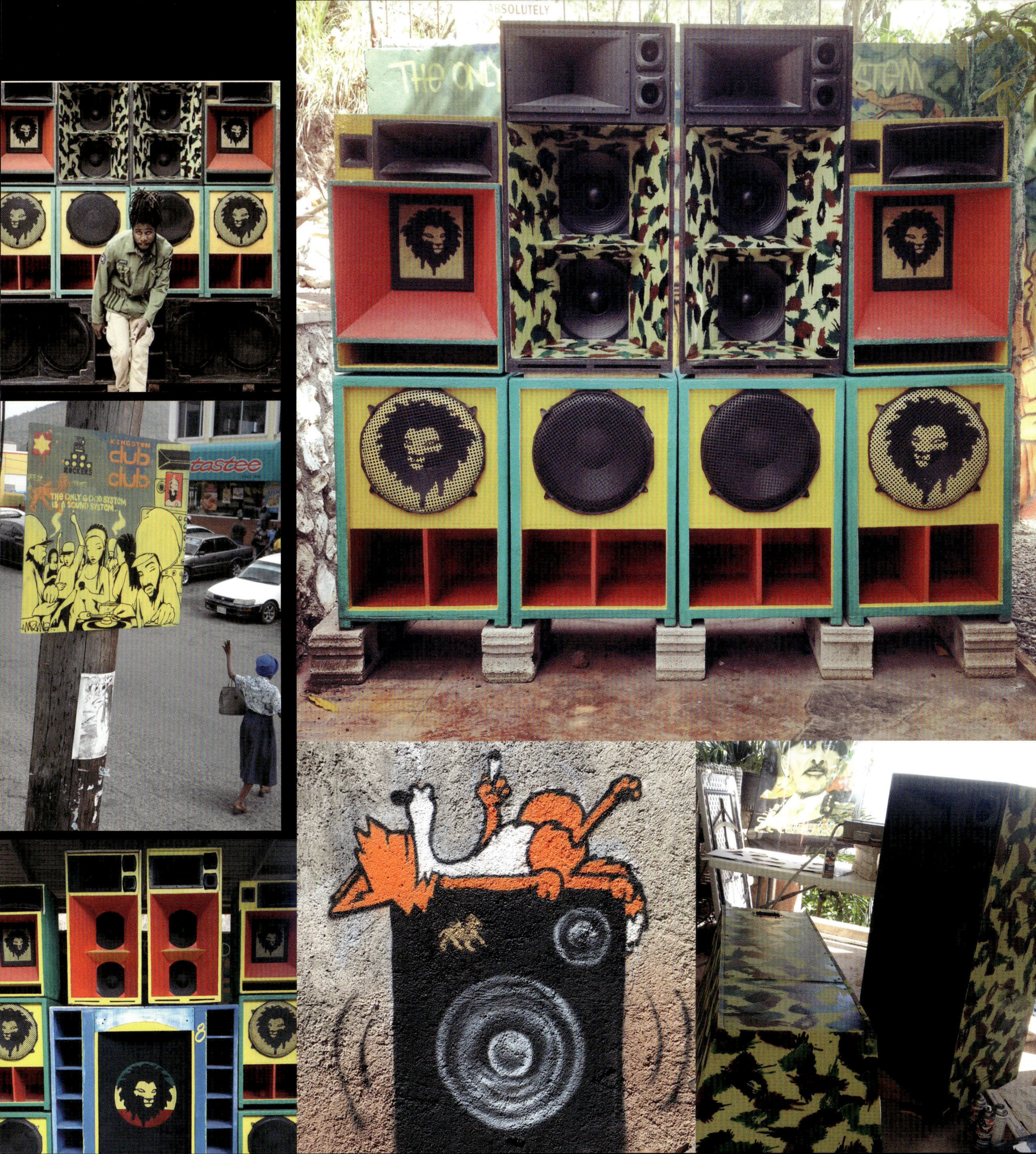
ABSOLUTELY
ROCKERS
KINGSTON
dub
club
THE ONLY GOOD SYSTEM
IS A SOUND SYSTEM...
tastee

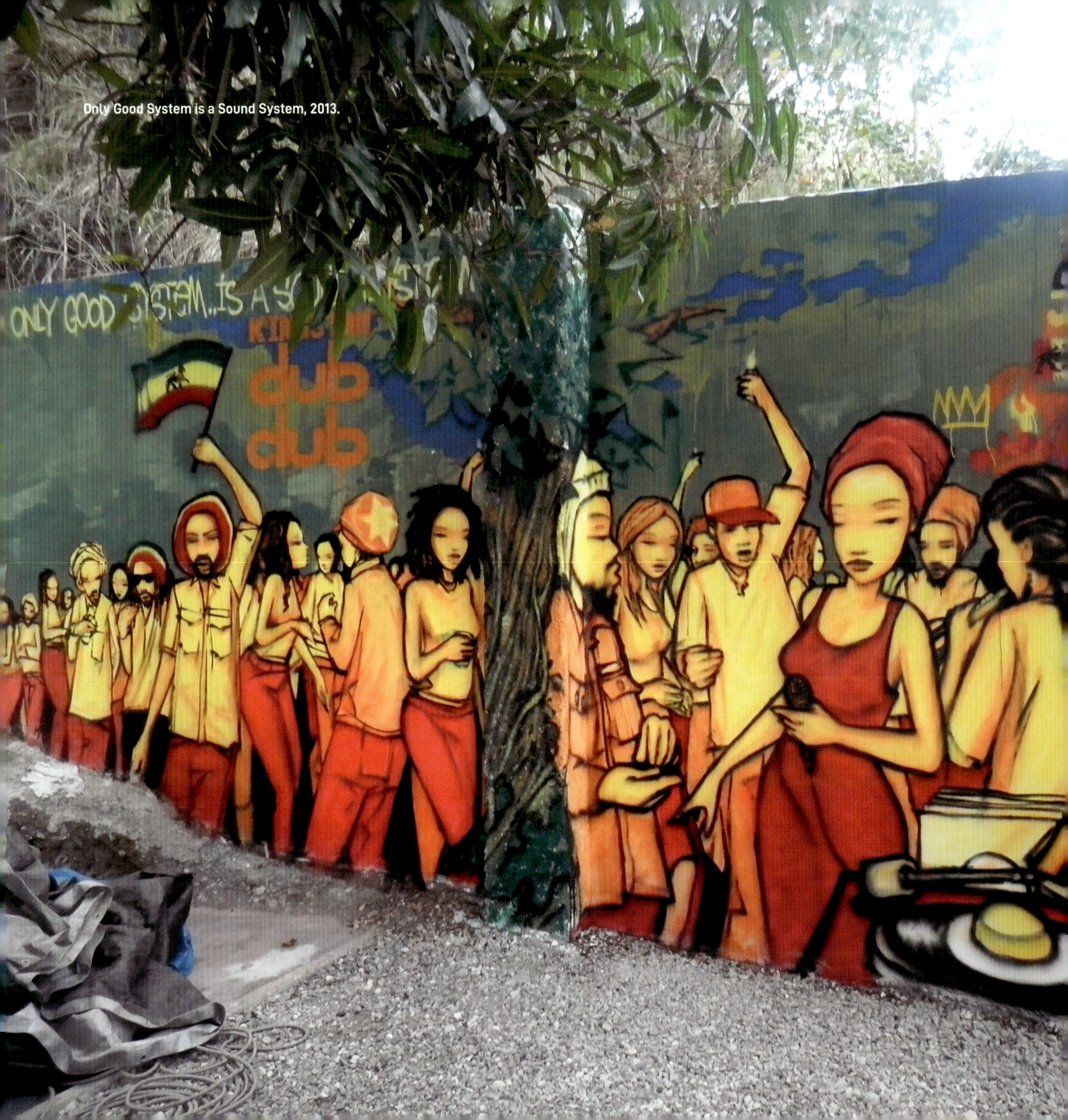

Only Good System is a Sound System, 2013.

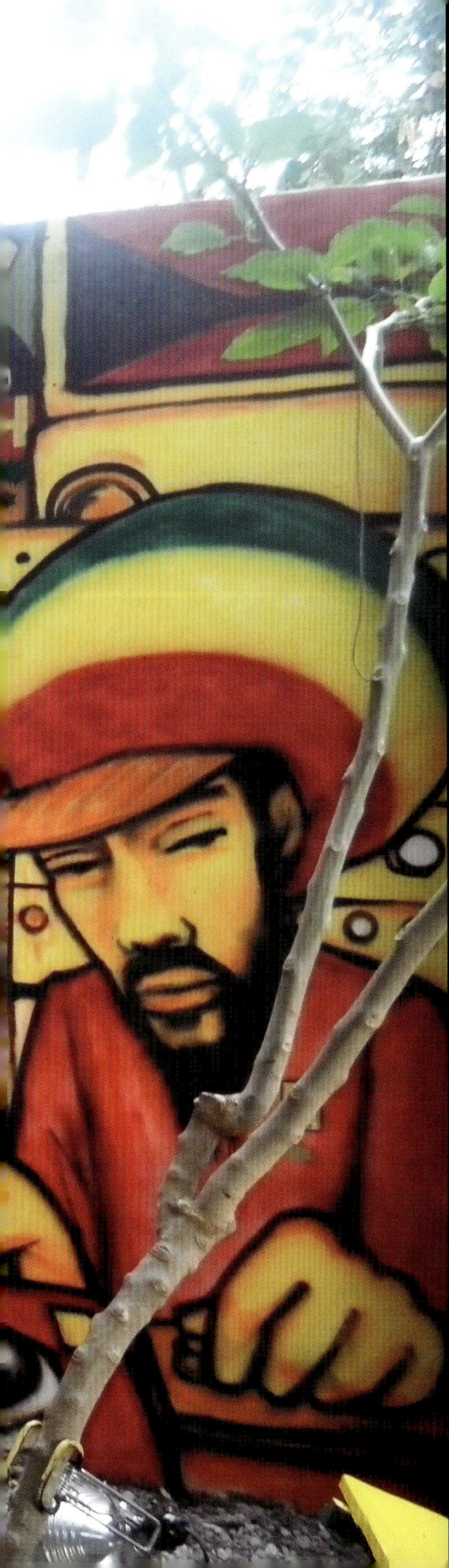

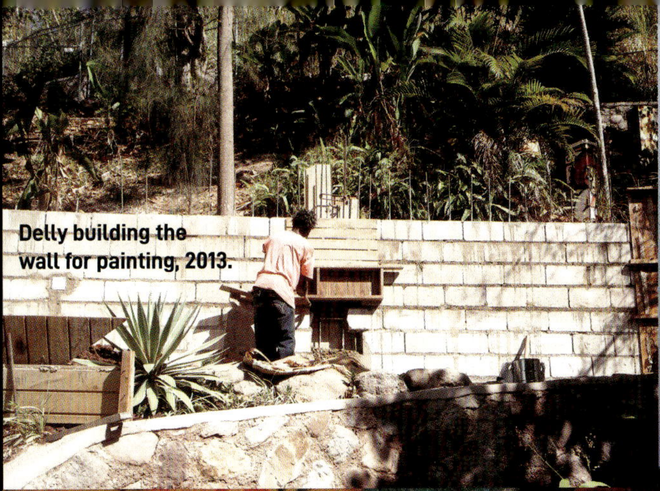

Delly building the wall for painting, 2013.

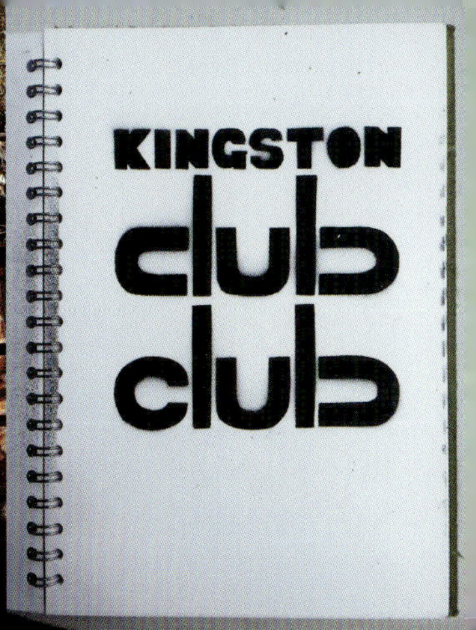

KINGSTON
dub
club

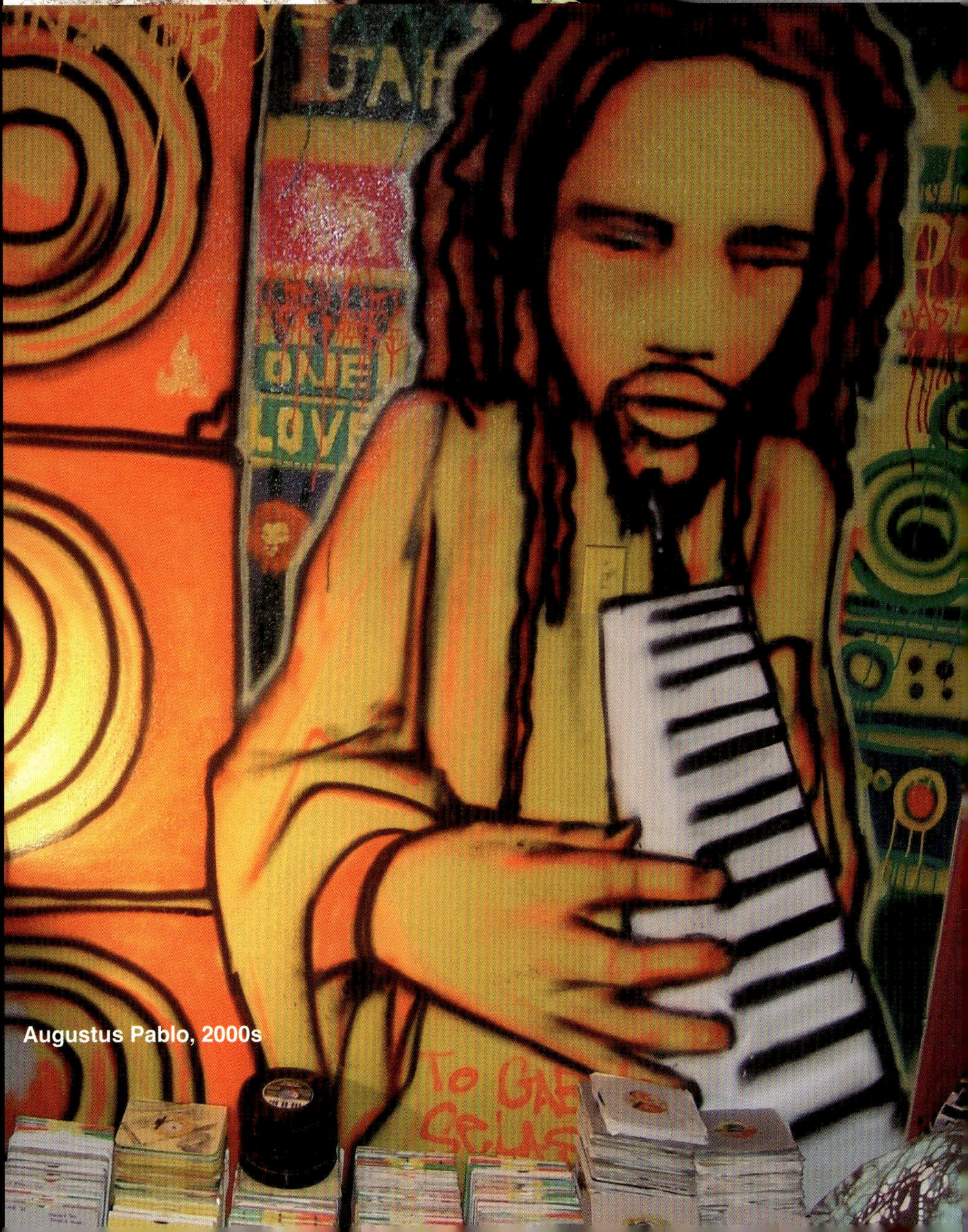

Augustus Pablo, 2000s

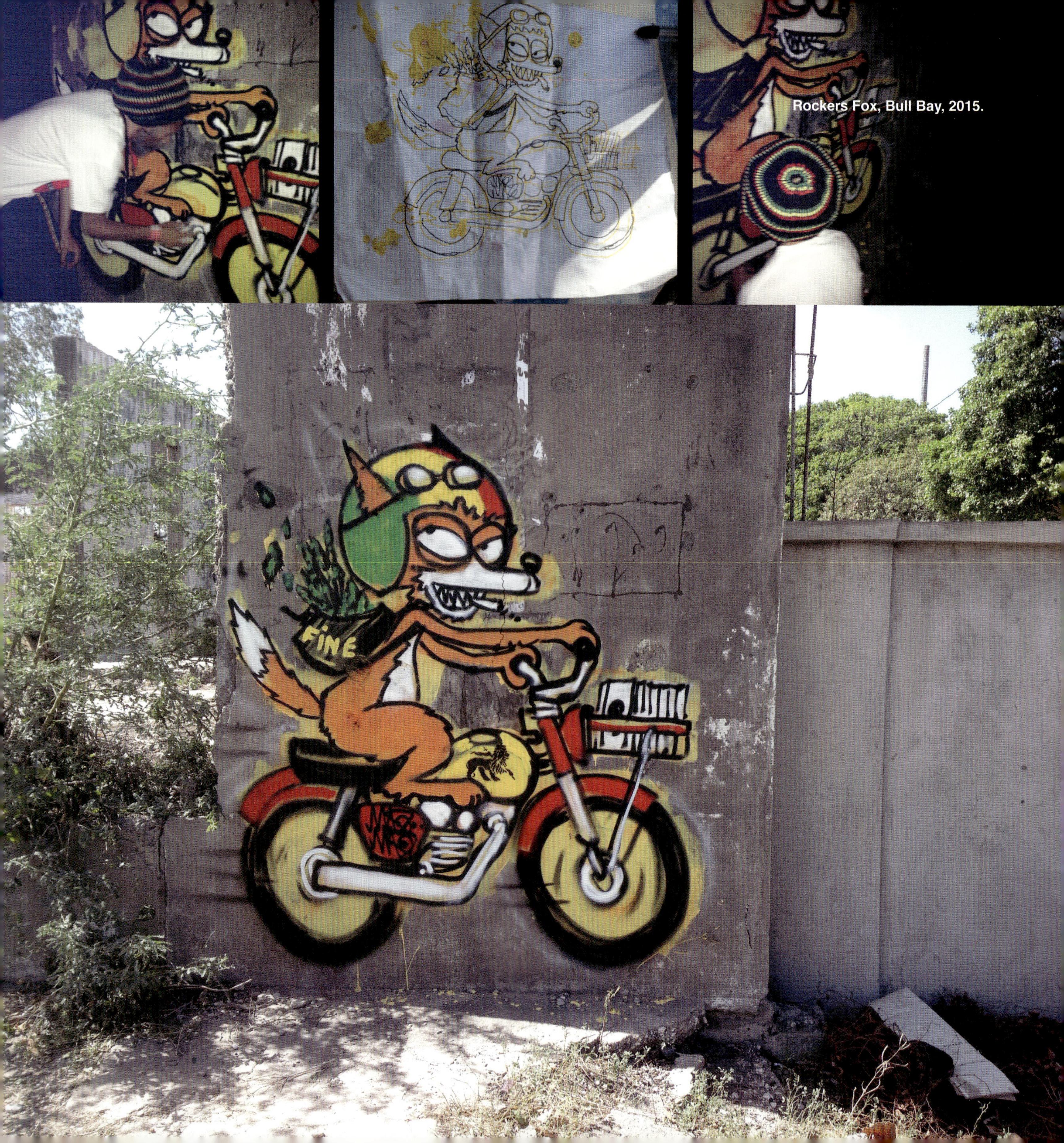

Rockers Fox, Bull Bay, 2015.

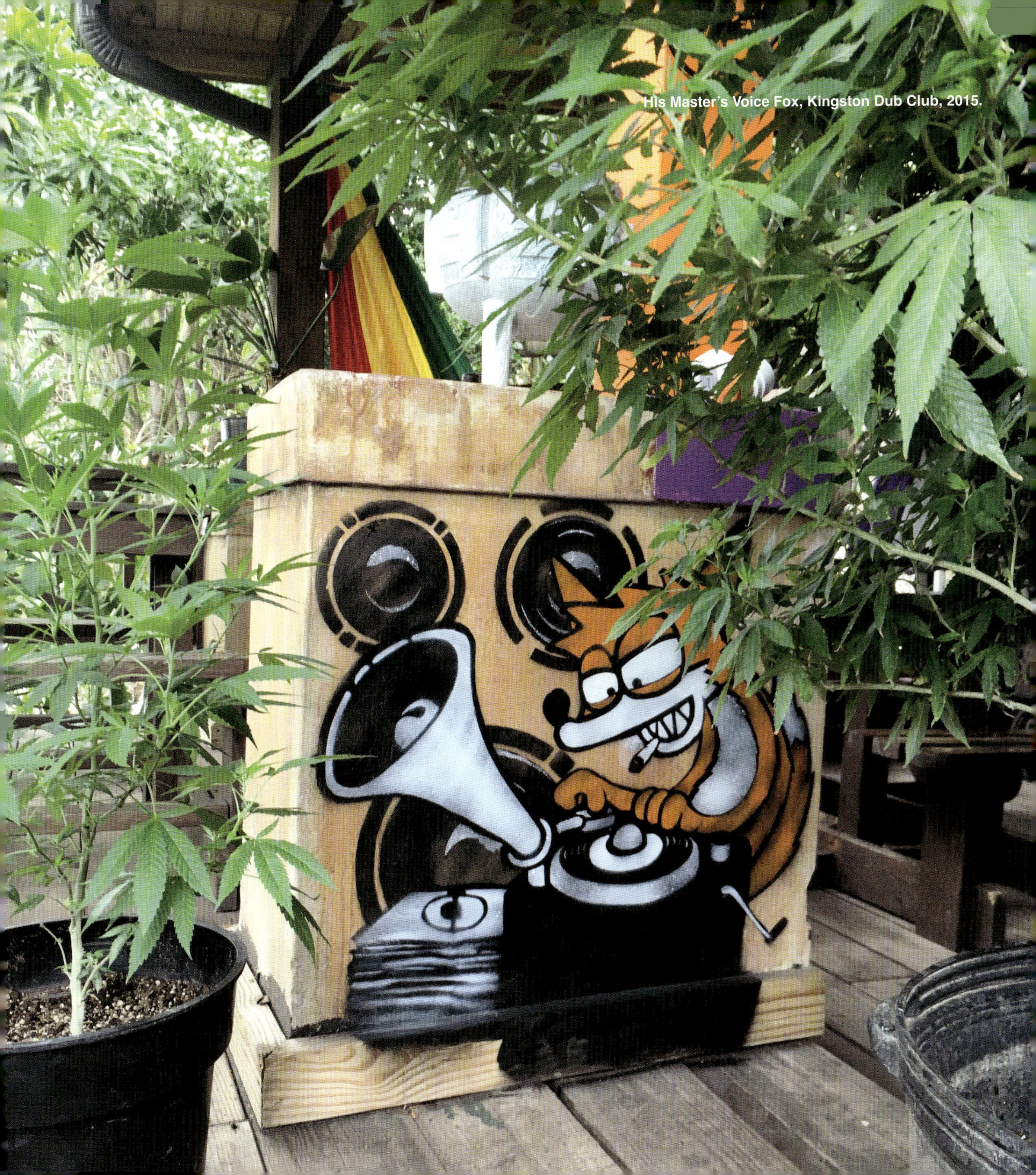

His Master's Voice Fox, Kingston Dub Club, 2015.

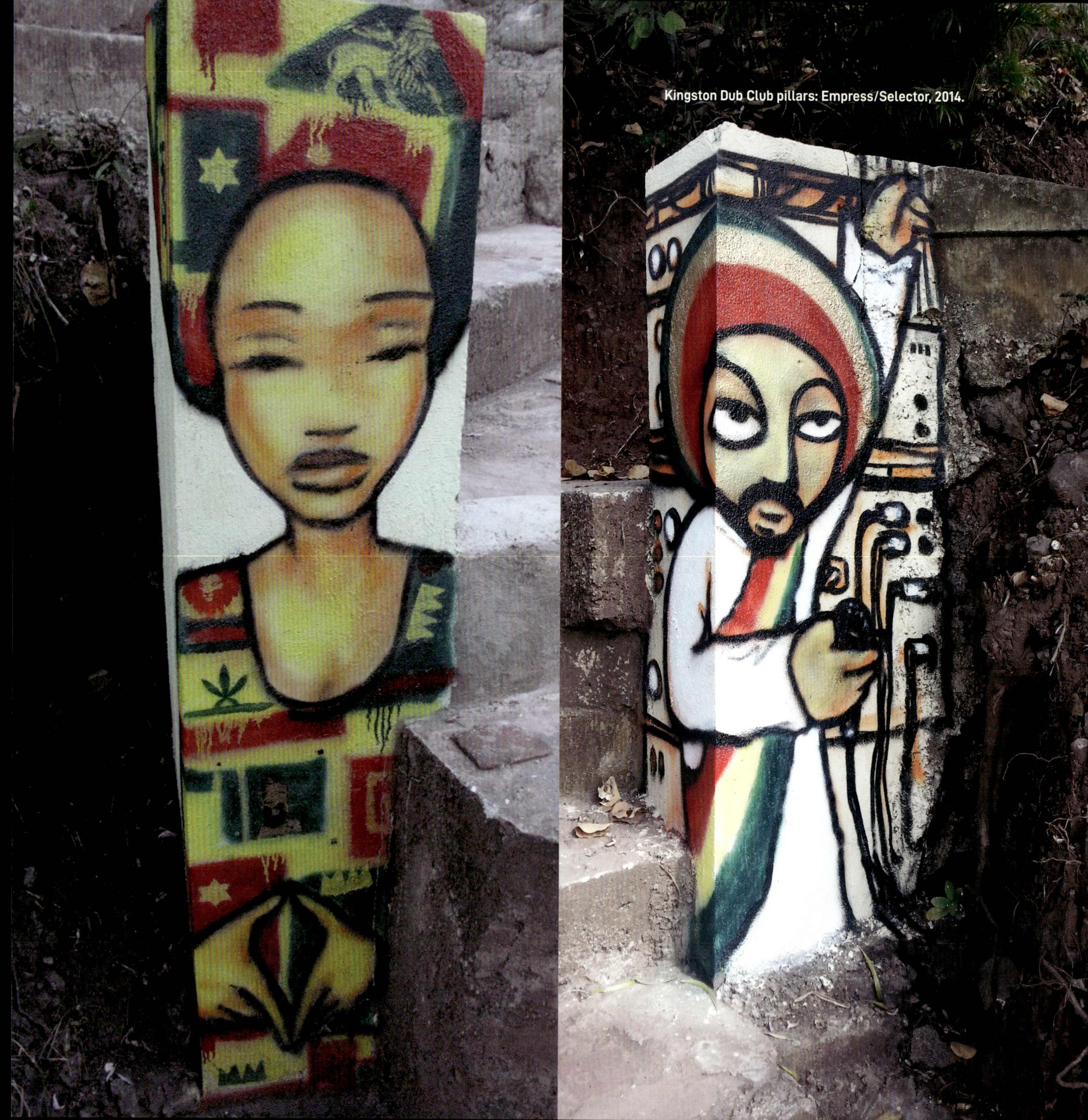

Kingston Dub Club pillars: Empress/Selector, 2014.

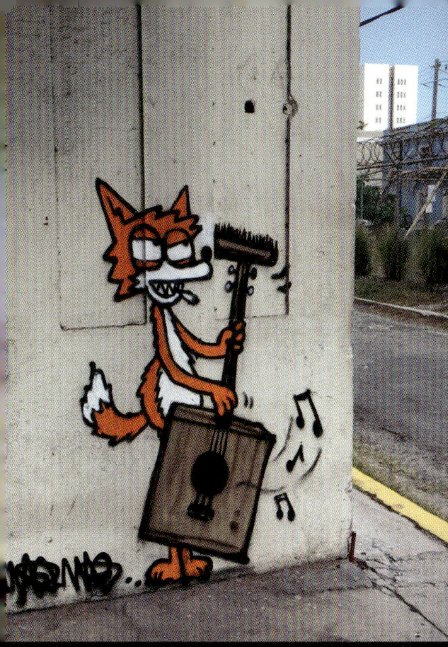

Mr Bassie Fox, Downtown Kingston, 2015.

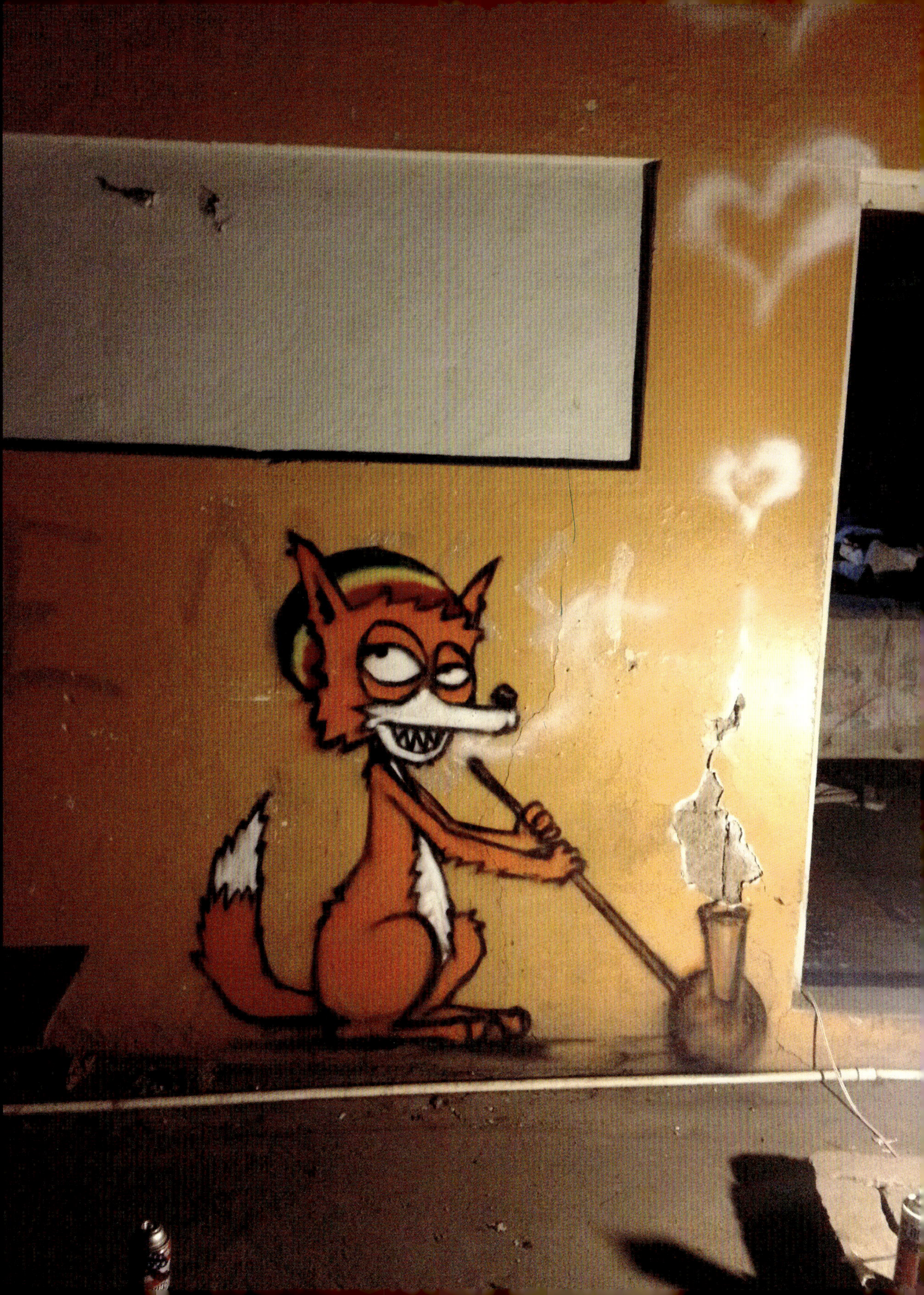

Steamer's Fox, 10½ Jah Ova Evil HQ, Kingston, 2015.

Between the music, the people, the sunshine and the herb, Jamaica is one of my favourite places to paint.

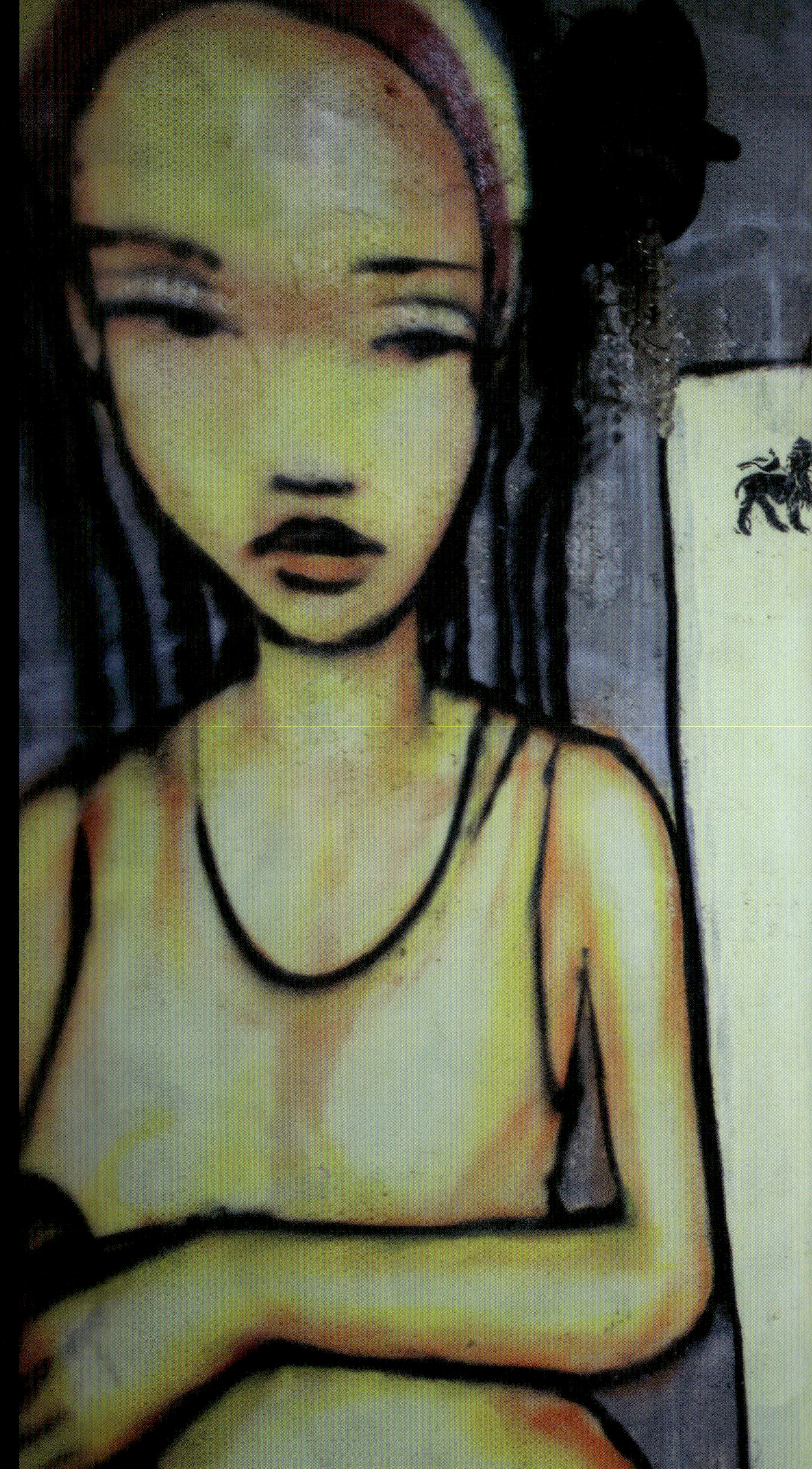

EDB Studios, Papine, Kingston, 2015.

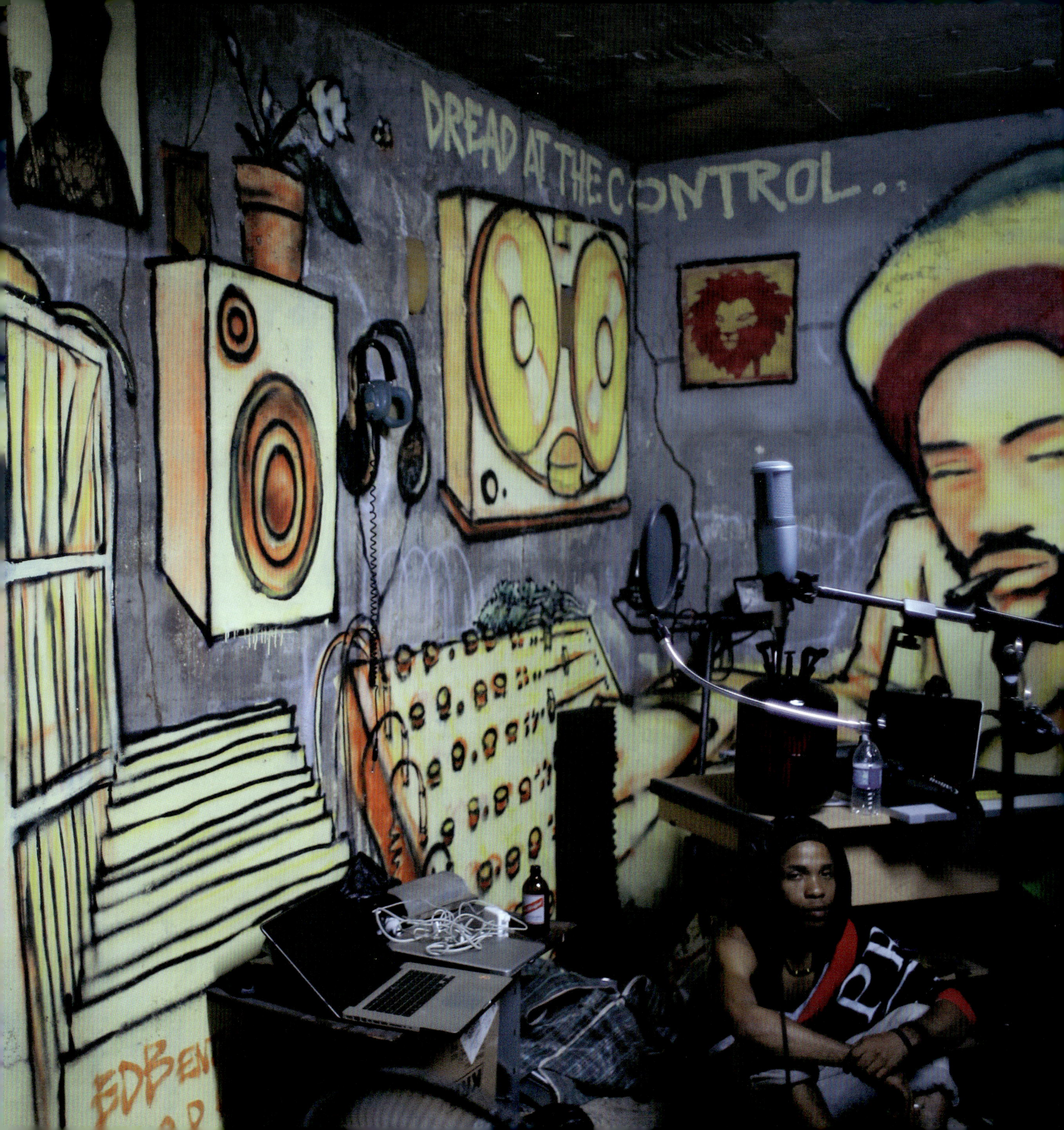
DREAD AT THE CONTROL . .

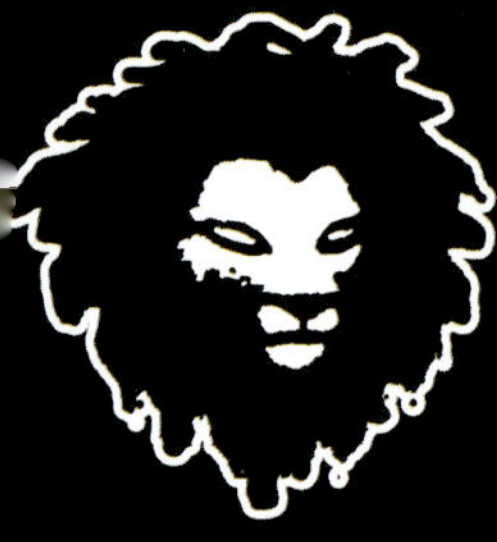

Photography -
Jonas Schaul, Eddie Otchere,
Graham Zzzz, Jeremy Gibbs,
Delete, Danial Turner,
Tim Lay, Radski,
Carlo Less, Beejoir,
Richard Braine, Chu,
Paula Davie, Joe Epstein.

Artwork and layouts -
Mau Mau

Words -
Tim Lay

Publisher Designer -
Robert Ayton
Sk8winemedia

First published by Velocity Press 2024

velocitypress.uk
mau-mau.co.uk

Printed and bound in Poland by
Interak Printing House.

ISBN: 9781913231545

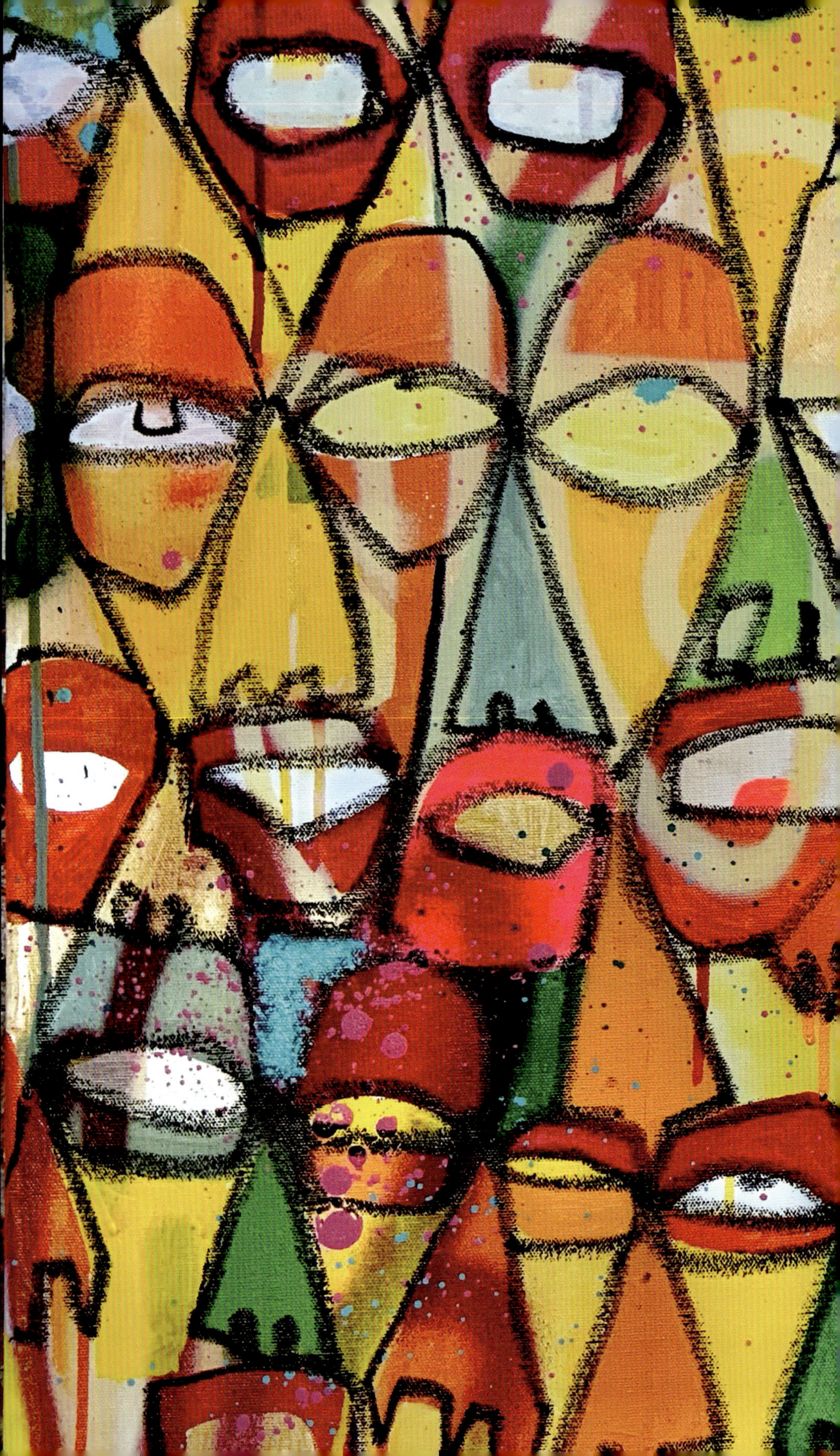

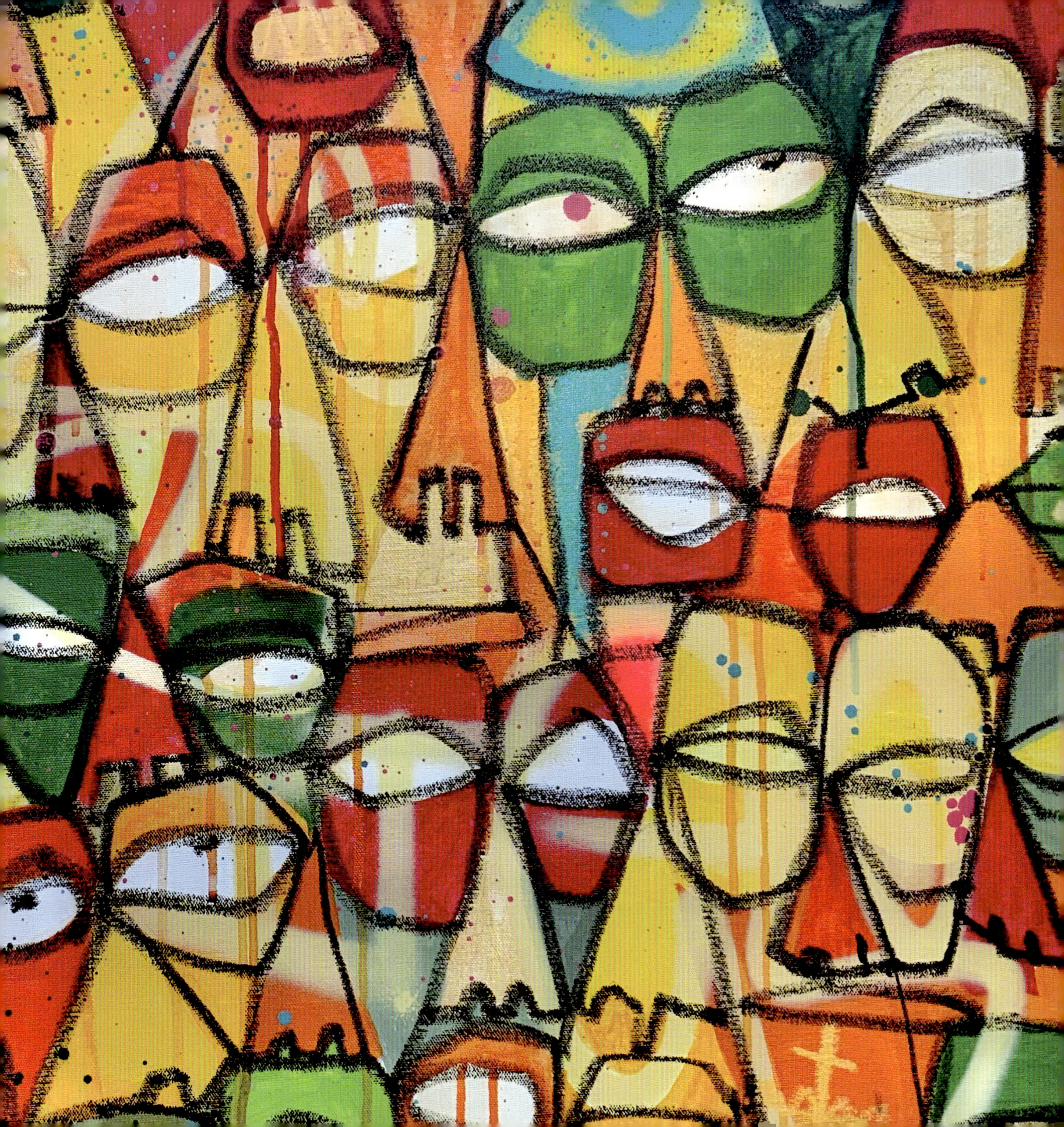

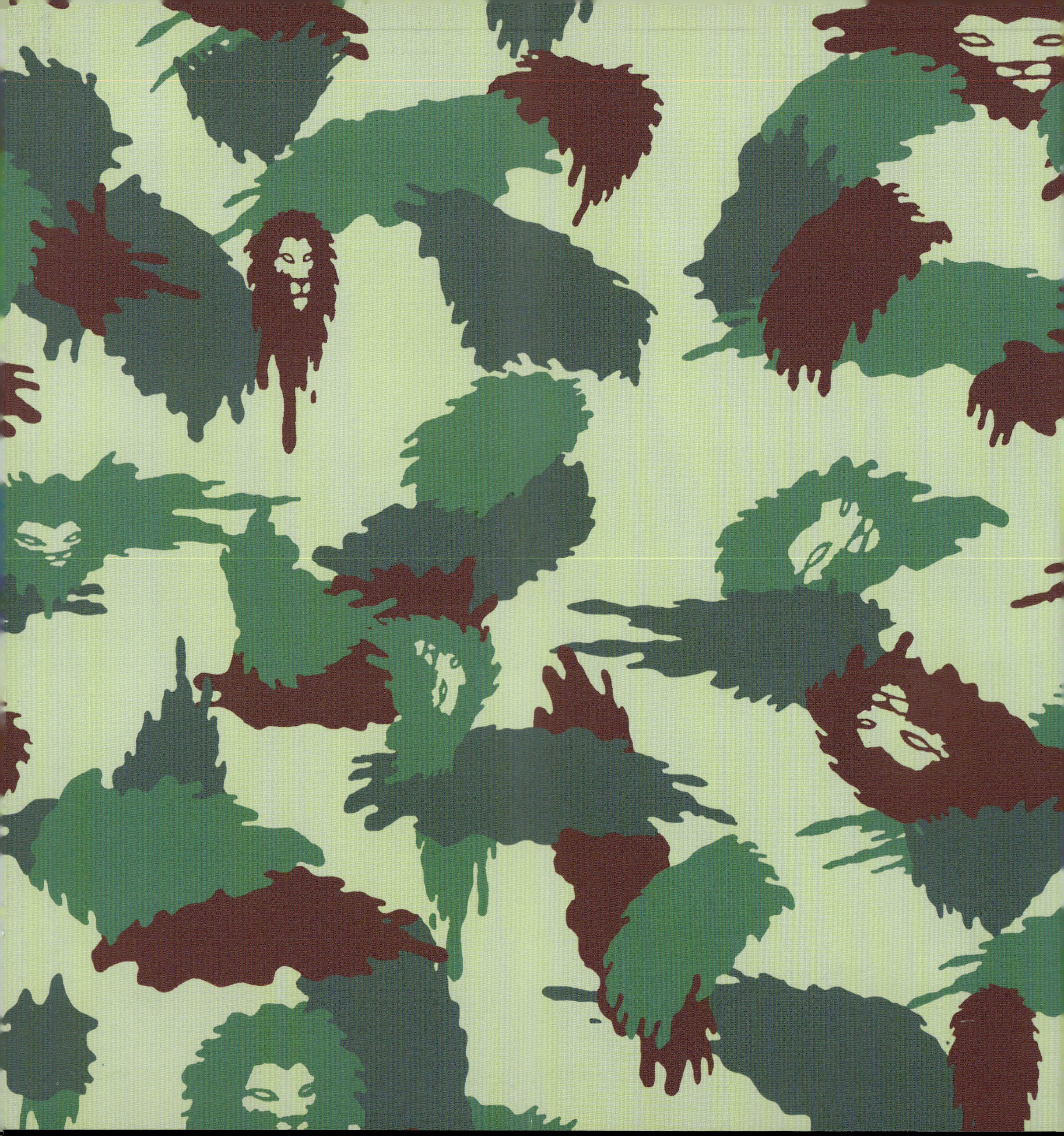